# CHILTON'S
REPAIR MANUAL

# BUICK SKYLARK
# BUICK SOMERSET
# OLDSMOBILE CALAIS
# PONTIAC GRAND AM
# 1985–92
All U.S. and Canadian front wheel drive models

| | |
|---|---|
| **Senior Vice President** | Ronald A. Hoxter |
| **Publisher and Editor-In-Chief** | Kerry A. Freeman, S.A.E. |
| **Executive Editors** | Dean F. Morgantini, S.A.E., W. Calvin Settle, Jr., S.A.E. |
| **Managing Editor** | Nick D'Andrea |
| **Special Products Manager** | Ken Grabowski, A.S.E., S.A.E. |
| **Senior Editors** | Jacques Gordon, Michael L. Grady, Debra McCall, Kevin M. G. Maher, Richard J. Rivele, S.A.E., Richard T. Smith, Jim Taylor, Ron Webb |
| **Project Managers** | Martin J. Gunther, Will Kessler, A.S.E., Richard Schwartz |
| **Production Manager** | Andrea Steiger |
| **Product Systems Manager** | Robert Maxey |
| **Director of Manufacturing** | Mike D'Imperio |
| **Editors** | Steve Horner, John Rutter |

**CHILTON BOOK COMPANY**

# CONTENTS

## 1 GENERAL INFORMATION and MAINTENANCE

**1** How to use this book
**2** Tools and Equipment
**9** Routine Maintenance

## 2 ENGINE PERFORMANCE and TUNE-UP

**38** Tune-Up Performance
**39** Tune-Up Specifications

## 3 ENGINE and ENGINE OVERHAUL

**71** Engine Electrical System
**85** Engine Service
**86** Engine Specifications

## 4 EMISSION CONTROLS

**154** Emission Controls System and Service

## 5 FUEL SYSTEM

**169** TBI Fuel Injection System
**175** MFI Fuel Injection System
**186** Fuel Tank

## 6 CHASSIS ELECTRICAL

**187** Heating and Air Conditioning
**191** Entertainment Systems
**194** Windshield Wipers and Washers
**196** Instruments and Switches
**200** Lighting
**203** Circuit Protection

## DRIVE TRAIN

**206** Manual Transaxle
**209** Halfshafts
**212** Clutch
**216** Automatic Transaxle

## SUSPENSION and STEERING

**220** Wheels
**221** Front Suspension
**230** Rear Suspension
**233** Steering

## BRAKES

**246** Brake Systems
**252** Front Disc Brakes
**255** Rear Drum Brakes
**257** Parking Brake
**258** Anti-Lock Brakes

## BODY

**274** Exterior
**290** Interior

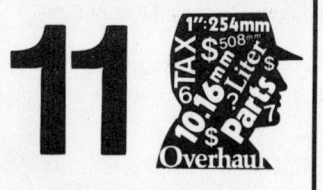
## MECHANIC'S DATA

**316** Mechanic's Data
**318** Glossary
**324** Abbreviations
**326** Index

**173** Chilton's Fuel Economy and Tune-Up Tips

**301** Chilton's Body Repair Tips

## SAFETY NOTICE

Proper service and repair procedures are vital to the safe, reliable operation of all motor vehicles, as well as the safety of those performing repairs. This book outlines procedures for servicing and repairing vehicles using safe effective methods. The procedures contain many NOTES, CAUTIONS and WARNINGS which should be followed along with standard safety procedures to eliminate the possibility of personal injury or improper service which could damage the vehicle or compromise its safety.

It is important to note that repair procedures and techniques, tools and parts for servicing motor vehicles, as well as the skill and experience of the individual performing the work vary widely. It is not possible to anticipate all of the conceivable ways or conditions under which vehicles may be serviced, or to provide cautions as to all of the possible hazards that may result. Standard and accepted safety precautions and equipment should be used during cutting, grinding, chiseling, prying, or any other process that can cause material removal or projectiles.

Some procedures require the use of tools specially designed for a specific purpose. Before substituting another tool or procedure, you must be completely satisfied that neither your personal safety, nor the performance of the vehicle will be endangered.

Although the information in this guide is based on industry sources and is as complete as possible at the time of publication, the possibility exists that the manufacturer made later changes which could not be included here. While striving for total accuracy, Chilton Book Company cannot assume responsibility for any errors, changes, or omissions that may occur in the compilation of this data.

## PART NUMBERS

Part numbers listed in the reference are not recommendations by Chilton for any product by brand name. They are references that can be used with interchange manuals and aftermarket supplier catalogs to locate each brand supplier's discrete part number.

## SPECIAL TOOLS

Special tools are recommended by the vehicle manufacturer to perform their specific job. Use has been kept to a minimum, but where absolutely necessary, they are referred to in the text by the part number of the tool manufacturer. These tools can be purchased, under the appropriate part number, from the Service Tool Division, Kent-Moore Corporation, 1501 South Jackson Street, Jackson, MI 49203 or an equivalent tool can be purchased locally from a tool supplier or parts outlet. Before substituting any tool for the one recommended, read the SAFETY NOTICE at the top of this page.

## ACKNOWLEDGEMENTS

Chilton Book Company expresses appreciation to Chevrolet Motor Division, General Motors Corporation, Detroit, Michigan for their generous assistance.

Copyright © 1992 by Chilton Book Company
All Rights Reserved
Published in Radnor, Pennsylvania 19089 by Chilton Book Company

Manufactured in the United States of America
    67890   10987

Chilton's Repair Manual: Buick Skylark, Buick Somerset, Oldsmobile Calais, Pontiac Grand AM
ISBN 0-8019-8303-7 pbk.
Library of Congress Catalog Card No. 91-058846

# General Information and Maintenance

## HOW TO USE THIS BOOK

Chilton's Repair Manual for Buick Skylark, Buick Somerset, Oldsmobile Calais and Pontiac Grand Am is intended to teach you more about the inner workings of your car and save you money on its upkeep. The first two Chapters will be used the most, since they contain maintenance and tune-up information and procedures. The following Chapters concern themselves with the more complex systems. Operating systems from engine through brakes are covered to the extent that we feel the average do-it-yourselfer should get involved as well as more complex procedures that will benefit both the advanced do-it-yourselfer mechanic as well as the professional.

A secondary purpose of this book is as a reference for owners who want to understand their car and/or their mechanics better. In this case, no tools at all are required.

Before attempting any repairs or service on your car, read through the entire procedure outlined in the appropriate Chapter. This will give you the overall view of what tools and supplies will be required. There is nothing more frustrating than having to walk to the bus stop on Monday morning because you were short one gasket on Sunday afternoon. So read ahead and plan ahead. Each operation should be approached logically and all procedures thoroughly understood before attempting any work. Some special tools that may be required can often be rented from local automotive jobbers or places specializing in renting tools and equipment. Check the yellow pages of your phone book.

All Chapters contain adjustments, maintenance, removal and installation procedures, and overhaul procedures. When overhaul is not considered practical, we tell you how to remove the failed part and then how to install the new or rebuilt replacement. In this way, you at least save the labor costs. Backyard overhaul of some components is just not practical, but the removal and installation procedure is often simple and well within the capabilities of the average car owner.

Two basic mechanic's rules should be mentioned here. First, whenever the LEFT side of the car or engine is referred to, it is meant to specify the DRIVER'S side of the car. Conversely, the RIGHT side of the car means the PASSENGER'S side. Second, all screws and bolts are removed by turning counterclockwise, and tightened by turning clockwise, unless otherwise noted.

Safety is always the most important rule. Constantly be aware of the dangers involved in working on or around an automobile and take proper precautions to avoid the risk of personal injury or damage to the vehicle. See the section in this Chapter, Servicing Your Vehicle Safely, and the SAFETY NOTICE on the acknowledgment page before attempting any service procedures and pay attention to the instructions provided. There are 3 common mistakes in mechanical work:

1. Incorrect order of assembly, disassembly or adjustment. When taking something apart or putting it together, doing things in the wrong order usually just costs you extra time; however it CAN break something. Read the entire procedure before beginning disassembly. Do everything in the order in which the instructions say you should do it, even if you can't immediately see a reason for it. When you're taking apart something that is very intricate, you might want to draw a picture of how it looks when assembled at one point in order to make sure you get everything back in its proper position. We will supply exploded views whenever possible, but sometimes the job requires more attention to detail than an illustration provides. When making adjustments (especially tune-up adjustments), do them in order. One adjustment often

# 2  GENERAL INFORMATION AND MAINTENANCE

affects another and you cannot expect satisfactory results unless each adjustment is made only when it cannot be changed by any other.

2. Overtorquing (or undertorquing) nuts and bolts. While it is more common for overtorquing to cause damage, undertorquing can cause a fastener to vibrate loose and cause serious damage, especially when dealing with aluminum parts. Pay attention to torque specifications and utilize a torque wrench in assembly. If a torque figure is not available remember that, if you are using the right tool to do the job, you will probably not have to strain yourself to get a fastener tight enough. The pitch of most threads is so slight that the tension you put on the wrench will be multiplied many times in actual force on what you are tightening. A good example of how critical torque is can be seen in the case of spark plug installation, especially where you are putting the plug into an aluminum cylinder head. Too little torque can fail to crush the gasket, causing leakage of combustion gases and consequent overheating of the plug and engine parts. Too much torque can damage the threads or distort the plug, which changes the spark gap at the electrode. Since more and more manufacturers are using aluminum in their engine and chassis parts to save weight, a torque wrench should be in any serious do-it-yourselfer's tool box.

There are many commercial chemical products available for ensuring that fasteners won't come loose, even if they are not torqued just right (a very common brand is Loctite®). If you're worried about getting something together tight enough to hold, but loose enough to avoid mechanical damage during assembly, one of these products might offer substantial insurance. Read the label on the package and make sure the product is compatible with the materials, fluids, etc. involved before choosing one.

3. Crossthreading. This occurs when a part such as a bolt is screwed into a nut or casting at the wrong angle and forced, causing the threads to become damaged. Crossthreading is more likely to occur if access is difficult. It helps to clean and lubricate fasteners, and to start threading with the part to be installed going straight in, using your fingers. If you encounter resistance, unscrew the part and start over again at a different angle until it can be inserted and turned several times without much effort. Keep in mind that many parts, especially spark plugs, use tapered threads so that gentle turning will automatically bring the part you're threading to the proper angle if you don't force it or resist a change in angle. Don't put a wrench on the part until it's been turned in a couple of times by hand. If you suddenly encounter resistance and the part has not seated fully, don't force it. Pull it back out and make sure it's clean and threading properly.

Always take your time and be patient; once you have some experience, working on your car will become an enjoyable hobby.

## TOOLS AND EQUIPMENT

NOTE: *Special tools are occasionally necessary to perfrom a specific job or are recommended to make a job easier. The requirement for those tools to do jobs described in this book has been kept to a minimum. When a special tool is indicated, it will be referred to by manufacturer's part number and, where possible, an illustration of the tool will be probided so that an equibalent tool may be found.*

Naturally, without the proper tools and equipment it is impossible to properly service your vehicle. It would be impossible to catalog each tool that you would need to perform each or every operation in this book. It would also be unwise for the amateur to rush out and buy an expensive set of tools on the theory that he may need one or more of them at sometime.

The best approach is to proceed slowly, gathering together a good quality set of those tools that are used most frequently. Don't be misled by the low cost of bargain tools. It is far better to spend a little more for better quality. Forged wrenches, 6- or 12-point sockets and fine tooth ratchets are by far preferable to their less expensive counterparts. As any good mechanic can tell you, there are few worse experiences than trying to work on a truck with bad tools. Your monetary savings will be far outweighed by frustration and mangled knuckles.

Certain tools, plus a basic ability to handle tools, are required to get started. A basic mechanics tool set, a torque wrench, and a Torx bits set. Torx bits are hexlobular drivers which fit both inside and outside on special Torx head fasteners used in various places on your vehicle.

Begin accumulating those tools that are used most frequently; those associated with routine maintenance and tune-up.

In addition to the normal assortment of screwdrivers and pliers you should have the following tools for routine maintenance jobs (your vehicle, depending on the model year, uses both SAE and metric fasteners):

1. SAE/Metric wrenches, sockets and combination open end/box end wrenches in sizes from $\frac{1}{8}$ in. (3mm) to $\frac{3}{4}$ in. (19mm); and a spark plug socket ($\frac{13}{16}$ in.) If possible, buy various length socket drive extensions. One break in this department is that the metric sockets available in the U.S. will all fit the ratchet handles and ex-

# GENERAL INFORMATION AND MAINTENANCE 3

tensions you may already have (¼ in., ⅜ in., and ½ in. drive).
2. Jackstands for support
3. Oil filter wrench
4. Oil filter spout for pouring oil
5. Grease gun for chassis lubrication
6. Hydrometer for checking the battery
7. A container for draining oil
8. Many rags for wiping up the inevitable mess.

In addition to the above items there are several others that are not absolutely necessary, but handy to have around. These include oil-dry (cat box litter works just as well and may be cheaper), a transmission funnel and the usual supply of lubricants, antifreeze and fluids, although these can be purchased as needed. This is a basic list for routine maintenance, but only your personal needs and desires can accurately determine your list of necessary tools.

The second list of tools is for tune-ups. While the tools involved here are slightly more sophisticated, they need not be outrageously expensive. There are several inexpensive tach/dwell meters on the market that are every bit as good for the average mechanic as a $100.00 professional model. Just be sure that it goes to at least 1,200–1,500 rpm on the tach scale and that it works on 4, 6 and 8 cylinder engines. A basic list of tune-up equipment could include:
1. Tach-dwell meter
2. Spark plug wrench
3. Timing light (a DC light that works from the vehicle's battery is best, although an AC light that plugs into 110V house current will suffice at some sacrifice in brightness)
4. Wire spark plug gauge/adjusting tools

In addition to these basic tools, there are several other tools and gauges you may find useful. These include:
1. A compression gauge. The screw-in type is slower to use, but eliminates the possibility of a faulty reading due to escaping pressure
2. A manifold vacuum gauge
3. A test light
4. An induction meter. This is used for determining whether or not there is current in a wire. These are handy for use if a wire is broken somewhere in a wiring harness.

Normally, the use of special factory tools is avoided for repair procedures, since these are not readily available for the do-it-yourself mechanic. When it is possible to perform the job with more commonly available tools, it will be pointed out, but occasionally, a special tool was designed to perform a specific function and should be used. Before substituting another tool, you should be convinced that neither your safety nor the performance of the vehicle will be compromised.

When a special tool is indicated, it will be referred to by the manufacturer's part number. Some special tools are available commercially from major tool manufacturers. Others for your car can be purchased from your GM dealer.

As a final note, you will probably find a torque wrench necessary for all but the most basic work. The beam type models are perfectly adequate, although the newer click (break-away) type are more precise, and you don't have to crane your neck to see a torque reading in awkward situations. The breakaway torque wrenches are more expensive and should be recalibrated periodically.

Torque specification for each fastener will be given in the procedure in any case that a specific torque value is required. If no torque specifications are given, use the following values as a guide, based upon fastener size:

**Bolts marked 6T**
  6mm bolt/nut – 5–7 ft. lbs.
  8mm bolt/nut – 12–17 ft. lbs.
  10mm bolt/nut – 23–34 ft. lbs.
  12mm bolt/nut – 41–59 ft. lbs.
  14mm bolt/nut – 56–76 ft. lbs.

**Bolts marked 8T**
  6mm bolt/nut – 6–9 ft. lbs.
  8mm bolt/nut – 13–20 ft. lbs.
  10mm bolt/nut – 27–40 ft. lbs.
  12mm bolt/nut – 46–69 ft. lbs.
  14mm bolt/nut – 75–101 ft. lbs.

## SERVICING YOUR VEHICLE SAFELY

It is virtually impossible to anticipate all of the hazards involved with automotive maintenance and service but care and common sense will prevent most accidents.

The rules of safety for mechanics range from "don't smoke around gasoline," to "use the proper tool for the job." The trick to avoid injuries is to develop safe work habits and take every possible precaution.

### Do's

• Do keep a fire extinguisher and first aid kit within easy reach.
• Do wear safety glasses or goggles when cutting, drilling, grinding or prying. If you wear glasses for the sake of vision, then they should be made of hardened glass that can serve also as safety glasses, or wear safety goggles over your regular glasses.
• Do wear safety glasses whenever you work around the battery. Batteries contain sulphuric acid. In case of contact with the eyes or skin, flush the area with water or a mixture of water

# 4 GENERAL INFORMATION AND MAINTENANCE

and baking soda and get medical attention immediately.

• Do use safety stands for any under-car service. Jacks are for raising vehicles; safety stands are for making sure the vehicle stays raised until you want it to come down. Whenever the vehicle is raised, block the wheels remaining on the ground and set the parking brake.

• Do use adequate ventilation when working with any chemicals. Asbestos dust resulting from brake lining wear can cause cancer.

• Do disconnect the negative battery cable when working on the electrical system. The primary ignition system can contain up to 40,000 volts.

• Do follow manufacturer's directions whenever working with potentially hazardous materials. Both brake fluid and antifreeze are poisonous if taken internally.

• Do properly maintain your tools. Loose hammerheads, mushroomed punches and chisels, frayed or poorly grounded electrical cords, excessively worn screwdriver, spread wrenches (open end), cracked sockets can cause accidents.

• Do use the proper size and type of tool for the job being done.

• Do when possible, pull on a wrench handle rather than push on it, and adjust your stance to prevent a fall.

• Do be sure that adjustable wrenches are tightly adjusted on the nut or bolt and pulled so that the face is on the side of the fixed jaw.

• Do select a wrench or socket that fits the nut or bolt. The wrench or socket should sit straight, not cocked.

• Do strike squarely with a hammer to avoid glancing blows.

• Do set the parking brake and block the drive wheels if the work requires that the engine is running.

## Don'ts

• Don't run an engine in a garage or anywhere else without proper ventilation – EVER! Carbon monoxide is poisonous. It is absorbed by the body 400 times faster than oxygen. It takes a long time to leave the human body and you can build up a deadly supply of it in you system by simply breathing in a little every day. You may not realize you are slowly poisoning yourself. Always use power vents, windows, fans or open the garage doors.

• Don't work around moving parts while wearing a necktie or other loose clothing. Short sleeves are much safer than long, loose sleeves. Hard-toed shoes with neoprene soles protect your toes and give a better grip on slippery surfaces. Jewelry such as watches, fancy belt buckles, beads or body adornment of any kind is not safe working around a car. Long hair should be hidden under a hat or cap.

• Don't use pockets for tool boxes. A fall or bump can drive a screwdriver deep into you body. Even a wiping cloth hanging from the back pocket can wrap around a spinning shaft or fan.

• Don't smoke when working around gasoline, cleaning solvent or other flammable material.

• Don't smoke when working around the battery. When the battery is being charged, it gives off explosive hydrogen gas.

• Don't use gasoline to wash your hands. There are excellent soaps available. Gasoline may contain lead, and lead can enter the body through a cut, accumulating in the body until you are very ill. Gasoline also removes all the natural oils from the skin so that bone dry hands will suck up oil and grease.

• Don't service the air conditioning system unless you are equipped with the necessary tools and training. Do wear safety glasses, the refrigerant, is extremely cold and when exposed to the air, will instantly freeze any surface it comes in contact with, including your eyes. Although the refrigerant is normally nontoxic, it becomes a deadly poisonous gas in the presence of an open flame. One good whiff of the vapors from burning refrigerant can be fatal.

## MODEL IDENTIFICATION

General Motors introduced the N body line of vehicles in 1985 to three of its divisions: Buick, Oldsmobile and Pontiac. The Buick models included the Somerset and Skylark. The Somerset was discontinued after 1987. The Oldsmobile version was the Cutlass Calais until 1992 and the Pontiac model remains the Grand Am. General Motors did a body redesign for all three N body vehicles in 1992, with the Oldsmobile model changing its name from Cutlass Calais to Achieva.

## SERIAL NUMBER IDENTIFICATION

### Vehicle

The VIN plate which contains the Vehicle Identification Number (VIN) is located at the top and back of the instrument panel on the left side and is visible from outside the vehicle on the lower left (driver's) side of the windshield. The VIN consists of 17 characters which represent codes supplying important information

# GENERAL INFORMATION AND MAINTENANCE

VIN number plate location

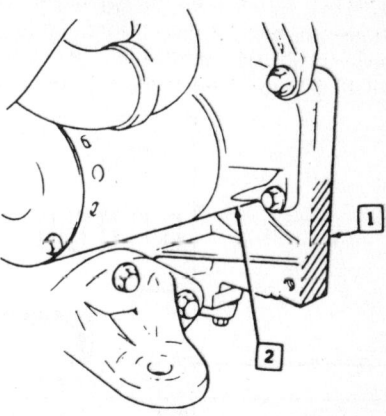

Partial engine identification number location—2.3L engine

about your vehicle. The first character represents the nation of origin. The second character identifies the manufacturer. The third character represents a code used by the manufacturer to identify the division. The fourth character represents a code used to establish the car line or series. The fifth character is a code which identifies the model. On vehicles from model years 1985–87, the sixth and seventh characters combined represent a code which identifies the body type. On vehicles from model years 1988–92, the sixth character is a code which identifies the body type and the seventh character identifies the type of restraint system used on the vehicle. The eighth character represents the engine code. The ninth character is a check digit. The tenth character is a code which represents the model year of the vehicle. The eleventh character is a code which represents the plant in which the vehicle was assembled. Char-

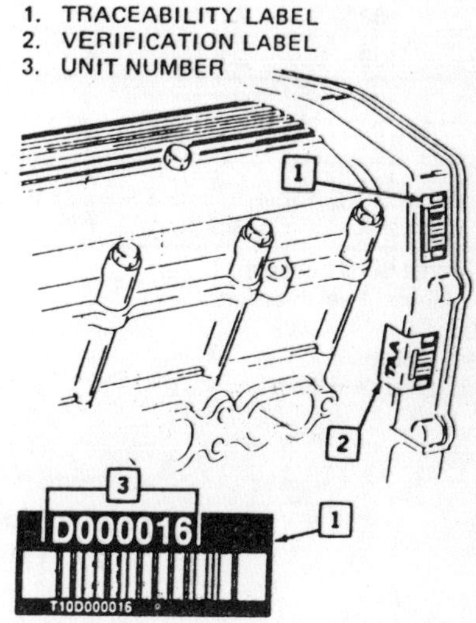

Engine code label location—2.3L engine

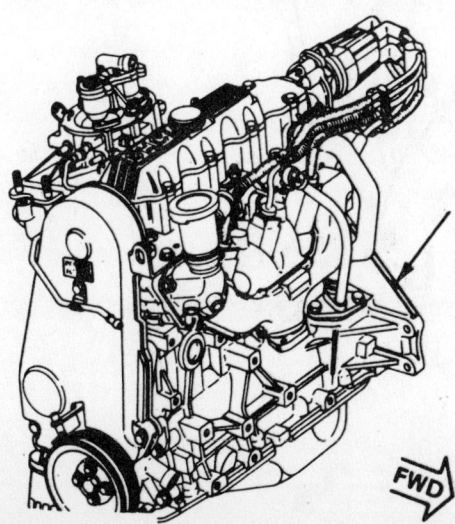

Engine identification number location—2.0L engine

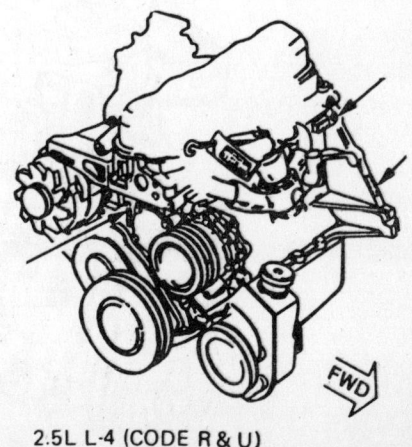

Engine identification number location—1985–87 2.5L engine

# 6 GENERAL INFORMATION AND MAINTENANCE

## VEHICLE IDENTIFICATION CHART

It is important for servicing and ordering parts to be certain of the vehicle and engine identification. The VIN (vehicle identification number) is a 17 digit number visible through the windshield on the driver's side of the dash and contains the vehicle and engine identification codes. The tenth digit indicates model year and the eighth digit indicates engine code. It can be interpreted as follows:

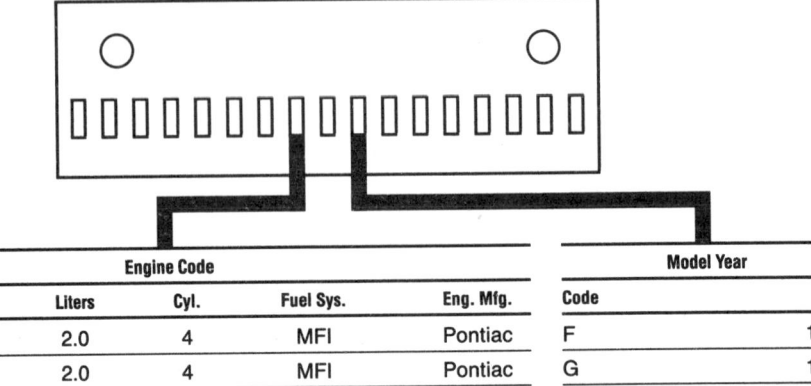

| Engine Code ||||||| Model Year ||
| --- | --- | --- | --- | --- | --- | --- | --- |
| Code | Cu. In. | Liters | Cyl. | Fuel Sys. | Eng. Mfg. | Code | Year |
| K | 122 | 2.0 | 4 | MFI | Pontiac | F | 1985 |
| M① | 122 | 2.0 | 4 | MFI | Pontiac | G | 1986 |
| A② | 138 | 2.3 | 4 | MFI | Oldsmobile | H | 1987 |
| D② | 138 | 2.3 | 4 | MFI | Oldsmobile | J | 1988 |
| 3③ | 138 | 2.3 | 4 | MFI | Oldsmobile | K | 1989 |
| U | 151 | 2.5 | 4 | TBI | Pontiac | L | 1990 |
| L | 181 | 3.0 | 6 | MFI | Buick | M | 1991 |
| N | 204 | 3.3 | 6 | MFI | Buick | N | 1992 |

TBI—Throttle Body Injection
MFI—Multi-port Fuel Injection
① Turbo
② Quad-4 engine
③ Single Overhead Cam

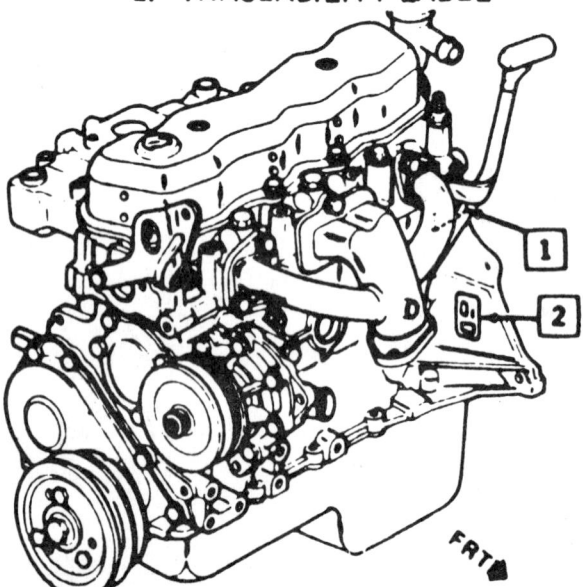

1. PARTIAL VIN LOCATION
2. TRACEABILITY LABEL

Engine code label and partial engine identification number location—1988–92 2.5L engine

# GENERAL INFORMATION AND MAINTENANCE

acters twelve through seventeen are the plant sequence number or the number of the vehicle of that model produced at that plant for the model year.

## Engine

The engine code is represented by the eighth character in the VIN and identifies the engine type, displacement, fuel system type and manufacturing division.

The engine identification code is either stamped onto the engine block or found on a label affixed to the engine. This code supplies information about the manufacturing plant location and time of manufacture. The location for a particular engine is shown in the illustrations.

## Transaxle

Similar the engine identification code, the transaxle identification code supplies information about the transaxle such as manufacturing plant, Julian date of manufacture, shift number and model. The location for the transaxle code is shown in the illustrations.

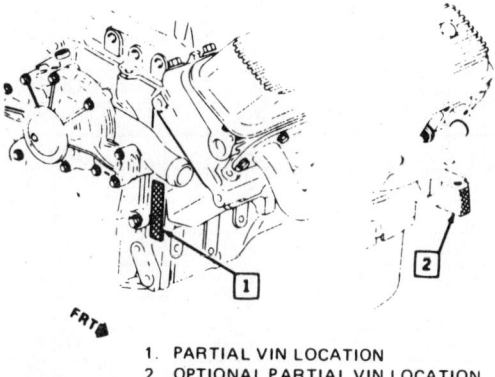

1. PARTIAL VIN LOCATION
2. OPTIONAL PARTIAL VIN LOCATION

Partial engine identification number location—3.0L and 3.3L engines

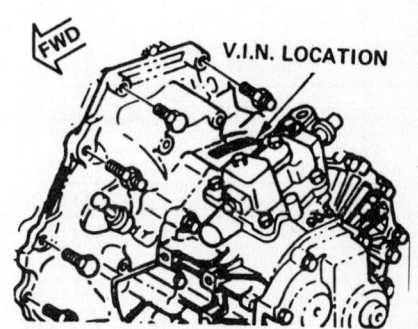

Manual transaxle identification number location—Isuzu 76MM manual transaxle

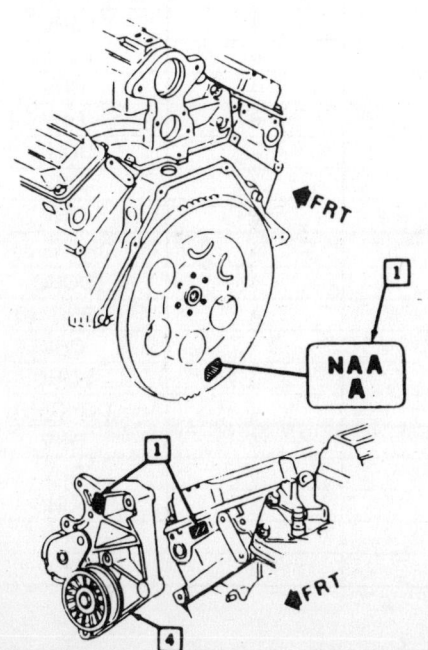

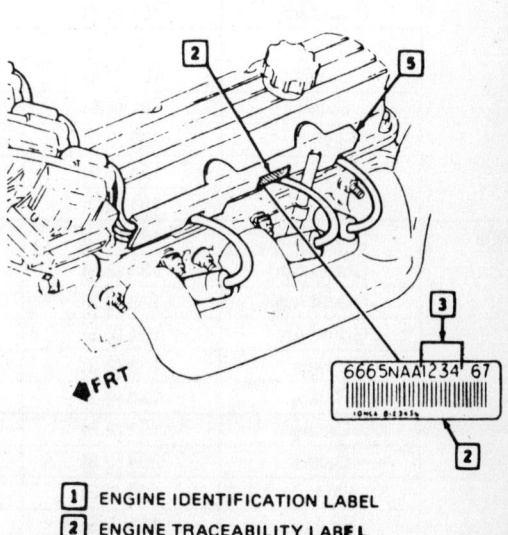

[1] ENGINE IDENTIFICATION LABEL
[2] ENGINE TRACEABILITY LABEL
[3] UNIT NUMBER
[4] DRIVE BELT TENSIONER
[5] SPARK PLUG WIRING HARNESS

Engine code label locations—3.3L engine

# 8  GENERAL INFORMATION AND MAINTENANCE

## ENGINE IDENTIFICATION

| Year | Model | Engine Displacement cu. in. (liter) | Engine Series Identification (VIN) | No. of Cylinders | Engine Type |
|---|---|---|---|---|---|
| 1985 | Grand Am | 151 (2.5) | U | 4 | OHV |
|  | Grand Am | 181 (3.0) | L | 6 | OHV |
|  | Calais | 151 (2.5) | U | 4 | OHV |
|  | Calais | 181 (3.0) | L | 6 | OHV |
|  | Somerset | 151 (2.5) | U | 4 | OHV |
|  | Somerset | 181 (3.0) | L | 6 | OHV |
| 1986 | Grand Am | 151 (2.5) | U | 4 | OHV |
|  | Grand Am | 181 (3.0) | L | 6 | OHV |
|  | Calais | 151 (2.5) | U | 4 | OHV |
|  | Calais | 181 (3.0) | L | 6 | OHV |
|  | Somerset | 151 (2.5) | U | 4 | OHV |
|  | Somerset | 181 (3.0) | L | 6 | OHV |
|  | Skylark | 151 (2.5) | U | 4 | OHV |
|  | Skylark | 181 (3.0) | L | 6 | OHV |
| 1987 | Grand Am | 122 (2.0) | K | 4 | OHC |
|  | Grand Am | 122 (2.0) | M | 4 | OHC Turbo |
|  | Grand Am | 151 (2.5) | U | 4 | OHV |
|  | Grand Am | 181 (3.0) | L | 6 | OHV |
|  | Calais | 151 (2.5) | U | 4 | OHV |
|  | Calais | 181 (3.0) | L | 6 | OHV |
|  | Somerset | 151 (2.5) | U | 4 | OHV |
|  | Somerset | 181 (3.0) | L | 6 | OHV |
|  | Skylark | 151 (2.5) | U | 4 | OHV |
|  | Skylark | 181 (3.0) | L | 6 | OHV |
| 1988 | Grand Am | 122 (2.0) | M | 4 | OHC Turbo |
|  | Grand Am | 138 (2.3) | D | 4 | DOHC |
|  | Grand Am | 151 (2.5) | U | 4 | OHV |
|  | Calais | 138 (2.3) | D | 4 | DOHC |
|  | Calais | 151 (2.5) | U | 4 | OHV |
|  | Calais | 181 (3.0) | L | 6 | OHV |
|  | Skylark | 138 (2.3) | D | 4 | DOHC |
|  | Skylark | 151 (2.5) | U | 4 | OHV |
|  | Skylark | 181 (3.0) | L | 6 | OHV |
| 1989 | Grand Am | 122 (2.0) | M | 4 | OHC Turbo |
|  | Grand Am | 138 (2.3) | D | 4 | DOHC |
|  | Grand Am | 138 (2.3) | A | 4 | DOHC-HO |
|  | Grand Am | 151 (2.5) | U | 4 | OHV |
|  | Calais | 138 (2.3) | D | 4 | DOHC |
|  | Calais | 138 (2.3) | A | 4 | DOHC-HO |
|  | Calais | 151 (2.5) | U | 4 | OHV |
|  | Calais | 204 (3.3) | N | 6 | OHV |
|  | Skylark | 138 (2.3) | D | 4 | DOHC |
|  | Skylark | 151 (2.5) | U | 4 | OHV |
|  | Skylark | 204 (3.3) | N | 6 | OHV |

## GENERAL INFORMATION AND MAINTENANCE

### ENGINE IDENTIFICATION

| Year | Model | Engine Displacement cu. in. (liter) | Engine Series Identification (VIN) | No. of Cylinders | Engine Type |
|---|---|---|---|---|---|
| 1990 | Grand Am | 138 (2.3) | D | 4 | DOHC |
| | Grand Am | 138 (2.3) | A | 4 | DOHC-HO |
| | Grand Am | 151 (2.5) | U | 4 | OHV |
| | Calais | 138 (2.3) | D | 4 | DOHC |
| | Calais | 138 (2.3) | A | 4 | DOHC-HO |
| | Calais | 151 (2.5) | U | 4 | OHV |
| | Calais | 204 (3.3) | N | 6 | OHV |
| | Skylark | 138 (2.3) | D | 4 | DOHC |
| | Skylark | 151 (2.5) | U | 4 | OHV |
| | Skylark | 204 (3.3) | N | 6 | OHV |
| 1991 | Grand Am | 138 (2.3) | D | 4 | DOHC |
| | Grand Am | 138 (2.3) | A | 4 | DOHC-HO |
| | Grand Am | 151 (2.5) | U | 4 | OHV |
| | Calais | 138 (2.3) | D | 4 | DOHC |
| | Calais | 138 (2.3) | A | 4 | DOHC-HO |
| | Calais | 151 (2.5) | U | 4 | OHV |
| | Calais | 204 (3.3) | N | 6 | OHV |
| | Skylark | 138 (2.3) | D | 4 | DOHC |
| | Skylark | 151 (2.5) | U | 4 | OHV |
| | Skylark | 204 (3.3) | N | 6 | OHV |
| 1992 | Grand Am | 138 (2.3) | 3 | 4 | SOHC |
| | Grand Am | 138 (2.3) | D | 4 | DOHC |
| | Grand Am | 138 (2.3) | A | 4 | DOHC-HO |
| | Grand Am | 151 (2.5) | U | 4 | OHV |
| | Achieva | 138 (2.3) | 3 | 4 | SOHC |
| | Achieva | 138 (2.3) | D | 4 | DOHC |
| | Achieva | 138 (2.3) | A | 4 | DOHC-HO |
| | Achieva | 151 (2.5) | U | 4 | OHV |
| | Achieva | 204 (3.3) | N | 6 | OHV |
| | Skylark | 138 (2.3) | 3 | 4 | SOHC |
| | Skylark | 138 (2.3) | D | 4 | DOHC |
| | Skylark | 151 (2.5) | U | 4 | OHV |
| | Skylark | 204 (3.3) | N | 6 | OHV |

DOHC—Double Overhead Cam
OHV—Overhead Valve
HO—High Output
SOHC—Single Overhead Cam

## ROUTINE MAINTENANCE

### Air Cleaner

The air cleaner keeps airborne dust and dirt from flowing into the engine. If allowed to enter the engine, dust and dirt combine with engine oil to create an abrasive compound which can drastically shorten engine life. Accordingly, the engine should never be run for a prolonged period without the air cleaner in place. A dirty air cleaner blocks the flow of air into the engine and can artificially richen the air/fuel mixture

## 10 GENERAL INFORMATION AND MAINTENANCE

### ISUZU 5-SPEED TRANSAXLE

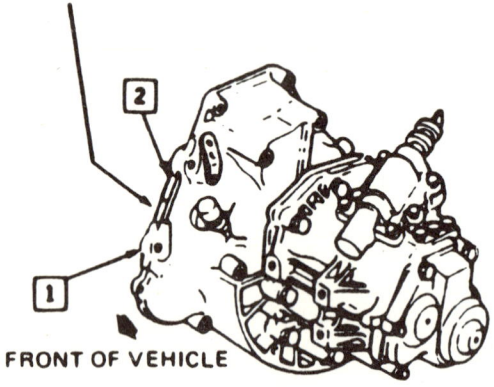

1. VIN LOCATION
2. OPTIONAL VIN LOCATION

Manual transaxle identification number and partial VIN location—Isuzu 76MM manual transaxle

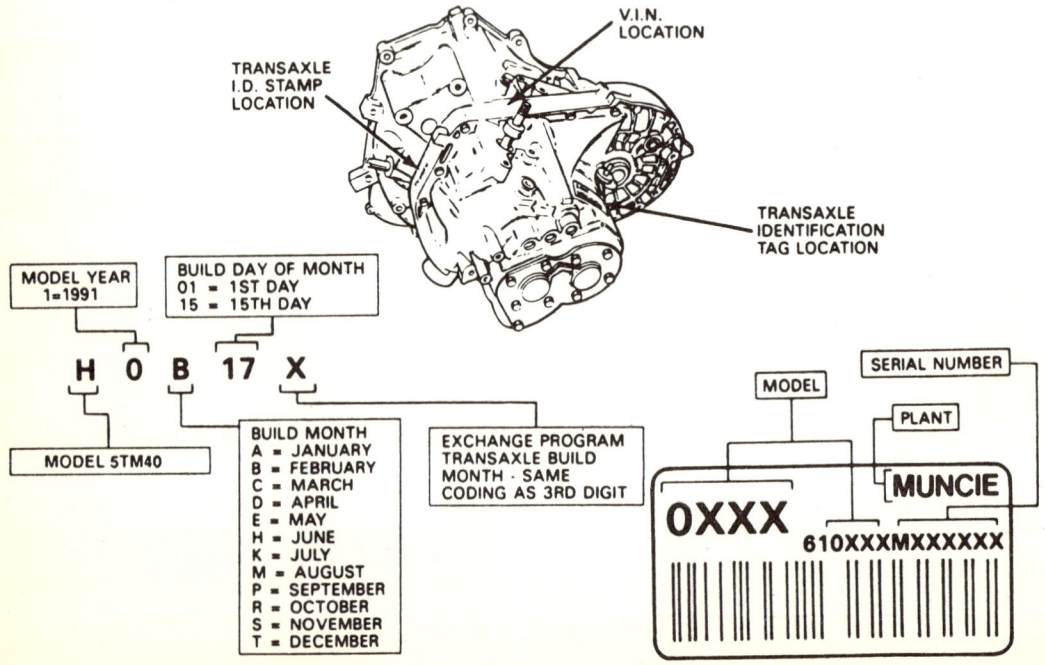

Manual transaxle identification number and partial VIN location—5T40 manual transaxle

## GENERAL INFORMATION AND MAINTENANCE

### TRANSAXLE IDENTIFICATION CHART

| Year | Engine Liter (cu. in.) | Manual 4-Spd. | Manual 5-Spd. | Automatic |
|---|---|---|---|---|
| 1987–89 | 2.0 (122) | — | HM-282 | 125C |
| 1988–89 | 2.3 (138) | — | HM-282 | |
| 1990–92 | 2.3 (138) | — | 5T40 | |
| 1988–89 | 2.3 (138) | — | — | 125C |
| 1990–92 | 2.3 (138) | — | — | 3T40 |
| 1985–92 | 2.5 (151) | | Isuzu 76 MM | |
| 1985–89 | 2.5 (151) | — | — | 125C |
| 1990–92 | 2.5 (151) | — | — | 3T40 |
| 1985–88 | 3.0 (181) | — | — | 125C |
| 1989 | 3.3 (204) | — | — | 125C |
| 1990–92 | 3.3 (204) | — | — | 3T40 |

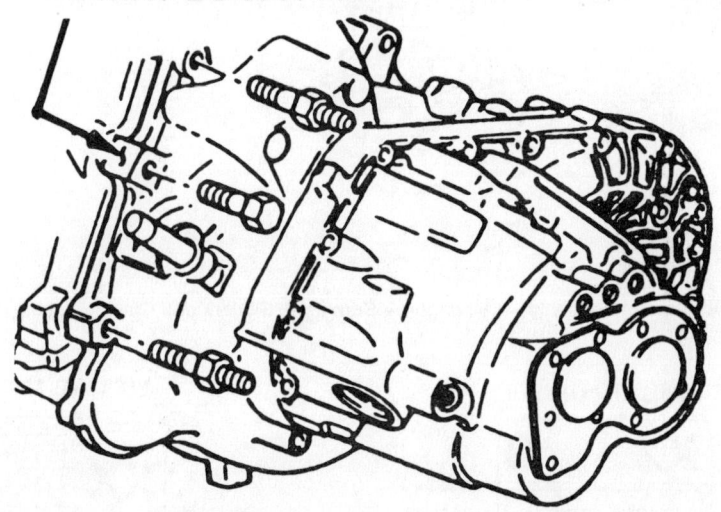

Manual transaxle identification number location—HM-282 manual transaxle

adversely affecting fuel economy and can even lead to damage to the catalytic converter.

The air cleaner should be checked periodically and replaced at least every 30,000 miles, more frequently in dusty driving conditions. Be sure the replacement air cleaner provides a proper fit and is not loose so that air is able to flow around the air cleaner instead of through it.

### REMOVAL AND INSTALLATION
#### 2.0L (VIN K and M), 2.5 (VIN U)

1. Remove the wing nut(s) and the air cleaner cover.

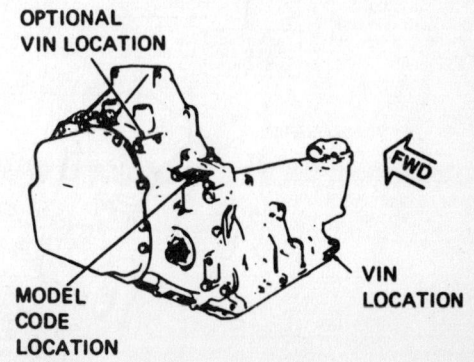

Automatic transaxle identification number location—125C automatic transaxle

## 12 GENERAL INFORMATION AND MAINTENANCE

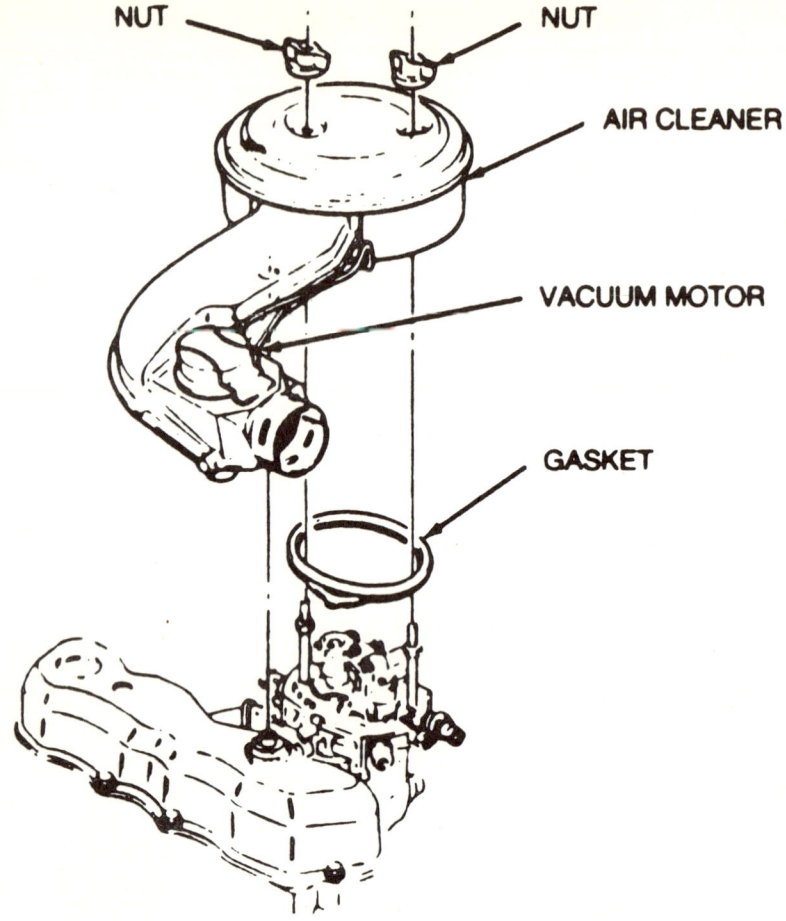

Air cleaner assembly—2.5L engine—Somerset, Skylark and Cutlass Calais

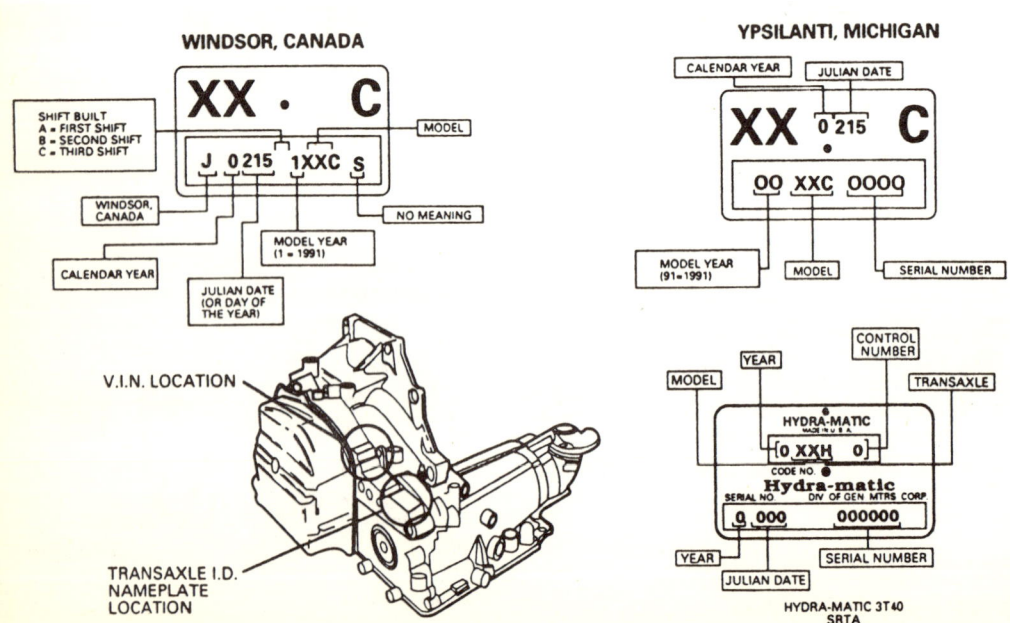

Automatic transaxle identification number and partial VIN location—3T40 automatic transaxle

## GENERAL INFORMATION AND MAINTENANCE 13

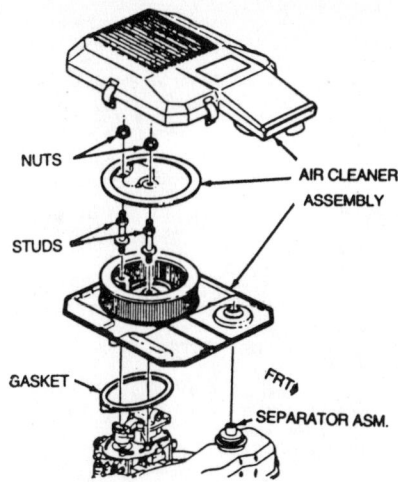

Air cleaner assembly—2.5L engine—Grand Am

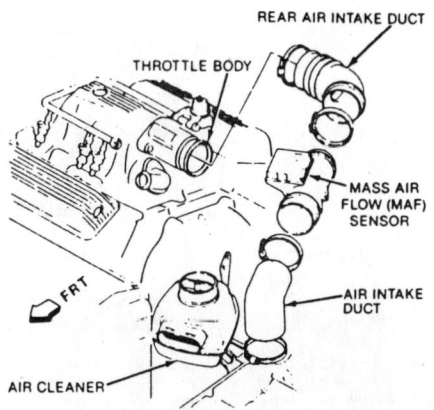

Air cleaner assembly—3.0L and 3.3L engines—Somerset and Skylark

2. Remove the old air cleaner element.
3. Wipe remaining dirt from the air cleaner housing.

**To install:**
4. Install the new air cleaner element
5. Install the air cleaner cover and wing nut(s).

### 2.3L (VIN D and A)

1. Remove the upper and lower duct clamps.
2. Disconnect the intake duct-to-oil/air separator hose.
3. Disconnect the air duct from the throttle body and air filter housing.
4. Remove the 2 hold-down clips on the air filter housing to cover and separate.
5. Remove the old air cleaner element and clean the air cleaner housing to remove remaining dirt.

**To install:**
6. Install the new air cleaner element into the air cleaner housing.
7. Install the air cleaner housing cover.
8. Install the 2 hold-down clips to the cover.
9. Connect the upper air filter duct with clamps to the air filter housing inlet and throttle body.
10. Connect the intake duct-to-oil/air separator hose.
11. Install the upper and lower duct clamps.

### 3.0L (VIN L) and 3.3L (VIN N)

1. Remove the air cleaner cover.
2. Remove the old air cleaner element
3. Wipe the inside of the air cleaner housing to remove dirt.

**To install:**
4. Install the new air cleaner element.
5. Install the air cleaner cover.

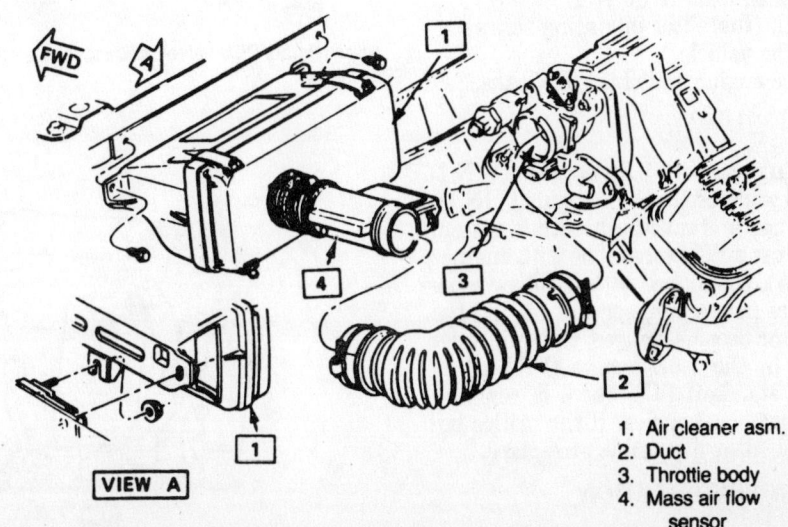

1. Air cleaner asm.
2. Duct
3. Throttle body
4. Mass air flow sensor

Air cleaner assembly—3.0L and 3.3L engines—Cutlass Calais

## 14 GENERAL INFORMATION AND MAINTENANCE

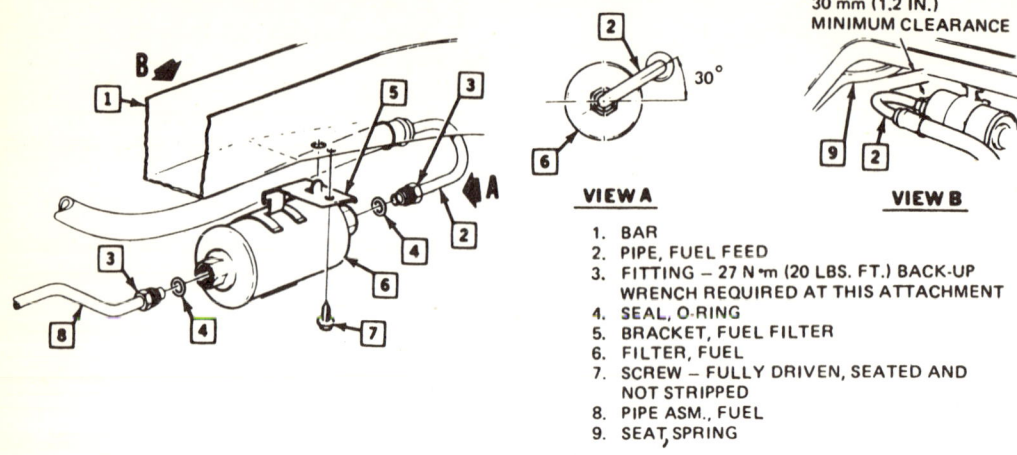

1. BAR
2. PIPE, FUEL FEED
3. FITTING – 27 N·m (20 LBS. FT.) BACK-UP WRENCH REQUIRED AT THIS ATTACHMENT
4. SEAL, O-RING
5. BRACKET, FUEL FILTER
6. FILTER, FUEL
7. SCREW – FULLY DRIVEN, SEATED AND NOT STRIPPED
8. PIPE ASM., FUEL
9. SEAT, SPRING

Fuel filter installation

## Fuel Filter

The fuel filter is located near the rear of the vehicle, forward of the fuel tank.

### REMOVAL AND INSTALLATION

1. Relieve the fuel system pressure.
2. Raise and safely support the vehicle.
3. Using a backup wrench, remove the fuel line fittings from the fuel filter.
4. Remove the fuel filter mounting screws and remove the filter from the vehicle.
5. Discard the fuel line O-rings.

**To install:**

6. Install new O-rings to the fuel line fittings.
7. Connect the fuel lines to the fuel filter.
8. Using a backup wrench, tighten the fuel lines to 20–22 ft. lbs. (27–30 Nm).
9. Install the fuel filter mounting screws.
10. Lower the vehicle.
11. Start the engine and check for leaks.

## PCV Valve

Vehicles equipped with 2.3L engines (VIN D and A) for all years or the 2.5L engine (VIN U) for 1991–92 use a crankcase breather system that does not use a PCV valve. The 2.3L engines (VIN D and A) are equipped with an oil/air separator that does not require service. Should the oil/air separator become clogged, the unit must be replaced. In the 2.5L engine (VIN U) in 1991–92 the standard PCV valve is replaced with a constant bleed orifice. If the orifice becomes clogged, clear if possible or replace.

### REMOVAL AND INSTALLATION

1. Remove the PCV valve from the grommet in the valve cover.

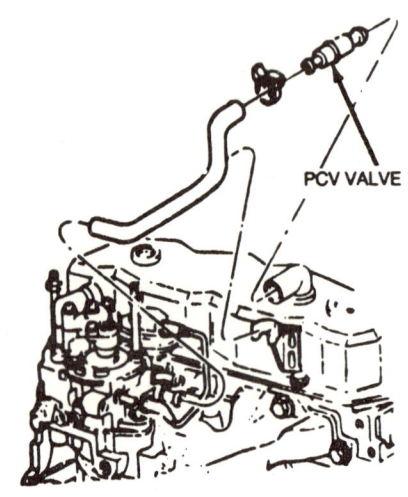

Approximate PCV valve/orifice location—2.0L and 2.5L engines

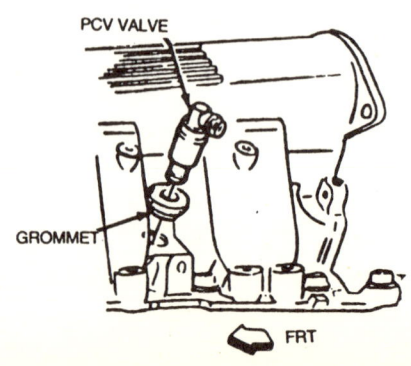

PCV valve location—3.0L and 3.3L engines

# GENERAL INFORMATION AND MAINTENANCE

2. Remove the PCV valve from the breather hose.

**To install:**

3. Install the new PCV valve into the breather hose.
4. Install the PCV valve into the grommet in the valve cover.

## Evaporative Canister

### REMOVAL AND Installation

1. Label and disconnect the hoses from the canister.
2. Remove the charcoal canister retaining nut.

1. TBI
2. Canister purge port
3. Vacuum signal
4. Purge valve
5. Vapor storage canister
6. Purge air
7. Fuel tank
8. Fuel
9. Vapor
10. Pressure-vacuum relief gas cap
11. Vent restrictor
12. Fuel tank vent
13. Purge line

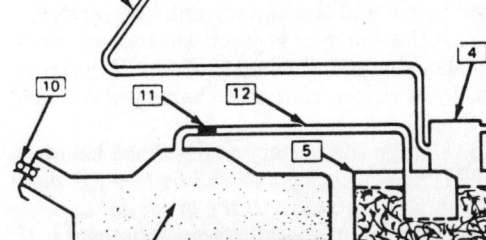

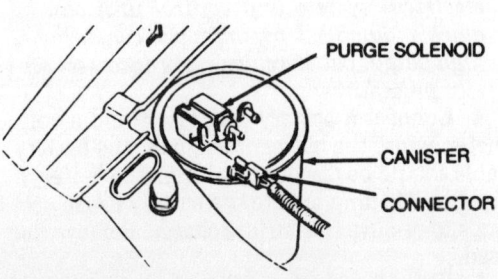

Typical TBI evaporative control system

3. Remove the canister from the vehicle.
4. Installation is the reverse of the removal procedure. Refer to the Vehicle Emission Control Information label, located in the engine compartment, for proper routing of the vacuum hoses.

## Battery

### GENERAL MAINTENANCE

Original equipment batteries are maintenance-free and do not require checking the electrolyte level. In fact, the cells are sealed on most batteries. As a result, there should be little or no build-up of corrosion on the battery posts, terminals or cables.

If equipped with a replacement battery that is not maintenance-free or has become corroded, proceed as follows.

### FLUID LEVEL

1. Remove the cell caps from the top of the battery.
2. Check the electrolyte level and add distilled water as necessary to bring the level up to the bottom of the cell filler opening. Some batteries have a fill level marking or a split ring inside the opening.
3. Replace the cell caps, making sure they are properly seated.
4. Wipe up any spilled electrolyte with a shop towel and dispose of the towel in case some of the electrolyte became mixed with the water and was absorbed by the towel.

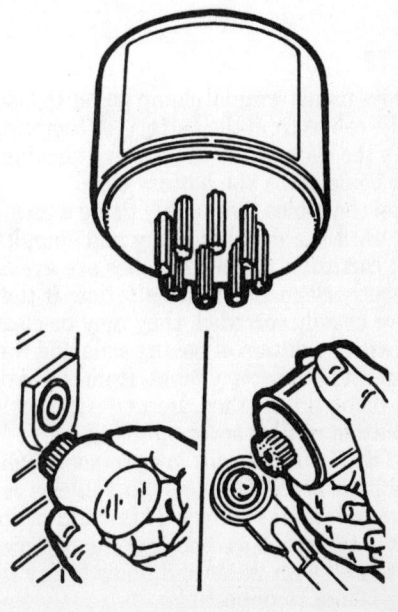

Special tool for cleaning side post battery terminals and clamps

# 16 GENERAL INFORMATION AND MAINTENANCE

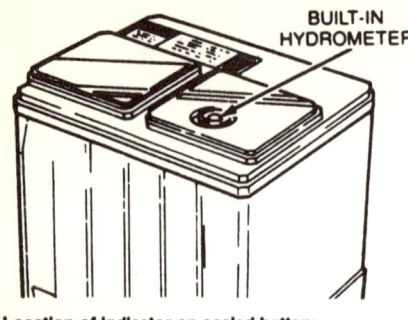

Location of indicator on sealed battery

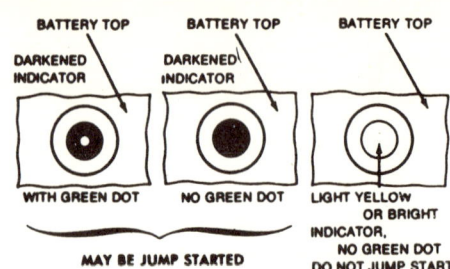

Check the appearance of the charge indicator on top of the battery before attempting a jump start; if it's not green or dark, do not jump start the car

Original equipment maintenance-free battery with built-in hydrometer

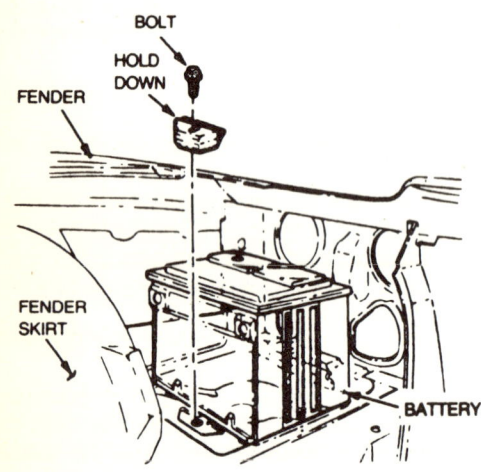

Typical battery installation

## CABLES

Always use a terminal clamp puller to disconnect the cables from the battery. Attempting to remove the clamp from the battery terminal by prying could crack the battery case.

Clean the cables thoroughly using a terminal brush until the metal is shiny and completely free of corrosion. Special brushes are available to properly clean side-post batteries. If the cables are heavily corroded, they may be cleaned using with a solution of baking soda and water. Disconnect both battery cables from the battery before using this method. Immerse the cable in the solution until it stops bubbling.

NOTE: *If the cell caps are removable, make sure none of the baking soda solution is allowed to enter the battery. This could neutralize the electrolyte and destroy the battery.*

Rinse well with water and allow to dry thoroughly before reconnecting.

Before reconnecting the cables, it is a good idea to remove the battery and inspect the condition of the battery tray. Remove any debris that may have collected under the battery. If the battery tray shows signs of corrosion, remove using a wire brush and apply a coat of acid-resistant paint to protect the tray.

After the cables have been reconnected, apply a thin coat of non-conductive grease to the terminal connection to retard corrosion.

### TESTING

Some maintenance-free batteries are equipped with a built-in hydrometer. To check the condition of the battery, observe the "eye" on the top of the battery case for the following conditions:

1. If the indicator is dark, the battery has enough fluid. If the eye is light, the electrolyte level is low and the battery must be replace.
2. If the indicator is green, the battery is sufficiently charged. Proceed to Step 4. If the green dot is not visible, charge the battery as outlined in Step 3.
3. Charge the battery as described below.

NOTE: *Do not charge the battery for more than 50 amp-hours. If the green dot appears or if the electrolyte squirts out of the vent hole, stop the charge and proceed to Step 4.*

It may be necessary to tip the battery from side-to-side in order to get the green dot to appear after charging.

WARNING: *When charging the battery, the electrical system and control unit can be quickly damaged by improper connections, high output battery chargers or incorrect service procedures.*

4. Connect a battery load tester and a voltmeter across the battery terminals (the battery cable should be disconnected from the battery). Apply a 300 amp load to the battery for 15 seconds to remove the surface charge. Remove the load.
5. Wait 15 seconds to allow the battery to recover. Apply the appropriate test load for 15

# GENERAL INFORMATION AND MAINTENANCE

## JUMP STARTING A DEAD BATTERY

The chemical reaction in a battery produces explosive hydrogen gas. This is the safe way to jump start a dead battery, reducing the chances of an accidental spark that could cause an explosion.

### Jump Starting Precautions

1. Be sure both batteries are of the same voltage.
2. Be sure both batteries are of the same polarity (have the same grounded terminal).
3. Be sure the vehicles are not touching.
4. Be sure the vent cap holes are not obstructed.
5. Do not smoke or allow sparks around the battery.
6. In cold weather, check for frozen electrolyte in the battery.
7. Do not allow electrolyte on your skin or clothing.
8. Be sure the electrolyte is not frozen.

### Jump Starting Procedure

1. Determine voltages of the two batteries; they must be the same.
2. Bring the starting vehicle close (they must not touch) so that the batteries can be reached easily.
3. Turn off all accessories and both engines. Put both cars in Neutral or Park and set the handbrake.
4. Cover the cell caps with a rag—do not cover terminals.
5. If the terminals on the run-down battery are heavily corroded, clean them.
6. Identify the positive and negative posts on both batteries and connect the cables in the order shown.
7. Start the engine of the starting vehicle and run it at fast idle. Try to start the car with the dead battery. Crank it for no more than 10 seconds at a time and let it cool off for 20 seconds in between tries.
8. If it doesn't start in 3 tries, there is something else wrong.
9. Disconnect the cables in the reverse order.
10. Replace the cell covers and dispose of the rags.

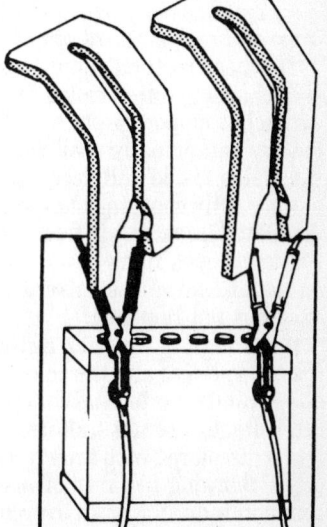

Side terminal batteries occasionally pose a problem when connecting jumper cables. There frequently isn't enough room to clamp the cables without touching sheet metal. Side terminal adaptors are available to alleviate this problem and should be removed after use.

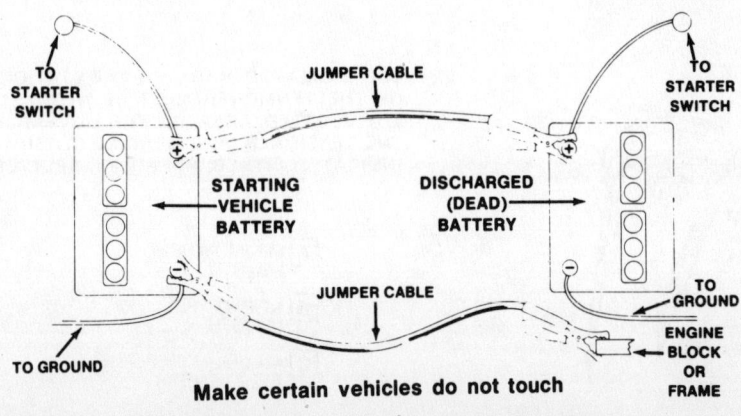

Make certain vehicles do not touch
This hook-up for negative ground cars only

# 18 GENERAL INFORMATION AND MAINTENANCE

seconds while reading the voltage. Disconnect the load.

6. Check the results against specifications. If the voltage is at or above the specified voltage for the temperature listed, the battery is good. If the voltage falls below specification, the battery should be replace.

## CHARGING

CAUTION: *Batteries give off hydrogen gas, which is explosive. DO NOT SMOKE around the battery while it is being charged. The battery electrolyte contains sulfuric acid. If any of the electrolyte should come in contact with the eyes or skin, flush with plenty of clear water and seek medical attention immediately.*

The best method for charging a battery is slow charging (often called "trickle charging"), with a low amperage charger. Quick charging a battery can actually cook the battery, damage the plates inside and decreasing the life of the battery. Any charging should be done in a well ventilated area away from the possibility of sparks or open flame. The cell caps (not found on maintenance-free batteries) should be loosened but not removed.

If the battery must be quick-charged, check the cell voltages and the color of the electrolyte a few minutes after the charge is begun. if the cell voltages are not uniform or if the electrolyte is discolored with brown sediment, stop the quick charging in favor of a trickle charge. A common indicator of an overcharged battery is the frequency need to add water to the battery.

## REPLACEMENT

If the battery is to be removed or replaced always disconnect the negative cable from the battery first using a battery clamp puller. Disconnect the positive cable next. Remove the battery hold-down clamp. Using a battery puller, remove the battery from the vehicle.

Charge the replacement battery, as required, using the slow charge method discussed above.

Inspect the battery terminals and cables, and service as required.

Install the battery into the vehicle and install the battery hold-down clamp, making sure not to overtighten the clamp. Overtightening the battery hold-down clamp could crack the battery case.

Connect the positive battery cable to the positive battery post and tighten the clamp.

NOTE: *Once the negative battery cable has been connected, do not go back to retighten the positive post. Since the electrical path is now complete, should you accidentally touch the body of the vehicle while touching the positive post an electrical short will occur.*

Connect the negative battery cable and tighten the clamp.

## Belts
### INSPECTION

Belt tension and condition should be checked at least every 30,000 miles or 24 month. Check

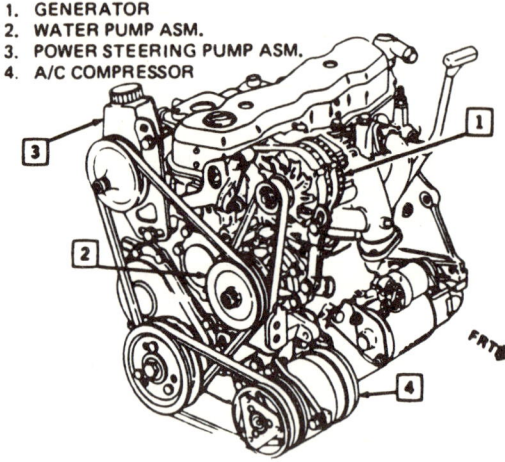

1. GENERATOR
2. WATER PUMP ASM.
3. POWER STEERING PUMP ASM.
4. A/C COMPRESSOR

**V-belt routing—2.5L engine**

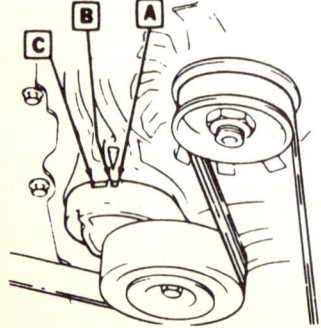

THE INDICATOR MARK ON THE STATIONARY PORTION OF THE TENSIONER MUST BE WITHIN THE LIMITS OF THE SLOTTED AREA ON THE MOVEABLE PORTION OF THE TENSIONER. ANY READING OUTSIDE THESE LIMITS INDICATES EITHER A FAULTY BELT OR TENSIONER.

A MINIMUM BELT LENGTH
B NORMAL BELT LENGTH
C MAXIMUM (REPLACE) BELT LENGTH

**Serpentine drive belt tensioner markings**

# GENERAL INFORMATION AND MAINTENANCE

the condition of both serpentine and V-belts for cracking, fraying and splitting on the inside of the belt.

A quick check for V-belt tension is to grasp the belt with the thumb and forefinger at the mid-point of the longest belt run and twist the belt. The belt should rotate no more than 90°. To properly check V-belt tension use a belt tension gauge and adjust to the specified tension.

Serpentine belts use a spring-loaded tensioner and do not need periodic adjustment.

## ADJUSTING

### V-Belt

1. Loosen the alternator mounting bolts.
2. Using a standard belt tension gauge, install it to the center of the longest span of the drive belt.
3. Use a medium prybar on the adjustment lug of the accessory (alternator, compressor or power steering pump) to adjust the belt tension to specification. Tighten the mounting and adjusting bolts.
4. Adjust the V-belts on the 2.5L (VIN U) engine as follows:
   - Alternator — 90–100 lbs. (41–45 kg) for a used belt or 165–175 lbs. (77–79 kg) for a new belt.
   - Power steering/coolant pumps — 90–100 lbs. (41–45 kg) for a used belt or 180 lbs. (81 kg) for a new belt.
   - Air conditioning compressor — 90–100 lbs. (41–45 kg) for a used belt or 165 lbs. (77 kg) for a new belt.

### Serpentine Belt

A single serpentine belt may be used to drive engine-mounted accessories. Drive belt tension is maintained by a spring loaded tensioner. The drive belt tensioner can control belt tension over a broad range of belt lengths, however, there are limits to the tensioner's ability to compensate.

A belt squeak when the engine in started or stopped is normal and does not necessarily indicate a worn belt. If the squeak persists or worsens, inspect the belt for wear and replace as necessary.

1. Inspect the tensioner markings to see if the belt is within operating lengths. Replace the belt if the belt is excessively worn or is outside of the tensioner's operating range.
2. Run the engine until operating temperature is reached. Be sure all accessories are off. Turn the engine off and read the belt tension using a belt tension gauge tool placed halfway between the alternator and the air conditioning compressor. If not equipped with air conditioning, read the tension between the power steering pump and crankshaft pulley. Remove the tool.
3. Run the engine for 15 seconds and turn it off. Using a box-end wrench, apply clockwise force to tighten to the tensioner pulley bolt. Release the force and immediately take a tension reading without disturbing belt tensioner position.
4. Using the same wrench, apply a counterclockwise force to the tensioner pulley bolt and raise the pulley to its fully raised position. Slowly lower the pulley to engage the belt. Take a tension reading without disturbing the belt tensioner position.
5. Average the 3 readings. If their average is lower than specifications, replace the tensioner:
   - 2.0L and 2.3L engines — 50 lbs. (23 kg)
   - 3.0L engine — 79 lbs. (36 kg)
   - 3.3L engine — 67 lbs. (30 kg)

## REMOVAL AND INSTALLATION

### V-belt

1. Loosen the accessory-to-mounting bracket bolt(s) and adjusting bolt.
2. Rotate the accessory to relieve the belt tension.
3. Slip the drive belt from the accessory pulley and remove it from the engine.

NOTE: *If the engine uses more than 1 belt, it may be necessary to remove belts that are in front of the belt being removed.*

**To install:**

4. Place the new belt over the crankshaft or drive pulley and stretch over the driven (accessory) pulley.
5. If removed, install the other belts in the same way.
6. Adjust the belts to the proper tension.
7. Tighten the adjusting and mounting bolts.

[A] ROTATE TENSIONER IN DIRECTION OF ARROW TO REMOVE OR INSTALL BELT

**Serpentine belt routing—2.3L engine**

## 20  GENERAL INFORMATION AND MAINTENANCE

### Serpentine Belt

1. Insert a ½ in. drive breaker bar into the adjuster arm on the tensioner pulley. Later models require an 18mm box end wrench.

NOTE: *Make sure the drive end of the breaker bar is long enough to fully seat in the tensioner pulley and that both the breaker bar and box wrench are long enough to provide the proper leverage.*

2. Rotate the tensioner to the left (counterclockwise) and remove the belt.
3. Slowly rotate the tensioner to the right (clockwise) to release the tension.

**To install:**

4. Route the belt over the pulleys following the diagram found in the engine compartment.
5. Rotate the tensioner to the left (counterclockwise) and install the belt over the remaining pulley.
6. Inspect the belt positioning over each pulley to ensure the belt is seated properly in all the grooves.

### Hoses

The hoses should be checked for deterioration, leaks and loose hose clamps every 12,000 miles or 12 months.

#### REMOVAL AND INSTALLATION

1. Drain the cooling system into a clean container to a level that is below the hose being removed. Save the coolant for reuse.
2. Loosen the hose clamps.

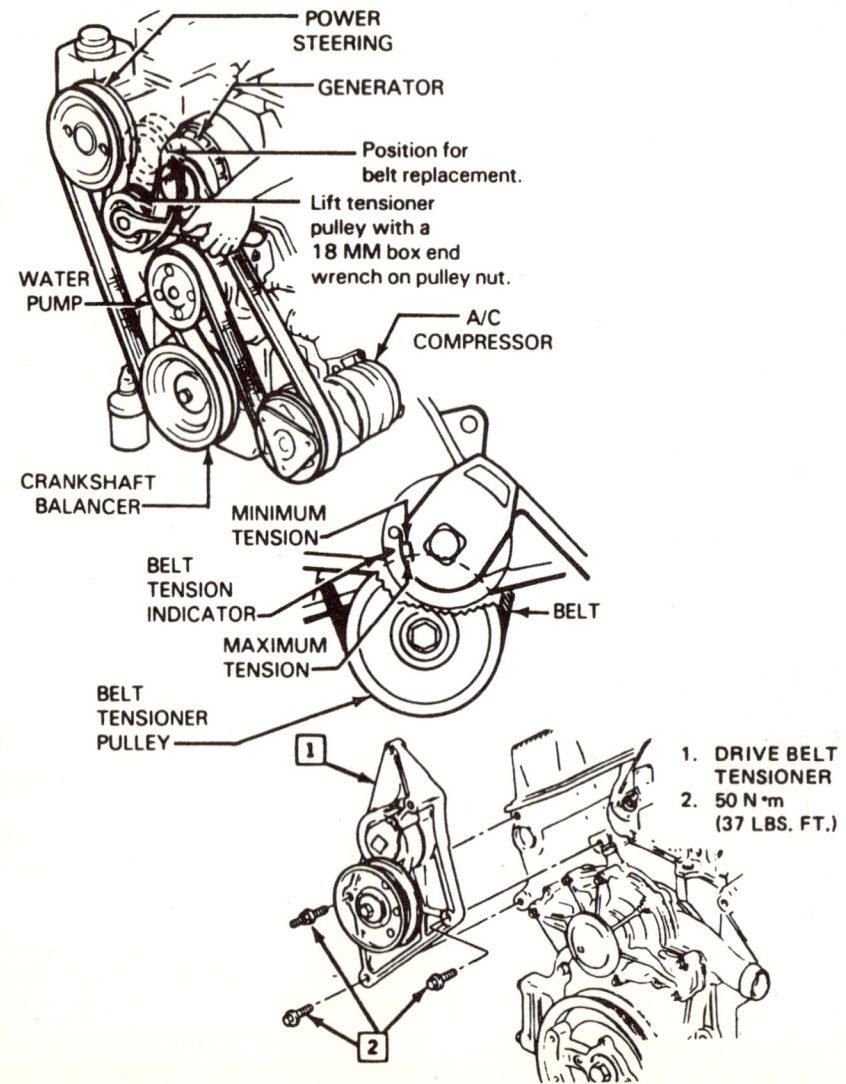

**Serpentine belt routing and tensioner installation—3.0L and 3.3L engines**

## GENERAL INFORMATION AND MAINTENANCE 21

## HOW TO SPOT WORN V-BELTS

V-Belts are vital to efficient engine operation—they drive the fan, water pump and other accessories. They require little maintenance (occasional tightening) but they will not last forever. Slipping or failure of the V-belt will lead to overheating. If your V-belt looks like any of these, it should be replaced.

**Cracking or weathering**

This belt has deep cracks, which cause it to flex. Too much flexing leads to heat build-up and premature failure. These cracks can be caused by using the belt on a pulley that is too small. Notched belts are available for small diameter pulleys.

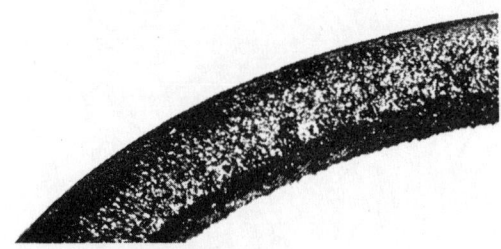

**Softening (grease and oil)**

Oil and grease on a belt can cause the belt's rubber compounds to soften and separate from the reinforcing cords that hold the belt together. The belt will first slip, then finally fail altogether.

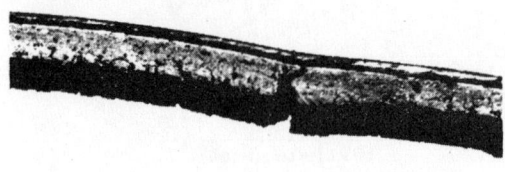

**Glazing**

Glazing is caused by a belt that is slipping. A slipping belt can cause a run-down battery, erratic power steering, overheating or poor accessory performance. The more the belt slips, the more glazing will be built up on the surface of the belt. The more the belt is glazed, the more it will slip. If the glazing is light, tighten the belt.

**Worn cover**

The cover of this belt is worn off and is peeling away. The reinforcing cords will begin to wear and the belt will shortly break. When the belt cover wears in spots or has a rough jagged appearance, check the pulley grooves for roughness.

**Separation**

This belt is on the verge of breaking and leaving you stranded. The layers of the belt are separating and the reinforcing cords are exposed. It's just a matter of time before it breaks completely.

## 22 GENERAL INFORMATION AND MAINTENANCE

3. Disconnect the inlet hose from the radiator and thermostat housing.
4. Disconnect the outlet hose from the radiator and coolant pump or cylinder block.

**To install:**

NOTE: *If installing original equipment hoses, make sure to align the reference marks on the hose with the marks on the radiator. A twist in the hose will place a strain on the radiator fitting and could cause the fitting to crack or break.*

5. Connect the outlet hose to the radiator and coolant pump or cylinder block.
6. Connect the radiator hose to the radiator and thermostat.
7. Refill the cooling system to a level just below the filler neck. Install the radiator cap.

NOTE: *The cooling systems on later models may use a surge tank instead of an overflow bottle. The overflow bottle has 1 small hose coming from the radiator filler neck. The*

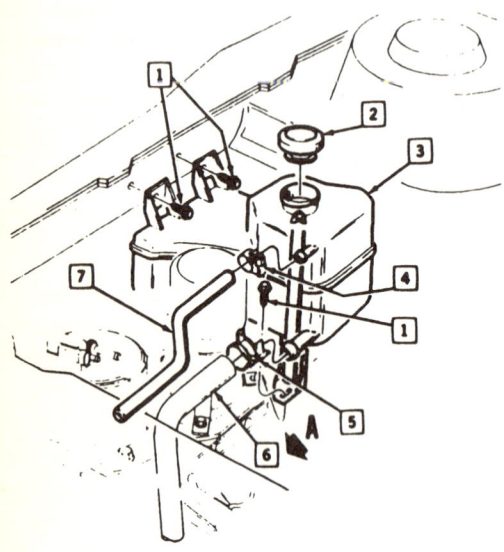

1. BOLT/SCREW – 4 N·m (35 LBS. IN.)
2. SURGE TANK CAP
3. SURGE TANK
4. CLAMP
5. CLAMP, SPRING
6. HOSE ASM., OUTLET
7. HOSE ASM., INLET

**Radiator surge tank and hose installation—2.3L engine**

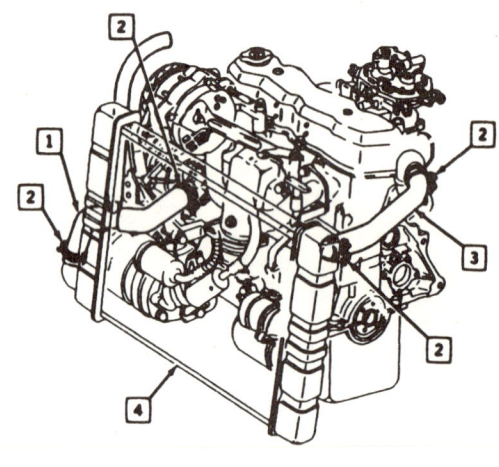

1. HOSE ASM., OUTLET
2. CLAMP
3. HOSE, INLET
4. RADIATOR

**Coolant hose locations—2.5L engine**

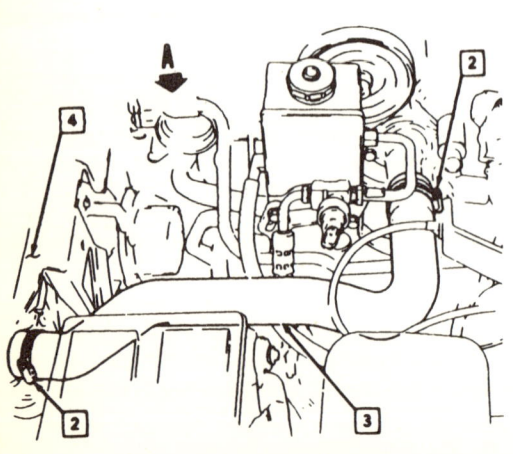

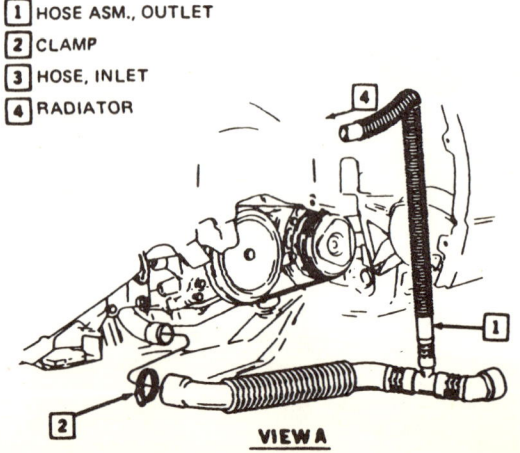

1. HOSE ASM., OUTLET
2. CLAMP
3. HOSE, INLET
4. RADIATOR

**Coolant hose locations—2.3L engine**

## GENERAL INFORMATION AND MAINTENANCE

## HOW TO SPOT BAD HOSES

Both the upper and lower radiator hoses are called upon to perform difficult jobs in an inhospitable environment. They are subject to nearly 18 psi at under hood temperatures often over 280°F., and must circulate nearly 7500 gallons of coolant an hour—3 good reasons to have good hoses.

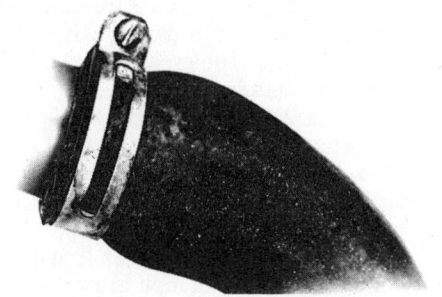

**Swollen hose**

A good test for any hose is to feel it for soft or spongy spots. Frequently these will appear as swollen areas of the hose. The most likely cause is oil soaking. This hose could burst at any time, when hot or under pressure.

**Cracked hose**

Cracked hoses can usually be seen but feel the hoses to be sure they have not hardened; a prime cause of cracking. This hose has cracked down to the reinforcing cords and could split at any of the cracks.

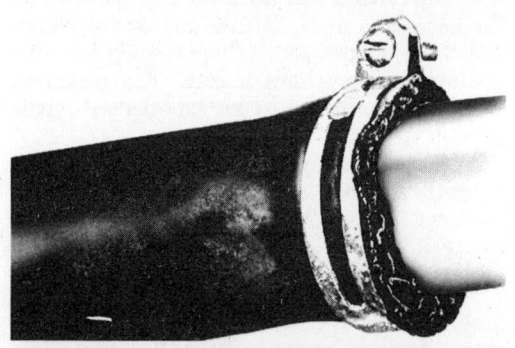

**Frayed hose end (due to weak clamp)**

Weakened clamps frequently are the cause of hose and cooling system failure. The connection between the pipe and hose has deteriorated enough to allow coolant to escape when the engine is hot.

**Debris in cooling system**

Debris, rust and scale in the cooling system can cause the inside of a hose to weaken. This can usually be felt on the outside of the hose as soft or thinner areas.

surge tank can be recognized by the presence of 2 hoses, 1 from the radiator cap and 1 outlet to the lower radiator hose. The surge tank is also mounted above the level of the radiator cap, making it the highest point in the cooling system.

8. If equipped with an overflow bottle, perform the following:

  a. Fill the overflow bottle to the "Full Hot" mark.

  b. Start the engine and allow to come to normal operating temperature.

  c. Stop the engine and refill the overflow bottle to the "Full Hot" mark.

  d. Check the coolant level frequently over the next couple of days.

9. If equipped with a surge tank, perform the following:

  a. Fill the surge tank to the base of the filler neck.

  b. Install the pressure cap on the surge tank. Start the engine and allow to come to normal operating temperature or until the upper radiator hose is hot.

  c. Stop the engine and check the level of coolant in the surge tank. If the level is not above the "full" line, allow the engine to cool enough to slowly remove the pressure cap.

  d. Add coolant to bring the level up to the "full" line.

  e. Install the pressure cap. Make sure the arrows on the cap line up with the overflow hose.

## Air Conditioning System

### SAFETY WARNINGS

The refrigerant used in this air conditioning system must not be discharged into the air. Discharging and refilling the refrigerant can only be done properly with approved freon recovery and evacuation equipment. Since this is specialized equipment not normally available outside a professional repair facility, air conditioning service that requires discharging the freon is considered beyond the scope of this book. If it is necessary to remove a component from the air conditioning system, have the system properly discharged at a shop that has recovery equipment. Working around automotive air conditioning systems requires a great deal of care due to the nature of the refrigerant and the system pressures, both operating and static. Review the safety precautions listed below carefully.

• DO NOT attempt to discharge the system by merely loosening a fitting or opening a service valve. If you do not have an approved R-12 Recovery/Recycling machine to remove the refrigerant refrigerant, the system properly discharged at a shop that has refrigerant recovery equipment.

• ALWAYS wear protective goggles when connecting or disconnecting any fitting of the refrigerant system. Even a discharged system may still have some slight pressure. refrigerant contacting the eyes could freeze the eyes causing permanent eye damage. If refrigerant should contact the eyes, seek medical attention immediately.

• Avoid contact with a charged refrigeration system when working on other parts of the vehicle. If a heavy tool or sharp object should come in contact with a section of the tubing or heat exchanger, a rupture could occur.

• Work in a well ventilated area free of open flame or other source of high heat. If a refrigerant leak occurs, do not run the engine. If refrigerant contacts open flame or is drawn into a running engine, deadly phosgene gas will be produced.

• Always have the system discharged if the vehicle is to be painted using a baked-on finish or before welding anywhere near the refrigerant lines.

### SYSTEM INSPECTION
#### Checking For Oil Leaks

Refrigerant leaks show up as oily areas on the various components because the compressor oil is transported through the entire system along with the refrigerant. Look for oily spots on all the hoses and lines, fittings and on the clutch end of the compressor. If there are oily deposits, the system may have a leak. The diagnosis should be confirmed by an experienced repair person.

NOTE: *A small area of oil on the front of the compressor is normal and no cause for alarm.*

#### Checking The Compressor Belt

Refer to the Belts portion of this Chapter. Beginning in 1987, except for the 2.5L (VIN U), a serpentine belt is used to drive all engine accessories. The tension is maintained automatically and no adjustment is needed.

#### Keep The Condenser Clear

Periodically, inspect the front of the condenser for bent fins or foreign matter, such as dirt, leaves, cigarette butts, etc. Straighten bent fins carefully using the edge of a small slotted screwdriver or purchase a coil comb. Remove any debris by first directing water from a hose through the back of the condenser fins. Avoid using a hose with excessive water pressure. Remove the remaining debris with a stiff bristle brush (not a wire brush).

## GENERAL INFORMATION AND MAINTENANCE

**Operate The System Periodically**

This step is accomplished automatically in later model vehicles due to the fact that the compressor is automatically engaged when the defrost mode is selected. In the colder weather, be sure to run the defroster for at least 5 minutes, once a week to make sure the refrigerant and, especially, the lubricant are circulated completely.

### REFRIGERANT LEVEL CHECKS

Neither the CCOT (Cycling Clutch Orifice Tube) nor VDOT (Variable Displacement Orifice Tube) air conditioning system uses a sight glass to indicate the refrigerant level. The level must be determined indirectly, using a set of manifold gauges.

1. Connect the manifold gauges to the system. Start the engine and run the air conditioning system. Observe the gauge pressures. if the air conditioner is working properly, the pressures will fall within the specifications shown in the performance chart.
2. Cycle the air conditioner **ON** and **OFF** to make sure you are seeing actual pressures in the system. Turn the system **OFF** and watch the manifold gauges. If there is refrigerant in the system, you should see the low side pressure rise and the high side pressure fall during the **OFF** cycle. If the system pressures are fluctuating when the compressor cycles and the operating pressure is within specification and the system is delivering cool air, everything is functioning normally.
3. If you observe low pressures on the high and low sides while the system is operating the system may be low on refrigerant.

## Windshield Wipers

Intense heat from the sun, snow and ice, road oils and the chemicals used in windshield washer solvents combine to deteriorate the rubber wiper refills. The refills should be replaced about twice a year or whenever the blades begin to streak or chatter.

For maximum effectiveness and longest element life, the windshield and wiper blades should be kept clean. Dirt, tree sap, road tar and so on will cause streaking, smearing and blade deterioration if left on the glass. It is advisable to wash the windshield carefully with a commercial glass cleaner at least once a month. Wipe off the rubber blades with the wet rag afterwards. Do not attempt to move the wipers by hand as damage to the motor and drive mechanism will result.

If the blades are found to be cracked, broken or torn, they should be replaced immediately. Replacement intervals will vary with usage, although ozone deterioration usually limits blade life to about 1 year at the maximum. If the wiper pattern is smeared or streaked, or if the blade chatters across the glass, the elements should be replaced. It is easiest and most sensible to replace the elements in pairs.

There are 3 different types of refills, which differ in their method of replacement. One type has 2 release buttons, approximately 1/3 of the way up from each end of the blade frame. Pushing the buttons down releases a lock and allows the rubber filler to be removed from the frame. The new blade slides back into the frame and locks into place.

The second type of refill has 2 metal tabs which are unlocked by squeezing them together. The rubber blade can then be withdrawn from the frame jaws. A new refill is installed by inserting the refill into the front frame jaws and sliding it rearward to engage the remaining frame jaws. There are usually 4 jaws. Be certain when installing that the refill is engaged in all of them. At the end of its travel, the tabs will lock into place on the front jaws of the wiper blade frame.

The third type is a refill made from polycarbonate. The refill has a simple locking device at 2 end which flexes downward out of the groove into which the jaws of the holder fit, allowing easy release. By sliding the new refill through all the jaws and pushing through the slight resistance when it reaches the end of its travel, the refill will lock into position.

Regardless of the type of refill used, make sure that all of the frame jaws are engaged as the refill is pushed into place and locked. The metal blade holder and frame will scratch the glass if allowed to touch it.

### WIPER REFILL REPLACEMENT

Normally, if the wipers are not cleaning the windshield properly, only the refill has to be replaced. The blade and arm usually require replacement only in the event of damage. It is only necessary to remove the arm or blade to replace the refill (except on Tridon® refills). The job may be made easier by turning the ignition switch to the **ON** position, then turn the wiper switch **ON**. When the wiper arms reach the center of the windshield, turn the ignition switch to the **OFF** position.

There are several types of refills and your vehicle could have any kind, since aftermarket blades and arms may not use exactly the same type of refill as the original equipment.

The original equipment wiper elements can be replaced as follows:

1. Lift the wiper arm off the glass.
2. Depress the release lever on the center bridge and remove the blade from the arm.

# 26 GENERAL INFORMATION AND MAINTENANCE

### TRICO
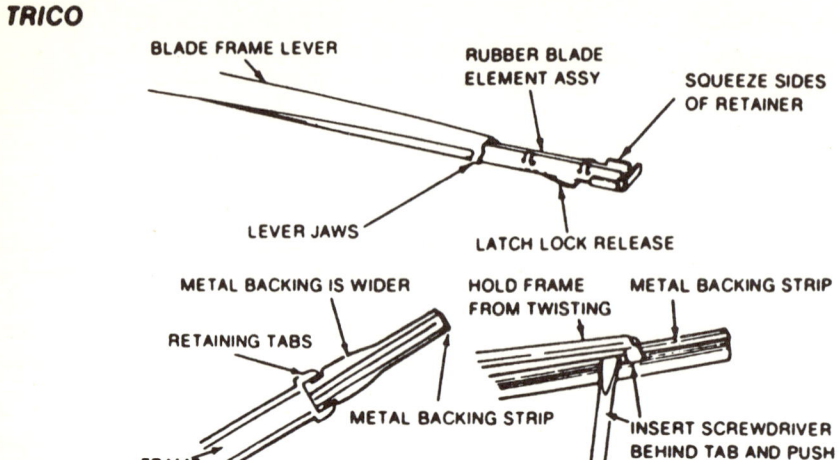

### ANCO
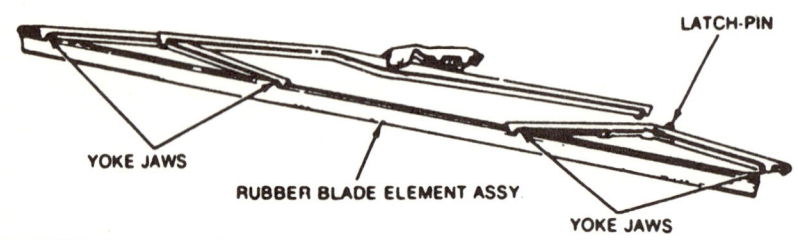

### POLYCARBONATE
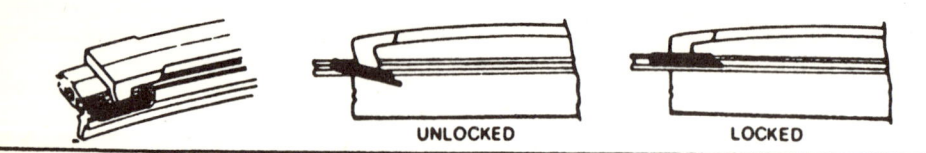

### TRIDON
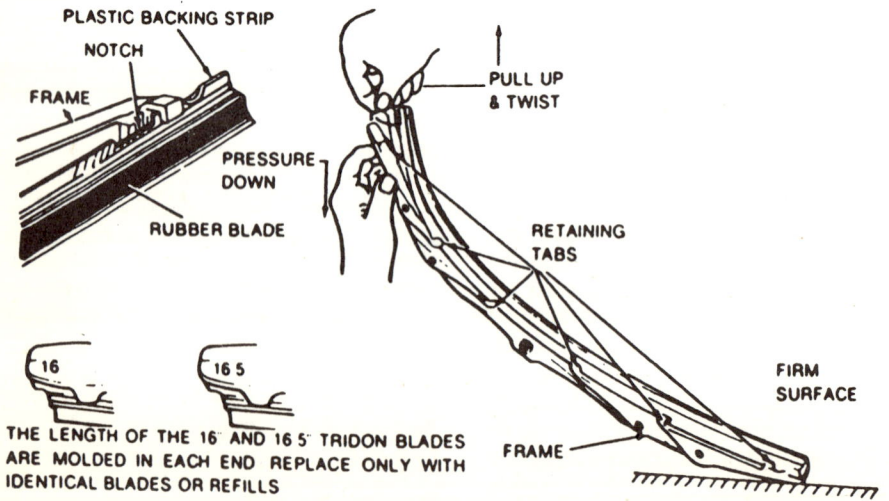

**Wiper insert replacement**

# GENERAL INFORMATION AND MAINTENANCE

3. Lift the tab and pinch the end bridge to release it from the center bridge.
4. Slide the end bridge from the wiper blade and the wiper blade from the opposite end bridge.
5. Install a new element and be sure the tab on the end bridge is down to lock the element into place. Check each release point for positive engagement.

## Tires and Wheels

### TIRE ROTATION

Tire wear can be equalized by switching the position of the tires at 6000 miles for new tires and then every 15,000 miles. Including a conventional spare in the rotation pattern can give up to 20% more life to a set of tires.

CAUTION: *DO NOT include the temporary use spare in the rotation pattern.*

There are certain exceptions to tire rotation, however. Studded snow tires should not be rotated. Radials should be kept on the same side of the vehicle (maintain the same direction or rotation). The belts on radial tires develop a set pattern. If the direction of rotation is reversed, it can cause a rough ride and vibration.

NOTE: *When radials or studded snows are removed for the season, mark them so they can be reinstalled on the same side of the vehicle.*

### TIRE DESIGN

For maximum service life tires should be used in sets of five, except on vehicles equipped with a space-saver spare tire. Do not mix tires of different designs, such as steel belted radial, fiberglass belted or bias/belted, or tires of different sizes, such as P165SR-14 and P185SR-14.

Conventional bias ply tires are constructed so that the cords run bead-to-bead at an angle (bias). Alternate plies run at an opposite angle. This type of construction gives rigidity to both tread and sidewall. Bias/belted tires are similar in construction to conventional bias ply tires. Belts run at an angel and also at a 90° angle to the bead, as in the radial tire. Tread life in improved considerably over the conventional bias tire. The radial tire differs in construction, but instead of the carcass plies running at an angle of 90° to each other, they run at an angle of 90° to the bead. This gives the tread a great deal of rigidity and the sidewall a great deal of flexibility and accounts for the characteristic bulge associated with radial tires.

All General Motors vehicles are capable of using radial tires and they are the recommended

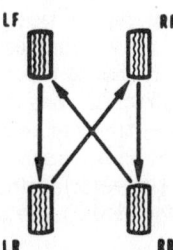

RECOMMENDED ROTATION PATTERN FOR FRONT WHEEL DRIVE CARS

DO NOT INCLUDE "TEMPORARY USE ONLY" SPARE TIRE IN ROTATION

**Possible tire rotation pattern**

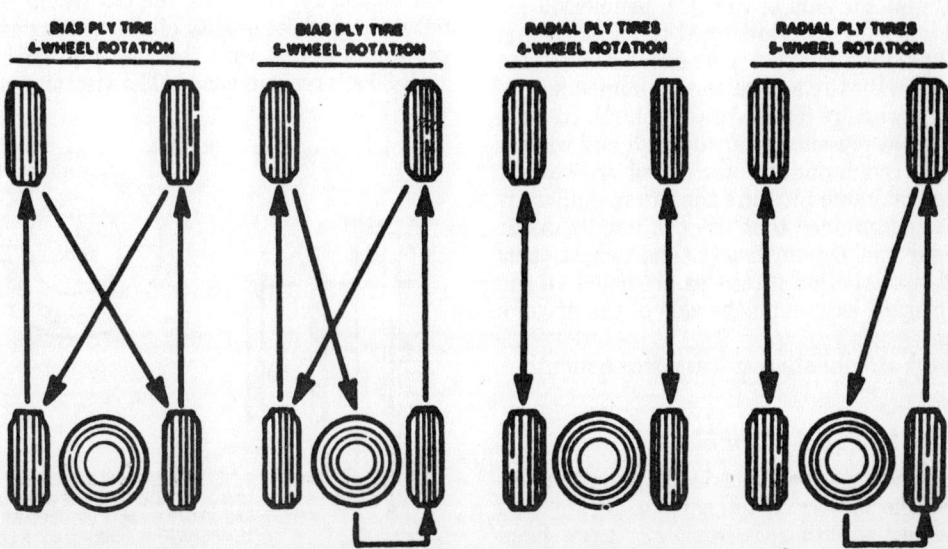

Tire rotation patterns; note that some manufacturers recommend that radials not be cross-switched

# GENERAL INFORMATION AND MAINTENANCE

type for all years. If radial tires are used, tires sizes and wheel diameters should be selected to maintain ground clearance and tire load capacity equivalent to the minimum specified tire. Radial tires should always be used in sets of 5 if the spare is a conventional tire. In an emergency, radial tires can be used with caution on the rear axle only. If this is done, both tires on the rear should be of radial design.

NOTE: *Radial tires should never be used on only the front axle as they can adversely effect steering if tires of different designs are mixed.*

## TIRE STORAGE

Store the tires at the proper inflation pressures, if they are mounted. All tires should be stored in a cool, dry place. If the tires are stored in a garage or basement, DO NOT, let them stand on a concrete floor. Instead, set them on blocks of wood.

## TIRE INFLATION

Factory installed wheels and tires are designed to handle loads up to and including their rated load capacity when inflated to the recommended inflation pressures. Correct tire pressure and driving techniques have an important influence on tire life. Heavy cornering, excessively rapid acceleration and unnecessary braking increase tire wear. Underinflated tires can cause handling problems, poor fuel economy, shortened tire life and tire overloading.

Maximum axle load must never exceed the value shown on the side of the tire. The inflation pressure should never exceed the value shown on the side of the tire, usually 35 psi (241kpa) for conventional tires or 60 psi (414kpa) for a compact spare tire. The pressure shown on the tire is NOT the recommended operating pressure for the tire or vehicle. In most cases, that pressure is far too high and will result in a rough ride and accelerated tire wear. It is the maximum pressure the tire manufacturer has determined that tire can handle under extreme load circumstances. The correct operating tire inflation pressures are listed on the tire placard located on the side of the driver's door.

Check tire inflation at least once a month.

## CARE OF SPECIAL WHEELS

If the vehicle is equipped with aluminum alloy wheels, be very careful when using any type of cleaner on either the wheels or tires. Read the label on the package of the cleaner to make sure that it will not damage aluminum.

## FLUIDS AND LUBRICANTS

### Fuel and Engine Oil Recommendations

*FUEL*

NOTE: *Some fuel additives contain chemicals that can damage the catalytic converter and/or oxygen sensor. Read all of the labels carefully before using any additive in the engine or fuel system.*

All engines require the use of unleaded fuel only. The octane rating required will vary according to the compression ratio of the engine. For the most part, if the compression ration is 9.0:1 or lower, the vehicle will perform satisfactorily on regular unleaded gasoline. If the compression ratio is greater than 9.0:1, premium unleaded is required. Check the owner's manual for specific guidelines for the engine in your vehicle.

Fuel should be selected for the brand and octane which performs best in your engine. Judge a gasoline by its ability to prevent ping, its engine starting capabilities (both cold and hot) and general all weather performance.

In general, choose the octane the manufacturer recommends. Regardless of the claims made by advertisers as to the improved performance delivered by the use of premium fuel, in most cases the vehicle runs best on the octane fuel recommended by the manufacturer.

*OIL*

Use only SG/CC, SG/CD, SF, SG, CC rated oils of the recommended viscosity. Under the classification system developed by the American Petroleum Institute, the SG rating designates the highest quality oil for use in passenger vehicles. Oils with the viscosity 5W-30 or 10W-30 are recommended. The viscosity of the

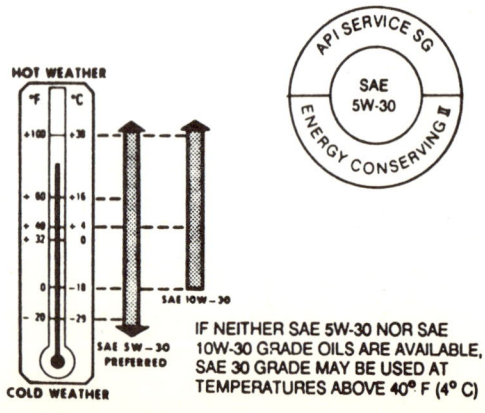

Oil viscosity chart

## GENERAL INFORMATION AND MAINTENANCE

engine oil has an effect on fuel economy and cold weather operation (starting and oil flow). Lower viscosity oil can provide better fuel economy and cold weather performance, however higher temperature weather conditions require higher viscosity engine oils for satisfactory lubrication.

Choose your oil with regard to the anticipated temperatures during the period before the next oil change. Using the accompanying chart, choose the oil viscosity of the lowest expected temperature.

### Engine
*OIL LEVEL CHECK*

The engine oil level is checked using the dipstick.

NOTE: *The oil should be checked before the engine is started or 5 minutes after the engine has been shut OFF. This gives the oil time to drain back into the oil pan and prevents an inaccurate oil level reading.*

Remove the dipstick from its tube, wipe it clean and insert it back into the tube all the way. Remove it again and observe the oil level. It should be maintained between the Full and Add marks without going above the Full or below the Add marks.

WARNING: *DO NOT overfill the crankcase. It may result in oil-fouled spark plugs, oil leaks cause by oil seal failure or engine damage due to oil foaming.*

*OIL AND FILTER CHANGE*

The manufacturer's recommended oil change interval is 7500 miles under normal operating conditions. We recommend an oil change interval of 3000–3500 miles under normal conditions; more frequently under severe conditions such as when the average trip is less than 4 miles, the engine is operated for extended periods at idle or low-speed, when towing a trailer or operating is dusty areas.

In addition, we recommend that the filter be replaced EVERY time the oil is changed.

NOTE: *Please be considerate of the environment. Dispose of waste oil properly by taking it to a service station, municipal facility or recycling center.*

1. Run the engine until it reaches normal operating temperature.
2. Raise and safely support the front of the vehicle using jackstands.
3. Slide a drain pan of at least 5 quarts capacity under the oil pan.
4. Loosen the drain plug. Turn it out by hand by keeping an inward pressure on the plug as you unscrew it. This will prevent hot oil from escaping past the threads until the plug is completely out of the threads.
5. Allow the oil to drain completely and then reinstall the drain plug. Do not overtighten the plug.
6. Using an oil filter wrench, remove the oil filter. Be aware, that the filter contains about 1 quart of hot, dirty oil.
7. Empty the old oil filter into the drain pan and dispose of the filter properly.
8. Using a clean shop towel, wipe off the filter adapter on the engine block. Be sure the towel does not leave any lint which could clog an oil passage.
9. Coat the rubber gasket on the new filter with fresh oil. Spin the filter onto the adapter by hand until it contacts the mounting surface. Tighten the filter ¾ to 1 full turn.
10. Refill the crankcase with the specified amount of engine oil.
11. Crank the engine over several times, then start it. After approximately 3–5 seconds, if the pressure gauge shows zero or the oil pressure warning indicator fails to go out, shut the engine OFF and investigate the problem.
12. If the oil pressure is OK and there are no leaks, shut the engine OFF and lower the vehicle.
13. Wait for a few minutes and check the oil level. Add oil, as necessary, to bring the level up to the **FULL** mark.

### Manual Transaxle
*FLUID RECOMMENDATIONS*

The recommended fluid is synchromesh transaxle fluid. The manual transaxle fluid does not require changing.

*LEVEL CHECK*

Check fluid level only when the engine is OFF, the vehicle is level and the transaxle is cold. To check the fluid level, remove and read the fluid level indicator/filler plug. If the indicator reads low, add the appropriate amount of synchromesh transaxle fluid to fill the transaxle to the FULL level.

### Automatic Transaxle
*FLUID RECOMMENDATIONS*

When adding fluid or refilling the transaxle, use Dexron®II automatic transmission fluid.

*LEVEL CHECK*

1. Start the engine and drive the vehicle for a minimum of 15 miles.

NOTE: *The automatic transmission fluid level must be checked with the vehicle at normal operating temperature; 180–200°F*

# 30  GENERAL INFORMATION AND MAINTENANCE

(82–93°C). Temperature will greatly affect transaxle fluid level.

2. Park the vehicle on a level surface.
3. Place the transaxle gear selector in **P**.
4. Apply the parking brake and block the drive wheels.
5. Let the vehicle idle for 3 minutes with the accessories OFF.
6. With the engine running, check the fluid level, color and condition.
7. Inaccurate fluid level readings may result if the fluid is checked immediately after the vehicle has been operated under any or all of the following conditions:
   a. In high ambient temperatures above 90°F (32°C).
   b. At sustained high speeds.
   c. In heavy city traffic during hot weather.
   d. As a towing vehicle.
   e. In commercial service (taxi or police use).
8. If the vehicle has been operated under these conditions, shut the engine OFF and allow the vehicle to cool for 30 minutes. After the cooldown period, restart the vehicle and continue from Step 2 above.

### DRAIN AND REFILL

1. Raise and safely support the vehicle.
2. Place the drain pan under the transaxle fluid pan.
3. Remove the fluid pan bolts from the front and sides only.
4. Loosen, but do not remove the 4 bolts at the rear of the fluid pan.
   NOTE: *Do not damage the transaxle case or fluid pan sealing surfaces.*
5. Lightly tap the fluid pan with a rubber mallet or pry to allow the fluid to partially drain from the pan.

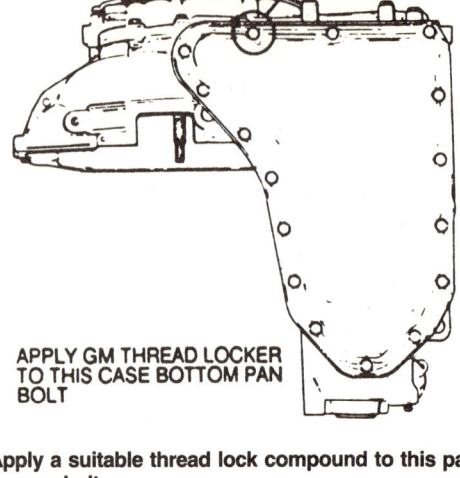

Apply a suitable thread lock compound to this pan-to-case bolt

6. Remove the remaining fluid pan bolts, fluid pan and gasket.

**To install:**

7. Install a new gasket to the fluid pan.
8. Install the fluid pan to the transaxle.
NOTE: *Apply a suitable sealant compound to the bolt shown in the illustration to prevent fluid leaks.*
9. Install the pan bolts. Tighten to 133 inch lbs. (11 Nm).
10. Lower the vehicle.
11. Fill the transaxle to the proper level with Dexron® II fluid. Check cold level reading. Do not overfill.
12. Follow the fluid check procedure in this section.
13. Check the pan for leaks.

### PAN AND FILTER SERVICE

1. With the pan removed from the vehicle and the fluid completely drained, thoroughly clean the inside of the pan to remove all old fluid and residue.
2. Inspect the gasket sealing surface on the fluid pan and remove any remaining gasket fragments with a scraper.
3. Remove the fluid filter, O-ring and seal from the case.

**To install:**

4. Apply a small amount of Transjel to the new seal and install the seal.
5. Install a new filter O-ring and filter.
6. Install the new gasket to the pan.

## Cooling System

### FLUID RECOMMENDATIONS

The cooling system should be inspected, flushed and refilled with fresh coolant at least

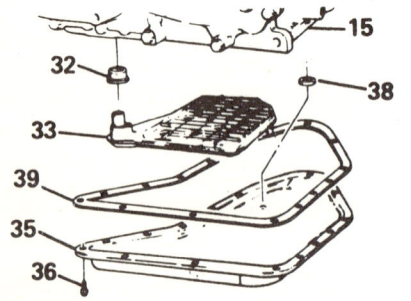

1. Transaxle assembly
2. Seal
3. Transaxle fluid strainer
4. Transaxle fluid pan
5. Transaxle fluid pan screw
6. Chip collector magnet
7. Transaxle fluid pan gasket

Automatic transaxle pan, screen and gasket installation

## GENERAL INFORMATION AND MAINTENANCE

every 30,000 miles or 24 months. If the coolant is left in the system too long, it loses its ability to prevent rust and corrosion.

When the coolant is being replaced, use a good quality ethylene glycol antifreeze that is safe to be used with aluminum cooling system components. The ratio of ethylene glycol to water should always be a 50/50 mixture. This ratio will ensure the proper balance of cooling ability, corrosion protection and antifreeze protection. At this ratio, the antifreeze protection should be good to −34°F (−37°C). If greater antifreeze protection is needed, the ratio should not exceed 70% antifreeze.

### LEVEL CHECK

NOTE: *When checking the coolant level, the radiator cap need not be removed. Simply check the coolant level in the recovery bottle or surge tank.*

Check the coolant level in the recovery bottle or surge tank, usually mounted on the inner fender. With the engine cold, the coolant level should be at the ADD or COLD level. With the engine at normal operating temperature, the coolant level should be at the FULL mark. Add coolant, as necessary.

### DRAIN AND REFILL

CAUTION: *When draining the coolant, keep in mind that cats and dogs are attracted by the ethylene glycol antifreeze and are quite likely to drink any that is left in an uncovered container or in puddles on the ground. This will prove fatal in sufficient quantity. Always drain the coolant into a sealable container. Coolant should be reused unless it is contaminated or several years old. To avoid injuries from scalding fluid and steam, DO NOT remove the radiator cap while the engine and radiator are still HOT.*

1. With the engine cool, remove the radiator cap by performing the following:
    a. Slowly rotate the cap counterclockwise to the detent.
    b. If any residual pressure is present, WAIT until the hissing stops.
    c. After the hissing noise has ceased, press down on the cap and continue rotating it counterclockwise to remove it.
2. Place a fluid catch pan under the radiator, open the radiator drain valve and drain the coolant from the system.
3. Close the drain valve.
4. Empty the coolant reservoir or surge tank and flush it.
5. Using the correct mixture of antifreeze, fill the radiator to the bottom of the filler neck and the coolant tank to the FULL mark.
6. Install the radiator cap, making sure the arrows line up over the overflow tube leading the reservoir or surge tank.
7. Start the engine. Select heat on the climate control panel and turn the temperature valve to full warm. Run the engine until it reaches normal operating temperature. Check to make sure there is hot air flowing from the floor ducts.
8. Check the fluid level in the reservoir or surge tank and add as necessary.

### FLUSHING AND CLEANING THE SYSTEM

1. Refer to the Drain and Refill procedure in this section and drain the cooling system.
2. Close the drain valve.

NOTE: *A flushing solution may be used. Ensure it is safe for use with aluminum cooling system components. Follow the directions on the container.*

3. If using a flushing solution, remove the thermostat. Reinstall the thermostat housing.
4. Add sufficient water to fill the system.
5. Start the engine and run for a few minutes. Drain the system.

NOTE: *This next step can get messy, so perform the work in a place where the water can drain away easily.*

6. If using a flushing solution, disconnect the heater hose that connects the cylinder head to the heater core (that end of the hose will clamp to a fitting on the firewall. Connect a water hose to the end of the heater hose that runs to the cylinder head and run water into the system until it begins to flow out of the top of the radiator.
7. Allow the water to flow out of the radiator until it is clear.
8. Reconnect the heater hose.
9. Drain the cooling system.
10. Reinstall the thermostat.
11. Empty the coolant reservoir or surge tank and flush it.
12. Fill the cooling system, using the correct ratio of antifreeze and water, to the bottom of the filler neck. Fill the reservoir or surge tank to the FULL mark.
13. Install the radiator cap, making sure that the arrows align with the overflow tube.

## Brake Master Cylinder

### FLUID RECOMMENDATION

Use only Heavy Duty Brake Fluid meeting DOT 3 specifications. Do NOT use any other fluid because severe brake system damage will result.

### LEVEL CHECK

The brake fluid in the master cylinder should be checked every 6 months/6,000 miles (9656km).

# GENERAL INFORMATION AND MAINTENANCE

Check the fluid level on the side of the reservoir. If fluid is required, remove the screw on filler cap and gasket from the master cylinder. Fill the reservoir to the full line in the reservoir with Heavy Duty Brake Fluid meeting DOT 3 specifications ONLY. Install the filler cap, making sure the gasket is properly seated in the cap. Make sure no dirt enters the system when adding fluid.

If fluid has to be added frequently, the system should be checked for a leak. Check for leaks at the master cylinder, calipers, proportioning valve and brake lines. If a leak is found, replace the component and bleed the system as outlined in Chapter 9.

## Clutch Master Cylinder

### FLUID RECOMMENDATION

Use only Heavy Duty Brake Fluid meeting DOT 3 specifications. Do NOT use any other fluid because severe clutch system damage will result.

### LEVEL CHECK

The clutch system fluid in the master cylinder should be checked every 6 months/6,000 miles.

The clutch master cylinder reservoir is located on top of the left (driver) strut tower. Check the fluid level on the side of the reservoir. If fluid is required, remove the screw on filler cap and gasket from the master cylinder. Fill the reservoir to the full line in the reservoir with Heavy Duty Brake Fluid meeting DOT 3 specifications ONLY. Install the filler cap, making sure the gasket is properly seated in the cap. Make sure no dirt enters the system when adding fluid.

If fluid has to be added frequently, the system should be checked for a leak. Check for leaks at the master cylinder, slave cylinder and hose. If a leak is found, replace the component and bleed the system as outlined in Chapter 7.

## Power Steering

### FLUID RECOMMENDATIONS

When adding fluid or making a complete fluid change, always use GM P/N 1050017 power steering fluid or equivalent. Do NOT use automatic transmission fluid. Failure to use the proper fluid may cause hose and seal damage and fluid leaks.

### LEVEL CHECK

The power steering fluid reservoir is directly above the steering pump. The pump is located on top of the engine on the right (passenger's) side.

Power steering fluid level is indicated either by marks on a see through reservoir or by marks on a fluid level indicator in the reservoir cap.

If the fluid is warmed up (about 150°F), the level should be between the HOT and COLD marks.

If the fluid is cooler than above, the level should be between the ADD and COLD marks.

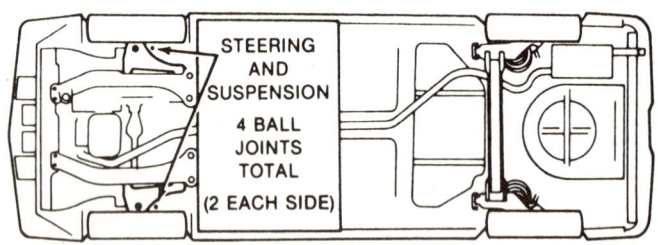

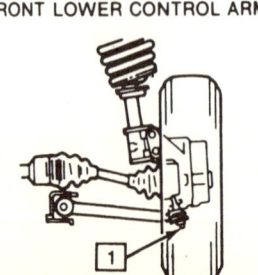

BALL JOINT
FRONT LOWER CONTROL ARM

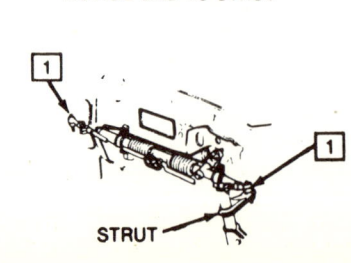

BALL JOINT
TIE ROD END-TO-STRUT

**Lubrication points**

# GENERAL INFORMATION AND MAINTENANCE

## Chassis Greasing

Lubricate the chassis lubrication points every 7,500 miles or 12 months. If your vehicle is equipped with grease fittings, lubricate the suspension and steering linkage with heavy duty chassis grease. Lubricate the transaxle shift linkage, parking cable guides, under body contact points and linkage with white lithium grease.

## Body Lubrication and Maintenance

### Lock Cylinders

Apply graphite lubricant sparingly through the key slot. Insert the key and operate the lock several times to be sure that the lubricant is worked into the lock cylinder.

### Door Hinges and Hinge Checks

Spray a silicone lubricant on the hinge pivot points to eliminate any binding conditions. Open and close the door several times to be sure that the lubricant is evenly and thoroughly distributed.

### Trunk lid or Tailgate

Spray a silicone lubricant on all of the pivot and friction surfaces to eliminate any squeaks or binds. Work the tailgate to distribute the lubricant

### Body Drain Holes

Be sure that the drain holes in the doors and rocker panels are cleared of obstruction. A small screwdriver can be used to clear them of any debris.

## Wheel Bearings (Rear)

CAUTION: *Some brake pads contain asbestos, which has been determined to be a cancer causing agent. Never clean the brake surfaces with compressed air! Avoid inhaling any dust from any brake surface! When cleaning brake surfaces, use a commercially available brake cleaning fluid.*

The N body models are equipped with sealed hub and bearing assemblies for the rear wheels. The hub and bearing assemblies are nonserviceable. If the assembly is damaged, the complete unit must be replaced. Refer to Chapter 8 for the hub and bearing removal and installation procedure.

## TRAILER TOWING

### General recommendations

Your vehicle is designed and intended to be used mainly to carry people. Towing a trailer will affect handling, durability and economy. Your safety and satisfaction depend upon proper use of correct equipment. Also, you should avoid overloads and other abusive use.

Factory trailer towing packages are available on most cars. However, if you are installing a trailer hitch and wiring on your car, there are a few things you should know.

Information on trailer towing, special equipment and optional equipment is available at your local dealership. You can write to Oldsmobile Customer Service Department, P.O. Box 30095, Lansing, MI 48909. In Canada, General Motors of Canada Limited, Customer Service Department, Oshawa, Ontario L1J 5Z6.

### Trailer Weight

Trailer weight is the first, and most important, factor in determining whether or not your vehicle is suitable for towing the trailer you have in mind. The horsepower-to-weight ratio should be calculated. The basic standard is a ratio of 35:1. That is, 35 pounds of GVW (gross vehicle weight) for every horsepower.

To calculate this ratio, multiply you engine's rated horsepower by 35, then subtract the weight of the vehicle, including passengers and luggage. The resulting figure is the ideal maximum trailer weight that you can tow.

### Hitch Weight

There are three kinds of hitches: bumper mounted, frame mounted, and load equalizing.

Bumper mounted hitches are those which attach solely to the vehicle's bumper. Many states prohibit towing with this type of hitch, when it attaches to the vehicle's stock bumper, since it subjects the bumper to stresses for which it was not designed. Aftermarket rear step bumpers, designed for trailer towing, are acceptable for use with bumper mounted hitches.

NOTE: *Do NOT attach any hitch to the bumper bar on the vehicle. A hitch attachment may be made through the bumper mounting locations, but only if an additional attachment is also made. Frame mounted hitches can be of the type which bolts to two or more points on the frame, plus the bumper, or just to several points on the frame. Frame mounted hitches can also be of the tongue type, for Class I towing, or, of the receiver type, for classes II and III.*

Load equalizing hitches are usually used for large trailers. Most equalizing hitches are welded in place and use equalizing bars and chains to level the vehicle after the trailer is hooked up.

The bolt-on hitches are the most common, since they are relatively easy to install.

Check the gross weight rating of your trailer. Tongue weight is usually figured as 10% of gross trailer weight. Therefore, a trailer with a maximum gross weight of 2,000 lbs. (907 kg) will have a maximum tongue weight of 200 lbs. (91 kg) Class I trailers fall into this category. Class II trailers are those with a gross weight rating of 2,000–3,500 lbs. (907–1588 kg), while Class III trailers fall into the 3,500–6,000 lbs. (1588–2722 kg) category. Class IV trailers are those over 6,000 lbs. (2722 kg) and are for use with fifth wheel trucks, only.

When you have determined the hitch that you'll need, follow the manufacturer's installation instructions, exactly, especially when it comes to fastener torques. The hitch will subjected to a lot of stress and good hitches come with hardened bolts. Never substitute an inferior bolt for a hardened bolt.

## Wiring

Wiring the car for towing is fairly easy. There are a number of good wiring kits available and these should be used, rather than trying to design your own. All trailers will need brake lights and turn signals as well as tail lights and side marker lights. Most states require extra marker lights for overly wide trailers. Also, most states have recently required back-up lights for trailers, and most trailer manufacturers have been building trailers with back-up lights for several years.

Additionally, some Class I, most Class II and just about all Class III trailers will have electric brakes.

Add to this number an accessories wire, to operate trailer internal equipment or to charge the trailer's battery, and you can have as many as seven wires in the harness.

Determine the equipment on your trailer and buy the wiring kit necessary. The kit will contain all the wires needed, plus a plug adapter set which included the female plug, mounted on the bumper or hitch, and the male plug, wired into, or plugged into the trailer harness.

When installing the kit, follow the manufacturer's instructions. The color coding of the wires is standard throughout the industry.

One point to note is that some domestic vehicles, and most imported vehicles, have separate turn signals. On most domestic vehicles, the brake lights and rear turn signals operate with the same bulb. For those vehicles with separate turn signals, you can purchase an isolation unit so that the brake lights won't blink whenever the turn signals are operated, or, you can go to your local electronics supply house and buy four diodes to wire in series with the brake and turn signal bulbs. Diodes will isolate the brake and turn signals. The choice is yours. The isolation units are simple and quick to install, but far more expensive than the diodes. The diodes, however, require more work to install properly, since they require the cutting of each bulb's wire and soldering the diode in place.

One final point, the best kits are those with a spring loaded cover on the vehicle mounted socket. This cover prevents dirt and moisture from corroding the terminals. Never let the vehicle socket hang loosely. Always mount it securely to the bumper or hitch.

## PUSHING AND TOWING

WARNING: *Push starting is not recommended for cars equipped with a catalytic converter, which represents ALL N Body cars. Raw gas collecting in the converter may cause damage. Jump starting is recommended.*

To push start your manual transaxle-equipped car (automatic transaxle-equipped models cannot be push started), make sure of bumper alignment. If the bumper of the car pushing does not match with your car's bumper, it would be wise to tie an old tire either on the back of your car, or on the front of the pushing car. Switch the ignition to ON and depress the clutch pedal. Shift the transaxle to third gear and hold the accelerator pedal about halfway down. Signal the push car to proceed. When the car speed reaches about 10 mph, signal the push car to brake. When your car has coasted a safe distance ahead, gradually release the clutch pedal. The engine should start, if not have the car towed.

Towing the vehicle on a flat bed ("roll back") truck is the most desirable option. The car is safest and the wheels do not have to turn. It is also the most expensive way to tow and not always available.

The vehicle must be towed with the drive wheels off the ground. If the transaxle is in proper working order, the car can be flat-towed with the front wheels on the ground (front wheel drive) for distances under 15 miles at speeds no greater then 30 mph.

If the transaxle is known to be damaged or if the car must be towed over 15 miles or over 30 mph, the car must be dollied or towed with the front wheels raised.

## JACKING

The jack that is furnished with the vehicle is ONLY to be used in an emergency to remove a flat tire. Never get beneath the car or, start or

# GENERAL INFORMATION AND MAINTENANCE

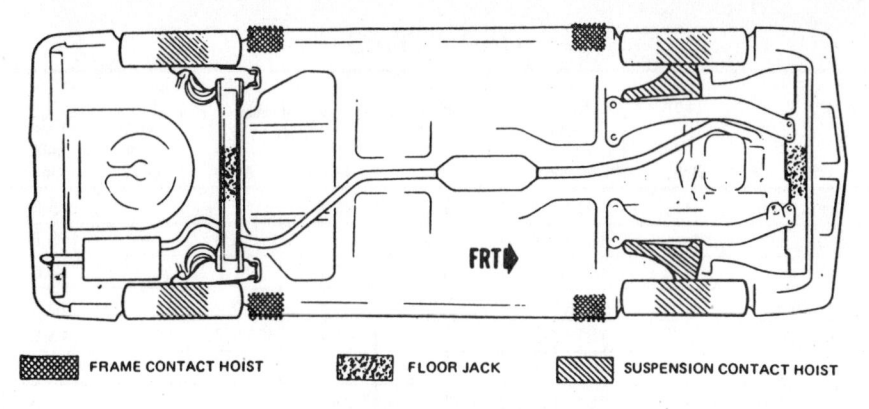

**Vehicle lifting points**

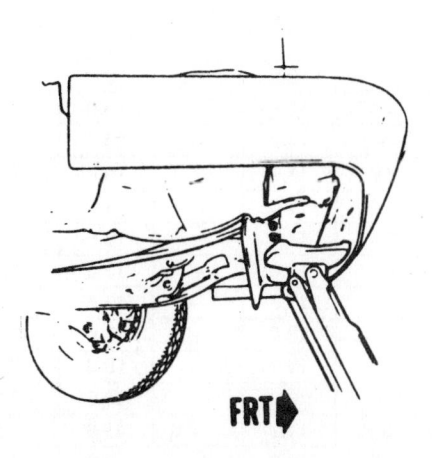

FRAME CONTACT HOIST    FLOOR JACK    SUSPENSION CONTACT HOIST

**WHEN USING FLOOR JACK, LIFT ON CENTER OF FRONT SUPPORT**

Lift point for the front of the vehicle

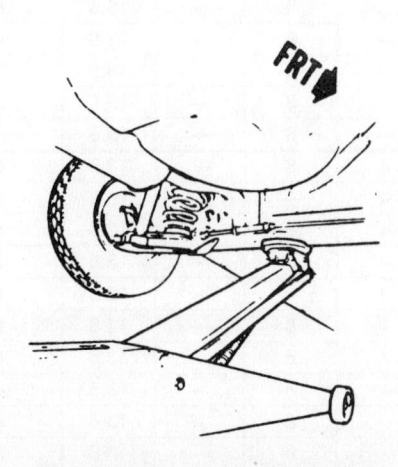

**WHEN USING FLOOR JACK, LIFT ON CENTER OR REAR TORQUE ARM**

Lift point for the rear of the vehicle

run the engine while the vehicle is supported by the jack. Front wheel drive cars have a center line of gravity that is far forward. Take the proper precautions to make sure the car does not fall forward while it is suspended. Personal injury may result if these procedures are not followed exactly.

When using a floor jack to lift the front of the car, lift from the center of the front crossmember. When using floor jack to lift the rear of the car, lift from the center of the rear jack pad.

After lifting the car, place jackstands under the body side pinch welds or similar strong and stable structure. Lower the car onto the jackstands slowly and carefully and check for stability before getting under the car.

## CHANGING A FLAT TIRE

1. Park on a level surface and apply the parking brake firmly.
2. If you are in a public or in a potentially dangerous location, turn the 4-way hazard flashers ON.
3. Shift the transaxle gear selector into the PARK position.
4. Remove the jacking tools and spare tire from the stowage area.
5. Connect the socket with side of ratchet marked UP/ON. Raise the jack slowly.
6. Position the jack head under the vehicle closest to the tire to be changed.
7. Raise the jack until the lift head mates with the vehicle notches as shown in the jacking previous illustration. Do NOT raise the vehicle.
8. Remove the wheel cover using the wedge end of ratchet. Connect the DOWN/OFF side of the ratchet to the socket and loosen, but do not remove the wheel nuts.
9. Connect the UP/ON side of the ratchet to the jack.
10. Raise the vehicle so the inflated spare will clear the surface when installed.

## GENERAL INFORMATION AND MAINTENANCE

## CAPACITIES

| Year | Model | VIN | No. Cylinder Displacement cu. in. (liter) | Engine Crankcase with Filter | Transmission (pts.) 5-Spd | Transmission (pts.) Auto. | Drive Axle (pts.) | Fuel Tank (gal.) | Cooling System (qts.) |
|---|---|---|---|---|---|---|---|---|---|
| 1985 | Grand Am | U | 151 (2.5) | 3.5 | 5.4 | 11.7 | — | 13.6 | 7.9① |
|  | Grand Am | L | 181 (3.0) | 4.5 | — | 18.0 | — | 13.6 | 10.3 |
|  | Calais | U | 151 (2.5) | 3.5 | 5.4 | 11.7 | — | 13.6 | 7.9① |
|  | Calais | L | 181 (3.0) | 4.5 | — | 18.0 | — | 13.6 | 10.3 |
|  | Somerset | U | 151 (2.5) | 3.5 | 5.4 | 11.7 | — | 13.6 | 7.9① |
|  | Somerset | L | 181 (3.0) | 4.5 | — | 18.0 | — | 13.6 | 10.3 |
| 1986 | Grand Am | U | 151 (2.5) | 3.5 | 5.4 | 11.7 | — | 13.6 | 7.9① |
|  | Grand Am | L | 181 (3.0) | 4.5 | — | 18.0 | — | 13.6 | 10.3 |
|  | Calais | U | 151 (2.5) | 3.5 | 5.4 | 11.7 | — | 13.6 | 7.9① |
|  | Calais | L | 181 (3.0) | 4.5 | — | 18.0 | — | 13.6 | 10.3 |
|  | Somerset | U | 151 (2.5) | 3.5 | 5.4 | 11.7 | — | 13.6 | 7.9① |
|  | Somerset | L | 181 (3.0) | 4.5 | — | 18.0 | — | 13.6 | 10.3 |
|  | Skylark | U | 151 (2.5) | 3.5 | 5.4 | 11.7 | — | 13.6 | 7.9① |
|  | Skylark | L | 181 (3.0) | 4.5 | — | 18.0 | — | 13.6 | 10.3 |
| 1987 | Grand Am | K | 122 (2.0) | 4.0 | 6.0 | 11.0 | — | 13.6 | 7.8① |
|  | Grand Am | M | 122 (2.0) | 4.0 | 6.0 | 11.0 | — | 13.6 | 7.8① |
|  | Grand Am | U | 151 (2.5) | 3.5 | 5.4 | 11.7 | — | 13.6 | 7.9 |
|  | Grand Am | L | 181 (3.0) | 4.5 | — | 18.0 | — | 13.6 | 10.3 |
|  | Calais | U | 151 (2.5) | 3.5 | 5.4 | 11.7 | — | 13.6 | 7.9① |
|  | Calais | L | 181 (3.0) | 4.5 | — | 18.0 | — | 13.6 | 10.3 |
|  | Somerset | U | 151 (2.5) | 3.5 | 5.4 | 11.7 | — | 13.6 | 7.9① |
|  | Somerset | L | 181 (3.0) | 4.5 | — | 18.0 | — | 13.6 | 10.3 |
|  | Skylark | U | 151 (2.5) | 3.5 | 5.4 | 11.7 | — | 13.6 | 7.9① |
|  | Skylark | L | 181 (3.0) | 4.5 | — | 18.0 | — | 13.6 | 10.3 |
| 1988 | Grand Am | M | 4-122 (2.0) | 4 | 4 | 8 | — | 13.6 | 8 |
|  | Grand Am | D | 4-138 (2.3) | 4 | 4 | 8 | — | 13.6 | 8 |
|  | Grand Am | U | 4-151 (2.5) | 4 | 5.3 | 8 | — | 13.6 | 8 |
|  | Calais | D | 4-138 (2.3) | 4 | 4 | 8 | — | 13.6 | 8 |
|  | Calais | U | 4-151 (2.5) | 4 | 5.3 | 8 | — | 13.6 | 8 |
|  | Calais | L | 6-181 (3.0) | 4 | — | 8 | — | 13.6 | 10 |
|  | Skylark | D | 4-138 (2.3) | 4 | — | 8 | — | 13.6 | 8 |
|  | Skylark | U | 4-151 (2.5) | 4 | — | 8 | — | 13.6 | 8 |
|  | Skylark | L | 6-181 (3.0) | 4 | — | 8 | — | 13.6 | 10 |
| 1989 | Grand Am | M | 4-122 (2.0) | 4 | 4 | 8 | — | 13.6 | 8 |
|  | Grand Am | A | 4-138 (2.3) | 4 | 4 | — | — | 13.6 | 8 |
|  | Grand Am | D | 4-138 (2.3) | 4 | 4 | 8 | — | 13.6 | 8 |
|  | Grand Am | U | 4-151 (2.5) | 4 | 4 | 8 | — | 13.6 | 8 |
|  | Calais | A | 4-138 (2.3) | 4 | 4 | — | — | 13.6 | 8 |
|  | Calais | D | 4-138 (2.3) | 4 | 4 | 8 | — | 13.6 | 8 |
|  | Calais | U | 4-151 (2.5) | 4 | 4 | 8 | — | 13.6 | 8 |
|  | Calais | N | 6-204 (3.3) | 4 | — | 8 | — | 13.6 | 10 |
|  | Skylark | D | 4-138 (2.3) | 4 | — | 8 | — | 13.6 | 8 |
|  | Skylark | U | 4-151 (2.5) | 4 | — | 8 | — | 13.6 | 8 |
|  | Skylark | N | 6-204 (3.3) | 4 | — | 8 | — | 13.6 | 10 |

## CAPACITIES

| Year | Model | VIN | No. Cylinder Displacement cu. in. (liter) | Engine Crankcase with Filter | Transmission (pts.) 5-Spd | Transmission (pts.) Auto. | Drive Axle (pts.) | Fuel Tank (gal.) | Cooling System (qts.) |
|---|---|---|---|---|---|---|---|---|---|
| 1990 | Grand Am | A | 4-138 (2.3) | 4 | 4 | — | — | 13.6 | 8 |
| | Grand Am | D | 4-138 (2.3) | 4 | 4 | 8 | — | 13.6 | 8 |
| | Grand Am | U | 4-151 (2.5) | 4 | 4 | 8 | — | 13.6 | 8 |
| | Calais | A | 4-138 (2.3) | 4 | 4 | — | — | 13.6 | 8 |
| | Calais | D | 4-138 (2.3) | 4 | 4 | 8 | — | 13.6 | 8 |
| | Calais | U | 4-151 (2.5) | 4 | 4 | 8 | — | 13.6 | 8 |
| | Calais | N | 6-204 (3.3) | 4 | — | 8 | — | 13.6 | 10 |
| | Skylark | D | 4-138 (2.3) | 4 | — | 8 | — | 13.6 | 8 |
| | Skylark | U | 4-151 (2.5) | 4 | — | 8 | — | 13.6 | 8 |
| | Skylark | N | 6-204 (3.3) | 4 | — | 8 | — | 13.6 | 10 |
| 1991 | Grand Am | A | 4-138 (2.3) | 4 | 4 | 8 | — | 13.6 | 10.4 |
| | Grand Am | D | 4-138 (2.3) | 4 | 4 | 8 | — | 13.6 | 10.4 |
| | Grand Am | U | 4-151 (2.5) | 4 | 4 | 8 | — | 13.6 | 10.7 |
| | Calais | A | 4-138 (2.3) | 4 | 4 | — | — | 13.6 | 10.4 |
| | Calais | D | 4-138 (2.3) | 4 | 4 | 8 | — | 13.6 | 10.4 |
| | Calais | U | 4-151 (2.5) | 4 | 4 | 8 | — | 13.6 | 10.7 |
| | Calais | N | 6-204 (3.3) | 4 | — | 8 | — | 13.6 | 12.7 |
| | Skylark | D | 4-138 (2.3) | 4 | — | 8 | — | 13.6 | 10.4 |
| | Skylark | U | 4-151 (2.5) | 4 | — | 8 | — | 13.6 | 10.7 |
| | Skylark | N | 6-204 (3.3) | 4 | — | 8 | — | 13.6 | 12.7 |
| 1992 | Grand Am | A | 4-138 (2.3) | 4 | 4 | 8 | — | 13.6 | 10.4 |
| | Grand Am | D | 4-138 (2.3) | 4 | 4 | 8 | — | 13.6 | 10.4 |
| | Grand Am | U | 4-151 (2.5) | 4 | 4 | 8 | — | 13.6 | 10.7 |
| | Achieva | A | 4-138 (2.3) | 4 | 4 | — | — | 13.6 | 10.4 |
| | Achieva | D | 4-138 (2.3) | 4 | 4 | 8 | — | 13.6 | 10.4 |
| | Achieva | 3 | 4-138 (2.3) | 4 | 4 | 8 | — | 13.6 | 10.4 |
| | Achieva | N | 6-204 (3.3) | 4 | — | 8 | — | 13.6 | 12.7 |
| | Skylark | 3 | 4-138 (2.3) | 4 | — | 8 | — | 13.6 | 10.4 |
| | Skylark | N | 6-204 (3.3) | 4 | — | 8 | — | 13.6 | 12.7 |

11. Remove the wheel nuts and wheel.

**To install:**

12. Install the spare tire and loosely tighten the wheel nuts.

13. Connect the UP/ON side of the ratchet to the socket and tighten the wheel nuts in a criss-cross sequence.

14. Lower the vehicle and remove the jack.

15. Retighten the wheel nuts securely to 100 ft. lbs. (140 Nm).

16. Install the wheel cover and securely store all jacking equipment.

17. Start driving the vehicle slowly to see if everything is secure.

# Engine Performance and Tune-Up 2

## TUNE-UP PROCEDURES

To get the best performance and fuel economy, it is essential that the engine be properly tuned at regular intervals. A periodic tune-up will keep your vehicle's engine running smoothly and will prevent annoying minor breakdowns and poor performance associated with a poorly tuned engine.

Before the days of unleaded fuel, electronic fuel injection, and electronically controlled ignition systems which, initially, did away with mechanical breaker points and has, on most of the newer engines, done away with the distriubor altogether, the tune-up was a much more involved process, requiring a delicate ear and just the right touch in order to fine tune an engine. On today's engines, ignition timing, and idle speed and mixture are controlled electronically, by the Electronic Control Module (ECM) and are not adjustable. The choke function has been incorporated into the fuel injection system and is no longer a separate component requiring periodic service and adjustment. In addition, with the advent of unleaded fuel and improved manufacturing techniques, spark plugs last longer. In fact, if your vehicle is equipped with the 2.3L engine, the Integrated Direct Ignition (IDI) system has even eliminated the spark plugs wires, and with them, the need for periodic inspection and replacement. Accordingly, whereas in the 'old days' the engine might have received a seasonal tune-up, one for the winter months and another for summer, the tune-up now consists of replacing the spark plugs, changing the air, fuel and PCV breather filters and performing a detailed visual inspection of the spark plug wires (if equipped!), vacuum, fuel and air lines and coolant hoses every 30,000 miles (48,300km).

This Chapter will include information about the ignition systems for the engines that may be installed in your Skylark, Somerset, Calais, Achieva or Grand Am. Although, as mentioned, not much of what you will read about is dealt with in the tune-up.

Under normal driving conditions, the tune-up should be performed every 30,000 miles (48,300km). This interval should be halved if the vehicle is operated under severe conditions, such as trailer towing, prolonged idling, continual stop and start driving, or if starting or running problems are noticed. It is assumed that the routine maintenance described in Chapter 1 has been kept up, as this will have a decided effect on the results of a tune-up. Follow the tune-up steps in order.

If the specifications listed in the on the Tune-Up Specifications chart in this Chapter differ from those found on the Vehicle Emission Control Information (VECI) label located in the engine compartment (usually on the radiator support) follow the specs on the VECI label. The VECI label often reflects changes made during the production run.

### Spark Plugs

A typical spark plug consists of a metal shell surrounding a ceramic insulator. A metal electrode extends downward through the center of the insulator and protrudes a small distance. Located at the end of the plug and attached to the side of the outer metal shell is the side electrode. The side electrode bends in at a 90 angle so that its tip is even with, and parallel to, the tip of the center electrode. The distance between these two electrodes (measured in thousandths of an inch or hundreths of a millimeter) is called the spark plug gap.

The spark plug in no way produces a spark but merely provides a gap across which the current can arc. The coil produces 20,000–40,000 volts or more, which travels from the coils, through the spark plug wires to the spark

# ENGINE PERFORMANCE AND TUNE-UP

## TUNE-UP SPECIFICATIONS

| Year | VIN | No. Cylinder Displacement cu. in. (liter) | Spark Plugs Gap (in.) | Ignition Timing (deg.) MT | Ignition Timing (deg.) AT | Fuel Pump (psi) | Idle Speed (rpm) MT | Idle Speed (rpm) AT | Valve Clearance In. | Valve Clearance Ex. |
|---|---|---|---|---|---|---|---|---|---|---|
| 1985 | U | 4-151 (2.5) | 0.060 | 8B | 8B | 12 | ① | ① | Hyd. | Hyd. |
|  | L | 6-181 (3.0) | 0.040 | 15B | 15B | 34–44 | ① | ① | Hyd. | Hyd. |
| 1986 | U | 4-151 (2.5) | 0.060 | 8B | 8B | 12 | ① | ① | Hyd. | Hyd. |
|  | L | 6-181 (3.0) | 0.040 | 15B | 15B | 34–44 | ① | ① | Hyd. | Hyd. |
| 1987 | K | 4-122 (2.0)④ | 0.035 | 8B | 8B | — | ① | ① | Hyd. | Hyd. |
|  | M | 4-122 (2.0)② | 0.035 | 8B | 8B | — | ① | ① | Hyd. | Hyd. |
|  | D | 4-138 (2.3) | 0.035 | — | — | 34–44 | — | — | Hyd. | Hyd. |
|  | U | 4-151 (2.5) | 0.060 | 8B | 8B | 12 | ① | ① | Hyd. | Hyd. |
|  | L | 6-181 (3.0) | 0.040 | 15B | 15B | 34–44 | ① | ① | Hyd. | Hyd. |
| 1988 | K | 4-122 (2.0)④ | 0.035 | 8B | 8B | — | ① | ① | Hyd. | Hyd. |
|  | M | 4-122 (2.0)② | 0.035 | 8B | 8B | — | ① | ① | Hyd. | Hyd. |
|  | D | 4-138 (2.3) | 0.035 | — | — | 34–44 | — | — | Hyd. | Hyd. |
|  | U | 4-151 (2.5) | 0.060 | — | — | 9–13 | ① | ① | Hyd. | Hyd. |
|  | L | 6-181 (3.0) | 0.045 | ③ | ③ | 34–44 | ① | ① | Hyd. | Hyd. |
| 1989 | M | 4-122 (2.0)② | 0.035 | 8B | 8B | — | ① | ① | Hyd. | Hyd. |
|  | A | 4-138 (2.3) | 0.035 | — | — | 34–44 | ① | — | Hyd. | Hyd. |
|  | D | 4-138 (0.3) | 0.035 | — | — | 34–44 | — | — | Hyd. | Hyd. |
|  | U | 4-151 (2.5) | 0.060 | — | — | 9–13 | ① | ① | Hyd. | Hyd. |
|  | N | 6-204 (3.3) | 0.060 | — | — | 36–43 | ① | ① | Hyd. | Hyd. |
| 1990 | A | 4-138 (2.3) | 0.035 | ⑤ | ⑤ | ⑦ | ⑥ | ⑥ | Hyd. | Hyd. |
|  | D | 4-138 (2.3) | 0.035 | ⑤ | ⑤ | ⑦ | ⑥ | ⑥ | Hyd. | Hyd. |
|  | U | 4-151 (2.5) | 0.060 | ⑤ | ⑤ | 9–13 | ⑥ | ⑥ | Hyd. | Hyd. |
|  | N | 6-204 (3.3) | 0.060 | — | ⑤ | ⑦ | — | ⑥ | Hyd. | Hyd. |
| 1991 | A | 4-138 (2.3) | 0.035 | ⑤ | ⑤ | ⑦ | ⑥ | ⑥ | Hyd. | Hyd. |
|  | D | 4-138 (2.3) | 0.035 | ⑤ | ⑤ | ⑦ | ⑥ | ⑥ | Hyd. | Hyd. |
|  | U | 4-151 (2.5) | 0.060 | ⑤ | ⑤ | 9–13 | ⑥ | ⑥ | Hyd. | Hyd. |
|  | N | 6-204 (3.3) | 0.060 | — | ⑤ | ⑦ | ⑥ | ⑥ | Hyd. | Hyd. |
| 1992 | A | 4-138 (2.3) | 0.035 | ⑤ | ⑤ | ⑦ | ⑥ | ⑥ | Hyd. | Hyd. |
|  | D | 4-138 (2.3) | 0.035 | ⑤ | ⑤ | ⑦ | ⑥ | ⑥ | Hyd. | Hyd. |
|  | 3 | 4-138 (2.3) | 0.035 | ⑤ | ⑤ | ⑦ | ⑥ | ⑥ | Hyd. | Hyd. |
|  | U | 4-151 (2.5) | 0.060 | ⑤ | ⑤ | 9–13 | ⑥ | ⑥ | Hyd. | Hyd. |
|  | N | 6-204 (3.3) | 0.060 | — | ⑤ | ⑦ | — | ⑥ | Hyd. | Hyd. |

**NOTE:** The Underhood Specifications sticker often reflects tune-up specification changes in production. Sticker figures must be used if they disagree with those in this chart.
B—Before Top Dead Center
Hyd.—Hydraulic
① See Underhood Specifications sticker
② Turbocharged
③ No timing adjustment required with C³I ignition
④ Non-Turbocharged
⑤ Ignition timing is controlled by the ECM and is not adjustable
⑥ Idle speed is controlled by the ECM and is not adjustable
⑦ 1—Connect fuel pressure gauge, engine at normal operating temperature.
   2—Turn ignition switch on.
   3—After approx. 2 seconds; pressure should read 41–47 psi and hold steady.
   4—Start engine and idle; pressure should drop 3–10 psi fropm static pressure.

## ENGINE PERFORMANCE AND TUNE-UP

plugs. The current passes along the center electrode and jumps the gap to the side electrode, and, in so doing, ignites the air/fuel mixture in the combustion chamber.

### SPARK PLUG HEAT RANGE

Spark plug heat range is the ability of the plug to dissipate heat. The longer the insulator (or the farther it extends into the engine), the hotter the plug will operate; the shorter the insulator the cooler it will operate. A plug that absorbs little heat and remains too cool will quickly accumulate deposits of oil and carbon since it is not hot enough to burn them off. This leads to plug fouling and consequently to misfiring. A plug that absorbs too much heat may have deposits also, but due to the higher temperatures, the electrodes will burn away quickly. In some instances, the higher temperatures may lead to preignition. Preignition takes place when plug tips get so hot that they glow sufficiently to ignite the fuel/air mixture before the actual spark occurs. This early ignition will usually result in the 'pinging' experienced during low speeds and heavy loads.

The general rule of thumb for choosing the correct heat range when picking a spark plug is, if most of your driving is long distance, high speed travel, use a colder plug; if most of your driving is stop and go, use a hotter plug. In general, however, unless you are experiencing a problem use the factory recommended spark plugs.

A set of spark plugs usually requires replacement after about 30,000 miles (48,300km) on cars with electronic ignition, depending on your style of driving. In normal operation, plug gap increases about 0.001 in. (0.0254mm) for every 1,000–2,500 miles (1600–4000km). As the gap increases, the plug's voltage requirement also increases. It requires a greater voltage to jump the wider gap and about two to three times as much voltage to fire a plug at high speeds than at idle.

### REMOVAL AND INSTALLATION

#### 2.0L (VIN K and M) Engine

NOTE: *To avoid engine damage, do NOT remove spark plugs when the engine is warm. When you're removing spark plugs, you should work on one at a time. Don't start by removing the plug wires all at once, because unless you number them, they may become mixed up. Take a minute before you begin and number the wires with tape. The best location for numbering is as near as possible to the spark plug boot.*

1. Disconnect the negative battery cable.
2. Remove air cleaner components in order to gain access to the spark plugs.
3. Remove the first spark plug cable by pulling and twisting the boot; then remove the spark plug.
4. The 2.0L (VIN K and M) engines use AC Type R42XLS plugs. Properly gap them to 0.035 in. (0.89mm) prior to installation.
5. Lubricate the threads lightly with an anti-seize compound and install the spark plug. Torque to 20 ft. lbs. (27 Nm). Install the cable on the plug. Make sure it snaps in place.
5. Repeat for the remaining spark plugs.
6. Install the air cleaner components.
7. Connect the negative battery cable.

#### 2.3L Engine

The spark plugs on this engine are located under the ignition coil and module assembly.

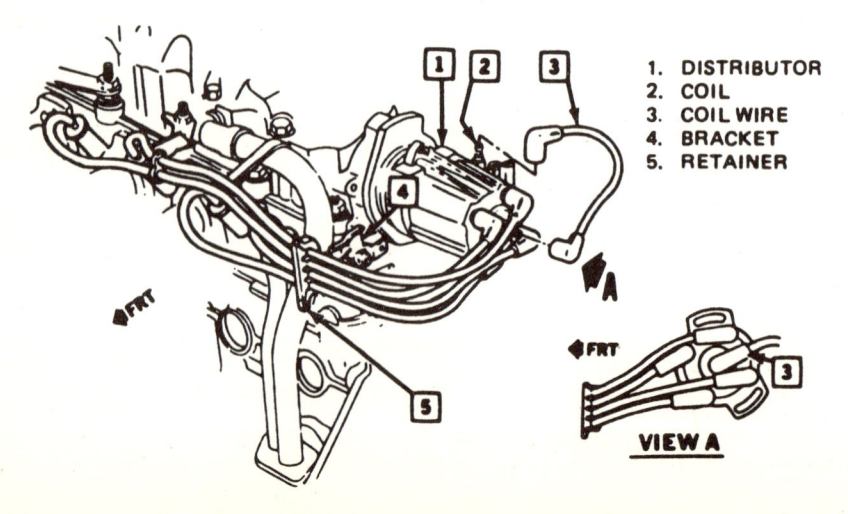

1. DISTRIBUTOR
2. COIL
3. COIL WIRE
4. BRACKET
5. RETAINER

**Spark plugs and cable routing—2.0L engine**

# ENGINE PERFORMANCE AND TUNE-UP

To gain access to the spark plugs, the coil and module assembly must be removed.

NOTE: *To avoid engine damage, do NOT remove spark plugs when the engine is warm. When you're removing spark plugs, you should work on one at a time. Don't start by removing the plug wires all at once, because unless you number them, they may become mixed up. Take a minute before you begin and number the wires with tape. The best location for numbering is as near as possible to the spark plug boot.*

1. Disconnect the negative battery cable.
2. Remove the air cleaner assembly.
3. Remove the four ignition cover-to-cylinder head bolts.
4. If the spark plug boot sticks, use a spark plug connector removing tool J-36011 or equivalent to remove with a twisting motion.
5. Remove the ignition cover and set aside.
6. Clean any dirt away from the spark plug recess area.
7. Remove the spark plugs with a spark plug socket.

**To install:**

8. The 2.3L engine uses AC Type FR3LS plugs. Properly gap them to 0.035 in. (0.89mm) prior to installation.
9. Lubricate the threads lightly with anti-seize compound and install the four spark plugs. Tighten the plugs to 17 ft. lbs. (23 Nm).
10. If removed, install the plug boots and retainers-to-ignition cover.
11. Apply dielectric compound to the plug boot.
12. Install the ignition cover-to-engine while carefully aligning the boots with the spark plug terminals.
13. Apply Loctite® thread locking compound, or equivalent to the ignition cover bolts. Install the bolts and tighten to 15 ft. lbs. (20 Nm).
14. If removed, connect the ignition cover electrical connectors.
15. Install the air cleaner and connect the negative battery cable.

### 2.5L Engine

1. Disconnect the negative battery cable.
2. Remove air cleaner components in order to gain access to the spark plugs.
3. Remove the first spark plug cable by pulling and twisting the boot; then remove the spark plug.
4. The 2.5L engine uses AC Type R43TSX or R43TS6 plugs. Properly gap them to 0.060 in. (1.5mm) prior to installation.
5. Lubricate the threads lightly with an anti-seize compound and install the spark plug. Torque to 20 ft. lbs. (27 Nm). Install the cable on the plug. Make sure it snaps in place.
5. Repeat for the remaining spark plugs.
6. Install the air cleaner components.
7. Connect the negative battery cable.

### 3.0L (VIN L) and 3.3L (VIN N) Engines

1. Disconnect the negative battery cable.
2. Remove the first spark plug cable by twisting the boot half a turn, then pulling up.
3. Remove the spark plug.
4. The 3.0L (VIN L) engine uses AC Type R44LTS plugs and they should be gapped to 0.045 in. (1.1mm) prior to installation. The 3.3L (VIN N) engine uses AC Type R44LTS6 plugs for 1989-90 and R45LTS6 plugs for 1991-92. Gap both types to 0.060 in. (1.5mm).
5. Lubricate the threads lightly with an anti-seize compound and install the spark plug. Torque to 20 ft. lbs. (27 Nm).
6. Install the cable to the plug and snap it in place.
7. Repeat for the remaining spark plugs.
8. Connect the negative battery cable.

## CHECKING AND REPLACING SPARK PLUG CABLES

Your vehicle is equipped with an electronic ignition system which utilizes 8mm wires to conduct the hotter spark produced (except 2.3L engine). The boots on these wires are designed to cover the spark plug cavities on the cylinder head. The 2.3L doesn't use spark plug wires. The coil assembly is connected directly to the spark plug with rubber connectors.

Visually inspect the spark plug cables for burns, cuts, or breaks in the insulation. Check the spark plug boots and the nipples on the distributor cap and coil. Replace any damaged wiring. If no physical damage is obvious, the wires can be checked with an ohmmeter for excessive

1. Ignition coil and module assembly
2. Module assembly, retaining bolts
3. Camshaft housing cover
4. Spark plug

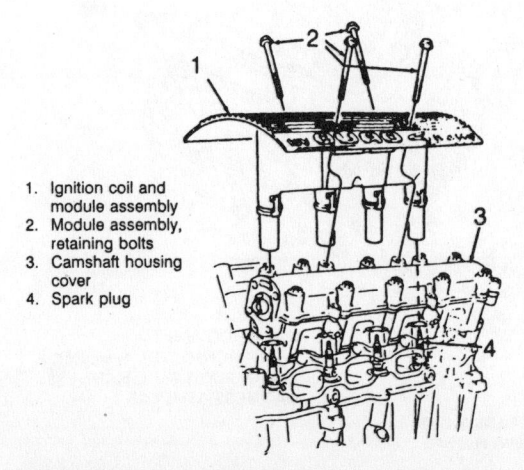

Remove the entire ignition cover to gain access to the spark plugs—2.3L engine

## 42  ENGINE PERFORMANCE AND TUNE-UP

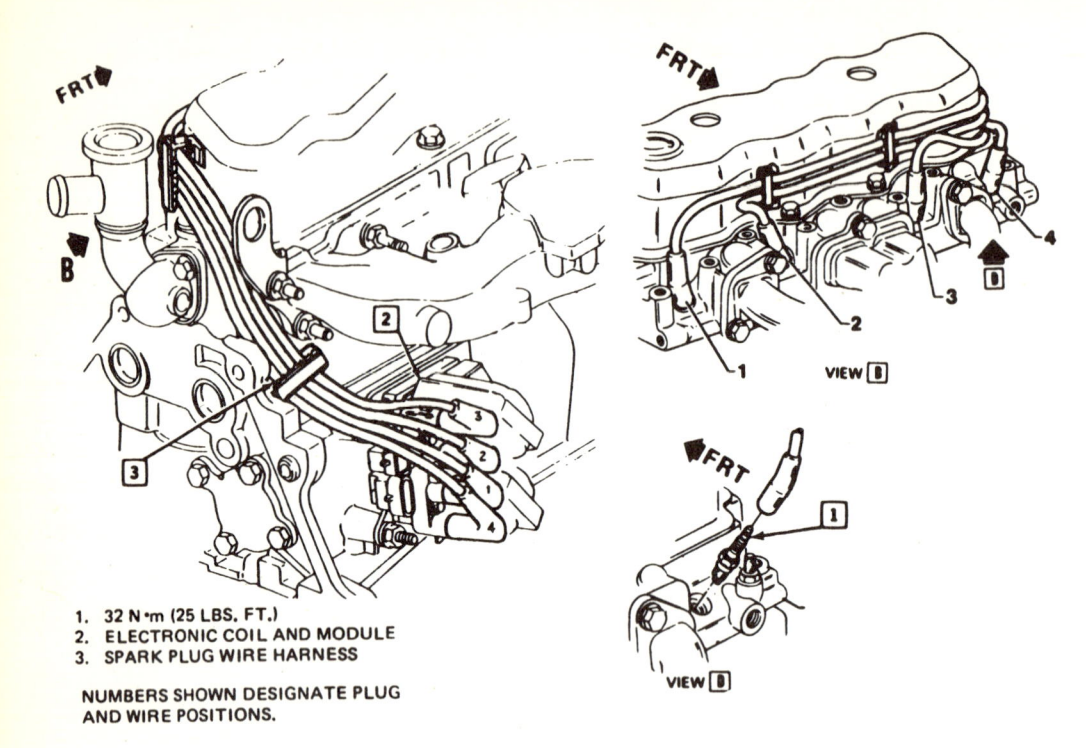

1. 32 N·m (25 LBS. FT.)
2. ELECTRONIC COIL AND MODULE
3. SPARK PLUG WIRE HARNESS

NUMBERS SHOWN DESIGNATE PLUG AND WIRE POSITIONS.

**Spark plugs and cable routing—2.5L engine**

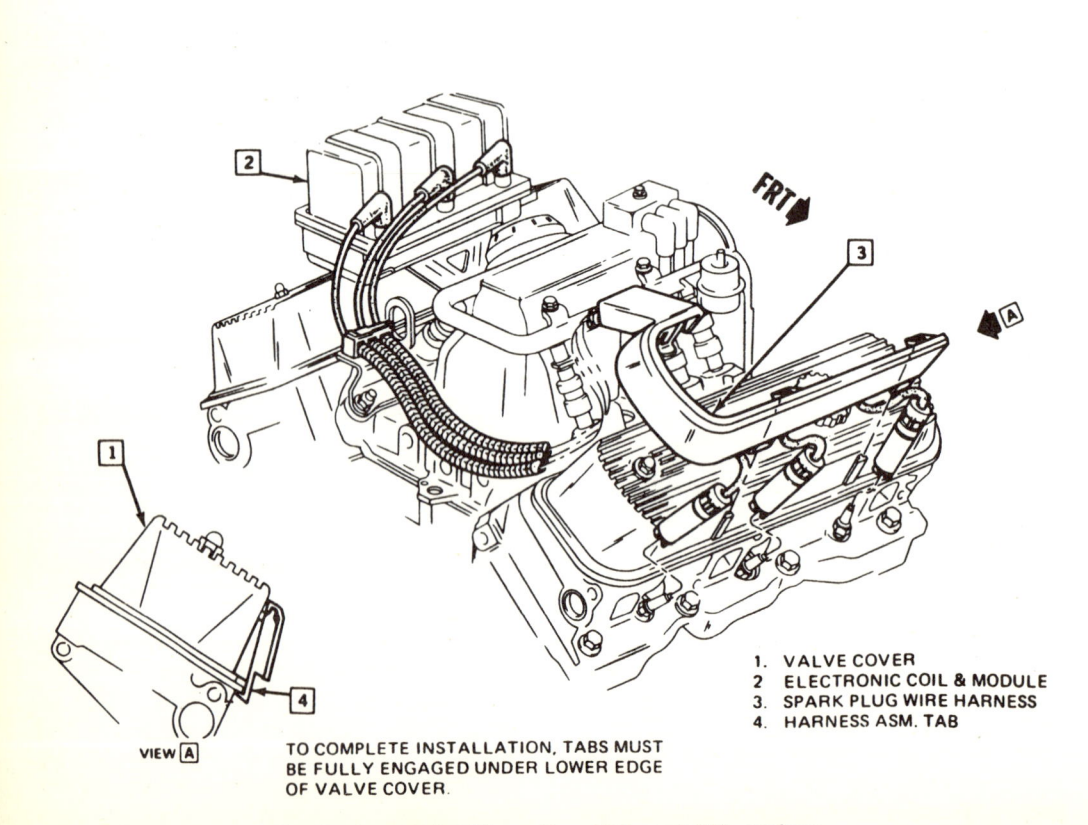

TO COMPLETE INSTALLATION, TABS MUST BE FULLY ENGAGED UNDER LOWER EDGE OF VALVE COVER.

1. VALVE COVER
2. ELECTRONIC COIL & MODULE
3. SPARK PLUG WIRE HARNESS
4. HARNESS ASM. TAB

**Spark plugs and cable routing—3.0L and 3.3L engines**

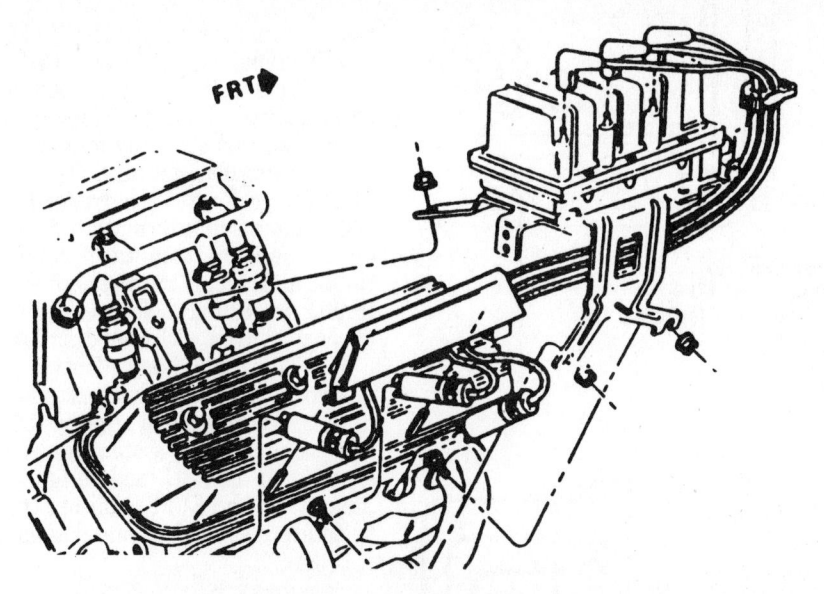

Spark plugs and cable routing—3.0L and 3.3L engines

resistance or an open. The resistance specification is 30,000 ohms or less. Always coat the terminals of any wire removed or replaced with a thin layer of dielectric compound.

When installing a new set of spark plug cables, replace the cables one at a time so there will be no mix-up. Start by replacing the longest cable first. Install the boot firmly over the spark plug. Route the wire exactly the same as the original, through all convolute tubing. Make sure the wire is clamped in all holders. Make sure ends snap into place. Repeat the process for each cable.

## FIRING ORDERS

NOTE: *To avoid confusion label, remove, and replace spark plug cables one at a time.*

## HIGH ENERGY IGNITION (HEI) SYSTEM
## 2.0L (VIN K AND M) ENGINES AND 2.5L (VIN U) ENGINE
### 1985-86

### General Description

The High Energy Ignition (HEI) system controls fuel combustion by providing a spark to ignite the air/fuel mixture at the appropriate time. This system consists of a modified module, which is used in conjunction with the Electronic Spark Timing (EST) function of the Electronic Control Module (ECM).

The HEI system installed on the 2.5L (VIN U) engine is equipped with an externally mounted ignition coil.

The HEI system features a longer spark duration which is essential in firing lean and EGR-diluted air/fuel mixtures. The condenser (capacitor) located within the HEI distributor is provided for noise (static) suppression purposes only and is not a regularly replaced igni-

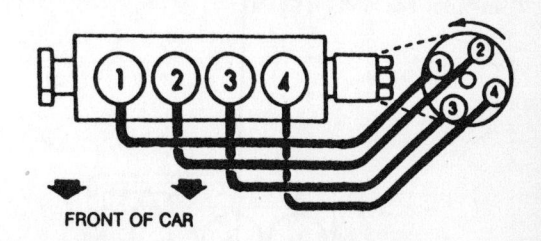

**2.0L Engine**
Engine Firing Order: 1-3-4-2
Distributor Rotation: Counterclockwise

**2.3L Engine**
Engine Firing Order: 1-3-4-2
Distributorless Ignition System

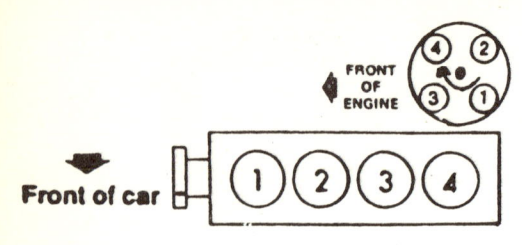

# 44 ENGINE PERFORMANCE AND TUNE-UP

**2.5L Engine (1985–86)**
Engine Firing Order: 1-3-4-2
Distributor Rotation: Clockwise

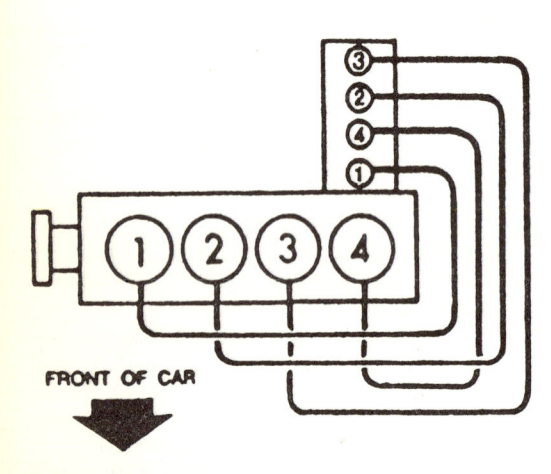

**2.5L Engine (1987–92)**
Engine Firing Order: 1-3-4-2
Distributorless Ignition System

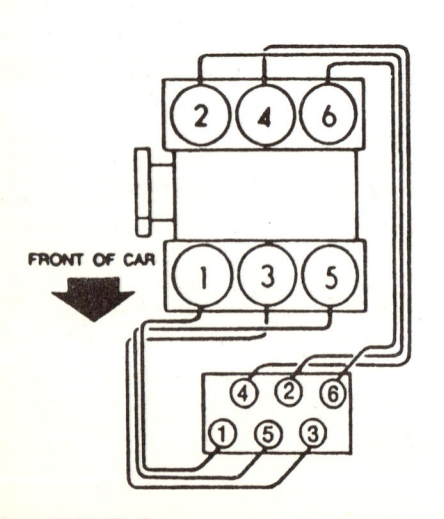

**3.0L and 3.3L Engines**
Enging Firing Order: 1-6-5-4-3-2
Distributorless Ignition System

tion system component. Dwell is controlled by the ECM and cannot be adjusted.

The HEI distributor is equipped to aid in spark timing changes necessary for optimum emissions, fuel economy and performance. All spark timing changes in the HEI (EST) distributors are performed electronically by the ECM, which monitors information from the various engine sensors, computes the desired spark timing and signals the distributor to change the timing accordingly. No vacuum or centrifugal advance is used with this distributor.

The Electronic Spark Control (ESC) system is used to control spark knock and enable maximum spark advance to improve driveability and fuel economy. This system consists of a knock sensor and an ESC module (generally part of Mem-Cal). The ECM monitors the ESC signal to determine when engine detonation occurs.

## SYSTEM OPERATION

The HEI distributor uses a magnetic pickup assembly, located inside the distributor containing a permanent magnet, a pole piece with internal teeth and a pickup coil. When the teeth of the rotating timer core and pole piece align, an induced voltage in the pickup coil signals the electronic module to open the coil primary circuit. As the primary current decreases, a high voltage is induced in the secondary windings of the ignition coil, directing a spark through the rotor and high voltage leads to fire the appropriate spark plug. The dwell period is automatically controlled by the ECM and increases with engine rpm.

To control ignition timing, the ECM receives information about the following conditions:
- Engine speed (rpm)
- Crankshaft position
- Engine load (manifold pressure or vacuum)
- Atmospheric (barometric) pressure
- Engine temperature
- Exhaust Gas Recirculation (EGR)

The ESC system is designed to retard spark timing 8–10° to reduce spark knock in the engine. When the knock sensor detects spark knock in the engine, it sends an AC voltage signal to the ECM, which increases with the severity of the knock. The ECM then signals the ESC circuit to adjust timing to reduce spark knock.

To control EST, the HEI module uses 4 connecting terminals. These terminals provide the following:
- Distributor reference circuit
- Reference ground circuit
- Bypass circuit
- EST circuit

# ENGINE PERFORMANCE AND TUNE-UP

## SYSTEM COMPONENTS

### Electronic Control Module (ECM)

The ECM is the control center of the fuel injection system. It constantly monitors information from various sensors and controls the system. The ECM has 2 replaceable parts. These parts are as follows:
- The controller — ECM without the MEM-CAL.
- The MEM-CAL.

### Memory Calibration (MEM-CAL) Unit

The MEM-CAL, located inside the ECM, allows the ECM to be installed in several different vehicles. It has calibration information based on the vehicle's weight, engine, transmission, axle ratio and several other factors.

### Pickup Coil

The pickup coil is a device which generates an alternating current signal to determine crankshaft position.

### HEI Module

The HEI module is a switching device which operates the primary circuit of the ignition coil.

### Ignition Secondary

The ignition secondary consists of the ignition coil, rotor, distributor cap, plugs wires and spark plug. These components supply the high voltage to fire the spark plugs.

### Electronic Spark Timing (EST)

The EST system consists of the distributor module, ECM and connecting wires. This system includes the following circuits:
- Distributor reference circuit — provides the ECM with rpm and crankshaft position information.
- Bypass signal — above 500 rpm, the ECM applies 5 volts to this circuit to switch spark timing control from the HEI module to the ECM.
- EST signal — the ECM uses this circuit to trigger the HEI module, after by-pass voltage is applied to the HEI module.
- Reference ground circuit — this wire is grounded through the module and insures that the ground circuit has no voltage drop between the ignition module and the ECM which could affect performance.

## Diagnosis and Testing

### SERVICE PRECAUTIONS

CAUTION: *The HEI coil secondary voltage output capabilities can exceed 40,000 volts. Avoid body contact with the HEI high voltage secondary components when the engine is running, or personal injury may result.*

NOTE: *To avoid damage to the ECM or other ignition system components, do not use electrical test equipment such as battery or AC powered voltmeter, ohmmeter, etc. or any type of tester other than specified.*

- When making compression checks, disconnect the ignition switch feed wire at the distributor.
- Never allow the tachometer terminal to touch ground, as damage to the module and/or ignition coil can result.
- To prevent Electrostatic Discharge damage, when working with the ECM, do not touch the connector pins or soldered components on the circuit board.
- When handling a PROM, CAL-PAK or MEM-CAL, do not touch the component leads. Also, do not remove the integrated circuit from the carrier.
- Never allow welding cables to lie on, near or across any vehicle electrical wiring.
- Leave new components and modules in the shipping package until ready to install them.
- When performing electrical tests on the system, use a high impedance multimeter, digital voltmeter (DVM) J–34029–A or equivalent.
- Never pierce a high tension lead or boot for any testing purpose; otherwise, future problems are guaranteed.

### READING CODES

The Assembly Line Diagnostic Link (ALDL) connector is used for communicating with the ECM. It is usually located under the instrument panel and is sometimes covered by a plastic cover labeled DIAGNOSTIC CONNECTOR. Codes stored in the ECM's memory can be read through a hand-held diagnostic scanner plugged into the ALDL connector. Codes can also be read by connecting a jumper wires between terminals A and B of the ALDL connector and counting the number of flashes of the SERVICE ENGINE SOON light, with the ignition switch turned **ON** and the engine **NOT** running.

### CLEARING CODES

To clear codes from the ECM memory, the ECM power feed must be disconnected for at least 30 seconds. Depending on the vehicle, the ECM power feed can be disconnected at the positive battery terminal pigtail, the inline fuseholder that originates at the positive connection at the battery or the ECM fuse in the fuse block. The negative battery cable may also be disconnected; however, other on-board memory data, such as radio station presets will also be lost.

## SYMPTOM DIAGNOSIS

An open or ground in the EST circuit, will set a Code 42 and cause the engine to run on the HEI module timing. This will cause poor performance and poor fuel economy.

Loss of the ESC signal, to the ECM, would cause the ECM to constantly retard the EST. This could result in sluggish performance and cause a Code 43 to set.

## ENGINE CRANKS BUT WILL NOT RUN

1. Check that the fuel quantity is ok.
2. Turn the ignition switch **ON**. Verify that the SERVICE ENGINE SOON light is ON.
3. Install the scan tool and check the following:
Throttle Position Sensor (TPS) — if over 2.5 volts, at closed throttle, check TPS for intermittent, open or short to ground, or faulty TPS.
Coolant — if less than 86°F (30°C), check Coolant Temperature Sensor (CTS) for intermittent, open or short to ground, or faulty CTS.
4. Connect spark checker, J 26792 or equivalent, and check for spark while cranking. Check at least 2 wires.
   a. If spark occurs, reconnect the spark plug wires and check for fuel spray at the injector(s) while cranking. If no spark is visible, go to the fuel system Chapter in this manual.
   b. If no spark occurs, check for battery voltage to the ignition system. If ok, use the ignition diagnosis chart.

## ELECTRONIC SPARK TIMING (EST) CIRCUIT

### TESTING

1. Clear codes.
2. Idle the engine for approximately 1 minute or until Code 42 sets. If Code 42 does not set, Code 42 is intermittent.
3. If Code 42 sets, turn the ignition **OFF** and disconnect the ECM connectors.
   a. Turn the ignition switch **ON**.
   b. Using an ohmmeter to ground, probe the ECM harness connector, at the EST circuit. Place the ohmmeter selector switch in the 1000–2000 ohms range. The meter should read less than 1000 ohms.
4. If not, check for a faulty connection, open circuit or faulty ignition module.
5. If ok, probe the bypass circuit with a test light to battery voltage.
6. If the test light is ON, disconnect the igni-tion 4-way connector and observe the test light.
   a. If the test light goes OFF, the problem is a faulty ignition module.
   b. If the test light stays ON, the bypass circuit is shorted to ground.
7. If the test light remains OFF, from Step 5, again probe the bypass circuit with the test light connected to battery voltage, and the ohmmeter still connected to the EST circuit and ground. As the test light contacts the bypass circuit, resistance should switch from under 1000 to over 2000 ohms.
   a. If it does, reconnect the ECM and idle the engine for approximately 1 minute or until Code 42 sets. If Code 42 sets, its a faulty ECM.
   b. If not, Code 42 is intermittent.
8. If the results are not as indicated in Step 7, disconnect the distributor 4-way connector. With the ohmmeter still connected to the bypass circuit, resistance should have gone high (open circuit).
9. If not, the EST circuit is shorted to ground.
10. If ok, the bypass circuit is open, faulty connections or faulty ignition module.
   NOTE: *When the problem has been corrected, clear codes and confirm Closed Loop operation and no SERVICE ENGINE SOON light.*

## PICKUP COIL

1. Remove the rotor and pickup coil leads from the module.
2. Using an ohmmeter, test as follow:
   a. Connect 1 lead of the ohmmeter between the distributor housing and 1 of the pickup coil lead. Meter should read infinity. Flex the leads by hand while observing the ohmmeter, to check for intermittent opens.

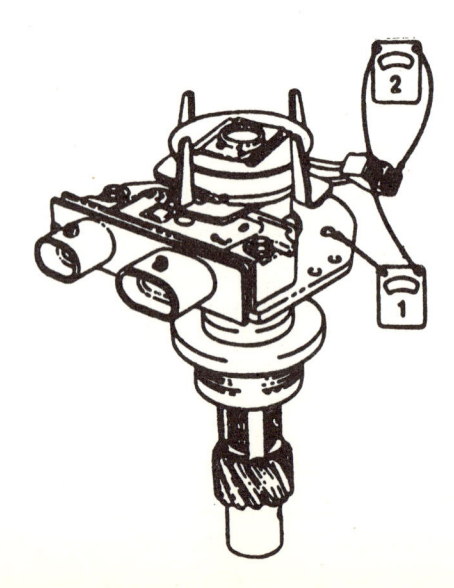

**Testing the HEI pick-up coil**

# ENGINE PERFORMANCE AND TUNE-UP

b. Connect the ohmmeter between leads between both of the pickup coil leads. Meter should read a steady value between 500–1500 ohms.

3. If the readings are not as specified, the pickup coil is defective and should be replaced.

## IGNITION COIL

1. Remove the ignition coil and check the coil with an ohmmeter for an open or ground.
2. Connect the meter as indicated in Step 1 (meter on the high scale). Should read very high or infinite. If not, replace the coil.
3. Connect the meter as indicated in Step 2 (meter on the low scale). Should read low or zero ohms. If not, replace the coil.
4. Connect the meter as indicated in Step 3 (meter on the high scale). Should not read infinite. If it does, replace the coil.

## Parts Replacement

### CAPACITOR

The capacitor, if equipped, is part of the coil wire harness assembly. The capacitor is used only for radio noise suppression, it will seldom need replacement.

### HEI DISTRIBUTOR

#### 2.0L Engine

1. Disconnect the negative battery cable.
2. Label and disconnect the coil and spark plug wires from the distributor cap.
3. Disconnect the coil and EST connectors.
4. Remove the distributor to cam carrier nuts.
5. Remove the distributor, marking the tang drive and camshaft for correct positioning upon reassembly.

**To install:**

6. Align the tang drive to the camshaft markings made upon removal.
7. Install the distributor-to-cam carrier nuts. Tighten to 13 ft. lbs. (18 Nm).
8. Connect the coil and EST connectors.
9. Connect the coil and spark plug wires to the cap.
10. Connect the negative battery cable.
11. Check and adjust ignition timing, as required.

#### 2.5L Engine

1. Disconnect the negative battery cable.
2. Remove the air cleaner assembly.
3. Disconnect the 2 electrical connectors from the side of the distributor.
4. Remove the distributor cover and wire retainer, if equipped. Turn the retaining screws counterclockwise and remove the cap.
5. Mark the relationship of the rotor to the distributor housing and the housing relationship to the engine.
6. Remove the distributor retaining bolt and hold-down clamp.
7. Pull the distributor up until the rotor just stops turning counterclockwise and again note the position of the rotor.
8. Remove the distributor from the engine.

**To install:**

9. Insert the distributor into the engine,

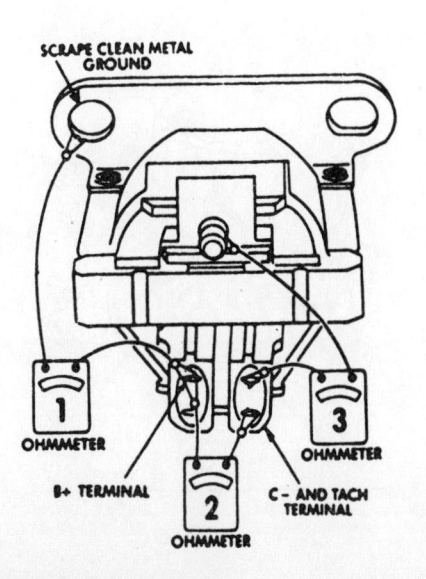

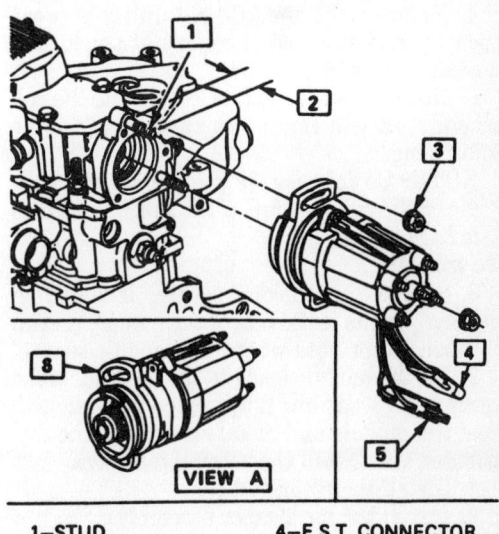

Testing the HEI ignition coil

Distributor installation—2.0L engine

1—STUD
2—20.5 ±1.0 (BOTH STUDS)
3—NUT ASM.
4—E.S.T. CONNECTOR
5—COIL CONNECTOR
6—DISTRIBUTOR ASM.

# ENGINE PERFORMANCE AND TUNE-UP

with the rotor aligned to the marks made previously.

10. Install the distributor hold-down clamp and retaining bolt.
11. If removed, install the wiring harness retainer and secondary wires.
12. Install the distributor cap.
13. Reconnect the 2 connectors to the side of the distributor. Make certain the connectors are fully seated and latched.
14. Reconnect the negative battery cable.

NOTE: *If the engine was accidentally cranked after the distributor was removed, the following procedure can be used during installation.*

15. Remove the No. 1 spark plug.
16. Place a finger over the spark plug hole and have a helper crank the engine slowly until compression is felt.
17. Align the timing mark on the pulley to **0** on the engine timing indicator. This will indicate that the engine is near TDC of the compression stroke.
18. Turn the rotor to point between No. 2 and No. 1 spark plug towers on the distributor cap.
19. Install the distributor assembly in the engine.
20. Install the cap and spark plug wires.
21. Check and adjust engine timing.

## HEI MODULE

1. Disconnect the negative battery cable.
2. Remove the air cleaner assembly.
3. Remove the distributor cap and rotor.
4. Remove the module retaining screws, then lift the stamped sheet metal shield and module upwards.
5. Disconnect the module leads. Note the color code on the leads, as these cannot be interchanged.

NOTE: *Do not wipe the grease from the module or distributor base, if the same module is to be replaced.*

**To install:**
6. Spread the silicone grease, included in package, on the metal face of the module and on the distributor base where the module seats.
7. Fit the module leads to the module. Make certain the leads are fully seated and latched. Seat the module and metal shield into the distributor and install the retaining screws.
8. Install the rotor and cap.
9. Install the air cleaner assembly.
10. Reconnect the negative battery cable.

## PICKUP COIL

1. Disconnect the negative battery cable.
2. Remove the distributor assembly.
3. Support the distributor assembly in a vice and drive the roll pin from the gear. Remove the shaft assembly.
4. To remove the pickup coil, remove the retainer and shield.
5. Lift the pickup coil assembly straight up to remove from the distributor.

**To install:**
6. Assembly the pickup coil, shield and retainer.
7. Install the shaft.
8. Install the gear and roll pin to the shaft. Make certain the matchmarks are aligned.
9. Spin the shaft and verify that the teeth do not touch the pole piece.
10. Reinstall the distributor.
11. Reconnect the negative battery cable.

## IGNITION COIL

1. Disconnect the negative battery cable.
2. Remove the secondary coil lead. Pull on the boot while a twisting.
3. Disconnect the harness connectors from the coil.
4. Remove the coil mounting screws.
5. Remove the ignition coil. If necessary, drill and punch out the rivets holding the coil to the bracket.

**To install:**
6. Place the ignition coil into position and install the mounting screws.
7. Reconnect the harness connector to the coil. Make certain the connectors are fully seated and latched.
8. Install the secondary lead to the coil tower.
9. Reconnect the negative battery cable.

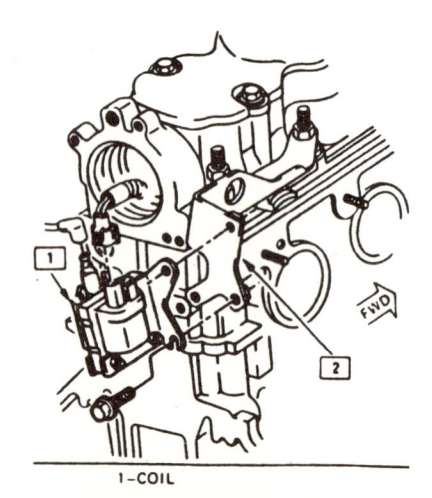

1-COIL
2-LIFT (COIL) BRACKET

**Ignition coil and mounting—2.0L engine**

# ENGINE PERFORMANCE AND TUNE-UP

## ELECTRONIC CONTROL MODULE (ECM) PROM CARRIER, CAL-PAK OR MEM-CAL
**Removal and Installation**

1. Turn the ignition switch **OFF**.
2. Disconnect the negative battery cable.
3. Remove the right side hush panel, as required.
4. Disconnect the harness connectors from the ECM.
5. Remove the ECM-to-bracket retaining screws and remove the ECM.
6. If replacement of the calibration unit is required, remove the access cover retaining screws and cover from the ECM. Carefully remove the calibration unit from the ECM, as follows:

    a. If the ECM contains a PROM carrier, use the rocker type PROM removal tool.
    b. If the ECM contains a Cal-Pak, grasp the Cal-Pak carrier (at the narrow end only), using the removal tool. Remove the Cal-Pak carrier.
    c. If the ECM contains a Mem-Cal, push both retaining clips back away from the Mem-Cal. At the same time, grasp it at both ends and lift it up out of the socket. Do not remove the cover of the Mem-Cal.

**To install:**

7. Fit the replacement calibration unit into the socket.
    NOTE: *The small notch of the carrier should be aligned with the small notch in the socket. Press on the ends of the carrier until it is firmly seated in the socket. Do not press on the calibration unit, only the carrier.*
8. Install the access cover and retaining screws.
9. Position the ECM in the vehicle and install the ECM-to-bracket retaining screws.
10. Reconnect the ECM harness connectors.
11. Install the right side hush panel, as required.
12. Check that the ignition switch is **OFF**. Then reconnect the negative battery cable.
    NOTE: *Before replacement of a defective ECM first check the resistance of each ECM controlled solenoid. This can be done at the ECM connector, using an ohmmeter and the ECM connector wiring diagram. Any ECM controlled device with low resistance will damage the replacement ECM due to high current flow through the ECM internal circuits.*

## PROGRAMMABLE READ ONLY MEMORY (PROM)
**Functional Check**

1. Turn the ignition switch **ON**.
2. Enter diagnostics, by grounding the appropriate ALDL terminals.

    a. Allow Code 12 to flash 4 times to verify that no other codes are present. This indicates the PROM is installed properly.
    b. If trouble Code 51 is present or if the SERVICE ENGINE SOON light is ON constantly with no codes, the PROM is not fully seated, installed backward, has bent pins or is defective.
    NOTE: *Anytime the calibration unit is installed backward and the ignition switch is turned ON, the unit is destroyed.*

## ESC KNOCK SENSOR
**Removal and Installation**

1. Disconnect the negative battery cable.
2. Raise and support the vehicle safely.
3. Disconnect the ESC wiring harness connector from the ESC sensor.
4. Remove the ESC sensor from the engine block.

**To install:**

5. Install the ESC sensor into the engine block. Tighten and torque to 14 ft. lbs. (19 Nm).
6. Reconnect the ESC wiring harness connector to the ESC sensor.
7. Lower the vehicle.
8. Reconnect the negative battery cable.

## INTEGRATED DIRECT IGNITION SYSTEM (IDI) 2.3L ENGINE

### General Description

The IDI ignition system features a distributorless ignition engine. The IDI system consists of 2 separate ignition coils, an ignition module and a secondary conductor housing mounted to an aluminum cover plate. The system also consists of a crankshaft sensor, connecting wires and the Electronic Spark Timing (EST) portion of the Electronic Control Module (ECM).

The IDI ignition system uses a magnetic crankshaft sensor (mounted remotely from the ignition module) and a reluctor to determine crankshaft position and engine speed. The reluctor is a special wheel cast into the crankshaft, with 7 slots machined into it. Six of the slots are equally spaced 60° apart and the seventh slot is spaced 10° from 1 of the other slots. This seventh slot is used to generate a sync-pulse.

The IDI system uses the same Electronic Spark Timing (EST) circuits as the distributor-type ignition. The ECM uses the EST circuit to control spark advance and ignition dwell, when the ignition system is operating in the EST mode.

# 50 ENGINE PERFORMANCE AND TUNE-UP

The Electronic Spark Control (ESC) system is used to control spark knock and enable maximum spark advance to improve driveability and fuel economy, . This system consists of a knock sensor and an ESC module (part of Mem-Cal). The ECM monitors the ESC signal to determine when engine detonation occurs.

## System Operation

The IDI ignition system uses a waste spark distribution method. Each cylinder is paired with the cylinder opposite it (i.e. 1–4, 2–3). The end of each coil secondary is attached to a spark plug. These 2 plugs are on companion cylinders, meaning they are at top dead center at the same time. The one that is on compression is said to be the event cylinder and the one on the exhaust stroke, the waste cylinder. When the coil discharges, both plugs fire at the same time to complete the series circuit.

Since the polarity of the primary and the secondary windings are fixed, one plug always fires in a forward direction and the other in reverse. This differs from a conventional system in which all plugs fire in the same direction each time. Because of the demand for additional energy; the coil design, saturation time and primary current flow are also different. This redesign of the system allows higher energy to be available from the distributorless coils, greater than 40 kilovolts at all rpm ranges.

The IDI ignition system uses a magnetic crankshaft sensor mounted remotely from the ignition module. It protrudes into the block to within approximately 0.050 in. (1.3mm) of the crankshaft reluctor. As the crankshaft rotates, the slots of the reluctor cause a changing magnetic field at the crankshaft sensor, creating an induced voltage pulse.

The IDI module sends reference signals to the ECM, based on the crankshaft sensor pulses, which are used to determine crankshaft position and engine speed. Reference pulses to the ECM occur at a rate of 1 per each 180° of crankshaft rotation. This signal is called the 2X reference because it occurs 2 times per crankshaft revolution.

A second reference signal is sent to the ECM

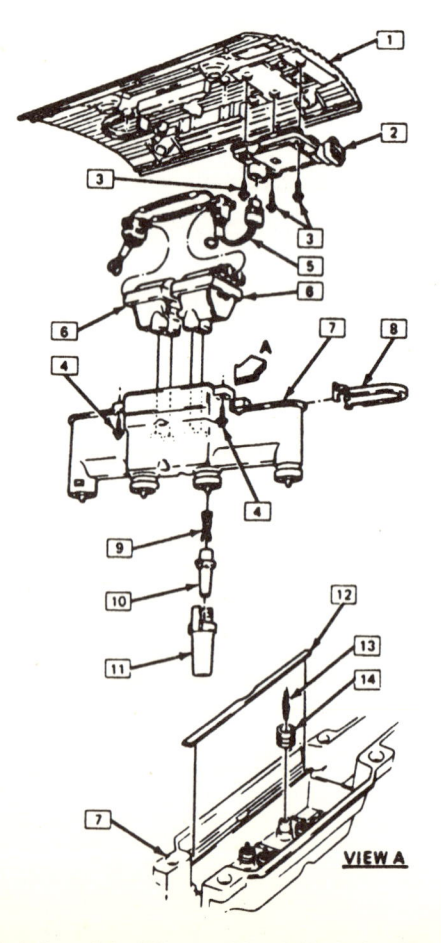

1. Ignition module cover
2. Ignition module assembly
3. Retaining bolt and screw, ignition module
4. Retaining bolt and screw, coil housing
5. Wiring harness, ignition module
6. Ignition coil assembly
7. Ignition coil, housing assembly
8. Ignition coil, housing cover
9. Connector, spark plug
10. Boot, spark plug
11. Retainer, spark plug
12. Spacer, ignition coil
13. Contact, ignition coil
14. Seal, ignition coil terminal

**Exploded view of the IDI assembly—2.3L engine. The entire unit is removed as an assembly**

## ENGINE PERFORMANCE AND TUNE-UP

which occurs at the same time as the sync-pulse, from the crankshaft sensor. This signal is called the 1X reference because it occurs 1 time per crankshaft revolution.

By comparing the time between the 1X and 2X reference pulses, the ignition module can recognize the sync-pulse (the seventh slot) which starts the calculation of the ignition coil sequencing. The second crank pulse following the sync-pulse signals the ignition module to fire No. 2-3 ignition coil and the fifth crank pulse signals the module to fire the No. 1-4 ignition coil.

During cranking, the ignition module monitors the sync-pulse to begin the ignition firing sequence and below 700 rpm the module controls spark advance by triggering each of the 2 coils at a pre-determined interval based on engine speed only. Above 700 rpm, the ECM controls the spark timing (EST) and compensates for all driving conditions. The ignition module must receive a sync-pulse and then a crank signal in that order to enable the engine to start.

To control EST the ECM uses the following inputs:

- Crankshaft position
- Engine speed (rpm)
- Engine coolant temperature
- Manifold air temperature
- Engine load (manifold pressure or vacuum)

The ESC system is designed to retard spark timing up to 15° to reduce spark knock in the engine. When the knock sensor detects spark knocking in the engine, it sends an AC voltage signal to the ECM, which increases with the severity of the knock. The ECM then adjusts the EST to reduce spark knock.

### SYSTEM COMPONENTS

#### Crankshaft Sensor

The crankshaft sensor, mounted remotely from the ignition module on an aluminum cover plate, is used to determine crankshaft position and engine speed.

#### Ignition Coil

The ignition coil assemblies are mounted inside the module assembly housing. Each coil distributes the spark for 2 plugs simultaneously.

#### Electronic Spark Timing (EST)

The EST system is basically the same EST to ECM circuit used on the distributor type ignition systems with EST. This system includes the following circuits:

- Reference circuit – provides the ECM with rpm and crankshaft position information from the IDI module. The IDI module receives this signal from the crank sensor.
- Bypass signal – above 700 rpm, the ECM applies 5 volts to this circuit to switch spark timing control from the IDI module to the ECM.
- EST signal – reference signal is sent to the ECM via the DIS module during cranking. Under 700 rpm, the IDI module controls the ignition timing. Above 700 rpm, the ECM applies 5 volts to the bypass line to switch the timing to the ECM control.
- Reference ground circuit – this wire is grounded through the module and insures that the ground circuit has no voltage drop between the ignition module and the ECM which could affect performance.

#### ESC Sensor

The ESC sensor, mounted in the engine block near the cylinders, detects abnormal vibration (spark knock) in the engine.

### Diagnosis and Testing

#### SERVICE PRECAUTIONS

NOTE: *To avoid damage to the ECM or other ignition system components, do not use electrical test equipment such as battery or AC powered voltmeter, ohmmeter, etc. or any type of tester other than specified.*

- When performing electrical tests on the system, use a high impedance multimeter, digital voltmeter (DVM) J-34029-A or equivalent. Use of a 12 volt test light is not recommended.
- To prevent Electrostatic Discharge damage, when working with the ECM, do not touch the connector pins or soldered components on the circuit board.
- When handling a PROM, CAL-PAK or MEM-CAL, do not touch the component leads. Also, do not remove the integrated circuit from the carrier.
- Never pierce a high tension lead or boot for any testing purpose; otherwise, future problems are guaranteed.
- Leave new components and modules in the shipping package until ready to install them.
- Never disconnect any electrical connection with the ignition switch ON unless instructed to do so in a test.

#### READING CODES

The Assembly Line Diagnostic Link (ALDL) connector is used for communicating with the ECM. It is usually located under the instrument panel and is sometimes covered by a plastic cover labeled "DIAGNOSTIC CONNECTOR." Codes stored in the ECM's memory can be read through a hand-held diagnostic scanner

# 52 ENGINE PERFORMANCE AND TUNE-UP

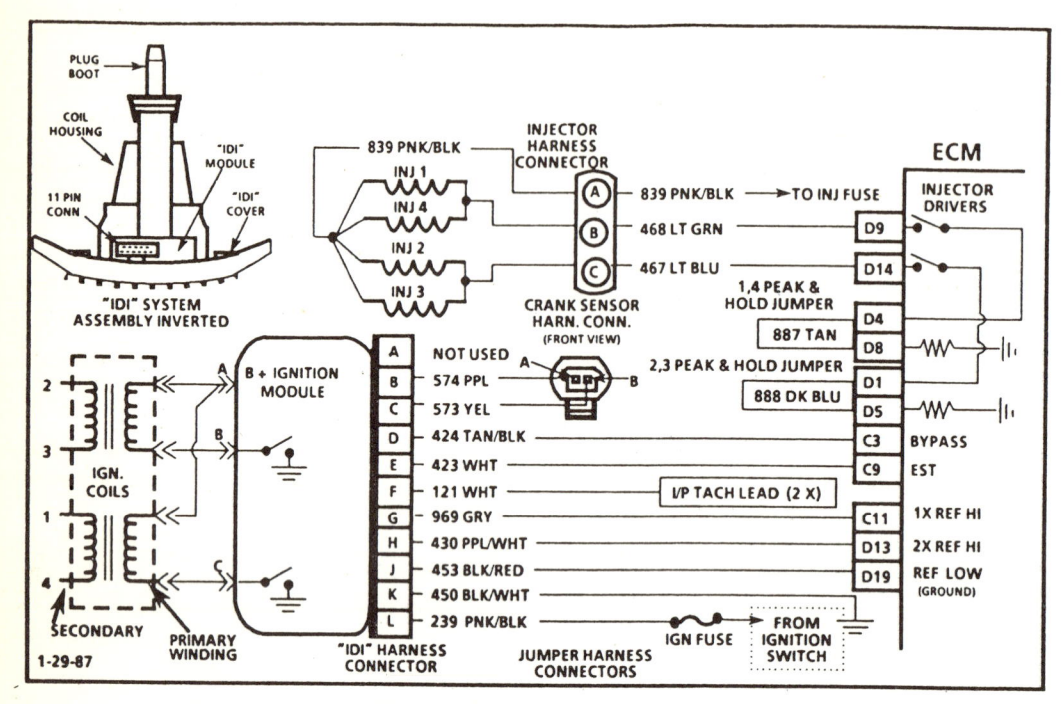

## INTEGRATED DIRECT IGNITION (IDI) MISFIRE DIAGNOSIS
## 2.3L (VIN D) (PORT)

### Circuit Description:
The "Integrated Direct Ignition" (IDI) system uses a waste spark method of distribution. In this type of system the ignition module triggers the #1-4 coil pair resulting in both #1 and #4 spark plugs firing at the same time. #1 cylinder is on the compression stroke at the same time #4 is on the exhaust stroke, resulting in a lower energy requirement to fire #4 spark plug. This leaves the remainder of the high voltage to be used to fire #1 spark plug. On this application, the crank sensor is mounted to, and protrudes through the block to within approximately 0.050" of the crankshaft reluctor. Since the reluctor is a machined portion of the crankshaft and the sensor is mounted in a fixed position on the block, timing adjustments are not possible or necessary.

### Test Description:
Numbers below refer to circled numbers on the diagnostic chart.
1. This checks for equal relative power output between the cylinders. Any injector which when disconnected did not result in an rpm drop approximately equal to the others, is located on the misfiring cylinder.
2. If a plug boot is burned, the other plug on that coil may still fire at idle. This step tests the system's ability to produce at least 25,000 volts at each spark plug.
3. No spark, on one coil, may be caused by an open secondary circuit. Therefore, the coil's secondary resistance should be checked. Resistance readings above 20,000 ohms, but not infinite, will probably not cause a no start but may cause an engine miss under certain conditions.
4. If the no spark condition is caused by coil connections, a coil or a secondary boot assembly, the test light will blink. If the light does not blink, the fault is module connections or the module.
5. Checks for ignition voltage feed to injector and for an open injector driver circuit.
6. An injector driver circuit shorted to ground would result in the test light "ON" steady, and possibly a flooded condition which could damage engine. A shorted injector (less than 2 ohms) could cause incorrect ECM operation.

### Diagnostic Aid:
Verify IDI connector terminal "K", CKT 450 resistance to ground is less than .5 ohm.

**Ignition system diagnosis—2.3L engine**

# ENGINE PERFORMANCE AND TUNE-UP

## INTEGRATED DIRECT IGNITION (IDI) MISFIRE DIAGNOSIS
## 2.3L (VIN D)     (PORT)

**(1)**
- ENGINE AT NORMAL OPERATING TEMPERATURE DISCONNECT IAC.
- REMOVE CV OIL/AIR SEPARATOR TO GAIN ACCESS TO INJECTOR. CONNECTORS.
- MOMENTARILY DISCONNECT EACH INJECTOR CONNECTOR WHILE OBSERVING ENGINE RPM.
- NOTE ANY INJECTOR(S) NOT RESULTING IN AN RPM DROP.
- INSTALL INJECTOR TEST LIGHT J-34730-2 IN INJ. HARN. CONN. FOR INJ. WHICH DID NOT RESULT IN RPM DROP. LIGHT SHOULD BLINK.
  DOES IT?

**YES** → (2) / **NO** → LIGHT "OFF" (5) or STEADY LIGHT (6)

**(2)**
- TEMPORARILY REMOVE IGNITION MODULE / COIL ASSEMBLY AND INSTALL SPARK PLUG JUMPER WIRES (J-36012)
- CHECK FOR SPARK WITH SPARK TESTER J-26792, (ST-125) OR EQUIVALENT ON PLUG JUMPER WIRE FOR CYLINDER(S) NOTED ABOVE WHILE CRANKING WITH <u>REMAINING PLUG WIRES STILL CONNECTED</u>.
- SPARK SHOULD JUMP TESTER GAP.
  DOES IT?

**(5) LIGHT "OFF"**
- DISCONNECT INJ. TEST LIGHT.
- PROBE INJ. HARNESS CONN. IGN FEED (PNK/BLK WIRE) TERMINAL AT INJ. WITH A TEST LIGHT TO GROUND.
- IGNITION "ON".
- TEST LIGHT SHOULD BE "ON". IS IT?

**(6) STEADY LIGHT**
- CHECK INJECTOR DRIVER CIRCUIT WHICH HAD THE STEADY LIGHT, FOR A SHORT TO GROUND.
- IF CIRCUIT IS NOT SHORTED, CHECK RESISTANCE ACROSS EACH INJECTOR IN THE CIRCUIT.
- RESISTANCE SHOULD BE BETWEEN 1.8 AND 2.2 OHMS FOR EACH INJECTOR.
  IS IT?

**(3) NO**
- REMOVE BOOT ASSYS. FOR AFFECTED COIL (1-4 OR 2-3)
- CONNECT DVM (20K OHMS SCALE) BETWEEN SECONDARY "IDI" COIL TERMINALS AND THEN FROM ONE COIL TERMINAL TO COVER PLATE.
- RESISTANCE SHOULD BE LESS THAN 10K OHMS BETWEEN TERMINALS AND INFINITE (OPEN CIRCUIT) TO COVER.
  IS IT?

**YES (from 2):** INSPECT SPARK PLUG AND BOOT FOR DAMAGE. IF OK, SUBSTITUTE A KNOWN GOOD INJ.,

**YES (from 5):** CHECK CKT 467 OR 468 FOR SHORT TO VOLTAGE, OPEN OR POOR CONNECTIONS AT ECM TERMINAL "D9" OR "D14". IF OK, CHECK FOR OPEN PEAK AND HOLD JUMPER CKT 887 OR 888. IF OK, REPLACE ECM.

**NO (from 5):** REPAIR OPEN OR GROUNDED CIRCUIT BETWEEN CAVITY "A" OF 3 TERMINAL INJECTOR HARNESS CONNECTOR AND INJECTOR CONNECTOR.

**NO (from 6):** REPLACE ANY INJECTOR THAT MEASURES UNDER 1.8 OHMS AND RECHECK FOR MISFIRE BEGINNING WITH STEP 1 AGAIN.

**YES (from 6):** FAULTY ECM.

**(4) YES**
- REMOVE COIL HOUSING AND DISCONNECT COIL HARNESS AT MODULE.
- OBSERVE A TEST LIGHT CONNECTED BETWEEN MODULE TO COIL POWER TERMINAL "A" (PURPLE WIRE) & DRIVER TERMINAL ("B" OR "C") FOR AFFECTED COIL, WHILE CRANKING ENGINE.
- SHOULD BLINK.
  DOES IT?

**NO (from 3):** CHECK FOR CORROSION AT COIL SECONDARY TERMINALS. IF TERMINALS ARE OK, THE IGNITION COIL IS FAULTY.

**NO (from 4):** POOR CONNECTION OR FAULTY IDI MODULE.

**YES (from 4):** OPEN OR SHORTED COIL HARNESS, POOR COIL CONNECTION, FAULTY COIL OR BOOT ASSEMBLY.

Ignition system diagnosis—2.3L engine

# 54  ENGINE PERFORMANCE AND TUNE-UP

plugged into the ALDL connector. If a scanner is not available, the codes can also be read by jumping from terminals **A** to **B** of the ALDL connector and counting the number of flashes of the Service Engine Soon light, with the ignition switch turned **ON**.

Refer to Chapter 4 for a more detailed look at diagnostic codes, what they mean and how to diagnose them.

### CLEARING CODES

To clear codes from the ECM memory, the ECM power feed must be disconnected for at least 30 seconds. Depending on the vehicle, the ECM power feed can be disconnected at the positive battery terminal pigtail, the inline fuseholder that originates at the positive connection at the battery or the ECM fuse in the fuse block. The negative battery cable may also be disconnected; however, other on-board memory data, such as preset radio tuning, will also be lost.

Also, if battery power is lost, computer re-learn time is approximately 5–10 minutes. This means the computer may have to re-calibrate components which set up the idle speed and the idle may fluctuate while this is occurring.

### SYMPTOM DIAGNOSIS

The ECM uses information from the MAP and coolant sensors, in addition to rpm to calculate spark advance as follows:
1. Low MAP output voltage – more spark advance
2. Cold engine – more spark advance
3. High MAP output voltage – less spark advance
4. Hot engine – less spark advance

Therefore, briefly, detonation could be caused by low MAP output or high resistance in the coolant sensor circuit. And poor performance could be caused by high MAP output or low resistance in the coolant sensor circuit.

The best way to diagnose what may be an ignition-related problem, first check for codes. If codes, exist, refer to the corresponding diagnostic charts in Chapter 4. Otherwise, the following charts may be helpful.

## Ignition Timing Adjustment

Because the reluctor wheel is an integral part of the crankshaft and the crankshaft sensor is mounted in a fixed position, timing adjustment is not possible or necessary.

## Parts Replacement

### IGNITION COIL AND MODULE ASSEMBLY

1. Turn the ignition switch **OFF**.
2. Disconnect the negative battery cable.
3. Disconnect the 11-pin IDI ignition harness connector.
4. Remove the ignition system assembly-to-camshaft housing bolts.
5. Remove the ignition system assembly from the engine.

NOTE: *If the boots are difficult to remove from the spark plugs, use tool J36011 or equivalent, to remove. First twist and then pull upward on the retainers. Reinstall the boots and retainers on the IDI housing secondary terminals. The boots and retainers must be in place on the IDI housing secondary terminals prior to ignition system assembly installation or ignition system damage may result.*

**To install:**

6. Install the spark plug boots and retainers to the housing.
7. Carefully aligned the boots to the spark plug terminals, while installing the ignition system assembly to the engine.
8. Coat the threads of the retaining bolts with 1052080 or equivalent and install. Tighten and torque to 19 ft. lbs. (26 Nm).
9. Reconnect the 11-pin IDI harness connector.
10. Check that the ignition switch is **OFF**. Then reconnect the negative battery cable.

### IGNITION COIL

1. Disconnect the negative battery cable.
2. Remove the IDI assembly from the engine.
3. Remove the housing to cover screws.
4. Remove the housing from the cover.
5. Remove the coil harness connector.
6. Remove the coils, contacts and seals from the cover.

**To install:**

7. Install the coil to the cover.
8. Install the coil harness connectors.
9. Install new seals to the housing.
10. Install the contacts to the housing. Use petroleum jelly to retain the contacts.
11. Install the housing cover and retaining screws. Tighten and torque to 35 inch lbs. (4 Nm).
12. Fit the spark plug boots and retainers to the housing.
13. Install the IDI assembly to the engine.
14. Reconnect the negative battery cable.

### IGNITION MODULE

1. Disconnect the negative battery cable.
2. Remove the IDI assembly from the engine.
3. Remove the housing to cover screws.
4. Remove the housing from the cover.
5. Remove the coil harness connector from the module.
6. Remove the module-to-cover retaining screws and remove the module from the cover.

## ENGINE PERFORMANCE AND TUNE-UP

NOTE: *Do not wipe the grease from the module or coil, if the same module is to be replaced. If a new module is to be installed, spread the grease (included in package) on the metal face of the new module and on the cover where the module seats. This grease is necessary from module cooling.*

**To install:**

7. Position the module to the cover and install the retaining screws. Tighten and torque to 35 inch lbs. (4 Nm).
8. Reconnect the coil harness connector to the module.
9. Install the housing cover and retaining screws. Tighten and torque to 35 inch lbs. (4 Nm).
10. Fit the spark plug boots and retainers to the housing.
11. Install the IDI assembly to the engine.
12. Reconnect the negative battery cable.

### CRANKSHAFT SENSOR

1. Disconnect the negative battery cable.
2. Disconnect the sensor harness connector at the sensor.
3. Remove the sensor retaining bolts and pull the sensor from the engine.

**To install:**

4. Fit a new O-ring to the sensor and lubricate with engine oil. Install the sensor into the engine.
5. Install the sensor retaining bolt. Tighten and torque to 88 inch lbs. (10 Nm).

6. Reconnect the sensor harness connector.
7. Reconnect the negative battery cable.

### ELECTRONIC CONTROL MODULE (ECM) OR MEM-CAL

1. Turn the ignition switch **OFF**.
2. Disconnect the negative battery cable.
3. Remove the right side hush panel.
4. Disconnect the harness connectors from the ECM.
5. Remove the ECM-to-bracket retaining screws and remove the ECM.

NOTE: *Before replacement of a defective ECM first check the resistance of each ECM controlled solenoid. This can be done at the ECM connector, using an ohmmeter and the ECM connector wiring diagram. Any ECM controlled device with low resistance will damage the replacement ECM due to high current flow through the ECM internal circuits.*

6. If replacement of the Mem-Cal is required, remove the access cover retaining screws and cover from the ECM. Note the position of the Mem-Cal for proper installation in the new ECM. Using 2 fingers, carefully push both retaining clips back away from the Mem-Cal. At the same time, grasp it at both ends and lift it up out of the socket. Do not remove the cover of the Mem-Cal.

**To install:**

7. Fit the replacement Mem-Cal into the socket.

NOTE: *The small notches in the Mem-Cal must be aligned with the small notches in the socket. Press only on the ends of the Mem-Cal until the retaining clips snap into the ends of the Mem-Cal. Do not press on the middle of the Mem-Cal, only the ends.*

8. Install the access cover and retaining screws.
9. Position the ECM in the vehicle and install the ECM-to-bracket retaining screws.
10. Reconnect the ECM harness connectors.
11. Install the hush panel.
12. Check that the ignition switch is **OFF**. Then reconnect the negative battery cable.

**Functional Check**

1. Turn the ignition switch **ON**.
2. Enter diagnostics.
   a. Allow Code 12 to flash 4 times to verify no other codes are present. This indicates the Mem-Cal is installed properly and the ECM is functioning.
   b. If trouble Codes 42, 43 or 51 occur, or if the **SERVICE ENGINE SOON** light is ON constantly with no codes, the Mem-Cal is not fully seated or is defective.
   c. If it is not fully seated, press firmly on the ends of the Mem-Cal.

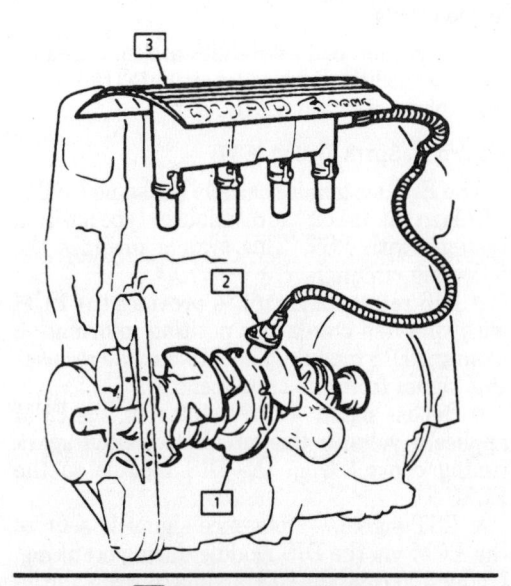

| 1 | CRANKSHAFT RELUCTOR |
| 2 | SENSOR ASM, CRANKSHAFT |
| 3 | IGNITION COIL AND MODULE ASM |

Crankshaft sensor—2.3L engine

# ENGINE PERFORMANCE AND TUNE-UP

## ESC KNOCK SENSOR

1. Disconnect the negative battery cable.
2. Raise and support the vehicle safely.
3. Disconnect the harness connector from the knock sensor.
4. Remove the sensor from the engine block.

**To install:**

5. Clean the threads on the engine block, where the sensor was installed. Install the sensor. Tighten to 11–16 ft. lbs. (15–22 Nm).
6. Reconnect the harness connector to the knock sensor.
7. Lower the vehicle.
8. Reconnect the negative battery cable.

## DIRECT IGNITION SYSTEM (DIS) – 2.5L (VIN U) – 1987–92 ENGINE

### General Description

The DIS ignition system features a distributorless ignition engine. The DIS system consists of 2 separate ignition coils on the 2.5L engine, a DIS ignition module, a crankshaft sensor, crankshaft reluctor ring, connecting wires and the Electronic Spark Timing (EST) portion of the Electronic Control Module (ECM).

The DIS ignition system uses a magnetic crankshaft sensor and a reluctor to determine crankshaft position and engine speed. The reluctor is a special wheel cast into the crankshaft with several machined slots. A specific slot, on the reluctor wheel, is used to generate a sync-pulse.

The DIS system uses the same Electronic Spark Timing (EST) circuits as the distributor-type ignition. The ECM uses the EST circuit to control spark advance and ignition dwell, when the ignition system is operating in the EST mode.

### System Operation

The DIS ignition system uses a waste spark distribution method. Each cylinder is paired with its companion cylinder (i.e. 1–4, 2–3. on a 4-cylinder engine). The end of each coil secondary is attached to a spark plug. These 2 plugs, being companion cylinders, are at top dead center at the same time. The one that is on compression is said to be the event cylinder and the one on the exhaust stroke, the waste cylinder. When the coil discharges, both plugs fire at the same time to complete the series circuit.

Since the polarity of the primary and the secondary windings are fixed, one plug always fires in a forward direction and the other in reverse. This is differs from a conventional system in which all plugs fire in the same direction each time. Because of the demand for additional energy; the coil design, saturation time and primary current flow are also different. This redesign of the system allows higher energy to be available from the distributorless coils, greater than 40 kilovolts at all rpm ranges.

The DIS ignition system uses a magnetic crankshaft sensor which protrudes into the engine block to within approximately 0.050 in. (1.3mm) of the crankshaft reluctor. As the crankshaft rotates, the slots of the reluctor cause a changing magnetic field at the crankshaft sensor, creating an induced voltage pulse. By counting the time between pulses, the ignition module can recognize the specified slot (sync pulse). Based on this sync pulse, the module sends reference signals to the ECM to calculate crankshaft position and engine speed.

To control EST the ECM uses the following inputs:
- Crankshaft position
- Engine Speed (rpm)
- Engine temperature
- Manifold air temperature
- Atmospheric (barometric) pressure
- Engine load (manifold pressure or vacuum)

### SYSTEM COMPONENTS

**Crankshaft Sensor**

The crankshaft sensor is mounted to the bottom of the DIS module. It is used determine crankshaft position and engine speed.

**Ignition Coils**

The ignition coil assemblies are mounted on the DIS module. Each coil distributes the spark for 2 plugs simultaneously.

**Electronic Spark Timing (EST)**

The EST system is basically the same EST to ECM circuit use on the distributor type ignition systems with EST. This system includes the following circuits:

- DIS reference circuit – provides the ECM with rpm and crankshaft position information from the DIS module. The DIS module receives this signal from the crank sensor.
- Bypass signal – above 400 rpm, the ECM applies 5 volts to this circuit to switch spark timing control from the DIS module to the ECM.
- EST signal – reference signal is sent to the ECM via the DIS module during cranking. Under 400 rpm, the DIS module controls the ignition timing. Above 400 rpm, the ECM applies 5 volts to the bypass line to switch the timing to the ECM control.
- Reference ground circuit – this wire is

# ENGINE PERFORMANCE AND TUNE-UP

grounded through the module and insures that the ground circuit has no voltage drop between the ignition module and the ECM which could affect performance.

## Diagnosis and Testing
### SERVICE PRECAUTIONS

NOTE: *To avoid damage to the ECM or other ignition system components, do not use electrical test equipment such as battery or AC powered voltmeter, ohmmeter, etc. or any type of tester other than specified.*

- When performing electrical tests on the system, use a high impedance multimeter or quality digital voltmeter (DVM). Use of a 12 volt test light is not recommended.
- To prevent electrostatic discharge damage, when working with the ECM, do not touch the connector pins or soldered components on the circuit board.
- When handling a PROM, CAL-PAK or MEM-CAL, do not touch the component leads. Also, do not remove the integrated circuit from the carrier.
- When performing electrical tests on the system, use a high impedance multimeter, digital voltmeter (DVM) J–34029–A or equivalent.
- Never pierce a high tension lead or boot for any testing purpose; otherwise, future problems are guaranteed.
- Leave new components and modules in the shipping package until ready to install them.
- Never disconnect any electrical connection with the ignition switch ON unless instructed to do so in a test.

### READING CODES

The Assembly Line Diagnostic Link (ALDL) connector is used for communicating with the ECM. It is usually located under the instrument panel and is sometimes covered by a plastic cover labeled "DIAGNOSTIC CONNECTOR." Codes stored in the ECM's memory can be read through a hand-held diagnostic scanner plugged into the ALDL connector. If a scanner is not available, the codes can also be read by jumping from terminals **A** to **B** of the ALDL connector and counting the number of flashes of the SERVICE ENGINE SOON light, with the ignition switch turned **ON**.

Refer to Chapter 4 for a more detailed look diagnostic codes, what they mean and how to diagnose them.

### CLEARING CODES

To clear codes from the ECM memory, the ECM power feed must be disconnected for at least 30 seconds. Depending on the vehicle, the ECM power feed can be disconnected at the positive battery terminal pigtail, the inline fuseholder that originates at the positive connection at the battery or the ECM fuse in the fuse block. The negative battery cable may also be disconnected; however, other on-board memory data, such as radio station presets, will also be lost.

### SYMPTOM DIAGNOSIS

The ECM uses information from the MAP and coolant sensors, in addition to rpm to calculate spark advance as follows:

1. Low MAP output voltage – more spark advance
2. Cold engine – more spark advance
3. High MAP output voltage – less spark advance
4. Hot engine – less spark advance

Therefore, briefly, detonation could be caused by low MAP output or high resistance in the coolant sensor circuit. And poor performance could be caused by high MAP output or low resistance in the coolant sensor circuit.

The best way to diagnose what may be an ignition-related problem, first check for codes. Otherwise, the following charts may be helpful.

## Parts Replacement
### IGNITION COIL

1. Disconnect the negative battery cable.
2. Disconnect the spark plug wires.
3. Remove the coil retaining nuts.
4. Separate and remove the coils from the module.

**To install:**

5. Fit the coils to the module and install the retaining nuts. Tighten and torque the retaining nuts 40 inch lbs. (4.5 Nm).
6. Install the spark plug wires.
7. Reconnect the negative battery cable.

### DIS ASSEMBLY

1. Disconnect the negative battery cable.
2. Disconnect the DIS electrical connectors.

**TERMINAL IDENTIFICATION**

| A | GROUND | E | SERIAL DATA |
| B | DIAGNOSTIC TERMINAL | F | TCC (IF USED) |
| C | A.I.R. (IF USED) | G | FUEL PUMP (IF USED) |
| D | SERVICE ENGINE SOON LIGHT (IF USED) | M | SERIAL DATA (IF USED) |

**ALDL connector terminals**

# 58 ENGINE PERFORMANCE AND TUNE-UP

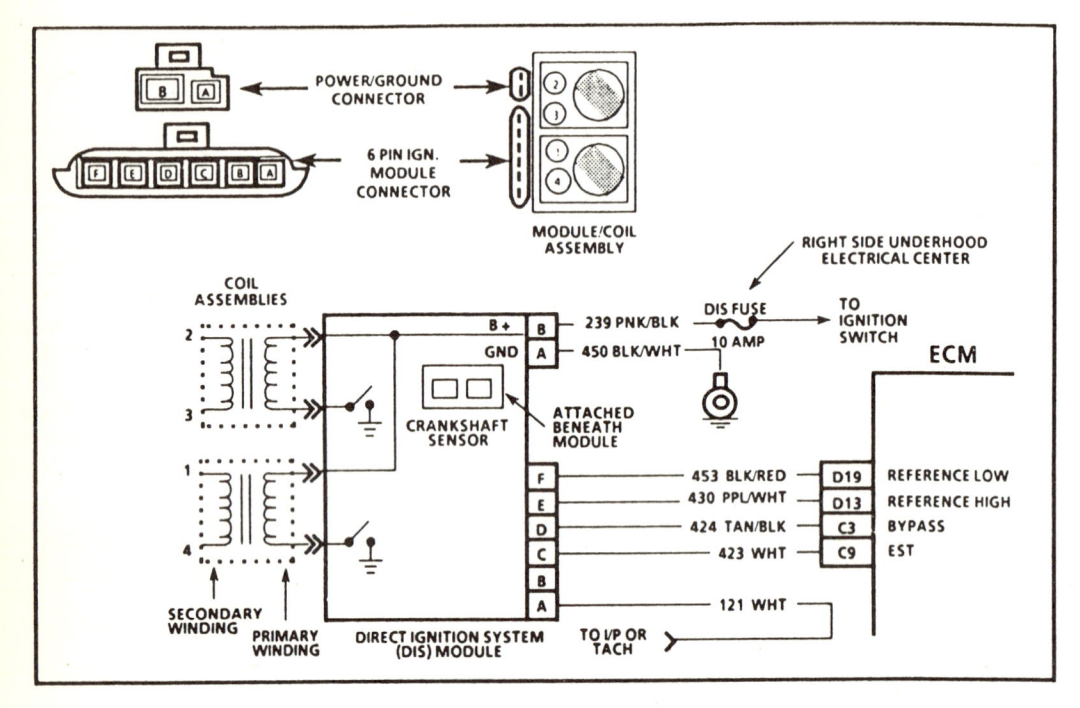

## "DIS" MISFIRE UNDER LOAD
## 2.5L (VIN R) (TBI)

**Circuit Description:**
The Direct Ignition System (DIS) uses a waste spark method of distribution. In this type of system, the ignition module triggers a dual coil, resulting in both connected spark plugs firing at the same time. One cylinder is on its compression stroke at the same time that the other is on its exhaust stroke, resulting in a lower energy requirement to fire the spark plug in the cylinder on its exhaust stroke. This leaves the remainder of the high voltage to be used to fire the spark plug which is in the cylinder on its compression stroke. On this application, the crank sensor is mounted to the bottom of the coil/module assembly and protrudes through the block to within approximately .050" of the crankshaft reluctor. Since the reluctor is a machined portion of the crankshaft and the crank sensor is mounted in a fixed position on the block, timing adjustments are not possible or necessary.

**Test Description:** Number(s) below refer to circled number(s) on the diagnostic chart.
1. If the "Misfire" complaint exists <u>at idle only</u>, CHART C-4D-1 must be used. Engine rpm should drop approximately equally on all plug leads. A spark tester such as a ST-125 must be used because it is essential to verify adequate available secondary voltage at the spark plug (25,000 volts).
2. If the spark jumps the test gap after grounding the opposite plug wire, it indicates excessive resistance in the plug which was bypassed. A faulty or poor connection at that plug could also result in the miss condition. Also check for carbon deposits inside the spark plug boot.
3. If carbon tracking is evident, replace coil and be sure plug wires relating to that coil are clean and tight. Excessive wire resistance or faulty connections could have caused the coil to be damaged.
4. If the no spark condition follows the suspected coil, that coil is faulty. Otherwise, the ignition module is the cause of no spark. This test could also be performed by substituting a known good coil for the one causing the no spark condition.

**Ignition system diagnosis—2.5L engine**

# ENGINE PERFORMANCE AND TUNE-UP 59

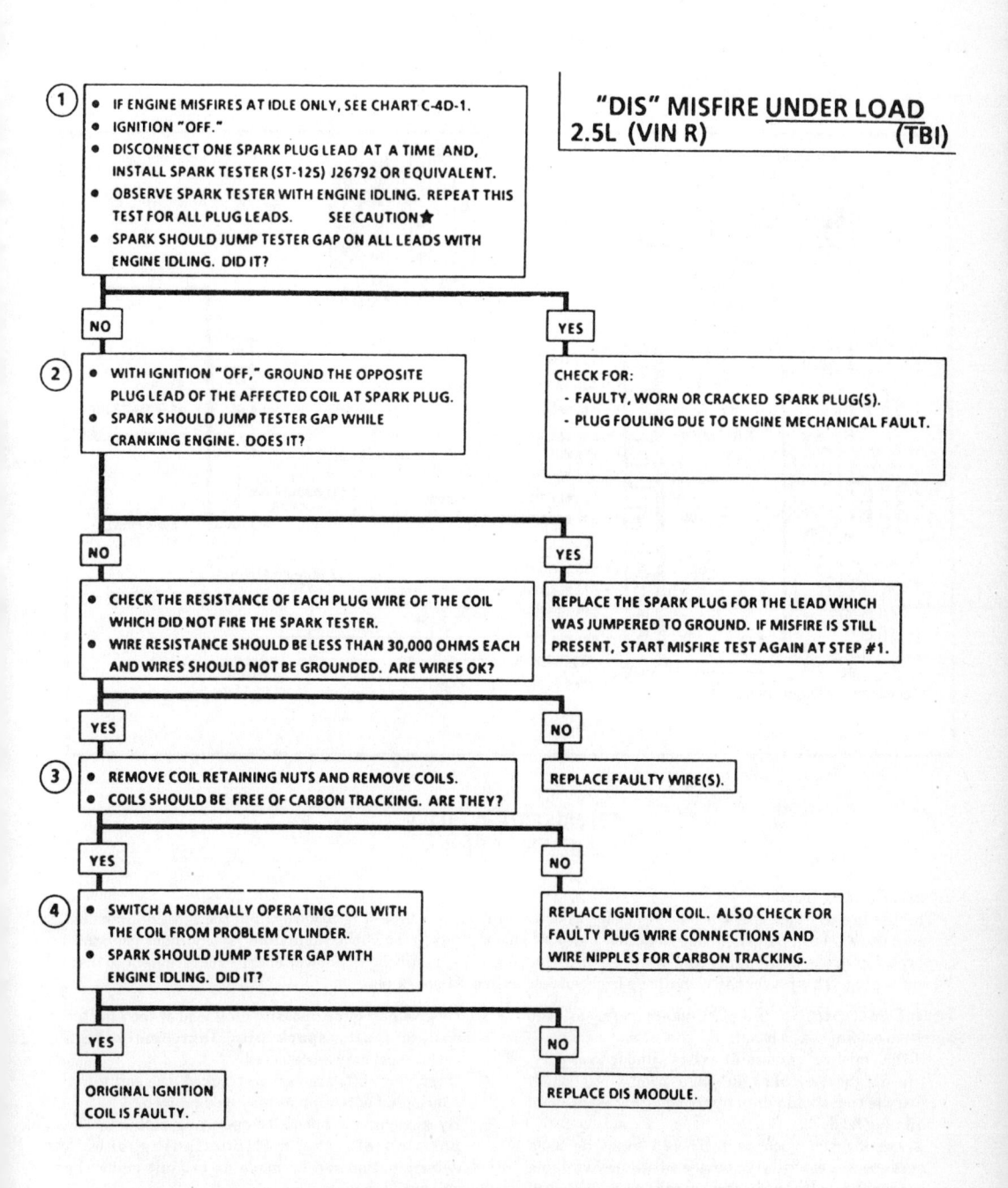

**"DIS" MISFIRE UNDER LOAD**
**2.5L (VIN R)**                                  **(TBI)**

**(1)**
- IF ENGINE MISFIRES AT IDLE ONLY, SEE CHART C-4D-1.
- IGNITION "OFF."
- DISCONNECT ONE SPARK PLUG LEAD AT A TIME AND, INSTALL SPARK TESTER (ST-125) J26792 OR EQUIVALENT.
- OBSERVE SPARK TESTER WITH ENGINE IDLING. REPEAT THIS TEST FOR ALL PLUG LEADS.    SEE CAUTION ★
- SPARK SHOULD JUMP TESTER GAP ON ALL LEADS WITH ENGINE IDLING. DID IT?

**NO** → **(2)**
- WITH IGNITION "OFF," GROUND THE OPPOSITE PLUG LEAD OF THE AFFECTED COIL AT SPARK PLUG.
- SPARK SHOULD JUMP TESTER GAP WHILE CRANKING ENGINE. DOES IT?

**YES** → CHECK FOR:
- FAULTY, WORN OR CRACKED SPARK PLUG(S).
- PLUG FOULING DUE TO ENGINE MECHANICAL FAULT.

**NO** →
- CHECK THE RESISTANCE OF EACH PLUG WIRE OF THE COIL WHICH DID NOT FIRE THE SPARK TESTER.
- WIRE RESISTANCE SHOULD BE LESS THAN 30,000 OHMS EACH AND WIRES SHOULD NOT BE GROUNDED. ARE WIRES OK?

**YES** → REPLACE THE SPARK PLUG FOR THE LEAD WHICH WAS JUMPERED TO GROUND. IF MISFIRE IS STILL PRESENT, START MISFIRE TEST AGAIN AT STEP #1.

**YES** → **(3)**
- REMOVE COIL RETAINING NUTS AND REMOVE COILS.
- COILS SHOULD BE FREE OF CARBON TRACKING. ARE THEY?

**NO** → REPLACE FAULTY WIRE(S).

**YES** → **(4)**
- SWITCH A NORMALLY OPERATING COIL WITH THE COIL FROM PROBLEM CYLINDER.
- SPARK SHOULD JUMP TESTER GAP WITH ENGINE IDLING. DID IT?

**NO** → REPLACE IGNITION COIL. ALSO CHECK FOR FAULTY PLUG WIRE CONNECTIONS AND WIRE NIPPLES FOR CARBON TRACKING.

**YES** → ORIGINAL IGNITION COIL IS FAULTY.

**NO** → REPLACE DIS MODULE.

★**CAUTION:** When handling secondary spark plug leads with engine running, insulated pliers must be used and care exercised to prevent a possible electrical shock.

"AFTER REPAIRS," CONFIRM "CLOSED LOOP" OPERATION AND NO "SERVICE ENGINE SOON" LIGHT.

**Ignition system diagnosis—2.5L engine**

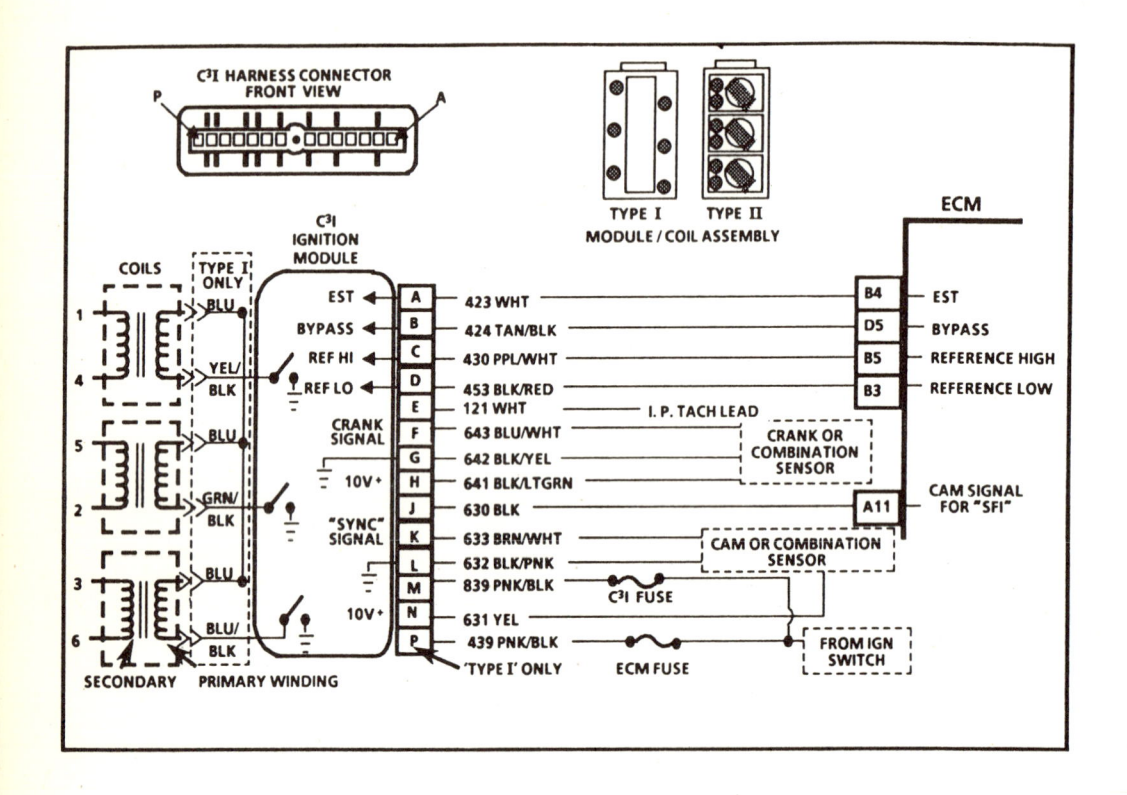

# ENGINE PERFORMANCE AND TUNE-UP

## C³I MISFIRE AT IDLE
## 3.0L "N" SERIES

### Circuit Description:
The C³I uses a waste spark method of spark distribution. In this type of ignition system the ignition module triggers the #1/4 coil pair resulting in both #1 and #4 spark plugs firing at the same time. #1 cylinder is on the compression stroke at the same time #4 is on the exhaust stroke, resulting in a lower energy requirement to fire #4 spark plug. This leaves the remaining high voltage to fire #1 spark plug.

### Test Description:
Step numbers refer to step numbers on diagnostic chart.
1. If the "misfire" complaint exists <u>under load only</u>, the diagnostic chart on page 2 must be used. Engine rpm should drop approximately equally on all plug leads.
2. A spark tester such as a ST-125 must be used because it is essential to verify adequate available secondary voltage at the spark plug. (25,000 volts.).
3. By grounding the opposite plug lead of the affected coil, a faulty spark plug (extremely high resistance) may be detected.
4. If ignition coils are carbon tracked, the coil tower spark plug wire nipples may be damaged.
5. By switching a normally operating coil into the position of the malfunctioning one, a determination can be made as to fault being the coil or C³I module.

**Ignition system diagnosis—3.0L engine**

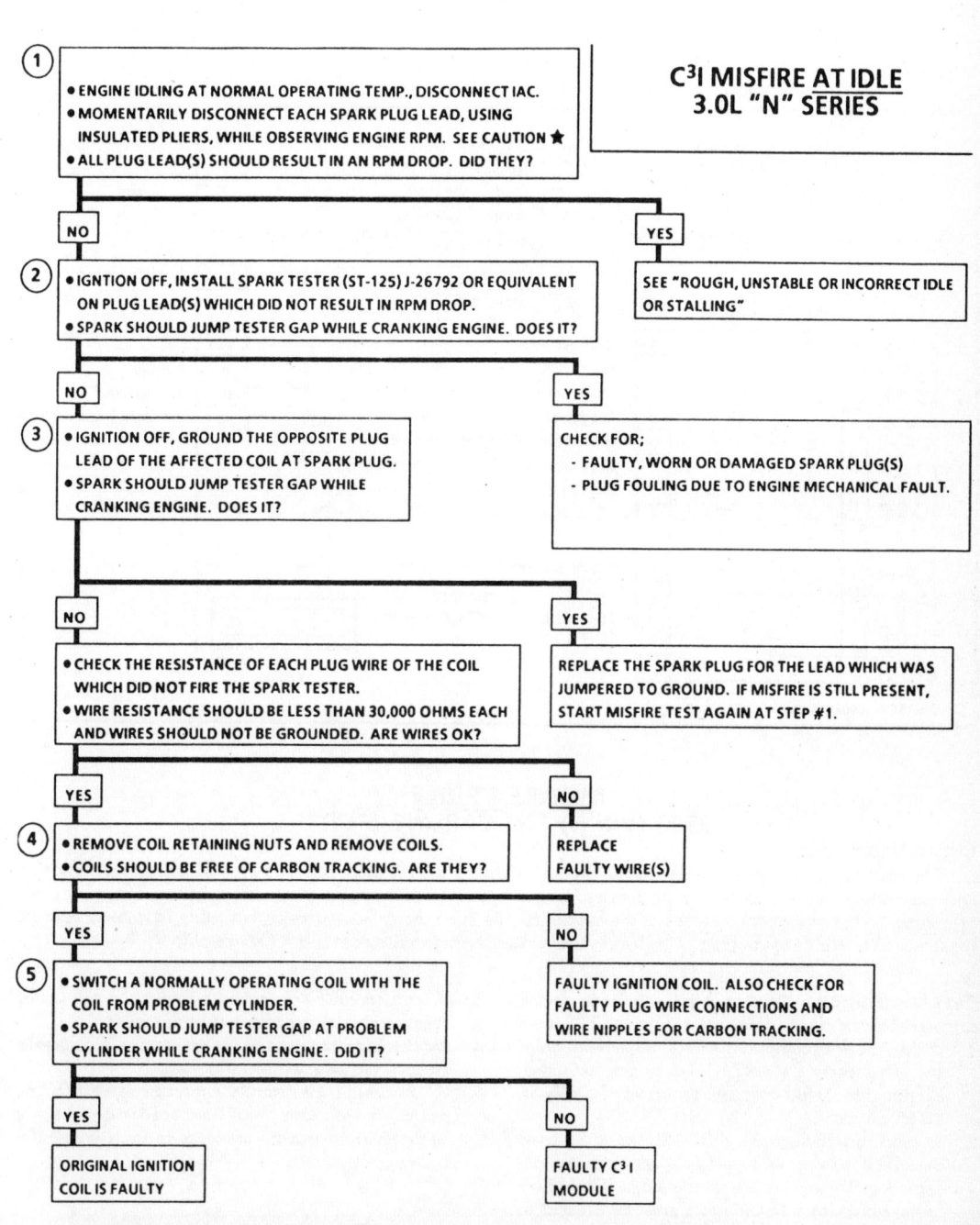

# ENGINE PERFORMANCE AND TUNE-UP

**C³I MISFIRE AT IDLE**
**3.0L "N" SERIES**

**1.**
- ENGINE IDLING AT NORMAL OPERATING TEMP., DISCONNECT IAC.
- MOMENTARILY DISCONNECT EACH SPARK PLUG LEAD, USING INSULATED PLIERS, WHILE OBSERVING ENGINE RPM. SEE CAUTION ★
- ALL PLUG LEAD(S) SHOULD RESULT IN AN RPM DROP. DID THEY?

**NO** →

**YES** → SEE "ROUGH, UNSTABLE OR INCORRECT IDLE OR STALLING"

**2.**
- IGNITION OFF, INSTALL SPARK TESTER (ST-125) J-26792 OR EQUIVALENT ON PLUG LEAD(S) WHICH DID NOT RESULT IN RPM DROP.
- SPARK SHOULD JUMP TESTER GAP WHILE CRANKING ENGINE. DOES IT?

**NO** →

**YES** → CHECK FOR;
- FAULTY, WORN OR DAMAGED SPARK PLUG(S)
- PLUG FOULING DUE TO ENGINE MECHANICAL FAULT.

**3.**
- IGNITION OFF, GROUND THE OPPOSITE PLUG LEAD OF THE AFFECTED COIL AT SPARK PLUG.
- SPARK SHOULD JUMP TESTER GAP WHILE CRANKING ENGINE. DOES IT?

**NO** →

**YES** → REPLACE THE SPARK PLUG FOR THE LEAD WHICH WAS JUMPERED TO GROUND. IF MISFIRE IS STILL PRESENT, START MISFIRE TEST AGAIN AT STEP #1.

- CHECK THE RESISTANCE OF EACH PLUG WIRE OF THE COIL WHICH DID NOT FIRE THE SPARK TESTER.
- WIRE RESISTANCE SHOULD BE LESS THAN 30,000 OHMS EACH AND WIRES SHOULD NOT BE GROUNDED. ARE WIRES OK?

**YES** →

**NO** → REPLACE FAULTY WIRE(S)

**4.**
- REMOVE COIL RETAINING NUTS AND REMOVE COILS.
- COILS SHOULD BE FREE OF CARBON TRACKING. ARE THEY?

**YES** →

**NO** → FAULTY IGNITION COIL. ALSO CHECK FOR FAULTY PLUG WIRE CONNECTIONS AND WIRE NIPPLES FOR CARBON TRACKING.

**5.**
- SWITCH A NORMALLY OPERATING COIL WITH THE COIL FROM PROBLEM CYLINDER.
- SPARK SHOULD JUMP TESTER GAP AT PROBLEM CYLINDER WHILE CRANKING ENGINE. DID IT?

**YES** → ORIGINAL IGNITION COIL IS FAULTY

**NO** → FAULTY C³I MODULE

★**CAUTION:** When handling secondary spark plug leads with engine running, insulated pliers must be used and care exercised to prevent a possible electrical shock.

CLEAR CODES AND CONFIRM "CLOSED LOOP" OPERATION AND NO "SERVICE ENGINE SOON" LIGHT.

**Ignition system diagnosis—3.0L engine**

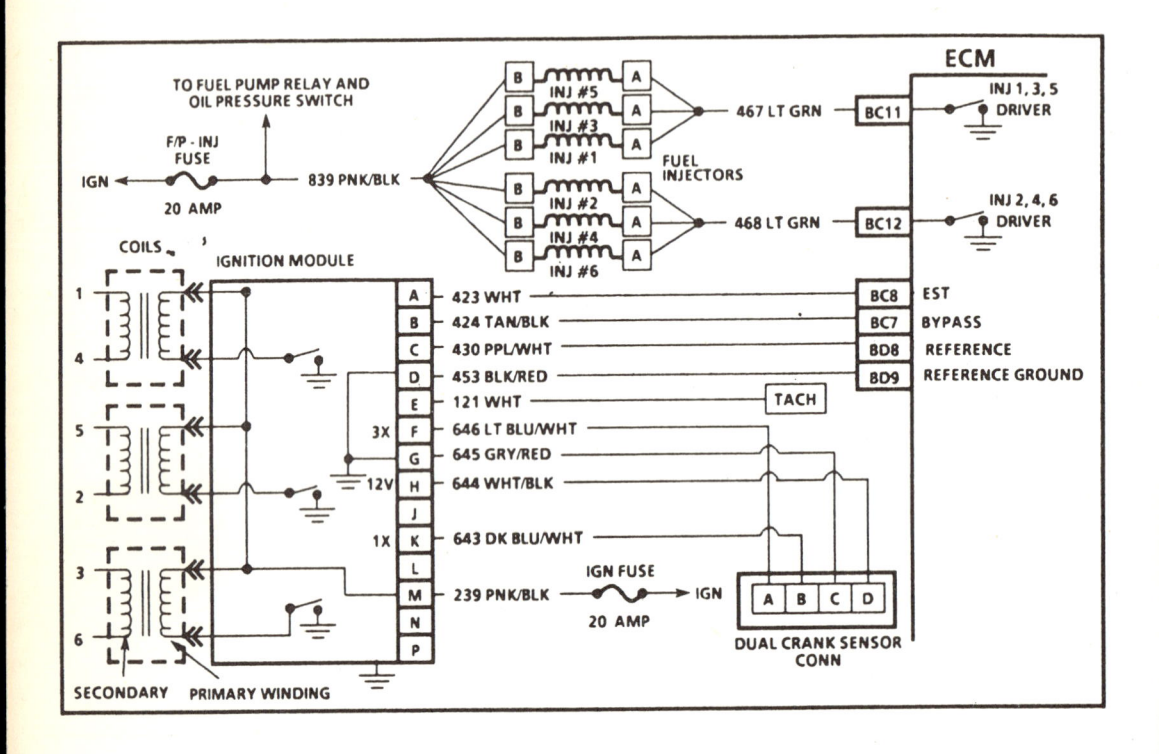

## 62 ENGINE PERFORMANCE AND TUNE-UP

## MISFIRE AT IDLE
### 3300 (VIN N) "N" CARLINE (PORT)

**Circuit Description:**
The ignition system uses a waste spark method of spark distribution. In this type of ignition system the ignition module triggers the #1/4 coil pair resulting in both #1 and #4 spark plugs firing at the same time. #1 cylinder is on the compression stroke at the same time #4 is on the exhaust stroke, resulting in a lower energy requirement to fire #4 spark plug. This leaves the remaining high voltage to fire #1 spark plug.

**Test Description:** Number(s) below refer to circled number(s) on the diagnostic chart.
1. If the "misfire" complaint exists under load only, the diagnostic CHART C-4-2 must be used. Engine rpm should drop approximately equally on all plug leads.
2. A spark tester such as a ST-125 must be used because it is essential to verify adequate available secondary voltage at the spark plug. Secondary voltage of at least 25,000 volts must be present to jump the gap of a ST-125.
3. If ignition coils are carbon tracked, the coil tower spark plug wire nipples may be damaged.
4. By checking the secondary resistance, a coil with an open secondary may be located.
5. By switching a normally operating coil into the position of the malfunctioning one, a determination can be made as to fault being the coil or ignition module.

**Ignition system diagnosis—3.3L engine**

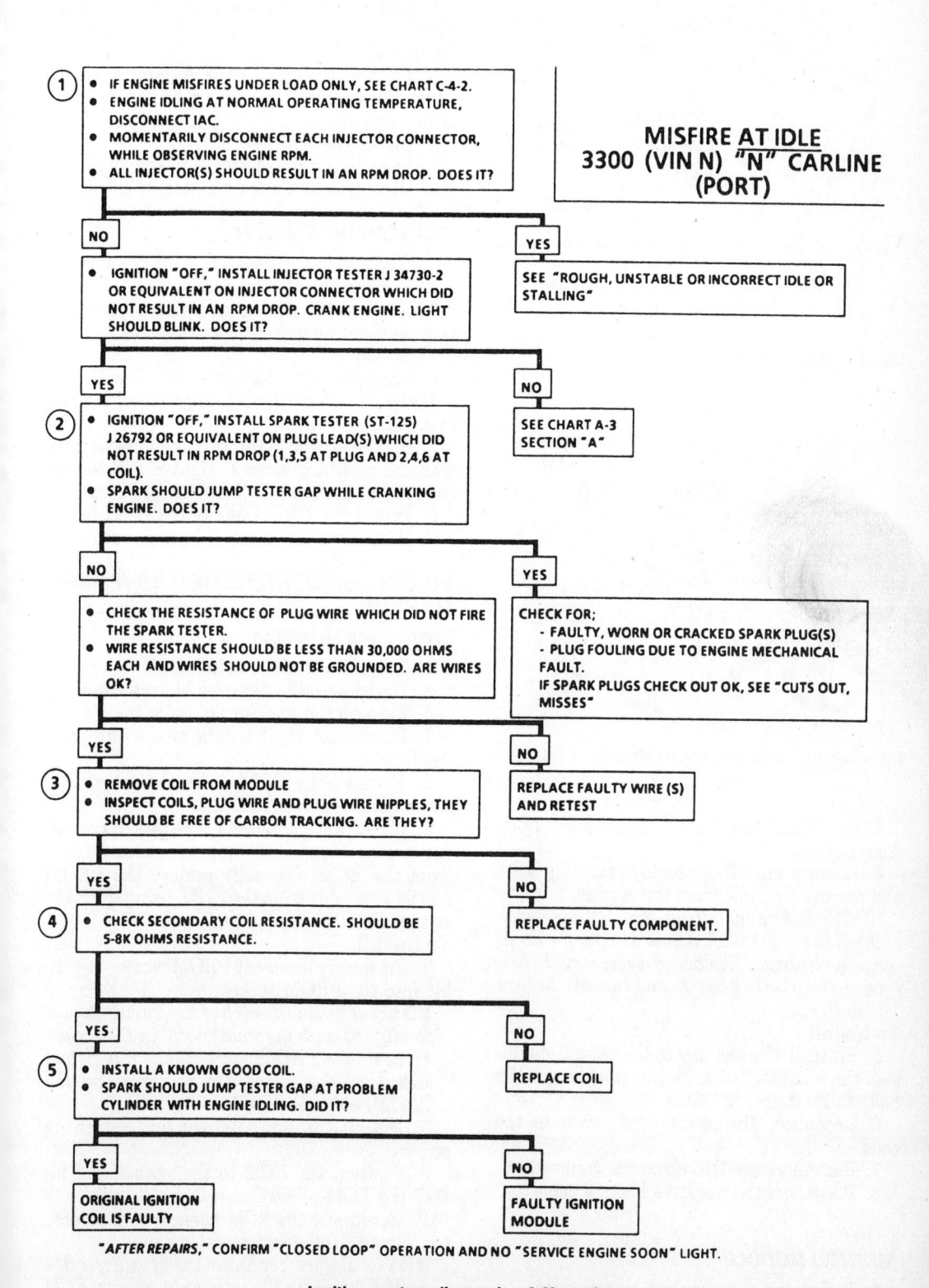

# ENGINE PERFORMANCE AND TUNE-UP 63

**MISFIRE AT IDLE**
**3300 (VIN N) "N" CARLINE**
**(PORT)**

**(1)**
- IF ENGINE MISFIRES UNDER LOAD ONLY, SEE CHART C-4-2.
- ENGINE IDLING AT NORMAL OPERATING TEMPERATURE, DISCONNECT IAC.
- MOMENTARILY DISCONNECT EACH INJECTOR CONNECTOR, WHILE OBSERVING ENGINE RPM.
- ALL INJECTOR(S) SHOULD RESULT IN AN RPM DROP. DOES IT?

**NO** →
- IGNITION "OFF," INSTALL INJECTOR TESTER J 34730-2 OR EQUIVALENT ON INJECTOR CONNECTOR WHICH DID NOT RESULT IN AN RPM DROP. CRANK ENGINE. LIGHT SHOULD BLINK. DOES IT?

**YES** → SEE "ROUGH, UNSTABLE OR INCORRECT IDLE OR STALLING"

**YES** →
**(2)**
- IGNITION "OFF," INSTALL SPARK TESTER (ST-125) J 26792 OR EQUIVALENT ON PLUG LEAD(S) WHICH DID NOT RESULT IN RPM DROP (1,3,5 AT PLUG AND 2,4,6 AT COIL).
- SPARK SHOULD JUMP TESTER GAP WHILE CRANKING ENGINE. DOES IT?

**NO** → SEE CHART A-3 SECTION "A"

**NO** →
- CHECK THE RESISTANCE OF PLUG WIRE WHICH DID NOT FIRE THE SPARK TESTER.
- WIRE RESISTANCE SHOULD BE LESS THAN 30,000 OHMS EACH AND WIRES SHOULD NOT BE GROUNDED. ARE WIRES OK?

**YES** →
CHECK FOR;
- FAULTY, WORN OR CRACKED SPARK PLUG(S)
- PLUG FOULING DUE TO ENGINE MECHANICAL FAULT.
IF SPARK PLUGS CHECK OUT OK, SEE "CUTS OUT, MISSES"

**YES** →
**(3)**
- REMOVE COIL FROM MODULE
- INSPECT COILS, PLUG WIRE AND PLUG WIRE NIPPLES, THEY SHOULD BE FREE OF CARBON TRACKING. ARE THEY?

**NO** → REPLACE FAULTY WIRE (S) AND RETEST

**YES** →
**(4)**
- CHECK SECONDARY COIL RESISTANCE. SHOULD BE 5-8K OHMS RESISTANCE.

**NO** → REPLACE FAULTY COMPONENT.

**YES** →
**(5)**
- INSTALL A KNOWN GOOD COIL.
- SPARK SHOULD JUMP TESTER GAP AT PROBLEM CYLINDER WITH ENGINE IDLING. DID IT?

**NO** → REPLACE COIL

**YES** → ORIGINAL IGNITION COIL IS FAULTY

**NO** → FAULTY IGNITION MODULE

"AFTER REPAIRS," CONFIRM "CLOSED LOOP" OPERATION AND NO "SERVICE ENGINE SOON" LIGHT.

**Ignition system diagnosis—3.3L engine**

# 64 ENGINE PERFORMANCE AND TUNE-UP

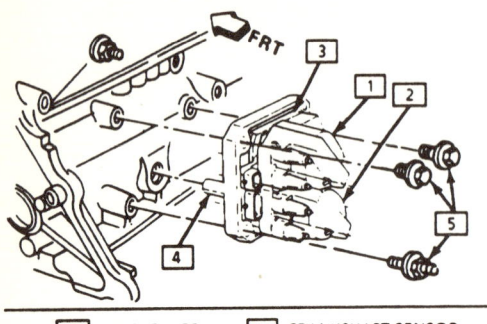

| 1 | #2/3 IGN COIL | 4 | CRANKSHAFT SENSOR |
| 2 | #1/4 IGN COIL | 5 | BOLT (3) 27 N·m (20 lb. ft.) |
| 3 | IGN MODULE | | |

**DIS assembly—2.5L engine**

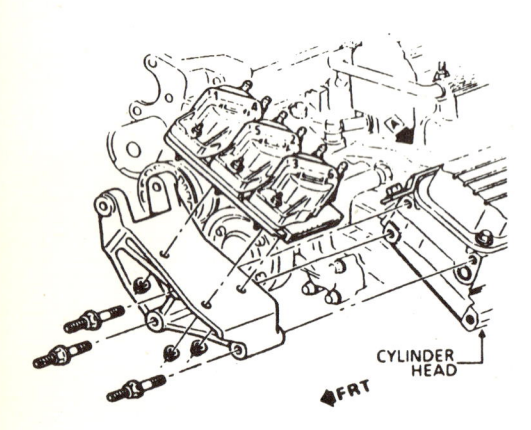

**DIS assembly—3.0L and 3.3L engines**

3. Disconnect and tag the spark plugs leads from the coils.
4. Remove the DIS assembly retaining bolts and remove the unit from the engine.
   NOTE: *Before installing the DIS assembly, check the crankshaft sensor O-ring for damage or leakage. Replace if necessary. Lubricate the O-ring with engine oil before installing.*

**To install:**
5. Fit the DIS assembly to the engine and install the retaining bolts. Tighten and torque the bolts to 20 ft. lbs. (27 Nm).
6. Reconnect the spark plug wires to the coils.
7. Reconnect the DIS electrical connectors.
8. Reconnect the negative battery cable.

## IGNITION MODULE

1. Disconnect the negative battery cable.
2. Remove the DIS assembly from the engine.
3. Remove the ignition coils.
4. Remove the module from the assembly plate.

**To install:**
5. Fit the module to the assembly plate. Carefully engage the sensor to the module terminals.
6. Install the ignition coils.
7. Install the DIS assembly to the engine.
8. Reconnect the negative battery cable.

## CRANKSHAFT SENSOR

1. Disconnect the negative battery cable.
2. Remove the DIS assembly.
3. Remove the sensor retaining screws and remove the sensor from DIS assembly.

**To install:**
4. Replace the crankshaft sensor O-ring. Lubricate the O-ring with engine oil before installing.
5. Fit the sensor to the DIS assembly and install the retaining screws. Tighten and torque the retaining screws 20 inch lbs. (2.3 Nm).
6. Install the DIS assembly to the engine.
7. Reconnect the negative battery cable.

## ELECTRONIC CONTROL MODULE (ECM) OR PROM

### Removal and Installation

1. Turn the ignition switch **OFF**.
2. Disconnect the negative battery cable.
3. Remove the interior access panel.
4. Disconnect the harness connectors from the ECM.
5. Remove the ECM-to-bracket retaining screws and remove the ECM.
6. If PROM replacement is required, remove the access cover retaining screws and cover from the ECM. Carefully remove the PROM carrier assembly from the ECM, using the rocker type PROM removal tool.

**To install:**
7. Fit the replacement PROM carrier assembly into the PROM socket.
   NOTE: *The small notch of the carrier should be aligned with the small notch in the socket. Press on the PROM carrier until if is firmly seated in the socket. Do not press on the PROM, only the carrier.*
8. Install the access cover and retaining screws.
9. Position the ECM in the vehicle and install the ECM-to-bracket retaining screws.
10. Reconnect the ECM harness connectors.
11. Install the interior access panel.
    NOTE: *Before replacement of a defective ECM first check the resistance of each ECM controlled solenoid. This can be done at the ECM connector, using an ohmmeter and the ECM connector wiring diagram. Any ECM*

*controlled device with low resistance will damage the replacement ECM due to high current flow through the ECM internal circuits.*

12. Check that the ignition switch is **OFF**. Then, reconnect the negative battery cable.

## COMPUTER CONTROLLED COIL IGNITION (C$^3$I) SYSTEM – 3.0L (VIN L) AND 3.3L (VIN N) ENGINES

### General Description

The Computer Controlled Coil Ignition (C$^3$I) system features a distributorless ignition engine. The C$^3$I system consists of 3 ignition coils, a C$^3$I ignition module, a dual crank sensor, camshaft sensor, connecting wires, and the Electronic Spark Timing (EST) portion of the Electronic Control Module (ECM).

The C$^3$I system uses the same Electronic Spark Timing (EST) circuits as the distributor-type ignition. The ECM uses the EST circuit to control spark advance and ignition dwell, when the ignition system is operating in the EST mode. There are 2 modes of ignition system operation. These modes are as follows:

- Module mode – the ignition system operates independently of the ECM, with module mode spark advance always at 10° BTDC. The ECM have no control of the ignition system when in this mode.
- EST mode – the ignition spark timing and ignition dwell time is fully controlled by the ECM. EST spark advance and ignition dwell is calculated by the ECM.

To control spark knock, and enable maximum spark advance to improve driveability and fuel economy, an Electronic Spark Control (ESC) system is used. This system is consists of a knock sensor and an ESC module (part of Mem-Cal). The ECM monitors the ESC signal to determine when engine detonation occurs.

### System Operation

The C$^3$I system uses a waste spark distribution method. Each cylinder is paired with the cylinder opposite it (i.e. 1–4, 2–5, 3–6). The ends of each coil secondary is attached to a spark plug. These 2 plugs, being on companion cylinders, are at top dead center at the same time. The one that is on compression is said to be the event cylinder and the one on the exhaust stroke, the waste cylinder. When the coil discharges, both plugs fire at the same time to complete the series circuit. Therefore, each pair of cylinders is fired for each crankshaft revolution.

Since the polarity of the primary and the secondary windings are fixed, one plug always fires in a forward direction and the other in reverse. This differs from a conventional system in which all plugs fire in the same direction each time. Because of the demand for additional energy; the coil design, saturation time and primary current flow are also different. This redesign of the system allows higher energy to be available from the distributorless coils, greater than 40 kilovolts at all rpm ranges.

During cranking, when the engine speed is beneath 400 rpm, the C$^3$I module monitors the dual crank sensor sync signal. The sync signal is used to determine the correct pair of cylinders to be sparked first. Once the sync signal has been processed by the ignition module, it sends a fuel control reference pulse to the ECM.

During the cranking period, the ECM will also receive a cam pulse signal and will operate the injectors sequentially, based on true camshaft position only.

The sync signal, or pulse, is used only by the ignition module. It is used for spark synchronization at start-up only.

When the engine speed is beneath 400 rpm (during cranking), the C$^3$I module controls the spark timing. Once the engine speed exceeds 400 rpm (engine running) spark timing is controlled by the EST signal from the ECM. To control EST the ECM uses the following inputs:

- Crankshaft position
- Engine speed (rpm)
- Engine coolant (Coolant Temperature Sensor – CTS)
- Intake air (Mass Air Flow – MAF)
- Throttle valve position (Throttle Position Sensor – TPS)
- Gear shift lever position (Park/Neutral Switch – P/N)
- Vehicle speed (Vehicle Speed Sensor – VSS)
- ESC signal (Knock Sensor)

The C$^3$I ignition module provides proper ignition coil sequencing during both the module and the EST modes.

The ESC system is designed to retard spark timing up to 10° to reduce spark knock in the engine. When the knock sensor detects spark knocking in the engine, it sends an AC voltage signal to the ECM, which increases with the severity of the knock. The ECM then adjusts the EST to reduce spark knock.

### SYSTEM COMPONENTS

#### C$^3$I Module

The C$^3$I module monitors the sync-pulse and the crank signal. During cranking the C$^3$I module monitors the sync-pulse to begin the ignition firing sequence. During this time, each of the 3 coils are fired at a pre-determined interval based on engine speed only. Above 400 rpm, the C³I module is only use as a reference signal.

### Ignition Coil

The ignition coil assemblies are mounted on the C³I module. Each coil distributes the spark for 2 plugs simultaneously.

### Electronic Spark Control (ESC)

The ESC system incorporates a knock sensor and the ECM. The knock sensor detects engine detonation. When engine detonation occurs, the ECM receives the ESC signal and retards EST to reduce detonation.

### Electronic Spark Timing (EST)

The EST system is basically the same EST to ECM circuit use on the distributor type ignition systems with EST. This system includes the following circuits:
- Reference circuit – provides the ECM with rpm and crankshaft position information from the C³I module. The C³I module receives this signal from the crank sensor hall-effect switch.
- Bypass signal – above 400 rpm, the ECM applies 5 volts to this circuit to switch spark timing control from the C³I module to the ECM.
- EST signal – reference signal is sent to the ECM via the C³I module during cranking. Under 400 rpm, the C³I module controls the ignition timing. Above 400 rpm, the ECM applies 5 volts to the bypass line to switch the timing to the ECM control.

### Electronic Control Module (ECM)

The ECM is responsible for maintaining proper spark and fuel injection timing for all driving conditions.

### Dual Crank Sensor

The dual crank sensor is mounted in a pedestal on the front of the engine near the harmonic balancer. The sensor consists of 2 hall-effect switches, which depend on 2 metal interrupter rings mounted on the balancer to activate them. Windows in the interrupters activate the hall-effect switches as they provide a path for the magnetic field between the switches transducers and magnets.

## Diagnosis and Testing
### SERVICE PRECAUTIONS

CAUTION: *The ignition coil's secondary voltage output capabilities can exceed 40,000 volts. Avoid body contact with the C³I high voltage secondary components when the engine is running, or personal injury may result.*

NOTE: *To avoid damage to the ECM or other ignition system components, do not use electrical test equipment such as battery or AC-powered voltmeter, ohmmeter, etc. or any type of tester other than specified.*

- To properly diagnosis the ignition systems and their problems, it will be necessary to refer to the diagnostic charts in the fuel injection chapter.
- When performing electrical tests on the system, use a high impedance multimeter or quality digital voltmeter (DVM). Use of a 12 volt test light is not recommended.
- To prevent electrostatic discharge damage, when working with the ECM, do not touch the connector pins or soldered components on the circuit board.
- When handling a PROM, CAL-PAK or MEM-CAL, do not touch the component leads. Also, do not remove the integrated circuit from the carrier.
- Never pierce a high tension lead or boot for any testing purpose; otherwise, future problems are guaranteed.
- Do not allow extension cords for power tools or droplights to lie on, near or across any vehicle electrical wiring.
- Leave new components and modules in the shipping package until ready to install them.

### READING CODES

The Assembly Line Diagnostic Link (ALDL) connector is used for communicating with the ECM. It is usually located under the instrument panel and is sometimes covered by a plastic cover labeled "DIAGNOSTIC CONNECTOR." Codes stored in the ECM's memory can be read through a hand-held diagnostic scanner plugged into the ALDL connector. If a scanner is not available, the codes can also be read by jumping from terminal **A** to **B** of the ALDL connector and counting the number of flashes of the Service Engine Soon light, with the ignition switch turned **ON**.

Refer to Chapter 4 for a more detailed look diagnostic codes, what they mean and how to diagnose them.

### CLEARING CODES

To clear codes from the ECM memory, the ECM power feed must be disconnected for at least 30 seconds. Depending on the vehicle, the ECM power feed can be disconnected at the positive battery terminal pigtail, the inline fuseholder that originates at the positive connection at the battery or the ECM fuse in the fuse block. The negative battery cable may also be disconnected; however, other on-board memory data, such as radio station presets, will also be lost.

Also, if battery power is lost, computer relearn time is approximately 5–10 minutes. This means the computer may have to re-calibrate components which set up the idle speed and the idle may fluctuate while this is occurring.

## BASIC IGNITION SYSTEM CHECK

1. Check for codes. If any are found, refer to the appropriate chart in Chapter 4.
2. Turn the ignition switch **ON**. Verify that the Service Engine Soon light is ON.
3. Install the scan tool and check the following:

Throttle Position Sensor (TPS) — if over 2.5 volts, at closed throttle, check the TPS and circuit.

Coolant — if not between −22°F (−30°C) and 266°F (130°C), check the sensor and circuit.

4. Disconnect all injector connectors and install injector test light (J–34730–2 or equivalent) in injector harness connector. Test light should be OFF.

NOTE: *Perform this test on 1 injector from each bank.*

5. Connect spark checker, (J 26792 or equivalent), and check for spark while cranking. Check at least 2 wires.

   a. If spark occurs, reconnect the spark plug wires and check for fuel spray at the injector(s) while cranking.
   b. If no spark occurs, check for battery voltage to the ignition system. If OK, substitute known good parts for possible faulty ignition parts. If not, refer to the wiring diagrams to track down loss of voltage.

## Parts Replacement

### IGNITION COIL

1. Disconnect the negative battery cable.
2. Disconnect the spark plug wires.
3. Remove the 2 retaining screws securing the coil to the ignition module.
4. Remove the coil assembly.

**To install:**

5. Fit the coil assembly to the ignition module.
6. Install the retaining screws and torque to 40 inch lbs. (4–5 Nm).
7. Install the spark plug wires.
8. Reconnect the negative battery cable.

### C³I MODULE

1. Disconnect the negative battery cable.
2. Disconnect the 14-way connector at the ignition module.
3. Disconnect the spark plug wires at the coil assembly.
4. Remove the nuts and washers that retains the module to the bracket.
5. Remove the coil-to-module retaining bolts.
6. Note the lead colors or mark for reassembly.
7. Disconnect the connectors between the coil and ignition module.
8. Remove the ignition module.

**To install:**

9. Fit the coils and connectors to the ignition module and install the retaining bolts. Tighten and torque the retaining bolts to 27 inch lbs. (3 Nm).
10. Fit the module assembly to the bracket and install the nuts and washers.
11. Reconnect the 14-way connector to the module.
12. Reconnect the negative battery cable.

### DUAL CRANK SENSOR

1. Disconnect the negative battery cable.
2. Remove the belt(s) from the crankshaft pulley.
3. Raise and support the vehicle safely.
4. Remove the right front wheel and inner fender access cover.
5. Remove the crankshaft harmonic balancer retaining bolt, then remove the harmonic balancer.
6. Disconnect the sensor electrical connector.
7. Remove the sensor and pedestal from the engine block, then separate the sensor from the pedestal.

**To install:**

8. Loosely install the crankshaft sensor to the pedestal.
9. Using tool J–37089 or equivalent, position the sensor with the pedestal attached, on the crankshaft.
10. Install the pedestal-to-block retaining bolts. Tighten and torque to 14–28 ft. lbs. (20–40 Nm).
11. Torque the pedestal pinch bolt 30–35 inch lbs. (20–40 Nm).
12. Remove tool J–37089 or equivalent.
13. Place tool J–37089 or equivalent, on the harmonic balancer and turn. If any vane of the harmonic balancer touches the tool, replace the balancer assembly.

NOTE: *A clearance of 0.025 in. (0.635mm) is required on either side of the interrupter ring. Be certain to obtain the correct clearance. Failure to do so will damage the sensor. A misadjusted sensor or bent interrupter ring could cause rubbing of the sensor, resulting in potential driveability problems, such as rough idle, poor performance, or a no start condition.*

# 68 ENGINE PERFORMANCE AND TUNE-UP

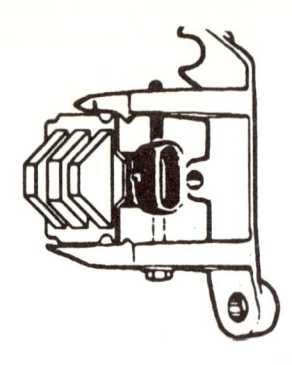

**Dual crankshaft sensor—3.0L and 3.3L engines**

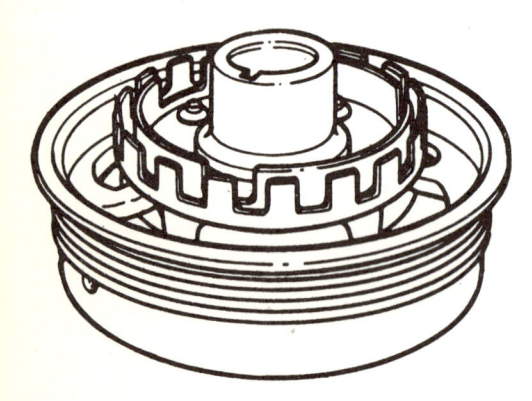

**Harmonic balancer assembly with interrupter rings—3.0L and 3.3L engines**

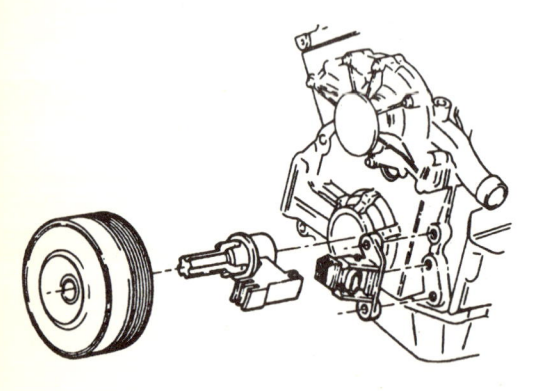

**Positioning crankshaft sensor on the engine block using special tool**

14. Install the balancer on the crankshaft. Install the balancer retaining bolt. Tighten and torque the retaining bolt to 200–239 ft. lbs. (270–325 Nm).
15. Install the inner fender shield.
16. Install the right front wheel assembly. Tighten and torque the wheel nuts to 100 ft. lbs. (140 Nm).
17. Lower the vehicle.
18. Install the belt(s).
19. Reconnect the negative battery cable.

### ESC KNOCK SENSOR

1. Disconnect the negative battery cable.
2. Raise and support the vehicle safely.
3. Disconnect the harness connector from the knock sensor.
4. Remove the sensor from the engine block.

**To install:**

5. Clean the threads on the engine block, where the sensor was installed. Install the sensor. Tighten to 11–16 ft. lbs. (15–22 Nm).
6. Reconnect the harness connector to the knock sensor.
7. Lower the vehicle.
8. Reconnect the negative battery cable.

### ELECTRONIC CONTROL MODULE (ECM) AND/OR MEM-CAL

1. Turn the ignition switch **OFF**.
2. Disconnect the negative battery cable.
3. Remove the right side hush panel.
4. Disconnect the harness connectors from the control unit.
5. Remove the control unit-to-bracket retaining screws and remove the control unit.
6. If replacement of the Mem-Cal is required, remove the access cover retaining screws and cover from the control unit. Note the position of the Mem-Cal for proper installation in the new ECM. Using 2 fingers, carefully push both retaining clips back away from the Mem-Cal. At the same time, grasp it at both ends and lift it up out of the socket. Do not remove the cover of the Mem-Cal.

**To install:**

7. Fit the replacement Mem-Cal into the socket.

NOTE: *The small notches in the Mem-Cal must be aligned with the small notches in the socket. Press only on the ends of the Mem-Cal until the retaining clips snap into the ends of the Mem-Cal. Do not press on the middle of the Mem-Cal, only the ends.*

8. Install the access cover and retaining screws.
9. Position the control unit in the vehicle and install the control unit-to-bracket retaining screws.
10. Reconnect the control unit harness connectors.
11. Install the hush panel.
12. Check that the ignition switch is **OFF**. Then reconnect the negative battery cable.

**Functional Check**

1. Turn the ignition switch **ON**.
2. Enter diagnostics.
   a. Allow Code 12 to flash 4 times to verify

# ENGINE PERFORMANCE AND TUNE-UP

no other codes are present. This indicates the Mem-Cal is installed properly and the control unit is functioning.

b. If trouble Codes 42, 43 or 51 occur, or if the Service Engine Soon light is ON constantly with no codes, the Mem-Cal is not fully seated or is defective.

c. If it is not fully seated, press firmly on the ends of the Mem-Cal.

## IGNITION TIMING

Ignition timing can be set on the 2.0L (VIN K and M) engines and the 2.5L (VIN U) engine equipped with the HEI ignition system only. The 2.5L (VIN U) engine was equipped with HEI in 1985–86 only. From 1987 on, the 2.5L (VIN U) engine was equipped with the Direct Ignition System (DIS) which is distributorless.

All other engines are distributorless. Accordingly, ignition timing is controlled by the ECM and is not adjustable.

NOTE: *If the following procedures vary from the Vehicle Emission Control Information (VECI) label located in the engine compartment, set the timing according to the procedure indicated on the VECI label.*

### 2.0L (VIN K and M) Engines

1. Start the engine, set the parking brake and run the engine until at normal operating temperature. Keep all lights and accessories off.
2. Connect the red lead of a tachometer to the terminal of the coil labeled **TACH** and connect the black lead to a good ground.

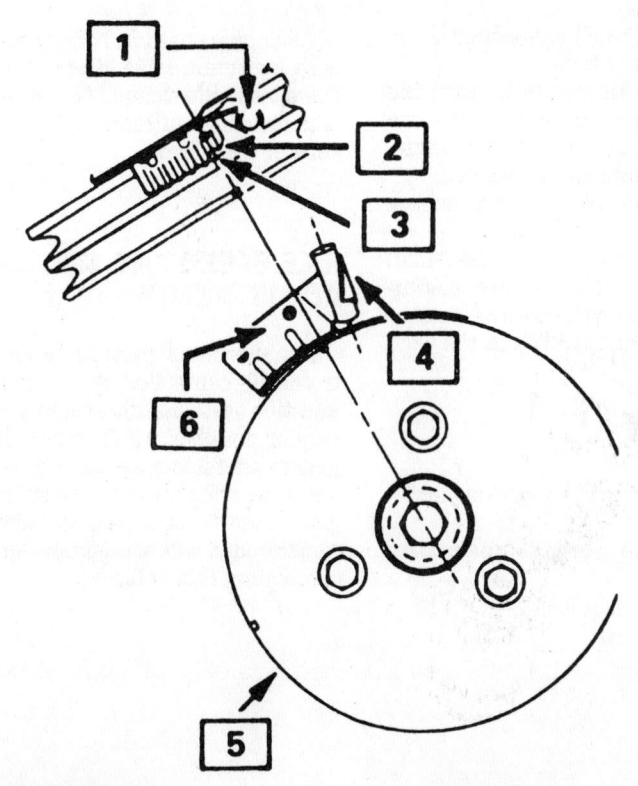

1— MAGNETIC TIMING PROBE HOLE

2— "O" STAMP ON POINTER

3— NOTCH IN PULLEY

4— MAGNETIC TIMING PROBE HOLE ASM.

5— PULLEY

6— ASM. MOUNTED TO FRONT COVER

**Typical ignition timing marker with magnetic pick-up**

# ENGINE PERFORMANCE AND TUNE-UP

3. If a magnetic timing unit is available, insert the probe into the receptacle near the timing scale.

4. If a magnetic timing unit is not available, connect a conventional power timing light to the No. 1 cylinder spark plug wire.

5. With parking brake safely set, place automatic transaxle in **D** or leave manual transaxle in neutral.

6. Ground the ALDL connector under the dash by installing a jumper wire between the **A** and **B** terminals. The CHECK ENGINE light should begin flashing.

7. Aim the timing light at the timing scale or read the magnetic timing unit. Record the reading.

8. Repeat Steps 3–6 using the No. 4 spark plug wire. Record the reading.

9. Use the average of the 2 readings to derive an average timing value.

10. Loosen the distributor hold-down nuts so the distributor can be rotated.

11. Using the average timing value, turn the distributor in the proper direction until the specified timing according to the Vehicle Emission Control Information label is reached.

12. Tighten the hold-down nuts and recheck the timing values.

13. Remove the jumper wire from the ALDL connector. To clear the ECM memory, disconnect the ECM harness from the positive battery pigtail for 10 seconds with the key in the OFF position.

## 2.5L (VIN U) Engine
### 1985–86

1. Place transmission in **P**, set parking brake and block wheels.

2. Bring engine to normal operating temperature.

3. Turn air conditioning **OFF**.

4. Connect a jumper between terminals A and B of the ALDL connector.

5. Connect an inductive timing light to the coil wire and check the ignition timing. Compare the reading to the specified setting on the VECI label.

6. If adjustment is necessary, loosen the distributor hold-down bolt and adjust the timing by rotating the distributor while observing the timing light.

7. When the timing is set to specification, tighten the hold-down bolt.

8. Disconnect the timing light.

9. Remove jumper wire.

## VALVE LASH

All engines used in N body cars are equipped with hydraulic valve lifters that do not require valve lash adjustment. Adjustment to zero lash is maintained automatically by hydraulic pressure in the lifters.

## IDLE SPEED AND MIXTURE ADJUSTMENTS

Idle speed and mixture for all engines is electronically controlled by the computerized fuel injection system. Adjustment are neither necessary or possible. All threaded throttle stop adjusters are factory set and capped to discourage any tampering; in some areas, tampering is illegal. In most cases, proper diagnosis and parts replacement will straighten out any problems concerning this subject.

# Engine and Engine Overhaul

# 3

## ENGINE ELECTRICAL

### Understanding the Engine Electrical System

The engine electrical system can be broken down into three systems:
1. The starting system.
2. The charging system.
3. The ignition system.

### BATTERY AND STARTING SYSTEM

#### Basic Operating Principles

The battery is the first link in the chain of mechanisms which work together to provide cranking of the automobile engine. In most modern cars, the battery is a lead/acid electrochemical device consisting of six 2v subsections connected in series so the unit is capable of producing approximately 12v of electrical pressure. Each subsection, or cell, consists of a series of positive and negative plates held a short distance apart in a solution of sulfuric acid and water. The two types of plates are of dissimilar metals. This causes a chemical reaction to be set up, and it is this reaction which produces current flow from the battery when its positive and negative terminals are connected to an electrical appliance such as a lamp or motor. The continued transfer of electrons would eventually convert the sulfuric acid in the electrolyte to water, and make the two plates identical in chemical composition. As electrical energy is removed from the battery, its voltage output tends to drop. Thus, measuring battery voltage and battery electrolyte composition are two ways of checking the ability of the unit to supply power. During the starting of the engine, electrical energy is removed from the battery. However, if the charging circuit is in good condition and the operating conditions are normal, the power removed from the battery will be replaced by the generator (or alternator) which will force electrons back through the battery, reversing the normal flow, and restoring the battery to its original chemical state.

The battery and starting motor are linked by very heavy electrical cables designed to minimize resistance to the flow of current. Generally, the major power supply cable that leaves the battery goes directly to the starter, while other electrical system needs are supplied by a smaller cable. During starter operation, power flows from the battery to the starter and is grounded through the car's frame and the battery's negative ground strap.

The starting motor is a specially designed, direct current electric motor capable of producing a very great amount of power for its size. One thing that allows the motor to produce a great deal of power is its tremendous rotating speed. It drives the engine through a tiny pinion gear (attached to the starter's armature), which drives the very large flywheel ring gear at a greatly reduced speed. Another factor allowing it to produce so much power is that only intermittent operation is required of it. Little allowance for air circulation is required, and the windings can be built into a very small space.

The starter solenoid is a magnetic device which employs the small current supplied by the starting switch circuit of the ignition switch. This magnetic action moves a plunger which mechanically engages the starter and electrically closes the heavy switch which connects it to the battery. The starting switch circuit consists of the starting switch contained within the ignition switch, a transmission neutral safety switch or clutch pedal switch, and the wiring necessary to connect these in series with the starter solenoid or relay.

A pinion, which is a small gear, is mounted to a one-way drive clutch. This clutch is splined to the starter armature shaft. When the ignition switch is moved to the **START** position, the solenoid plunger slides the pinion toward the fly-

# 72 ENGINE AND ENGINE OVERHAUL

wheel ring gear via a collar and spring. If the teeth on the pinion and flywheel match properly, the pinion will engage the flywheel immediately. If the gear teeth butt one another, the spring will be compressed and will force the gears to mesh as soon as the starter turns far enough to allow them to do so. As the solenoid plunger reaches the end of its travel, it closes the contacts that connect the battery and starter and then the engine is cranked.

As soon as the engine starts, the flywheel ring gear begins turning fast enough to drive the pinion at an extremely high rate of speed. At this point, the one-way clutch begins allowing the pinion to spin faster than the starter shaft so that the starter will not operate at excessive speed. When the ignition switch is released from the starter position, the solenoid is de-energized, and a spring contained within the solenoid assembly pulls the gear out of mesh and interrupts the current flow to the starter.

Some starter employ a separate relay, mounted away from the starter, to switch the motor and solenoid current on and off. The relay thus replaces the solenoid electrical switch, buy does not eliminate the need for a solenoid mounted on the starter used to mechanically engage the starter drive gears. The relay is used to reduce the amount of current the starting switch must carry.

## THE CHARGING SYSTEM
### Basic Operating Principles

The automobile charging system provides electrical power for operation of the vehicle's ignition and starting systems and all the electrical accessories. The battery services as an electrical surge or storage tank, storing (in chemical form) the energy originally produced by the engine driven generator. The system also provides a means of regulating generator output to protect the battery from being overcharged and to avoid excessive voltage to the accessories.

The storage battery is a chemical device incorporating parallel lead plates in a tank containing a sulfuric acid/water solution. Adjacent plates are slightly dissimilar, and the chemical reaction of the two dissimilar plates produces electrical energy when the battery is connected to a load such as the starter motor. The chemical reaction is reversible, so that when the generator is producing a voltage (electrical pressure) greater than that produced by the battery, electricity is forced into the battery, and the battery is returned to its fully charged state.

The vehicle's generator is driven mechanically, through V-belts, by the engine crankshaft. It consists of two coils of fine wire, one stationary (the stator), and one movable (the rotor). The rotor may also be known as the armature, and consists of fine wire wrapped around an iron core which is mounted on a shaft. The electricity which flows through the two coils of wire (provided initially by the battery in some cases) creates an intense magnetic field around both rotor and stator, and the interaction between the two fields creates voltage, allowing the generator to power the accessories and charge the battery.

There are two types of generators: the earlier is the direct current (DC) type. The current produced by the DC generator is generated in the armature and carried off the spinning armature by stationary brushes contacting the commutator. The commutator is a series of smooth metal contact plates on the end of the armature. The commutator plates, which are separated from one another by a very short gap, are connected to the armature circuits so that current will flow in one directions only in the wires carrying the generator output. The generator stator consists of two stationary coils of wire which draw some of the output current of the generator to form a powerful magnetic field and create the interaction of fields which generates the voltage. The generator field is wired in series with the regulator.

Newer automobiles use alternating current generators or alternators, because they are more efficient, can be rotated at higher speeds, and have fewer brush problems. In an alternator, the field rotates while all the current produced passes only through the stator winding. The brushes bear against continuous slip rings rather than a commutator. This causes the current produced to periodically reverse the direction of its flow. Diodes (electrical one-way switches) block the flow of current from traveling in the wrong direction. A series of diodes is wired together to permit the alternating flow of the stator to be converted to a pulsating, but unidirectional flow at the alternator output. The alternator's field is wired in series with the voltage regulator.

The regulator consists of several circuits. Each circuit has a core, or magnetic coil of wire, which operates a switch. Each switch is connected to ground through one or more resistors. The coil of wire responds directly to system voltage. When the voltage reaches the required level, the magnetic field created by the winding of wire closes the switch and inserts a resistance into the generator field circuit, thus reducing the output. The contacts of the switch cycle open and close many times each second to precisely control voltage.

While alternators are self-limiting as far as maximum current is concerned, DC generators

# ENGINE AND ENGINE OVERHAUL

employ a current regulating circuit which responds directly to the total amount of current flowing through the generator circuit rather than to the output voltage. The current regulator is similar to the voltage regulator except that all system current must flow through the energizing coil on its way to the various accessories.

## ENGINE ELECTRICAL

### Ignition Coil

#### TESTING

Check the ignition coil for opens and ground with an ohmmeter.

1. Connect the negative lead of the ohmmeter, set at a high scale to a good metal ground and the positive lead to the B+ terminal of the coil. The reading should be infinite, if not replace the coil.

2. Use the low scale and connect the negative lead of the ohmmeter to the B- terminal of the coil. Connect the positive lead to the C-/tach terminal. the reading should be very low or zero. If not replace the coil.

3. Using the high scale, connect the negative lead of the ohmmeter to the C+ coil terminal and the positive lead to the coil tower. The reading should not be infinite; if it is, replace the coil.

#### REMOVAL AND INSTALLATION

**2.0L Engine**

1. Disconnect the negative battery cable.
2. Remove the air cleaner assembly.
3. Remove the coil mounting nut and bolt.
4. Disconnect the electrical connectors and remove the coil.
5. Installation is the reverse of removal procedure.

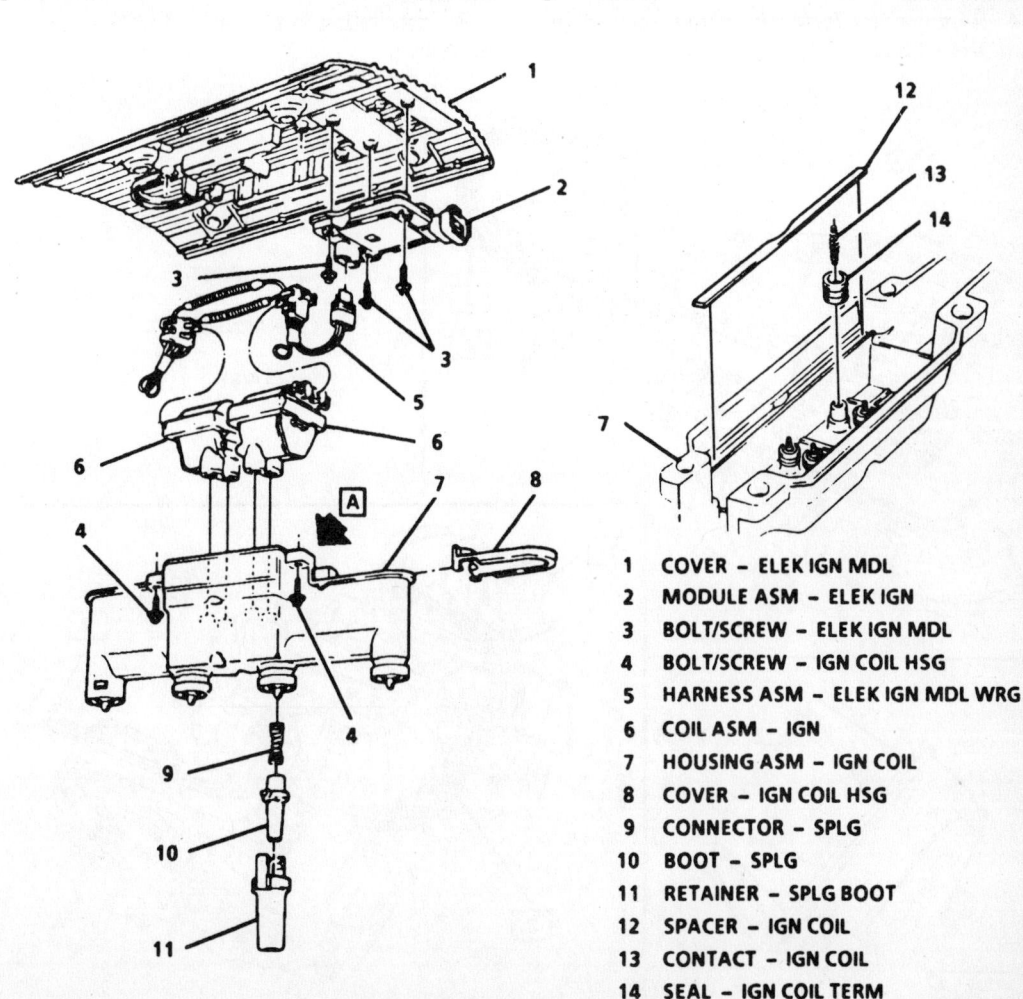

| | |
|---|---|
| 1 | COVER – ELEK IGN MDL |
| 2 | MODULE ASM – ELEK IGN |
| 3 | BOLT/SCREW – ELEK IGN MDL |
| 4 | BOLT/SCREW – IGN COIL HSG |
| 5 | HARNESS ASM – ELEK IGN MDL WRG |
| 6 | COIL ASM – IGN |
| 7 | HOUSING ASM – IGN COIL |
| 8 | COVER – IGN COIL HSG |
| 9 | CONNECTOR – SPLG |
| 10 | BOOT – SPLG |
| 11 | RETAINER – SPLG BOOT |
| 12 | SPACER – IGN COIL |
| 13 | CONTACT – IGN COIL |
| 14 | SEAL – IGN COIL TERM |

Ignition Coil and Module assembly—2.3L

## 74 ENGINE AND ENGINE OVERHAUL

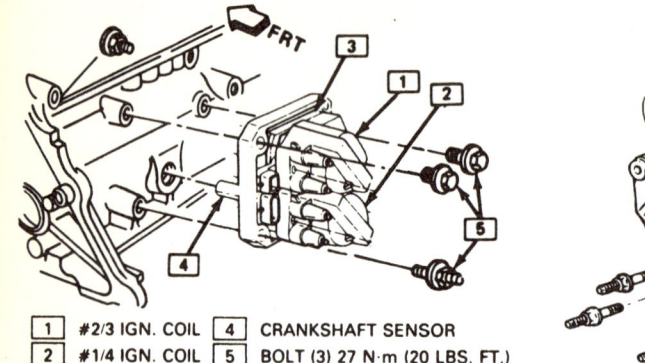

| 1 | #2/3 IGN. COIL | 4 | CRANKSHAFT SENSOR |
| 2 | #1/4 IGN. COIL | 5 | BOLT (3) 27 N·m (20 LBS. FT.) |
| 3 | IGN. MODULE | | |

**Ignition Coil, Module and Crankshaft Sensor—2.5L**

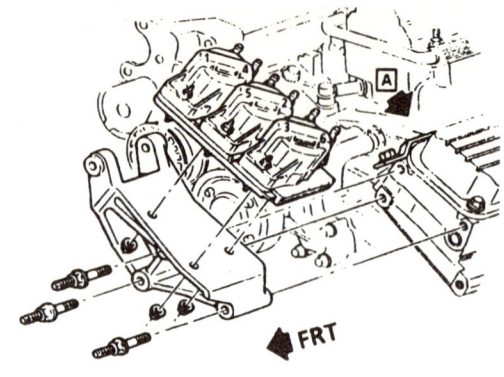

**3.3L Ignition Coil and Module assembly**

### 2.3L Engine

1. Disconnect the negative battery cable.
2. Disconnect the 11 pin harness connector.
3. Remove the 4 ignition assembly to cam housing bolts.
4. Remove the ignition system assembly from the engine.
5. Remove the 4 housing to cover screws and remove the housing from the cover.
6. Remove the 2 coil harness connectors.
7. Remove the coils, contacts, and seals from the cover.
8. Installation is the reverse of the removal procedure.

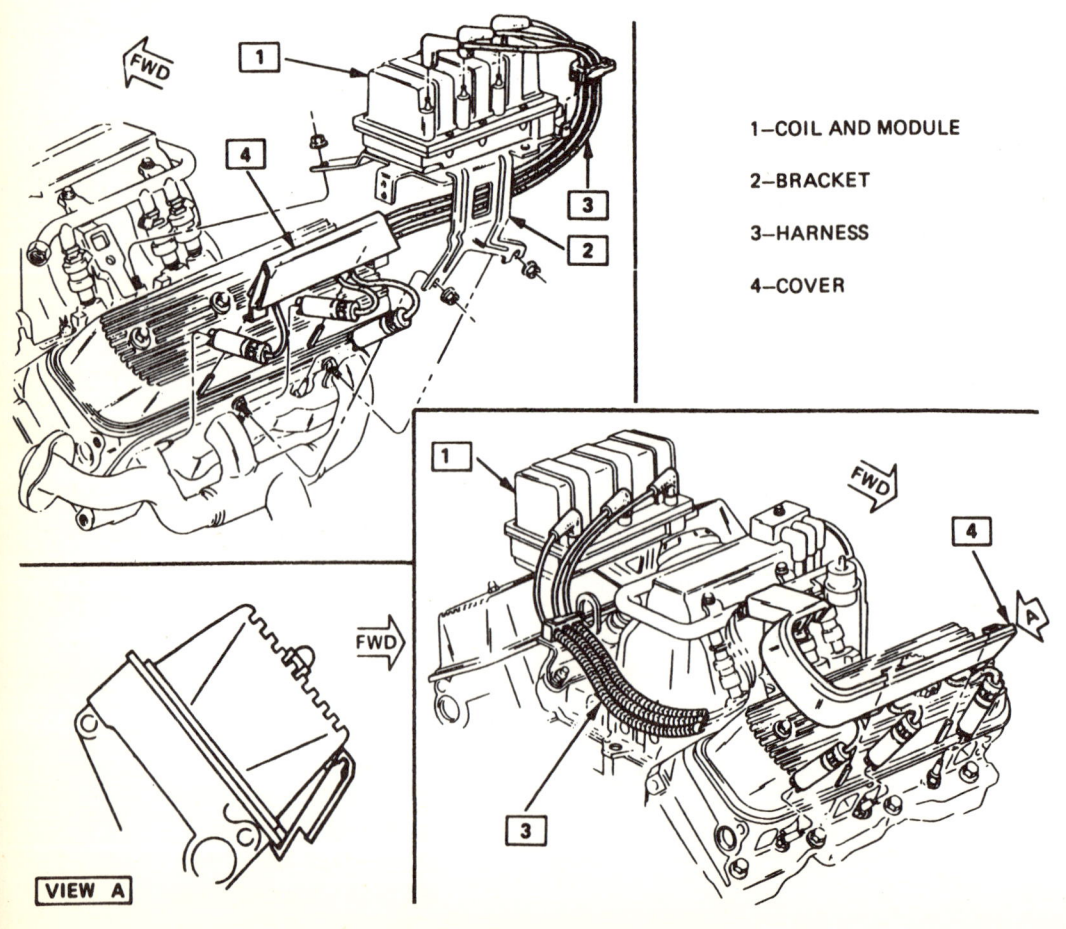

1—COIL AND MODULE

2—BRACKET

3—HARNESS

4—COVER

**3.0L Ignition Coil and Module assembly**

# ENGINE AND ENGINE OVERHAUL

## 2.5L, 3.0L and 3.3L Engines
1. Disconnect the negative battery cable.
2. Disconnect the spark plug and coil wires.
3. Remove the coil bolts that secure it to the ignition module.
4. Remove the coil assembly.
5. Installation is the reverse of the removal procedure.

## Ignition Module
### REMOVAL AND INSTALLATION
1. Disconnect the negative battery cable.
2. Disconnect the 14-pin connector at the ignition module.
3. Remove the spark plug wires at the coil assembly.
4. Remove the nuts and washers securing the ignition module assembly to the mounting bracket.
5. Remove the screws securing the ignition module to the coil.
6. Tilt the coil and disconnect the coil to module connectors.
7. Separate the coil and module.
8. Installation is the reverse of removal.

The ignition module on the N-Body engines monitors the crank signals and the "Sync-Pulse". The ECM then recieves this information and makes adjustments so that the spark and fuel injector timing is correct for all driving conditions. While cranking, the ignition module monitors the "Sync-Pulse" to begin the ignition firing sequence. When the engine is running below 400 RPM the ignition module controls spark advance by actuating each of the coils at a pre-determined interval based solely on engine speed. When the engine is running above 400 RPM, the ignition module sends the crank signal to the ECM as a reference signal. Then the ECM controls the spark timing and compensates for all operating conditions. The ignition module must first recieve a "Sync-Pulse" and then a crank signal in order to start the engine. The ignition module is not repairable and if it tests bad it must be replaced.

## Computer Controlled Coil Ignition (C³I)
### COMPONENT REMOVAL
#### V6 Engines
##### IGNITION COIL
1. Disconnect the negative battery cable.
2. Remove the spark plug wires.
3. Remove the screws holding the coil to the ignition module.
4. Tilt the coil assembly to the rear and remove the coil to module connectors.
5. Remove the coil assembly.
6. Installation is the reverse of removal.

##### IGNITION MODULE
1. Disconnect the negative battery cable.
2. Disconnect the 14-pin connector at the ignition module.
3. Remove the spark plug wires at the coil assembly.
4. Remove the nuts and washers securing the ignition module assembly to the mounting bracket.
5. Remove the screws securing the ignition module to the coil.
6. Tilt the coil and disconnect the coil to module connectors.
7. Separate the coil and module.
8. Installation is the reverse of removal.

##### CRANKSHAFT SENSOR
NOTE: *It is not necessary to remove the sensor bracket.*
1. Disconnect the negative battery cable.
2. Disconnect the sensor 3-way connector.
3. Raise the vehicle and support it safely.
4. Rotate the harmonic balancer so the slot in the disc is aligned with the sensor.
5. Loosen the sensor retaining bolt.
6. Slide the sensor outboard and remove through the notch in the sensor housing.
7. Install the new sensor in the housing and rotate the harmonic balancer so that the disc is positioned in the sensor.
8. Adjust the sensor so that there is an equal distance on each side of the disc. There should be approximately .030 in. (.76mm) clearance between the disc and the sensor.
9. Tighten the retaining bolt and recheck the clearance.
10. Install remaining components in the reverse order of removal.

##### CAMSHAFT POSITION SENSOR
NOTE: *If only the camshaft sensor is being replaced, it is not necessary to remove the entire assembly. The sensor is replaceable separately.*
1. Disconnect the negative battery cable.
2. Disconnect the ignition module 14-pin connector.
3. Remove the spark plug wires at the coil assembly.
4. Remove the ignition module bracket assembly.
5. Disconnect the sensor 3-way connector.
6. Remove the sensor mounting screws, then remove the sensor.
7. Installation is the reverse of removal.

# 76  ENGINE AND ENGINE OVERHAUL

*CAMSHAFT POSITION SENSOR DRIVE ASSEMBLY*

1. Follow steps 1–6 of the cam sensor removal procedure. Note the position of the slot in the rotating vane.
2. Remove the bolt securing the drive assembly to the engine.
3. Remove the drive assembly.
4. Install the drive assembly with the slot in the vane. Install mounting bolt.
5. Install the camshaft sensor.
6. Rotate the engine to set the No. 1 cylinder at TDC/compression.
7. Mark the harmonic balancer and rotate the engine to 25 degrees after top dead center.
8. Remove the plug wires from the coil assembly.
9. Using weatherpack removal tool J-28742-A, or equivalent, remove terminal B of the sensor 3-way connector on the module side.
10. Probe terminal B by installing a jumper and reconnecting the wire removed to the jumper wire.
11. Connect a voltmeter between the jumper wire and ground.
12. With the key ON and the engine stopped, rotate the camshaft sensor counterclockwise until the sensor switch just closes. This is indicated by the voltage reading going from a high 5–12 volts to a low 0–2 volts. The low voltage indicates the switch is closed.
13. Tighten the retaining bolt and reinstall the wire into terminal B.
14. Install remaining components.

## Distributor

### REMOVAL

*2.0L ENGINE*

1. Disconnect the negative battery cable.
2. Disconnect the coil and Electronic Spark Timing (EST) connectors.
3. Remove the coil wire. Unscrew the distributor cap hold-down screws and lift off the distributor cap with all ignition wires still connected.
4. Matchmark the rotor to the distributor housing and the distributor housing to the cam carrier.
   NOTE: *Do not crank the engine during this procedure. If the engine is cranked, the rotor's matchmark must be disregarded.*
5. Remove the hold-down nuts.
6. Remove the distributor from the engine.

### INSTALLATION

*TIMING NOT DISTURBED*

1. Install a new distributor housing O-ring.
2. Install the distributor in the cam carrier

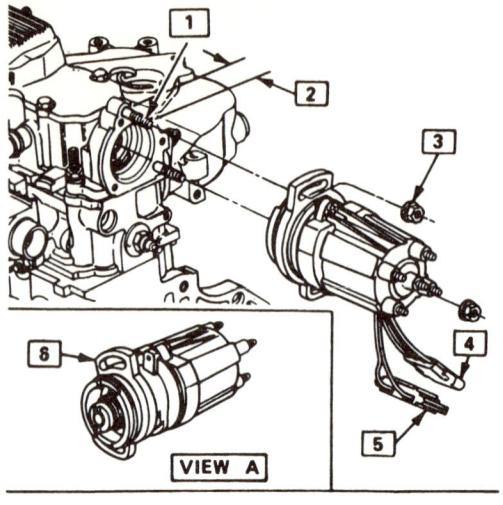

1—STUD
2—20.5 ±1.0 (BOTH STUDS)
3—NUT ASM.
4—E.S.T. CONNECTOR
5—COIL CONNECTOR
6—DISTRIBUTOR ASM.

Distributor—2.0L

so the rotor is aligned with the matchmark on the housing and the housing is aligned with the matchmark on the cam carrier. Make sure the distributor is fully seated and the distributor tang drive is fully engaged.
3. Install the hold-down nuts.
4. Install the distributor cap and attaching screws. Install the coil wire.
5. Connect the coil and EST connectors.
6. Connect the negative battery cable.
7. Adjust the ignition timing and tighten the hold-down nuts.

*TIMING DISTURBED*

1. Install a new distributor housing O-ring.
2. Position the engine so the No. 1 piston is at TDC of the compression stroke and the mark on the vibration damper is aligned with **0** on the timing indicator.
3. Install the distributor in the cam carrier so the rotor is aligned with the matchmark on the housing and the housing is aligned with the matchmark on the cam carrier. Make sure the distributor is fully seated and the distributor tang drive is fully engaged.
4. Install the hold-down nuts.
5. Install the distributor cap and attaching screws. Install the coil wire.
6. Connect the coil and EST connectors.
7. Connect the negative battery cable.
8. Adjust the ignition timing and tighten the hold-down nuts.

## HEI Distributor

### REMOVAL AND INSTALLATION

#### 2.5L Engine

1. Disconnect the ignition switch battery feed wire from the distributor.
2. Remove the distributor cap with the spark plug wires attached by releasing the two locking tabs and removing the coil wire. Move the cap out of the way.
3. Disconnect the 4-terminal ECM harness connector from the distributor. Release the locking tabs and remove the coil connector from the distributor.
4. Remove the distributor clamp screw and hold-down clamp.
5. Note the position of the rotor and scribe an alignment mark on the distributor base. Pull the distributor slowly up until the rotor stops turning counterclockwise and again scribe an alignment mark on the distributor base.
6. Installation is the reverse of removal. Set the rotor at the second alignment mark and lower the distributor into the engine. The rotor should rotate clockwise to the first alignment mark when the distributor is installed.

NOTE: *The engine should not be rotated while the distributor is removed. If the engine was accidentally cranked with the distributor out, proceed as follows.*

7. Remove the No. 1 spark plug.
8. Place your finger over the No. 1 spark plug hole and rotate the engine slowly in the normal direction or rotation until compression is felt.
9. Align the timing mark on the pulley to TDC (0) on the engine timing indicator.
10. Turn the distributor rotor so it points between the No. 1 and No. 3 spark plug towers.
11. Install the distributor and connect all wiring, then install the distributor cap.
12. Start the engine and check the timing as outlined in Chapter 2.

## Distributorless Ignition

### REMOVAL AND INSTALLATION

#### 2.3L Engine

INTEGRATED DIRECT IGNITION (IDI) COIL AND MODULE ASSEMBLY

1. Disconnect the negative battery cable.
2. Disconnect 11-pin IDI harness connector.
3. Remove the bolts that fasten the assembly to the camshaft housing.
4. Remove the IDI assembly. If the boots adhere to the spark plugs, remove them by twisting and pulling up on the retainers.

**To install:**

5. Install the boots and retainers to the housing, if they were separated during removal.
6. Align the spark plug boots with the plugs and place the assembly on the camshaft housing.
7. Install the mounting bolts and tighten to 19 ft. lbs. (26 Nm).
8. Connect the harness connector.
9. Connect the negative battery cable and check for proper operation.

## Alternator

All N-Body models use a Delco SI integral regulator charging system. Although several models of alternators are available with different idle and maximum outputs, their basic operating principles are the same.

A solid state regulator is mounted inside the alternator. All regulator components are mounted in a solid mold and this unit along with the brush holder assembly is attached to the slip ring end frame. The regulator voltage cannot be adjusted. If found to be defective, the regulator must be replaced as an assembly.

The alternator rotor bearings contain enough grease to eliminate the need for periodic lubrication. Two brushes carry current through two slip rings to the field coil mounted on the rotor. Stator windings are assembled inside a laminated core that forms part of the alternator frame. A rectifier bridge connected to the stator windings contains six diodes and electrically changes stator AC voltage to DC voltage, which is fed through the alternator output terminal. Alternator field current is supplied through a diode trio which is also connected to the stator windings. A capacitor or condenser mounted in the end frame protects the rectifier bridge and diode trio from high voltages and also suppresses radio noise. No periodic adjustment or maintenance of any kind is required on the entire alternator assembly.

### ALTERNATOR PRECAUTIONS

To prevent damage to the alternator, regulator and on-board computer, the following precautions should be taken when working with the electrical system.

1. Never reverse the battery connections or attempt to disconnect or reconnect them with the ignition key ON. Take care not to let metal tools touch ground when disconnecting the positive battery cable.
2. Booster batteries for starting must be connected properly — positive-to-positive and negative-to-negative with the ignition turned OFF. Do not attempt to connect jumper cables from another vehicle while its engine is running.
3. Disconnect the battery cables before using a fast charger; the charger has a tendency to

# 78 ENGINE AND ENGINE OVERHAUL

force current through the diodes in the opposite direction for which they were designed. This burns out the diodes.

4. Never use a fast charger as a booster for starting the vehicle.

5. Never disconnect the alternator connectors while the engine is running.

6. Do not short across or ground any of the terminals on the AC generator.

7. Never operate the alternator on an open circuit. Make sure that all connections within the circuit are clean and tight.

8. Disconnect the battery terminals when performing any service on the electrical system. This will eliminate the possibility of accidental reversal of polarity.

9. Disconnect the battery ground cable if arc welding is to be done on any part of the car.

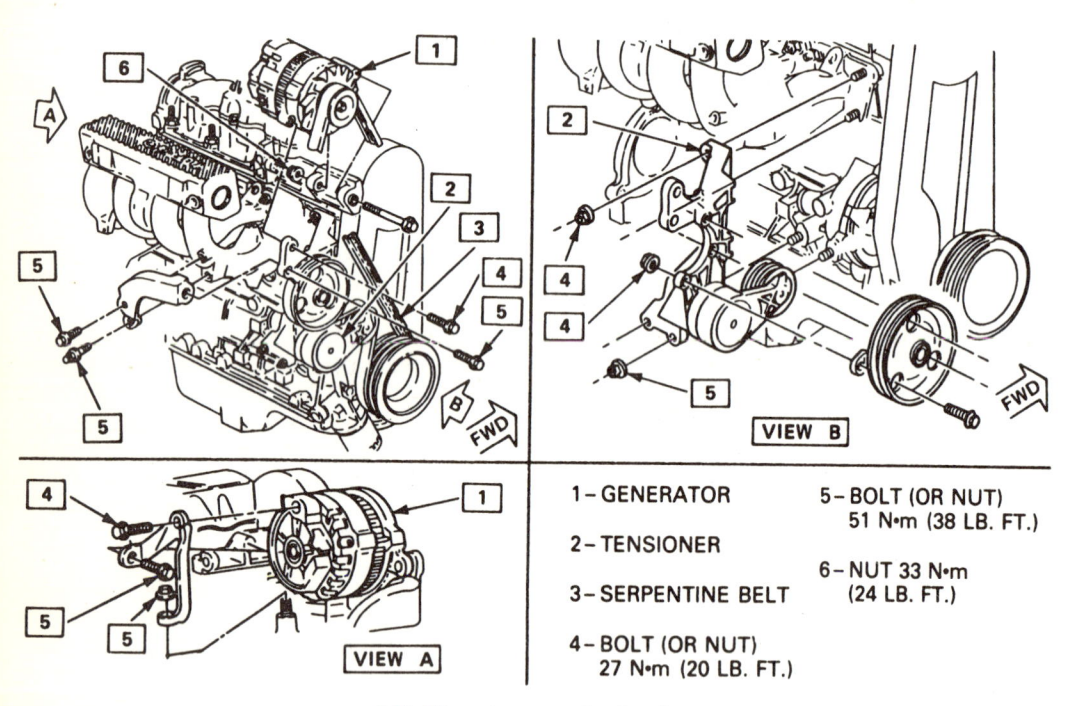

1 – GENERATOR
2 – TENSIONER
3 – SERPENTINE BELT
4 – BOLT (OR NUT) 27 N•m (20 LB. FT.)
5 – BOLT (OR NUT) 51 N•m (38 LB. FT.)
6 – NUT 33 N•m (24 LB. FT.)

**2.0L Alternator mounting bracket**

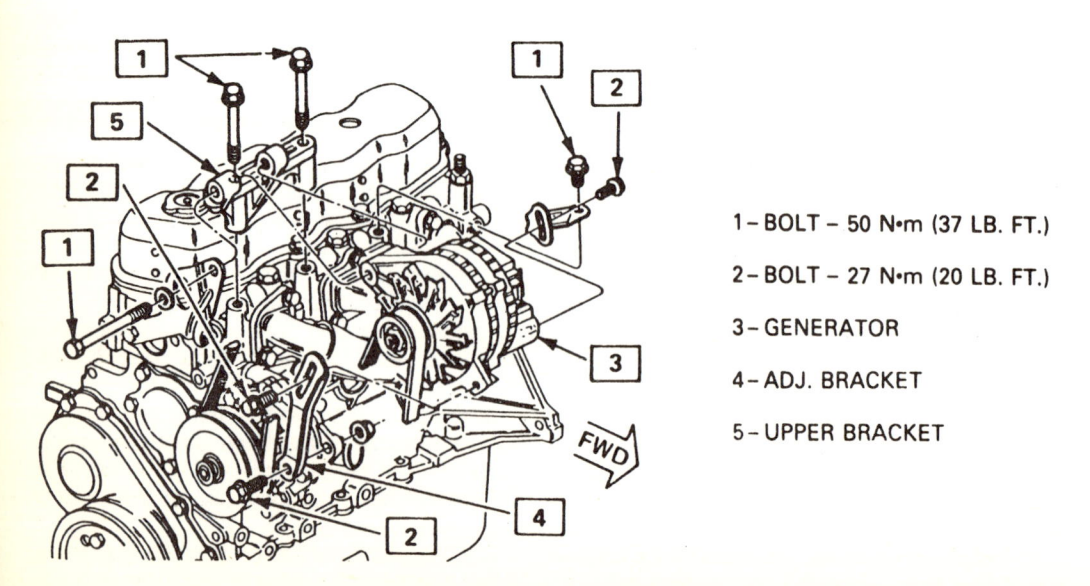

1 – BOLT – 50 N•m (37 LB. FT.)
2 – BOLT – 27 N•m (20 LB. FT.)
3 – GENERATOR
4 – ADJ. BRACKET
5 – UPPER BRACKET

**2.3L Alternator mounting bracket (VIN U)**

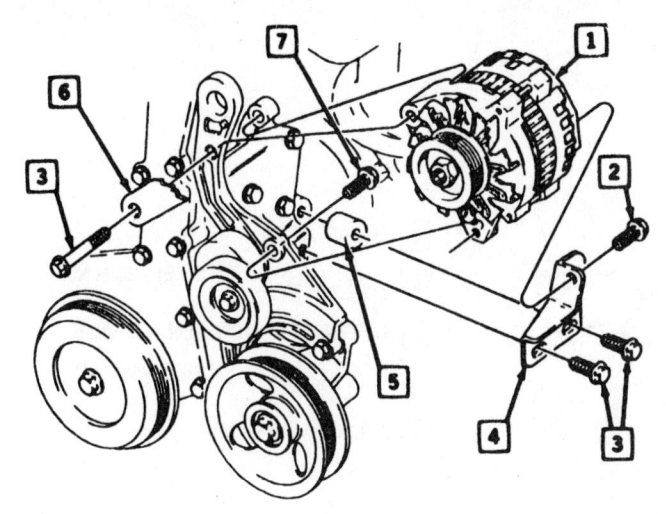

# ENGINE AND ENGINE OVERHAUL 79

1. GENERATOR ASM.
2. 26 N·m (20 LBS. FT.)
3. 50 N·m (37 LBS. FT.)
4. BRACE
5. SPACER
6. CLIP ASM.

2.3L Alternator mounting without A/C (VIN D)

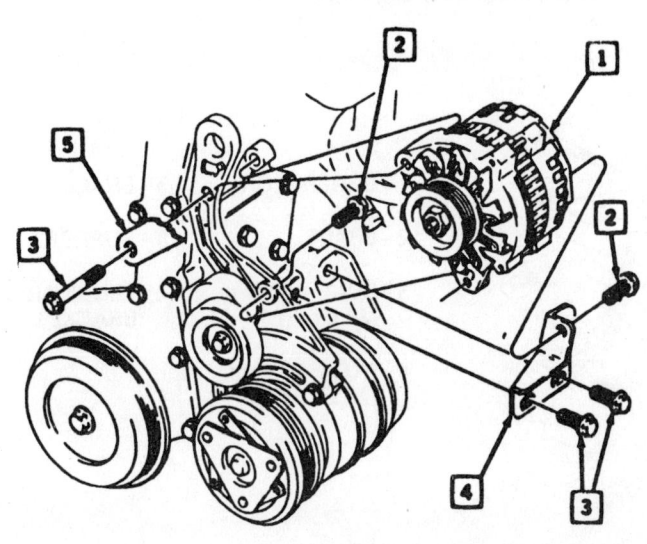

1. GENERATOR ASM.
2. 26 N·m (20 LBS. IN.)
3. 50 N·m (37 LBS. IN.)
4. BRACE
5. CLIP ASM.

2.3L Alternator mounting with A/C (VIN D)

## REMOVAL AND INSTALLATION

### All Engines except 2.3L (VIN A,D and 3)

1. Disconnect the negative battery cable.
2. Label and disconnect the wiring from the back of the alternator.
3. On the 2.5L engine, loosen the adjusting bolts and remove the alternator belt. If equipped with a serpentine belt, loosen the tesioner and turn it counterclockwise to remove the belt.
4. Remove the alternator mounting bolts and lift the alternator clear.
5. Installation is the reverse of the removal procedure.

6. Check and/or adjust the belt tesion.
7. Connect the negative battery cable and check the alternator for proper operation.

### 2.3L (VIN A,D and 3) Engines

1. Disconnect the negative battery cable.
2. Loosen the tensioner pulley bolt, turn the pulley counterclockwise and remove the belt from the alternator pulley.
3. Label and disconnect the two vacuum lines at the front of the engine.
4. Disconnect the vacuum line bracket and push to the side.
5. Disconnect the injector harness connector and the alternator electrical connectors.
6. Remove the two rear alternator mounting bolts.

## 80  ENGINE AND ENGINE OVERHAUL

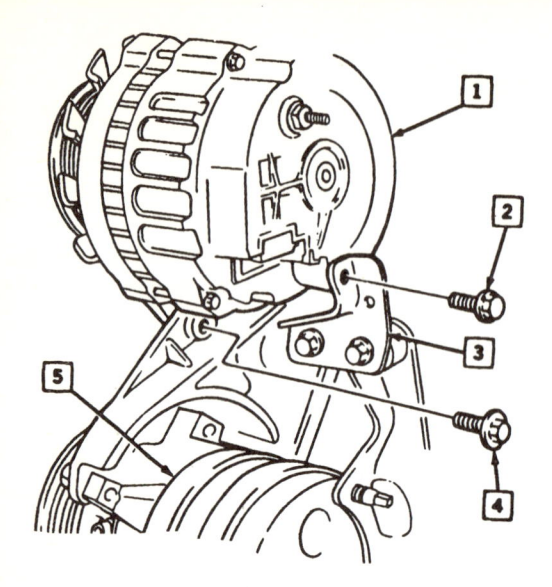

1. GENERATOR
2. BOLT (13 MM HEX SIZE) - 26 N.M (19 LBS. FT.)
3. GENERATOR TO ENGINE BRACE
4. BOLT (10 MM HEX SIZE) - 26 N.M (19 LBS. FT.)
5. A/C COMPRESSOR

Rear view of Alternator mounting—2.3L

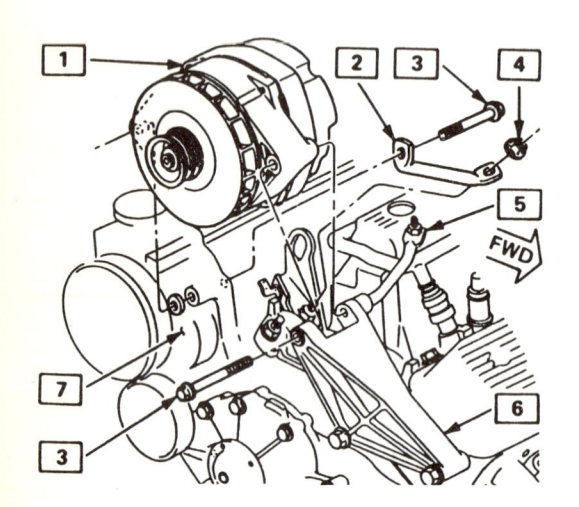

1 - GENERATOR
2 - BRACE
3 - BOLT - 27 N•m (20 LB. FT.)
4 - NUT - 27 N•m (20 LB. FT.)
5 - BRACE
6 - SUPPORT
7 - TENSIONER BRACKET

3.0L Alternator mounting

7. Remove the front alternator mounting bolt and engine harness clip.
8. Lift the alternator out, being careful not to damage the A/C lines.

**To install:**
9. Install the alternator into the engine compartment and hand tighten the front bolt.
10. Connect the front harness clip and install the two rear alternator bolts. Tighten the bolts to 20 ft. lbs. (26 Nm)
11. Tighten the front alternator bolt to 37 ft. lbs. (50 Nm) and install the serpentine belt.
12. Connect the electrical connectors and install the vacuum harness and retaining clip.
13. Connect the two hoses to the vacuum harness and connect the negative battery cable.

NOTE: *When adjusting belt tension, apply pressure at the center of the alternator, not against either end frame.*

### Regulator

The alternator used in this vehicle has an internal regulator. The alternator is serviced as a complete unit and cannot be overhauled.

### Battery

#### REMOVAL AND INSTALLATION

NOTE: *Always turn off the ignition switch when connecting or disconnecting the battery cables or a battery charger. Failure to do so could damage the ECM or other electronic components.*

*Disconnecting the battery cable may in-*

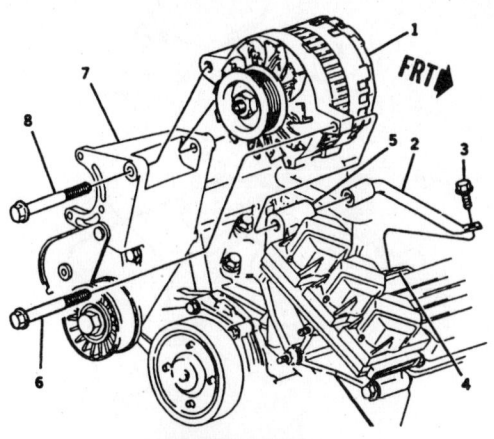

# ENGINE AND ENGINE OVERHAUL

## Starter

### REMOVAL AND INSTALLATION

*EXCEPT 2.3L ENGINE*

1. Disconnect the negative battery cable.
2. Raise and safely support the vehicle. Disconnect the electrical wiring from the starter.
3. Remove the dust cover bolts and pull the dust cover back to gain access to the front starter bolt and remove the front starter bolt.
4. Remove the rear support bracket.
5. Pull the rear dust cover back to gain access to the rear starter bolt and remove the rear bolt.
6. Note the number and location of any shims.

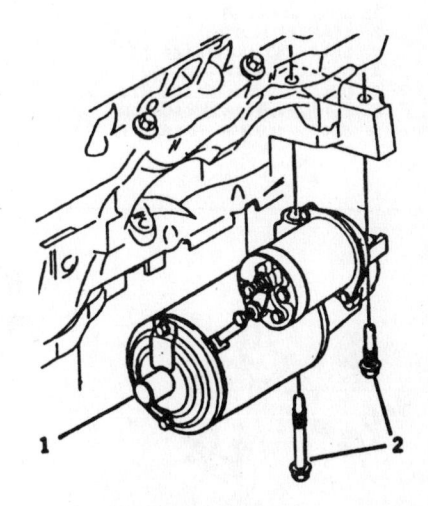

1. GENERATOR ASM.
2. GENERATOR SUPPORT
3. BOLT - 27 N•m (20 LBS. FT.)
4. GENERATOR BRACKET
5. GENERATOR SUPPORT
6. BOLT - 27 N•m (20 LBS. FT.)
7. TENSIONER ASM.
8. BOLT - 27 N•m (20 LBS. FT.)

**3.3L Alternator mounting**

terfere with the functions of the on board computer systems and may require the computer to undergo a complete relearning process once the negative battery cable is connected.

Refer to Chapter 1 for details on battery maintenance.

1. Disconnect the negative (ground) cable from the terminal and then the positive cable. Special pullers are available to remove the cable clamps. To avoid sparks, always disconnect the ground cable first and connect it last.
2. Remove the battery holddown clamp.
3. Remove the battery, being careful not to spill the acid.

NOTE: *Spilled acid can be neutralized with a baking soda/water solution. If you somehow get acid into your eyes, flush it out with lots of water and get to a doctor.*

4. Clean the battery posts thoroughly before reinstalling or when installing a new battery.
5. Clean the cable clamps, using a wire brush, both inside and out.
6. Install the battery and the holddown clamp or strap. Connect the positive, and then the negative cable. DO NOT hammer them in place.

NOTE: *The terminals should be coated lightly (externally) with a petroleum type jelly to prevent corrosion. Make absolutely sure that the battery is connected properly before you turn on the ignition switch. Reversed polarity can burn out your alternator and regulator within a matter of a split second.*

1. STARTER MOTOR
2. BOLT - 43 N•m (32 LBS. FT.)

**3.3L Starter mounting**

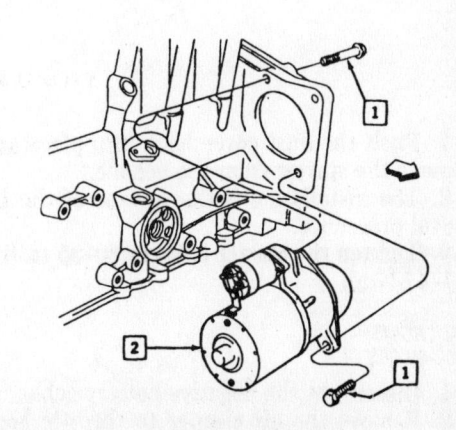

1. 100 N•m (74 LBS. FT.)
2. STARTER ASM.

**2.3L Starter mounting**

# 82  ENGINE AND ENGINE OVERHAUL

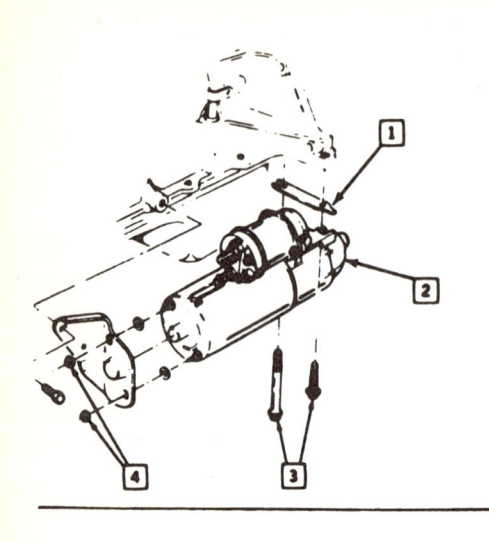

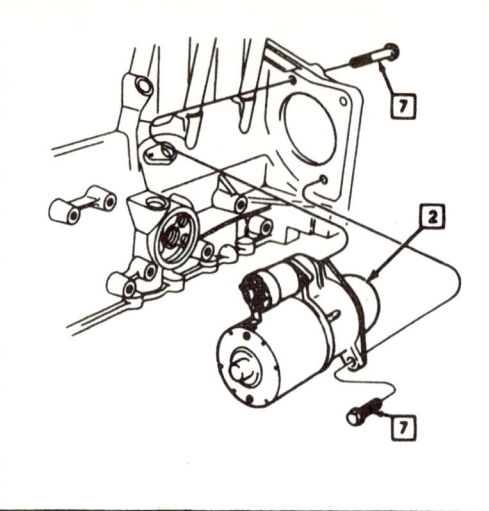

1. SHIM, STARTER
2. STARTER MOTOR
3. BOLT — 43 N·m (32 LBS. FT.)
4. NUT — 8 N·m (71 LBS. IN.)
5. BOLT — 50 N·m (37 LBS. FT.)
6. SUPPORT, STARTER MOTOR
7. BOLT — 100 N·m (74 LBS. FT.)

STARTER NOISE DIAGNOSTIC PROCEDURE

STARTER NOISE DURING CRANKING: REMOVE 1 — .015" DOUBLE SHIM OR ADD SINGLE .015" SHIM TO OUTER BOLT ONLY.

HIGH PITCHED WHINE AFTER ENGINE FIRES: ADD .015" DOUBLE SHIMS UNTIL NOISE DISAPPEARS (NOT TO EXCEED .045").

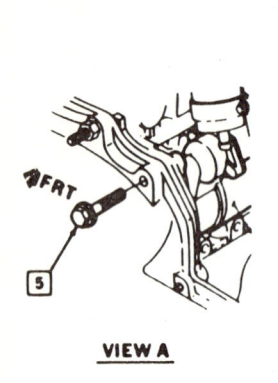

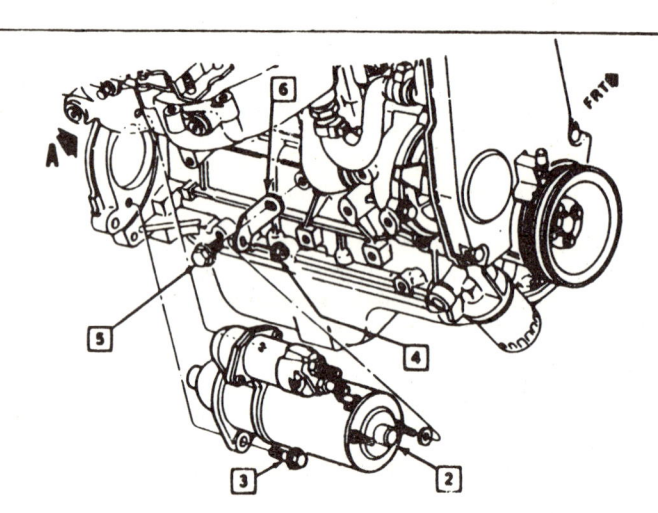

VIEW A

VIN U, D, M Starter mounting

7. Push the dust cover back into place and remove the starter from the vehicle.
8. The installation is the reverse of the removal procedure.
9. Tighten the starter bolts to 30–35 ft. lbs. (41–47 Nm).

## 2.3L ENGINE
### 1988–89 (VIN D)

1. Disconnect the negative battery cable.
2. Remove the air cleaner to throttle body duct.
3. Label and disconnect the TPS, IAC and MAP sensor connectors.
4. Remove vacuum harness assembly from intake and position aside.
5. Remove cooling fan shroud attaching bolts and remove the shroud.
6. Remove upper radiator support.
7. Disconnect the connector from the cooling fan and remove the fan assembly. Do not damage the lock tang on the TPS with the fan bracket.
8. Remove the starter mounting bolts.
9. Tilt the rear of starter towards the radiator, pull the starter out and rotate solenoid towards the radiator to gain access to the electrical connections.

NOTE: *If present, do not to damage the crank sensor mounted directly to the rear of the starter.*

10. Disconnect the connectors from the solenoid.
11. Move the starter toward the driver's side of the vehicle and remove.

**To install:**

12. Lower the starter and connect the solenoid connectors.
13. Rotate the starter into installation position, properly install any shims that were removed and install the mounting bolts. Tighten to 74 ft. lbs. (100 Nm).
14. Install the fan, support and shroud.
15. Install the vacuum harness assembly and connect the TPS, IAC and MAP sensor connectors.
16. Install the air cleaner to throttle body duct.
17. Connect the negative battery cable and check the starter for proper operation.

*2.3L ENGINE*
*1990–92 (VIN D)*
*1989–92 (VIN A)*

1. Disconnect the negative battery cable.
2. Remove the cooling fan assembly.
3. Remove the oil filter, if necessary.
4. Remove the intake manifold brace.
5. Remove the mounting bolts; some engines may have 3 starter mounting bolts. Pull the starter out of the hole and move toward the front of the vehicle.
6. Disconnect the wiring from the solenoid.
7. Remove the starter by lifting it between the intake manifold and the radiator.

**To install:**

8. Lower the starter between the intake manifold and the radiator and connect the wiring to the solenoid.
9. Rotate the starter into installation position and install the mounting bolts. Tighten to 74 ft. lbs. (100 Nm).
10. Install the intake manifold brace and oil filter.
11. Install the cooling fan assembly.
12. Connect the negative battery cable and check the starter for proper operation.

## Sending Units and Sensors

### REMOVAL AND INSTALLATION

**Coolant Temperature sensor**

1. Properly relieve cooling system pressure.
2. Make sure ignition is in the OFF position.
3. Disconnect the electrical connector to the coolant temperature sensor.
4. Remove sensor carefully.

**To install:**

5. Coat threads of sensor with proper type sealant.

### STARTER SPECIFICATIONS

| Year(s) | Engine No. Cyl. (cu. in.) | Series | Type | No-Load Test Amps | Volts | RPM |
|---|---|---|---|---|---|---|
| 1985–86 | 4-151 | 5 MT | 101 | 50–75 | 10 | 6,000–11,900 |
|  | 6-181 | 5 MT | 101 | 50–75 | 10 | 6,000–11,900 |
| 1987–88 | 4-122 | 5 MT | 101 | 55–85 | 10 | 6,000–12,000 |
|  | 4-138 | 5 MT | 101 | 52–76 | 10 | 6,000–12,000 |
|  | 4-151 | 5 MT | 101 | 55–85 | 10 | 6,000–12,000 |
|  | 6-181 | 5 MT | 101 | 55–85 | 10 | 6,000–12,000 |
| 1989 | 4-122 | SD-200 | — | 55–85 | 10 | 6,000–12,000 |
|  | 4-138 | SD-200 | — | 52–76 | 10 | 6,000–12,000 |
|  | 4-151 | SD-200 | — | 55–85 | 10 | 6,000–12,000 |
|  | 6-204 | SD-200 | — | 48–75 | 10 | 9,000–13,000 |
| 1990 | 4-138 | SD-200 | — | 52–76 | 10 | 6,000–12,000 |
|  | 4-151 | SD-200 | — | 55–85 | 10 | 6,000–12,000 |
|  | 6-204 | SD-250 | — | 45–74 | 10 | 8,600–12,900 |
| 1991 | 4-138 | SD-200 | — | 52–76 | 10 | 6,000–12,000 |
|  | 4-151 | SD-200 | — | 55–85 | 10 | 6,000–12,000 |
|  | 6-204 | SD-250 | — | 45–74 | 10 | 8,600–12,900 |
| 1992 | 4-138 | SD-200 | — | 52–76 | 10 | 6,000–12,000 |
|  | 6-204 | SD-250 | — | 45–74 | 10 | 8,600–12,900 |

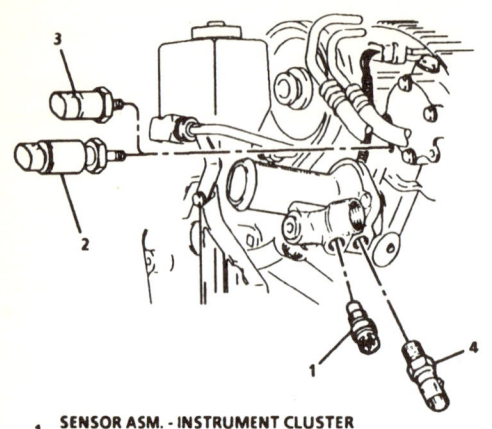

# 84  ENGINE AND ENGINE OVERHAUL

1. SENSOR ASM. - INSTRUMENT CLUSTER
   30 N·m (22 lb. in.)
2. SENSOR ASM. - FUEL PUMP SWITCH AND OIL PRESSURE
   (U21/U52) 13 N·m (115 lb. in.)
3. SWITCH ASM. - OIL PRESSURE (EXC. U21/U52)
   13 N·m (115 lb. in.)
4. SENSOR ASM. - ECM COOLANT TEMP.
   13 N·m (115 lb. in.)

APPLY 1052080 OR EQUIVALENT TO THREADS OF SENSORS OR SWITCH

**Coolant Sensor**

6. Install sensor to engine and tighten to 22 ft. lbs.(30 Nm).
7. Connect electrical connector to sensor.
8. Check coolant level and refill if necessary.

**Intake Air Temperature sensor**

1. Make sure ignition switch is in the OFF position.
2. Disconnect the electrical connector to the IAT sensor.
3. Carefully remove the sensor from the intake manifold.

**To install:**

4. Install the IAT sensor in the intake manifold.
5. Tighten the sensor to 6 ft. lbs.(8 Nm)
6. Connect the electrical connector to the sensor.

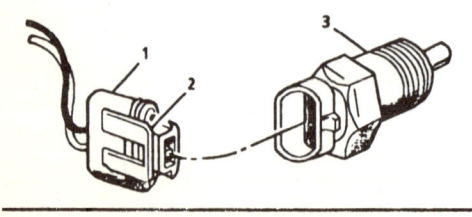

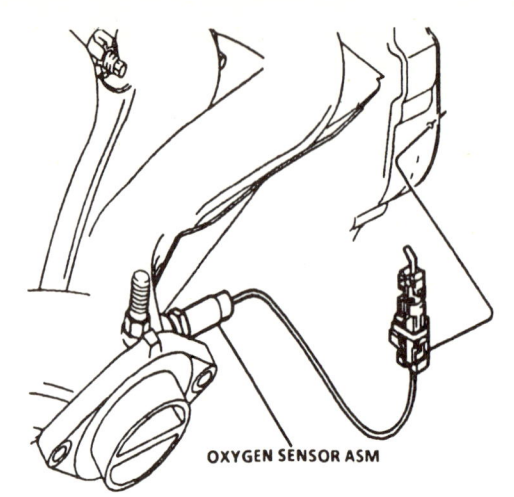

NOTICE: SHOWN WITH HEAT SHIELD REMOVED FOR CLARITY. DO NOT OPERATE CAR WITH HEAT SHIELD REMOVED.

OXYGEN SENSOR ASM

Oxygen Sensor

**Oxygen sensor**

1. Make sure ignition is OFF. Disconnect sensor connector.
2. Remove sensor assembly very carefully.
NOTE: *Excessive force may damage the threads in the intake manifold or exhaust pipe.*
**To install:**
3. Coat threads of Oxygen sensor with Anti-seize compound.
4. Install sensor and torque to 30 ft. lbs.(41 Nm.)
5. Connect electrical connector.

**Throttle Position sensor**

1. Disconnect the throttle cable.
2. Remove the throttle body air duct.
3. Disconnect the throttle body vacuum line connector.
4. Disconnect the sensor connector.

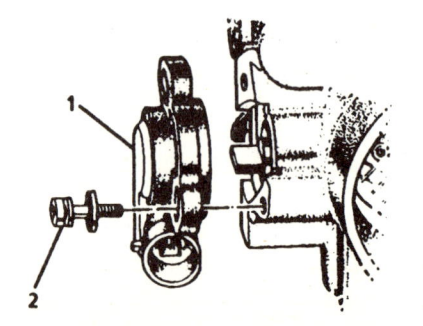

1. HARNESS CONNECTOR TO ECM
2. LOCKING TAB
3. TEMPERATURE SENSOR

**Intake Air Temperature Sensor**

1. THROTTLE POSITION SENSOR (TPS)
2. TPS ATTACHING SCREW ASSEMBLY

**Throttle Position Sensor**

# ENGINE AND ENGINE OVERHAUL

**1 MAP SENSOR**

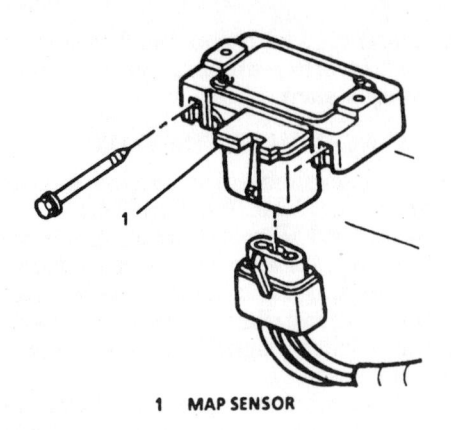

**MAP Sensor**

5. Remove the throttle cable bracket and the throttle body bolts.
6. Lift the throttle body until the TPS clears the fuel line.
7. Remove the TPS attaching screws and retainers.
8. Remove the sensor.

**To install:**

9. Make sure the throttle valve is in the CLOSED position and install the sensor. The remaining steps are the reversal of the removal procedure.

### MAP sensor

1. Disconnect the vacuum hose.
2. Disconnect the electrical connector and remove the atttaching screws.
3. Remove the sensor.

**To install:**

4. Installation is the reverse of the removal procedure.

## ENGINE MECHANICAL

### Engine Overhaul Tips

Most engine overhaul procedures are fairly standard. In addition to specific parts replacement procedures and complete specifications for your individual engine, this Chapter also is a guide to accept rebuilding procedures. Examples of standard rebuilding practice are shown and should be used along with specific details concerning your particular engine.

Competent and accurate machine shop services will ensure maximum performance, reliability and engine life.

In most instances it is more profitable for the do-it-yourself mechanic to remove, clean and inspect the component, buy the necessary parts and deliver these to a shop for actual machine work.

On the other hand, much of the rebuilding work (crankshaft, block, bearings, piston rods, and other components) is well within the scope of the do-it-yourself mechanic.

### TOOLS

The tools required for an engine overhaul or parts replacement will depend on the depth of your involvement. With a few exceptions, they will be the tools found in a mechanic's tool kit (see Chapter 1). More in-depth work will require any or all of the following:

- a dial indicator (reading in thousandths) mounted on a universal base
- micrometers and telescope gauges
- jaw and screw-type pullers
- scraper
- valve spring compressor
- ring groove cleaner
- piston ring expander and compressor
- ridge reamer
- cylinder hone or glaze breaker
- Plastigage®
- engine stand

The use of most of these tools is illustrated in this Chapter. Many can be rented for a one-time use from a local parts jobber or tool supply house specializing in automotive work.

Occasionally, the use of special tools is called for. See the information on Special Tools and Safety Notice in the front of this book before substituting another tool.

### INSPECTION TECHNIQUES

Procedures and specifications are given in this Chapter for inspecting, cleaning and assessing the wear limits of most major components. Other procedures such as Magnaflux® and Zyglo® can be used to locate material flaws and stress cracks. Magnaflux® is a magnetic process applicable only to ferrous materials. The Zyglo® process coats the material with a fluorescent dye penetrant and can be used on any material. Check for suspected surface cracks can be more readily made using spot check dye. The dye is sprayed onto the suspected area, wiped off and the area sprayed with a developer. Cracks will show up brightly.

### OVERHAUL TIPS

Aluminum has become extremely popular for use in engines, due to its low weight. Observe the following precautions when handling aluminum parts:

- Never hot tank aluminum parts (the caustic hot tank solution will eat the aluminum.
- Remove all aluminum parts (identification tag, etc.) from engine parts prior to the tanking.
- Always coat threads lightly with engine oil

or anti-seize compounds before installation, to prevent seizure.

- Never overtorque bolts or spark plugs especially in aluminum threads.

Stripped threads in any component can be repaired using any of several commercial repair kits (Heli-Coil®, Microdot®, Keenserts®, etc.).

When assembling the engine, any parts that will be frictional contact must be prelubed to provide lubrication at initial start-up. Any product specifically formulated for this purpose can be used, but engine oil is not recommended as a prelube.

When semi-permanent (locked, but removable) installation of bolts or nuts is desired, threads should be cleaned and coated with Loctite® or other similar, commercial non-hardening sealant.

### REPAIRING DAMAGED THREADS

Several methods of repairing damaged threads are available. Heli-Coil® (shown here), Keenserts® and Microdot® are among the most widely used. All involve basically the same principle — drilling out stripped threads, tapping the hole and installing a prewound insert — making welding, plugging and oversize fasteners unnecessary.

Two types of thread repair inserts are usually supplied: a standard type for most Inch Coarse,

## GENERAL ENGINE SPECIFICATIONS

| Year | Engine VIN | Engine Displacement cu. in. (Liters) | Fuel System Type | Net Horsepower @ rpm | Net Torque @ rpm (ft. lbs.) | Bore × Stroke (in.) | Compression Ratio | Oil Pressure @ rpm |
|---|---|---|---|---|---|---|---|---|
| 1985–86 | U | 151 (2.5) | TBI | 92 @ 4500 | 138 @ 2400 | 4.00 × 3.00 | 9.0:1 | 36–41 @ 2000 |
| | L | 181 (3.0) | MFI | 125 @ 4900 | 150 @ 2400 | 3.80 × 2.66 | 8.45:1 | 37 @ 2400 |
| 1987 | M | 122 (2.0) | Turbo | 167 @ 4500 | 175 @ 4000 | 3.40 × 3.40 | 8.0:1 | NA |
| | D | 138 (2.3) | PFI | 150 @ 5200 | 160 @ 4000 | 3.62 × 3.35 | 9.5:1 | 30 @ 2000 |
| | U | 151 (2.5) | TBI | 98 @ 4300 | 135 @ 3200 | 4.00 × 3.00 | 8.3:1 | 37 @ 2000 |
| | L | 181 (3.0) | PFI | 125 @ 4900 | 150 @ 2400 | 3.80 × 2.70 | 9.0:1 | 37 @ 2400 |
| 1988 | M | 122 (2.0) | Turbo | 167 @ 4500 | 175 @ 4000 | 3.40 × 3.40 | 8.0:1 | NA |
| | D | 138 (2.3) | PFI | 150 @ 5200 | 160 @ 4000 | 3.62 × 3.35 | 9.5:1 | 30 @ 2000 |
| | U | 151 (2.5) | TBI | 98 @ 4300 | 135 @ 3200 | 4.00 × 3.00 | 8.3:1 | 37 @ 2000 |
| | L | 181 (3.0) | PFI | 125 @ 4900 | 150 @ 2400 | 3.80 × 2.70 | 9.0:1 | 37 @ 2400 |
| 1989 | M | 122 (2.0) | Turbo | 167 @ 4500 | 175 @ 4000 | 3.40 × 3.40 | 8.0:1 | NA |
| | A | 138 (2.3) | PFI | 180 @ 6200 | 160 @ 5200 | 3.62 × 3.35 | 10.0:1 | 30 @ 2000 |
| | D | 138 (2.3) | PFI | 160 @ 6200 | 155 @ 5200 | 3.62 × 3.35 | 9.5:1 | 30 @ 2000 |
| | U | 151 (2.5) | TBI | 110 @ 5200 | 135 @ 3200 | 4.00 × 3.00 | 8.3:1 | 37 @ 2000 |
| | N | 204 (3.3) | PFI | 160 @ 5200 | 185 @ 3200 | 3.70 × 3.16 | 9.0:1 | 45 @ 2000 |
| 1990 | A | 138 (2.3) | PFI | 180 @ 6200 | 160 @ 5200 | 3.62 × 3.35 | 10.0:1 | 30 @ 2000 |
| | D | 138 (2.3) | PFI | 160 @ 6200 | 155 @ 5200 | 3.62 × 3.35 | 9.5:1 | 30 @ 2000 |
| | U | 151 (2.5) | TBI | 110 @ 5200 | 135 @ 3200 | 4.00 × 3.00 | 8.3:1 | 37 @ 2000 |
| | N | 204 (3.3) | PFI | 160 @ 5200 | 185 @ 3200 | 3.70 × 3.16 | 9.0:1 | 45 @ 2000 |
| 1991 | A | 138 (2.3) | PFI | 180 @ 6200 | 160 @ 5200 | 3.62 × 3.35 | 10.0:1 | 30 @ 2000 |
| | D | 138 (2.3) | PFI | 160 @ 6200 | 155 @ 5200 | 3.62 × 3.35 | 9.5:1 | 30 @ 2000 |
| | U | 151 (2.5) | TBI | 110 @ 5200 | 135 @ 3200 | 4.00 × 3.00 | 8.3:1 | 26 @ 800 |
| | N | 204 (3.3) | PFI | 160 @ 5200 | 185 @ 3200 | 3.70 × 3.16 | 9.0:1 | 60 @ 1850 |
| 1992 | 3 | 138 (2.3) | PFI | 180 @ 6200 | 160 @ 5200 | 3.62 × 3.35 | 9.5:1 | 30 @ 2000 |
| | A | 138 (2.3) | PFI | 180 @ 6200 | 160 @ 5200 | 3.62 × 3.35 | 10.0:1 | 30 @ 2000 |
| | D | 138 (2.3) | PFI | 160 @ 6200 | 155 @ 5200 | 3.62 × 3.35 | 9.5:1 | 30 @ 2000 |
| | N | 204 (3.3) | PFI | 160 @ 5200 | 185 @ 3200 | 3.70 × 3.16 | 9.0:1 | 60 @ 1850 |

**NOTE:** Horsepower and torque are SAE net figures. They are measured at the rear of the transmission with all accessories installed and operating. Since the figures vary when a given engine is installed in different models, some are representative rather than exact.

TBI—Throttle Body Injection
MFI—Multi-Port Fuel Injection
PFI—Port Fuel Injection
Turbo—Turbocharged

## ENGINE AND ENGINE OVERHAUL

## VALVE SPECIFICATIONS

| Year | VIN | No. Cylinder Displacement cu. in. (Liters) | Seat Angle (deg.) | Face Angle (deg.) | Spring Test Pressure (lbs. @ in.) | Spring Installed Height (in.) | Stem-to-Guide Clearance (in.) Intake | Stem-to-Guide Clearance (in.) Exhaust | Stem Diameter (in.) Intake | Stem Diameter (in.) Exhaust |
|---|---|---|---|---|---|---|---|---|---|---|
| 1985 | U | 4-151 (2.5) | 46 | 45 | 82 @ | 1.66 | 0.0010–0.0027 | 0.0010–0.0027 | 0.3420–0.3430 | 0.3420–0.3430 |
|  | L | 6-181 (3.0) | 45 | 45 | 220 @ | 1.34 | 0.0015–0.0035 | 0.0015–0.0032 | 0.3401–0.3412 | 0.3401–0.3412 |
| 1986 | U | 4-151 (2.5) | 46 | 45 | 82 @ | 1.66 | 0.0010–0.0027 | 0.0010–0.0027 | 0.3130–0.3140 | 0.3120–0.3130 |
|  | L | 6-181 (3.0) | 45 | 45 | 220 @ | 1.34 | 0.0015–0.0035 | 0.0015–0.0032 | 0.3401–0.3412 | 0.3405–0.3412 |
| 1987–88 | M | 4-122 (2.0) | 45 | 46 | NA | NA | 0.0006–0.0020 | 0.0010–0.0024 | — | — |
|  | D | 4-138 (2.3) | 45 | 44 | 64–70 @ 1.4370 in. | 1.423–1.443 | 0.0009–0.0027 | 0.0015–0.0032 | 0.2751–0.2744 | 0.2754–0.2739 |
|  | U | 4-151 (2.5) | 46 | 45 | 158–170 @ 1.040 in. | 1.44 | 0.0010–0.0026 | 0.0013–0.0041 | 0.3130–0.3140 | 0.3120–0.3130 |
|  | L | 6-181 (3.0) | 45 | 45 | 175–195 @ 1.340 in. | 1.73 | 0.0015–0.0035 | 0.0015–0.0032 | 0.3401–0.3412 | 0.3405–0.3412 |
| 1989 | M | 4-122 (2.0) | 45 | 46 | 165–179 @ 1.043 in. | NA | 0.0006–0.0017 | 0.0010–0.0024 | 0.2755–0.2760 | 0.2747–0.2753 |
|  | A | 4-138 (2.3) | 45 | ① | 188–202 @ 1.043 in. | 1.42–1.44 | 0.0009–0.0027 | 0.0015–0.0032 | 0.2744–0.2751 | 0.2740–0.2747 |
|  | D | 4-138 (2.3) | 45 | ① | 159–173 @ 1.043 in. | 1.42–1.44 | 0.0009–0.0027 | 0.0015–0.0032 | 0.2744–0.2751 | 0.2740–0.2747 |
|  | U | 4-151 (2.5) | 46 | 45 | 173 @ 1.24 in. | 1.68 | 0.0010–0.0026 | 0.0013–0.0041 | NA | NA |
|  | N | 6-204 (3.3) | 45 | 45 | 200–220 @ 1.315 in. | 1.69–1.75 | 0.0015–0.0035 | 0.0015–0.0032 | NA | NA |
| 1990 | A | 4-138 (2.3) | 45 | ① | 193–207 @ 1.043 in. | 1.42–1.44 | 0.0009–0.0027 | 0.0015–0.0032 | 0.2744–0.2751 | 0.2740–0.2747 |
|  | D | 4-138 (2.3) | 45 | ① | 193–207 @ 1.043 in. | 1.42–1.44 | 0.0009–0.0027 | 0.0015–0.0032 | 0.2744–0.2751 | 0.2740–0.2747 |
|  | U | 4-151 (2.5) | 46 | 45 | 173 @ 1.24 in. | 1.68 | 0.0010–0.0026 | 0.0013–0.0041 | NA | NA |
|  | N | 6-204 (3.3) | 45 | 45 | 200–220 @ 1.315 in. | 1.69–1.75 | 0.0015–0.0035 | 0.0015–0.0032 | NA | NA |
| 1991 | A | 4-138 (2.3) | 45 | 44 | 193–207 @ 1.043 in. | 0.98–1.00② | 0.0010–0.0027 | 0.0015–0.0032 | 0.2744–0.2751 | 0.2740–0.2747 |
|  | D | 4-138 (2.3) | 45 | 44 | 193–207 @ 1.043 in. | 0.98–1.00② | 0.0010–0.0027 | 0.0015–0.0032 | 0.2744–0.2751 | 0.2740–0.2747 |
|  | U | 4-151 (2.5) | 46 | 45 | 173 @ 1.24 in. | 1.68 | 0.0010–0.0026 | 0.0013–0.0041 | NA | NA |
|  | N | 6-204 (3.3) | 45 | 45 | 210 @ 1.315 in. | 1.69–1.72 | 0.0015–0.0035 | 0.0015–0.0035 | NA | NA |
| 1992 | A | 4-138 (2.3) | 45 | 44 | 193–207 @ 1.043 in. | 0.98–1.00② | 0.0015–0.0032 | 0.0015–0.0032 | 0.2740–0.2747 | 0.2740–0.2747 |
|  | D | 4-138 (2.3) | 45 | 44 | 193–207 @ 1.043 in. | 0.98–1.00② | 0.0015–0.0032 | 0.0015–0.0032 | 0.2740–0.2747 | 0.2740–0.2747 |
|  | 3 | 4-138 (2.3) | 45 | 44 | 193–207 @ 1.043 in. | 0.98–1.00② | 0.0015–0.0032 | 0.0015–0.0032 | 0.2740–0.2747 | 0.2740–0.2747 |
|  | N | 6-204 (3.3) | 45 | 45 | 210 @ 1.315 in. | 1.69–1.72 | 0.0015–0.0032 | 0.0015–0.0035 | NA | NA |

① Intake: 45°
Exhaust: 44.5°
② Measured from top of valve stem to top of camshaft housing mounting surface

# 88  ENGINE AND ENGINE OVERHAUL

Inch Fine, Metric Coarse and Metric Fine thread sizes and a spark plug type to fit most spark plug port sizes. Consult the individual manufacturer's catalog to determine exact applications. Typical thread repair kits will contain a selection of prewound threaded inserts, a tap (corresponding to the outside diameter threads of the insert) and an installation tool. Spark plug inserts usually differ because they require a tap equipped with pilot threads and a

## CAMSHAFT SPECIFICATIONS
All measurements given in inches.

| Year | Engine ID/VIN | Engine Displacement Liters (cc) | Journal Diameter 1 | 2 | 3 | 4 | 5 | Elevation In. | Ex. | Bearing Clearance | Camshaft End Play |
|---|---|---|---|---|---|---|---|---|---|---|---|
| 1985–86 | U | 4-151 (2.5) | 1.8690 | 1.8690 | 1.8690 | 1.8690 | 1.8690 | 0.3980 | 0.3980 | 0.0007–0.0027 | 0.0015–0.0050 |
| | L | 6-181 (3.0) | 1.7850–1.7860 | 1.7850–1.7860 | 1.7850–1.7860 | 1.7850–1.7860 | — | 0.3580 | 0.3840 | 0.0005–0.0025 | NA |
| 1987–88 | M | 4-122 (2.0) | 1.6714–1.6720 | 1.6812–1.6816 | 1.6911–1.6917 | 1.7009–1.7015 | 1.7108–1.7114 | 0.2409 | NA | 0.0008 | 0.0016–0.0064 |
| | D | 4-138 (2.3) | 1.3751–1.3760 | 1.3751–1.3760 | 1.3751–1.3760 | 1.3751–1.3760 | 1.3751–1.3760 | 0.3400 | 0.3500 | 0.0019–0.0043 | 0.0014–0.0060 |
| | U | 4-151 (2.5) | 1.8690 | 1.8690 | 1.8690 | 1.8690 | 1.8690 | 0.3980 | 0.3980 | 0.0007–0.0027 | 0.0015–0.0050 |
| | L | 6-181 (3.0) | 1.7850–1.7860 | 1.7850–1.7860 | 1.7850–1.7860 | 1.7850–1.7860 | — | 0.3580 | 0.3840 | 0.0005–0.0025 | NA |
| 1989 | M | 4-122 (2.0) | 1.6706–1.6712 | 1.6812–1.6818 | 1.6911–1.6917 | 1.7009–1.7015 | 1.7100–1.7106 | 0.2625 | 0.2625 | 0.0011–0.0035 | 0.0016–0.0064 |
| | D | 4-138 (2.3) | 1.3751–1.3760 | 1.3751–1.3760 | 1.3751–1.3760 | 1.3751–1.3760 | 1.3751–1.3760 | 0.3400 | 0.3500 | 0.0019–0.0043 | 0.0014–0.0060 |
| | A | 4-138 (2.3) | 1.3751–1.3760 | 1.3751–1.3760 | 1.3751–1.3760 | 1.3751–1.3760 | 1.3751–1.3760 | 0.4100 | 0.4100 | 0.0019–0.0043 | 0.0014–0.0060 |
| | U | 4-151 (2.5) | 1.8690 | 1.8690 | 1.8690 | 1.8690 | 1.8690 | 0.2480 | 0.2480 | 0.0007–0.0027 | 0.0020–0.0090 |
| | N | 6-204 (3.3) | 1.7850–1.7860 | 1.7850–1.7860 | 1.7850–1.7860 | 1.7850–1.7860 | — | 0.2500 | 0.2550 | 0.0005–0.0035 | NA |
| 1990 | D | 4-138 (2.3) | 1.5720–1.5728 | 1.3751–1.3760 | 1.3751–1.3760 | 1.3751–1.3760 | 1.3751–1.3760 | 0.3400 | 0.3500 | 0.0019–0.0043 | 0.0014–0.0060 |
| | A | 4-138 (2.3) | 1.5720–1.5728 | 1.3751–1.3760 | 1.3751–1.3760 | 1.3751–1.3760 | 1.3751–1.3760 | 0.4100 | 0.4100 | 0.0019–0.0043 | 0.0014–0.0060 |
| | U | 4-151 (2.5) | 1.8690 | 1.8690 | 1.8690 | 1.8690 | 1.8690 | 0.2480 | 0.2480 | 0.0007–0.0027 | 0.0020–0.0090 |
| | N | 6-204 (3.3) | 1.7850–1.7860 | 1.7850–1.7860 | 1.7850–1.7860 | 1.7850–1.7860 | — | 0.2500 | 0.2550 | 0.0005–0.0035 | NA |
| 1991 | D | 4-138 (2.3) | 1.5720–1.5728 | 1.3751–1.3760 | 1.3751–1.3760 | 1.3751–1.3760 | 1.3751–1.3760 | 0.3750 | 0.3750 | 0.0019–0.0043 | 0.0009–0.0088 |
| | A | 4-138 (2.3) | 1.5720–1.5728 | 1.3751–1.3760 | 1.3751–1.3760 | 1.3751–1.3760 | 1.3751–1.3760 | 0.4100 | 0.4100 | 0.0019–0.0043 | 0.0009–0.0088 |
| | U | 4-151 (2.5) | 1.8690 | 1.8690 | 1.8690 | 1.8690 | 1.8690 | 0.2480 | 0.2480 | 0.0007–0.0027 | 0.0020–0.0090 |
| | N | 6-204 (3.3) | 1.7850–1.7860 | 1.7850–1.7860 | 1.7850–1.7860 | 1.7850–1.7860 | — | 0.2500 | 0.2550 | 0.0005–0.0035 | NA |
| 1992 | A | 4-138 (2.3) | 1.5720–1.5728 | 1.3751–1.3760 | 1.3751–1.3760 | 1.3751–1.3760 | 1.3751–1.3760 | 0.4100 | 0.4100 | 0.0019–0.0043 | 0.0009–0.0088 |
| | D | 4-138 (2.3) | 1.5720–1.5728 | 1.3751–1.3760 | 1.3751–1.3760 | 1.3751–1.3760 | 1.3751–1.3760 | 0.3750 | 0.3750 | 0.0019–0.0043 | 0.0009–0.0088 |
| | 3 | 4-138 (2.3) | 1.5720–1.5728 | 1.3751–1.3760 | 1.3751–1.3760 | 1.3751–1.3760 | 1.3751–1.3760 | 0.4100 | 0.4100 | 0.0019–0.0043 | 0.0009–0.0088 |
| | N | 6-204 (3.3) | 1.7850–1.7860 | 1.7850–1.7860 | 1.7850–1.7860 | 1.7850–1.7860 | — | 0.2500 | 0.2550 | 0.0005–0.0035 | NA |

## ENGINE AND ENGINE OVERHAUL

combined reamer/tap section. Most manufacturers also supply blister-packed thread repair inserts separately in addition to a master kit containing a variety of taps and inserts plus installation tools.

Before effecting a repair to a threaded hole, remove any snapped, broken or damaged bolts or studs. Penetrating oil can be used to free frozen threads. The offending item can be removed with locking pliers or with a screw or

### CRANKSHAFT AND CONNECTING ROD SPECIFICATIONS
All measurements are given in inches.

| Year | Engine ID/VIN | Engine Displacement Liters (cc) | Main Brg. Journal Dia. | Main Brg. Oil Clearance | Shaft End-play | Thrust on No. | Journal Diameter | Oil Clearance | Side Clearance |
|---|---|---|---|---|---|---|---|---|---|
| 1985–86 | U | 4-151 (2.5) | 2.3000 | 0.0005–0.0022 | 0.0035–0.0085 | 5 | 2.0000 | 0.0005–0.0022 | 0.0060–0.0020 |
| | L | 6-181 (3.0) | 2.4995 | 0.0003–0.0018 | 0.0030–0.0150 | 2 | 2.4870 | 0.0005–0.0026 | 0.0030–0.0150 |
| 1987 | M | 4-122 (2.0) | 2.2830–2.2833① | 0.0006–0.0016 | 0.0030–0.0120 | 3 | 1.9278–1.9286 | 0.0007–0.0024 | 0.0027–0.0095 |
| | D | 4-138 (2.3) | 2.0470–2.0474 | 0.0005–0.0020 | 0.0034–0.0095 | 3 | 1.8887–1.8897 | 0.0005–0.0025 | 0.0059–0.0177 |
| | U | 4-151 (2.5) | 2.3000 | 0.0005–0.0022 | 0.0035–0.0085 | 5 | 2.0000 | 0.0005–0.0022 | 0.0060–0.0220 |
| | L | 6-181 (3.0) | 2.4995 | 0.0003–0.0018 | 0.0030–0.0085 | 2 | 2.4870 | 0.0005–0.0026 | 0.0030–0.0150 |
| 1988 | M | 4-122 (2.0) | 2.2830–2.2833① | 0.0006–0.0016 | 0.0030–0.0120 | 3 | 1.9278–1.9286 | 0.0007–0.0024 | 0.0027–0.0095 |
| | D | 4-138 (2.3) | 2.0470–2.0474 | 0.0005–0.0022 | 0.0034–0.0095 | 3 | 1.8887–1.8897 | 0.0005–0.0025 | 0.0059–0.0177 |
| | U | 4-151 (2.5) | 2.3000 | 0.0005–0.0022 | 0.0035–0.0085 | 5 | 2.0000 | 0.0005–0.0026 | 0.0060–0.0220 |
| | L | 6-181 (3.0) | 2.4988–2.4998 | 0.0003–0.0018 | 0.0030–0.0110 | 2 | 2.2487–2.2495 | 0.0003–0.0028 | 0.0030–0.0150 |
| 1989 | M | 4-122 (2.0) | 2.2828–2.2833① | 0.0006–0.0016 | 0.0028–0.0118 | 3 | 1.9279–1.9287 | 0.0007–0.0025 | 0.0028–0.0095 |
| | A | 4-138 (2.3) | 2.0470–2.0480 | 0.0005–0.0023 | 0.0034–0.0095 | 3 | 1.8887–1.8897 | 0.0005–0.0020 | 0.0059–0.0177 |
| | D | 4-138 (2.3) | 2.0470–2.0480 | 0.0005–0.0023 | 0.0034–0.0095 | 3 | 1.8887–1.8897 | 0.0005–0.0020 | 0.0059–0.0177 |
| | U | 4-151 (2.5) | 2.3000 | 0.0005–0.0020 | 0.0006–0.0110 | 5 | 2.0000 | 0.0005–0.0030 | 0.0060–0.0240 |
| | N | 6-204 (3.3) | 2.4988–2.4998 | 0.0003–0.0018 | 0.0030–0.0110 | 2 | 2.2487–2.2499 | 0.0003–0.0026 | 0.0030–0.0150 |
| 1990 | A | 4-138 (2.3) | 2.0470–2.0480 | 0.0005–0.0023 | 0.0034–0.0095 | 3 | 1.8887–1.8897 | 0.0005–0.0020 | 0.0059–0.0177 |
| | D | 4-138 (2.3) | 2.0470–2.0480 | 0.0005–0.0023 | 0.0034–0.0095 | 3 | 1.8887–1.8897 | 0.0005–0.0020 | 0.0059–0.0177 |
| | U | 4-151 (2.5) | 2.3000 | 0.0005–0.0020 | 0.0006–0.0110 | 5 | 2.0000 | 0.0005–0.0030 | 0.0060–0.0240 |
| | N | 6-204 (3.3) | 2.4988–2.4998 | 0.0003–0.0018 | 0.0030–0.0110 | 2 | 2.2487–2.2499 | 0.0003–0.0026 | 0.0030–0.0150 |
| 1991 | A | 4-138 (2.3) | 2.0470–2.0480 | 0.0005–0.0023 | 0.0034–0.0095 | 3 | 1.8887–1.8897 | 0.0005–0.0020 | 0.0059–0.0177 |
| | D | 4-138 (2.3) | 2.0470–2.0480 | 0.0005–0.0023 | 0.0034–0.0095 | 3 | 1.8887–1.8897 | 0.0005–0.0020 | 0.0059–0.0177 |
| | U | 4-151 (2.5) | 2.3000 | 0.0005–0.0022 | 0.0059–0.0110 | 5 | 2.0000 | 0.0005–0.0030 | 0.0060–0.0240 |
| | N | 6-204 (3.3) | 2.4988–2.4998 | 0.0003–0.0018 | 0.0030–0.0110 | 2 | 2.2487–2.2499 | 0.0003–0.0026 | 0.0030–0.0150 |

## ENGINE AND ENGINE OVERHAUL

### CRANKSHAFT AND CONNECTING ROD SPECIFICATIONS
All measurements are given in inches.

| Year | Engine ID/VIN | Engine Displacement Liters (cc) | Crankshaft Main Brg. Journal Dia. | Main Brg. Oil Clearance | Shaft End-play | Thrust on No. | Connecting Rod Journal Diameter | Oil Clearance | Side Clearance |
|---|---|---|---|---|---|---|---|---|---|
| 1992 | A | 4-138 (2.3) | 2.0470–2.0480 | 0.0005–0.0023 | 0.0034–0.0095 | 3 | 1.8887–1.8897 | 0.0005–0.0020 | 0.0059–0.0177 |
|  | D | 4-138 (2.3) | 2.0470–2.0480 | 0.0005–0.0023 | 0.0034–0.0095 | 3 | 1.8887–1.8897 | 0.0005–0.0020 | 0.0059–0.0177 |
|  | 3 | 4-138 (2.3) | 2.0470–2.0480 | 0.0005–0.0023 | 0.0034–0.0095 | 3 | 1.8887–1.8897 | 0.0005–0.0020 | 0.0059–0.0177 |
|  | N | 6-204 (3.3) | 2.4988–2.4998 | 0.0003–0.0018 | 0.0030–0.0110 | 2 | 2.2487–2.2499 | 0.0003–0.0026 | 0.0030–0.0150 |

① Brown: 2.2830–2.2833
   Green: 2.2827–2.2830

### PISTON AND RING SPECIFICATIONS
All measurements are given in inches.

| Year | VIN | No. Cylinder Displacement Liters (cc) | Piston Clearance | Ring Gap Top Compression | Bottom Compression | Oil Control | Ring Side Clearance Top Compression | Bottom Compression | Oil Control |
|---|---|---|---|---|---|---|---|---|---|
| 1985 | U | 4-151 (2.5) | 0.0014–0.0022① | 0.0100–0.0200 | 0.0100–0.0200 | 0.0200–0.0600 | 0.00200–0.00300 | 0.00100–0.00300 | 0.01500–0.05500 |
|  | L | 6-181 (3.0) | 0.0008–0.0020② | 0.0130–0.0280 | 0.0130–0.0230 | 0.0150–0.0350 | 0.00300–0.00500 | 0.00300–0.00500 | 0.00350 |
| 1986 | U | 4-151 (2.5) | 0.0014–0.0022① | 0.0100–0.0200 | 0.0100–0.0200 | 0.0200–0.0600 | 0.00200–0.00300 | 0.00100–0.00300 | 0.01500–0.05500 |
|  | L | 6-181 (3.0) | 0.0008–0.0020② | 0.0130–0.0280 | 0.0130–0.0230 | 0.0150–0.0350 | 0.00300–0.00500 | 0.00300–0.00500 | 0.00350 |
| 1987 | M | 4-122 (2.0) | 0.0012–0.0020 | 0.0120–0.0200 | 0.0120–0.0200 | 0.0160–0.0550 | 0.00200–0.00300 | 0.00100–0.00240 | — |
|  | D | 4-138 (2.3) | 0.0007–0.0020 | 0.0160–0.0250 | 0.0160–0.0250 | 0.0160–0.0550 | 0.00200–0.00350 | 0.00160–0.00310 | — |
|  | U | 4-151 (2.5) | 0.0014–0.0022① | 0.0100–0.0200 | 0.0100–0.0200 | 0.0200–0.0600 | 0.00200–0.00300 | 0.00100–0.00300 | 0.01500–0.05500 |
|  | L | 6-181 (3.0) | 0.0008–0.0020② | 0.0130–0.0280 | 0.0130–0.0230 | 0.0150–0.0350 | 0.00300–0.00500 | 0.00300–0.00500 | 0.00350 |
| 1988 | M | 4-122 (2.0) | 0.0012–0.0020 | 0.0120–0.0200 | 0.0120–0.0200 | 0.0160–0.0550 | 0.00200–0.00300 | 0.00100–0.00300 | NA |
|  | D | 4-138 (2.3) | 0.0007–0.0020 | 0.0160–0.0250 | 0.0160–0.0250 | 0.0160–0.0550 | 0.00200–0.00400 | 0.00160–0.00310 | NA |
|  | U | 4-151 (2.5) | 0.0014–0.0022 | 0.0100–0.0200 | 0.0100–0.0200 | 0.0200–0.0600 | 0.00200–0.00300 | 0.00100–0.00300 | 0.01500–0.05500 |
|  | L | 6-181 (3.0) | 0.0010–0.0045 | 0.0100–0.0200 | 0.0100–0.0220 | 0.0150–0.0550 | 0.00100–0.00300 | 0.00100–0.00300 | 0.00050–0.00650 |
| 1989 | M | 4-122 (2.0) | 0.0012–0.0020 | 0.0100–0.0200 | 0.0120–0.0200 | 0.0160–0.0550 | 0.00200–0.00400 | 0.00200–0.00300 | NA |
|  | A | 4-138 (2.3) | 0.0007–0.0020 | 0.0140–0.0240 | 0.0160–0.0260 | 0.0160–0.0550 | 0.00200–0.00400 | 0.00200–0.00300 | NA |
|  | D | 4-138 (2.3) | 0.0007–0.0020 | 0.0140–0.0240 | 0.0160–0.0260 | 0.0160–0.0550 | 0.00200–0.00400 | 0.00200–0.00300 | NA |
|  | U | 4-151 (2.5) | 0.0014–0.0022 | 0.0100–0.0200 | 0.0100–0.0200 | 0.0200–0.0600 | 0.00200–0.00300 | 0.00100–0.00300 | 0.01500–0.05500 |
|  | N | 6-204 (3.3) | 0.0004–0.0022 | 0.0100–0.0250 | 0.0100–0.0250 | 0.0100–0.0400 | 0.00100–0.00300 | 0.00100–0.00300 | 0.00100–0.00800 |

## ENGINE AND ENGINE OVERHAUL 91

### PISTON AND RING SPECIFICATIONS
All measurements are given in inches.

| Year | VIN | No. Cylinder Displacement Liters (cc) | Piston Clearance | Ring Gap Top Compression | Ring Gap Bottom Compression | Ring Gap Oil Control | Ring Side Clearance Top Compression | Ring Side Clearance Bottom Compression | Ring Side Clearance Oil Control |
|---|---|---|---|---|---|---|---|---|---|
| 1990 | A | 4-138 (2.3) | 0.0007–0.0020 | 0.0140–0.0240 | 0.0160–0.0260 | 0.0160–0.0550 | 0.00300–0.00500 | 0.00200–0.00300 | NA |
|  | D | 4-138 (2.3) | 0.0007–0.0020 | 0.0140–0.0240 | 0.0160–0.0260 | 0.0160–0.0550 | 0.00200–0.00400 | 0.00200–0.00300 | NA |
|  | U | 4-151 (2.5) | 0.0014–0.0022 | 0.0100–0.0200 | 0.0100–0.0200 | 0.0200–0.0600 | 0.00200–0.00300 | 0.00100–0.00300 | 0.01500–0.05500 |
|  | N | 6-204 (3.3) | 0.0004–0.0022 | 0.0100–0.0250 | 0.0100–0.0250 | 0.0100–0.0400 | 0.00100–0.00300 | 0.00100–0.00300 | 0.00100–0.00800 |
| 1991 | A | 4-138 (2.3) | 0.0007–0.0020 | 0.0140–0.0240 | 0.0160–0.0260 | 0.0160–0.0550 | 0.00300–0.00500 | 0.00200–0.00300 | NA |
|  | D | 4-138 (2.3) | 0.0007–0.0020 | 0.0140–0.0240 | 0.0160–0.0260 | 0.0160–0.0550 | 0.00200–0.00400 | 0.00200–0.00300 | NA |
|  | U | 4-151 (2.5) | 0.0014–0.0022 | 0.0100–0.0200 | 0.0100–0.0200 | 0.0200–0.0600 | 0.00200–0.00300 | 0.00100–0.00300 | 0.01500–0.05500 |
|  | N | 6-204 (3.3) | 0.0004–0.0022① | 0.0100–0.0250 | 0.0100–0.0250 | 0.0100–0.0400 | 0.00100–0.00300 | 0.00100–0.00300 | 0.00100–0.00800 |
| 1992 | D | 4-138 (2.3) | 0.0007–0.0020 | 0.0138–0.0236 | 0.0157–0.0256 | 0.0157–0.0551 | 0.00197–0.00394 | 0.00157–0.00315 | 0.01957–0.02060 |
|  | A | 4-138 (2.3) | 0.0007–0.0020 | 0.0138–0.0236 | 0.0157–0.0256 | 0.0157–0.0551 | 0.00270–0.00470 | 0.00157–0.00315 | 0.01957–0.02060 |
|  | 3 | 4-138 (2.3) | 0.0007–0.0020 | 0.0138–0.0236 | 0.0157–0.0256 | 0.0157–0.0551 | 0.00197–0.00394 | 0.00157–0.00315 | 0.01957–0.02060 |
|  | N | 6-204 (3.3) | 0.0004–0.0022 | 0.0100–0.0250 | 0.0100–0.0250 | 0.0150–0.0550 | 0.00130–0.00310 | 0.00130–0.00310 | 0.00110–0.00810 |

NA—Not available
① Measured 1.8 in. (44mm) down from top of piston
② Measured at top of piston skirt

stud extractor. After the hole is clear, the thread can be repaired, as shown in the series of accompanying illustrations.

## Checking Engine Compression

A noticeable lack of engine power, excessive oil consumption and/or poor fuel mileage measured over an extended period are all indicators of internal engine war. Worn piston rings, scored or worn cylinder bores, blown head gaskets, sticking or burnt valves and worn valve seats are all possible culprits here. A check of each cylinder's compression will help you locate the problems.

As mentioned in the Tools and Equipment section of Chapter 1, a screw-in type compression gauge is more accurate that the type you simply hold against the spark plug hole, although it takes slightly longer to use. It's worth it to obtain a more accurate reading. Follow the procedures below.

Testing the compression on diesel engines requires the use of special adapters and pressure gauges. Consult a tool distributor or dealership for the proper tools.

## Engine

### REMOVAL AND INSTALLATION

CAUTION: *When draining the coolant, keep in mind that cats and dogs are attracted by the ethylene glycol antifreeze, and are quite likely to drink any that is left in an uncovered container or in puddles on the ground. This will prove fatal in sufficient quantity. Always drain the coolant into a sealable container. Coolant should be reused unless it is contaminated or several years old.*

#### 2.0L AND 2.5L ENGINES

1. Relieve the fuel system pressure.
2. Disconnect both battery cables and ground straps.
3. Drain the cooling system and remove the cooling fan.

## ENGINE AND ENGINE OVERHAUL

## TORQUE SPECIFICATIONS
All readings in ft. lbs.

| Year | VIN | No. Cylinder Displacement Liters (cc) | Cylinder Head Bolts | Main Bearing Bolts | Rod Bearing Bolts | Crankshaft Pulley Bolts | Flywheel Bolts | Manifold Intake | Manifold Exhaust | Spark Plugs |
|------|-----|---------------------------------------|---------------------|--------------------|--------------------|-------------------------|----------------|-----------------|------------------|-------------|
| 1985 | U | 4-151 (2.5) | 92 | 70 | 32 | 200 | 44 | 38 | 44 | 15 |
|      | L | 6-181 (3.0) | 80 | 100 | 40 | 200 | 60 | 45 | 25 | 15 |
| 1986 | U | 4-151 (2.5) | 92 | 70 | 32 | 162 | 44 | 38 | 44 | 15 |
|      | L | 6-181 (3.0) | 80 | 100 | 40 | 225 | 60 | 45 | 25 | 15 |
| 1987 | U | 4-151 (2.5) | 92 | 70 | 32 | 162 | 44 | 38 | 44 | 15 |
|      | M | 4-122 (2.0) | ① | 44② | 26⑯ | 34 | 48 | 16 | 16 | 15 |
|      | D | 4-140 (2.3) | — | — | — | — | — | — | — | — |
|      | L | 6-181 (3.0) | 80 | 100 | 40 | 225 | 60 | 45 | 25 | 15 |
| 1988 | M | 4-122 (2.0) | ① | 44② | 26② | 20 | 48③ | 16 | 16 | 15 |
|      | D | 4-140 (2.3) | ④ | 15⑤ | 15⑥ | 74⑤ | 22② | 18 | 27 | 17 |
|      | U | 4-151 (2.5) | ⑫ | 70 | 32 | 162 | ⑨ | 25 | ⑩ | 15 |
|      | L | 6-181 (3.0) | ⑪ | 100 | 45 | 219 | 60 | 32 | 37 | 20 |
| 1989 | M | 4-122 (2.0) | ① | 44② | 26② | 20 | 63③ | 18 | 10 | 15 |
|      | A | 4-138 (2.3) | ④ | 15⑤ | 18⑬ | 74⑤ | 22② | 18 | 27 | 17 |
|      | D | 4-138 (2.3) | ④ | 15⑤ | 18⑬ | 74⑤ | 22② | 18 | 27 | 17 |
|      | U | 4-151 (2.5) | ⑫ | 65 | 29 | 162 | ⑨ | 25 | ⑩ | 15 |
|      | N | 6-204 (3.3) | ⑭ | 90 | 20② | 219 | 61 | 7 | 30 | 20 |
| 1990 | A | 4-138 (2.3) | ⑮ | 15⑤ | 18⑬ | 74⑤ | 22② | 18 | ⑦ | 17 |
|      | D | 4-138 (2.3) | ⑮ | 15⑤ | 18⑬ | 74⑤ | 22② | 18 | ⑦ | 17 |
|      | U | 4-151 (2.5) | ⑫ | 65 | 29 | 162 | ⑨ | 25 | ⑩ | 15 |
|      | N | 6-204 (3.3) | ⑭ | 90 | 20② | 219 | 61 | 7 | 30 | 20 |
| 1991 | A | 4-138 (2.3) | ⑮ | 15⑤ | 18⑬ | 74⑤ | 22② | 18 | ⑦ | 17 |
|      | D | 4-138 (2.3) | ⑮ | 15⑤ | 18⑬ | 74⑤ | 22② | 18 | ⑦ | 17 |
|      | U | 4-151 (2.5) | ⑫ | 65 | 29 | 162 | ⑨ | 25 | ⑩ | 15 |
|      | N | 6-204 (3.3) | ⑭ | 26⑯ | 20② | 105⑰ | 89⑧⑤ | 89⑧ | 41 | 20 |
| 1992 | A | 4-138 (2.3) | ⑮ | 15⑤ | 18⑬ | 74⑤ | 22② | 18 | ⑦ | 17 |
|      | D | 4-138 (2.3) | ⑮ | 15⑤ | 18⑬ | 74⑤ | 22② | 18 | ⑦ | 17 |
|      | 3 | 4-138 (2.3) | ⑮ | 15⑤ | 18⑬ | 74⑤ | 22② | 18 | ⑦ | 17 |
|      | N | 6-204 (3.3) | ⑭ | 26⑯ | 20② | 105⑰ | 89⑧⑤ | 89⑧ | 41 | 20 |

① Step 1: 18 ft. lbs.
  Step 2: 3 rounds of 60° turns in sequence
  Step 3: An additional 30-50° turn after engine warm up
② Plus an additional 40–50° turn
③ Plus an additional 30° turn
④ Short bolts: 26 ft. lbs. plus an additional 80° turn
  Long bolts: 26 ft. lbs. plus an additional 90° turn
⑤ Plus an additional 90° turn
⑥ Plus an additional 75° turn
⑦ Nuts: 27 ft. lbs.
  Studs: 106 inch lbs.
⑧ Inch lbs.
⑨ Manual transaxle: 69 ft. lbs.
  Automatic transaxle: 55 ft. lbs.
⑩ Outer bolts: 26 ft. lbs.
  Inner bolts: 37 ft. lbs.
⑪ Step 1: 25 ft. lbs.
  Step 2: 2 rounds of 90° turns in sequence, not to exceed 60 ft. lbs.
⑫ Step 1: 18 ft. lbs.
  Step 2: 26 ft.lbs., except front bolt/stud
  Step 3: Front bolt/stud to 18 ft. lbs.
  Step 4: An additional 90° turn
⑬ Plus an additional 80° turn
⑭ Step 1: 35 ft. lbs.
  Step 2: An additional 130° turn
  Step 3: An additional 30° turn on center 4 bolts
⑮ Short bolts: 26 ft. lbs. plus an additional 100° turn
  Long bolts: 26 ft. lbs. plus an additional 110° turn
⑯ Plus an additional 45° turn
⑰ Plus an additional 56° turn

## ENGINE AND ENGINE OVERHAUL 93

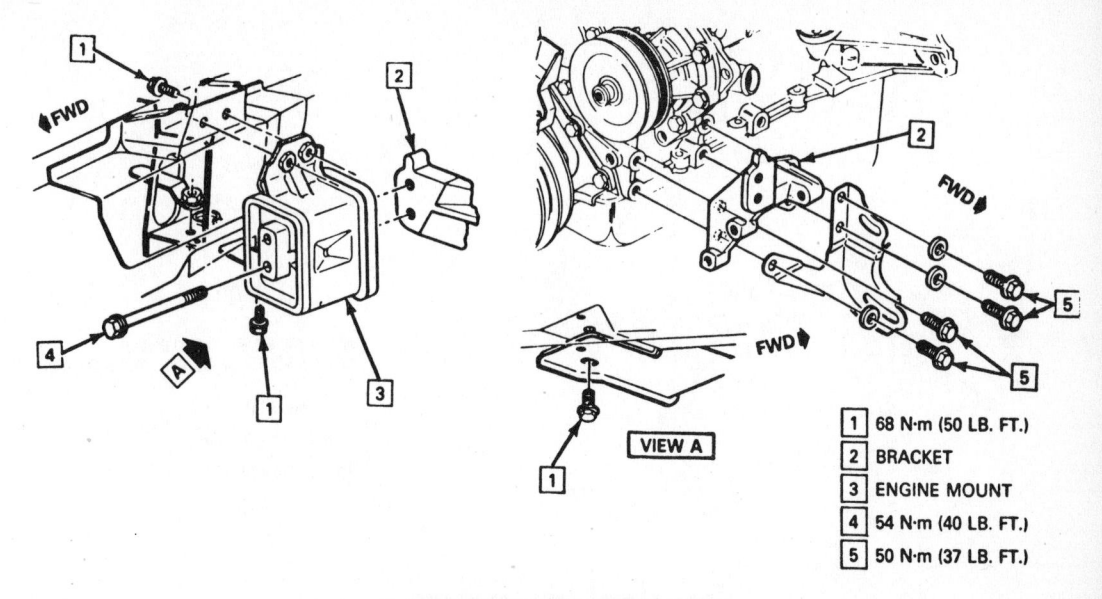

| 1 | 68 N·m (50 LB. FT.) |
|---|---|
| 2 | BRACKET |
| 3 | ENGINE MOUNT |
| 4 | 54 N·m (40 LB. FT.) |
| 5 | 50 N·m (37 LB. FT.) |

**Front Engine Mounts—2.0L and 2.5L**

4. Remove the air cleaner assembly.
5. Disconnect the ECM connections and feed harness through the bulkhead. Lay the harness across the engine.
6. Label and disconnect the engine wiring harness and all engine-related connectors and lay across the engine.
7. Label and disconnect the radiator hoses and vacuum lines. Disconnect and plug the fuel lines.
8. On 2.5L engine, remove the air conditioning compressor from the engine and lay it aside, without disconnecting the refrigerant lines. Remove the transaxle struts.
9. If equipped with power steering, remove the power steering pump from its mount and

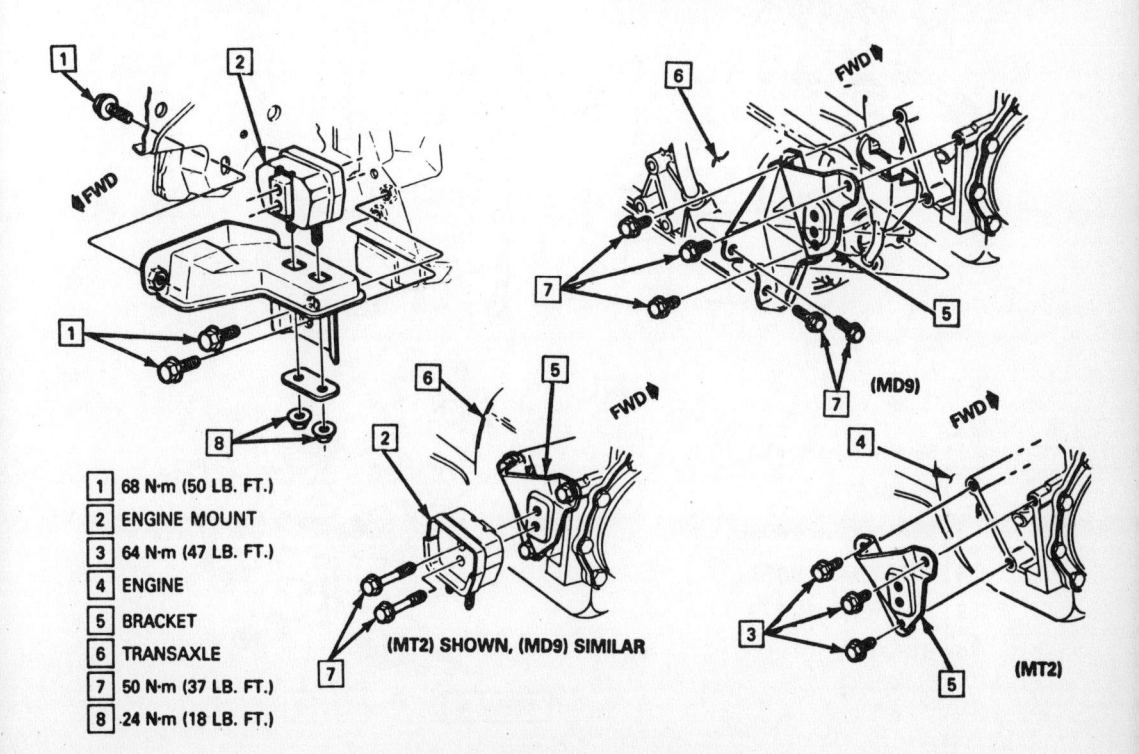

| 1 | 68 N·m (50 LB. FT.) |
|---|---|
| 2 | ENGINE MOUNT |
| 3 | 64 N·m (47 LB. FT.) |
| 4 | ENGINE |
| 5 | BRACKET |
| 6 | TRANSAXLE |
| 7 | 50 N·m (37 LB. FT.) |
| 8 | 24 N·m (18 LB. FT.) |

**Rear Engine Mounts—2.0L and 2.5L**

# 94 ENGINE AND ENGINE OVERHAUL

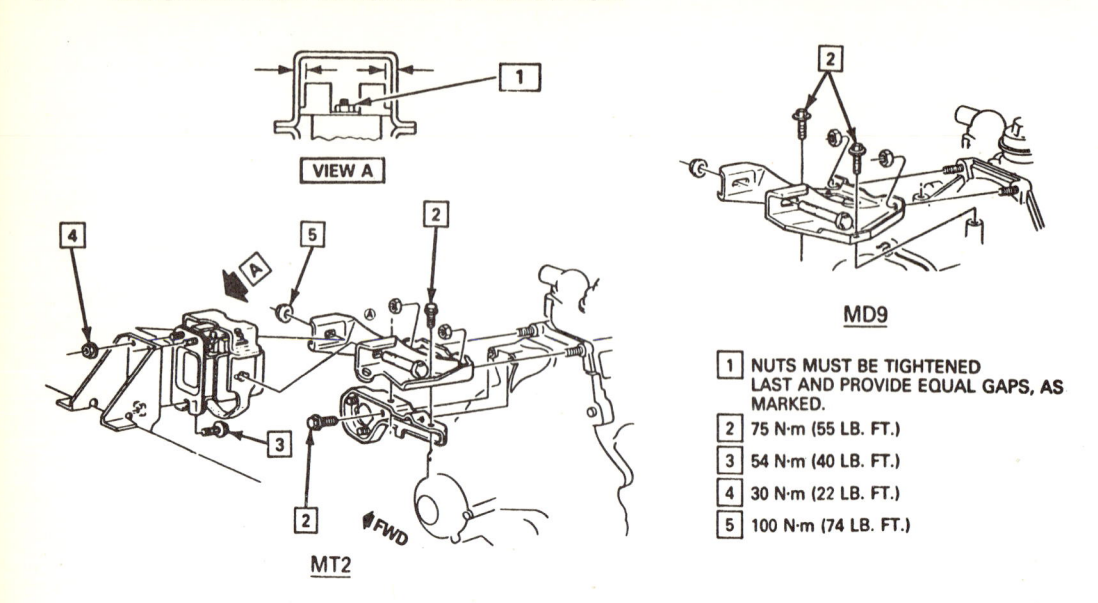

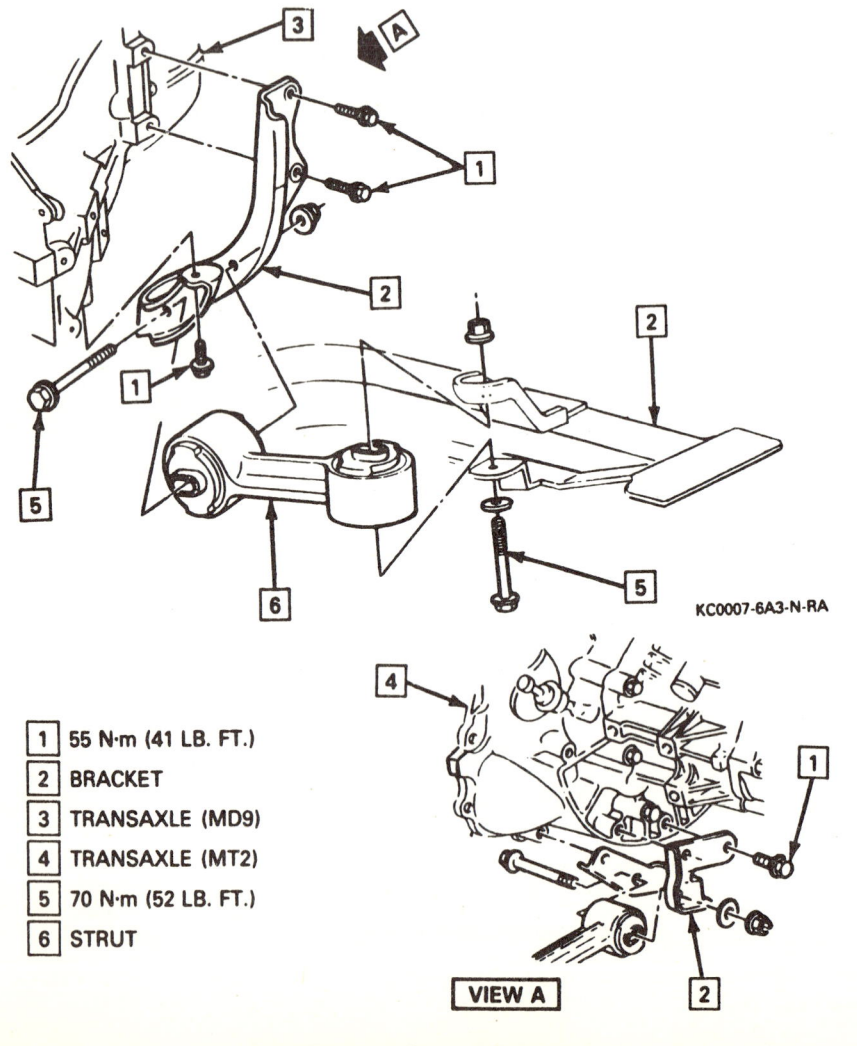

**VIEW A**

**MD9**

| 1 | NUTS MUST BE TIGHTENED LAST AND PROVIDE EQUAL GAPS, AS MARKED. |
|---|---|
| 2 | 75 N·m (55 LB. FT.) |
| 3 | 54 N·m (40 LB. FT.) |
| 4 | 30 N·m (22 LB. FT.) |
| 5 | 100 N·m (74 LB. FT.) |

**MT2**

**Transaxle Mounts—2.0L and 2.5L**

| 1 | 55 N·m (41 LB. FT.) |
|---|---|
| 2 | BRACKET |
| 3 | TRANSAXLE (MD9) |
| 4 | TRANSAXLE (MT2) |
| 5 | 70 N·m (52 LB. FT.) |
| 6 | STRUT |

**VIEW A**

**Front Transaxle Strut—2.0L and 2.5L**

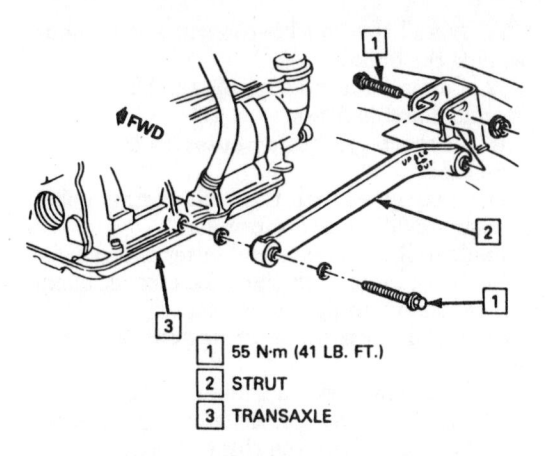

## ENGINE AND ENGINE OVERHAUL

lay it aside. Remove the power steering pump bracket from the engine.

10. If equipped with a manual transaxle, disconnect the clutch and transaxle linkage. Remove the throttle cable from the throttle body.
11. If equipped with an automatic transaxle, disconnect the transaxle cooler lines, shifter linkage, downshift cable and throttle cable from the throttle body.
12. Raise and safely support the vehicle.
13. Disconnect all wiring from the transaxle.
14. On 2.0L engine, properly discharge the air conditioning system and remove the compressor. Remove the transaxle strut(s).
15. Disconnect the exhaust pipe from the exhaust manifold and hangers.
16. Disconnect the heater hoses from the heater core tubes and plug them.

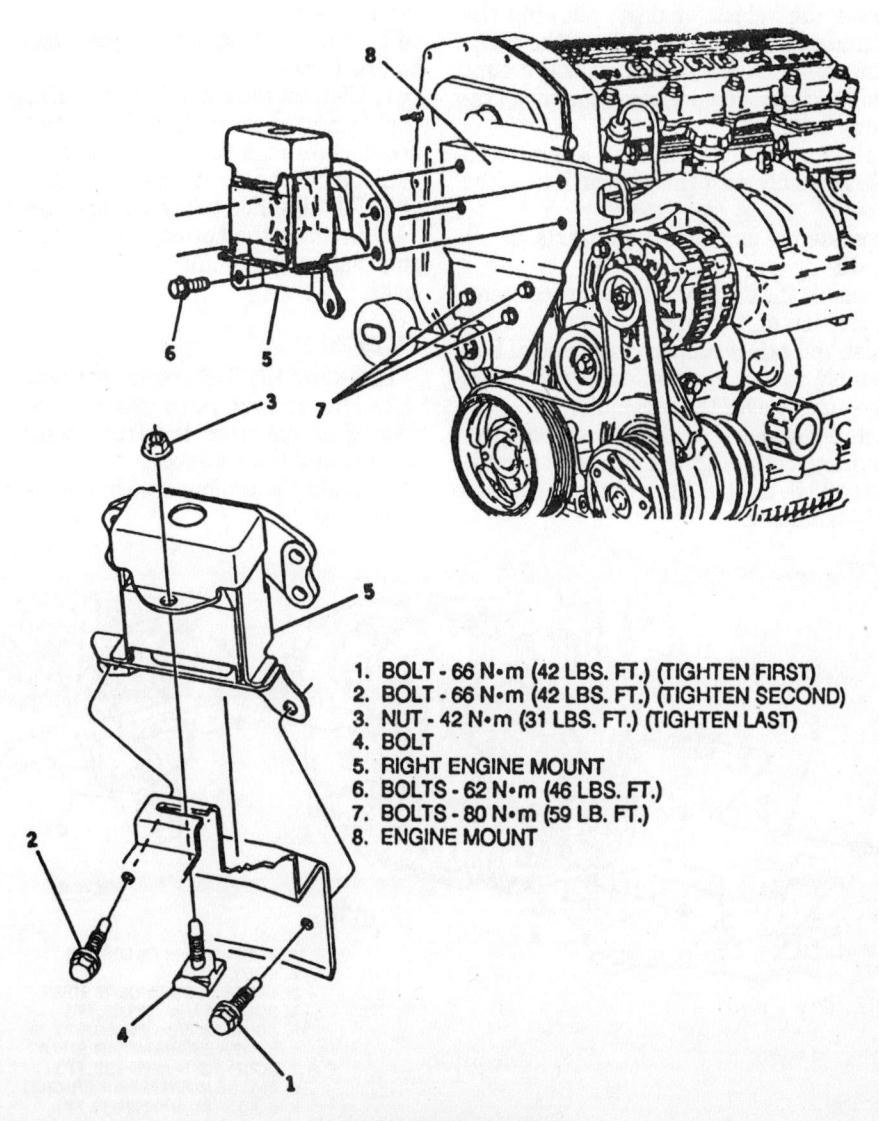

1. 55 N·m (41 LB. FT.)
2. STRUT
3. TRANSAXLE

**Automatic Transaxle Strut—2.0L and 2.5L**

1. BOLT - 66 N·m (42 LBS. FT.) (TIGHTEN FIRST)
2. BOLT - 66 N·m (42 LBS. FT.) (TIGHTEN SECOND)
3. NUT - 42 N·m (31 LBS. FT.) (TIGHTEN LAST)
4. BOLT
5. RIGHT ENGINE MOUNT
6. BOLTS - 62 N·m (46 LBS. FT.)
7. BOLTS - 80 N·m (59 LB. FT.)
8. ENGINE MOUNT

**Right Engine Mount—2.3L**

# 96 ENGINE AND ENGINE OVERHAUL

17. Remove the front wheels. Remove the calipers and wire them up aside. Remove the brake rotors.
18. Matchmark and remove the knuckle-to-strut bolts.
19. Remove the body-to-cradle bolts at the lower control arms. Loosen the remaining body-to-cradle bolts. Remove a bolt at each cradle side, leaving 1 bolt per corner.
20. Using the proper equipment, support the vehicle under the radiator frame support.
21. Position a jack to the rear of the body pan with a 4 in. (102mm) × 4 in. (102mm) × 6 ft. (1.8m) timber spanning the vehicle.
22. Raise the vehicle enough to remove the support equipment.
23. Position a dolly under the engine/transaxle assembly with 3 blocks of wood for additional support.
24. Lower the vehicle slightly, allowing the engine/transaxle assembly to rest on the dolly.
25. Remove all engine and transaxle mount bolts and brackets. Remove the remaining cradle-to-body bolts.
26. Raise the vehicle, leaving engine and transaxle assembly with the suspension on the dolly.
27. Separate the engine and transaxle.

**To install:**

28. Assemble the engine and transaxle assembly and position on the dolly.
29. Raise and safely support the vehicle. Roll the assembly to the installation position and lower the vehicle over the assembly.
30. Install all engine, transaxle and suspension mounting bolts. Tighten all cradle mounting bolts to 65 ft. lbs. (88 Nm). Connect the wiring to the transaxle.
31. Install the knuckle-to-strut bolts and assemble the brakes.
32. Connect the exhaust pipe to the exhaust manifold and hangers.
33. Connect the heater hoses to the heater core tubes.
34. If equipped with the 2.0L engine, install the air conditioning compressor.
35. Install the wheels and lower the vehicle.
36. If equipped with the 2.5L engine, install the air conditioning compressor.
37. Install the power steering pump and related parts.
38. If equipped with a manual transaxle, connect the clutch and transaxle linkage. Connect the throttle cable to the throttle body.
39. If equipped with an automatic transaxle, connect the transaxle cooler lines, shifter linkage, downshift cable and throttle cable to the throttle body.
40. Connect the radiator hoses, vacuum lines and fuel lines.
41. Connect the engine wiring harness and all engine-related connectors. Feed the ECM connections through the bulkhead and connect.
42. Install the air cleaner assembly.
43. Fill all fluids to their proper levels.
44. Connect the battery cables, start the engine and set the timing, if necessary. Check for leaks.

*2.3L ENGINE*

1. Relieve the fuel system pressure.
2. Disconnect both battery cables and ground straps from the front engine mount bracket and the transaxle.
3. Drain the cooling system and remove the cooling fan.

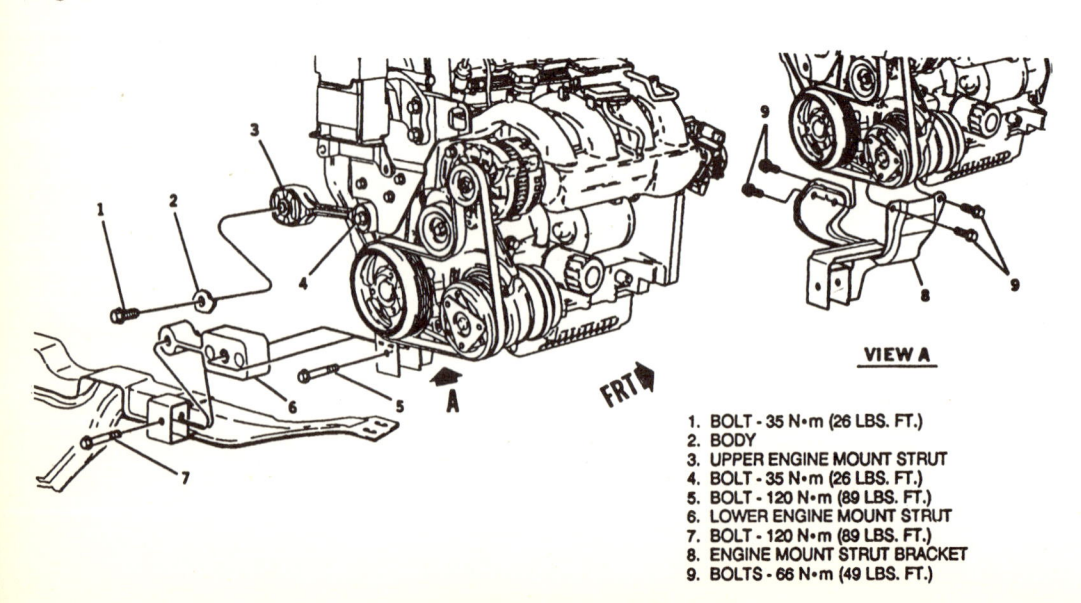

1. BOLT - 35 N•m (26 LBS. FT.)
2. BODY
3. UPPER ENGINE MOUNT STRUT
4. BOLT - 35 N•m (26 LBS. FT.)
5. BOLT - 120 N•m (89 LBS. FT.)
6. LOWER ENGINE MOUNT STRUT
7. BOLT - 120 N•m (89 LBS. FT.)
8. ENGINE MOUNT STRUT BRACKET
9. BOLTS - 66 N•m (49 LBS. FT.)

**2.3L Engine Mount Strut and Bracket**

## ENGINE AND ENGINE OVERHAUL

4. Remove the air cleaner duct.
5. Disconnect the heater and radiator hoses from the thermostat housing.
6. Properly discharge the air conditioning system and disconnect the hoses from the compressor.
7. Remove the upper radiator support.
8. Disconnect the 2 vacuum hoses from the front of the engine.
9. Label and disconnect all electrical connectors from engine and transaxle-mounted devices.
10. Unplug the wires at the starter solenoid.
11. Disconnect the power brake vacuum hose from the throttle body.
12. Disconnect the throttle cable and remove the bracket.
13. Remove the power steering pump bracket and lay the pump aside with the lines attached.
14. Disconnect and plug the fuel lines.
15. If equipped with a manual transaxle, disconnect the shifter cables and the clutch actuator cylinder.
16. If equipped with an automatic transaxle, disconnect the shift and TV cables.
17. Disconnect the transaxle and engine oil cooler pipes, if equipped.
18. Remove the exhaust manifold and heat shield.
19. Remove the lower radiator hose and front engine mount.
20. Install engine support fixture tool J-28467-A.
21. Raise and safely support the vehicle.
22. Remove the wheels, right side splash shield and radiator air deflector.
23. Separate the ball joints from the steering knuckles.
24. Using the proper equipment, support the suspension supports, crossmember and stabilizer shaft. Remove the attaching bolts and remove as an assembly.
25. Disconnect the heater hose from the radiator outlet pipe.
26. Remove the halfshafts from the transaxle.
27. Remove the nut from the transaxle mount through bolt.
28. Remove the nut from the rear engine mount through bolt.
29. Remove the rear engine mount body bracket.
30. Position a suitable support fixture below the engine/transaxle assembly and lower the vehicle so the weight of the engine/transaxle assembly is on the support fixture.
31. Remove the transaxle mount through bolt.
32. Mark the threads on fixture tool J-28467-A so the setting can be duplicated when installing the engine/transaxle assembly. Remove the fixture.
33. Move the engine/transaxle assembly rearward and slowly raise the vehicle from the engine/transaxle assembly.

NOTE: *Many of the bell housing bolts are of different lengths; note their locations before removing. It is imperative that these bolts go back in their original locations when assembling the engine and transaxle or engine damage could result.*

34. Separate the engine from the transaxle.

**To install:**
35. Assemble the engine and transaxle. If equipped with an automatic transaxle, thoroughly clean and dry the torque converter bolts and bolt holes, apply thread locking compound to the threads and tighten the bolts to 46 ft. lbs. (63 Nm). If equipped with a manual transaxle, tighten the clutch cover bolts to 22 ft. lbs. (30 Nm).
36. Raise and safely support the vehicle. Position the engine/transaxle assembly and lower the vehicle over the assembly until the transaxle mount is indexed, then install the bolt.
37. Install the engine support fixture and adjust to previously indexed setting. Raise the vehicle off the support fixture.
38. Install the rear mount to body bracket and tighten the bolts to 55 ft. lbs. (75 Nm).
39. Install the rear mount nut and tighten to 55 ft. lbs. (75 Nm).
40. Install the transaxle mount through bolt and tighten the nut to 55 ft. lbs. (75 Nm). Tighten so equal gaps are maintained.
41. Install the halfshafts.
42. Connect the heater hose to the the radiator outlet pipe.
43. Install the suspension supports, crossmember and stabilizer shaft assembly. Tighten the center bolts first, then front, then rear, to 65 ft. lbs. (90 Nm).
44. Install the ball joints and tighten the nuts to a maximum of 50 ft. lbs. (68 Nm).
45. Install the radiator air deflector and splash shield.
46. Install the wheels and lower the vehicle.
47. Install the front engine mount nut and tighten to 41 ft. lbs. (56 Nm). Remove the engine support fixture. Connect the lower radiator hose.
48. Install the exhaust manifold and heat shield.
49. Connect the transaxle and engine oil cooler pipes, if equipped.
50. If equipped with a manual transaxle, connect the shifter cables and the clutch actuator cylinder.
51. If equipped with an automatic transaxle, connect the shift and TV cables.
52. Connect the fuel lines.
53. Install the power steering pump and related parts.

# 98 ENGINE AND ENGINE OVERHAUL

54. Connect the throttle cable and install the bracket.
55. Connect the power brake vacuum hose to the throttle body.
56. Connect the starter wires.
57. Connect all electrical connectors and cables to the proper engine and transaxle-mounted devices.
58. Connect the 2 vacuum hoses at the front of the engine.
59. Install the upper radiator support.
60. Using new seals, connect the air conditioning hoses to the compressor.
61. Connect the heater and radiator hoses at the thermostat housing.
62. Install the air cleaner duct.
63. Fill all fluids to their proper levels.
64. Connect the battery cables, start the engine and check for leaks.

## 3.0L AND 3.3L ENGINES (EXCEPT 1992)

1. Disconnect the negative battery cable. Relieve the fuel pressure.
2. Matchmark the hinge-to-hood position and remove the hood.
3. Drain the cooling system. Disconnect and label all electrical connectors from the engine, alternator and fuel injection system, vacuum hoses, and engine ground straps. Remove the alternator.
4. Remove the coolant hoses from the radiator and engine. Remove the radiator and cooling fan assembly.

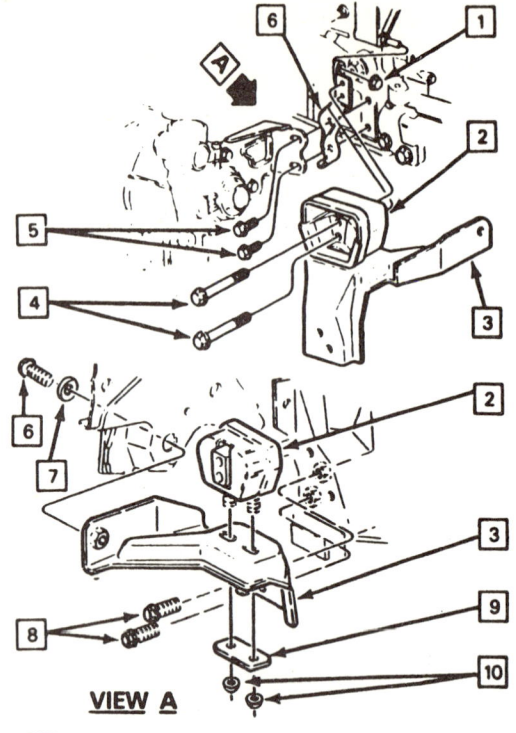

VIEW A

| 1 | NUT 45 N•M (33 LBS-FT) | 6 | BOLT 56 N•M (41 LBS-FT) |
| 2 | MOUNT | 7 | WASHER |
| 3 | BRACKET | 8 | BOLT 56 N•M (41 LBS-FT) |
| 4 | BOLT 54 N•M (40 LBS-FT) | 9 | PLATE |
| 5 | BOLT 95 N•M (70 LBS-FT) | 10 | NUTS 24 N•M (18 LBS-FT) |

**3.3L Engine Rear Mount**

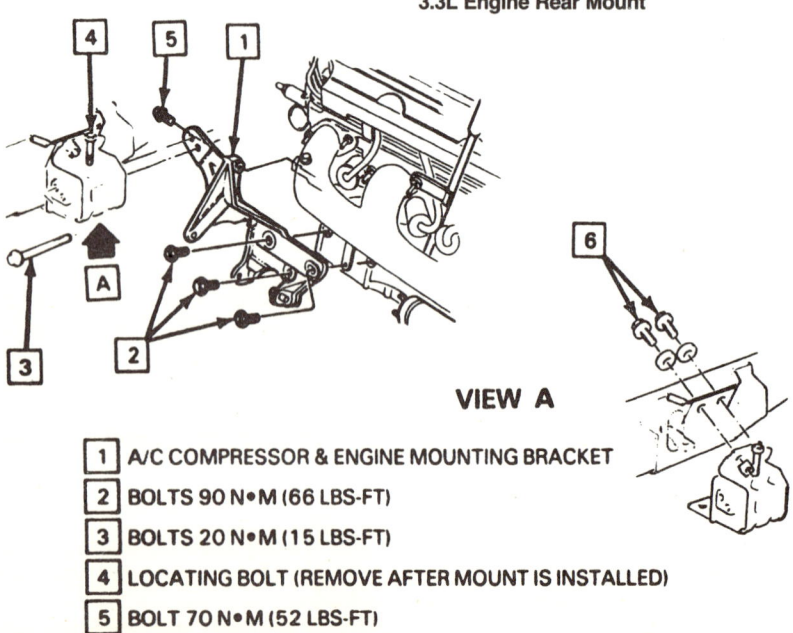

VIEW A

| 1 | A/C COMPRESSOR & ENGINE MOUNTING BRACKET |
| 2 | BOLTS 90 N•M (66 LBS-FT) |
| 3 | BOLTS 20 N•M (15 LBS-FT) |
| 4 | LOCATING BOLT (REMOVE AFTER MOUNT IS INSTALLED) |
| 5 | BOLT 70 N•M (52 LBS-FT) |
| 6 | BOLT 73 N•M (54 LBS-FT) |

**3.3L Engine Front Mount**

# ENGINE AND ENGINE OVERHAUL

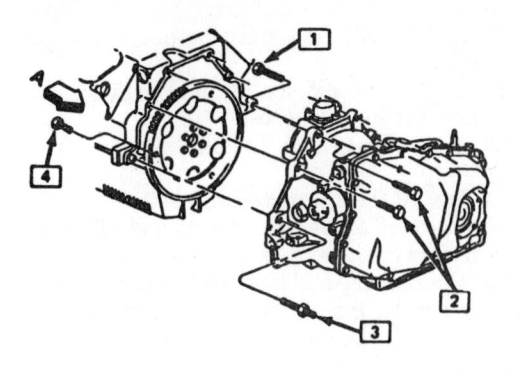

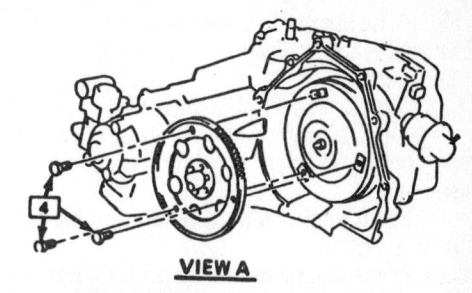

**VIEW A**

| 1 | BOLT (LOCATED BETWEEN TRANSAXLE AND ENGINE AND INSTALLED IN OPPOSITE DIRECTION) 75 N·m (55 LBS. FT.) |
| 2 | BOLT 75 N·m (55 LBS. FT.) |
| 3 | STUD 75 N·m (55 LBS. FT.) |
| 4 | BOLT TIGHTEN TWICE IN SEQUENCE TO 62 N·m (46 LBS. FT.) |

3.3L Engine to Transaxle Mounting

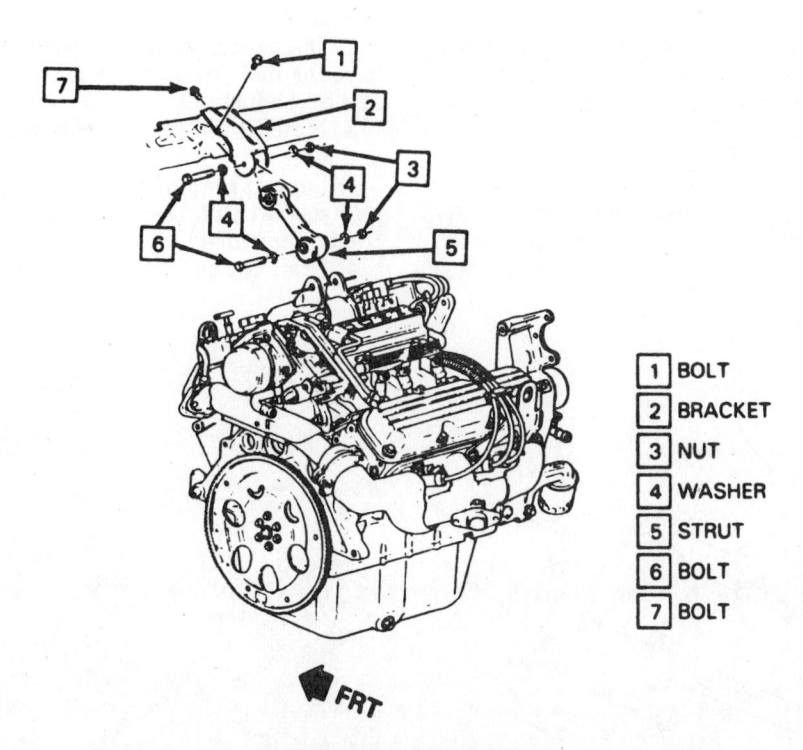

| 1 | BOLT |
| 2 | BRACKET |
| 3 | NUT |
| 4 | WASHER |
| 5 | STRUT |
| 6 | BOLT |
| 7 | BOLT |

3.3L Engine to Strut Bracket

5. Remove the air intake duct. Disconnect the fuel lines from the fuel rail. Disconnect the throttle, TV and cruise control cables from the throttle body.

6. Raise and safely support the vehicle. Drain the engine oil. Disconnect the exhaust pipe from the exhaust manifold.

7. Remove the air conditioning compressor mounting bolts, and position it aside.

8. Disconnect the heater hoses.

9. Remove the transaxle inspection cover, matchmark the converter to the flexplate and remove the torque converter bolts.

10. Remove the rear engine mount bolts.

11. Remove the lower bell housing bolts. Label and disconnect the starter motor wiring and remove the starter motor from the engine.

12. Lower the vehicle. Remove the power steering pump mounting bolts and set the pump aside.

13. Support the transaxle with a floor jack or equivalent. Attach an engine lifting device to the engine.

14. Remove the upper bell housing bolts.

15. Remove the front engine mount bolts.

16. Lift and remove the engine from the vehi-

# ENGINE AND ENGINE OVERHAUL

cle. If the master cylinder is preventing removal, remove it and plug the brake lines.

**To install:**

17. Lower the engine into the engine compartment. Align the engine mounts and install the bolts. Tighten the bolts to their proper values:
- Front engine mount bracket to block — 66 ft. lbs. (90 Nm)
- Front engine mount to underbody — 54 ft. lbs. (73 Nm)
- Front engine mount to engine bracket — 15 ft. lbs. (20 Nm)
- Rear engine mount to bracket — 18 ft. lbs. (24 Nm)
- Rear engine mount bracket to underbody — 41 ft. lbs. (56 Nm)
- Rear engine mount to engine bracket — 40 ft. lbs. (54 Nm)

18. Install the upper transaxle-to-engine mounting bolts and tighten to 55 ft. lbs. (75 Nm). Remove the engine lifting fixture from the engine.
19. Raise and safely support the vehicle.
20. Align the converter marks, install the torque converter bolts and tighten to 46 ft. lbs. (63 Nm). Install the transaxle inspection cover.
21. Connect the exhaust pipe to the exhaust manifold. Install the starter motor and connect the wiring.
22. Install the air conditioning compressor. Connect the heater hoses.
23. Lower the vehicle. Install the power steering pump.
24. Install the alternator and belt.
25. Connect all vacuum hoses and electrical connectors to the engine.
26. Connect the fuel lines and all cables to the throttle body. Install the air intake duct.
27. Install the radiator and fan assembly. Connect the fan motor wiring. Connect the radiator hoses and refill the cooling system.
28. Fill all fluids to their proper levels.
29. Connect the battery cables, start the engine and check for leaks.

*1992 3.3L ENGINE*

1. Disconnect the negative battery cable. Relieve the fuel pressure and disconnect the fuel line to the fuel rail.
2. Matchmark the hinge-to-hood position and remove the hood.
3. Support the engine using a proper type engine support tool. Disconnect the exhaust pipe from the manifold.
4. Drain the cooling system. Disconnect and

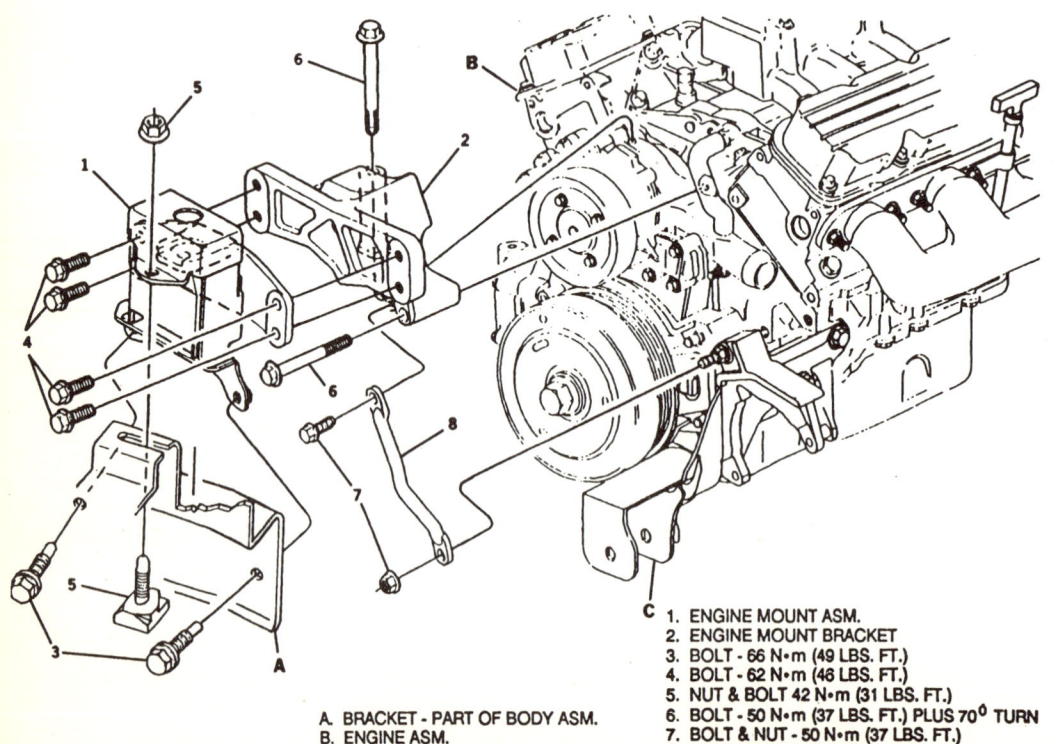

A. BRACKET - PART OF BODY ASM.
B. ENGINE ASM.
C. ENGINE MOUNT STRUT BRACKET
1. ENGINE MOUNT ASM.
2. ENGINE MOUNT BRACKET
3. BOLT - 66 N•m (49 LBS. FT.)
4. BOLT - 62 N•m (46 LBS. FT.)
5. NUT & BOLT 42 N•m (31 LBS. FT.)
6. BOLT - 50 N•m (37 LBS. FT.) PLUS 70° TURN
7. BOLT & NUT - 50 N•m (37 LBS. FT.)
8. ENGINE MOUNT BRACE

**1992 3.3L Engine Right Mount**

## ENGINE AND ENGINE OVERHAUL  101

label all electrical connectors from the engine, alternator and fuel injection system, vacuum hoses, and engine ground straps.

5. Remove the coolant hoses from the radiator and engine. Remove the radiator and cooling fan assembly.

6. Remove the air intake duct. Disconnect the fuel lines from the fuel rail. Disconnect the throttle, TV and cruise control cables from the throttle body.

7. Disconnect the vacuum lines from the brake power booster and the evaporative canister.

8. Remove the accessory drive belt and disconnect the power steering pump and place to the side.

9. Remove the upper transaxle to engine bolts.

10. Raise and safely support the vehicle. Drain the engine oil. Disconnect the exhaust pipe from the exhaust manifold.

11. Remove the air conditioning compressor mounting bolts, and position it aside.

12. Remove the right engine mount and engine mount torque strut assembly.

13. Remove the transaxle inspection cover,

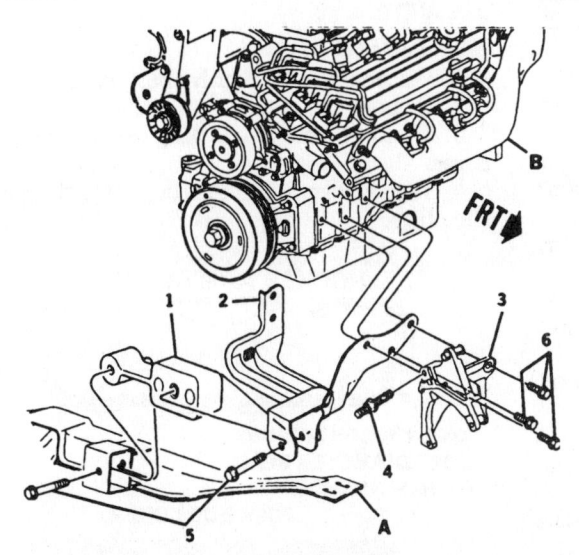

A. FRONT SUSPENSION SUPPORT
B. ENGINE ASM.

1. ENGINE MOUNT STRUT ASSEMBLY
2. ENGINE MOUNT STRUT BRACKET ASM.
3. A/C COMPRESSOR BRACKET ASM.
4. STUD - 50 N·m (37 LBS. FT.)
5. BOLT - 120 N·m (89 LBS. FT.)
6. BOLT - 90 N·m (66 LBS. FT.)

**1992 3.3L Engine Mount Strut and Bracket**

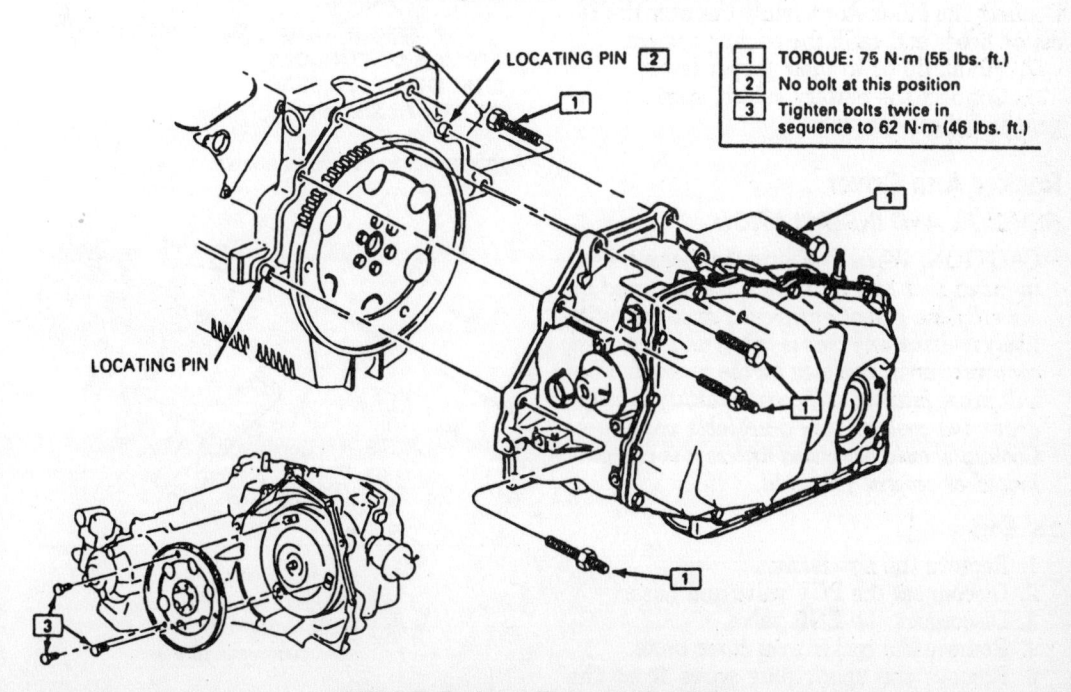

LOCATING PIN [2]

[1] TORQUE: 75 N·m (55 lbs. ft.)
[2] No bolt at this position
[3] Tighten bolts twice in sequence to 62 N·m (46 lbs. ft.)

LOCATING PIN

**1992 3.3L Engine to Transaxle Mounting**

# 102  ENGINE AND ENGINE OVERHAUL

matchmark the converter to the flexplate and remove the flywheel to converter bolts.
14. Lower the engine and remove the transaxle bolts.
NOTE: *One of the transaxle bolts is located between the transaxle case and the engine block. This bolt is installed in the opposite direction.*
15. Lower the vehicle and remove the engine assembly.

**To install:**
16. Lower the engine into the engine compartment. Align the engine with the transaxle and install the bolts. Tighten the bolts to 55 ft. lbs. (75 Nm).
17. Raise and safely support the vehicle.
18. Align and install the flywheel to converter bolts and tighten to 46 ft. lbs. (62 Nm).
19. Install the right engine mount and torque strut. Tighten the bolts to 89 ft. lbs. (120 Nm) Install the transaxle inspection cover.
20. Install the air conditioning compressor. Connect the heater hoses.
21. Connect the exhaust pipe to the exhaust manifold. Install the starter motor and connect the wiring.
22. Lower the vehicle. Install the power steering pump.
23. Install the alternator and belt.
24. Connect all vacuum hoses and electrical connectors to the engine.
25. Connect the fuel lines and all cables to the throttle body. Install the air intake duct.
26. Install the radiator and fan assembly. Connect the fan motor wiring. Connect the radiator hoses and refill the cooling system.
27. Fill all fluids to their proper levels.
28. Connect the battery cables, start the engine and check for leaks.

## Rocker Arm Cover

### REMOVAL AND INSTALLATION

CAUTION: *When draining the coolant, keep in mind that cats and dogs are attracted by the ethylene glycol antifreeze, and are quite likely to drink any that is left in an uncovered container or in puddles on the ground. This will prove fatal in sufficient quantity. Always drain the coolant into a sealable container. Coolant should be reused unless it is contaminated or several years old.*

#### 2.5L Engine

1. Remove the air cleaner.
2. Disconnect the PCV valve and hose.
3. Disconnect the EGR valve.
4. Remove the rocker arm cover bolts.
5. Remove the spark plug wires from the spark plugs and clips.
6. Tap the rocker arm cover gently with a rubber mallet to break the gasket loose then remove the cover. Do not pry on the cover or damage to the sealing surfaces may result.
7. Clean the sealing surfaces of all old gasket material.
8. Installation is the reverse of removal. Apply a continuous 3/16 in. (5mm) bead of RTV sealant around the cylinder head sealing surface inboard at the bolt holes. Keep sealant out of the bolt holes. Torque the rocker arm cover mounting bolts to 6 ft. lbs. (8 Nm).

#### 3.0L AND 3.3L V6

*FRONT ROCKER ARM COVER*

1. Disconnect the negative battery cable.
2. Remove the crankcase ventilation hose.
3. Remove the spark plug wire harness cover.
4. Tag and disconnect the spark plug wires at the plugs.

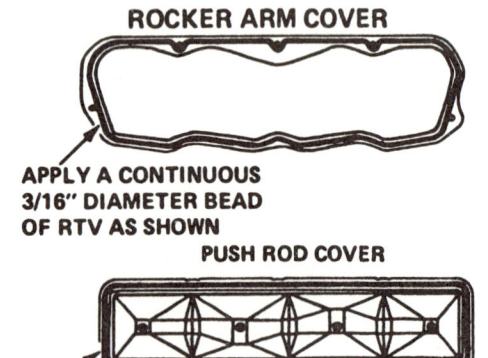

**ROCKER ARM COVER**

APPLY A CONTINUOUS
3/16" DIAMETER BEAD
OF RTV AS SHOWN

**PUSH ROD COVER**

APPLY A CONTINUOUS
3/16" DIAMETER BEAD
OF RTV AS SHOWN

Apply sealer to covers as shown

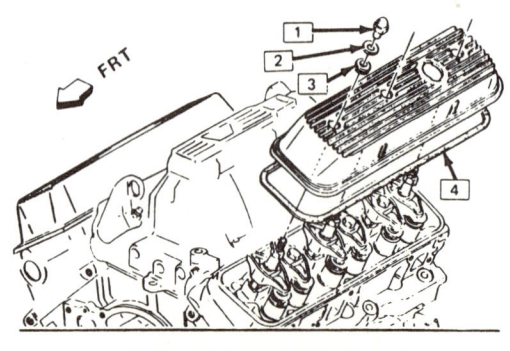

| 1 | NUT 10 N·m (88 LB. IN.) |
| 2 | WASHER |
| 3 | RUBBER GRAMMET |
| 4 | FORMED RUBBER GASKET |

3.0L Valve Cover Gasket

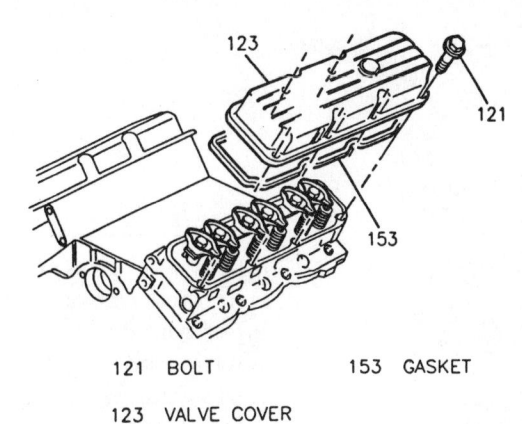

## ENGINE AND ENGINE OVERHAUL 103

| | |
|---|---|
| 121 | BOLT |
| 123 | VALVE COVER |
| 153 | GASKET |

**1992 3.3L Valve Cover Removal**

5. Remove the rocker cover nuts, washers and seals.
6. Remove the rocker cover and gasket. Clean all sealing surfaces of old gasket material.
7. Installation is the reverse of removal. Torque the mounting nuts to 7 ft. lbs. (10 Nm).

### REAR ROCKER COVER

1. Disconnect the negative battery cable.
2. Remove the C3I ignition coil and module (if so equipped) with the spark plug wires attached.
3. Disconnect the EGR solenoid wiring and vacuum hoses after tagging them for installation.
4. Disconnect the serpentine drive belt.
5. Tag and disconnect the alternator wiring.
6. Remove the rear alternator mounting bolt and rotate the alternator toward the front of the vehicle.
7. Disconnct the power steering pump from the belt tensioner and remove the belt tensioner assembly.
8. Remove the engine lifting bracket and the rear alternator brace.
9. Drain the engine coolant below the heater hose level, then remove the throttle body heater hoses.
10. Remove the rocker cover nuts, washers and seals.
11. Remove the rocker cover and gasket. Clean all mating surfaces of old gasket material.
12. Installation is the reverse of removal. Torque the mounting nuts to 7 ft. lbs. (10 Nm).

## Rocker Arm Assembly

### REMOVAL AND INSTALLATION

#### 2.0L Engine

1. Disconnect the negative battery cable. Remove the camshaft carrier cover.
2. Hold the valves in place with compressed air, using an air adapter in the spark plug hole.
3. Compress the valve springs using a suitable valve spring compressor.
4. Remove rocker arms. Keep them in order if they are being reused.
5. The installation is the reverse of the removal procedure.
6. Connect the negative battery cable and check for proper operation.

#### 2.5L Engine

1. Remove the rocker arm cover.
2. Remove the rocker arm bolt and ball. If replacing the pushrod only, loosen the rocker arm bolt and swing the arm clear of the pushrod.
3. Remove the rocker arm, pushrod and guide. Store all components in order so they can be reassembled in their original location. Pushrod guides are different and must be reassembled in the previous location.
4. Installation is the reverse of removal. When new rocker arms or balls are used, coat the bearing surfaces with Molykote® or equivalent. Torque the rocker arm bolt to 20 ft. lbs. (27 Nm).

#### 3.0L and 3.3L V6

1. Remove the rocker arm cover as previously described.

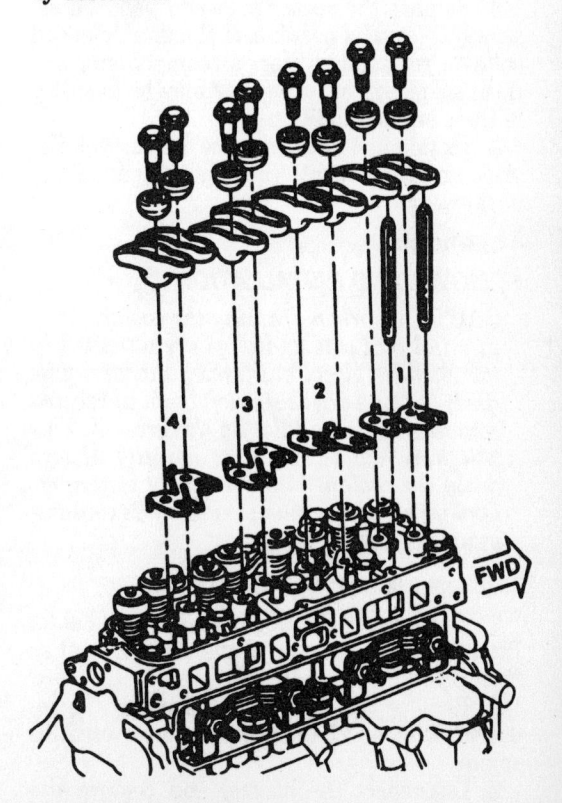

**2.5L Rocker Arm Removal**

# 104 ENGINE AND ENGINE OVERHAUL

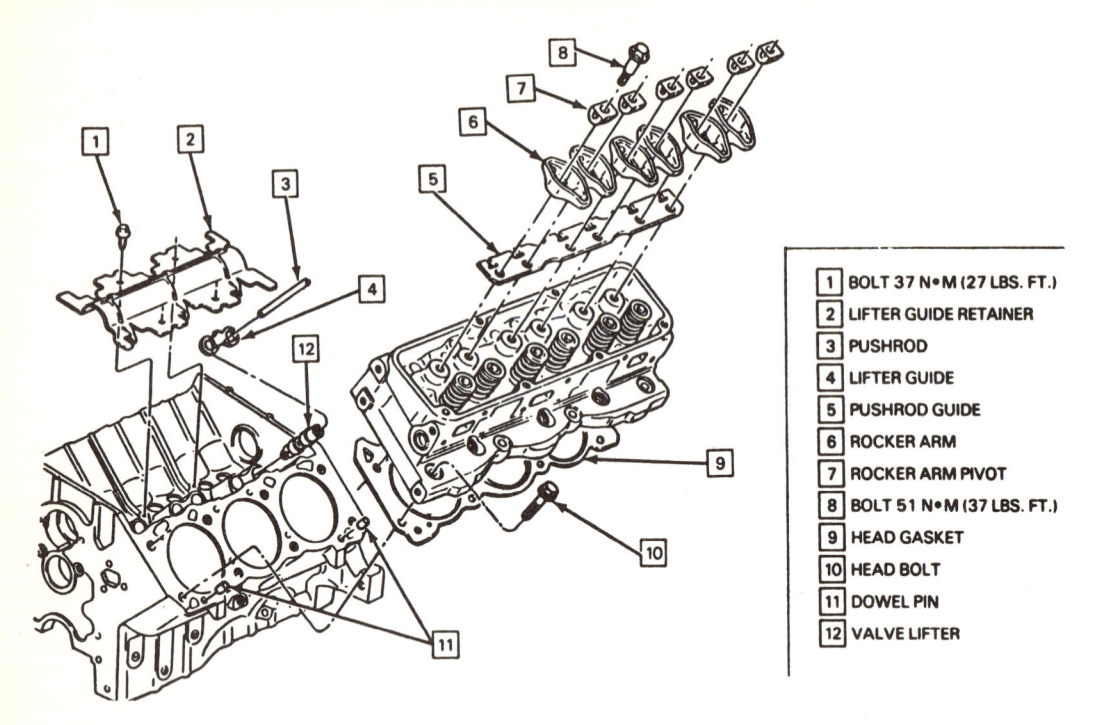

| | |
|---|---|
| 1 | BOLT 37 N•M (27 LBS. FT.) |
| 2 | LIFTER GUIDE RETAINER |
| 3 | PUSHROD |
| 4 | LIFTER GUIDE |
| 5 | PUSHROD GUIDE |
| 6 | ROCKER ARM |
| 7 | ROCKER ARM PIVOT |
| 8 | BOLT 51 N•M (37 LBS. FT.) |
| 9 | HEAD GASKET |
| 10 | HEAD BOLT |
| 11 | DOWEL PIN |
| 12 | VALVE LIFTER |

3.3L Rocker Arm and Cylinder Head Assembly (3.0L Similar)

2. Remove the rocker arm pedestal retaining bolts.
3. Remove the rocker arm and pedestal assembly. Note the position of the double ended bolts for reassembly. Store all components on a clean surface in order so they may be installed in their original locations.
4. Installation is the reverse of removal. Replace any components that show signs of unusual wear.

## Thermostat

### REMOVAL AND INSTALLATION

CAUTION: *When draining the coolant, keep in mind that cats and dogs are attracted by the ethylene glycol antifreeze, and are quite likely to drink any that is left in an uncovered container or in puddles on the ground. This will prove fatal in sufficient quantity. Always drain the coolant into a sealable container. Coolant should be reused unless it is contaminated or several years old.*

**All except 2.0L and 1988 2.5L Engines**

1. Disconnect the negative battery cable. Drain the coolant down to thermostat level or below.
2. Remove the air cleaner assembly, as required. Disconnect the coolant sensor on 2.3L engine.
3. Disconnect the hose(s) and remove the thermostat housing.

4. Remove the thermostat and discard the gasket.
5. Clean the housing mating surfaces and use a new gasket.
6. The installation is the reverse of the removal procedure.
7. Fill the system with coolant.

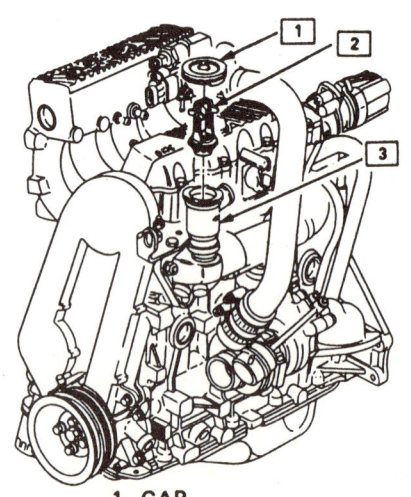

1—CAP

2—THERMOSTAT

3—HOUSING

2.0L Thermostat and Housing

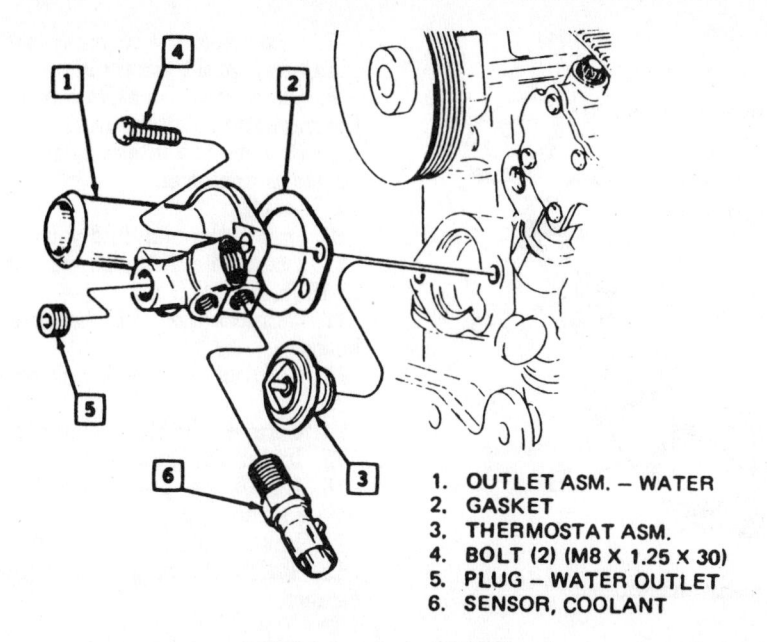

# ENGINE AND ENGINE OVERHAUL 105

1. OUTLET ASM. — WATER
2. GASKET
3. THERMOSTAT ASM.
4. BOLT (2) (M8 X 1.25 X 30)
5. PLUG — WATER OUTLET
6. SENSOR, COOLANT

**2.3L Thermostat and Housing**

8. Connect the negative battery cable, run the vehicle until the thermostat opens, fill the radiator and recovery tank completely.
9. Connect the negative battery cable.
10. Fill cooling system and check for leaks. Start the engine and allow to come to normal operating temperature. Recheck for leaks. Top-up coolant.

### 2.0L and 1988 2.5L Engines

1. Disconnect the negative battery cable.
2. Remove the thermostat housing cap.
3. Remove the thermostat and discard the gasket.
4. Clean the housing mating surfaces and use a new gasket.
5. The installation is the reverse of the removal procedure.

## Intake Manifold

### REMOVAL AND INSTALLATION

CAUTION: *When draining the coolant, keep in mind that cats and dogs are attracted by*

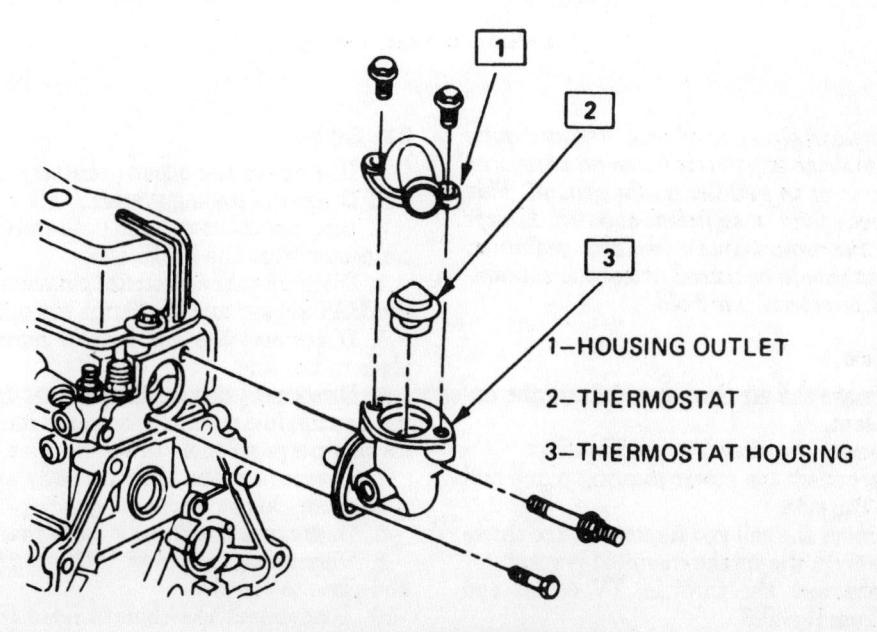

1—HOUSING OUTLET
2—THERMOSTAT
3—THERMOSTAT HOUSING

**2.5L and 3.0L Thermostat and Housing**

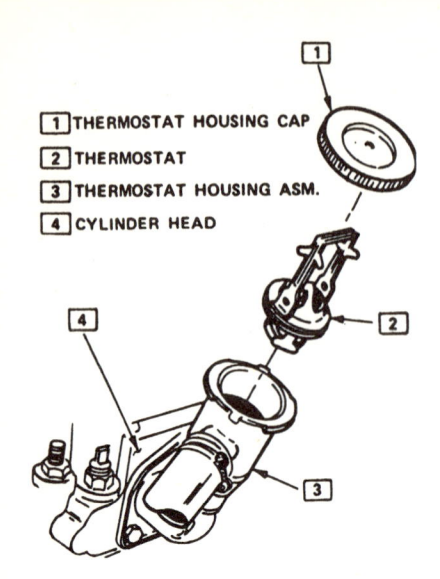

# 106 ENGINE AND ENGINE OVERHAUL

- 1 THERMOSTAT HOUSING CAP
- 2 THERMOSTAT
- 3 THERMOSTAT HOUSING ASM.
- 4 CYLINDER HEAD

**1988 2.5L Thermostat and Housing**

1. OUTLET
2. BOLT – 27 N·m (20 LBS. FT.)
3. STUD – 27 N·m (20 LBS. FT.)
4. GASKET
5. THERMOSTAT

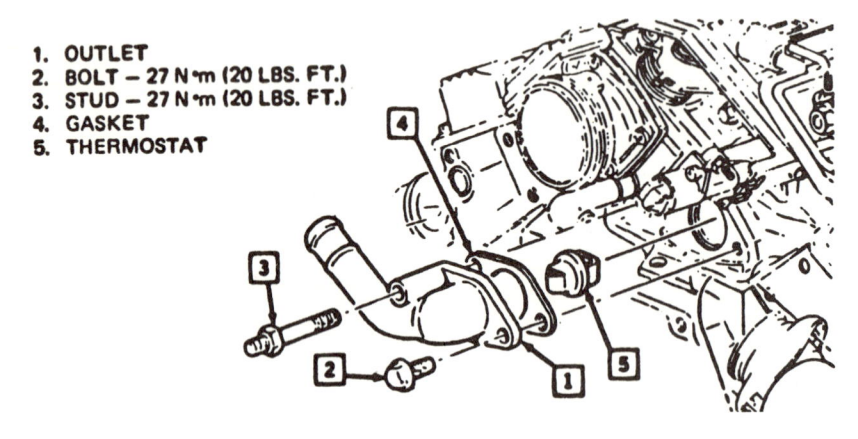

**3.3L Thermostat and Housing**

7. Disconnect the coolant hoses at the water pump and intake manifold.
8. Disconnect the ECM harness and remove the manifold retaining nuts.
9. Remove the intake manifold and remove all gasket material.

**To Install:**

10. Install the manifold with a new gasket.
11. Install the nuts and washers and tighten to 16 ft. lbs.(22 Nm).
12. Connect the ECM harness and coolamt hoses.
13. Connect the fuel lines and wiring to the TBI.
14. Connect the throttle and TV cables.
15. Install the ignition coil.
16. Install the power steering bracket and power steering pump.
17. Install the alternator and the bracket.
18. Refill the coolant and install the air cleaner.

*the ethylene glycol antifreeze, and are quite likely to drink any that is left in an uncovered container or in puddles on the ground. This will prove fatal in sufficient quantity. Always drain the coolant into a sealable container. Coolant should be reused unless it is contaminated or several years old.*

## 2.0L Engine

1. Remove the air cleaner and drain the engine coolant.
2. Remove the alternator and bracket.
3. Disconnect the power steering pump and place to the side.
4. Remove the coil and disconnect the throttle cable from the intake manifold bracket.
5. Disconnect the throttle, TV cables and wiring from the TBI.
6. Disconnect the inlet and return fuel lines.

## 2.3L Engine

1. Disconnect the negative battery cable.
2. Drain the cooling system.
3. Disconnect the vacuum hose and electrical connector from the MAP sensor.
4. Disconnect the electrical connectors from the MAT sensor and the Purge solenoid.
5. Disconnect the fuel injector harness and place to the side.
6. Disconnect the vacuum hosess from the intake manifold and the hose at the fuel regulator and purge solenoid to the canister.
7. Disconnect the throttle body and vent tube to air cleaner ducts.
8. Disconnect the throttle cable bracket.
9. Disconnect the power brake vacuum line and place to the side.
10. Disconnect the coolant lines from the throttle body.

# ENGINE AND ENGINE OVERHAUL 107

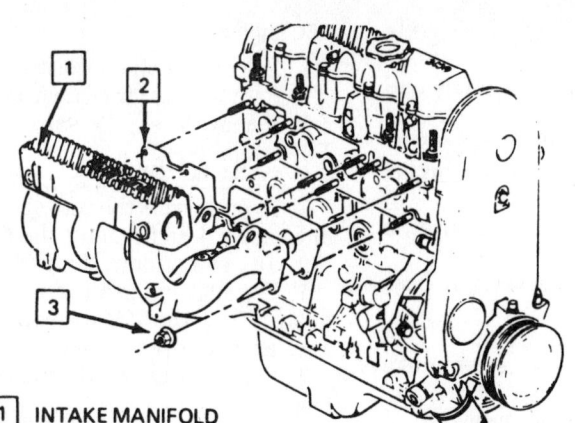

| 1 | INTAKE MANIFOLD |
| 2 | GASKET |
| 3 | NUT 25 N•M (18 LBS. FT.) |

**INLET MANIFOLD NUT TIGHTENING SEQUENCE**

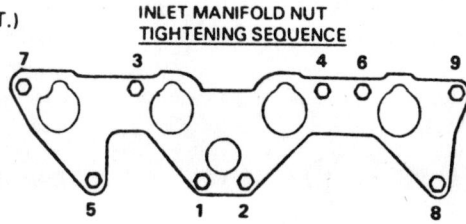

2.0L Intake Manifold

**TIGHTENING SEQUENCE**

99. STUD - 11 N.m (96 LBS. IN.)
100. INTAKE MANIFOLD GASKET
103. INTAKE MANIFOLD
104. BOLT - 25 N.m (18 LBS. FT.)
105. NUT - 25 N.m (18 LBS. FT.)

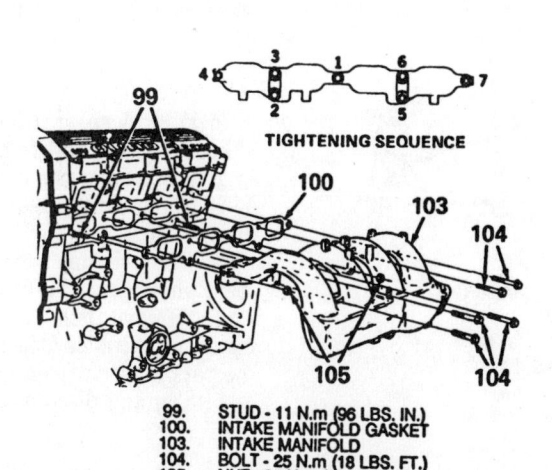

2.3L Intake Manifold

11. Remove the oil/air separator and leave the hoses connected.
12. Remove the oil fill cap and oil level indicator assembly.
13. Remove the oil fill tube bolt/screw and pull tube upward to remove.
14. Disconnect the injector harness connector.
15. Remove the intake manifold support brace and manifold retaining nuts and bolts.
16. Remove the intake manifold.

**To Install:**

17. Install the manifold with a new gasket.
NOTE: *Make sure that the numbers stamped on the gasket are facing towards the manifold surface.*
18. Follow the tightening sequence and tighten the bolts/nuts to 18 ft. lbs.(25 Nm).
19. Install the intake manifold brace and retainers.
20. Lubricate a new oil fill tube O-ring with engine oil and install tube down between intake manifold.
21. Place oil fill tube into it's normal position

## ENGINE AND ENGINE OVERHAUL

and press downward until it becomes properly seated.
22. Install the oil/air separator assembly and connect all hoses.
23. Install the oil fill tube bolt/screw.
24. Install the throttle body to the intake manifold using a new gasket.
25. Connect the coolant lines to the throttle body.
26. Connect the power brake vaccum hose and secure bracket.
27. Install the throttle cable bracket.
28. Connect the vacuum hoses to the intake manifold and connect the fuel regulator hose.
29. Connect all electrical connectors.
30. Install the coolant recovery tank and refill the coolant to its proper level.
31. Connect the negative battery cable.

### 2.5L Engine
1. Disconnect the negative battery cable.
2. Remove the air cleaner and hot air pipe.
3. Remove the PCV valve and hose at the TBI assembly.
4. Drain the cooling system.
5. Depressurize the fuel system as described in Chapter 4 and remove the fuel lines.
6. Tag and remove the vacuum hoses.
7. Tag and remove the wiring and throttle linkage from the TBI assembly.
8. Remove the transaxle downshift linkage.
9. Remove the cruise control and linkage if installed.
10. Remove the throttle linkage and bellcrank and lay aside for clearance.
11. Disconnect the heater hose.
12. Remove the upper power steering pump bracket.
13. Remove the ignition coil.
14. Remove the retaining bolts and lift off the intake manifold. Clean all gasket mating surfaces on the intake manifold and cylinder head.
15. Installation is the reverse of removal. Torque the intake manifold retaining bolts to 25 ft. lbs. (34 Nm) in the sequence illustrated. Note that the No. 7 bolt is torqued to 37 ft. lbs. (50 Nm).

### 3.0L V6

NOTE: *A special bolt wrench J-24394 or equivalent is required for this procedure.*
1. Disconnect the negative battery cable.
2. Remove the mass air flow sensor and air intake duct.
3. Remove the serpentine accessory drive belt, alternator and bracket.
4. Remove the C3I ignition module with the spark plug cables attached. Tag all wiring connectors before disconnecting.
5. Tag and disconnect all vacuum lines and

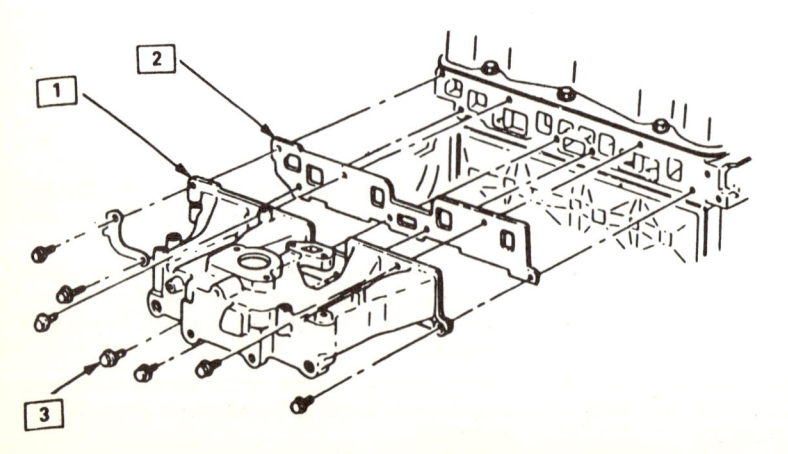

400. INTAKE MANIFOLD BRACE
401. BOLTS - 26 N.m (19 LBS. FT.)

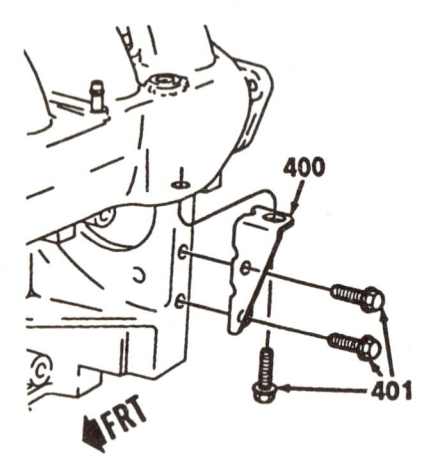

**2.3L Intake Manifold Brace**

1—INTAKE MANIFOLD

2—GASKET

3—BOLTS (7) 43 N m (25 LB. FT.)

**2.5L Intake Manifold**

# ENGINE AND ENGINE OVERHAUL 109

wiring connectors as necessary to gain clearance to remove the manifold.

6. Remove the throttle, cruise control and T.V. cables from the throttle body.
7. Drain the cooling system.
8. Remove the heater hoses from the throttle body.
9. Remove the upper radiator hose.
10. Depressurize the fuel system as described in Chapter 4, then remove the fuel lines, fuel rail and injectors.
11. Remove the intake manifold bolts. Loosen in reverse of the torque sequence to prevent manifold warping. Remove the intake manifold and gasket.
12. Installation is the reverse of removal. Clean all gasket mating surfaces and apply sealer No. 1050026 or equivalent if a steel gasket is used. Torque all manifold bolts in sequence to 32 ft. lbs. (44 Nm).

### 3.3L Engine

1. Disconnect the negative battery cable.
2. Depressurize and disconnect the fuel lines from the fuel rail.
3. Drain the coolant.
4. Disconnect the drive belt.
5. Remove the alternator and the supports.
6. Disconnect the power steering pump and the supports.
7. Disconnect the coolant bypass hose, the heater pipe and the upper radiator hose.
8. Disconnect the air inlet duct.
9. Remove the throttle cable bracket and remove the cables from the throttle body.
10. Remove the vacuum hoses from the intake manifold.

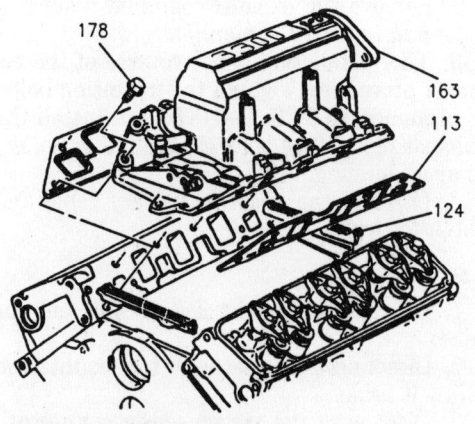

113 INTAKE MANIFOLD GASKET
124 INTAKE MANIFOLD SEAL
163 INTAKE MANIFOLD
178 BOLT 10 N·m (88 LB. IN.)
TIGHTEN TWICE IN GIVEN SEQUENCE. APPLY P/N 1052624 TO BOLTS BEFORE ASSEMBLY

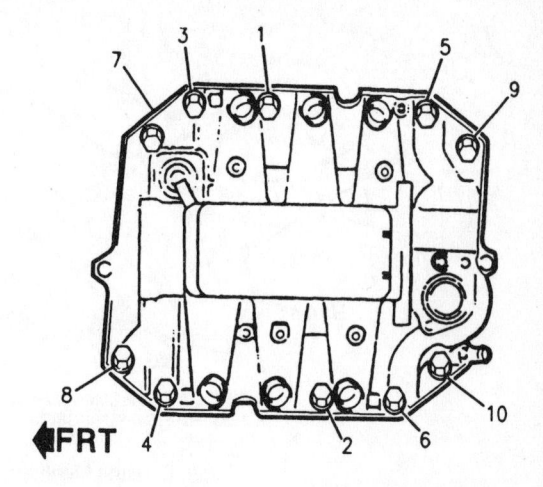

3.3L Intake Manifold (3.0L Similar)

3.0L and 3.3L Intake Manifold Bolt Tightening Sequence

2.0L Exhaust Manifold

11. Disconnect the electrical connectors and remove the fuel rail.
12. Disconnect the vapor canister purge line and the heater hose from the throttle body.
13. Disconnect the rear spark plug wires.
14. Remove the intake manifold bolts and remove the manifold.
15. Installation is the reverse of the removal procedure. Clean cylinder block, heads and intake manifold surfaces of all oil.
16. Apply RTV type sealer to the ends of the manifold seals.
17. Clean the intake manifold bolts and bolt holes of all adhesive compound.
18. Apply thread locking compound to the intake manifold bolts and tighten TWICE to 88 inch lbs.(10 Nm) in the proper sequence.

## Exhaust Manifold

### REMOVAL AND INSTALLATION

#### 2.0L Engine

1. Remove the air cleaner.
2. Number and remove the spark plug wires and retainers.

# 110  ENGINE AND ENGINE OVERHAUL

**TIGHTENING SEQUENCE**

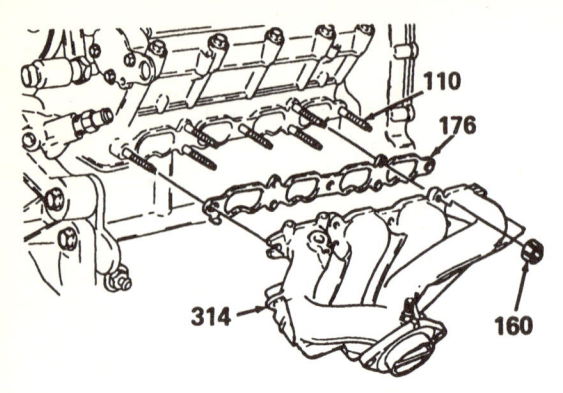

- 110. STUD - 12 N.m (106 LBS. IN)
- 160. NUT (7) - 42 N.m (31 LBS. FT.) SEE TIGHTENING SEQUENCE
- 176. GASKET
- 314. MANIFOLD ASSEMBLY

(HEAT SHIELD REMOVED FOR ILLUSTRATION PURPOSES)

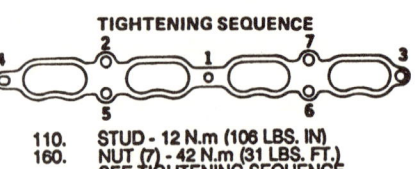

**2.3L Exhaust Manifold and Gasket Installation**

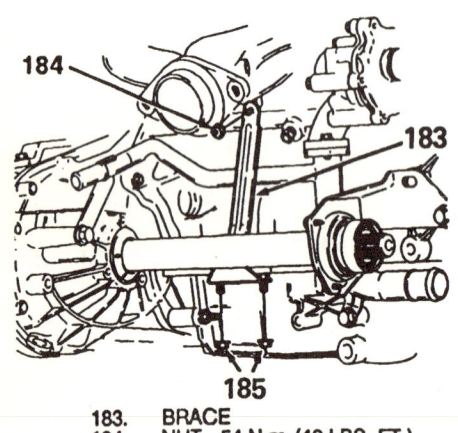

- 183. BRACE
- 184. NUT - 54 N.m (40 LBS. FT.)
- 185. NUTS - 26 N.m (19 LBS. FT.)

**2.3L Exhaust Manifold Brace**

3. Remove the oil dipstick tube and breather.
4. Disconnect the oxygen sensor wire.
5. Disconnect the exhaust pipe from the manifold.
6. Remove the nuts and remove the manifold and the gasket.

**To Install:**

7. Install the exhaust manifold with a new gasket. Tighten the nuts to 16 ft. lbs.(22 Nm).
8. Install the exhaust pipe to the exhaust manifold and tighten the nuts to 19 ft. lbs.(25 Nm).
9. Connect the wire to the oxygen sensor.
10. Install the oil dipstick tube and breather.
11. Install the spark plug wires and retainers.
12. Install the air cleaner.

## 2.3L ENGINE

1. Disconnect the negative battery cable and oxygen sensor connector.
2. Remove upper and lower exhaust manifold heat shields.
3. Remove the bolt that attaches the exhaust manifold brace to the manifold.
4. Break loose the manifold to exhaust pipe spring loaded bolts using a 13mm box wrench.
5. Raise and safely support the vehicle.

NOTE: *It is necessary to relieve the spring pressure from 1 bolt prior to removing the second bolt. If the spring pressure is not relieved it will cause the exhaust pipe to twist and bind up the bolt as it is removed.*

6. Remove the manifold to exhaust pipe bolts from the exhaust pipe flange as follows:
   a. Unscrew either bolt clockwise 4 turns.
   b. Remove the other bolt.
   c. Remove the first bolt.
7. Pull down and back on the exhaust pipe to disengage it from the exhaust manifold bolts.
8. Lower the vehicle.
9. Remove the exhaust manifold mounting bolts and remove the manifold.
10. The installation is the reverse of the removal procedure. Tighten the mounting bolts, in sequence, to 27 ft. lbs. (37 Nm). Install the exhaust pipe flange bolts evenly and gradually to avoid binding.
11. Connect the negative battery cable and check for leaks.

## 2.5L Engine

1. Disconnect the air cleaner and hot air tube.
2. Disconnect the alternator top mounts and swing it aside.
3. Disconnect the oxygen sensor connector.
4. Raise the vehicle and support it safely.
5. Disconnect the exhaust pipe from the manifold.
6. Lower the vehicle.
7. Remove the exhaust manifold retaining bolts, then remove the exhaust manifold and gasket.

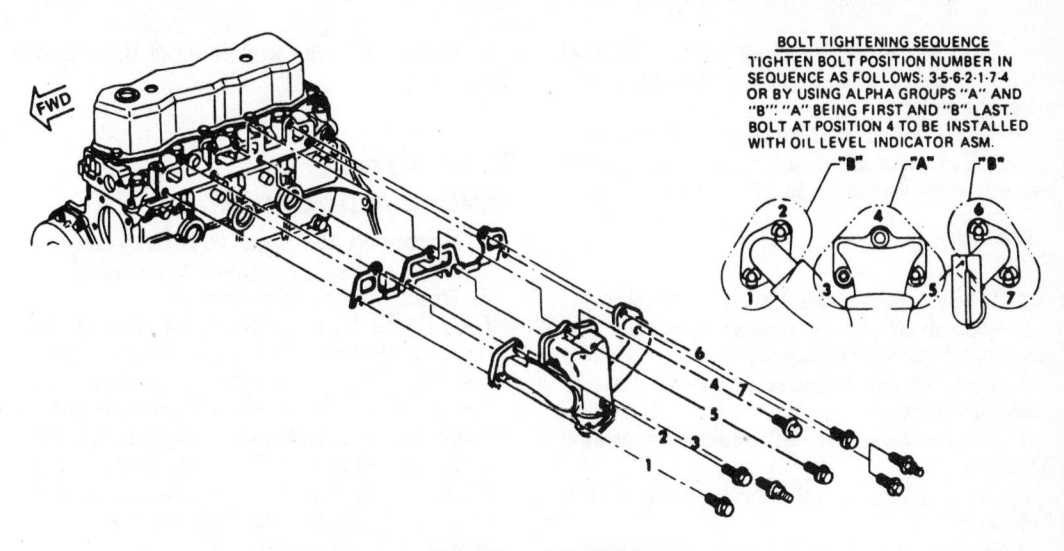

## ENGINE AND ENGINE OVERHAUL

**BOLT TIGHTENING SEQUENCE**
TIGHTEN BOLT POSITION NUMBER IN SEQUENCE AS FOLLOWS: 3-5-6-2-1-7-4 OR BY USING ALPHA GROUPS "A" AND "B"; "A" BEING FIRST AND "B" LAST. BOLT AT POSITION 4 TO BE INSTALLED WITH OIL LEVEL INDICATOR ASM.

**2.5L Exhaust Manifold**

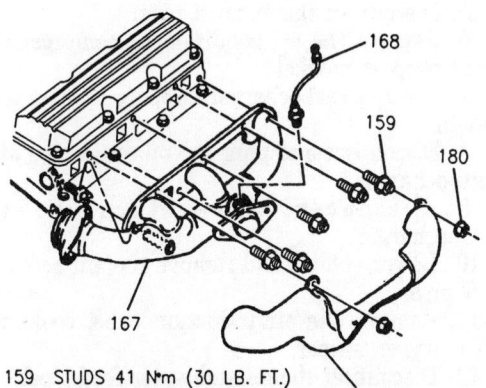

159 STUDS 41 N•m (30 LB. FT.)
164 EXHAUST MANIFOLD HEAT SHIELD 164
167 EXHAUST MANIFOLD
168 OXYGEN SENSOR
180 NUTS 26 N•m (19 LB. FT.)

**3.5L Right Exhaust Manifold (3.0L Similar)**

8. Clean all gasket mating surfaces on the cylinder head and manifold.
9. Installation is the reverse of removal. Torque all exhaust manifold mounting bolts to 44 ft. lbs. (60 Nm) in sequence.

**3.0L Engine**

1. Disconnect the negative battery cable.
2. Raise and support the vehicle safely.
3. Remove the bolts attaching the exhaust pipe to the manifold.
4. Lower the vehicle.
5. Disconnect the oxygen sensor connector.
6. Remove the spark plug wires. Tag them for installation.
7. Remove the two nuts retaining the crossover pipe to the manifold.

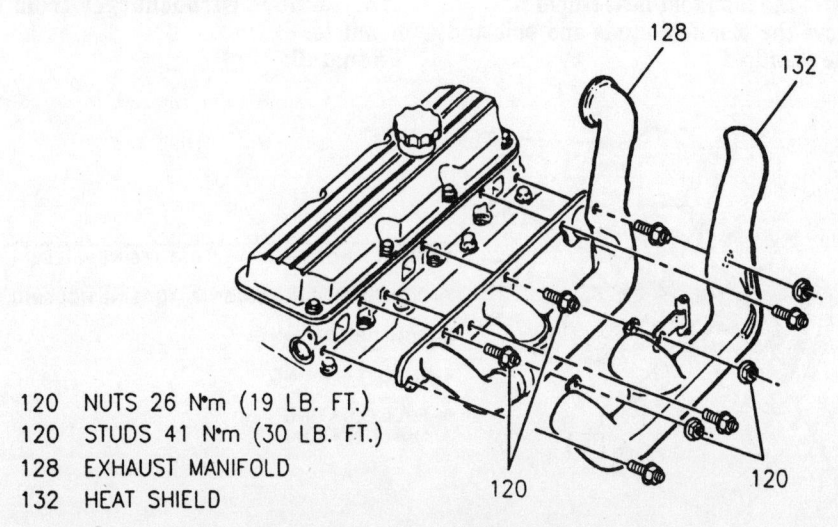

120 NUTS 26 N•m (19 LB. FT.)
120 STUDS 41 N•m (30 LB. FT.)
128 EXHAUST MANIFOLD
132 HEAT SHIELD

**3.3L Left Exhaust Manifold (3.0L Similar)**

# ENGINE AND ENGINE OVERHAUL

8. Remove the bolts attaching the exhaust manifold and remove the exhaust manifold from the engine.
9. Installation is the reverse of removal. Clean all gasket mating surfaces and torque the exhaust manifold bolts to 37 ft. lbs. (50 Nm).

### 3.3L Engine
#### Front

1. Disconnect the negative battery cable.
2. Disconnect the air cleaner inlet duct and disconnect the spark plug wires.
3. Remove the exhaust crossover pipe to manifold bolts.
4. Remove the engine lift hook and manifold heat shield.
5. Remove the oil level indicator tube and the indicator.
6. Remove the manifold studs and remove the manifold.
7. Installation is the reverse of the removal procedure.

#### Rear

1. Disconnect the negative battery cable.
2. Disconnect the spark plug wires.
3. Disconnect the wire from the oxygen sensor.
4. Remove the throttle cable bracket and remove the cables from the throttle body.
5. Remove the brake booster hose from the manifold.
6. Remove the two exhaust crossover pipe to manifold bolts.
7. Remove the exhaust pipe to manifold bolts.
8. Remove the engine lift hook.
9. Remove the transaxle oil level indicator tube.
10. Remove the manifold heat shield.
11. Remove the manifold studs and bolt and remove the manifold.

12. Installation is the reverse of the removal procedure.

## Turbocharger
### REMOVAL AND INSTALLATION

1. Disconnect the negative battery cable.
2. Raise and safely support the vehicle.
3. Drain the engine coolant.

CAUTION: *When draining the coolant, keep in mind that cats and dogs are attracted by the ethylene glycol antifreeze, and are quite likely to drink any that is left in an uncovered container or in puddles on the ground. This will prove fatal in sufficient quantity. Always drain the coolant into a sealable container. Coolant should be reused unless it is contaminated or several years old.*

4. Remove the fan attaching screws.
5. Disconnect the exhaust pipe.
6. Remove the air conditioning compressor rear support bracket.
7. Remove turbocharger support bracket to engine.
8. Disconnect and plug the oil drain pipe at turbocharger.
9. Disconnect water return pipe at turbocharger.
10. Lower vehicle and remove coolant recovery pipe.
11. Remove the air induction tube, coolant fan, oxygen sensor.
12. Disconnect the oil and water feed pipes.
13. Remove air intake duct and vacuum hose at actuator.
14. Remove the exhaust manifold attaching nuts and remove turbocharger and manifold as an assembly.
15. Remove turbocharger from exhaust manifold.

**To install:**

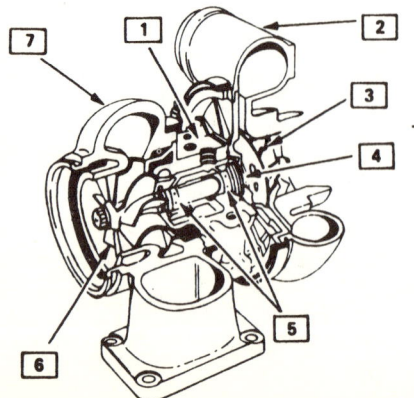

1—CENTER HOUSING
2—COMPRESSOR HOUSING
3—COMPRESSOR WHEEL
4—THRUST BEARING
5—FULL FLOATING SHAFT BEARING
6—TURBINE WHEEL
7—TURBINE HOUSING

Turbocharger

# ENGINE AND ENGINE OVERHAUL 113

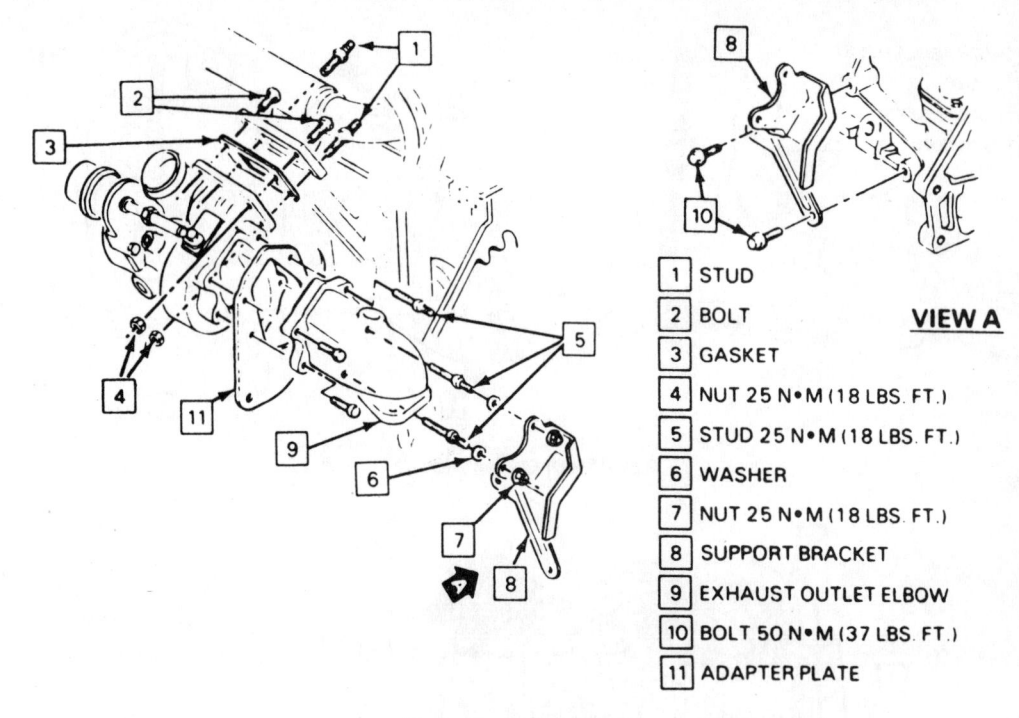

| | |
|---|---|
| 1 | STUD |
| 2 | BOLT |
| 3 | GASKET |
| 4 | NUT 25 N•M (18 LBS. FT.) |
| 5 | STUD 25 N•M (18 LBS. FT.) |
| 6 | WASHER |
| 7 | NUT 25 N•M (18 LBS. FT.) |
| 8 | SUPPORT BRACKET |
| 9 | EXHAUST OUTLET ELBOW |
| 10 | BOLT 50 N•M (37 LBS. FT.) |
| 11 | ADAPTER PLATE |

VIEW A

**Turbocharger Mounting**

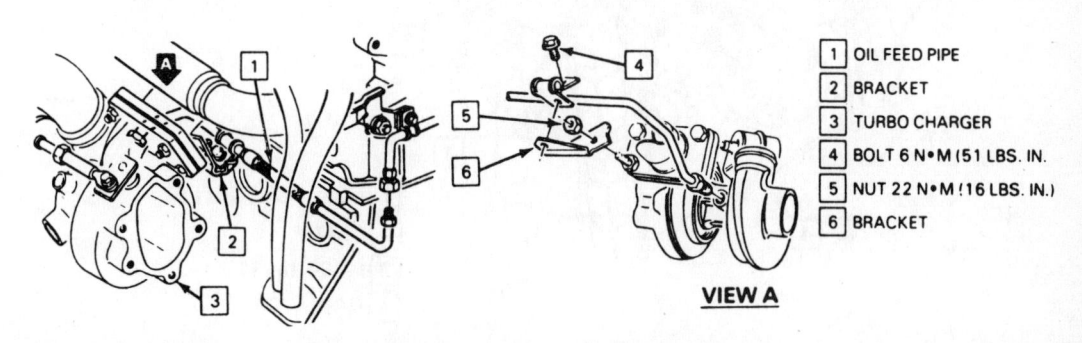

| | |
|---|---|
| 1 | OIL FEED PIPE |
| 2 | BRACKET |
| 3 | TURBO CHARGER |
| 4 | BOLT 6 N•M (51 LBS. IN.) |
| 5 | NUT 22 N•M (16 LBS. IN.) |
| 6 | BRACKET |

VIEW A

**Turbo Oil Feed Pipe Hose Assembly**

16. Assemble the turbocharger and exhaust manifold.
17. Clean the exhaust manifold and cylinder head mating surfaces.
18. Install a new gasket and install the manifold/turbocharger assembly to the engine. Tighten the Nos. 2 and 3 manifold runner nuts first, then Nos. 1 and 4, to 18 ft. lbs. (24 Nm).
19. Connect the oil and water feed and return lines.
20. Connect the oxygen sensor.
21. Install the air intake duct and connect the vacuum hose to the actuator.
22. Install the cooling fan.
23. Install the induction tube and coolant recovery tube.
24. Raise and safely support the vehicle.
25. Install the rear turbocharger support bolt.
26. Install the compressor support bracket.
27. Install the oil drain hose.
28. Connect the exhaust pipe.
29. Connect the negative battery cable and check the turbocharger for proper operation and the assembly for leaks.

## Radiator

### REMOVAL AND INSTALLATION

1. Disconnect the negative battery cable.
2. Drain the coolant. Disconnect the the engine strut brace at the radiator, loosen the engine side bolt and swing aside, if equipped.

CAUTION: *When draining the coolant, keep in mind that cats and dogs are attracted by the ethylene glycol antifreeze, and are quite likely to drink any that is left in an uncovered*

# 114  ENGINE AND ENGINE OVERHAUL

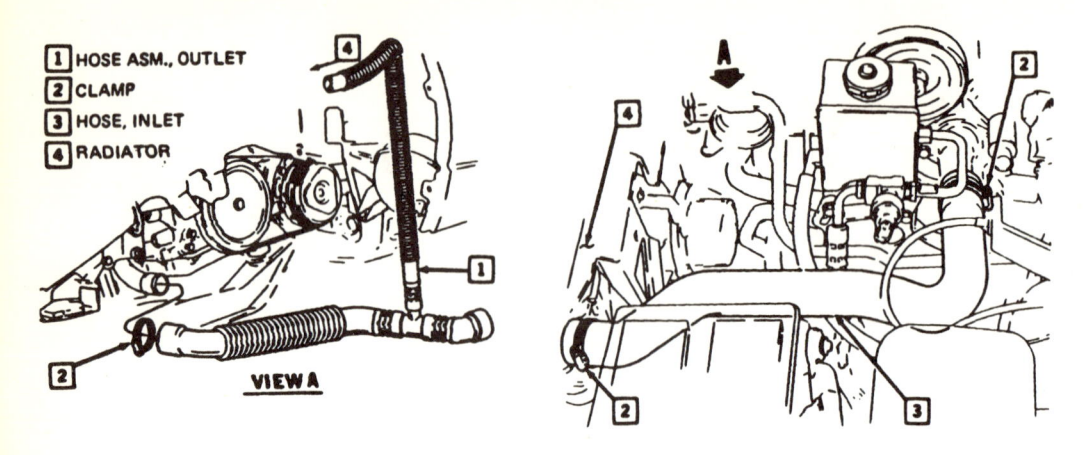

1. HOSE ASM., OUTLET
2. CLAMP
3. HOSE, INLET
4. RADIATOR

**2.3L (VIN D) Coolant Hoses**

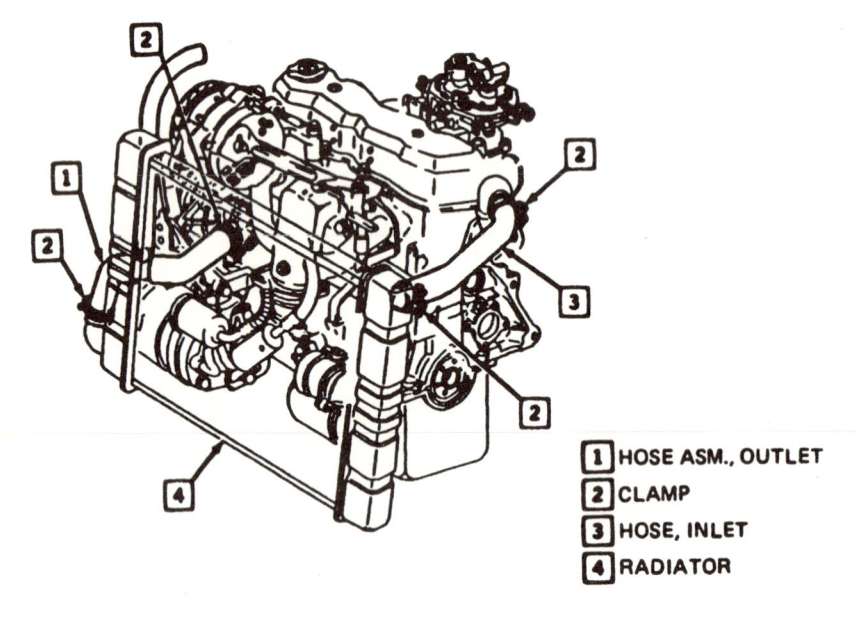

1. HOSE ASM., OUTLET
2. CLAMP
3. HOSE, INLET
4. RADIATOR

**2.5L Coolant Hoses**

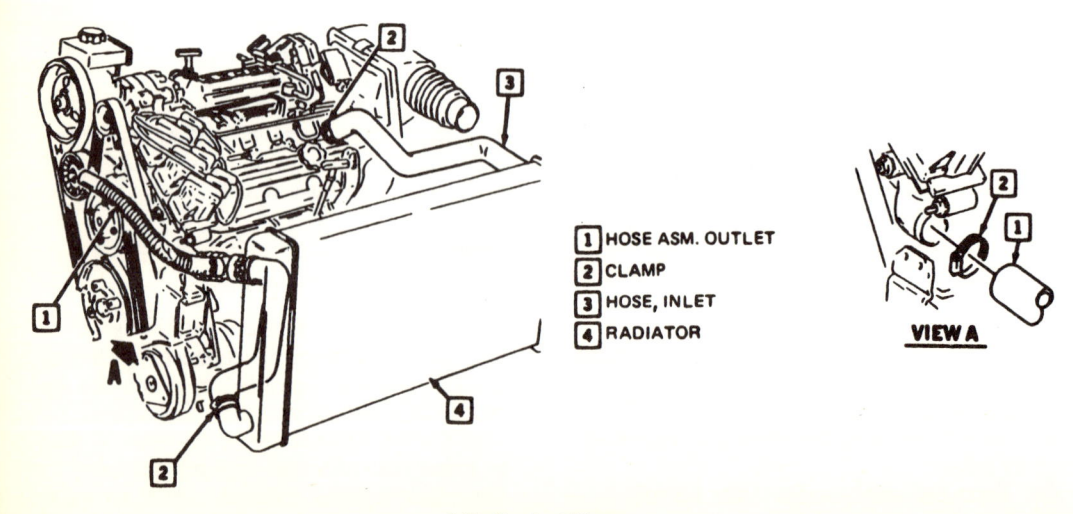

1. HOSE ASM. OUTLET
2. CLAMP
3. HOSE, INLET
4. RADIATOR

**3.3L Coolant Hoses**

# ENGINE AND ENGINE OVERHAUL 115

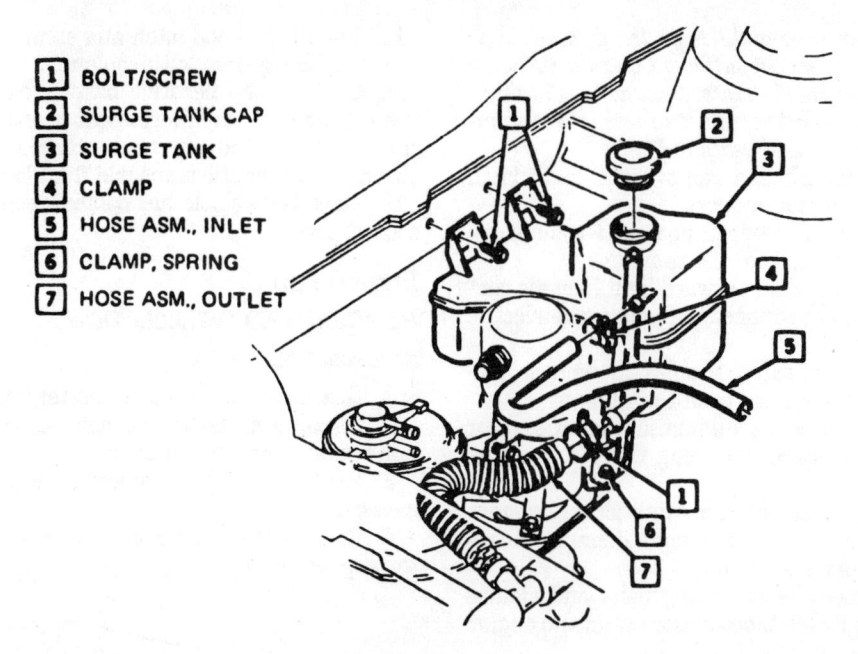

1. BOLT/SCREW
2. SURGE TANK CAP
3. SURGE TANK
4. CLAMP
5. HOSE ASM., INLET
6. CLAMP, SPRING
7. HOSE ASM., OUTLET

Radiator Surge Tank

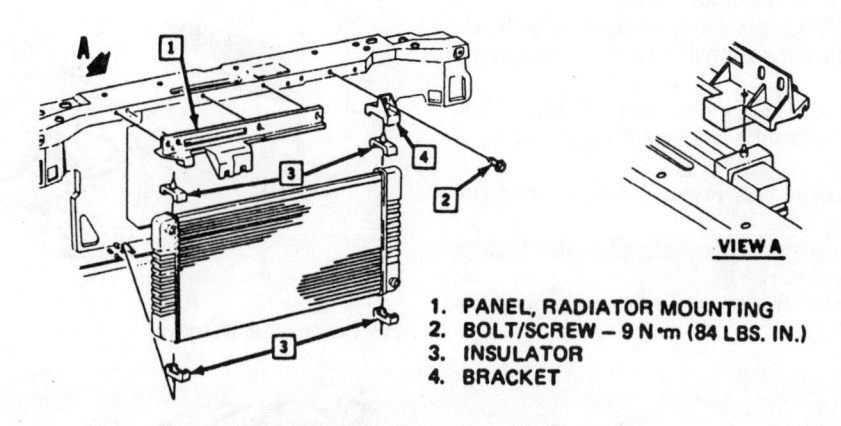

1. PANEL, RADIATOR MOUNTING
2. BOLT/SCREW — 9 N·m (84 LBS. IN.)
3. INSULATOR
4. BRACKET

Radiator Mounting (2.0L, 2.3L, 3.0L and 3.3L)

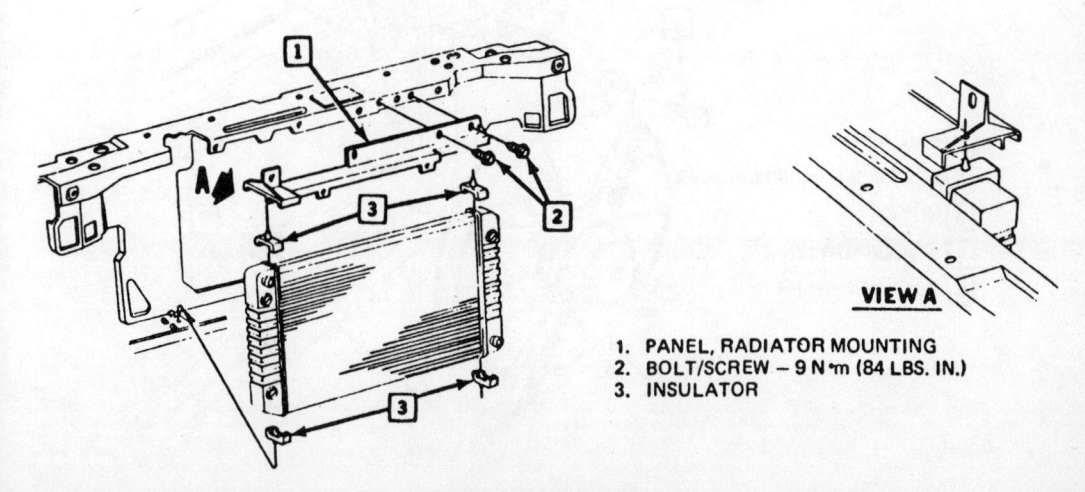

1. PANEL, RADIATOR MOUNTING
2. BOLT/SCREW — 9 N·m (84 LBS. IN.)
3. INSULATOR

Radiator Mounting—2.5L

# 116 ENGINE AND ENGINE OVERHAUL

*container or in puddles on the ground. This will prove fatal in sufficient quantity. Always drain the coolant into a sealable container. Coolant should be reused unless it is contaminated or several years old.*

3. Matchmark and remove the hood latch from the radiator support.
4. Remove the upper hose and coolant reserve tank hose from the radiator.
5. Disconnect the forward light harness connector and fan connector. Remove the electric cooling fan.
6. Raise and safely support the vehicle. Remove the lower hose from the radiator.
7. Disconnect the automatic transaxle cooler hoses, if equipped, and plug them. Lower the vehicle.
8. If equipped with air conditioning, remove the radiator to condenser bolts. Remove the refrigerant line clamp bolt.
9. Remove the mounting bolts and clamps and carefully lift the radiator out of the engine compartment.

**To install:**
10. Lower the radiator into position.
11. Install the mounting clamps and bolts, including those associated with air conditioning parts.
12. Raise and safely support the vehicle. Connect the automatic transaxle cooler lines, if equipped.
13. Connect the lower hose. Lower the vehicle.
14. Install the electric cooling fan and connect the connectors.
15. Connect the upper hose and coolant reserve tank hose.
16. Install the hood latch and strut brace.
17. Fill the system with coolant.
18. Connect the negative battery cable, run the vehicle until the thermostat opens, fill the radiator and recovery tank completely and check the automatic transaxle fluid level.
19. Once the vehicle has cooled, recheck the coolant level.

## Engine Fan

### REMOVAL AND INSTALLATION

#### All except 2.3L (VIN D)

1. Disconnect the negative battery cable.
2. Disconnect the wiring harness from the motor and from the fan frame.
3. Remove the fan guard and hose support if necessary.
4. Remove the fan assembly from the radiator support.

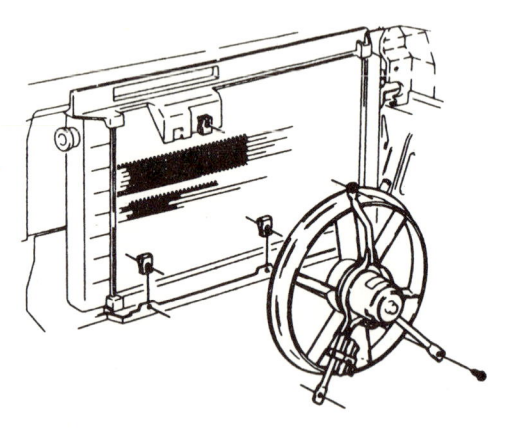

**2.0L Coolant Fan Mounting**

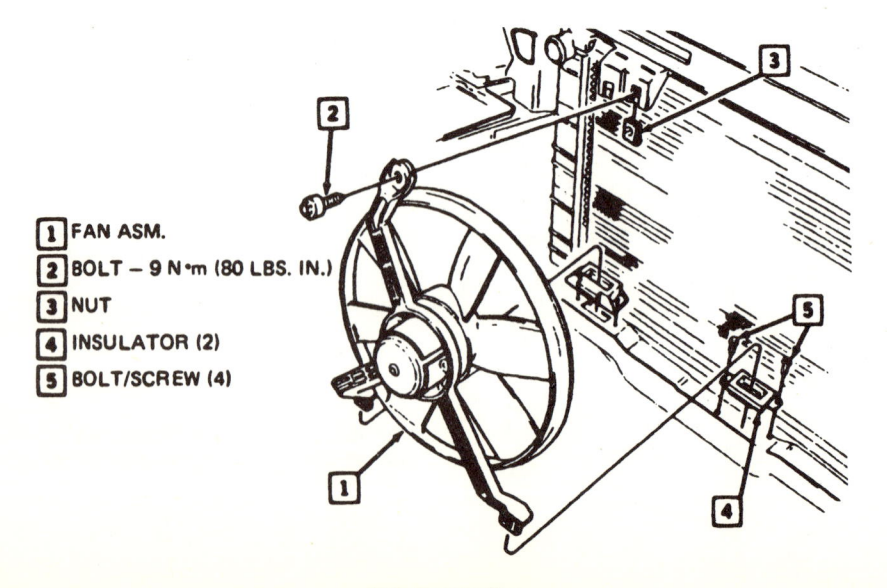

[1] FAN ASM.
[2] BOLT – 9 N•m (80 LBS. IN.)
[3] NUT
[4] INSULATOR (2)
[5] BOLT/SCREW (4)

**2.3L Engine Fan**

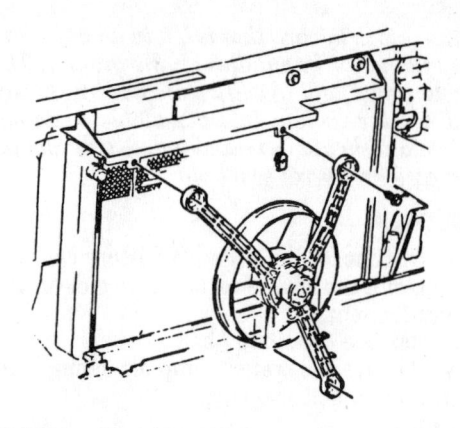

# ENGINE AND ENGINE OVERHAUL    117

**2.5L Engine Fan without A/C**

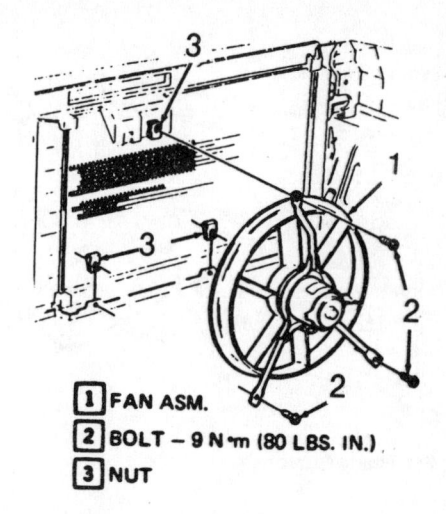

**1** FAN ASM.
**2** BOLT – 9 N·m (80 LBS. IN.)
**3** NUT

3.3L Engine Fan (3.0L Similar)

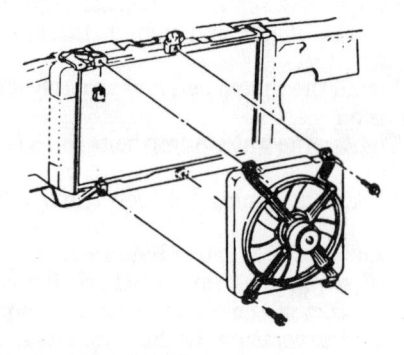

5. Installation is the reverse of the removal procedure.

### 2.3L Engine (VIN D)

1. Disconnect the negative battery cable.
2. Disconnect the air cleaner to the throttle body duct.
3. Disconnect the TPS, IAC, and MAP sensor connectors and position the harness off to the side.

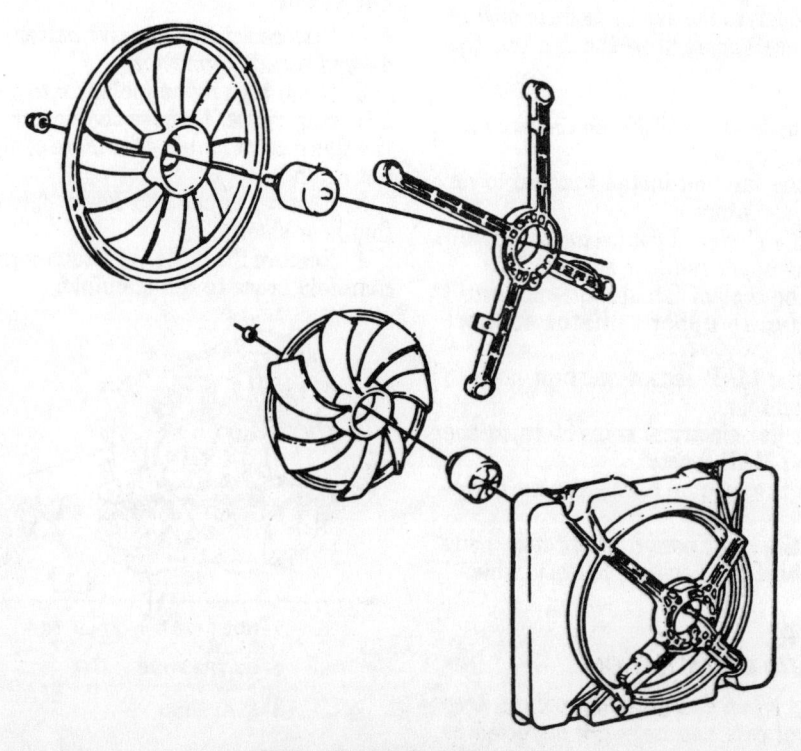

**2.5L Engine Fan with A/C**

**Typical Engine Fan Assembly**

# 118 ENGINE AND ENGINE OVERHAUL

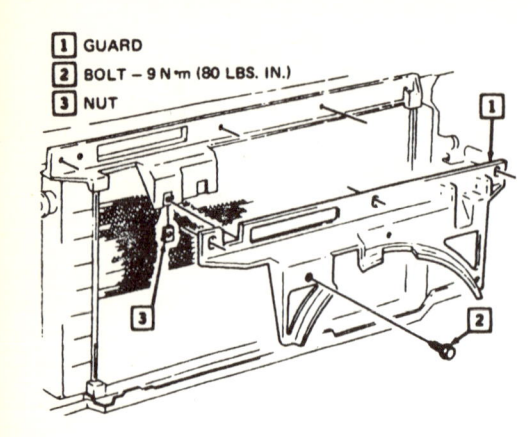

1 GUARD
2 BOLT – 9 N·m (80 LBS. IN.)
3 NUT

2.3L Fan Blade Guard

4. Disconnect the vacuum harness assembly from the throttle body and place to the side.
5. Disconnect the MAP sensor vacuum hose from the intake manifold.
6. Remove the coolant fan shroud bolts and remove the fan shroud.
7. Remove the coolant fan to upper radiator support bolt and remove the upper radiator support.
8. Disconnect the electrical connector from the coolant fan.
9. Lift the fan out from the lower insulators. Rotate the bracket so that the two lower legs point upward.
10. Move the fan to the driver's side to ensure proper clearance and remove the fan out the top.

To install:
11. Install the fan assembly with the two lower legs pointing upward.
12. Rotate the fan and install the two lower legs into the insulators.
13. Install the electrical connector to the fan and install the upper radiator support.
14. Install the coolant fan shroud and install the coolant fan to upper radiator support mounting bolt.
15. Install the MAP sensor vacuum hose to the intake manifold.
16. Connect the electrical connectors to the TPS, IAC, and MAP sensor.
17. Connect the vacuum harness to the throttle body.
18. Install the air cleaner to throttle body duct and connect the negative battery cable.

## Water Pump

### REMOVAL AND INSTALLATION

CAUTION: *When draining the coolant, keep in mind that cats and dogs are attracted by the ethylene glycol antifreeze, and are quite likely to drink any that is left in an uncovered container or in puddles on the ground. This will prove fatal in sufficient quantity. Always drain the coolant into a sealable container. Coolant should be reused unless it is contaminated or several years old.*

### 2.0L Engine

1. Disconnect the negative battery cable.
2. Drain the engine coolant into a clean container for reuse.
3. Remove the timing belt.
4. Remove the water pump attaching bolts, water pump and seal ring.

To install:
5. Thoroughly clean and dry the mounting surfaces, bolts and bolt holes.
6. Using a new sealing ring, install the water pump to the engine and tighten the bolts by hand.
7. Install the timing belt and properly adjust the tension.
8. Tighten the water pump bolts to 18 ft. lbs. (24 Nm).
9. Install the timing belt cover and related parts.
10. Connect the negative battery cable.
11. Fill cooling system and check for leaks. Start the engine and allow to come to normal operating temperature. Recheck for leaks. Top-up coolant.

### 2.3L Engine

1. Disconnect the negative battery cable and oxygen sensor connector.
2. Drain the engine coolant into a clean container for reuse. Remove the heater hose from the thermostat housing for more complete coolant drain.
3. Remove upper and lower exhaust manifold heat shields.
4. Remove the bolt that attaches the exhaust manifold brace to the manifold.

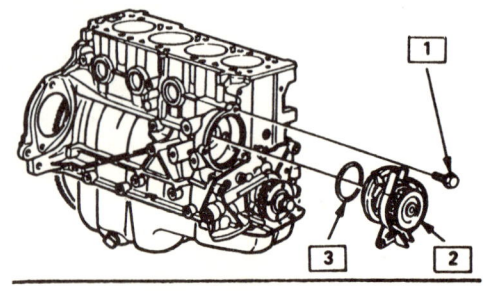

1—BOLT · 28 N·m (21 LB. FT.)
2—WATER PUMP
3—SEAL RING

2.0L Water Pump

# ENGINE AND ENGINE OVERHAUL 119

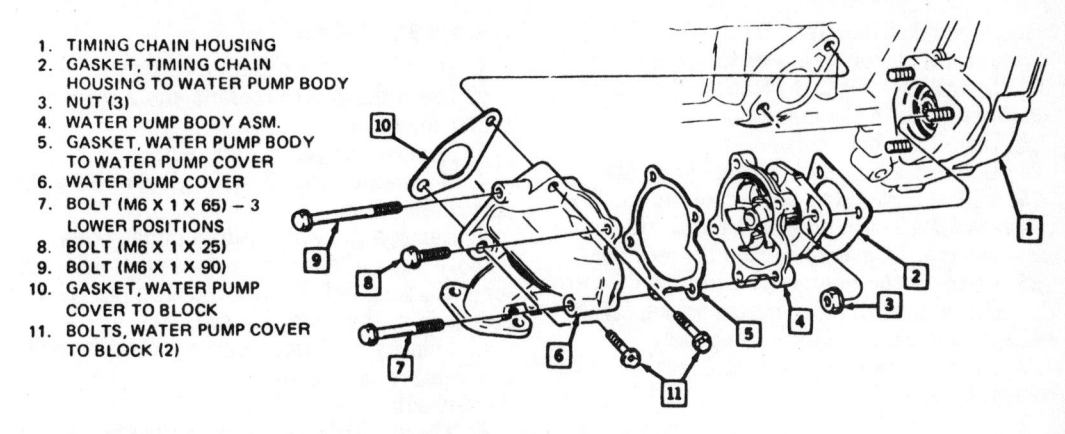

1. TIMING CHAIN HOUSING
2. GASKET, TIMING CHAIN HOUSING TO WATER PUMP BODY
3. NUT (3)
4. WATER PUMP BODY ASM.
5. GASKET, WATER PUMP BODY TO WATER PUMP COVER
6. WATER PUMP COVER
7. BOLT (M6 X 1 X 65) – 3 LOWER POSITIONS
8. BOLT (M6 X 1 X 25)
9. BOLT (M6 X 1 X 90)
10. GASKET, WATER PUMP COVER TO BLOCK
11. BOLTS, WATER PUMP COVER TO BLOCK (2)

2.3L Water Pump and Cover

5. Break loose the manifold to exhaust pipe spring loaded bolts using a 13mm box wrench.
6. Raise and safely support the vehicle.
NOTE: *It is necessary to relieve the spring pressure from 1 bolt prior to removing the second bolt. If the spring pressure is not relieved, it will cause the exhaust pipe to twist and bind up the bolt as it is removed.*
7. Remove the manifold to exhaust pipe bolts from the exhaust pipe flange as follows:
   a. Unscrew either bolt clockwise 4 turns.
   b. Remove the other bolt.
   c. Remove the first bolt.
8. Pull down and back on the exhaust pipe to disengage it from the exhaust manifold bolts.
9. Remove the radiator outlet pipe from the oil pan and transaxle. If equipped with a manual transaxle, remove the exhaust manifold brace. Leave the lower radiator hose attached and pull down on the outlet pipe to remove it from the water pump.
10. Lower the vehicle.
11. Remove the exhaust manifold, seals and gaskets.
12. Loosen and reposition the rear engine mount and bracket for clearance, as required.
13. Remove the water pump mounting bolts and nuts. Remove the water pump and cover assembly and separate the 2 pieces.

**To install:**
14. Thoroughly clean and dry all mounting surfaces, bolts and bolt holes. Using a new gasket, install the water pump to the cover and tighten the bolts finger tight.
15. Lubricate the splines of the water pump with clean grease and install the assembly to the engine using new gaskets. Install the mounting bolts and nuts finger tight.
16. Lubricate the radiator outlet pipe O-ring with antifreeze and install to the water pump with the bolts finger tight.
17. With all gaps closed, tighten the bolts, in the following sequence, to the proper values:
   a. Pump assembly to chain housing nuts – 19 ft. lbs. (26 Nm).
   b. Pump cover to pump assembly – 106 inch lbs. (12 Nm).
   c. Cover to block, bottom bolt first – 19 ft. lbs. (26 Nm).
   d. Radiator outlet pipe assembly to pump cover – 125 inch lbs. (14 Nm).
18. Install the exhaust manifold.
19. Raise and safely support the vehicle.
20. Install the exhaust pipe flange bolts evenly and gradually to avoid binding.
21. Connect the radiator outlet pipe to the

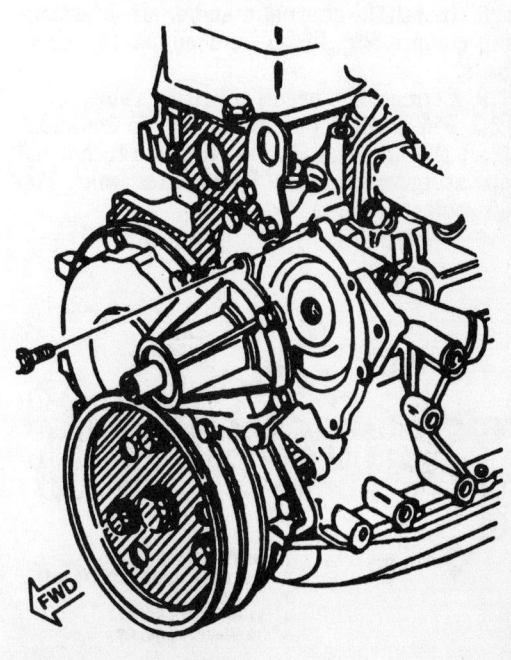

2.5L Water Pump Mounting

# ENGINE AND ENGINE OVERHAUL

transaxle and oil pan. Install the exhaust manifold brace, if removed. Lower the vehicle.
22. Install the bolt that attaches the exhaust manifold brace to the manifold.
23. Install the heat shields.
24. Connect the oxygen sensor connector.
25. Fill the radiator with coolant until it comes out the heater hose outlet at the thermostat housing. Then connect the heater hose.
26. Connect the negative battery cable, run the vehicle until the thermostat opens, fill the radiator and recovery tank completely.
27. Once the vehicle has cooled, recheck the coolant level.

## 2.5L Engine

1. Disconnect the negative battery cable.
2. Drain the engine coolant into a clean container for reuse.
3. Remove the drive belts, alternator and air conditioning compressor, as required.
4. Remove the water pump mounting bolts and remove the water pump from the vehicle.

**To install:**

5. Transfer the water pump pulley to the new pump using the proper pulley removal and installation tools.
6. Thoroughly clean and dry the mounting surfaces, bolts and bolt holes. Place a 1/8 in. (3mm) bead of RTV sealant on the pump's sealing surface.
7. Install the pump to the engine and coat the bolt threads with sealant as they are installed. Tighten the bolts to 25 ft. lbs. (34 Nm).
8. Install the alternator and/or air conditioning compressor. Install and adjust the drive belts.
9. Connect the negative battery cable.
10. Fill cooling system and check for leaks. Start the engine and allow to come to normal operating temperature. Recheck for leaks. Top off coolant level.

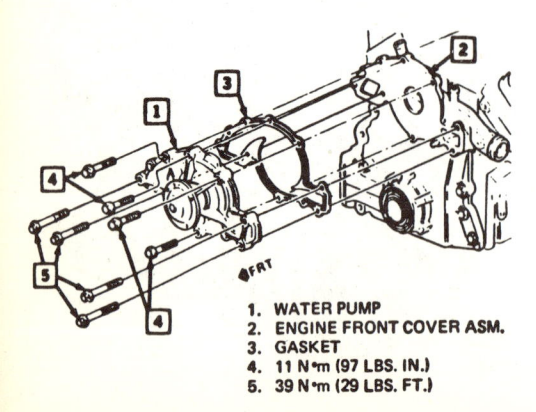

1. WATER PUMP
2. ENGINE FRONT COVER ASM.
3. GASKET
4. 11 N·m (97 LBS. IN.)
5. 39 N·m (29 LBS. FT.)

**3.3L Water Pump Mounting (3.0L Similar)**

## 3.0L and 3.3L Engines

1. Disconnect the negative battery cable.
2. Drain the engine coolant into a clean container for reuse.
3. Remove the serpentine belt.
4. If equipped with 3.3L engine, remove the idler pulley bolt.
5. Remove the water pump pulley bolts and remove the pulley. If equipped with 3.0L engine, the long bolt is removed through the access hole in the body side rail.
6. Remove the water pump mounting bolts and remove the pump.

**To install:**

7. Thoroughly clean and dry the mounting surfaces, bolts and bolt holes.
8. Using a new gasket, install the water pump to the engine and tighten pump to front cover bolts to 97 inch lbs. (11 Nm) and the pump to block bolts to 29 ft. lbs. (39 Nm).
9. Install the water pump pulley and tighten the bolts to 115 inch lbs. (13 Nm).
10. If equipped with 3.3L engine, install the idler pulley bolt.
11. Install the serpentine belt.
12. Fill the system with coolant.
13. Connect the negative battery cable, run the vehicle until the thermostat opens, fill the radiator and recovery tank completely.
14. Once the vehicle has cooled, recheck the coolant level.

## Cylinder Head

### REMOVAL AND INSTALLATION

CAUTION: *When draining the coolant, keep in mind that cats and dogs are attracted by the ethylene glycol antifreeze, and are quite likely to drink any that is left in an uncovered container or in puddles on the ground. This will prove fatal in sufficient quantity. Always drain the coolant into a sealable container. Coolant should be reused unless it is contaminated or several years old.*

## 2.0L Engine

NOTE: *Cylinder head gasket replacement is necessary if camshaft carrier/cylinder head bolts are loosened. The head bolts should only be loosened when the engine is cold and should never be reused.*

1. Relieve the fuel system pressure. Disconnect the negative battery cable.
2. Drain the coolant. Remove the induction tube.
3. Remove the alternator and bracket.
4. Remove the ignition coil.
5. Matchmark the rotor to the distributor housing and the distributor housing to the cam carrier. Remove the distributor and spark plug wires.

## ENGINE AND ENGINE OVERHAUL

6. Disconnect all cables from the throttle body.
7. Disconnect and tag all electrical connections from the throttle body and intake manifold.
8. Disconnect all vacuum lines and heater hoses.
9. Disconnect and plug the fuel lines.
10. Remove the breather from the camshaft carrier.
11. Remove the upper radiator support.
12. Disconnect the exhaust manifold from the turbocharger and disconnect the oxygen sensor.
13. Label and disconnect wiring at engine harness and thermostat housing.
14. Remove the timing belt.
15. Remove the camshaft carrier/cylinder head bolts in the reverse order of the installation sequence.

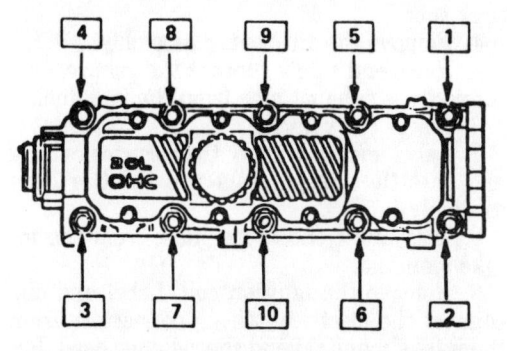

Cylinder Head/Camshaft Carrier Bolt Loosening Sequence—2.0L

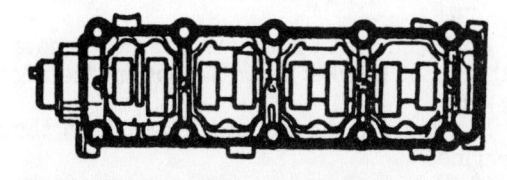

Applying Sealer to Camshaft Carrier—2.0L

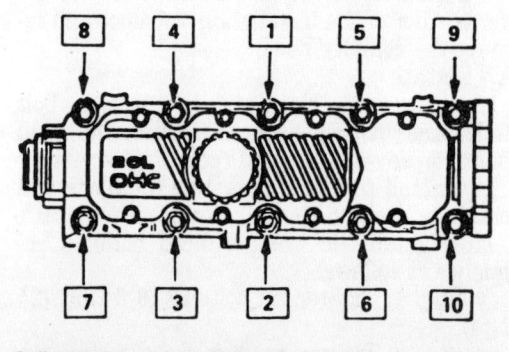

Cylinder Head/Camshaft Carrier Bolt Torque Sequence—2.0L

16. Remove camshaft carrier, rocker arms and valve lifters.
17. Remove cylinder head and manifolds as an assembly. Remove the head gasket.

**To install:**

18. Thoroughly clean and dry the mating surfaces and bolt holes. Apply a continuous bead of RTV sealant to the sealing surface of camshaft carrier.
19. Install a new head gasket and position the head on the engine block. Tighten the new head bolts in sequence as follows:
- Step 1 – Tighten to 18 ft. lbs. (25 Nm).
- Step 2 – Using a torque angle meter, tighten an additional 60 degrees.
- Step 3 – Tighten another additional 60 degrees.
- Step 4 – Tighten a third additional 60 degrees.
- Step 5 – Tighten and additional 30–50 degrees turn after engine warm up.

20. Install the rear cover and timing belt.
21. Connect all wiring to the engine harness and thermostat housing.
22. Install the exhaust manifold to turbo connection and connect the oxygen sensor.
23. Install the upper radiator support.
24. Install the breather on the camshaft carrier.
25. Connect all vacuum and fuel lines.
26. Connect the heater hoses.
27. Connect all electrical connectors to the throttle body and intake manifold.
28. Connect all cables to the throttle body.
29. Install the distributor and spark plug wires, aligning the matchmarks.
30. Install the ignition coil.
31. Install the alternator and bracket.
32. Fill all fluids to their proper levels.
33. Connect the battery cable, start the engine and check for leaks.
34. Tighten all head bolts another additional 30–50 degrees, in sequence, after full engine warm up.

### 2.3L Engine

1. Relieve the fuel system pressure. Disconnect the negative battery cable and drain cooling system.
2. Disconnect heater inlet and throttle body heater hoses from water outlet. Disconnect the upper radiator hose from the water outlet.
3. Remove the exhaust manifold.
4. Remove the intake and exhaust camshaft housings.
5. Remove the oil cap and dipstick. Pull oil fill tube upward to unseat from block.
6. Label and disconnect the injector harness electrical connector.

# ENGINE AND ENGINE OVERHAUL

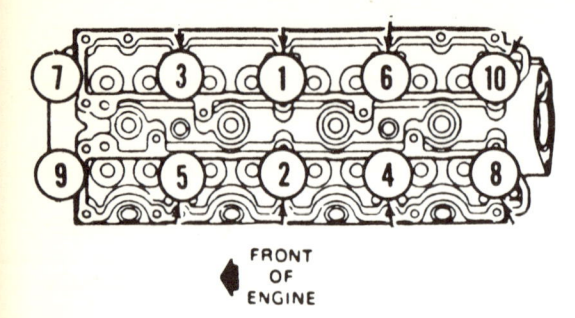

**2.3L Cylinder Head Bolt Torque Sequence**

7. Disconnect the throttle body air intake duct. Disconnect the cables and bracket and position aside.
8. Remove the throttle body from the intake manifold.
9. Matchmark and disconnect the vacuum hose from intake manifold.
10. Remove intake manifold bracket to block bolt.
11. Disconnect the coolant sensor connectors.
12. Remove the cylinder head bolts in reverse order of the installation sequence.
13. Remove the cylinder head and gasket. Inspect the oil flow check valve for freedom of movement.

**To install:**

14. Thoroughly clean and dry all bolts, bolt holes and mating surfaces. Inspect the head bolts for any damage and replace, if necessary.
15. Install the cylinder head gasket to the cylinder block and carefully position the cylinder head in place.
16. Coat the head bolt threads with clean engine oil and allow the oil to drain off before installing.
17. On 1988–89 engines, tighten the cylinder head bolts in sequence as follows:
   - Step 1 — Tighten all head bolts to 26 ft. lbs. (35 Nm).
   - Step 2 — Using a torque angle meter, tighten the short bolts an additional 80 degrees and the long bolts an additional 90 degrees.
18. On 1990–92 engines, tighten the cylinder head bolts in sequence as follows:
   - Step 1 — Tighten all head bolts to 26 ft. lbs. (35 Nm).
   - Step 2 — Using a torque angle meter, tighten the short bolts an additional 100 degrees and the long bolts an additional 110 degrees.
19. Install the intake manifold bracket.
20. Connect the MAP sensor vacuum hose to the intake manifold.
21. Install the throttle body to the intake manifold.
22. Connect the throttle body air intake duct. Install the throttle cable and bracket.
23. Connect the injector harness electrical connector.
24. Connect the 2 coolant sensor connections.
25. Install the oil cap and dipstick. Install the oil fill tube into the block.
26. Install the exhaust and intake camshaft housings.
27. Install the exhaust manifold.
28. Connect the heater inlet and throttle body heater hoses to the water outlet. Connect the upper radiator hose to the water outlet.
29. Fill all fluids to their proper levels.
30. Connect the battery cable, start the engine and check for leaks.

## 2.5L Engine

1. Relieve the fuel system pressure.
2. Disconnect the negative battery cable.
3. Drain the coolant and remove the oil dipstick tube.
4. Remove the air cleaner assembly.
5. Raise and safely support the vehicle. Disconnect the exhaust pipe from the manifold.
6. Lower the vehicle.
7. Label and disconnect the electrical wiring and throttle linkage from the throttle body assembly.
8. Disconnect the heater hose from the intake manifold.
9. Remove the ignition coil. Label and disconnect the electrical wiring connectors from the intake manifold and the cylinder head. Remove the alternator.
10. If equipped with a top-mounted air conditioning compressor, remove the compressor and lay it aside.
11. If equipped with power steering, remove the upper bracket from the power steering pump.
12. Remove the radiator hoses from the engine.
13. Remove the valve cover. Label and remove the rocker arms and pushrods.
14. Remove the cylinder head bolts in reverse order of the installation sequence and remove the cylinder head.

**To install:**

15. Thoroughly clean and dry all bolts, bolt holes and mating surfaces. Inspect the head bolts for any damage and replace if necessary.
16. Install the head gasket to the block and carefully position the cylinder head in place.
17. Tighten the cylinder head bolts in sequence as follows:
   - Step 1: Tighten all bolts to 18 ft. lbs. (25 Nm).
   - Step 2: Tighten to 26 ft. lbs. (35 Nm), except front bolt/stud.

# ENGINE AND ENGINE OVERHAUL 123

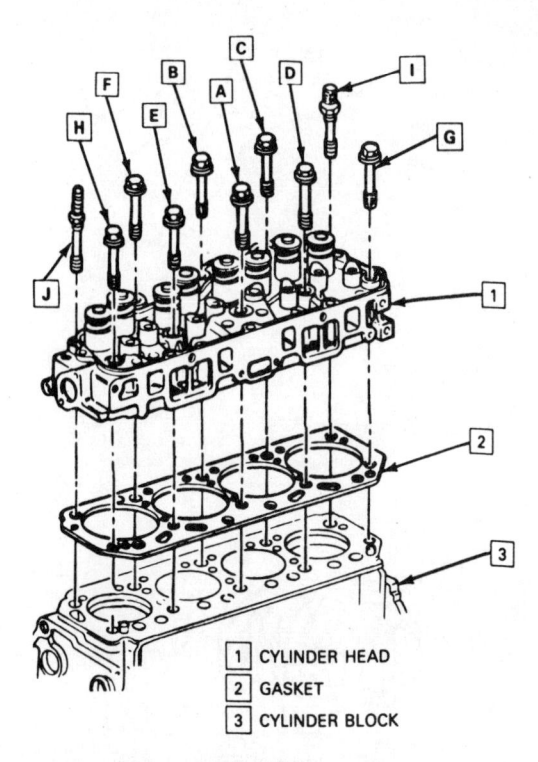

**2.5L Cylinder Head Assembly**

1. CYLINDER HEAD
2. GASKET
3. CYLINDER BLOCK

- Step 3: Tighten front bolt/stud to 18 ft. lbs. (25 Nm).
- Step 4: Using a torque angle meter, tighten all bolts an additional 90 degrees.

18. Install the pushrods and rocker arms in their original positions. Install the valve cover with a new gasket.
19. Install the radiator hoses. Install the power steering pump and upper bracket.
20. Install the air conditioning compressor, if removed.
21. Install the ignition coil and connect the electrical wiring connectors to the intake manifold and the cylinder head.
22. Install the alternator.
23. Install the heater hose to the intake manifold.
24. Connect the electrical wiring and throttle linkage to the throttle body assembly.
25. Raise and safely support the vehicle.
26. Install the exhaust pipe to the manifold.
27. Install the air cleaner assembly.
28. Adjust all belt tensions and fill all fluids to their proper levels.
29. Connect the battery cable, start the engine and check for leaks.

**3.0L and 3.3L Engines**

1. Relieve the fuel system pressure.
2. Disconnect the negative battery cable and drain the coolant.
3. Remove the mass air flow sensor and the air intake duct.
4. Remove ignition module and wiring.
5. Remove the serpentine drive belt, the alternator and bracket.
6. Label and remove all necessary vacuum lines and electrical connections.
7. Remove the fuel lines, the fuel rail and the spark plug wires.
8. Remove the heater/radiator hoses from the throttle body and intake manifold. Remove the cooling fan and the radiator.
9. Remove the intake manifold.
10. Remove the valve covers. Label and remove the rocker arms, pedestals and pushrods.

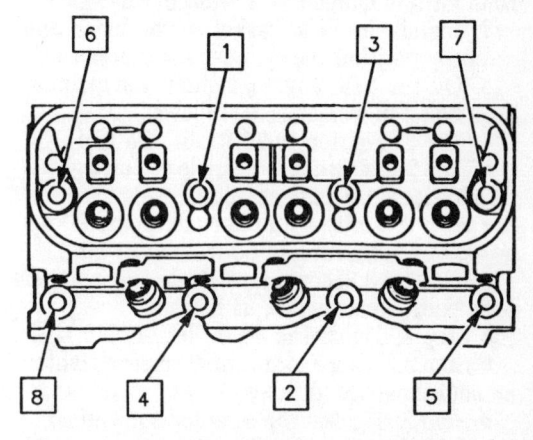

**3.0L and 3.3L Cylinder Head Torque Sequence**

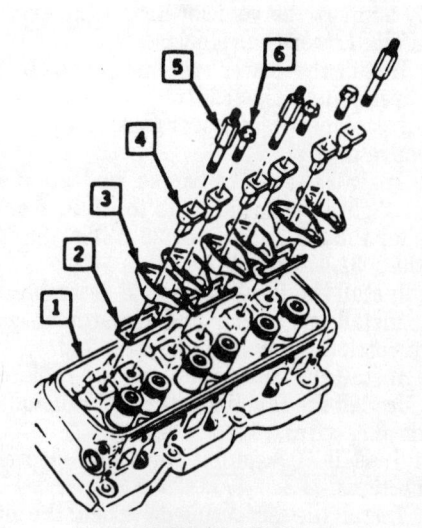

1. CYLINDER HEAD
2. PEDESTAL RETAINER
3. ROCKER ARM
4. PEDESTAL
5. DOUBLE ENDED BOLT
   60 N·m (45 LBS. FT.)
6. 60 N·m (45 LBS. FT.)

**3.0L Cylinder Head Assembly**

## 124 ENGINE AND ENGINE OVERHAUL

11. Remove the left side exhaust manifold.
12. Remove the power steering pump. Remove the dipstick and dipstick tube.
13. Remove the left side head bolts in reverse order of the installation sequence and lift the left cylinder head from the engine.
14. Raise and safely support the vehicle. Remove the right exhaust manifold-to-engine bolts.
15. Remove the right cylinder head-to-engine bolts in reverse of the installation sequence and lift the right cylinder head from the engine.

**To install:**
16. Thoroughly clean and dry all bolts, bolt holes and mating surfaces. Inspect the head bolts for any damage and replace if necessary.
17. Install the head gasket to the block and carefully position the cylinder head in place.
18. On the 3.0L engine, tighten the cylinder head bolts, in sequence, as follows:
 - Step 1: Tighten to 25 ft. lbs. (34 Nm).
 - Step 2: Using a torque angle meter, tighten an additional 90 degrees.
 - Step 3: Tighten another additional 90 degrees, to a maximum of 60 ft. lbs. (81 Nm).
19. On the 3.3L engine, tighten the cylinder head bolts, in sequence, as follows:
 - Step 1: Tighten to 35 ft. lbs. (47 Nm).
 - Step 2: Using a torque angle meter, tighten an additional 130 degrees.
 - Step 3: Tighten the 4 center bolts an additional 30 degrees.
20. Install the intake manifold. Raise and safely support the vehicle. Install the exhaust manifold. Lower the vehicle.
21. Install the power steering pump. Install the dipstick and dipstick tube.
22. Install new valve cover gaskets and install the valve covers.
23. Install the rocker arms, pedestals and bolts. Tighten pedestal bolts to 43 ft. lbs. (58 Nm) for the 3.0L engine or 28 ft. lbs. (38 Nm) for the 3.3L engine.
24. Install the intake manifold assembly.
25. Install the heater and radiator hoses to the throttle body and intake manifold.
26. Install the cooling fan and the radiator.
27. Install the fuel lines, the fuel rail and the spark plug wires.
28. Install all vacuum lines and electrical connections.
29. Install the serpentine drive belt, the alternator and bracket.
30. Install the ignition module and wiring.
31. Install the mass air flow sensor and the air intake duct.
32. Fill all fluids to their proper levels.
33. Connect the battery cable, start the engine and check for leaks.

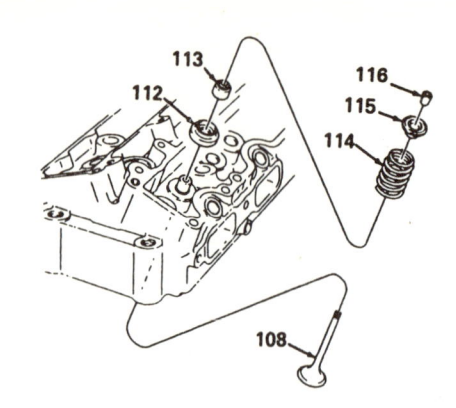

2.3L Valve Assembly

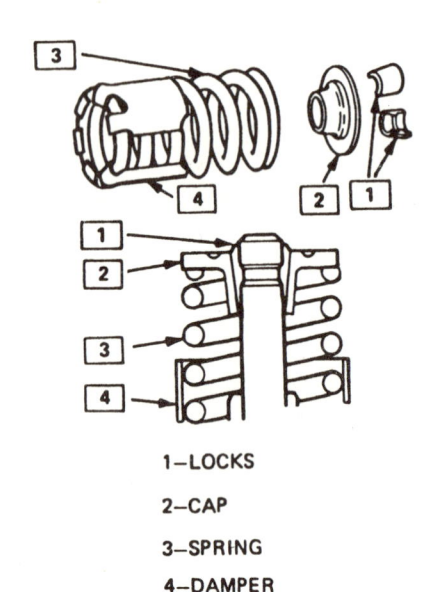

2.5L Upper Valve Assembly

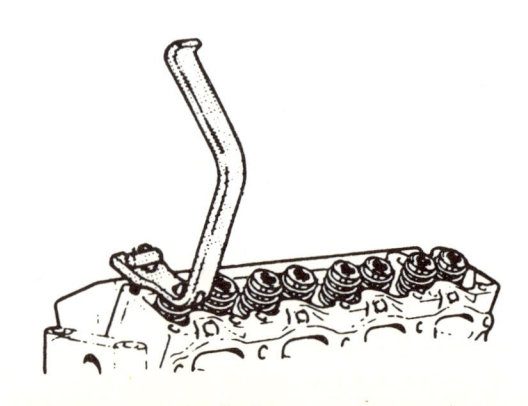

1—LOCKS
2—CAP
3—SPRING
4—DAMPER

Compressing Valve Springs

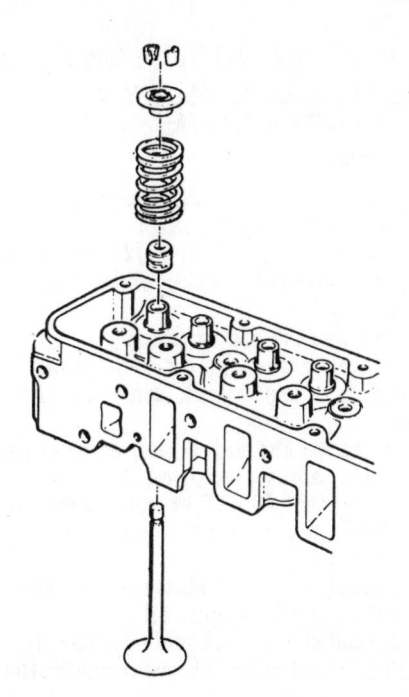

# ENGINE AND ENGINE OVERHAUL 125

**3.0L and 3.3L Valve Assembly**

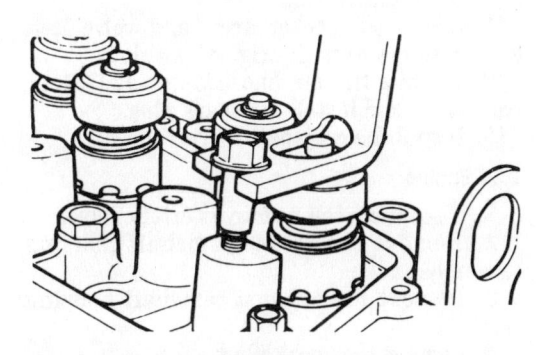

**Compressing Valve Springs**

## Valves

### REMOVAL AND INSTALLATION

1. Disconnect the negative battery cable.
2. Remove the cylinder head and gasket as previously outlined.
3. Using a valve spring compressing tool, compress the valve spring and remove the valve keys.
4. Remove the retainer and spring.
5. Remove the valve seal, using tool J36017 or equivalent.
6. Remove the rotator and the valve.

NOTE: *Make sure to keep all valve train components together and in order so that they may be reinstalled to their original position.*

**To install:**

7. Install the valve and rotator.
8. Install the valve seal and properly seat it, using tool J36007 or equivalent.
9. Install the spring and the retainer.
10. Using a valve spring compressing tool, compress the valve spring and install the valve keys.
11. Install cylinder head and gasket.
12. Connect the negative battery cable.

### INSPECTION

1. Inspect the valve stem tip for wear.
2. Inspect the lock/keeper grooves for chipping or wear. Replace the valve if chipped or severely worn.
3. Inspect the valve face for burn marks or cracks.
4. Inspect the valve stem for burrs and scratches. Minor scratches can be removed with an oil stone.
5. Inspect the valve stem for straightness. Bent valves must be replaced.
6. Inspect the valve face for grooves. If excessively grooved, the valve must be replaced.
7. If grinding the valves, measure the valve margin when done. If the margin is less that the minimum, replace the valve.

### REFACING

NOTE: *All machine work should be performed by a competent, professional machine shop. Valve face angle is not always identical to valve seat angle.*

A minimum margin of $\frac{1}{32}$ in. (0.8mm) should

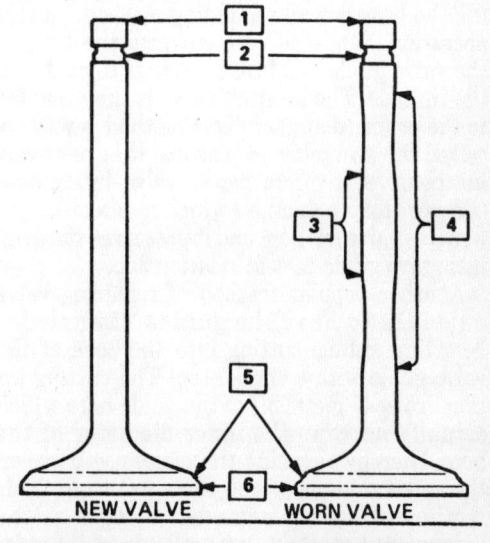

1—VALVE TIP
2—KEEPER GROOVE
3—STEM-LEAST WORN SECTION
4—STEM-MOST WORN SECTION
5—FACE
6—MARGIN

**Valve Inspection**

# ENGINE AND ENGINE OVERHAUL

remain after grinding the valve. The valve stem top should also be squared and resurfaced, by placing the stem in the V-block of the grinder, and turning it while pressing lightly against the grinding wheel. Be sure to chamfer the edge of the tip so that the squared edges don't dig into the rocker arm.

## LAPPING

This procedure should be performed after the valves and seats have been machined, to insure that each valve mates to each seat precisely.

1. Invert the cylinder head, lightly lubricate the valve stems, and install the valves in the head as numbered.
2. Coat valve seats with fine grinding compound, and attach the lapping tool suction cup to a valve head. Moisten the suction cup.
3. Rotate the tool between your palms, changing position and lifting the tool often to prevent grooving.
4. Lap the valve until a smooth, polished seat is evident.
5. Remove the valve and tool, and rinse away all traces of grinding compound.

## Valve Guide Service

The valve guides used in these engines are integral with the cylinder head, that is, they cannot be replaced. Refer to the previous "Valves — Removal and Installation" to check the valve guides for wear.

Valve guides are most accurately repaired using the bronze wall rebuilding method. In this operation, "threads" are cut into the bore of the valve guide and bronze wire is turned into the threads. The bronze "wall" is then reamed to the proper diameter. This method is well received for a number of reasons: it is relatively inexpensive, it offers better valve lubrication (the wire forms channels which retain oil), it offers less valve friction, and it preserves the original valve guide-to-seat relationship.

Another popular method of repairing valve guides is to have the guides "knurled." Knurling entails cutting into the bore of the valve guide with a special tool. The cutting action "raises" metal off of the guide bore which actually narrows the inner diameter of the bore, thereby reducing the clearance between the valve guide bore and the valve stem. This method offers the same advantages as the bronze wall method, but will generally wear faster.

Either of the above services must be performed by a professional machine shop which has the specialized knowledge and tools necessary to perform the service.

## Valve Springs and Valve Stem Seals

### REMOVAL AND INSTALLATION (WITH HEAD ON ENGINE)

**2.0L Engine**

1. Remove the camshaft carrier cover.
2. Remove the spark plugs.
3. Using air line adapter J22794 or equivalent, apply air pressure to cylinder to hold valve in place.
4. Remove the rocker arms.
5. Using valve spring compressing tool J33302-25 or equivalent, compress the valve spring.
6. Remove the valve lash compensators, valve locks, and valve spring.
7. Using tool J36017 or equivalent, remove the valve seal.

**To install:**

8. Install the plastic sleeve to the valve stem and lubricate with engine oil.
9. Install the new oil seal over the stem and install the seat over the valve guide. Remove the plastic sleeve.
10. Using tool J33302-25, install the valve springs, caps and locks.
11. Install the rocker arms and valve lash compensators to their original positions.
12. Remove the air line adapter J22794 or equivalent and install the spark plug.
13. Install the camshaft carrier cover.

**2.3L Engine**

1. Disconnect the negative battery cable.
2. Remove the intake camshaft housing assembly.
3. Remove the exhaust camshaft housing assembly.
4. Remove the spark plugs.
5. Using the proper adapter, apply continuous air pressure to the cylinder.
6. Using a valve spring compressing tool, compress the valve spring.
7. Remove the valve keys, retainer and spring.
8. Using tool J36017 or equivalent, remove the valve seal.
9. Remove the rotator assembly.

**To install:**

10. Install the rotator and a new valve seal, using tool J36007 or equivalent.
11. Install the spring and retainer.
12. Using a valve spring compressing tool, compress the valve spring and install the valve keys.
13. Remove the air pressure line and install the spark plugs.
14. Install the exhaust camshaft and housing.
15. Install the intake camshaft and housing.
16. Connect the negative battery cable.

# ENGINE AND ENGINE OVERHAUL

17. Start the car and inspect for any oil leakage.

### 3.0L and 3.3L Engine

1. Remove the negative battery cable.
2. Remove the valve cover.
3. Remove the rocker arm assemblies.
4. Remove the spark plugs.
5. Using an adaptor apply air pressure to the cylinder to hold the valve closed.
6. Using a valve spring compressing tool, compress the valve spring.
7. Remove the valve keys, retainer and spring.
8. Using tool J36017 or equivalent, remove the valve seal.

**To install:**
10. Install the new valve seal, using tool J36007 or equivalent.
11. Install the spring and retainer.
12. Using a valve spring compressing tool, compress the valve spring and install the valve keys.
13. Remove the air pressure line and install the spark plugs.
14. Install the spark plugs.
15. Install the rocker arm assemblies and the valve cover.
16. Connect the negative battery cable.

### *REMOVAL AND INSTALLATION (WITH HEAD OFF ENGINE)*

1. Using a valve spring compressing tool, compress the valve spring and remove the valve keys.
2. Remove the retainer and spring.
3. Remove the valve seal, using tool J36017 or equivalent.
4. Remove the rotator.

**To install:**
5. Install the rotator and install the valve seal, using tool J36007 or equivalent.
6. Install the spring and the retainer.
7. Using a valve spring compressing tool, compress the valve spring and install the valve keys.

## Valve Springs
### *INSPECTION*

1. Inspect the valve springs at their expanded height.
2. Inspect the spring ends, if not paralell, replace the spring.
3. Using tension tester tool J8056 or equivalent, check the spring tension. If not within specifications, replace the spring.

## Valve Lifters
### *REMOVAL AND INSTALLATION*

CAUTION: *When draining the coolant, keep in mind that cats and dogs are attracted by the ethylene glycol antifreeze, and are quite likely to drink any that is left in an uncovered container or in puddles on the ground. This will prove fatal in sufficient quantity. Always drain the coolant into a sealable container. Coolant should be reused unless it is contaminated or several years old.*

### 2.0L Engine

1. Disconnect the negative battery cable. Remove the camshaft carrier cover.
2. Hold the valves in place with compressed air, using an air adapter in the spark plug hole.
3. Compress the valve springs using a valve spring compressor.
4. Remove rocker arms; keep them in order for reassembly.
5. Remove the lifters.
6. The installation is the reverse of the removal procedure. Soak the lifters in clean engine oil prior to installation.

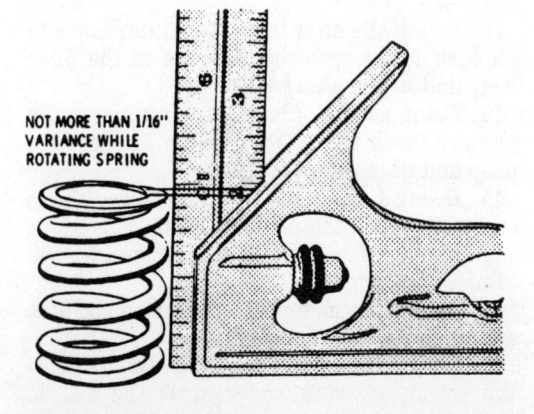

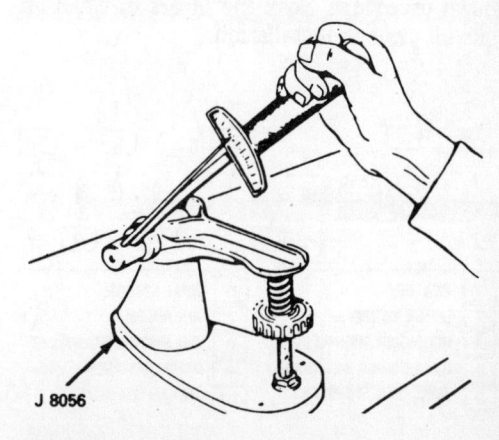

NOT MORE THAN 1/16" VARIANCE WHILE ROTATING SPRING

**Measuring Valve Springs**

J 8056

**Testing Valve Springs**

# ENGINE AND ENGINE OVERHAUL

7. Connect the negative battery cable and check the lifters for proper operation.

## 2.3L Engine

1. Disconnect the negative battery cable.
2. Remove the camshafts.
3. Remove the lifters from their bores.
4. The installation is the reverse of the removal procedure. Soak the lifters in clean engine oil prior to installation.
5. Connect the negative battery cable and check the lifters for proper operation.

## 2.5L Engine

1. Relieve the fuel system pressure.
2. Disconnect the negative battery cable.
3. Remove the valve cover and intake manifold.
5. Remove the side pushrod cover.
6. Loosen the rocker arms in pairs and rotate them in order to clear the pushrods.
7. Remove the pushrods, retainer and guide from each cylinder.
8. Remove the valve lifters.
9. The installation is the reverse of the removal procedure. Soak the lifters in clean engine oil prior to installation.
10. Connect the negative battery cable and check the lifters for proper operation.

## 3.0L and 3.3L Engines

1. Relieve the fuel system pressure.
2. Disconnect the negative battery terminal.
3. Disconnect and remove the fuel rail and the throttle body from the intake manifold.
4. Drain the cooling system.
5. Remove valve covers and the intake manifold.
6. Remove the rocker arms, pedestals and pushrods. Keep these components in order for accurate installation.
7. Remove the valve lifters.
8. The installation is the reverse of the removal procedure. Soak the lifters in clean engine oil prior to installation.

| 1 | ROLLER | 6 | BALL CHECK |
| 2 | LIFTER BODY | 7 | PLUNGER |
| 3 | PLUNGER SPRING | 8 | OIL METERING VALVE |
| 4 | BALL CHECK RETAINER | 9 | PUSH ROD SEAT |
| 5 | BALL CHECK SPRING | 10 | RETAINER RING |

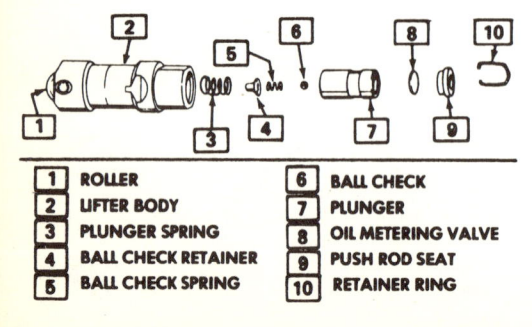

Roller Tappet Type Valve Lifter

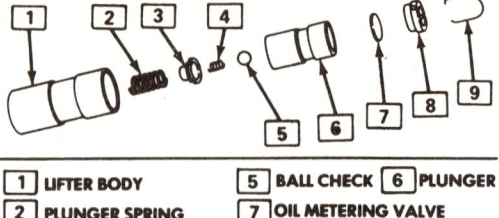

| 1 | LIFTER BODY | 5 | BALL CHECK | 6 | PLUNGER |
| 2 | PLUNGER SPRING | 7 | OIL METERING VALVE |
| 3 | BALL CHECK RETAINER | 8 | PUSH ROD SEAT |
| 4 | BALL CHECK SPRING | 9 | RETAINER RING    3B6A43 |

Flat Tappet Valve Lifter

9. Connect the negative battery cable and check the lifters for proper operation.

### OVERHAUL

1. Remove the push rod seat retainer by holding the plunger down and removing the reatiner with a small screwdriver.
2. Remove the push rod seat and the metering valve.
3. Remove the plunger. If plunger is stuck, tap the lifter upside down on a flat surface, if still stuck, soak in parts cleaning solvent.
4. Remove the ball check valve assembly.
5. Remove the plunger spring.
6. Clean lifter of all sludge and varnish build-up.
7. Inspect for excessive wear and scuffing. Replace if excessively worn or scuffed.
8. Inspect for flat spots on the bottom. If worn flat, replace the lifter.
9. If equipped with roller, inspect for freedom of movement, looseness, flat spots or pitting. If any detected, replace the lifter.
10. Install the check ball to the small hole in the bottom of the plunger.
11. Place ball retainer and spring over check ball and press into place using a small screwdriver.
12. Install the plunger spring over the ball retainer.
13. Install the lifter body over the spring and plunger. Make sure the oil holes in the lifter body and in the plunger line up.
14. Using a $\frac{1}{8}$ in. (3mm) drift pin, push the plunger down until the oil holes in the lifter body and plunger are aligned.
15. Insert a $\frac{1}{16}$ in. (1.6mm) pin through the oil holes to lock the plunger down.
16. Remove the $\frac{1}{8}$ in. (3mm) pin and fill the lifter with engine oil.
17. Install the metering valve, push rod seat and push rod seat retainer.
18. Push down on the push rod seat to relieve the spring pressure and remove the $\frac{1}{16}$ in. (1.6mm) pin.

# ENGINE AND ENGINE OVERHAUL 129

## Oil Pan

### REMOVAL AND INSTALLATION

#### 2.0L Engine

1. Disconnect the negative battery cable.
2. Raise and safely support the vehicle. Remove the right front wheel assembly and the splash shield.
3. Drain the engine oil.
4. Remove the exhaust pipe from the turbocharger.
5. Remove the flywheel inspection cover.
6. Remove the oil pan attaching bolts and remove the oil pan, scraper and gasket.
7. The installation is the reverse of the removal procedure. Use a new gasket and apply sealant at the 4 engine block seams. Use thread locking compound on the bolt threads and tighten to 4 ft. lbs. (6 Nm), starting from the middle and working outward.
8. Fill the crankcase with oil to specification.
9. Connect the negative battery cable and check for leaks.

#### 2.3L Engine

1. Disconnect the negative battery cable. Raise and safely support the vehicle.
2. Remove the flywheel inspection cover.
3. Remove the splash shield-to-suspension support bolt. Remove the exhaust manifold brace, if equipped.
4. Remove the radiator outlet pipe-to-oil pan bolt.
5. Remove the transaxle-to-oil pan nut and stud using a 7mm socket.

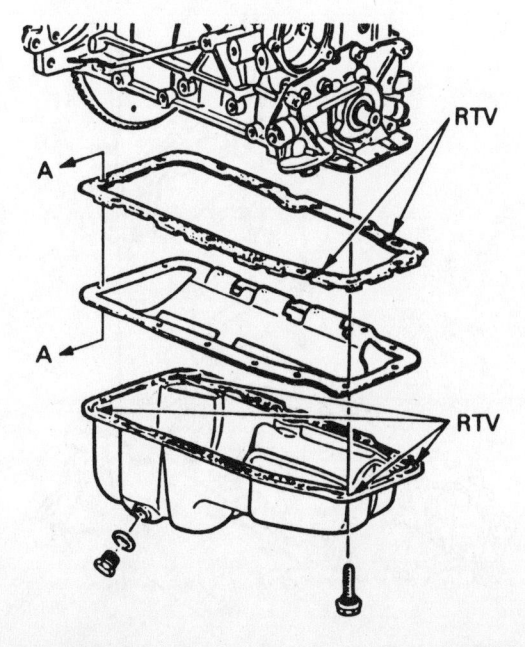

2.0L Oil Pan

2.3L Oil Pan Fasteners

6. Gently pry the spacer out from between oil pan and transaxle.
7. Remove the oil pan bolts. Rotate the crankshaft, if necessary, and remove the oil pan and gasket from the engine.
8. Inspect the silicone strips across the top of the aluminum carrier at the oil pan-cylinder block-seal housing 3-way joint. If damaged, these strips must be repaired with silicone sealer. Use only enough sealer to restore the strips to their original dimension; too much sealer could cause leakage.

**To install:**

9. Thoroughly clean and dry the mating surfaces, bolts and bolt holes. Install the oil pan with a new gasket; do not uses sealer on the gasket. Loosely install the pan bolts.
10. Place the spacer in its approximate installed position but allow clearance to tighten the pan bolt above it.
11. Tighten the pan to block bolts to 17 ft. lbs. (24 Nm) and the remaining bolts to 106 inch lbs. (12 Nm).
12. Install the spacer and stud.
13. Install the oil pan transaxle nut and bolt.
14. Install the slash shield to suspension support.
15. Install the radiator outlet pipe bolt.
16. Install the exhaust manifold brace, if removed.
17. Install the flywheel inspection cover.
18. Fill the crankcase with the proper oil.
19. Connect the negative battery cable and check for leaks.

#### 2.5L Engine

1. Disconnect the negative battery cable.
2. Raise and safely support the vehicle. Drain the engine oil.
3. Disconnect the exhaust pipe and hangers from the exhaust manifold and allow it to swing aside.
4. Disconnect electrical connectors from the starter. Remove the starter-to-engine bolts, the starter and the flywheel housing inspection cover from the engine.
5. Remove the oil pan-to-engine bolts and the oil pan.

# 130 ENGINE AND ENGINE OVERHAUL

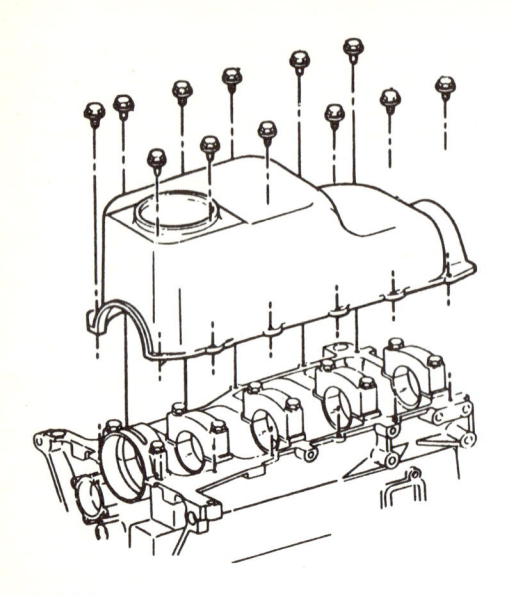

**2.5L Oil Pan**

**To install:**
6. Thoroughly clean the mating surfaces, bolts and bolt holes.
7. Apply sealant to the oil pan flange, surrounding all bolt holes. Also, apply sealant to the engine at the front and rear seams.
8. Install the oil pan and tighten the bolts to 20 ft. lbs. (27 Nm) for 1988 vehicles or 89 inch lbs. (10 Nm) for 1989–92 vehicles.
9. Install the flywheel housing cover and exhaust pipe.
10. Fill the crankcase with oil to specification.
11. Connect the negative battery cable and check for leaks.

### 3.0L and 3.3L Engines
1. Disconnect the negative battery cable.
2. Raise and safely support the vehicle.

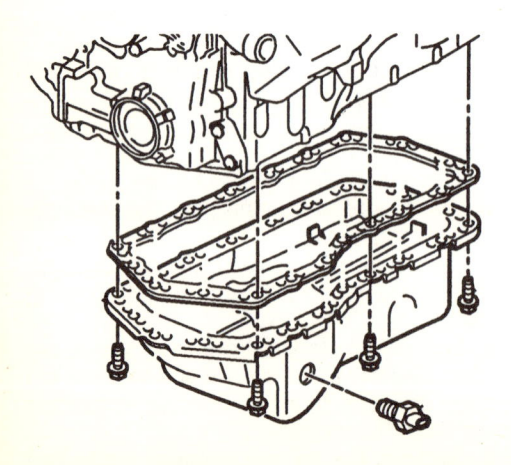

**3.0L and 3.3L Oil Pan**

3. Drain the engine oil and remove the oil filter.
4. Remove the flywheel cover and the starter.
5. Remove the oil pan, tensioner spring and formed rubber gasket.
6. The installation is the reverse of the removal procedure. Tighten the oil pan-to-engine bolts to 88 inch lbs. (10 Nm) for the 3.0L engine or 124 inch lbs. (14 Nm) for the 3.3L engine.
7. Fill the crankcase with the proper oil.
8. Connect the negative battery cable and check for leaks.

## Oil Pump

### REMOVAL AND INSTALLATION

#### 2.0L Engine
1. Disconnect negative battery cable.
2. Remove the timing belt and crankshaft sprocket.
3. Remove the rear timing belt cover.
4. Disconnect oil pressure sending unit connector.
5. Raise and safely support the vehicle.
6. Drain the engine oil.
7. Remove the oil pan and oil filter.
8. Remove the oil pump mounting bolts and remove the pump and pickup tube.

**To install:**
9. Prime the pump by pouring fresh oil into the pump intake and turning the driveshaft until oil comes out the pressure port. Repeat a few times until no air bubbles are present.

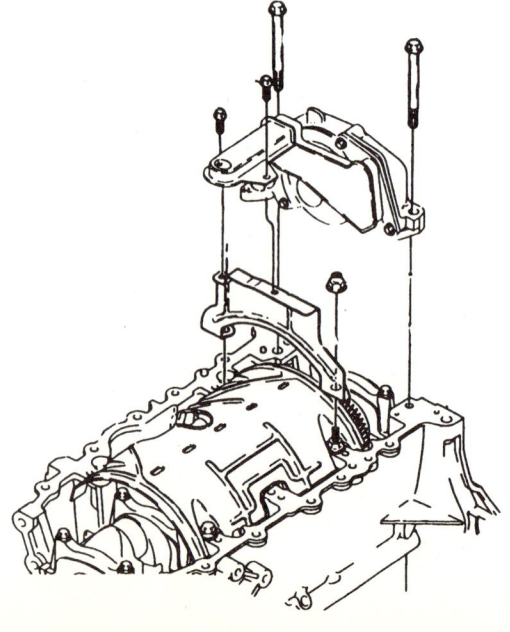

**Oil Pump to Block—2.3L**

# ENGINE AND ENGINE OVERHAUL

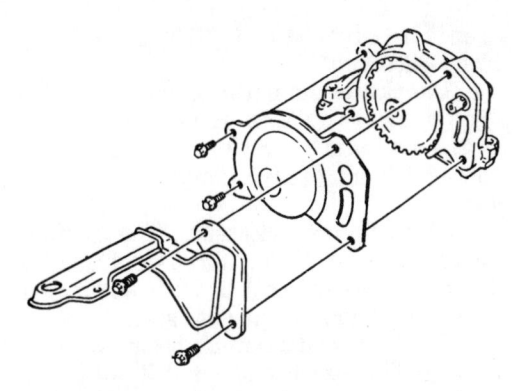

**2.3L Oil Pump Gear Cover and Screen**

10. The installation is the reverse of the removal procedure. Use a new gasket and seal and tighten the oil pump bolts to 5 ft. lbs. (7 Nm). Use a new ring for the pickup tube.
11. Fill the crankcase with the proper oil.
12. Connect the negative battery cable, check the oil pressure and check for leaks.

### 2.3L Engine

1. Disconnect the negative battery cable.
2. Raise and safely support the vehicle.
3. Drain the engine oil and remove the oil pan.
4. Remove the oil pump attaching bolts and nut.
5. Remove the oil pump assembly, shims if equipped, and screen.

**To install:**

6. With the oil pump assembly off the engine, remove 3 attaching bolts and separate the driven gear cover and screen assembly from the oil pump.
7. Install the oil pump on the block using the original shims, if equipped. Tighten the bolts to 33 ft. lbs. (45 Nm).
8. Mount a dial indicator assembly to measure backlash between oil pump to drive gear.
9. Record oil pump drive to driven gear backlash. Proper backlash is 0.010–0.018 in. (0.254–0.457mm). When measuring, do not allow the crankshaft to move.
10. If equipped with shims, remove shims to decrease clearance and add shims to increase clearance. If no shims were present, replace the assembly if proper backlash cannot be obtained.
11. When the proper clearance is reached, rotate crankshaft ½ turn and recheck clearance.
12. Remove oil pump from block, fill the cavity with petroleum jelly and reinstall driven gear cover and screen assembly to pump. Tighten the bolts to 106 inch lbs. (13 Nm).
13. Reinstall the pump assembly to the block. Tighten oil pump-to-block bolts 33 ft. lbs. (45 Nm).
14. Install the oil pan.
15. Fill the crankcase with the proper oil.
16. Connect the negative battery cable, check the oil pressure and check for leaks.

### 2.5L Engine

1. Disconnect the negative battery cable.
2. Drain the engine oil and remove the oil pan.
3. Remove the oil filter.
4. Remove the oil pump cover assembly.
5. Remove the gerotor pump gears.

CAUTION: *The pressure regulator valve spring is under pressure. Exercise caution when removing the pin or personal injury may result!*

6. Remove the pressure regulator pin, spring and valve.

**To install:**

7. Lubricate all internal parts with clean engine oil and fill all pump cavities with petroleum jelly.
8. Install the pressure regulator valve, spring and secure the pin.

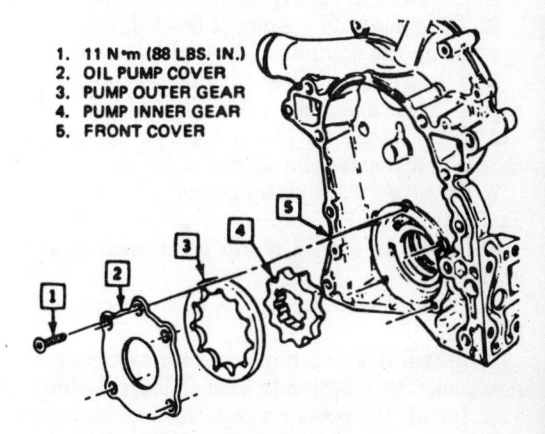

1. 11 N·m (88 LBS. IN.)
2. OIL PUMP COVER
3. PUMP OUTER GEAR
4. PUMP INNER GEAR
5. FRONT COVER

**3.0L and 3.3L Oil Pump and Housing**

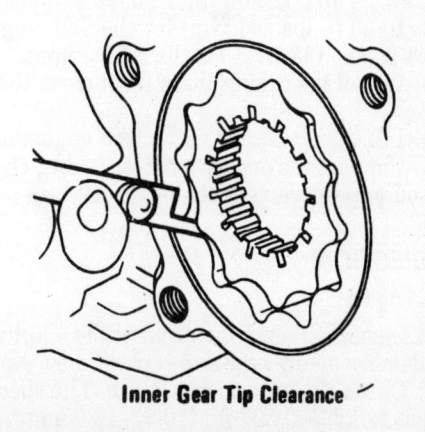

Inner Gear Tip Clearance

**Measuring Oil Pump Inner Gear Clearance**

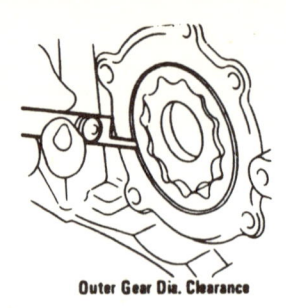

# 132 ENGINE AND ENGINE OVERHAUL

*Measuring Oil Pump Outer Gear Diameter Clearance*

9. Install the gerotor gears.
10. Install the pump cover and tighten the screws to 10 ft. lbs. (14 Nm).
11. Install the oil filter.
12. Install the oil pan.
13. Fill the crankcase with oil to specification.
14. Connect the negative battery cable, check the oil pressure and check for leaks.

### 3.0L and 3.3L Engines

1. Disconnect the negative battery cable.
2. Remove the timing chain front cover.
3. Raise and safely support the vehicle.
4. Drain the engine oil. Lower the vehicle.
5. Remove the oil filter adapter, the pressure regulator valve and the valve spring.
6. Remove the oil pump cover-to-oil pump screws and remove the cover.
7. Remove the oil pump gears.

**To install:**

8. Lubricate the oil pump gears with clean engine oil.
9. Pack the pump cavity with petroleum jelly.
10. Install the oil pump cover screws using a new gasket and tighten to 97 inch lbs. (11 Nm).
11. Install the pressure regulator spring and valve.
12. Install the oil filter adaptor using a new gasket. Tighten the oil filter adapter-to-engine bolts to 30 ft. lbs. (41 Nm) for the 3.0L engine or 24 ft. lbs. (33 Nm) for the 3.3L engine.
13. Install the timing chain front cover to the engine.
14. Fill the crankcase with clean engine oil.
15. Connect the negative battery cable, check the oil pressure and check for leaks.

### INSPECTION

#### 2.0L Engine

1. Inspect all components carefully for physical damage of any type and replace worn parts.
2. Check the gear pocket depth. The specification is 0.395–0.397 in. (10.03–10.08mm).
3. Check the gear pocket diameter. The specification is 3.230–3.235 in. (82.02–82.15mm).
4. Check the diameter of the gears. The specifications are 0.014–0.018 in. (0.35–0.45mm) for the drive gear and 0.004–0.007 in. (0.11–0.19mm) for the idler gear.
5. Check the side clearance. The specifications are 2.317–2.319 in. (58.85–58.90mm) for the drive gear and 3.225–3.227 in. (81.91–81.96mm) for the idler gear.
6. Check the end clearance below the pump housing. The specification is 0.001–0.004 in. (0.03–0.10mm).

#### 2.3L Engine

1. Inspect all components carefully for physical damage of any type and replace worn parts.
2. Check the gerotor cavity depth. The specification for 1988 is 0.689–0.691 in. (17.50–17.55mm). The specification for 1989–92 is 0.674–0.676 in. (17.11–17.16mm).
3. Check the gerotor cavity diameter. The specification for 1988 is 2.010–2.012 in. (51.054–51.104mm). The specification for 1989–92 is 2.127–2.129 in. (53.95–54.00mm).
4. Check the inner gerotor tip clearance. The maximum clearance is 0.006 in. (15mm).
5. Check the outer gerotor diameter clearance. The specification is 0.010–0.014 in. (0.254–0.354mm).

#### 2.5L Engine

1. Inspect all components carefully for physical damage of any type and replace worn parts.
2. Check the gerotor cavity depth. The specification for 1988 is 0.995–0.998 in. (25.27–25.35mm). The specification for 1989–92 is 0.514–0.516 in. (13.05–13.10mm).
3. Check the gear lash. The specification is 0.009–0.015 in. (0.23–0.38mm).
4. Check the clearance of both gears. The maximum clearance is 0.004 in. (0.10mm).

#### 3.0L and 3.3L Engines

1. Inspect all components carefully for physical damage of any type and replace worn parts.
2. Check the gear pocket depth. The specification is 0.461–0.463 in. (11.71–11.75mm).
3. Check the gear pocket diameter. The specification is 3.508–3.512 in. (89.10–89.20mm).
4. Check the inner gear tip clearance. The maximum clearance is 0.006 in. (0.152mm).
5. Check the outer gear diameter clearance. The specification is 0.008–0.015 in. (0.025–0.089mm).

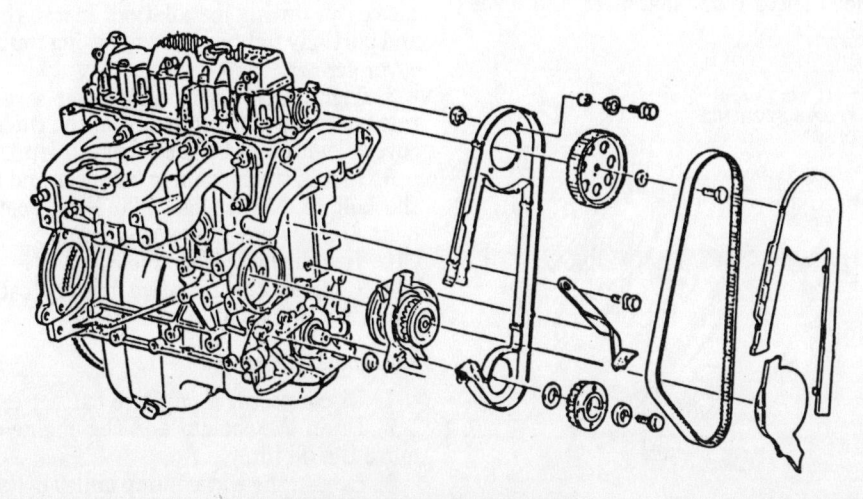

# ENGINE AND ENGINE OVERHAUL

## OVERHAUL

1. Remove the oil pan or front engine cover to gain access to the oil pump as previously described.
2. Remove the oil pump cover.
3. Remove the oil pump gears.
4. Remove the cotter pin or unscrew the plug from the pressure regulator valve bore and then remove the the spring and pressure regulator valve.

CAUTION: *The pressure regulator valve spring is under tension. Use extreme caution when removing the cotter pin or unscrewing the plug or bodily injury may result.*

5. Soak all oil pump parts in carburetor cleaning solvent to remove sludge, oil and varnish build-up.
6. Check the pump housing for cracks, scoring, damaged threads or casting flaws.
7. Check the oil pump gears for chipping, galling or wear and replace if necessary.
8. Install the gears to the oil pump housing and check clearances.
9. Lubricate all oil pump parts with clean engine oil and pack all oil pump cavities with petroleum jelly before final assembly to insure oil pump priming.
10. Install oil pump cover and screws. Torque screws to 97 inch lbs.
11. Install pressure regulator spring and valve.
12. Install oil filter adapter with new gasket and install front engine cover.

## Crankshaft Dampener

### REMOVAL AND INSTALLATION

1. Properly raise and support the vehicle.
2. Remove the crankshaft dampener bolt and washer.
3. Remove the dampener and key.
4. Installation is the reverse of the removal procedure.
5. Tighten the dampener bolt to proper torque specifications.

## Timing Belt Front Cover

### REMOVAL AND INSTALLATION

#### 2.0L Engine

1. Disconnect negative battery cable.
2. Remove tensioner and bolt.
3. Remove serpentine belt.
4. Unsnap upper and lower cover.
5. The installation is the reverse of the removal procedure.

#### Oil Seal Replacement

1. Disconnect the negative battery cable.
2. Remove the timing belt sprockets and the inner cover. Remove the crankshaft key and thrust washer.

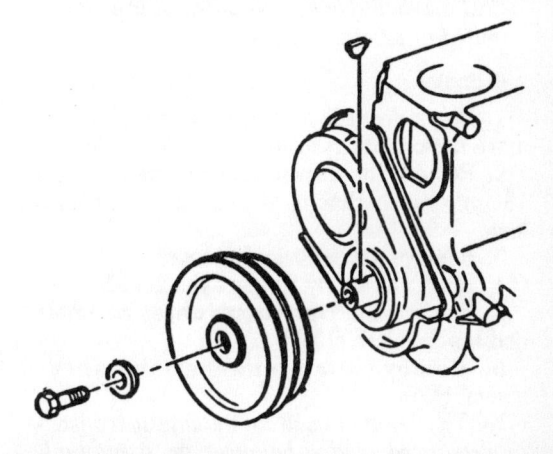

**Crankshaft Dampener**

**1988 2.0L Timing Belt Assembly**

# ENGINE AND ENGINE OVERHAUL

3. Using a small prybar, pry out the old oil seal.

NOTE: *Use care to avoid damage to seal bore and crankshaft.*

4. Thoroughly clean and dry the oil seal mounting surface.

5. Use the appropriate installation tool and drive the oil seal into the front cover.

6. The installation is the reverse of the removal procedure.

7. Connect the negative battery cable and check for leaks.

## Timing Chain Front Cover

### REMOVAL AND INSTALLATION

CAUTION: *When draining the coolant, keep in mind that cats and dogs are attracted by the ethylene glycol antifreeze, and are quite likely to drink any that is left in an uncovered container or in puddles on the ground. This will prove fatal in sufficient quantity. Always drain the coolant into a sealable container. Coolant should be reused unless it is contaminated or several years old.*

**2.3L Engine**

1. Disconnect the negative battery cable. Remove the coolant recovery reservoir.

2. Remove the serpentine drive belt using a 13mm wrench that is at least 24 in. (61cm) long.

3. Remove upper cover fasteners.

4. Raise and safely support the vehicle.

5. Remove the right front wheel assembly and lower splash shield.

6. Remove the crankshaft balancer assembly.

NOTE: *Do not install an automatic transaxle-equipped engine balancer on a manual-transaxle equipped engine or vice-versa.*

7. Remove lower cover fasteners and lower the vehicle.

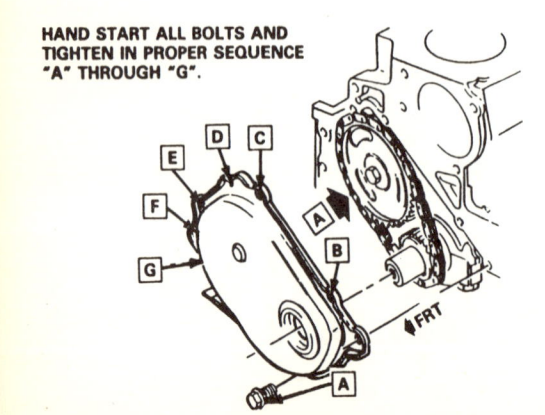

**HAND START ALL BOLTS AND TIGHTEN IN PROPER SEQUENCE "A" THROUGH "G".**

**2.5L Timing Chain Front Cover**

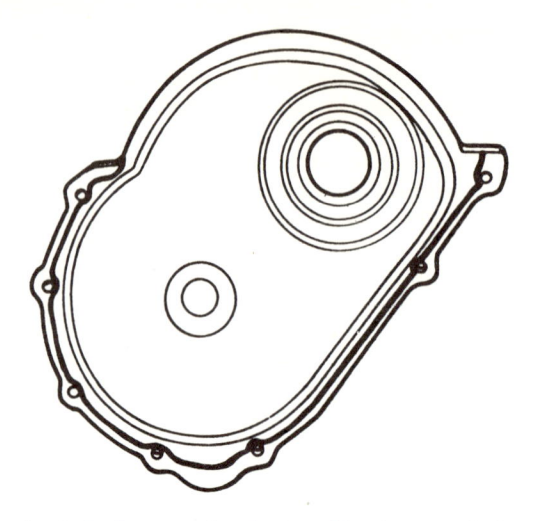

**Apply Sealer around perimeter of front cover—2.5L**

8. Remove the front cover.

9. The installation is the reverse of the removal procedure. Tighten the balancer attaching bolt to 74 ft. lbs. (100 Nm).

**1990–92 2.5L ENGINE**

1. Disconnect the negative battery cable.

2. Remove the belts. Remove the power steering pump mounting bolts and position it aside.

3. Raise and safely support the vehicle. Remove the inner fender splash shield.

4. Remove the crankshaft dampener.

5. Remove the timing chain cover-to-engine bolts and the timing case cover.

**To install:**

6. Thoroughly clean and dry all mating surfaces. Use RTV sealant to seal all mating surfaces.

7. A centering tool fits over the crankshaft seal and is used to correctly position the timing case cover during installation. Install the cover and partially tighten the 2 opposing timing case cover screws.

8. Tighten the remaining cover screws and remove the centering tool from the timing case cover. Tighten to 89 inch lbs. (10 Nm).

9. Install the harmonic balancer and tighten the bolt to 162 ft. lbs. (220 Nm). Install the belts and the power steering pump.

10. Install the splash shield.

11. Connect the negative battery cable and check for leaks.

**3.0L and 3.3L Engines**

1. Disconnect the negative battery cable.

2. Drain the coolant and the engine oil. Remove the oil filter.

3. Loosen the water pump pulley bolts but do not remove them. Remove the serpentine drive

## ENGINE AND ENGINE OVERHAUL 135

belt and the pulley. Remove the water pump-to-engine bolts and the water pump.

4. Raise and safely support the vehicle. Remove the right front wheel assembly and the right inner fender splash shield.
5. Remove the crankshaft harmonic balancer and the crankshaft sensor.
6. Remove the radiator and heater hoses.
7. Remove the timing case cover-to-engine bolts, the timing case cover and the gasket.
8. Clean the gasket mounting surfaces. Replace the front oil seal.
9. The installation is the reverse of the removal procedure. Coat all timing case cover bolts with thread sealer prior to installation.
10. Fill all fluids to their proper levels.
11. Connect the negative battery cable and check for leaks.

## Timing Gear Front Cover

### REMOVAL AND INSTALLATION

#### 1988–89 2.5L ENGINE

1. Disconnect the negative battery cable.
2. Remove the belts.
3. Raise and safely support the vehicle. Remove the inner fender splash shield.
4. Remove the harmonic balancer.
5. Remove the cover-to-engine bolts and the timing cover.

**To install:**

6. Thoroughly clean and dry all mating surfaces. Use RTV sealant to seal all mating surfaces.
7. A centering tool fits over the crankshaft seal and is used to correctly position the timing case cover during installation. Install the cover and partially tighten the 2 opposing timing case cover screws.
8. Tighten the remaining cover screws and remove the centering tool from the timing case cover. Final torque of all screws should be 89 inch lbs. (10 Nm).
9. Install the harmonic balancer and tighten the bolt to 162 ft. lbs. (220 Nm). Install the belts and the power steering pump.
10. Install the splash shield.
11. Connect the negative battery cable and check for leaks.

## Front Cover Oil Seal

### REPLACEMENT

1. Disconnect the negative battery cable.
2. Remove the front cover.
3. Using a small prybar, pry out the old oil seal.

NOTE: *Use care to avoid damage to seal bore or seal contact surfaces.*

4. Thoroughly clean and dry the oil seal mounting surface.
5. Use the appropriate installation tool and drive the oil seal into the front cover.
6. Lubricate balancer and seal lip with clean engine oil.
7. The installation is the reverse of the removal procedure.
8. Connect the negative battery cable and check for leaks.

## Timing Belt and Tensioner

Timing belts are made of rubber and do wear out. It is recommended that the belt be replaced after approximately 60,000 miles. Failure to do so may result in a broken belt which could cause further engine damage.

### REMOVAL AND INSTALLATION

#### 2.0L Engine

#### 1988

1. Disconnect the negative battery cable.
2. Remove the timing belt cover.
3. Remove the crankshaft pulley.
4. Remove the coolant reservoir.
5. Loosen the water pump mounting bolts and remove the timing belt.

**To install:**

6. Position the camshaft so the mark on its sprocket aligns with the mark on the rear timing belt cover.
7. Position the crankshaft so the mark on the pulley aligns with 10 degrees BTDC on the timing scale.
8. Install the timing belt.
9. Adjust the timing belt using tools J–26486–A and J–33039 to adjust the water pump. Increase the tension — with the gauge installed — to within the band on the gauge will ensure an initial over-tensioning.
10. Crank the engine without starting it about 10 revolutions; a substantial tension loss should occur.
11. Recheck the tension with the gauge. If a tension increase is needed, remove the gauge and adjust the water pump. Repeat until the tension is within specification.

NOTE: *Do not increase tension with the gauge installed or the resulting tension will be inaccurate.*

12. After the proper tension has been reached, tighten the water pump bolts to 19 ft. lbs. (25 Nm).
13. Install the timing belt cover and all related parts.
14. Install the coolant reservoir.
15. Connect the negative battery cable and road test the vehicle.

#### 1989

1. Disconnect the negative battery cable.
2. Remove the timing belt cover.

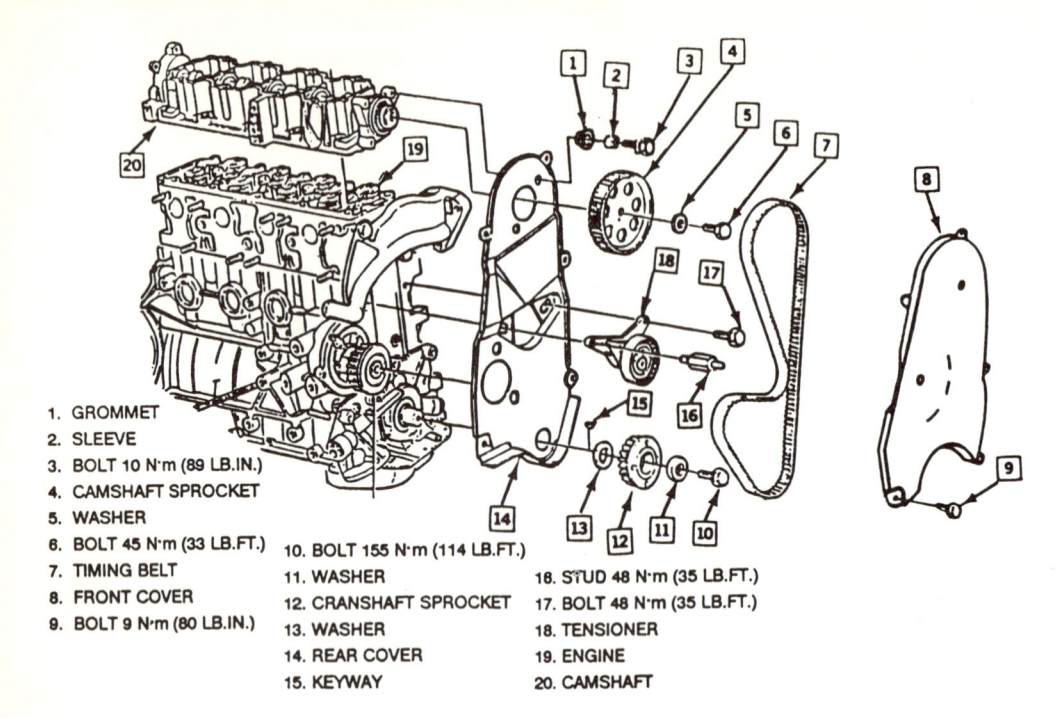

# ENGINE AND ENGINE OVERHAUL

1. GROMMET
2. SLEEVE
3. BOLT 10 N·m (89 LB.IN.)
4. CAMSHAFT SPROCKET
5. WASHER
6. BOLT 45 N·m (33 LB.FT.)
7. TIMING BELT
8. FRONT COVER
9. BOLT 9 N·m (80 LB.IN.)
10. BOLT 155 N·m (114 LB.FT.)
11. WASHER
12. CRANSHAFT SPROCKET
13. WASHER
14. REAR COVER
15. KEYWAY
16. STUD 48 N·m (35 LB.FT.)
17. BOLT 48 N·m (35 LB.FT.)
18. TENSIONER
19. ENGINE
20. CAMSHAFT

**1989 2.0L Timiing Belt Assembly**

3. Remove the crankshaft pulley.
4. Loosen the water pump mounting bolts and relieve the tension using tool J–33039.
5. Remove the timing belt.

**To install:**

6. Position the camshaft and crankshaft so the marks on their sprockets aligns with the marks on the rear cover.
7. Install the timing belt so the portion between the camshaft and crankshaft has no slack.
8. Adjust the timing belt using tool J–33039 to turn the water pump eccentric clockwise until the tensioner contacts the high torque stop. Temporarily tighten the water to prevent movement.
9. Turn the engine 2 revolutions to fully seat the belt into the gear teeth.
10. Turn the water pump eccentric counterclockwise until the hole in the tensioner arm is aligned with the hole in the base.
11. Tighten the water pump bolts to 19 ft. lbs. (25 Nm), making sure the tensioner hole remains aligned as in Step 10.
12. Install the timing belt cover and all related parts.
13. Install the crankshaft pulley.
14. Install the timing belt cover and all related parts.
15. Connect the negative battery cable and road test the vehicle.

## Timing Chain and Sprockets
### REMOVAL AND INSTALLATION

CAUTION: *When draining the coolant, keep in mind that cats and dogs are attracted by the ethylene glycol antifreeze, and are quite likely to drink any that is left in an uncovered container or in puddles on the ground. This will prove fatal in sufficient quantity. Always drain the coolant into a sealable container. Coolant should be reused unless it is contaminated or several years old.*

**2.3L Engine**

NOTE: *It is recommended that the entire procedure be reviewed before attempting to service the timing chain.*

1. Disconnect the negative battery cable.
2. Remove the front timing chain cover and crankshaft oil slinger.
3. Rotate the crankshaft clockwise, as viewed from front of engine (normal rotation) until the camshaft sprocket's timing dowel pin holes align with the holes in the timing chain housing. The mark on the crankshaft sprocket should align with the mark on the cylinder block. The crankshaft sprocket keyway should point upwards and align with the centerline of the cylinder bores. This is the normal timed position.
4. Remove the 3 timing chain guides.

# ENGINE AND ENGINE OVERHAUL 137

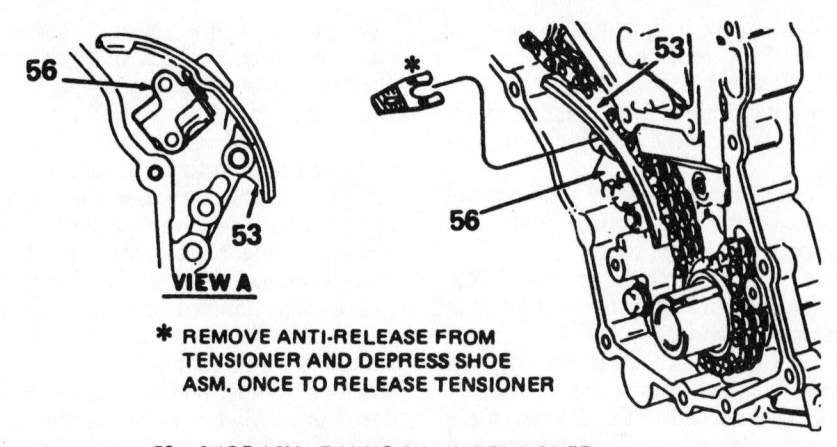

* REMOVE ANTI-RELEASE FROM TENSIONER AND DEPRESS SHOE ASM. ONCE TO RELEASE TENSIONER

53. SHOE ASM., TIMING CHAIN TENSIONER
56. TENSIONER, TIMING CHAIN

**2.3L Timing Chain Tensioner Spring and Retainer**

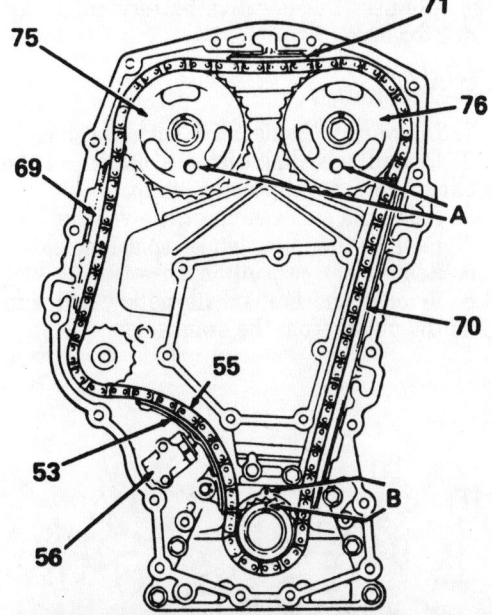

A. CAMSHAFT TIMING ALIGNMENT PIN LOCATIONS
B. CRANKSHAFT GEAR TIMING MARKS
53. SHOE ASM. TIMING CHAIN TENSIONER
55. TIMING CHAIN
56. TENSIONER, TIMING CHAIN
69. GUIDE – R.H. TIMING CHAIN
70. GUIDE – L.H. TIMING CHAIN
71. GUIDE – UPPER TIMING CHAIN
75. SPROCKET, EXHAUST CAMSHAFT
76. SPROCKET, INTAKE CAMSHAFT

**2.3L Timing Chain**

5. Raise and safely support the vehicle.
6. Gently pry off timing chain tensioner spring retainer and remove spring.
   NOTE: *Two styles of tensioner are used. Early production engines will have a spring post and late production ones will not. Both styles are identical in operation and are interchangeable.*
7. Remove the timing chain tensioner shoe retainer.
8. Make sure all the slack in the timing chain is above the tensioner assembly; remove the chain tensioner shoe. The timing chain must be disengaged from the wear grooves in the tensioner shoe in order to remove the shoe. Slide a prybar under the timing chain while pulling shoe outward.
9. If difficulty is encountered removing chain tensioner shoe, proceed as follows:
   a. Lower the vehicle.
   b. Hold the intake camshaft sprocket with a holding tool and remove the sprocket bolt and washer.
   c. Remove the washer from the bolt and re-thread the bolt back into the camshaft by hand, the bolt provides a surface to push against.
   d. Remove intake camshaft sprocket using a 3-jaw puller in the 3 relief holes in the sprocket. Do not attempt to pry the sprocket off the camshaft or damage to the sprocket or chain housing could occur.
10. Remove the tensioner assembly attaching bolts and the tensioner.
    CAUTION: *The tensioner piston is spring loaded and could fly out causing personal injury.*
11. Remove the chain housing to block stud, which is actually the timing chain tensioner shoe pivot.
12. Remove the timing chain.
**To install:**
13. Tighten intake camshaft sprocket attach-

# ENGINE AND ENGINE OVERHAUL

ing bolt and washer, while holding the sprocket with tool J-36013, if removed.

14. Install the special tool through holes in camshaft sprockets into holes in timing chain housing. This positions the camshafts for correct timing.

15. If the camshafts are out of position and must be rotated more than 1/8 turn in order to install the alignment dowel pins:

   a. The crankshaft must be rotated 90 degrees clockwise off of TDC in order to give the valves adequate clearance to open.

   b. Once the camshafts are in position and the dowels installed, rotate the crankshaft counterclockwise back to TDC. Do not rotate the crankshaft clockwise to TDC or valve and piston damage could occur.

16. Install the timing chain over the exhaust camshaft sprocket, around the idler sprocket and around the crankshaft sprocket.

17. Remove the alignment dowel pin from the intake camshaft. Using a dowel pin remover tool, rotate the intake camshaft sprocket counterclockwise enough to slide the timing chain over the intake camshaft sprocket. Release the camshaft sprocket wrench. The length of chain between the 2 camshaft sprockets will tighten. If properly timed, the intake camshaft alignment dowel pin should slide in easily. If the dowel pin does not fully index, the camshafts are not timed correctly and the procedure must be repeated.

18. Leave the alignment dowel pins installed.

19. With slack removed from chain between intake camshaft sprocket and crankshaft sprocket, the timing marks on the crankshaft and the cylinder block should be aligned. If marks are not aligned, move the chain 1 tooth forward or rearward, remove slack and recheck marks.

20. Tighten the chain housing to block stud. The stud is installed under the timing chain. Tighten to 19 ft. lbs. (26 Nm).

21. Reload timing chain tensioner assembly to its 0 position as follows:

   a. Assemble restraint cylinder, spring and nylon plug into plunger. Index slot in restraint cylinder with peg in plunger. While rotating the restraint cylinder clockwise, push the restraint cylinder into the plunger until it bottoms. Keep rotating the restraint cylinder clockwise but allow the spring to push it out of the plunger. The pin in the plunger will lock the restraint in the loaded position.

   b. Install tool J-36589 or equivalent, onto plunger assembly.

   c. Install plunger assembly into tensioner body with the long end toward the crankshaft when installed.

22. Install the tensioner assembly to the chain housing. Recheck plunger assembly installation. It is correctly installed when the long end is toward the crankshaft.

23. Install and tighten timing chain tensioner bolts and tighten to 10 ft. lbs. (14 Nm).

24. Install the tensioner shoe and tensioner shoe retainer. Remove special tool J-36589 and squeeze plunger assembly into the tensioner body to unload the plunger assembly.

25. Lower vehicle and remove the alignment dowel pins. Rotate crankshaft clockwise 2 full rotations. Align crankshaft timing mark with mark on cylinder block and reinstall alignment dowel pins. Alignment dowel pins will slide in easily if engine is timed correctly.

NOTE: *If the engine is not correctly timed, severe engine damage could occur.*

26. Install 3 timing chain guides and crankshaft oil slinger.
27. Install the timing chain front cover.
28. Connect the negative battery cable and check for leaks.

### 3.0L, 3.3L AND 1990-92 2.5L ENGINES

1. Disconnect the negative battery cable.
2. Drain the cooling system. Disconnect the cooling hose from the water pump.
3. Raise and safely support the vehicle.
4. Remove the inner fender splash shield.
5. Remove the serpentine drive belt.
6. Remove the crankshaft pulley bolt and slide the pulley from the crankshaft.

| | |
|---|---|
| 1 | KEY |
| 2 | DAMPNER |
| 3 | SPRING |
| 4 | BOLT 22 N•M (16 LBS-FT) |
| 5 | CRANKSHAFT SPROCKET |
| 6 | BOLTS 35 N•M (26 LBS-FT) |
| 7 | TIMING CHAIN |
| 8 | CAMSHAFT SPROCKET |

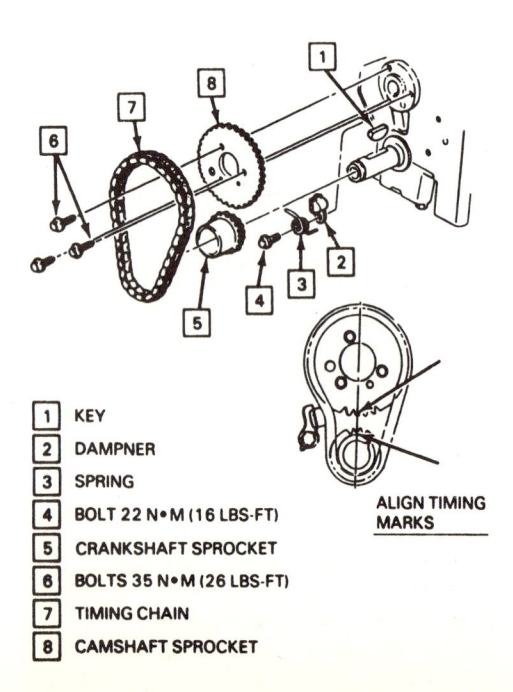

3.3L Timing Chain (3.0L and 2.5L Similar)

# ENGINE AND ENGINE OVERHAUL

7. Remove the front cover.
8. Rotate the crankshaft to align the timing marks on the sprockets. Remove the chain dampener assembly.
9. Remove the camshaft sprocket-to-camshaft bolt(s), remove the camshaft sprocket and chain and thrust bearing.
10. Remove the crankshaft gear by sliding it forward.
11. Clean the gasket mounting surfaces. Inspect the timing chain and the sprockets for damage and/or wear and replace damaged parts.

**To install:**
12. Position the crankshaft so the No. 1 piston is at TDC of its compression stroke. Install the thrust bearing on 2.5L engine.
13. Temporarily install the gear on the camshaft and position the camshaft so the timing mark on the gear is pointing straight down.
14. Assemble the timing chain to the gears so the timing marks are aligned, mark-to-mark.
15. Install the camshaft sprocket attaching bolt(s).
16. Install the camshaft thrust bearing, if not already done.
17. Install the timing chain dampener.
18. Install the front cover and all related parts.
19. Connect the negative battery cable and check for leaks.

## Timing Gears

### REMOVAL AND INSTALLATION

#### 1988–89 2.5L Engine

NOTE: *If the camshaft gear is to be replaced, the engine must be removed from the vehicle. The crankshaft gear may be replaced with the engine in the vehicle.*

1. Disconnect the negative battery cable.
2. Raise and safely support the vehicle.
3. Remove the inner fender splash shield.
4. Remove the accessory drive belts. Remove the crankshaft pulley-to-crankshaft pulley bolt and slide the pulley from the crankshaft.
5. If replacing the camshaft gear, perform the following procedures:
   a. Remove the engine from the vehicle and secure it onto a suitable holding fixture.
   b. Remove the camshaft from the engine.
   c. Using an arbor press, press the camshaft gear from the camshaft.
   d. To install the camshaft gear onto the camshaft, press the gear onto the shaft until a thrust clearance of 0.0015–0.0050 in. (0.0381–0.127mm) exists.
6. If removing the crankshaft gear, perform the following procedures:
   a. Remove the front cover-to-engine bolts.
   b. Remove the attaching bolt and slide the crankshaft gear forward off the crankshaft.
7. Clean the gasket mounting surfaces. Inspect the parts for damage and/or wear and replace damaged parts.
8. The installation is the reverse of the removal procedure. Make sure the timing marks are aligned mark-to-mark when installing.

## Timing Sprockets

### REMOVAL AND INSTALLATION

1. Disconnect the negative battery cable.
2. If removing the camshaft sprocket, remove the camshaft carrier cover.
3. Remove the timing belt cover.
4. Position the engine so the timing marks are aligned for belt installation.
5. Remove the timing belt.
6. If removing the camshaft sprocket, hold the camshaft with an open-end wrench.
7. Remove the camshaft or crankshaft sprocket attaching bolt, washer and the sprocket.
8. The installation is the reverse of the removal procedure. Tighten the camshaft sprocket bolt to 34 ft. lbs. (45 Nm). Tighten the crankshaft sprocket bolt to 114 ft. lbs. (155 Nm).
9. Connect the negative battery cable and road test the vehicle.

## Camshaft

### REMOVAL AND INSTALLATION

#### 2.0L Engine

1. Relieve the fuel system pressure.
2. Disconnect the negative battery cable.
3. Remove the camshaft carrier cover.
4. Hold the valves in place with compressed air, using air adapters in the spark plug holes.
5. Compress the valve springs with the special valve spring compressing tool.
6. Remove the rocker arms and lifters and keep them in order for reassembly. Hold the camshaft with an open-end wrench and remove the camshaft sprocket. Try to keep the valve timing by using a rubber cord, if possible. If the timing cannot be kept intact, the timing belt will have to be reset.
7. Matchmark and remove the distributor.
8. Remove the camshaft thrust plate from the rear of the carrier.
9. Remove the camshaft by sliding it toward the rear. Remove the front carrier seal.

**To install:**
10. Install a new carrier seal.
11. Thoroughly lubricate the camshaft and journals with clean oil and install the camshaft.
12. Install the rear thrust plate and tighten the bolts to 70 inch lbs. (8 Nm).

# 140   ENGINE AND ENGINE OVERHAUL

13. Install camshaft sprocket, timing belt and cover.
14. Install the distributor.
15. Hold the valves in place with compressed air as in Step 4, compress the valve springs and install the lifters and rocker arms.
16. Apply sealer to the camshaft carrier cover and install.
17. Connect the negative battery cable and road test the vehicle.

## 2.3L Engine

### INTAKE CAMSHAFT

NOTE: *Any time the camshaft housing to cylinder head bolts are loosened or removed, the camshaft housing to cylinder head gasket must be replaced.*

1. Relieve the fuel system pressure. Disconnect the negative battery cable.
2. Label and disconnect the ignition coil and module assembly electrical connections.
3. Remove 4 ignition coil and module assembly to camshaft housing bolts and remove assembly by pulling straight up. Use a special spark plug boot wire remover tool to remove connector assemblies, if they have stuck to the spark plugs.

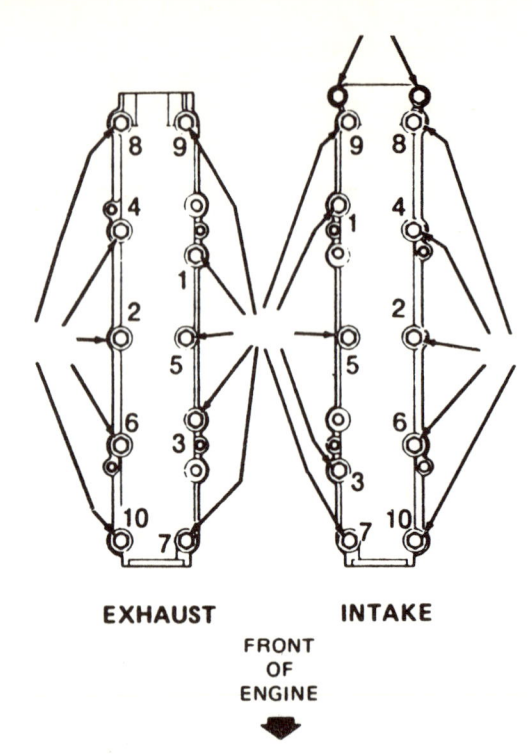

**2.3L Camshaft Bolt Torque sequence**

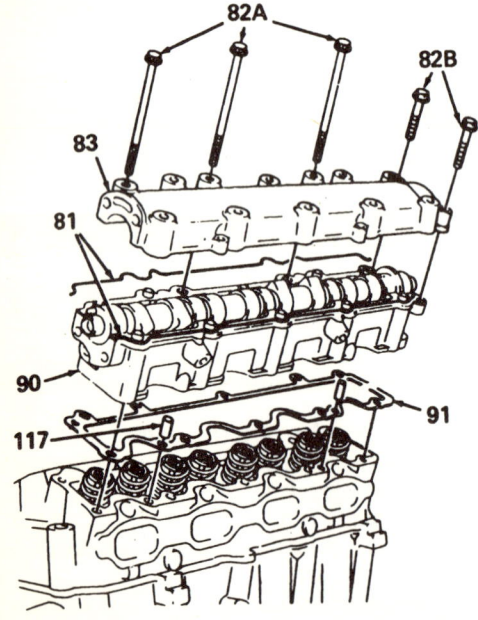

4. Remove the idle speed power steering pressure switch connector.
5. Loosen 3 power steering pump pivot bolts and remove drive belt.

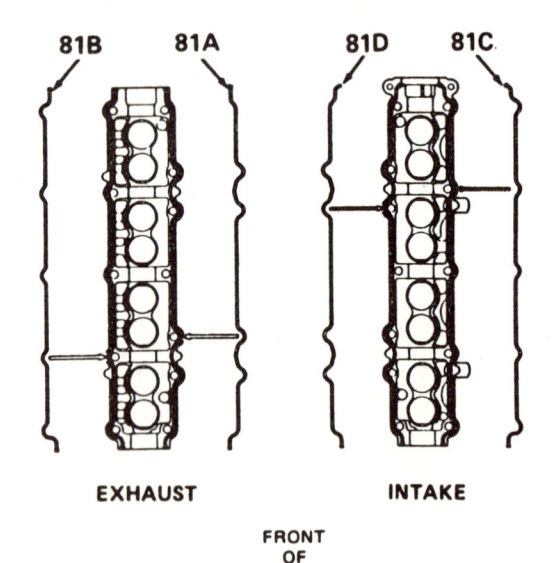

81. SEALS, CAMSHAFT HOUSING TO CAMSHAFT HOUSING COVER (EACH SEAL IS DIFFERENT)
82A. BOLT, CAMSHAFT HOUSING TO CYLINDER HEAD
82B. BOLT, CAMSHAFT HOUSING COVER TO CAMSHAFT HOUSING
83. COVER, CAMSHAFT
90. CAMSHAFT HOUSING (INTAKE SHOWN)
91. GASKET, CAMSHAFT HOUSING TO CYLINDER HEAD
117. DOWEL PIN (2)

**2.3L Camshaft, Housing and Assembly**

81A. SEAL-INNER (EXHAUST, RED)
81B. SEAL-OUTER (EXHAUST, RED)
81C. SEAL-OUTER (INTAKE, BLUE)
81D. SEAL-INNER (INTAKE, BLUE)

**Camshaft Housing to Cover Seals—2.3L**

## ENGINE AND ENGINE OVERHAUL    141

6. Disconnect the 2 rear power steering pump bracket to transaxle bolts.
7. Remove the front power steering pump bracket to cylinder block bolt.
8. Disconnect the power steering pump assembly and position aside.
9. Using the special tool, remove the power steering pump drive pulley from the intake camshaft.
10. Remove oil/air separator bolts and hoses. Leave the hoses attached to the separator, disconnect from the oil fill, chain housing and intake manifold. Remove as an assembly.
11. Remove vacuum line from fuel pressure regulator and disconnect the fuel injector harness connector.
12. Disconnect fuel line attaching clamp from bracket on top of intake camshaft housing.
13. Remove fuel rail to camshaft housing attaching bolts.
14. Remove the fuel rail from the cylinder head. Cover injector openings in cylinder head and cover injector nozzles. Leave fuel lines attached and position fuel rail aside.
15. Disconnect the timing chain and housing but do not remove from the engine.
16. Remove intake camshaft housing cover to camshaft housing attaching bolts.
17. Remove the intake camshaft housing to cylinder head attaching bolts. Use the reverse of the tightening sequence when loosening camshaft housing to cylinder head attaching bolts. Leave 2 bolts loosely in place to hold the camshaft housing while separating camshaft cover from housing.
18. Push the cover off the housing by threading 4 of the housing to head attaching bolts into the tapped holes in the cam housing cover. Tighten the bolts in evenly so the cover does not bind on the dowel pins.
19. Remove the 2 loosely installed camshaft housing to head bolts and remove the cover. Discard the gaskets.
20. Note the position of the chain sprocket dowel pin for reassembly. Remove the camshaft carefully; do not damage the camshaft oil seal.
21. Remove intake camshaft oil seal from camshaft and discard seal. This seal must be replaced any time the housing and cover are separated.
22. Remove the camshaft carrier from the cylinder head and remove the gasket.

**To install:**
23. Thoroughly clean the mating surfaces of the camshaft carrier and the cylinder head, bolts and bolt holes. Install a new gasket and place the housing on the head. Install 1 bolt loosely to hold in place.
24. Install the lifters into their bores. If the camshaft is being replaced, the lifters must also be replaced. Lubricate camshaft lobes, journals and lifters with camshaft and lifter prelube. The camshaft lobes and journals must be adequately lubricated or engine damage could occur upon start up.
25. Install the camshaft in the same position as when removed. The timing chain sprocket dowel pin should be straight up and align with the centerline of the lifter bores.
26. Install new camshaft housing to camshaft housing cover seals into cover; do not use sealer. Make sure the correct color seal is placed in each groove. Install the cover to the housing.
27. Apply thread locking compound to the camshaft housing and cover attaching bolt threads.
28. Install bolts and tighten to 11 ft. lbs. (15 Nm). Rotate the bolts, except the 2 rear bolts that hold the fuel pipe to the camshaft housing, an additional 75 degrees, in sequence. Tighten the excepted bolts to 16 ft. lbs. (15 Nm), then rotate an additional 25 degrees.
29. Install timing chain housing and timing chain.
30. Uncover fuel injectors and install new fuel injector O-ring seals lubricated with oil. Install the fuel rail.
31. Install the fuel line attaching clamp and retainer to bracket on top of the intake camshaft housing.
32. Connect the vacuum line to the fuel pressure regulator.
33. Connect the fuel injectors harness connector.
34. Install the oil/air separator assembly.
35. Lubricate the inner sealing surface of the intake camshaft seal with oil and install the seal to the housing.
36. Install the power steering pump pulley onto the intake camshaft.
37. Install the power steering pump assembly and drive belt.
38. Connect the idle speed power steering pressure switch connector.
39. Clean any loose lubricant that is present on the ignition coil and module assembly to camshaft housing bolts. Apply Loctite® 592 or equivalent, onto the ignition coil and module assembly to camshaft housing bolts. Install the bolts and tighten to 13 ft. lbs. (18 Nm).
40. Connect the electrical connectors to ignition coil and module assembly.
41. Connect the negative battery cable and road test the vehicle. Check for leaks.

*EXHAUST CAMSHAFT*

NOTE: *Any time the camshaft housing to cylinder head bolts are loosened or removed the camshaft housing to cylinder head gasket must be replaced.*

# 142 ENGINE AND ENGINE OVERHAUL

1. Relieve the fuel system pressure. Disconnect the negative battery cable.
2. Label and disconnect the ignition coil and module assembly electrical connections.
3. Remove 4 ignition coil and module assembly to camshaft housing bolts and remove assembly by pulling straight up. Use a special tool to remove connector assemblies if they have stuck to the spark plugs.
4. Remove the idle speed power steering pressure switch connector.
5. Remove the transaxle fluid level indicator tube assembly from exhaust camshaft cover and position aside.
6. Remove exhaust camshaft cover and gasket.
7. Disconnect the timing chain and housing but do not remove from the engine.
8. Remove exhaust camshaft housing to cylinder head bolts. Use the reverse of the tightening procedure when loosening camshaft housing while separating camshaft cover from housing.
9. Push the cover off the housing by threading 4 of the housing to head attaching bolts into the tapped holes in the camshaft cover. Tighten the bolts in evenly so the cover does not bind on the dowel pins.
10. Remove the 2 loosely installed camshaft housing to cylinder head bolts and remove cover, discard gaskets.
11. Loosely reinstall 1 camshaft housing to cylinder head bolt to retain the housing during camshaft and lifter removal.
12. Note the position of the chain sprocket dowel pin for reassembly. Remove camshaft being careful not to damage the camshaft or journals.
13. Remove the camshaft carrier from the cylinder head and remove the gasket.

**To install:**

14. Thoroughly clean the mating surfaces of the camshaft carrier and the cylinder head, bolts and bolt holes. Install a new gasket and place the housing on the head. Install 1 bolt loosely to hold in place.
15. Install the lifters into their bores. If the camshaft is being replaced, the lifters must also be replaced. Lubricate camshaft lobes, journals and lifters with camshaft and lifter prelube. The camshaft lobes and journals must be adequately lubricated or engine damage could occur upon start up.
16. Install camshaft in same position as when removed. The timing chain sprocket dowel pin should be straight up and align with the centerline of the lifter bores.
17. Install new camshaft housing to camshaft housing cover seals into cover; do not use sealer. Make sure the correct color seal is placed in each groove. Install the cover to the housing.
18. Apply thread locking compound to the camshaft housing and cover attaching bolt threads.
19. Install bolts and tighten, in sequence, to 11 ft. lbs. (15 Nm). Then rotate the bolts an additional 75 degrees, in sequence.
20. Install timing chain housing and timing chain.
21. Install the transaxle fluid level indicator tube assembly to exhaust camshaft cover.
22. Connect the idle speed power steering pressure switch connector.
23. Clean any loose lubricant that is present on the ignition coil and module assembly to camshaft housing bolts. Apply Loctite® 592 or equivalent, onto the ignition coil and module assembly to camshaft housing bolts. Install the bolts and tighten to 13 ft. lbs. (18 Nm).
24. Connect the electrical connectors to ignition coil and module assembly.
25. Connect the negative battery cable and road test the vehicle. Check for leaks.

## 2.5L Engine

1. Disconnect the negative battery cable. Relieve the fuel system pressure before disconnecting any fuel lines. Remove the engine from the vehicle and secure to a suitable holding fixture.
2. Remove the valve cover, rocker arms and

**Removing Camshaft Thrust Plate Screws—2.5L**

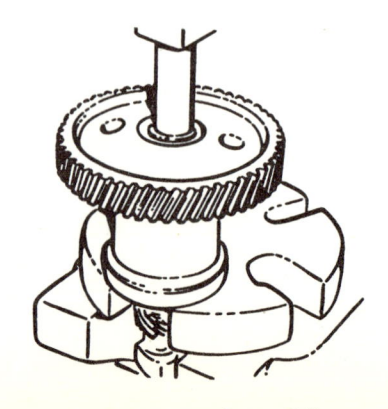

**Removing Camshaft Timing Gear—2.5L**

# ENGINE AND ENGINE OVERHAUL 143

pushrods. Keep all parts in order for reassembly.

3. Remove the distributor, spark plug wires and plugs.

4. Remove the pushrod cover, the gasket and the lifters. Keep all parts in order for reassembly.

5. Remove the alternator, alternator lower bracket and the front engine mount bracket assembly.

6. Remove the oil pump driveshaft and gear assembly.

7. Remove the crankshaft pulley and front cover Remove the timing chain and gears, if equipped.

8. Remove the 2 camshaft thrust plate screws by working through the holes in the gear.

9. Remove the camshaft, and gear assembly, if gear driven by pulling it through the front of the block. Take care not to damage the bearings while removing the camshaft.

**To install:**

10. The installation is the reverse of the removal procedure. Coat all parts with a liberal amount of clean engine oil supplement before installing.

11. Fill all fluids to their proper levels.

12. Connect the negative battery cable and check for leaks.

### 3.0L and 3.3L Engines

1. Disconnect the negative battery cable. Relieve the fuel system pressure before disconnecting any fuel lines. Remove the engine from the vehicle and secure to a suitable holding fixture.

2. Remove the intake manifold.

3. Remove the valve covers, rocker arm assemblies, pushrods and lifters. Keep all parts in order for reassembly.

4. Remove the crankshaft balancer from the crankshaft.

5. Remove the front cover.

6. Rotate the crankshaft to align the timing marks on the timing sprockets. Remove the camshaft sprocket and the timing chain.

7. Remove the camshaft retainer bolts and slide the camshaft forward out of the engine. Take care not to damage the bearings while removing the camshaft.

**To install:**

8. The installation is the reverse of the removal procedure. Coat all parts with a liberal amount of clean engine oil supplement before installing.

9. Fill all fluids to their proper levels.

10. Connect the negative battery cable and check for leaks.

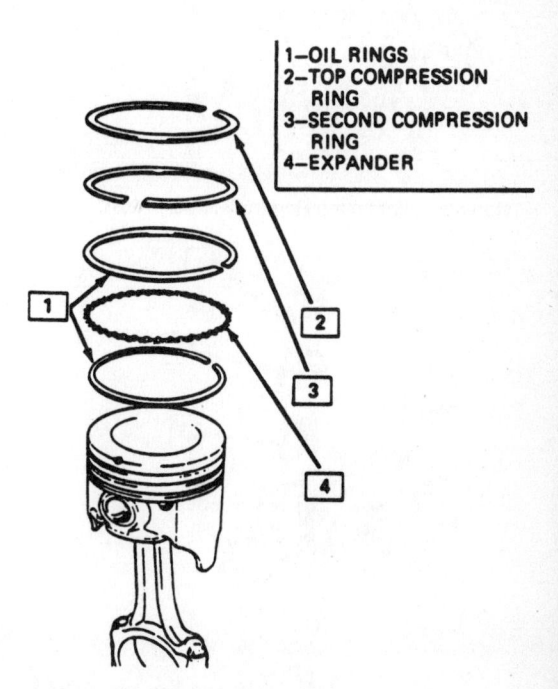

2.0L Piston and Rod Assembly

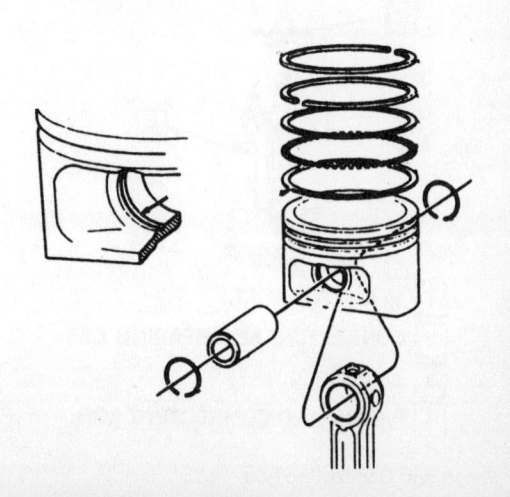

| 1 | BEARING AND SPRING ASSEMBLY |
| 2 | CAMSHAFT |
| 3 | BEARINGS |
| 4 | CUP PLUG |

3.0L and 3.3L Camshaft Assembly

2.3L Piston, Pin and Rings

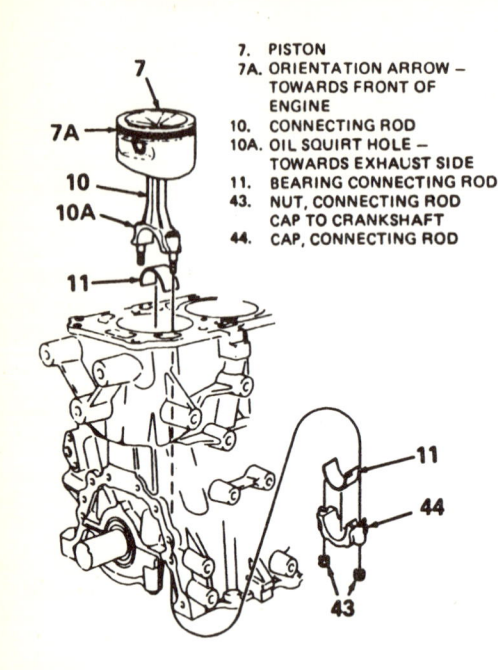

# ENGINE AND ENGINE OVERHAUL

7. PISTON
7A. ORIENTATION ARROW — TOWARDS FRONT OF ENGINE
10. CONNECTING ROD
10A. OIL SQUIRT HOLE — TOWARDS EXHAUST SIDE
11. BEARING CONNECTING ROD
43. NUT, CONNECTING ROD CAP TO CRANKSHAFT
44. CAP, CONNECTING ROD

Piston and Connecting Rod Installation—2.3L

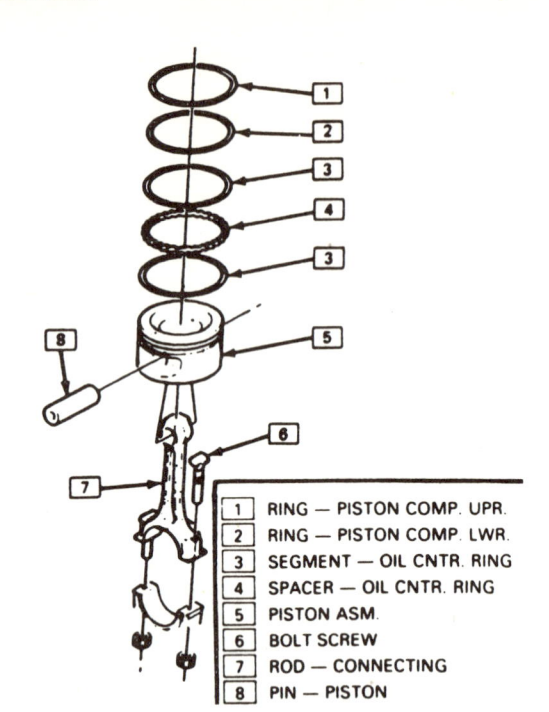

| 1 | RING — PISTON COMP. UPR. |
| 2 | RING — PISTON COMP. LWR. |
| 3 | SEGMENT — OIL CNTR. RING |
| 4 | SPACER — OIL CNTR. RING |
| 5 | PISTON ASM. |
| 6 | BOLT SCREW |
| 7 | ROD — CONNECTING |
| 8 | PIN — PISTON |

Piston and Rod Assembly—2.5L

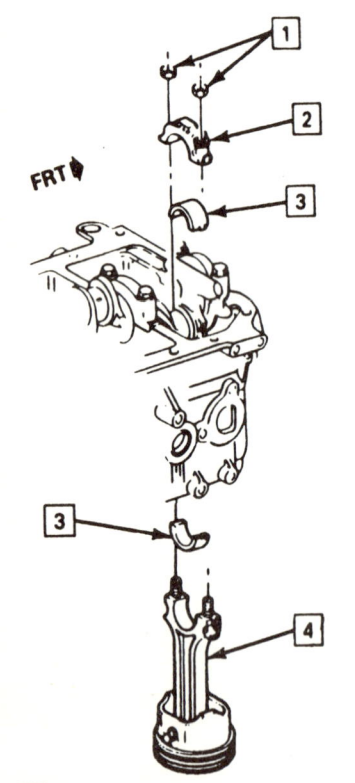

| 1 | 40 N·m (29 LB. FT.) |
| 2 | CONNECTING ROD BEARING CAP |
| 3 | BEARING |
| 4 | PISTON AND CONNECTING ROD |

Piston and Connecting Rod—2.5L

## Pistons and Connecting Rods

### REMOVAL

1. Disconnect the negative battery cable.
2. Remove the cylinder head and oil pan as previously described.
3. Mark the connecting rod and cap to ensure correct reassembly.
4. Remove the connecting rod bolts and cap.
5. Remove the piston and connecting rod assembly.

### CLEANING AND INSPECTION

1. Inspect the piston for cracked ring lands, skirts or pin bosses.
2. Inspect for wavy or worn ring lands, scuffed or damaged skirts and for eroded areas at the top of the piston.
3. Replace the pistons if damaged or excessively worn.
4. Inspect the grooves for knicks or burrs that may interfere with the rings.
5. Measure the piston diameter and the cylinder bore diameter.
6. Subtract the piston diameter from the cylinder bore diameter to determine piston-to-bore clearance. Compare this with the recommended clearances.

### RIDGE REMOVAL AND HONING

1. To hone cylinders, follow the manufacturer's recomendations for use of the hone.

# ENGINE AND ENGINE OVERHAUL 145

2. During the honing operation, the bore should be cleaned and the selected piston checked for proper fit.

3. During the finish-hone stage, move the hone up and down at a sufficent speed to obtain a uniform finish.

4. The finish marks should be clean but not sharp, free from impedded particles and torn or folded metal.

5. The bores MUST be thoroughly cleaned with hot water and detergent. This step is extremely important. If any abrasive material is left in the bore it will rapidly wear the new rings and the bores.

6. The bores should be swabbed several times with light engine oil and a clean cloth and then wiped with a clean dry cloth. THE CYLINDERS SHOULD NOT BE CLEANED WITH GASOLINE OR KEROSENE. Clean the cylinder block to remove excess material that may have been spread during the honing operation.

## PISTON PIN REPLACEMENT

1. Remove the piston rings using a suitable piston ring removal tool.

2. Remove the piston pin lockring, if used.

3. Install the guide bushing of the piston pin removal and installation tool.

4. Install the piston and rod assembly on a support and place the assembly in an arbor press. Press the pin out of the connecting rod using the proper piston pin tool.

5. Assembly is the reverse of the removal procedure.

## PISTON RING REPLACEMENT

1. Using a piston ring expander, install the lower oil control ring.

2. Install the upper oil control ring.

3. Making sure that the manufacturers marks are pointing upward, install the upper and lower compression rings.

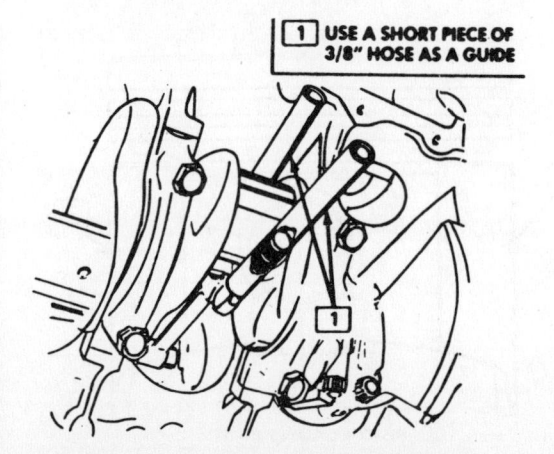

### INSTALLATION

1. Install the piston rings to the piston.
2. Turn the crankshaft to bottom dead center.
3. Lubricate the cylinder with engine oil.
4. Install the connecting rod bearing.
5. Using a ring compresser, install the piston and connecting rod assembly. Make sure that the ridges are toward the front of the engine.

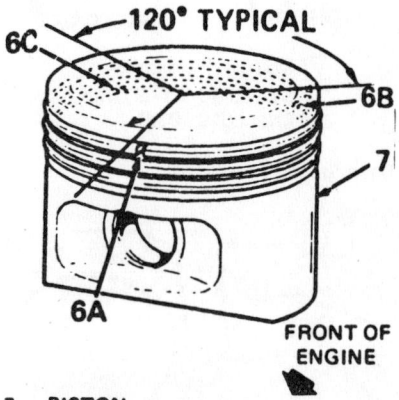

7. PISTON
6A. UPPER COMPRESSION RING GAP
6B. LOWER COMPRESSION RING GAP
6C. OIL RING ASM. GAP

Piston Pin Gap Locations—2.3L

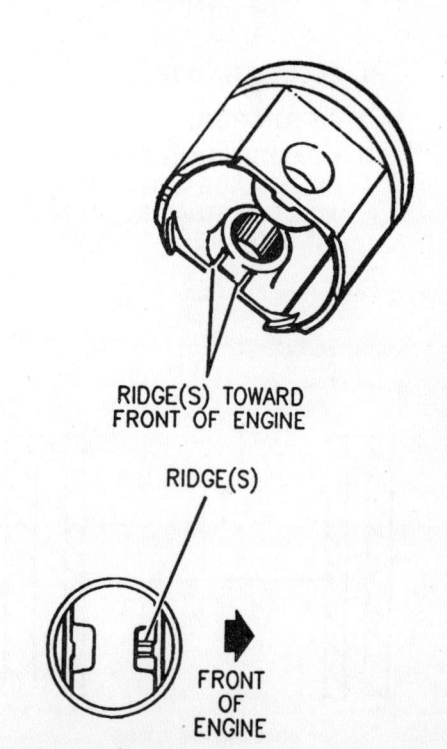

Using Pieces of Hose to Protect Connecting Rod

3.3L Piston Installation

# ENGINE AND ENGINE OVERHAUL

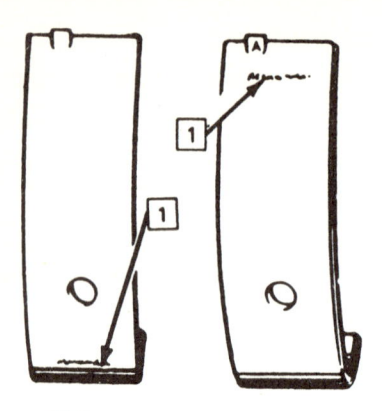

**1** AMOUNT UNDERSIZE STAMPED AT EITHER END (.016, .032)

**Main Bearing Insert Markings**

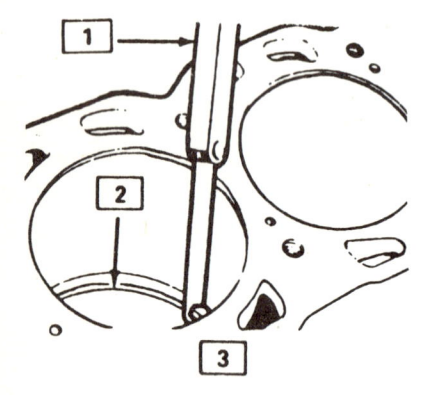

1—FEELER GAUGE

2—PISTON RING

3—MEASURE RING GAP CLEARANCE WITH RING POSITIONED AT BOTTOM RING TRAVEL AS SHOWN

**Measuring Piston Ring End Gap**

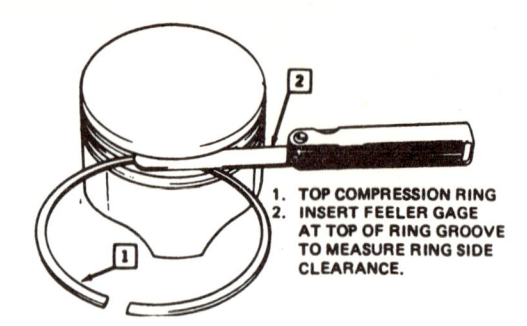

1. TOP COMPRESSION RING
2. INSERT FEELER GAGE AT TOP OF RING GROOVE TO MEASURE RING SIDE CLEARANCE.

**Measuring Piston Ring Side Clearance—2.0L**

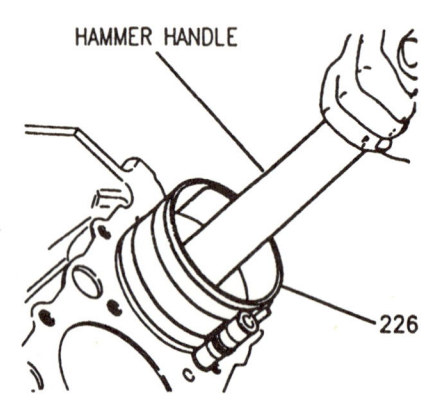

HAMMER HANDLE

226 RING COMPRESSOR

**Installing Piston Using a Ring Compressor**

6. Install the connecting rod cap and bolts and tighten to the specified torque.
7. Install the oil pan and cylinder head and connect the negative battery cable.

## Rear Main Bearing Oil Seal
### REMOVAL AND INSTALLATION
*2.0L AND 2.5L ENGINES*

1. Disconnect the negative battery cable.
2. Remove the transaxle.

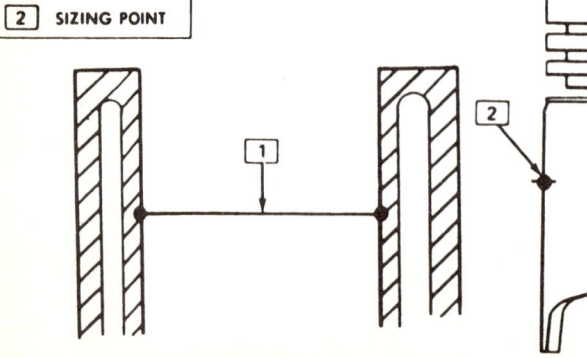

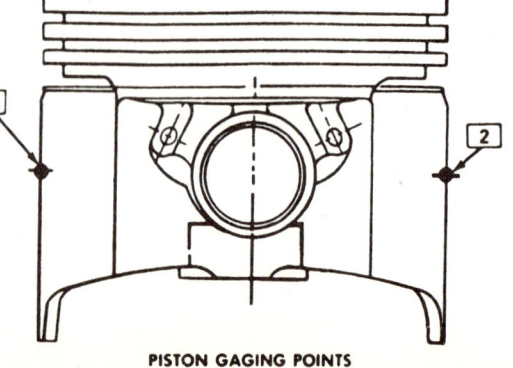

**1** GAGING POINT
**2** SIZING POINT

BORE GAGING POINTS

PISTON GAGING POINTS

**Piston to Cylinder Bore Gaging Points**

# ENGINE AND ENGINE OVERHAUL 147

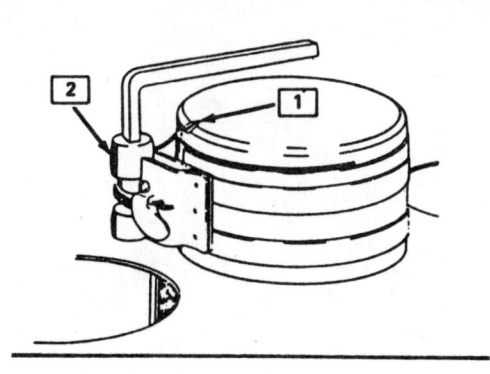

**1—NOTCH TOWARDS FRONT OF ENGINE**
**2—TOOL J-8037**

**Piston Installation Tool**

3. If equipped with a manual transaxle, remove the pressure plate and clutch disc.
4. Remove the flywheel-to-crankshaft bolts and the flywheel.
5. Using a medium prybar, pry out the old seal; be careful not to scratch the crankshaft surface.
6. Clean the block and crankshaft-to-seal mating surfaces.
7. Using the appropriate seal installation tool, install the new rear seal into the block. Lubricate the outside of the seal to aid installation and press the seal in evenly with the tool.
8. The installation is the reverse of the removal procedure.
9. Connect the negative battery cable and check for leaks.

### 2.3L ENGINE

1. Disconnect the negative battery cable.
2. Remove the transaxle.
3. If equipped with a manual transaxle, remove the pressure plate and clutch disc.
4. Remove the flywheel-to-crankshaft bolts and the flywheel.
5. Remove the oil pan-to-seal housing bolts and the block-to-seal housing bolts.
6. Remove the seal housing from the engine.
7. Place 2 blocks of equal thickness on a flat surface and position the seal housing on the 2 blocks. Remove the seal from the housing.
8. The installation is the reverse of the removal procedure. Use new gaskets when installing.
9. Connect the negative battery cable and for leaks.

### 3.0L AND 3.3L ENGINES

NOTE: *If replacing the entire 2-piece seal, the engine must be removed in order to remove the crankshaft. Use the following if only replacing the lower half of the seal.*

1. Disconnect the negative battery cable. Raise and safely support the vehicle.
2. Drain the oil and remove the oil pan.
3. Remove the rear main bearing cap-to-engine bolts and the bearing cap from the engine.
4. Remove the old seal from the bearing cap.

**To install:**

5. Using a seal packing tool, insert it against one end of the seal in the cylinder block. Pack the old seal into the groove until it is packed tightly. Repeat the procedure on the other end of the seal.
6. Measure the amount the seal was driven up and add approximately $1/16$ in. (1.6mm). Cut this length from the old seal removed from the lower bearing cap, repeat for the other side.

NOTE: *When cutting the seal into short lengths, use a double edged blade and the lower bearing cap as a holding fixture.*

7. Using a seal packer guide, install it onto the cylinder block.

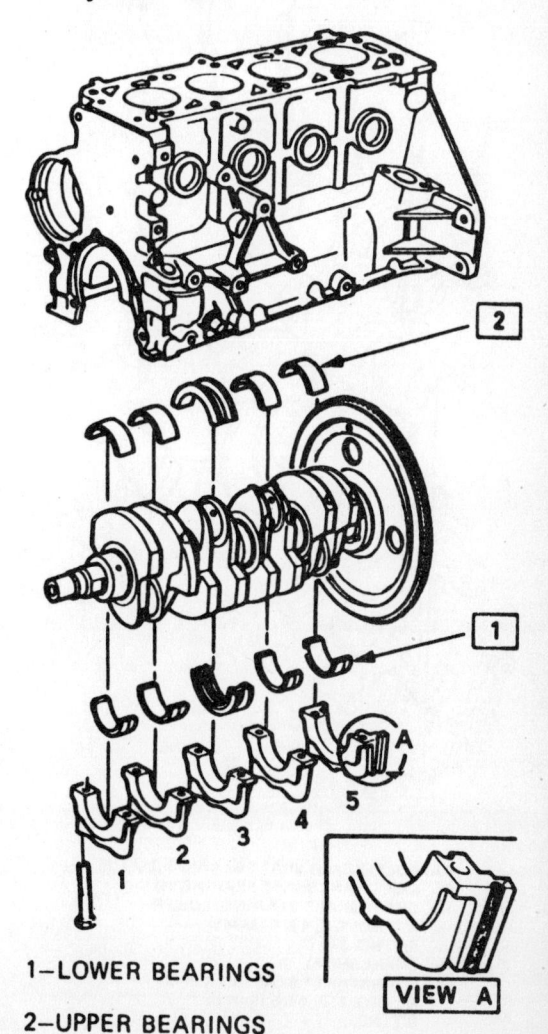

**1—LOWER BEARINGS**
**2—UPPER BEARINGS**

**2.0L Crankshaft Installation**

# 148 ENGINE AND ENGINE OVERHAUL

8. Using the packing tool, work the short pieces into the guide tool and pack into the cylinder block until the tool hits the built-in stop.

NOTE: *It may help to use oil on the short seal pieces when packing into the block.*

9. Repeat Steps 7 and 8 for the other side.
10. Remove the guide tool.
11. Install a new rope seal into the lower bearing cap.
12. Install the lower main bearing cap and tighten the main bearing cap bolts to 100 ft. lbs. (135 Nm) for 3.0L engine or 90 ft. lbs. (122 Nm) for 3.3L engine.
13. Install the oil pan.
14. Fill the crankcase with the proper engine oil.
15. Connect the negative battery cable and check for leaks.

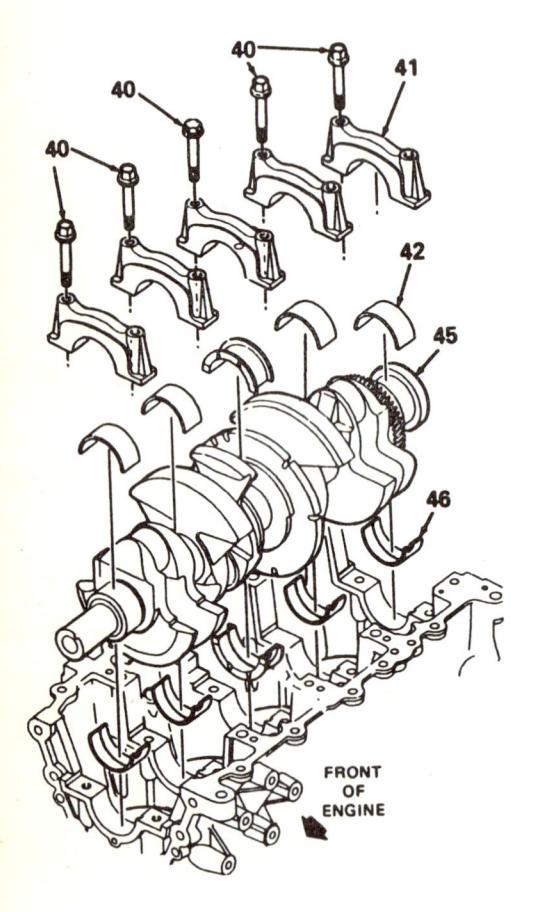

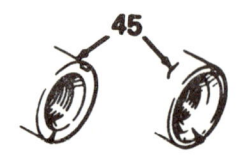

45. CRANKSHAFT
61. BALANCER ASM.
62. WASHER
63. BOLT

2.3L Crankshaft Identification

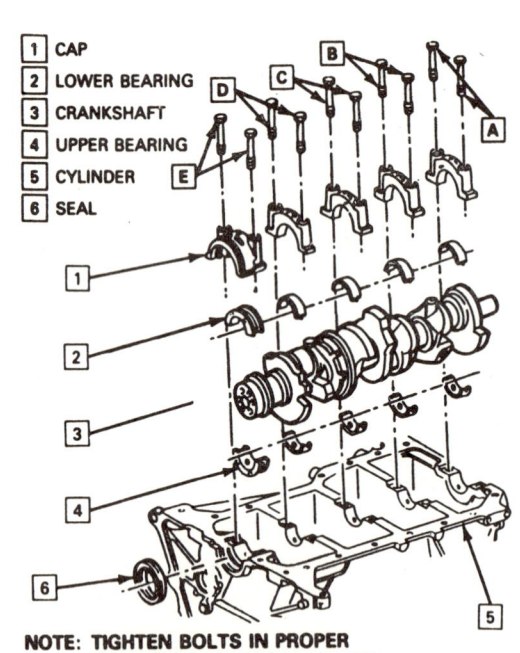

1. CAP
2. LOWER BEARING
3. CRANKSHAFT
4. UPPER BEARING
5. CYLINDER
6. SEAL

NOTE: TIGHTEN BOLTS IN PROPER SEQUENCE "A" THROUGH "E" TO 88 N·m (65 LB. FT.)

2.5L Crankshaft

40. BOLT, CRANKSHAFT BEARING CAP (10)
41. CAP, CRANKSHAFT BEARING (5)
42. CRANKSHAFT BEARING, LOWER
   A. NO. 1, 2, 4 & 5 (SAME)
   B. NO. 3
45. CRANKSHAFT
46. CRANKSHAFT BEARING, UPPER
   A. NO. 1, 2, 4 & 5 (SAME)
   B. NO. 3

2.3L Crankshaft and Bearings

## Crankshaft and Main Bearings
### REMOVAL AND INSTALLATION

1. Remove the engine from the vehicle as previously described.
2. Remove the front engine cover.

# ENGINE AND ENGINE OVERHAUL 149

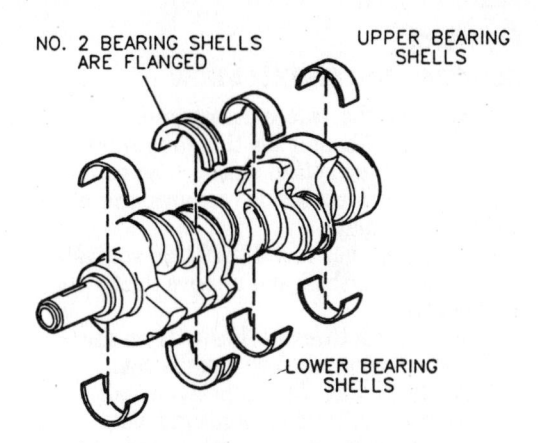

**3.0L and 3.3L Crankshaft and Bearings**

3. Remove the timing chain or belt and sprockets.
4. Remove the oil pan and the oil pump.
5. Mark the cylinder number on the machined surfaces of the bolt boses of the connecting rods and caps for identification purposes during installation.
6. Remove the connecting rod caps and store them so that they may be reinstalled to their original position.
7. Remove all of the main bearing caps.
8. Note the position of the keyway in the crankshaft, so that it may be reinstalled to it's original position.
9. Lift the crankshaft away from the block.
10. Remove the rear main oil seal.

**To install:**

11. Install sufficient oil pan bolts to the block to align with the connecting rod bolts. Use rubber bands between the bolts to hold the connecting rods in place.
12. Place the upper half of the main bearings in the block and lubricate them with clean engine oil.
13. Place the crankshaft keyway in the same position as removed and lower it into the block. The connecting rods should follow the crank pins into position as it is lowered.
14. Lubricate the thrust flanges with 10501609 lubricant or equivalent. Install caps with the lower half of the bearings lubricated with engine oil. Lubricate the cap bolts with engine oil and install, but do not tighten.
15. With a block of wood, tap the shaft in each direction to properly align the thrust flanges of the main bearing. Hold the shaft towards the front while torquing the thrust bearing cap bolts.
16. Torque all of the main bearing to specifications and check crankshaft endplay.
17. Lubricate the connecting rod bearings with clean oil. Install the connecting rod bearing caps to their original positions and tighten the nuts to specification.
18. Complete installation by reversing the removal steps.

## CLEANING AND INSPECTION

1. Clean all oil passages in the block and crankshaft.
2. Using a dial indicator, check the crankshaft journal runout. Measure the journals with a micrometer to determine the correct size rod and main bearings to be used.

## INSPECTING MAIN BEARING CLEARANCE

1. Remove the bearing cap and wipe the oil from the crankshaft journal and the outer and inner bearing shell surfaces.
2. Place a piece of plastic gauging material across the entire bearing width.
3. Using a suitable tool, lightly tap on the bearing cap to properly seat it.
4. Torque the bearing cap bolts to specifications.
5. Remove the bearing cap with the guaging material left intact.
6. Measure the plastic gauging material that is flattened at it's widest point. The scale printed on the gauging material package should be used. This will give you the bearing clearance measurement.
7. If the clearance is greater than allowed, replace both bearing shells as a set.

## CONNECTING ROD AND MAIN BEARING REPLACEMENT

Main bearing clearances must be corrected by the use of selective lower and upper shells. DO NOT USE shims behind the shells to compensate for wear.

1. Remove the oil pan as previously described.
2. If necessary, remove the oil pump assembly.
3. Loosen all of the main bearing caps and remove the main bearing caps and remove the lower shell.

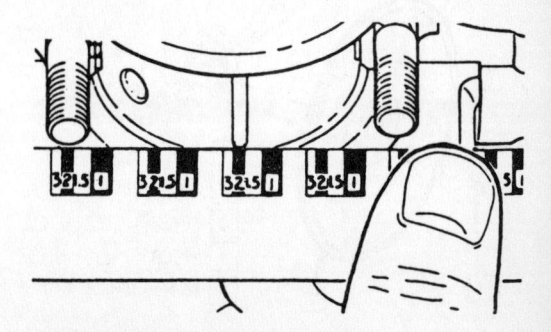

**Inspecting Bearing Clearance**

# ENGINE AND ENGINE OVERHAUL

4. Insert a bearing roll out pin or cotter pin into the oil passage hole in the crankshaft and rotate the crankshaft in the direction that is opposite of the normal cranking rotation. The pin should make contact with the upper shell and roll it out.

5. Inspect the main bearing journals for roughness and wear. Remove slight roughness with a fine grit polishing cloth saturated with engine oil.

6. If the journals are scored or ridged, the crankshaft must be replaced.

7. Thoroughly clean the crankshaft journals and bearing caps before installing new main bearings.

8. Apply special lubricant No. 1050169 or equivalent to the thrust flanges of the bearing shells.

9. Install a new upper shell on the crankshaft journal with the locating tang in the correct position and as in removal, rotate the shaft to turn it into place using a cotter pin or roll pin.

10. Install a new bearing shell to the bearing cap.

11. Install a new oil seal in the rear main bearing cap and block.

12. Lubricate the main bearings with engine oil and the thrust surface with special lubricant No. 1050169 or equivalent.

13. Lubricat the main bearing caps with engine oil and tighten the bolts to specifications.

## Flywheel
### REMOVAL AND INSTALLATION

1. Remove the transaxle assembly, refer to the transaxle Chapter for this procedure.
2. Remove the splash shield, if so equipped.
3. If manual transaxle, remove the clutch and pressure plate.
4. Using special tool J38122 or equivalent, secure the crankshaft and remove the flywheel.

**To Install:**

5. Remove all thread adhesive from the bolts and from the holes before installation.
6. Apply locking type adhesive to all of the flywheel to crankshaft mounting bolts.
7. The remaining installation steps are the reverse of the removal procedure. Tighten the flywheel bolts in stages to the specified torque.

## EXHAUST SYSTEM

## Front Exhaust Pipe with Flange
### REMOVAL AND INSTALLATION

1. Raise and safely support the vehicle.
2. Support the catalytic converter and remove the attaching bolts from between the exhaust pipe and the converter.
3. Remove the bolts from between the exhaust pipe and the manifold.
4. Remove the manifold and converter seals and remove the pipe.

**To Install:**

**Typical Flywheel—2.5L Shown**

| 1 | 75 N·m (55 LB. FT.) |
| 2 | FLYWHEEL |
| 3 | SPACER |
| 4 | INSERT |
| 5 | 95 N·m (69 LB. FT.) |

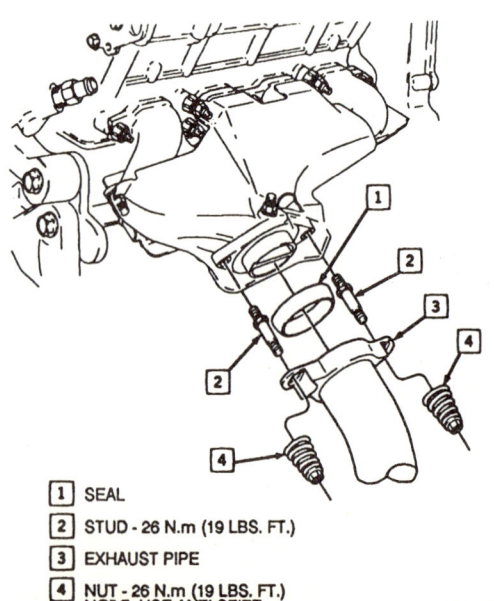

**Manifold Attachment—2.3L**

| 1 | SEAL |
| 2 | STUD - 26 N.m (19 LBS. FT.) |
| 3 | EXHAUST PIPE |
| 4 | NUT - 26 N.m (19 LBS. FT.) NOTE: USE ANTI-SEIZE COMPOUND ON NUTS |

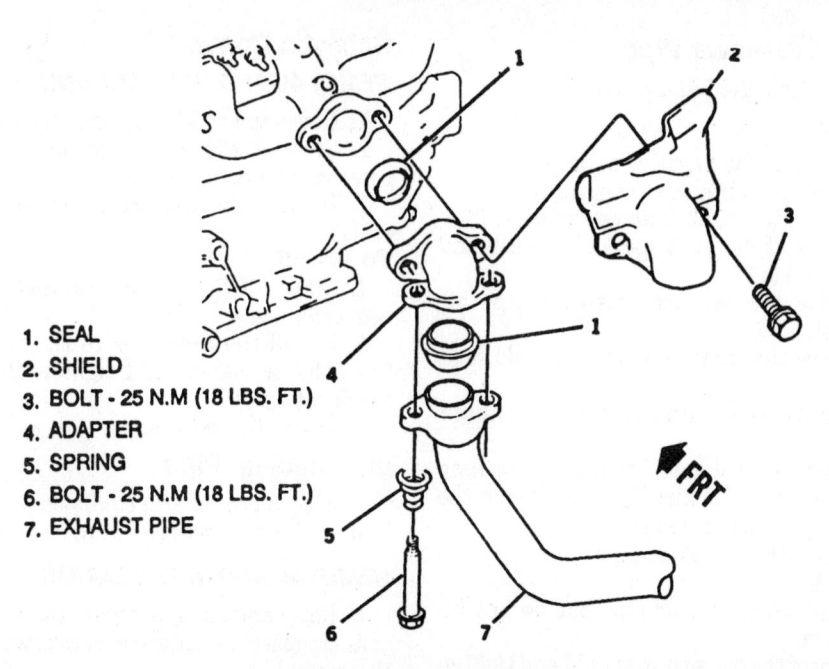

# ENGINE AND ENGINE OVERHAUL    151

1. SEAL
2. SHIELD
3. BOLT - 25 N.M (18 LBS. FT.)
4. ADAPTER
5. SPRING
6. BOLT - 25 N.M (18 LBS. FT.)
7. EXHAUST PIPE

Manifold Attachment—3.3L

5. Properly clean the flange surfaces and install the manifold and catalytic converter seals.
6. Install the exhaust pipe to the manifold with bolts and tighten the bolts to specifications.
7. Connect the exhaust pipe to the converter and install the bolts. Tighten the bolts to specifications.
8. Lower the vehicle.

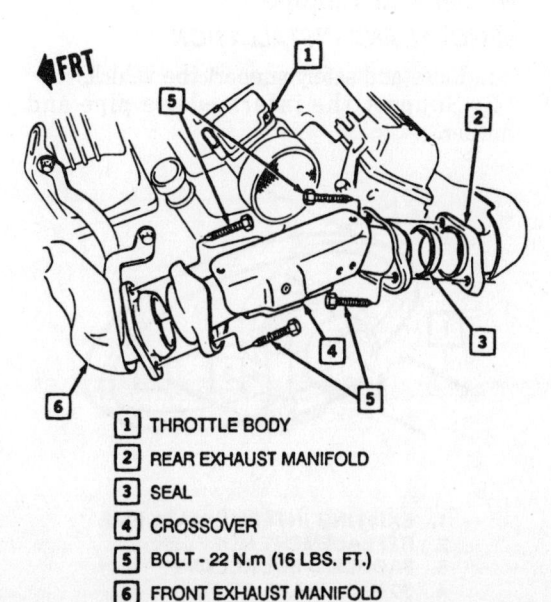

## Front Exhaust Pipe without Flange
### REMOVAL AND INSTALLATION

1. Raise and safely support the vehicle.
2. Support the catalytic converter.
3. Remove the clamps and disconnect the exhaust pipe from the catalytic converter.
4. Disconnect the exhaust pipe from the manifold and remove the pipe.
5. Remove the manifold seal.

**To Install:**

6. Connect the exhaust pipe to the catalytic converter and install the clamp.
7. Install the manifold seal and connect the exhaust pipe to the manifold. Lower the vehicle.

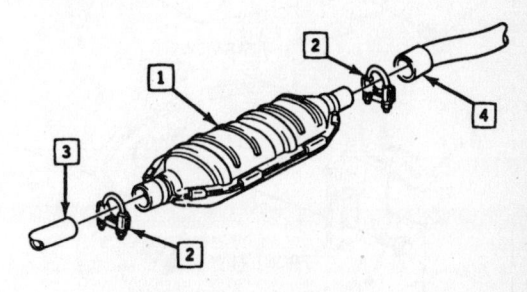

[1] THROTTLE BODY
[2] REAR EXHAUST MANIFOLD
[3] SEAL
[4] CROSSOVER
[5] BOLT - 22 N.m (16 LBS. FT.)
[6] FRONT EXHAUST MANIFOLD

[1] CATALYTIC CONVERTER
[2] GUILLOTINE CLAMP - 35 N.m (26 LBS. FT.)
[3] FRONT EXHAUST PIPE
[4] INTERMEDIATE PIPE

**3.3L Crossover Attachment**            **Catalytic Converter Without Flange**

## ENGINE AND ENGINE OVERHAUL

## Exhaust Crossover Pipe

### REMOVAL AND INSTALLATION

**3.3L Engine**

1. Disconnect the negative battery cable.
2. Remove the air cleaner assembly.
3. Remove the engine cooling fan assembly.
4. Disconnect the front spark plug wires and place to the side.
5. Remove the exhaust crossover pipe attaching bolts.
6. Remove the front exhaust manifold heat shield.
7. Remove the front exhaust support bracket.
8. Loosen the exhaust manifold attaching bolts and position the manifold away from the engine for clearance reasons.
9. Remove the crossover pipe.

**To Install:**

10. Install the crossover pipe but do not install bolts yet.
11. Connect the exhaust manifold and tighten the bolts.
12. Install the crossover pipe bolts and tighten to specifications.
13. Install the exhaust manifold support bracket and heat shield.
14. Install the engine cooling fan assembly.
15. Install the air cleaner assembly and connect the negative battery cable.

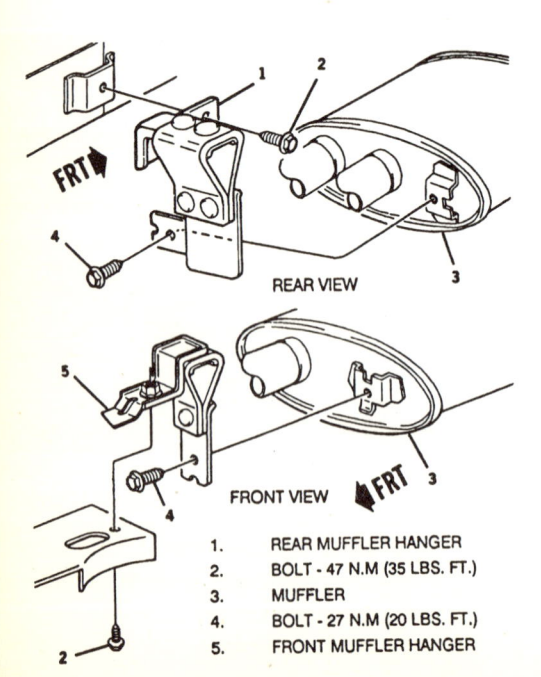

## Catalytic Converter

### REMOVAL AND INSTALLATION

1. Raise and safely support the vehicle.
2. Support the converter and remove the converter bolts or clamps.
3. Remove the converter and the converter seals.

**To Install:**

4. Clean all flange surfaces and install the converter seals.
5. Install the converter to the vehicle with the bolts or clamps and tighten the bolts to specifications.
6. Lower the vehicle.

## Intermediate Pipe

NOTE: *If vehicle still equipped with original welded system, a service muffler must be used.*

### REMOVAL AND INSTALLATION

1. Raise and safely support the vehicle.
2. Support the catalytic converter and muffler assembly.
3. Disconnect the intermediate pipe hanger.
4. Unbolt the pipe from the converter and disconnect the intermediate pipe.
5. Remove the muffler hangers and the muffler and remove the converter seal.

**To Install:**

6. Install the converter seal and install the muffler to the intermediate pipe and to the hanger.
7. Install the intermediate pipe to the converter and connect to the hanger.
8. Lower the vehicle.

## Muffler and Tailpipe

### REMOVAL AND INSTALLATION

1. Raise and safely support the vehicle.
2. Support the intermediate pipe and muffler.

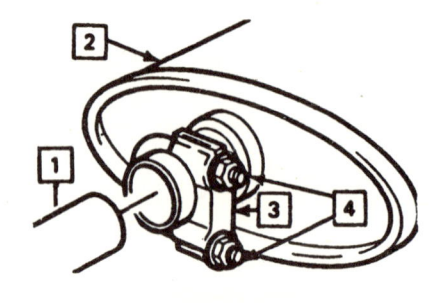

1. REAR MUFFLER HANGER
2. BOLT - 47 N.M (35 LBS. FT.)
3. MUFFLER
4. BOLT - 27 N.M (20 LBS. FT.)
5. FRONT MUFFLER HANGER

**Typical Muffler Attachment**

1. EXISTING INTERMEDIATE PIPE
2. REPLACEMENT MUFFLER
3. SADDLE/U BOLT CLAMP
4. 30 N·m (22 LBS. FT.)

**Muffler Installation**

# ENGINE AND ENGINE OVERHAUL 153

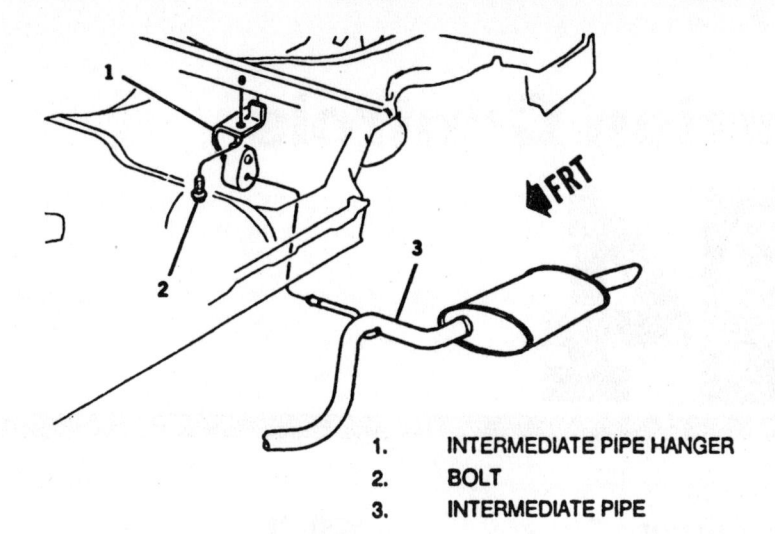

1. INTERMEDIATE PIPE HANGER
2. BOLT
3. INTERMEDIATE PIPE

**Typical Intermediate Pipe Hanger**

3. Using an exhaust pipe cutting tool, cut the intermediate pipe as close to the weld as possible.
4. Remove the muffler hangers and the muffler.

**To Install:**
5. Connect the muffler to the intermediate pipe and install the hangers.
6. Install a U-Bolt type clamp and tighten. Lower the vehicle.

# Emission Controls

## EMISSION CONTROLS

### Crankcase Ventilation System

#### OPERATION

The Crankcase Ventilation system is used on all vehicles to evacuate the crankcase vapors. There are 2 types of ventilation systems: Crankcase Ventilation (CV) and Positive Crankcase Ventilation (PCV).

Both systems purge crankcase vapors and differ only in the use of fresh air, circulated through the crankcase, in the case of PCV systems. The CV system, used on the 2.3L engine, allows crankcase vapors to escape but does not introduce fresh air into the crankcase.

The PCV system, used on all other engines, circulates fresh air from the air cleaner or intake duct through the crankcase, where it mixes with blow-by gases and then passes through the Positive Crankcase Ventilation (PCV) valve or constant bleed orifice into the intake manifold.

When manifold vacuum is high, such as at idle, the orifice or valve restricts the flow of blow-by gases into the intake manifold. If abnormal operating conditions occur, the system will allow excessive blow-by gases to back flow through the hose into the air cleaner. These blow-by gases will then be mixed with the intake air in the air cleaner instead of the manifold. The air cleaner has a small filter attached to the inside wall that connects to the breather hose to trap impurities flowing in either direction.

A plugged PCV valve, orifice or hose may cause rough idle, stalling or slow idle speed, oil leaks, oil in the air cleaner or sludge in the engine. A leak could cause rough idle, stalling or high idle speed. The condition of the grommets in the valve cover will also affect system and engine performance.

#### SERVICE

**PCV Valve**

1. Remove the PCV valve from the rocker arm cover.
2. With the engine at normal operating temperature, run at idle.
3. Remove the PCV valve or orifice from the grommet in the valve cover and place thumb over the end to check if vacuum is present. If vacuum is not present, check for plugged hoses or manifold port. Repair or replace as necessary.
4. If the engine is equipped with a PCV valve, stop the engine and remove the valve. Shake and listen for the rattle of the check valve needle. If no rattle is heard, replace the valve.

**PCV System**

1. Check to make sure the engine has the correct PCV valve or bleed orifice.
2. Start the engine and bring to normal operating temperature.
3. Block off PCV system fresh air intake passage.
4. Remove the engine oil dipstick and install a vacuum gauge on the dipstick tube.
5. Run the engine at 1500 rpm for 30 seconds

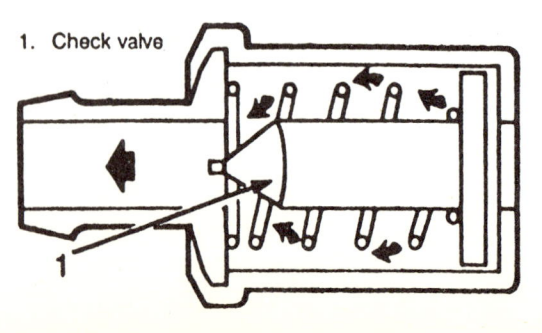

1. Check valve

**Standard PCV valve is also a check valve**

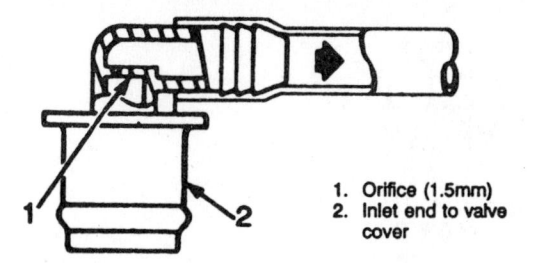

## EMISSION CONTROLS 155

**Standard PCV orifice—1991-92 2.5L engine**
1. Orifice (1.5mm)
2. Inlet end to valve cover

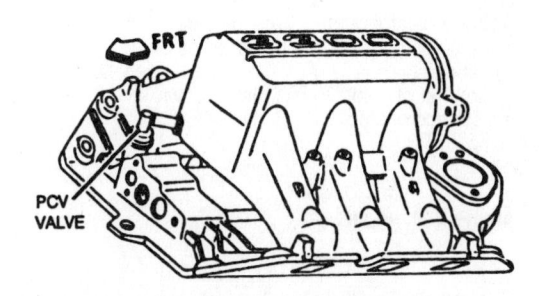

**Location of PCV valve on 3.3L engine**

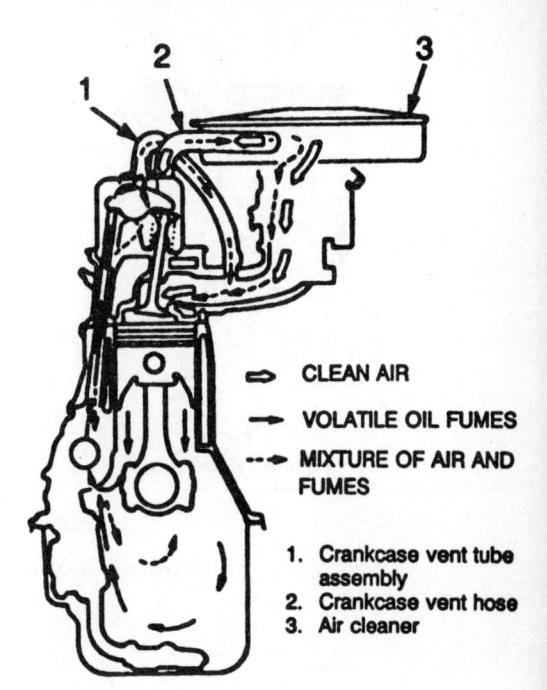

**Schematic of PCV system—2.0L and 2.5L engines**

⇨ CLEAN AIR
→ VOLATILE OIL FUMES
--▶ MIXTURE OF AIR AND FUMES

1. Crankcase vent tube assembly
2. Crankcase vent hose
3. Air cleaner

then read the vacuum gauge with the engine at 1500 rpm.
- If vacuum is present, the PCV system is functioning properly.
- If there is no vacuum, the engine may not be sealed and/or is drawing in outside air. Check the grommets and valve cover or oil pan gasket for leaks.

- If the vacuum gauge registers a pressure or the vacuum gauge is pushed out of the dipstick tube, check for the correct PCV valve or bleed orifice, a plugged hose or excessive engine blow-by.

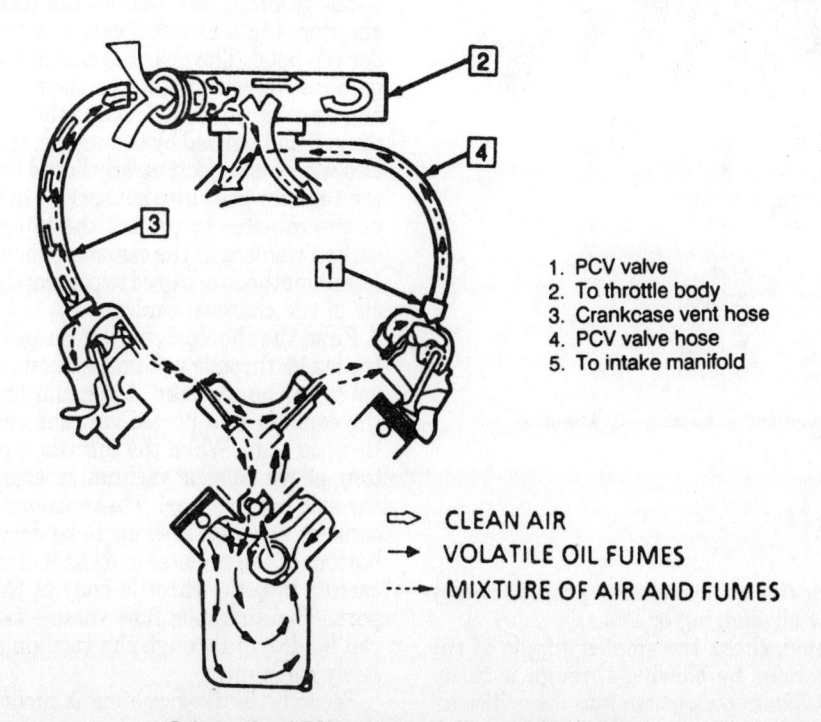

1. PCV valve
2. To throttle body
3. Crankcase vent hose
4. PCV valve hose
5. To intake manifold

⇨ CLEAN AIR
→ VOLATILE OIL FUMES
--▶ MIXTURE OF AIR AND FUMES

**Schematic of PCV system—3.0L and 3.3L engines**

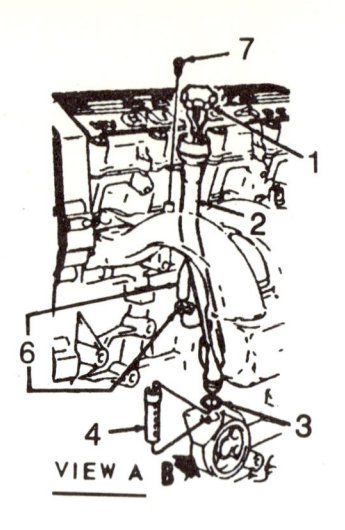

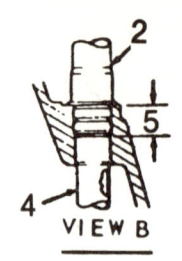

# EMISSION CONTROLS

1. Oil fill cap and indicator
2. Oil fill tube
3. O-ring
4. Oil level indicator guide. Holes in guide must face outboard 90° from centerline of crankshaft
5. Position top of guide 3/4 in. (19mm) down from surface of block
6. Clamp
7. Bolt

Crankcase ventilation system—2.3L engine

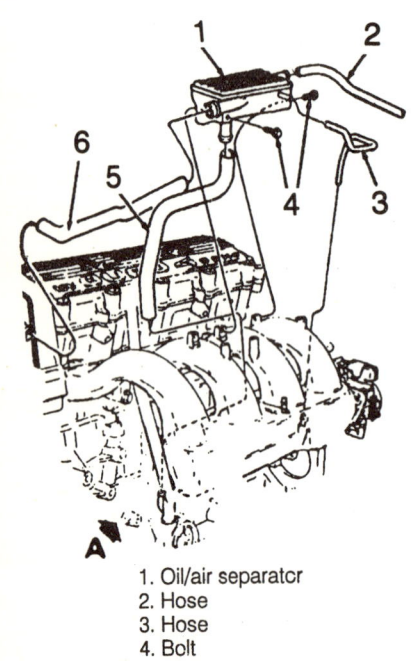

1. Oil/air separator
2. Hose
3. Hose
4. Bolt
5. Hose
6. Hose

Crankcase ventilation system—2.3L engine

## CV System

### 2.3L ENGINE

1. Check the CV system for proper flow by looking for oil sludging or leaks.
2. If noted, check the smaller nipple of the oil/air separator by blowing through it or inserting a 1.52mm plug gauge into the orifice inside the nipple.
3. If the orifice is plugged, replace the CV oil/air separator assembly.

## Fuel Evaporative Emission Control System

### OPERATION

The Evaporative Emission Control System is designed to prevent fuel tank vapors from being emitted into the atmosphere. When the engine is not running, gasoline vapors from the tank are stored in a charcoal canister, mounted under the hood. The charcoal canister absorbs the gasoline vapors and stores them until certain engine conditions are met and the vapors can be purged and burned by the engine. In some vehicles with fuel injection, any liquid fuel entering the canister goes into a reservoir in the bottom of the canister to protect the integrity of the carbon element in the canister above. Three different methods are used to control the purge cycle of the charcoal canister.

First, the charcoal canister purge cycle is controlled by throttle position without the use of a valve on the canister. A vacuum line connects the canister to a ported vacuum source on the throttle body. When the throttle is at any position above idle, a vacuum is created in the throttle body venturi. That vacuum acts on the canister causing fresh air to be drawn into the bottom of the canister and the fuel vapors to be carried into the throttle body at that vacuum port. The air/vapor flow volume is only what can be drawn through the vacuum port and is fairly constant.

Second, the flow volume is modulated with throttle position through a vacuum valve. The

# EMISSION CONTROLS 157

ported vacuum from the throttle body is used to open a diaphragm valve on top of the canister. When the valve is open, air and vapors are drawn into the intake manifold, usually through the same manifold port as the PCV system. With this method, the purge valve cycle is slaved to the throttle opening; more throttle opening, more purge air flow.

And third, the charcoal canister purge valve cycle is controlled by the ECM through a solenoid valve on the canister. When the solenoid is activated, full manifold vacuum is applied to the top of the purge valve diaphragm to open the valve all the way. A high volume of fresh air is drawn into the canister and the gasoline vapors are purged quickly. The ECM activates the solenoid valve when the following conditions are met:

- The engine is at normal operating temperature.
- After the engine has been running a specified period of time.
- Vehicle speed is above a predetermined speed.
- Throttle opening is above a predetermined value.
- A vent pipe allows fuel vapors to flow to the charcoal canister. On some vehicles, the tank is isolated from the charcoal canister by a tank pressure control valve, located either in the tank or in the vapor line near the canister. It is a combination roll-over, integral pressure and vacuum relief valve. When the vapor pressure in the tank exceeds 5kPa, the valve opens to allow vapors to vent to the canister. The valve also provides vacuum relief to protect against vacuum build-up in the fuel tank and roll-over spill protection.
- Poor engine idle, stalling and poor driveability can be caused by an inoperative canister purge solenoid, a damaged canister or split, damaged or improperly connected hoses.
- The most common symptom of problems in this system is fuel odors coming from under the hood. If there is no liquid fuel leak, check for a cracked or damaged vapor canister, inoperative or always open canister control valve, disconnected, mis-routed, kinked or damaged vapor pipe or canister hoses; or a damaged air cleaner or improperly seated air cleaner gasket.

## TESTING

### CHARCOAL CANISTER

1. Visually check the canister for cracks or damage.
2. If fuel is leaking from the bottom of the canister, replace canister and check for proper hose routing.
3. Check the filter at the bottom of the canister. If dirty, replace the filter.

### TANK PRESSURE CONTROL VALVE

1. Using a hand-held vacuum pump, apply a vacuum of 15 in. Hg (51kPa) through the control vacuum signal tube to the purge valve diaphragm. If the diaphragm does not hold vacuum for at least 20 seconds, the diaphragm is leaking. Replace the control valve.
2. With the vacuum still applied to the control vacuum tube, attach a short piece of hose to the valve's tank tube side and blow into the hose. Air should pass through the valve. If it does not, replace the control valve.

### CANISTER PURGE CONTROL VALVE

1. Connect a clean length of hose to the fuel tank vapor line connection on the canister and attempt to blow through the purge control valve. It should be difficult or impossible to blow through the valve. If air passes easily, the valve is stuck open and should be replaced.
2. Connect a hand-held vacuum pump to the top vacuum line fitting of the purge control

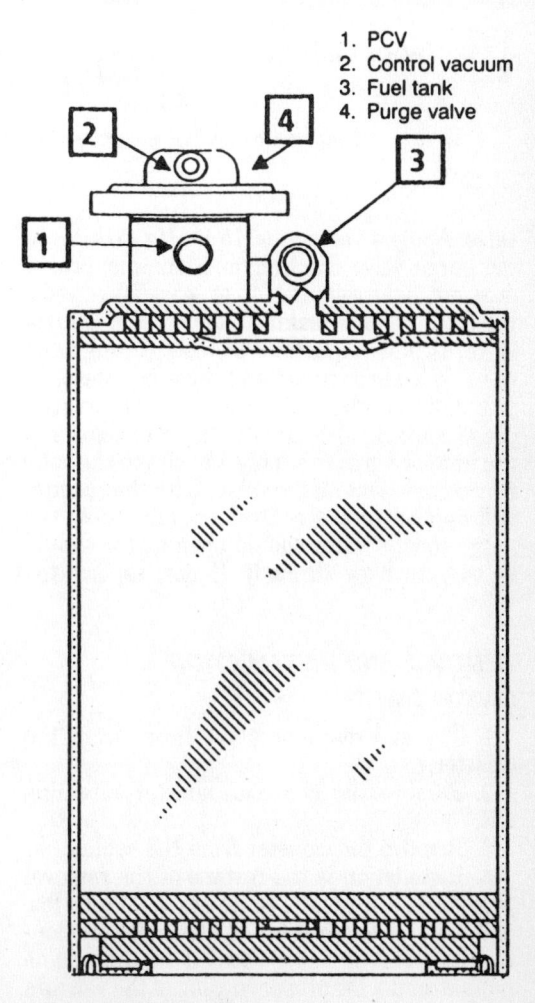

1. PCV
2. Control vacuum
3. Fuel tank
4. Purge valve

Vapor canister connections

# 158 EMISSION CONTROLS

| 1 | Throttle Body | 3 | Fuel Tank | 5 | Purge Solenoid Control Assembly |
| 2 | Vapor Canister | 4 | Vapor Restriction (.055" orifice) | 6 | Outside Air |

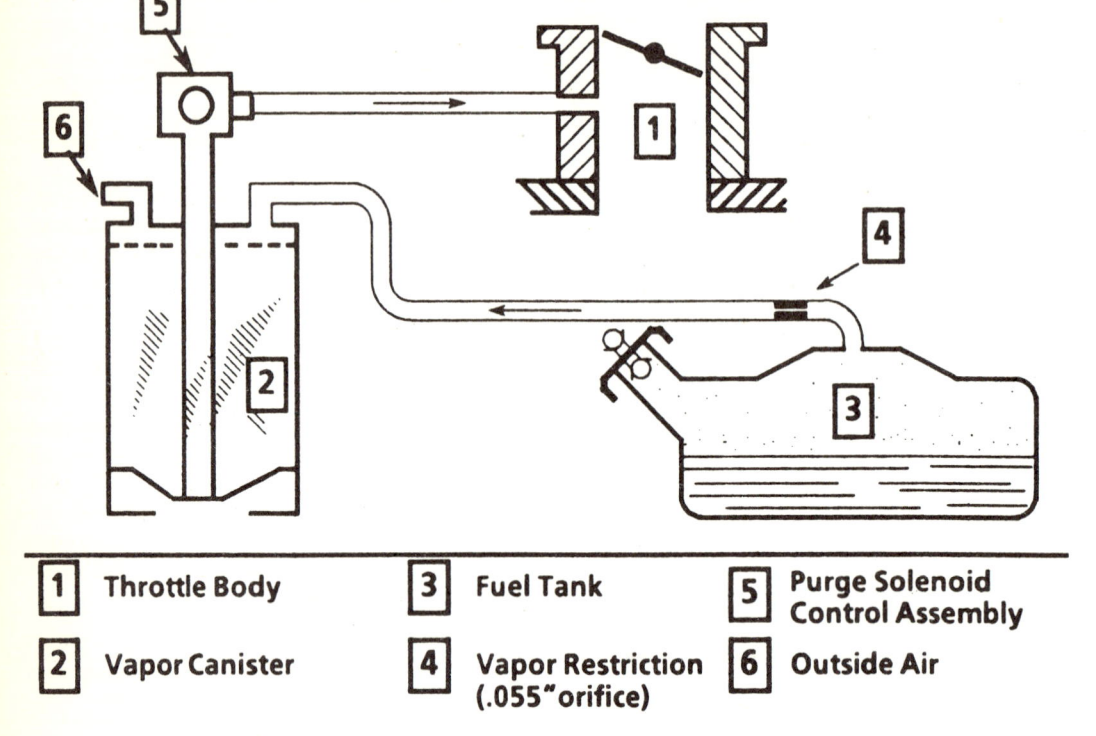

Evaporative emission control system schematic—3.3L engine—others similar

valve. Apply a vacuum of 15 in. Hg (51kPa) to the purge valve diaphragm. If the diaphragm does not hold vacuum for at least 20 seconds the diaphragm is leaking. Replace the control valve. If it is impossible to blow through the valve, it is stuck closed and must be replaced.

3. On vehicles with a solenoid activated purge control valve, unplug the connector and use jumper wires to supply 12 volts to the solenoid connections on the valve. With the vacuum still applied to the control vacuum tube, the purge control valve should open and it should be easy to blow through. If not, replace the valve.

## REMOVAL AND INSTALLATION
### CHARCOAL CANISTER

1. Tag and disconnect the hoses from the canister.
2. Remove the charcoal canister retaining nut.
3. Remove the canister from the vehicle.
4. Installation is the reverse of the removal procedure. Torque the retainers to 25 inch lbs. (2.8 Nm). Refer to the Vehicle Emission Control Information label, located in the engine compartment, for proper routing of the vacuum hoses.

### TANK PRESSURE CONTROL VALVE

1. Disconnect the hoses from the control valve.
2. Remove the mounting hardware.
3. Remove the control valve from the vehicle.
4. Installation is the reverse of the removal procedure. Refer to the Vehicle Emission Control Information label, located in the engine compartment, for proper routing of the vacuum hoses.

## Exhaust Gas Recirculation System
### OPERATION

NOTE: *The 2.3L and 3.3L engines do not use an EGR valve.*

The EGR system is used to reduce oxides of nitrogen (NOx) emission levels caused by high combustion chamber temperatures. This is accomplished by the use of an EGR valve which opens, under specific engine operating conditions, to admit a small amount of exhaust gas into the intake manifold, below the throttle plate. The exhaust gas mixes with the incoming air charge and displaces a portion of the oxygen in the air/fuel mixture entering the combustion chamber. The exhaust gas does not support combustion of the air/fuel mixture but it takes up volume, the net effect of which is to lower the temperature of the combustion process. This lower temperature also helps control detonation.

The EGR valve is a mounted on the intake manifold and has an opening into the exhaust manifold. The EGR valve is opened by ported vacuum and allows exhaust gases to flow into the intake manifold. If too much exhaust gas enters, combustion will not occur. Because of this, very little exhaust gas is allowed to pass through the valve. The EGR system will be activated once the engine reaches normal operating temperature and the EGR valve will open when engine operating conditions are above idle speed and below Wide Open Throttle (WOT). On California vehicles equipped with a Vehicle Speed Sensor (VSS), the EGR valve opens when the VSS signal is greater than 2 mph. The EGR system is deactivated on vehicles equipped with a Transmission Converter Clutch (TCC) when the TCC is engaged.

Too much EGR flow at idle, cruise, or during cold operation may result in the engine stalling after cold start, the engine stalling at idle after deceleration, vehicle surge during cruise and rough idle. If the EGR valve is always open, the vehicle may not idle. Too little or no EGR flow allows combustion temperatures to get too high which could result in spark knock (detonation), engine overheating and/or emission test failure.

The two types of EGR valves used on N body vehicles are ported and negative backpressure and differ mainly in the way EGR flow is modulated.

### Ported EGR Valve

The ported EGR valve takes its name from the fact that it uses a ported vacuum source to open the EGR valve and modulate the EGR flow. The ported vacuum source is a small opening just above the throttle blade in the throttle body. When the throttle begins to open the air passing through the venturi, creates a low pressure which draws on the EGR valve diaphragm causing it to open. As the throttle blade opens further, the ported vacuum increases and opens the valve further.

The ECM controls EGR operation through an EGR control solenoid. Ported vacuum must flow through the EGR control solenoid to open the EGR valve. The ECM uses information received from the Coolant Temperature Sensor (CTS), Throttle Position Sensor (TPS) and the Mass Air Flow (MAF) sensor to determine when to allow EGR operation. When certain parameters are met, such as engine at normal operating temperature and the engine speed is above idle, the ECM signals the solenoid to open, allowing EGR operation.

### Negative Backpressure EGR Valve

The negative backpressure EGR valve, used on the 2.5L engine, varies the amount of exhaust gas flow into the intake manifold depending on manifold vacuum and variations in exhaust backpressure. Like the ported EGR valve, the negative backpressure EGR valve uses a ported vacuum source. An air bleed valve, located inside the EGR valve assembly acts as a vacuum regulator. The bleed valve controls the amount of vacuum in the vacuum chamber by bleeding vacuum to outside air during the open phase of the cycle. The diaphragm on the valve has an internal air bleed hole which is held closed by a small spring when there is no exhaust backpressure. Engine vacu-

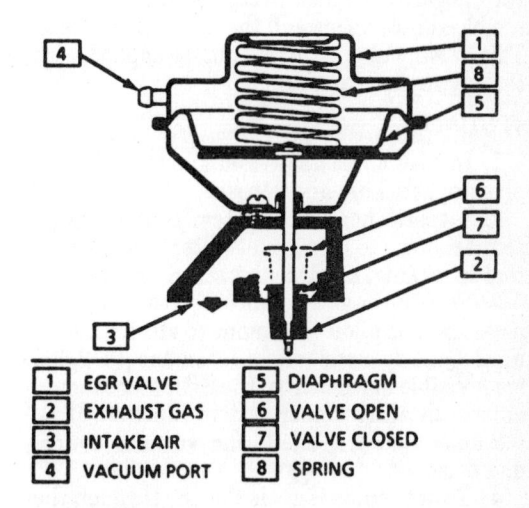

| 1 | EGR VALVE | 5 | DIAPHRAGM |
| 2 | EXHAUST GAS | 6 | VALVE OPEN |
| 3 | INTAKE AIR | 7 | VALVE CLOSED |
| 4 | VACUUM PORT | 8 | SPRING |

Port EGR valve

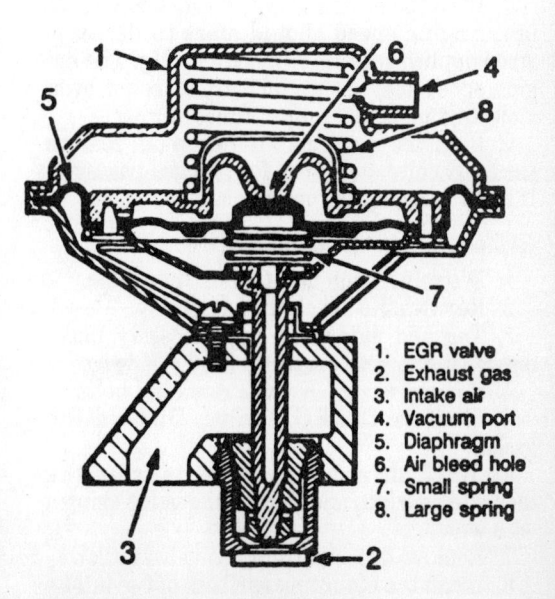

1. EGR valve
2. Exhaust gas
3. Intake air
4. Vacuum port
5. Diaphragm
6. Air bleed hole
7. Small spring
8. Large spring

Negative backpressure EGR valve

# 160 EMISSION CONTROLS

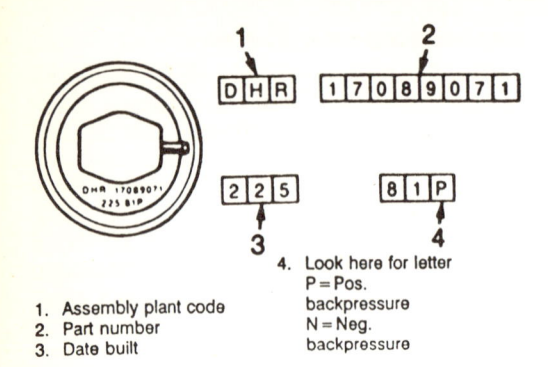

**Identification of EGR valve**

1. Assembly plant code
2. Part number
3. Date built
4. Look here for letter
   P = Pos. backpressure
   N = Neg. backpressure

um opens the EGR valve against the pressure of a spring. When manifold vacuum combines with negative exhaust backpressure, the vacuum bleed hole opens and the EGR valve closes. This valve will open if vacuum is applied with the engine not running.

## TESTING

1. Inspect all passages and moving parts for plugging, sticking and deposits.
2. Inspect the entire system (hoses, tubes, connections, etc.) for leakage. Replace any part that is leaking, hardened, cracked, or melted.
3. Run the engine to normal operating temperature, and allow the engine to idle for 2 minutes. Quickly accelerate the engine to 2,500 rpm. Visible movement of the EGR stem should occur indicating proper system function. If no movement occurs, check the vacuum source and hose.
4. To determine if gas is flowing through the system, connect a vacuum pump to the valve.
5. With the engine idling, slowly apply vacuum. Engine speed should start to decrease when applied vacuum reaches 3 in. Hg. The engine speed may drop quickly and could even stall; this indicated proper function.
6. If engine speed does not drop off, remove the EGR valve and check for plugged passages. If everything checks out, replace the valve.

## REMOVAL AND INSTALLATION

1. Disconnect the negative battery cable.
2. Remove the air cleaner assembly.
3. Tag and disconnect the necessary hoses and wiring to gain access to the EGR valve.
4. Remove the EGR valve retaining bolts.
5. Remove the EGR valve. Discard the gasket.
6. Buff the exhaust deposits from the mounting surface and around the valve using a wire wheel.
7. Remove deposits from the valve outlet.
8. Clean the mounting surfaces of the intake manifold and valve assembly.

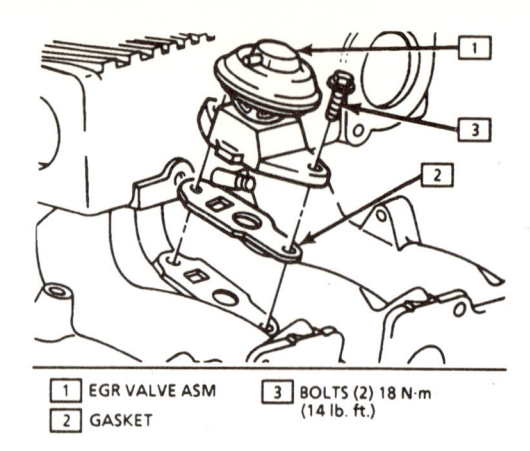

EGR valve location—2.0L engine
1. EGR VALVE ASM
2. GASKET
3. BOLTS (2) 18 N·m (14 lb. ft.)

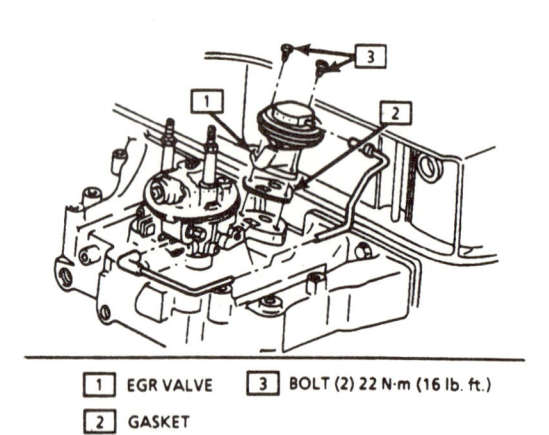

EGR valve location—2.5L engine
1. EGR VALVE
2. GASKET
3. BOLT (2) 22 N·m (16 lb. ft.)

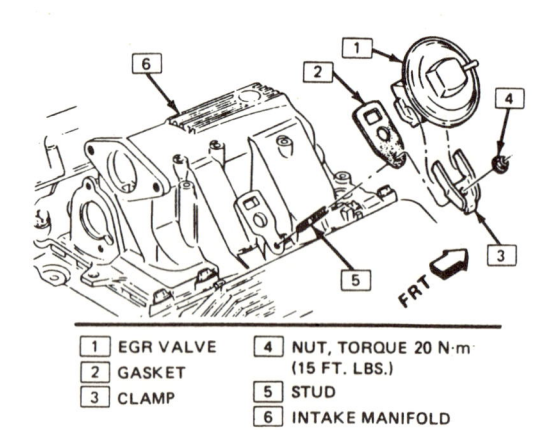

EGR valve location—3.0L engine
1. EGR VALVE
2. GASKET
3. CLAMP
4. NUT, TORQUE 20 N·m (15 FT. LBS.)
5. STUD
6. INTAKE MANIFOLD

**To install:**

9. Install a new EGR gasket.
10. Install the EGR valve to the manifold.
11. Install the retaining bolts and torque to 16 ft. lbs. (22 Nm).

# EMISSION CONTROLS

12. Connect the wiring and hoses.
13. Install the air cleaner assembly.
14. Connect the negative battery cable.

## Catalytic Converter

### OPERATION

The catalytic converter is mounted in the engine exhaust stream ahead of the muffler. Its function is to combine carbon monoxide (CO) and hydrocarbons (HC) with oxygen and break down nitrogen oxide (NOx) compounds. These gasses are converted to mostly $CO_2$ and water. It heats to operating temperature within about 1–2 minutes, depending on ambient temperature and driving conditions and will operate at temperatures up to about 1500°F. Inside the converter housing is a single or dual bed ceramic monolith, coated with various combinations of platinum, paladium and rhodium.

The catalytic converter is not serviceable. If tests and visual inspection show the converter to be damaged, it must be replaced. There are 2 types of failures: melting or fracturing. The most common failure is melting, resulting from unburned gasoline contacting the monolith, such as when a cylinder does not fire. Usually when the monolith melts, high backpressure results. When it cracks, it begins to break up into small particles that get blown out the tail pipe.

Poor fuel mileage and/or a lack of power can often be traced to a melted or plugged catalytic converter. The damage may be the result of engine malfunction or the use of leaded gasoline in the vehicle. Proper diagnosis for a restricted exhaust system is essential before any components are replaced. The following procedure that can be used to determine if the exhaust system is restricted.

### TESTING

#### Check at Oxygen Sensor

1. Carefully remove the oxygen sensor.
2. Install an adapter that has the same threads as the sensor and that will hook up to a pressure gauge. Install in place of the sensor.
3. Perform Backpressure Diagnosis Test.
4. When test is complete, remove the pressure gauge and adapter. Lightly coat the threads of the oxygen sensor with an anti-seize compound. Reinstall the oxygen sensor.

#### Backpressure Diagnosis Test

1. With engine idling at normal operating temperature, observe the backpressure reading on the gauge. The reading should not exceed 1.25 psi (8.6kPa).
2. Increase engine speed to 2000 rpm and observe gauge. The reading should not exceed 3 psi (20.7kPa).
3. If the backpressure at either speed exceeds specification, a restricted exhaust is indicated.
4. Inspect the entire exhaust system for a collapsed pipe, heat distress or possible internal muffler failure.
5. If there are no obvious reasons for the excessive backpressure, the catalytic converter is suspected and should be removed for inspection or replacement.

#### Inspection

1. Raise and safely support the vehicle.
2. Inspect the catalytic converter protector for any damage.
NOTE: *If any part of the protector is dented to the extent that is contacts the converter, replace the protector.*
3. Check the heat insulator for adequate clearance between the converter and the heat insulator. Repair or replace any damaged components.

### REMOVAL AND INSTALLATION

1. Raise and safely support the vehicle.
2. Remove the retaining bolts at the front and the rear and remove the converter.
3. On units with a ceramic monolith, it should be possible to look into the end of the housing and see light through the other end. If it is melted enough to cause high exhaust backpressure, it will be obvious.
4. Installation is the reverse of the removal procedure. Lower the vehicle, start the engine and check for exhaust leaks.

## ELECTRONIC ENGINE CONTROLS

### Fuel System

NOTE: *For removal and installation procedures and additional information, please refer to Chapter 5.*

### GENERAL INFORMATION

The basic function of the fuel metering system is to control the delivery of fuel to the meet all engine operating conditions. The fuel delivery system consists of the Throttle Body Injection (TBI) unit or fuel rail assembly with individual injectors and pressure regulator and throttle body assembly with Idle Air Control (IAC) valve and Throttle Position Sensor (TPS); the fuel pump, fuel pump relay, fuel tank, accelerator control, fuel lines, fuel filters and evaporative emission control system.

The fuel system is controlled by an Electronic Control Module (ECM) located in the passenger compartment. The ECM is the control center of

# EMISSION CONTROLS

the computer command control system processing information from various input sources to control certain engine functions. The ECM controls fuel delivery, ignition timing, electronic spark control, some emission control systems, engagement of the transmission converter clutch and downshift control or the manual transmission shift light. The ECM is also a valuable diagnostic tool in that it has the ability to store trouble codes which can by helpful in identifying malfunctioning systems. The ECM can also be used in conjunction with a SCAN tool to monitor values of engine sensors to see if they are within specification.

The ECM operates in 2 running mode conditions: open and closed loop. When the engine is cold and engine rpm is above a specified value, the ECM ignores any signal it may be receiving from the oxygen sensor and stays in open loop. The ECM will go into closed loop when the following conditions are met: the oxygen sensor is sending a fluctuating signal to the ECM (indicating that it is hot enough to operate properly and respond to changes in the oxygen content in the exhaust gas), the engine is at normal operating temperature and a specific amount of time has elapsed since engine start. When operating in closed loop, the ECM varies the injector on-time in order to maintain the ideal stoichiometric ratio of 14.7:1. This mixture ratio provides optimum fuel economy and engine performance as well as minimizing exhaust emissions.

## Fuel Injection System
### OPERATION

The fuel injection system uses a solenoid-operated fuel injector(s) mounted either on the throttle body (2.5L engine) or at the intake valve port of each cylinder (all other engines). The ECM controls the flow of fuel to the cylinders by varying the injector duty cycle or length of time the electrical solenoid is energized.

The TBI system used on the 2.5L (VIN U) uses model 700 fuel injector units. The model 700 unit consists of 2 major castings: the fuel meter assembly with pressure regulator and fuel injector, and the throttle body with the IAC valve and TPS.

MPFI systems deliver fuel to the intake port of each cylinder by a fuel injector which is controlled by the ECM.

## Coolant Temperature Sensor
### OPERATION

Most engine functions are affected by the coolant temperature. Determining whether the engine is hot or cold is largely dependent on the temperature of the coolant. An accurate temperature signal to the ECM is supplied by the coolant temperature sensor. The coolant temperature sensor is a thermistor mounted in the engine coolant stream. A thermistor is an electrical device that varies its resistance in relation to changes in temperature. Low coolant temperature produces a high resistance (100,000Ω at $-40°F/-40°C$) and high coolant temperature produces low resistance (70Ω at $266°F/130°C$). The ECM supplies a signal of 5 volts to the coolant temperature sensor through a resistor in the ECM and measures the voltage. The voltage will be high when the engine is cold and low when the engine is hot.

## Fuel Filter
### OPERATION

The in-line fuel filter is a paper element filter designed to trap particles that may damage the fuel injection system. The filter element must be replaced periodically. The fuel system pressure must be relieved before opening the system to replace the filter.

## Fuel Injector Assembly
### OPERATION

The fuel injector(s) are mounted on the fuel meter assembly or at the intake port of each cylinder. The fuel injector is a solenoid-operated device, controlled by the ECM. The ECM energizes the solenoid, which lifts a normally-closed ball valve off its seat. The fuel, which is under pressure, is injected in a conical spray pattern at the walls of the throttle body bore above the throttle valve. The amount of fuel sprayed is de-

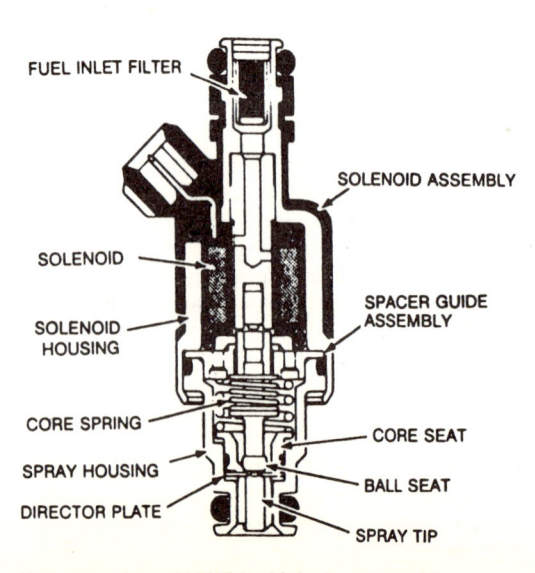

**Cutaway view of MPFI fuel injector assembly**

# EMISSION CONTROLS

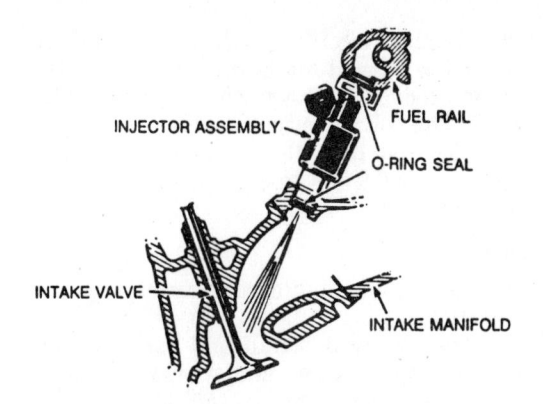

**MPFI fuel injector position and operation in the intake manifold**

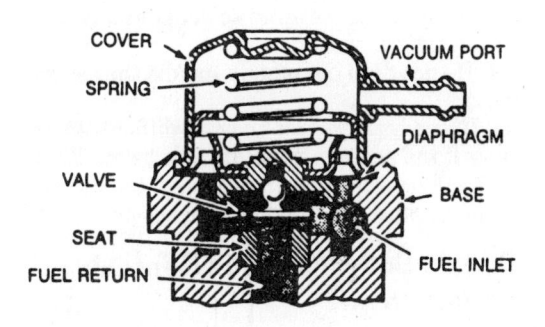

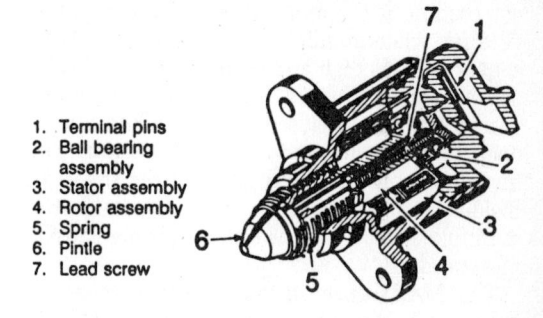

**Cutaway view of IAC valve**

1. Terminal pins
2. Ball bearing assembly
3. Stator assembly
4. Rotor assembly
5. Spring
6. Pintle
7. Lead screw

**Cutaway view of fuel regulator**

termined by the length of time the ECM energizes the injector solenoid, known as the pulse width.

The fuel which is not used by the injectors is cycled through the pressure regulator and back to the fuel tank; cycling the fuel helps prevent vapor lock.

## Fuel Pressure Regulator

### OPERATION

The fuel pressure regulator keeps the fuel available to the injectors within a specified pressure range. The pressure regulator is a diaphragm-operated relief valve with fuel pump pressure on one side and air cleaner pressure in vehicles equipped with TBI or intake manifold vacuum in others, acting on the other side. On some engines, the pressure regulator and fuel rail are serviced as an assembly, and the regulator cannot be removed from the fuel rail.

## Idle Air Control (IAC) Valve

### OPERATION

Engine idle speeds are controlled by the ECM through the IAC valve mounted on the throttle body. The ECM sends voltage pulses to the IAC motor windings causing the IAC motor shaft and pintle to move **IN** or **OUT** a given distance (number of steps) for each pulse (called counts). The movement of the pintle controls the airflow around the throttle plate, which in turn, controls engine idle speed. Idle Air Control valve pintle position counts can be observed using a Scan tool. Zero (0) counts corresponds to a fully closed passage, while 140 counts or more correspond to full flow.

Idle speed can be categorized in 2 ways: actual (controlled) idle speed and minimum idle speed. Controlled idle speed is obtained by the ECM positioning the IAC valve pintle. Resulting idle speed is determined by total air flow (IAC/passage + PCV + throttle valve + calibrated vacuum leaks). Controlled idle speed is specified at normal operating conditions, which consists of engine coolant at normal operating temperature, air conditioning compressor **OFF**, manual transmission in neutral or automatic transmission in **D**.

Minimum idle air speed is set at the factory with a stop screw. This setting allows enough air flow by the throttle valves to cause the IAC valve pintle to be positioned a calibrated number of steps (counts) from the seat during normal controlled idle operation.

The idle speed is controlled by the ECM through the IAC valve. No adjustment is required during routine maintenance. Tampering with the minimum idle speed adjustment is highly discouraged and may result in premature failure of the IAC valve.

## Manifold Absolute Pressure (MAP) Sensor

### OPERATION

**Except 3.0L (VIN L) and 3.3L (VIN N) Engines**

The MAP sensor measures the changes in intake manifold pressure, which result from engine load and speed changes and converts this information to a voltage output. The MAP sen-

# EMISSION CONTROLS

sor reading is the opposite of a vacuum gauge reading: when manifold pressure is high, MAP sensor value is high and vacuum is low. A MAP sensor will produce a low output on engine coastdown with a closed throttle while a wide open throttle will produce a high output. The high output is produced because the pressure inside the manifold is the same as outside the manifold, so 100% of the outside air pressure is measured.

The MAP sensor is also used to measure barometric pressure under certain conditions, which allows the ECM to automatically adjust for different altitudes.

The MAP sensor changes the 5 volt signal supplied by the ECM, which reads the change and uses the information to control fuel delivery and ignition timing.

## Mass Air Flow (MAF) Sensor
### OPERATION
#### 3.0L (VIN L) and 3.3L (VIN N) Engines

The Mass Air Flow sensor, used on 3.0L (VIN L) and 3.3L (VIN N) engines, replaces the MAP sensor used on other engines. The MAF sensor is located in the incoming air stream and measures the amount of air that passes through the electrical grid. The MAF indicates air flow to the ECM as an electrical value. The ECM uses this information to determine the operating condition of the engine in order to determine fuel requirements. A large quantity of air passing through the MAF will be read by the ECM as acceleration condition and a small quantity as deceleration or idle.

## Manifold Air Temperature (MAT)/Intake Air Temperature (IAT) Sensor
### OPERATION

The MAT/IAT sensor is a thermistor which supplies manifold air temperature information to the ECM. The MAT/IAT sensor produces high resistance (100,000Ω at −40°F/−40°C) at low temperatures and low resistance of 70Ω at 266°F (130°C) at high temperatures. The ECM supplies a 5 volt signal to the MAT sensor and measures MAT/IAT sensor output voltage. The voltage signal will be high when the air is cold and low when the air is hot.

## Oxygen Sensor
### OPERATION

The exhaust oxygen sensor or $O_2$ sensor, is mounted in the exhaust stream where it monitors oxygen content in the exhaust gas. The oxygen content in the exhaust is a measure of the air/fuel mixture going into the engine. The oxygen in the exhaust reacts with the oxygen sensor to produce a voltage which is read by the ECM. The voltage output is very low, ranging from 0.1 volt in a high oxygen-lean mixture condition to 0.9 volt in a low oxygen-rich mixture condition.

#### Precautions:

• Careful handling of the oxygen sensor is essential.

• The electrical pigtail and connector are permanently attached and should not be removed from the oxygen sensor.

• The in-line electrical connector and louvered end of the oxygen sensor must be kept free of grease, dirt and other contaminants.

• Avoid using cleaning solvents of any type on the oxygen sensor.

• Do not drop or roughly handle the oxygen sensor.

• The oxygen sensor may be difficult to remove if the engine temperature is below 120°F (48°C). Excessive force may damage the threads in the exhaust manifold or exhaust pipe.

## Throttle Body Injection (TBI) Unit
### OPERATION

The TBI unit is mounted on the intake manifold and contains the fuel injector(s), pressure regulator, IAC valve and fuel meter assembly. The fuel injector is/are solenoid-operated device, controlled by the ECM. The ECM energizes the solenoid, which lifts a normally closed ball valve off its seat. Fuel, under pressure, is injected in a conical spray pattern at the walls of the throttle body bore above the throttle valve. When the ECM de-energizes the solenoid, spring pressure closes the ball valve. The amount of fuel sprayed is determined by the length of time the injector is energized (pulse width) which is controlled by the ECM. The longer the injector solenoid is energized (greater the pulse width), the more fuel is injected.

## Throttle Position Sensor (TPS)
### OPERATION

The TPS is mounted to the throttle body, opposite the throttle lever and is connected to the throttle shaft. Its function is to sense the current throttle valve position and relay that information to the ECM. Throttle position information allows the ECM to generate the required injector control signals. The TPS consists of a potentiometer which alters the flow of voltage according to the position of a wiper on the variable resistor windings, in proportion to the movement of the throttle shaft.

## Vehicle Speed Sensor

### OPERATION

The VSS is located on the transmission and sends a pulsing voltage signal to the ECM which is converted to miles per hour. This sensor mainly controls the operation of the TCC system, shift light, cruise control and activation of the EGR system.

## SELF-DIAGNOSTIC SYSTEMS

### System Description

The Electronic Control Module (ECM) is required to maintain the exhaust emissions at acceptable levels. The module is a small, solid state computer which receives signals from many sources and sensors; it uses these data to make judgments about operating conditions and then control output signals to the fuel and emission systems to match the current requirements.

Inputs are received from many sources to form a complete picture of engine operating conditions. Some inputs are simply Yes or No messages, such as that from the Park/Neutral switch; the vehicle is either in gear or in Park/Neutral; there are no other choices. Other data is sent in quantitative input, such as engine RPM, coolant temperature and throttle position. The ECM is pre-programmed to recognize acceptable ranges or combinations of signals and control the outputs to control emissions while providing good driveability and economy. The ECM also monitors some output circuits, making sure that the components function as commanded. For proper engine operation, it is essential that all input and output components function properly and communicate properly with the ECM.

Since the control module is programmed to recognize the presence and value of electrical inputs, it will also note the lack of a signal or a radical change in values. It will, for example, react to the loss of signal from the vehicle speed sensor or note that engine coolant temperature has risen beyond acceptable (programmed) limits. Once a fault is recognized, a numeric code is assigned and held in memory. The dashboard warning lamp – CHECK ENGINE or SERVICE ENGINE SOON – will illuminate to advise the operator that the system has detected a fault.

More than one code may be stored. Although not every engine uses every code, possible codes range from 12 to 100. Additionally, the same code may carry different meanings relative to each engine or engine family.

In the event of an ECM failure, the system will default to a pre-programmed set of values. These are compromise values which allow the engine to operate, although possibly at reduced efficiency. This is variously known as the default, limp-in or back-up mode. Driveability is almost always affected when the ECM enters this mode.

### Learning Ability

The ECM can compensate for minor variations within the fuel system through the block learn and fuel integrator systems. The fuel integrator monitors the oxygen sensor output voltage, adding or subtracting fuel to drive the mixture rich or lean as needed to reach the ideal air fuel ratio of 14.7:1. The integrator values may be read with a scan tool; the display will range from 0–255 and should center on 128 if the oxygen sensor is seeing a 14.7:1 mixture.

The temporary nature of the integrator's control is expanded by the block learn function. The name is derived from the fact that the entire engine operating range (load vs. rpm) is divided into 16 sections or blocks. Within each memory block is stored the correct fuel delivery value for that combination of load and engine speed. Once the operating range enters a certain block, that stored value controls the fuel delivery unless the integrator steps in to change it. If changes are made by the integrator, the new value is memorized and stored within the block. As the block learn makes the correction, the integrator correction will be reduced until the integrator returns to 128; the block learn then controls the fuel delivery with the new value.

The next time the engine operates within the block's range, the new value will be used. The block learn data can also be read by a scan tool; the range is the same as the integrator and should also center on 128. In this way, the systems can compensate for engine wear, small air or vacuum leaks or reduced combustion.

Any time the battery is disconnected, the block learn values are lost and must be relearned by the ECM. This loss of corrected values may be noticed as a significant change in driveability. To re-teach the system, make certain the engine is fully warmed up. Drive the vehicle at part throttle using moderate acceleration and idle until normal performance is felt.

### Dashboard Warning Lamp

The primary function of the dash warning lamp is to advise the operator that a fault has been detected, and, in most cases, a code stored. Under normal conditions, the dash warning lamp will illuminate when the ignition

# EMISSION CONTROLS

is turned **ON**. Once the engine is started and running, the ECM will perform a system check and extinguish the warning lamp if no fault is found.

Additionally, the dash warning lamp can be used to retrieve stored codes after the system is placed in the Diagnostic Mode. Codes are transmitted as a series of flashes with short or long pauses. When the system is placed in the Field Service Mode, the dash lamp will indicate open loop or closed loop function to the technician.

## Intermittents

If a fault occurs intermittently, such as a loose connector pin breaking contact as the vehicle hits a bump, the ECM will note the fault as it occurs and energize the dash warning lamp. If the problem self-corrects, as with the terminal pin again making contact, the dash lamp will extinguish after 10 seconds but a code will remain stored in the ECM memory.

When an unexpected code appears during diagnostics, it may have been set during an intermittent failure that self-corrected; the codes are still useful in diagnosis and should not be discounted.

## Tools and Equipment

### SCAN TOOLS

Although stored codes may be read with only the use of a small jumper wire, the use of a hand-held scan tool such as GM's TECH 1 or equivalent is recommended. There are many manufacturers of these tools; a purchaser must be certain that the tool is proper for the intended use. If you own a Scan type tool, it probably came with comprehensive instructions on proper use. Be sure to follow the instructions that came with your unit if they differ from what is given here; this is a general guide with useful information included.

The scan tool allows any stored codes to be read from the ECM memory. The tool also allows the operator to view the data being sent to the ECM while the engine is running. This ability has obvious diagnostic advantages; the use of the scan tool is frequently required by the diagnostic charts. Use of the scan tool provides additional data but does not eliminate the need for use of the charts. The scan tool makes collecting information easier; the data must be correctly interpreted by an operator familiar with the system.

An example of the usefulness of the scan tool may be seen in the case of a temperature sensor which has changed its electrical characteristics. The ECM is reacting to an apparently warmer engine (causing a driveability problem), but the sensor's voltage has not changed enough to set a fault code. Connecting the scan tool, the voltage signal being sent to the ECM may be viewed; comparison to either a chart of normal values or a known good vehicle reveals the problem quickly.

The ECM is capable of communicating with a scan tool in 3 modes:

### Normal or Open Mode

This mode is not applicable to all engines. When engaged, certain engine data can be observed on the scanner without affecting engine operating characteristics. The number of items readable in this mode varies with engine family. Most scan tools are designed to change automatically to the ALDL mode if this mode is not available.

### ALDL Mode

Also referred to as the 10K or SPECIAL mode, the scanner will present all readable data as available. Certain operating characteristics of the engine are changed or controlled when this mode is engaged. The closed loop timers are bypassed, the spark (EST) is advanced and the PARK/NEUTRAL restriction is bypassed. If applicable, the IAC controls the engine speed to 1000 rpm ± 50, and, on some engines, the canister purge solenoid is energized.

### Factory Test

Sometimes referred to as BACK-UP mode, this level of communication is primarily used during vehicle assembly and testing. This mode will confirm that the default or limp-in system is working properly within the ECM. Other data obtainable in this mode has little use in diagnosis.

> NOTE: *A scan tool that is known to display faulty data should not be used for diagnosis. Although the fault may be believed to be in only one area, it can possibly affect many other areas during diagnosis, leading to errors and incorrect repair.*

To properly read system values with a scan tool, the following conditions must be met. All normal values given in the charts will be based on these conditions:
- Engine running at idle, throttle closed
- Engine warm, upper radiator hose hot
- Vehicle in park or neutral
- System operating in closed loop
- All accessories **OFF**

### ELECTRICAL TOOLS

The most commonly required electrical diagnostic tool is the Digital Multimeter, allowing voltage, ohmage (resistance) and amperage to be read by one instrument. The multimeter must be a high-impedance unit, with 10 megohms of impedance in the voltmeter. This type of meter will not place an additional load on the circuit it is testing; this is extremely important in low voltage circuits. The multimeter must be of high quality in all respects. It should be handled carefully and protected from impact or damage. Replace batteries frequently in the unit.

Other necessary tools include an unpowered test light, a quality tachometer with an inductive (clip-on) pick up, and the proper tools for releasing GM's Metri-Pack, Weather Pack and Micro-Pack terminals as necessary. The Micro-Pack connectors are used at the ECM connector. A vacuum pump/gauge may also be required for checking sensors, solenoids and valves.

## Diagnosis and Testing

### TROUBLESHOOTING

Diagnosis of a driveablility and/or emissions problems requires attention to detail and following the diagnostic procedures in the correct order. Resist the temptation to perform any repairs before performing the preliminary diagnostic steps. In many cases this will shorten diagnostic time and often cure the problem without electronic testing.

The proper troubleshooting procedure for these vehicles is as follows:

### Visual/Physical Underhood Inspection

This is possibly the most critical step of diagnosis. A detailed examination of connectors, wiring and vacuum hoses can often lead to a repair without further diagnosis. Performance of this step relies on the skill of the technician performing it; a careful inspector will check the undersides of hoses as well as the integrity of hard-to-reach hoses blocked by the air cleaner or other component. Wiring should be checked carefully for any sign of strain, burning, crimping, or terminal pull-out from a connector. Checking connectors at components or in harnesses is required; usually, pushing them together will reveal a loose fit.

### Diagnostic Circuit Check

This step is used to check that the on-board diagnostic system is working correctly. A system which is faulty or shorted may not yield correct codes when placed in the Diagnostic Mode. Performing this test confirms that the diagnostic system is not failed and is able to communicate through the dash warning lamp.

If the diagnostic system is not operating correctly, or if a problem exists without the dash warning lamp being lit, refer to the specific engine's A-Charts. These charts cover such conditions as Engine Cranks but Will Not Run or No Service Engine Soon Light.

### Reading Codes and Use of Scan Tool

Once the integrity of the system is confirmed, enter the Diagnostic Mode and read any stored codes. To enter the diagnostic mode:

1. Turn the ignition switch **OFF**. Locate the Assembly Line Diagnostic Link (ALDL), usually under the instrument panel. It may be within a plastic cover or housing labeled DIAGNOSTIC CONNECTOR. This link is used to communicate with the ECM.

2. The code(s) stored in memory may be read either through counting the flashes of the dashboard warning lamp or through the use of a hand-held scan tool. If using the scan tool, connect it correctly to the ALDL.

3. If reading codes via the dash warning lamp, use a small jumper wire to connect Terminal B to Terminal A of the ALDL. As the ALDL connector is viewed from the front, Terminal A is on the extreme right of the upper row; Terminal B is second from the right on the upper row.

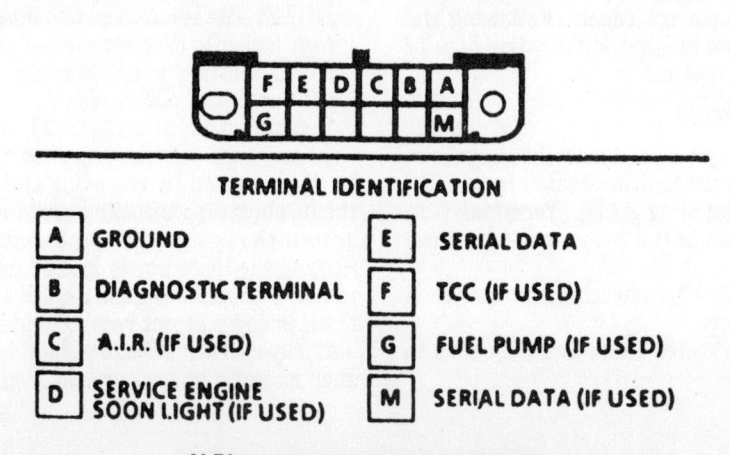

TERMINAL IDENTIFICATION

| A | GROUND | E | SERIAL DATA |
| B | DIAGNOSTIC TERMINAL | F | TCC (IF USED) |
| C | A.I.R. (IF USED) | G | FUEL PUMP (IF USED) |
| D | SERVICE ENGINE SOON LIGHT (IF USED) | M | SERIAL DATA (IF USED) |

ALDL connector terminal identification

# EMISSION CONTROLS

4. After the terminals are connected, turn the ignition switch to the **ON** position but do not start the engine. The dash warning lamp should begin to flash Code 12. The code will display as one flash, a pause and two flashes. Code 12 is not a fault code. It is used as a system acknowledgement or handshake code; its presence indicates that the ECM can communicate as requested. Code 12 is used to begin every diagnostic sequence. Some vehicles also use Code 12 after all diagnostic codes have been sent.

5. After Code 12 has been transmitted 3 times, the fault codes, if any, will each be transmitted 3 times. The codes are stored and transmitted in numeric order from lowest to highest.

NOTE: *The order of codes in the memory does not indicate the order of occurrence.*

6. If there are no codes stored, but a driveability or emissions problem is evident, refer to the Symptoms and Intermittents Chart for the specific fuel system.

7. If one or more codes are stored, record them. At the end of the procedure, refer to the applicable Diagnostic Code chart.

8. If no fault codes are transmitted, connect the scan tool (if not already connected). Use the scan functions to view the values being sent to the ECM. Compare the actual values to the typical or normal values for the engine.

9. Switch the ignition **OFF** when finished with code retrieval or scan tool readings.

### Circuit/Component Diagnosis and Repair

Using the appropriate chart(s) based on the Diagnostic Circuit Check, the fault codes and the scan tool data will lead to diagnosis and checking of a particular circuit or component. It is important to note that the fault code indicates a fault or loss of signal in an ECM-controlled system, not necessarily in the specific component. Detailed procedures to isolate the problem are included in each code chart; these procedures must be followed accurately to insure timely and correct repair. Following the procedure will also insure that only truly faulty components are replaced.

## DIAGNOSTIC MODE

The ECM may be placed into the diagnostic mode by turning the ignition switch from **OFF** to **ON**, then grounding ALDL Terminal B to Terminal A. When in the Diagnostic Mode, the ECM will:
• Display Code 12, indicating the system is operating correctly.
• Display any stored fault codes 3 times in succession.
• Energize all the relays controlled by the ECM except the fuel pump relay. This will allow the relays and circuits to be checked in the shop without recreating certain driving conditions.
• Move the IAC valve to its fully extended position, closing the idle air passage.

NOTE: *Due to increased battery draw, do not allow the vehicle to remain in the Diagnostic Mode for more than 30 minutes. If longer periods are necessary, connect a battery charger.*

## FIELD SERVICE MODE

If ALDL terminal B is grounded to terminal A with the engine running, the system enters the Field Service Mode. In this mode, the dash warning lamp will indicate whether the system is operating in open loop or closed loop.

If working in open loop, the dash warning lamp will flash rapidly 2½ times per second. In closed loop, the flash rate slows to once per second. Additionally, if the system is running lean in closed loop, the lamp will be off most of the cycle. A rich condition in closed loop will cause the lamp to remain lit for most of the 1 second cycle.

When operating in the Field Service Mode, additional codes cannot be stored by the ECM. The closed loop timer is bypassed in this mode.

## CLEARING THE TROUBLE CODES

Stored fault codes may be erased from memory at any time by removing power from the ECM for at least 30 seconds. It may be necessary to clear stored codes during diagnosis to check for any recurrence during a test drive, but the stored codes must be written down when retrieved. The codes may still be required for subsequent troubleshooting. Whenever a repair is complete, the stored codes must be erased and the vehicle test driven to confirm correct operation and repair.

NOTE: *The ignition switch must be OFF any time power is disconnected or restored to the ECM. Severe damage may result if this precaution is not observed.*

Depending on the electrical distribution of the particular vehicle, power to the ECM may be disconnected by removing the ECM fuse in the fusebox, disconnecting the in-line fuse holder near the positive battery terminal or disconnecting the ECM power lead at the battery terminal. Disconnecting the negative battery cable to clear codes is not recommended as this will also clear other memory data in the vehicle such as radio presets or seat memory.

# Fuel System

## THROTTLE BODY FUEL INJECTION SYSTEM (2.5L ENGINE)

### System Description

The electronic throttle body fuel injection system is a fuel metering system with the amount of fuel delivered by the throttle body injector(s) (TBI) determined by an electronic signal supplied by the Electronic Control Module (ECM). The ECM monitors various engine and vehicle conditions to calculate the fuel delivery time (pulse width) of the injector. The fuel pulse may be modified by the ECM to account for special operating conditions, such as cranking, cold starting, altitude, acceleration, and deceleration.

The Throttle Body Injection (TBI) system provides a means of fuel distribution for controlling exhaust emissions within legislated limits. The TBI system, by precisely controlling the air/fuel mixture under all operating conditions, provides as near as possible complete combustion.

This is accomplished by using an Electronic Control Module (ECM) (a small on-board microcomputer) that receives electrical inputs from various sensors about engine operating conditions. An oxygen sensor in the main exhaust stream functions to provide feedback information to the ECM as to the oxygen content, lean or rich, in the exhaust. The ECM uses this information from the oxygen sensor, and other sensors, to modify fuel delivery to achieve, as near as possible, an ideal air/fuel ratio of 14.7:1. This air/fuel ratio allows the 3-way catalytic converter to be more efficient in the conversion process of reducing exhaust emissions while at the same time providing acceptable levels of driveability and fuel economy.

The basic TBI model 700 is made up of 2 major casting assemblies: (1) a throttle body with a valve to control airflow and (2) a fuel body assembly with an integral pressure regulator and fuel injector to supply the required fuel. A device to control idle speed (IAC) and a device to provide information about throttle valve position (TPS) are included as part of the TBI unit.

### Service Precautions

When working around any part of the fuel system, take precautionary steps to prevent fire and/or explosion:
- Disconnect negative terminal from battery (except when testing with battery voltage is required).
- When ever possible, use a flashlight instead of a drop light.
- Keep all open flame and smoking material out of the area.
- Use a shop cloth or similar to catch fuel when opening a fuel system.
- Relieve fuel system pressure before servicing.
- Use eye protection.
- Always keep a dry chemical (class B) fire extinguisher near the area.

### Relieving Fuel System Pressure

1. Remove the fuel filler cap to relieve fuel tank vapor pressure.
2. Remove the fuel pump fuse from the fuse panel.
3. Start the engine and run until the engine stalls. Engage the starter an additional 3 seconds to assure complete relief.
4. Install the fuel filler cap.
5. Disconnect the negative battery cable and continue with fuel system work.

### Electric Fuel Pump

#### REMOVAL AND INSTALLATION

1. Disconnect the negative battery cable.
2. Relieve the fuel system pressure.

## 170  FUEL SYSTEM

| | |
|---|---|
| 1 | FUEL SENDER |
| 2 | PULSATOR |
| 3 | BUMPER |
| 4 | FUEL PUMP - ELECTRIC |
| 5 | INSULATOR |
| 6 | FUEL PUMP STRAINER |
| 7 | MOUNTING BRACKET |
| 8 | FUEL PUMP ELECTRICAL CONNECTOR |
| 9 | FUEL FEED TUBE |
| 10 | FUEL SENDER ASSEMBLY WIRING |

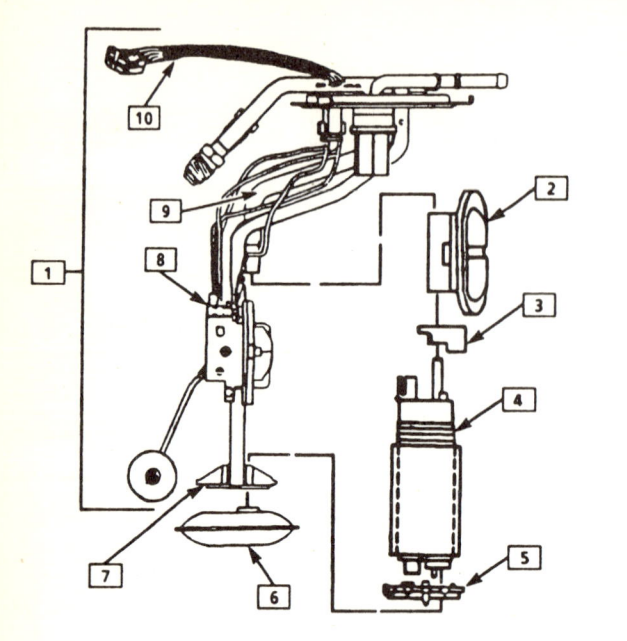

Fuel level meter assembly

3. Raise and safely support the vehicle with jackstands.
4. Safely drain and remove the fuel tank assembly as outlined in the "Fuel tank" removal procedures in this Chapter.
5. Turn the fuel pump cam lock ring counterclockwise and lift the assembly out of the tank.
6. Remove the fuel pump from the level sensor unit as follows:
   a. Pull the pump up into the attaching hose or pulsator while pulling outward away from the bottom support.
   b. Take care to prevent damage to the rubber insulator and strainer during removal.
   c. When the pump assembly is clear of the bottom support, pull the pump out of the rubber connector for removal.

**To install:**
7. Replace any attaching hoses or rubber sound insulator that show signs of deterioration.
8. Push the fuel pump into the attaching hoses and install the pump/sensor assembly into the tank. Always use a new O-ring seal.
Be careful not to fold over or twist the strainer when installing the sensor unit. Also, make sure the strainer does not block full travel of the float arm.
9. Install the cam lock and turn clockwise to lock.
10. Install the fuel tank as outlined in this Chapter.
11. Fill the tank with four gallons of gas and check for fuel leaks.

### FUEL PRESSURE CHECK

1. Relieve the fuel pressure from the fuel system.
2. Turn the ignition **OFF**.
3. Uncouple the fuel supply flexible hose in the engine compartment and install fuel pressure gauge J29658/BT8205 or equivalent in the pressure line.
4. Be sure to tighten the fuel line to the gauge to ensure that there no leaks during testing.
5. Start the engine and observe the fuel pressure reading. The fuel pressure should be 9–13 psi (62–90 kPa).
6. Relieve the fuel pressure. Remove the fuel pressure gauge and reinstall the fuel line. Be sure to install a new O-ring on the fuel feed line.
7. Start the engine and check for fuel leaks.

## Throttle Body

### REMOVAL AND INSTALLATION

1. Relieve the fuel system pressure. Raise the hood, install fender covers and remove the air cleaner assembly. Disconnect the negative battery cable.
2. Disconnect the electrical connectors for the idle speed control motor, the throttle position sensor, fuel injectors, EFE and any other component necessary in order to remove the throttle body.
3. Remove the throttle return spring, cruise control, throttle linkage and downshift cable.
4. Disconnect all necessary vacuum lines, the fuel inlet line, fuel return line, brake booster

line, MAP sensor hose and the AIR hose. Be sure to use a back-up wrench on all metal lines.

5. Remove the PCV, EVAP and/or EGR hoses from the front of the throttle body.

6. Remove the 3 throttle body mounting screws and remove the throttle body and gasket.

7. The installation is the reverse order of the removal procedure.

8. Torque the throttle body retaining screws to 18 ft. lbs. (24 Nm) and fuel lines to 20 ft. lbs. Always use new gaskets and O-rings.

9. Make certain cruise and shift cables do not hold the throttle above the idle stop. Reset the IAC by depressing the accelerator slightly, run engine for 3–4 seconds and turn ignition **OFF** for 10 seconds.

## Fuel Meter Body Assembly

### REMOVAL AND INSTALLATION

1. Relieve the fuel system pressure. Raise the hood, install fender covers and remove the air cleaner assembly. Disconnect the negative battery cable.

2. Remove the electrical connector from the injector. Remove the grommet with wires from the fuel meter assembly.

3. Remove the fuel inlet and outlet lines and O-rings. Be sure to use a back-up wrench to keep the TBI nuts from turning. Be sure to discard the old O-rings.

4. Remove the TBI mounting hardware. Remove the 2 fuel meter body attaching screws.

5. Remove the fuel meter assembly from the throttle body and remove the fuel meter to throttle body gasket, discard the gasket.

6. Install the new throttle body to fuel meter body gasket. Match the cut portions in the gasket with the opening in the throttle body.

7. Install the fuel meter body assembly onto the throttle body assembly.

8. Install the fuel meter body to the throttle body attaching screw assemblies, pre-coated with a suitable thread sealer.

9. Torque the screw assemblies to 53 inch lbs. Install the fuel inlet and outlet nuts with new gaskets to the fuel meter body assembly. Torque the inlet and outlet nut to 20 ft. lbs. (27 Nm).

10. Install the fuel inlet and return lines and new O-rings. Be sure to use a back-up wrench to keep the TBI nuts from turning.

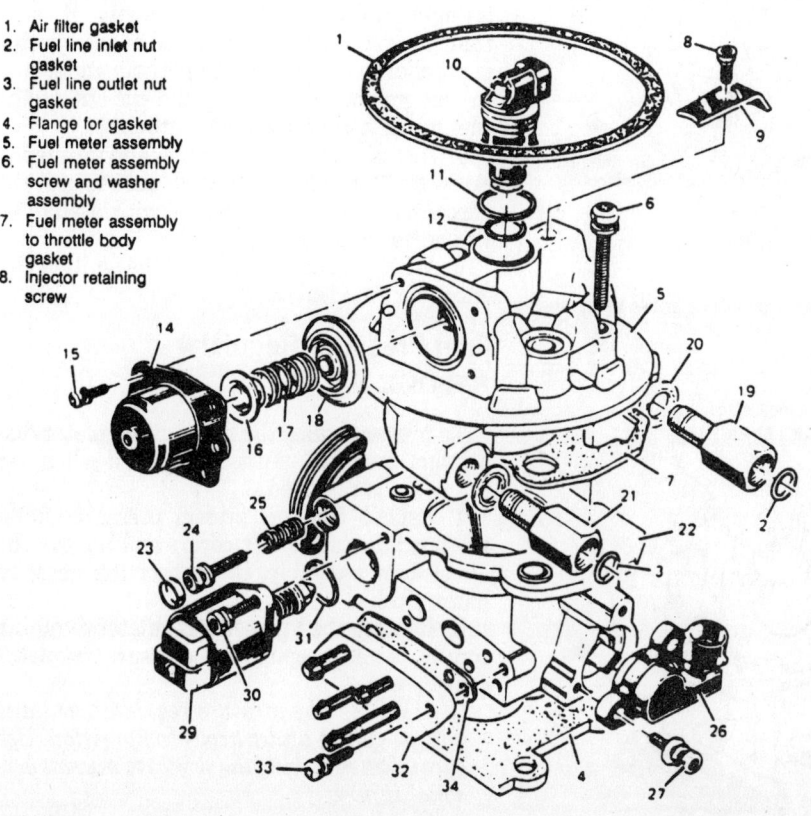

1. Air filter gasket
2. Fuel line inlet nut gasket
3. Fuel line outlet nut gasket
4. Flange for gasket
5. Fuel meter assembly
6. Fuel meter assembly screw and washer assembly
7. Fuel meter assembly to throttle body gasket
8. Injector retaining screw
9. Injector retainer
10. Fuel injector
11. Fuel injector upper O-ring
12. Fuel injector lower O-ring
13. Injector filter
14. Pressure regulator assembly cover
15. Pressure regulator attaching screw
16. Spring seat
17. Pressure regulator spring
18. Pressure regulator diaphragm assembly
19. Fuel inlet nut
20. Fuel nut seal
21. Fuel outlet nut
22. Throttle body assembly
23. Idle stop screw plug
24. Idle stop screw assembly
25. Idle stop screw spring
26. Throttle position sensor
27. Throttle position sensor screw
28. Throttle position sensor washer
29. Idle air control valve
30. Idle air control valve attaching screw
31. Idle air control valve O-ring
32. Tube module assembly
33. Manifold attaching screws
34. Tube manifold gasket

**Exploded view of the TBI model 700 assembly**

# 172 FUEL SYSTEM

11. Install the grommet with wires to the fuel meter assembly. Connect the electrical connector to the injector.

12. With the engine **OFF** and the ignition **ON** check for fuel leaks.

## Fuel Injector

Use care in removing the injector to prevent damage to the electrical connector pins on top of the injector, the injector fuel filter and the nozzle. The fuel injector is serviced as a complete assembly only. The fuel injector is an electrical component and should not be immersed in any type of cleaner.

### REMOVAL AND INSTALLATION

1. Relieve the fuel system pressure. Raise the hood, install fender covers and remove the air cleaner assembly. Disconnect the negative battery cable.

2. Disconnect electrical connector to injector by squeezing on tow tabs and pulling straight up.

3. Remove the injector retainer screw and retainer.

4. Use a suitable dowel rod and lay the dowel rod on top of the fuel meter body.

5. Insert a suitable pry tool into the small lip of the injector and pry against the dowel rod lifting the injector straight up. Tool J–26868 or equivalent can also be used.

6. Remove the injector from the throttle body. Remove the upper and lower O-ring from the injector cavity. Be sure to discard both O-rings.

NOTE: *Check the fuel injector filter for evidence of dirt and contamination. If present, check for presence of dirt in the fuel lines or fuel tank. Be sure to replace the injector with an identical part. Injectors from other models can fit in the TBI 700 unit, but are calibrated for different flow rates.*

**To install:**

7. Lubricate the new upper and lower O-rings with automatic transmission fluid. Make sure that the upper O-ring is in the groove and the lower one is flush up against the injector fuel filter.

8. Install the injector assembly, pushing it straight into the fuel injector cavity. Be sure that the electrical connector end of the injector is parallel to the casting support rib and facing in the general direction of the cut-out in the fuel meter body for the wire grommet.

9. Install the injector retainer and torque the screw to 27 inch lbs. (3 Nm). Be sure to coat the threads of the retainer screw with a suitable thread sealant.

10. With the engine **OFF** and the ignition **ON** check for fuel leaks.

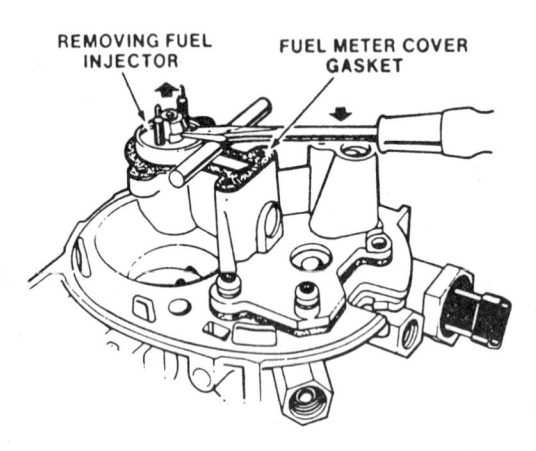

Removing the fuel injector from the throttle body assembly

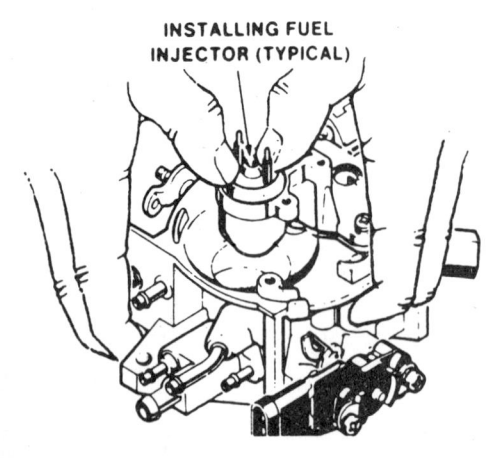

Installing the fuel injector into the throttle body assembly

## Fuel Pressure Regulator

### REMOVAL AND INSTALLATION

To prevent leaks, the pressure regulator diaphragm assembly must be replaced whenever the cover is removed.

1. Relieve the fuel system pressure. Raise the hood, install fender covers and remove the air cleaner assembly. Disconnect the negative battery cable.

2. Remove the 4 pressure regulator retaining screws, while keeping the pressure regulator compressed.

CAUTION: *The pressure regulator contains a large spring under heavy compression. Use care when removing the screws to prevent personal injury.*

3. Check the pressure regulator seat in the fuel meter body cavity for pitting, nicks or irregularities. Use a magnifying glass if neces-

# CHILTON'S
# FUEL ECONOMY & TUNE-UP TIPS

Tune-up • Spark Plug Diagnosis • Emission Controls

Fuel System • Cooling System • Tires and Wheels

General Maintenance

**55 WAYS TO IMPROVE FUEL ECONOMY**

# CHILTON'S FUEL ECONOMY & TUNE-UP TIPS

Fuel economy is important to everyone, no matter what kind of vehicle you drive. The maintenance-minded motorist can save both money and fuel using these tips and the periodic maintenance and tune-up procedures in this Repair and Tune-Up Guide.

There are more than 130,000,000 cars and trucks registered for private use in the United States. Each travels an average of 10-12,000 miles per year, and, and in total they consume close to 70 billion gallons of fuel each year. This represents nearly ⅔ of the oil imported by the United States each year. The Federal government's goal is to reduce consumption 10% by 1985. A variety of methods are either already in use or under serious consideration, and they all affect you driving and the cars you will drive. In addition to "down-sizing", the auto industry is using or investigating the use of electronic fuel delivery, electronic engine controls and alternative engines for use in smaller and lighter vehicles, among other alternatives to meet the federally mandated Corporate Average Fuel Economy (CAFE) of 27.5 mpg by 1985. The government, for its part, is considering rationing, mandatory driving curtailments and tax increases on motor vehicle fuel in an effort to reduce consumption. The government's goal of a 10% reduction could be realized — and further government regulation avoided — if every private vehicle could use just 1 less gallon of fuel per week.

## How Much Can You Save?

Tests have proven that almost anyone can make at least a 10% reduction in fuel consumption through regular maintenance and tune-ups. When a major manufacturer of spark plugs sur-

## TUNE-UP

1. Check the cylinder compression to be sure the engine will really benefit from a tune-up and that it is capable of producing good fuel economy. A tune-up will be wasted on an engine in poor mechanical condition.

2. Replace spark plugs regularly. New spark plugs alone can increase fuel economy 3%.

3. Be sure the spark plugs are the correct type (heat range) for your vehicle. See the Tune-Up Specifications.

Heat range refers to the spark plug's ability to conduct heat away from the firing end. It must conduct the heat away in an even pattern to avoid becoming a source of pre-ignition, yet it must also operate hot enough to burn off conductive deposits that could cause misfiring.

The heat range is usually indicated by a number on the spark plug, part of the manufacturer's designation for each individual spark plug. The numbers in bold-face indicate the heat range in each manufacturer's identification system.

| Manufacturer | Typical Designation |
|---|---|
| AC | R **45** TS |
| Bosch (old) | WA **145** T30 |
| Bosch (new) | HR **8** Y |
| Champion | RBL **15** Y |
| Fram/Autolite | **4**15 |
| Mopar | P-**62** PR |
| Motorcraft | BRF-**4**2 |
| NGK | BP **5** ES-15 |
| Nippondenso | W **16** EP |
| Prestolite | 14GR **5** 2A |

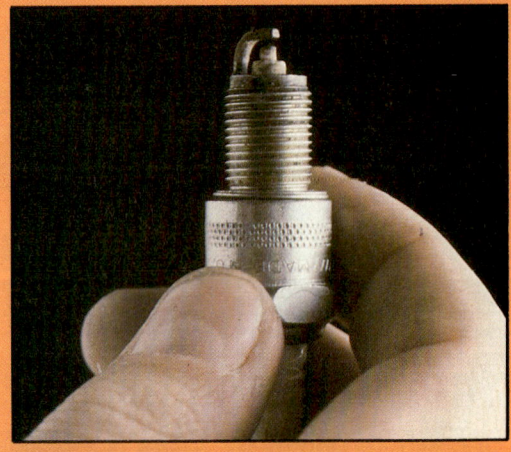

*Periodically, check the spark plugs to be sure they are firing efficiently. They are excellent indicators of the internal condition of your engine.*

On AC, Bosch (new), Champion, Fram/Autolite, Mopar, Motorcraft and Prestolite, a higher number indicates a hotter plug. On Bosch (old), NGK and Nippondenso, a higher number indicates a colder plug.

4. Make sure the spark plugs are properly gapped. See the Tune-Up Specifications in this book.

5. Be sure the spark plugs are firing efficiently. The illustrations on the next 2 pages show you how to "read" the firing end of the spark plug.

6. Check the ignition timing and set it to specifications. Tests show that almost all cars have incorrect ignition timing by more than 2°.

veyed over 6,000 cars nationwide, they found that a tune-up, on cars that needed one, increased fuel economy over 11%. Replacing worn plugs alone, accounted for a 3% increase. The same test also revealed that 8 out of every 10 vehicles will have some maintenance deficiency that will directly affect fuel economy, emissions or performance. Most of this mileage-robbing neglect could be prevented with regular maintenance.

Modern engines require that all of the functioning systems operate properly for maximum efficiency. A malfunction anywhere wastes fuel. You can keep your vehicle running as efficiently and economically as possible, by being aware of your vehicle's operating and performance characteristics. If your vehicle suddenly develops performance or fuel economy problems it could be due to one or more of the following:

| PROBLEM | POSSIBLE CAUSE |
| --- | --- |
| Engine Idles Rough | Ignition timing, idle mixture, vacuum leak or something amiss in the emission control system. |
| Hesitates on Acceleration | Dirty carburetor or fuel filter, improper accelerator pump setting, ignition timing or fouled spark plugs. |
| Starts Hard or Fails to Start | Worn spark plugs, improperly set automatic choke, ice (or water) in fuel system. |
| Stalls Frequently | Automatic choke improperly adjusted and possible dirty air filter or fuel filter. |
| Performs Sluggishly | Worn spark plugs, dirty fuel or air filter, ignition timing or automatic choke out of adjustment. |

*Check spark plug wires on conventional point type ignition for cracks by bending them in a loop around your finger.*

*Be sure that spark plug wires leading to adjacent cylinders do not run too close together. (Photo courtesy Champion Spark Plug Co.)*

7. If your vehicle does not have electronic ignition, check the points, rotor and cap as specified.

8. Check the spark plug wires (used with conventional point-type ignitions) for cracks and burned or broken insulation by bending them in a loop around your finger. Cracked wires decrease fuel efficiency by failing to deliver full voltage to the spark plugs. One misfiring spark plug can cost you as much as 2 mpg.

9. Check the routing of the plug wires. Misfiring can be the result of spark plug leads to adjacent cylinders running parallel to each other and too close together. One wire tends to pick up voltage from the other causing it to fire "out of time".

10. Check all electrical and ignition circuits for voltage drop and resistance.

11. Check the distributor mechanical and/or vacuum advance mechanisms for proper functioning. The vacuum advance can be checked by twisting the distributor plate in the opposite direction of rotation. It should spring back when released.

12. Check and adjust the valve clearance on engines with mechanical lifters. The clearance should be slightly loose rather than too tight.

# SPARK PLUG DIAGNOSIS

## Normal

APPEARANCE: This plug is typical of one operating normally. The insulator nose varies from a light tan to grayish color with slight electrode wear. The presence of slight deposits is normal on used plugs and will have no adverse effect on engine performance. The spark plug heat range is correct for the engine and the engine is running normally.

CAUSE: Properly running engine.

RECOMMENDATION: Before reinstalling this plug, the electrodes should be cleaned and filed square. Set the gap to specifications. If the plug has been in service for more than 10-12,000 miles, the entire set should probably be replaced with a fresh set of the same heat range.

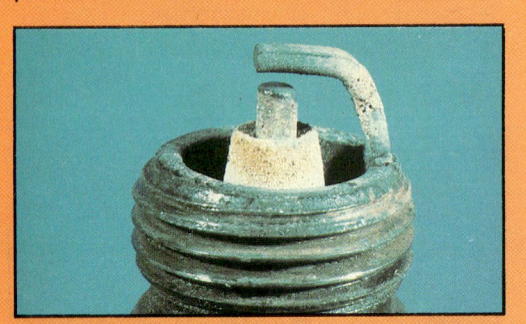

## Oil Deposits

APPEARANCE: The firing end of the plug is covered with a wet, oily coating.

CAUSE: The problem is poor oil control. On high mileage engines, oil is leaking past the rings or valve guides into the combustion chamber. A common cause is also a plugged PCV valve, and a ruptured fuel pump diaphragm can also cause this condition. Oil fouled plugs such as these are often found in new or recently overhauled engines, before normal oil control is achieved, and can be cleaned and reinstalled.

RECOMMENDATION: A hotter spark plug may temporarily relieve the problem, but the engine is probably in need of work.

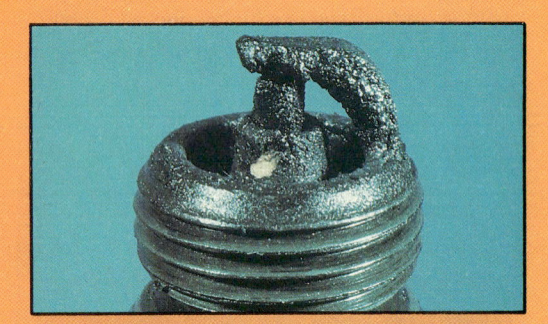

## Incorrect Heat Range

APPEARANCE: The effects of high temperature on a spark plug are indicated by clean white, often blistered insulator. This can also be accompanied by excessive wear of the electrode, and the absence of deposits.

CAUSE: Check for the correct spark plug heat range. A plug which is too hot for the engine can result in overheating. A car operated mostly at high speeds can require a colder plug. Also check ignition timing, cooling system level, fuel mixture and leaking intake manifold.

RECOMMENDATION: If all ignition and engine adjustments are known to be correct, and no other malfunction exists, install spark plugs one heat range colder.

## Carbon Deposits

APPEARANCE: Carbon fouling is easily identified by the presence of dry, soft, black, sooty deposits.

CAUSE: Changing the heat range can often lead to carbon fouling, as can prolonged slow, stop-and-start driving. If the heat range is correct, carbon fouling can be attributed to a rich fuel mixture, sticking choke, clogged air cleaner, worn breaker points, retarded timing or low compression. If only one or two plugs are carbon fouled, check for corroded or cracked wires on the affected plugs. Also look for cracks in the distributor cap between the towers of affected cylinders.

RECOMMENDATION: After the problem is corrected, these plugs can be cleaned and reinstalled if not worn severely.

Photos Courtesy Fram Corporation

## MMT Fouled

**APPEARANCE:** Spark plugs fouled by MMT (Methycyclopentadienyl Maganese Tricarbonyl) have reddish, rusty appearance on the insulator and side electrode.

**CAUSE:** MMT is an anti-knock additive in gasoline used to replace lead. During the combustion process, the MMT leaves a reddish deposit on the insulator and side electrode.

**RECOMMENDATION:** No engine malfunction is indicated and the deposits will not affect plug performance any more than lead deposits (see Ash Deposits). MMT fouled plugs can be cleaned, regapped and reinstalled.

## High Speed Glazing

**APPEARANCE:** Glazing appears as shiny coating on the plug, either yellow or tan in color.

**CAUSE:** During hard, fast acceleration, plug temperatures rise suddenly. Deposits from normal combustion have no chance to fluff-off; instead, they melt on the insulator forming an electrically conductive coating which causes misfiring.

**RECOMMENDATION:** Glazed plugs are not easily cleaned. They should be replaced with a fresh set of plugs of the correct heat range. If the condition recurs, using plugs with a heat range one step colder may cure the problem.

## Ash (Lead) Deposits

**APPEARANCE:** Ash deposits are characterized by light brown or white colored deposits crusted on the side or center electrodes. In some cases it may give the plug a rusty appearance.

**CAUSE:** Ash deposits are normally derived from oil or fuel additives burned during normal combustion. Normally they are harmless, though excessive amounts can cause misfiring. If deposits are excessive in short mileage, the valve guides may be worn.

**RECOMMENDATION:** Ash-fouled plugs can be cleaned, gapped and reinstalled.

## Detonation

**APPEARANCE:** Detonation is usually characterized by a broken plug insulator.

**CAUSE:** A portion of the fuel charge will begin to burn spontaneously, from the increased heat following ignition. The explosion that results applies extreme pressure to engine components, frequently damaging spark plugs and pistons.

Detonation can result by over-advanced ignition timing, inferior gasoline (low octane) lean air/fuel mixture, poor carburetion, engine lugging or an increase in compression ratio due to combustion chamber deposits or engine modification.

**RECOMMENDATION:** Replace the plugs after correcting the problem.

Photos Courtesy Champion Spark Plug Co.

## EMISSION CONTROLS

13. Be aware of the general condition of the emission control system. It contributes to reduced pollution and should be serviced regularly to maintain efficient engine operation.

14. Check all vacuum lines for dried, cracked or brittle conditions. Something as simple as a leaking vacuum hose can cause poor performance and loss of economy.

15. Avoid tampering with the emission control system. Attempting to improve fuel econ-

## FUEL SYSTEM

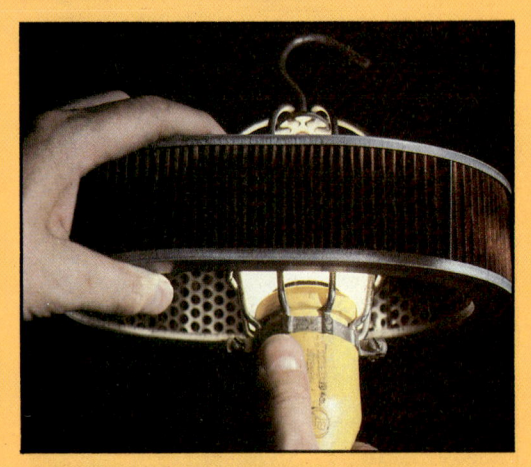

*Check the air filter with a light behind it. If you can see light through the filter it can be reused.*

*Extremely clogged filters should be discarded and replaced with a new one.*

18. Replace the air filter regularly. A dirty air filter richens the air/fuel mixture and can increase fuel consumption as much as 10%. Tests show that ⅓ of all vehicles have air filters in need of replacement.

19. Replace the fuel filter at least as often as recommended.

20. Set the idle speed and carburetor mixture to specifications.

21. Check the automatic choke. A sticking or malfunctioning choke wastes gas.

22. During the summer months, adjust the automatic choke for a leaner mixture which will produce faster engine warm-ups.

## COOLING SYSTEM

29. Be sure all accessory drive belts are in good condition. Check for cracks or wear.

30. Adjust all accessory drive belts to proper tension.

31. Check all hoses for swollen areas, worn spots, or loose clamps.

32. Check coolant level in the radiator or expansion tank.

33. Be sure the thermostat is operating properly. A stuck thermostat delays engine warm-up and a cold engine uses nearly twice as much fuel as a warm engine.

34. Drain and replace the engine coolant at least as often as recommended. Rust and scale

## TIRES & WHEELS

38. Check the tire pressure often with a pencil type gauge. Tests by a major tire manufacturer show that 90% of all vehicles have at least 1 tire improperly inflated. Better mileage can be achieved by over-inflating tires, but never exceed the maximum inflation pressure on the side of the tire.

39. If possible, install radial tires. Radial tires deliver as much as ½ mpg more than bias belted tires.

40. Avoid installing super-wide tires. They only create extra rolling resistance and decrease fuel mileage. Stick to the manufacturer's recommendations.

41. Have the wheels properly balanced.

omy by tampering with emission controls is more likely to worsen fuel economy than improve it. Emission control changes on modern engines are not readily reversible.

16. Clean (or replace) the EGR valve and lines as recommended.

17. Be sure that all vacuum lines and hoses are reconnected properly after working under the hood. An unconnected or misrouted vacuum line can wreak havoc with engine performance.

---

23. Check for fuel leaks at the carburetor, fuel pump, fuel lines and fuel tank. Be sure all lines and connections are tight.

24. Periodically check the tightness of the carburetor and intake manifold attaching nuts and bolts. These are a common place for vacuum leaks to occur.

25. Clean the carburetor periodically and lubricate the linkage.

26. The condition of the tailpipe can be an excellent indicator of proper engine combustion. After a long drive at highway speeds, the inside of the tailpipe should be a light grey in color. Black or soot on the insides indicates an overly rich mixture.

27. Check the fuel pump pressure. The fuel pump may be supplying more fuel than the engine needs.

28. Use the proper grade of gasoline for your engine. Don't try to compensate for knocking or "pinging" by advancing the ignition timing. This practice will only increase plug temperature and the chances of detonation or pre-ignition with relatively little performance gain.

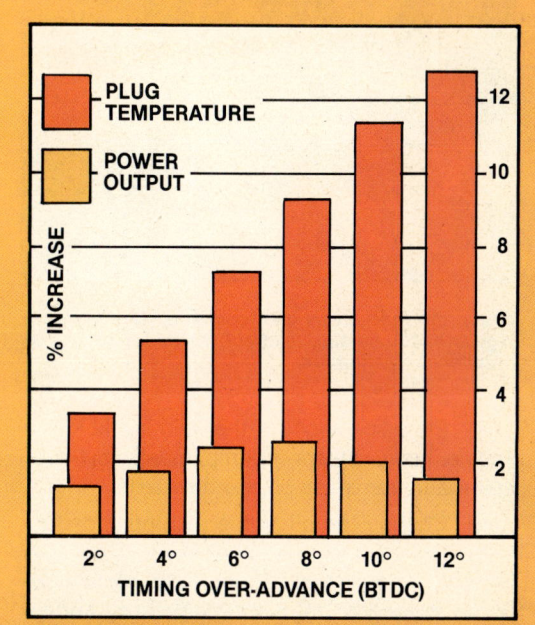

*Increasing ignition timing past the specified setting results in a drastic increase in spark plug temperature with increased chance of detonation or preignition. Performance increase is considerably less. (Photo courtesy Champion Spark Plug Co.)*

---

that form in the engine should be flushed out to allow the engine to operate at peak efficiency.

35. Clean the radiator of debris that can decrease cooling efficiency.

36. Install a flex-type or electric cooling fan, if you don't have a clutch type fan. Flex fans use curved plastic blades to push more air at low speeds when more cooling is needed; at high speeds the blades flatten out for less resistance. Electric fans only run when the engine temperature reaches a predetermined level.

37. Check the radiator cap for a worn or cracked gasket. If the cap does not seal properly, the cooling system will not function properly.

---

42. Be sure the front end is correctly aligned. A misaligned front end actually has wheels going in differed directions. The increased drag can reduce fuel economy by .3 mpg.

43. Correctly adjust the wheel bearings. Wheel bearings that are adjusted too tight increase rolling resistance.

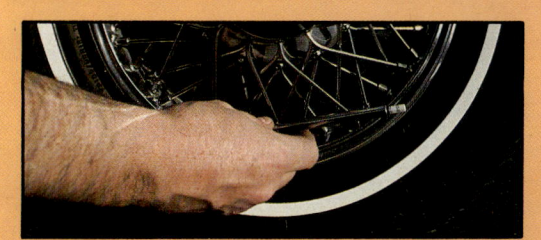

*Check tire pressures regularly with a reliable pocket type gauge. Be sure to check the pressure on a cold tire.*

# GENERAL MAINTENANCE

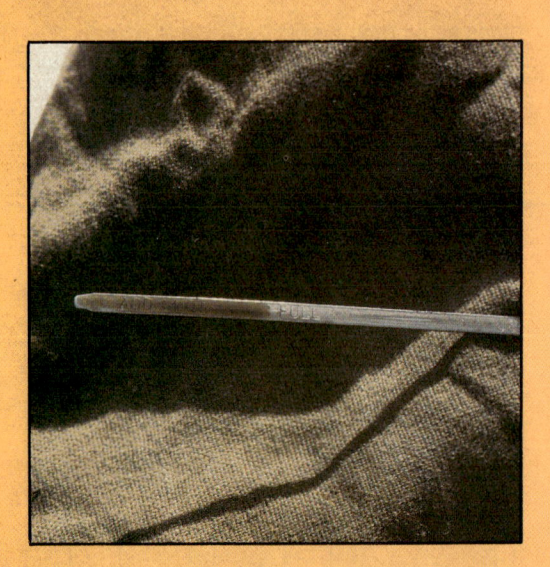

*Check the fluid levels (particularly engine oil) on a regular basis. Be sure to check the oil for grit, water or other contamination.*

*A vacuum gauge is another excellent indicator of internal engine condition and can also be installed in the dash as a mileage indicator.*

44. Periodically check the fluid levels in the engine, power steering pump, master cylinder, automatic transmission and drive axle.

45. Change the oil at the recommended interval and change the filter at every oil change. Dirty oil is thick and causes extra friction between moving parts, cutting efficiency and increasing wear. A worn engine requires more frequent tune-ups and gets progressively worse fuel economy. In general, use the lightest viscosity oil for the driving conditions you will encounter.

46. Use the recommended viscosity fluids in the transmission and axle.

47. Be sure the battery is fully charged for fast starts. A slow starting engine wastes fuel.

48. Be sure battery terminals are clean and tight.

49. Check the battery electrolyte level and add distilled water if necessary.

50. Check the exhaust system for crushed pipes, blockages and leaks.

51. Adjust the brakes. Dragging brakes or brakes that are not releasing create increased drag on the engine.

52. Install a vacuum gauge or miles-per-gallon gauge. These gauges visually indicate engine vacuum in the intake manifold. High vacuum = good mileage and low vacuum = poorer mileage. The gauge can also be an excellent indicator of internal engine conditions.

53. Be sure the clutch is properly adjusted. A slipping clutch wastes fuel.

54. Check and periodically lubricate the heat control valve in the exhaust manifold. A sticking or inoperative valve prevents engine warm-up and wastes gas.

55. Keep accurate records to check fuel economy over a period of time. A sudden drop in fuel economy may signal a need for tune-up or other maintenance.

© 1980 Chilton Book Company, Radnor, PA 19089

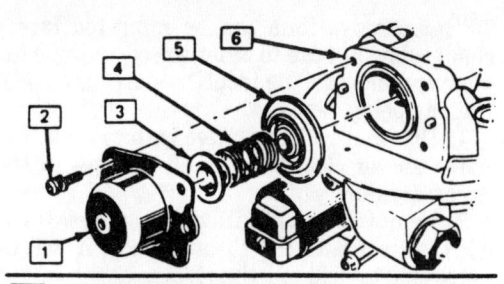

## FUEL SYSTEM 173

5. Install the regulator spring seat and spring into the cover assembly.
6. Install the cover assembly over the diaphragm, while aligning the mounting holes. Be sure to use care while installing the pressure regulator to prevent misalignment of the diaphragm and possible leaks.
7. Coat the 4 regulator retaining bolts with a suitable thread sealer and torque the screws to 22 inch lbs. (2.5 Nm).
8. With the engine **OFF** and the ignition **ON** check for fuel leaks.

## Idle Air Control (IAC) Valve
### REMOVAL AND INSTALLATION

1. Remove the air cleaner.
2. Disconnect the electrical connection from the idle air control assembly.
3. Remove the idle air control assembly from the throttle body. Clean the IAC valve O-ring sealing surface, pintle valve seat and air passage.
4. Use a suitable carburetor cleaner (be sure it is safe to use on systems equipped with a oxygen sensor) and a parts cleaning brush to remove the carbon deposits. Do not use a cleaner that contains methyl ethyl ketone. It is an extremely strong solvent and not necessary for this type of deposits. Shiny spots on the pintle or on the seat are normal and do not indicate a misalignment or a bent pintle shaft. If the air passage has heavy deposits, remove the throttle body for a complete cleaning.

NOTE: *Before installing a new idle air control valve, measure the distance that the valve is extended. This measurement should be made from motor housing to end of the cone. The distance should be no greater than 1⅛ in. (28mm). If the cone is extended too far damage to the valve may result. The IAC valve pintle may also be retracted by using IAC/ISC Motor Tester J-37027/BT-8256K. It is recommended not to push or pull on the IAC pintle. However, the force required to retract the pintle of a NEW valve should not cause damage. Do not soak the IAC valve in any liquid cleaner or solvent as damage may result.*

5. Be sure to identify the replacement idle air control valve and replace with an identical part. The IAC valve pintle shape and diameter are designed for specific applications.
6. Install the new idle air control valve and torque the retaining screws to 27 inch lbs. (3 Nm).
7. Reconnect all electrical connections.
8. The base idle will not be correct until the ECM resets the IAC.

---

| 1 | PRESSURE REGULATOR COVER |
| --- | --- |
| 2 | SCREW ASSEMBLY |
| 3 | SPRING - SEAT |
| 4 | SPRING |
| 5 | DIAPHRAGM |
| 6 | FUEL METER ASSEMBLY |

Exploded view of the pressure regulator—2.5L engine

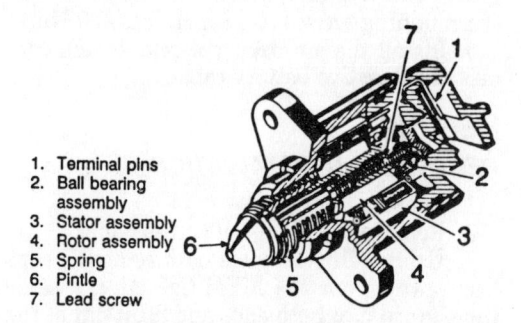

1. Terminal pins
2. Ball bearing assembly
3. Stator assembly
4. Rotor assembly
5. Spring
6. Pintle
7. Lead screw

Cutaway view of the IAC valve

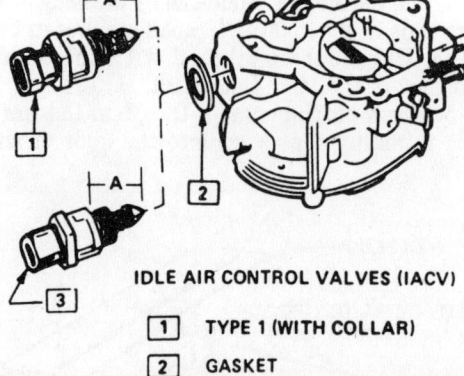

PRIOR TO INSTALLATION, DISTANCE AT DIMENSION "A" MUST NOT EXCEED SPECS.

IDLE AIR CONTROL VALVES (IACV)

| 1 | TYPE 1 (WITH COLLAR) |
| --- | --- |
| 2 | GASKET |
| 3 | TYPE 2 (WITHOUT COLLAR) |

Idle air control assembly

sary. If any of the above is present, the whole fuel body casting must be replaced.
**To install:**
4. Install the new pressure regulator diaphragm assembly making sure it is seated in the groove in the fuel meter body.

## Coolant Temperature Sensor

The coolant temperature sensor is located on the left side of the cylinder head. It may be necessary to drain some of the coolant from the coolant system.

### REMOVAL AND INSTALLATION

CAUTION: *When draining the coolant, keep in mind that cats and dogs are attracted by the ethylene glycol antifreeze, and are quite likely to drink any that is left in an uncovered container or in puddles on the ground. This will prove fatal in sufficient quantity. Always drain the coolant into a sealable container. Coolant should be reused unless it is contaminated or several years old.*

1. Disconnect the negative battery cable and disconnect the electrical connector at the sensor.
2. Remove the threaded temperature sensor from the engine.
3. Check the sensor with the tip immersed in water at 50°F (15°C). The resistance across the terminals should approximately 5600Ω. Check Code 14 or 15 engine chart for specific resistance on vehicle being serviced. If not within specifications, replace the sensor.
4. Apply some pipe tape to the threaded sensor and install the sensor.
5. Fill the cooling system if any coolant was removed. Reconnect the sensor connector and the negative battery cable.

## Torque Converter Clutch Solenoid

### REMOVAL AND INSTALLATION

1. Remove the negative battery cable. Raise and support the vehicle safely.
2. Drain the transmission fluid into a suitable drain pan. Remove the transmission pan.
3. Remove the TCC solenoid retaining screws and then remove the electrical connector, solenoid and check ball.
4. Clean and inspect all parts. Replace defective parts as necessary.

**To install:**

5. Install the check ball, TCC solenoid and electrical connector. Install the solenoid retaining screws and torque them to 10 ft. lbs. (14 Nm).
6. Install the transmission pan with a new gasket and torque the pan retaining bolts to 10 ft. lbs. (14 Nm).
7. Lower the vehicle and refill the transmission with the proper amount of the automatic transmission fluid.

## Throttle Position Sensor

### REMOVAL AND INSTALLATION

The TPS is not adjustable and is not supplied with attaching screw retainers. Since these TPS configurations can be mounted interchangeably, be sure to order the correct one for your engine with the identical part number of the one being replaced.

1. Disconnect the negative battery cable. Remove the air cleaner assembly along with the necessary duct work.
2. Remove the TPS attaching screws. If the TPS is riveted to the throttle body, it will be necessary to drill out the rivets.
3. Remove the TPS from the throttle body assembly.

NOTE: *The throttle position sensor is an electrical component and should not be immersed in any type of liquid solvent or cleaner, as damage may result.*

4. With the throttle valve closed, install the TPS onto the throttle shaft. Rotate the TPS counterclockwise to align the mounting holes. Install the retaining screws or rivets. Torque the retaining screws to 18 inch lbs. (2.0 Nm).
5. Install the air cleaner assembly and connect the negative battery cable.

## MEM-CAL

### REMOVAL AND INSTALLATION

1. Remove the ECM.
2. Remove the Mem-Cal access panel.
3. Using 2 fingers, push both retaining clips back away from the MEM-Cal. At the same time, grasp it at both ends and lift it out of the socket. Do not remove the cover of the Mem-Cal. Use of an unapproved Mem-Cal removal procedures may cause damage to the Mem-Cal or the socket.

**To install:**

4. Install the new Mem-Cal by pressing only the ends of the Mem-Cal. Small notches in the Mem-Cal must be aligned with the small notches in the Mem-Cal socket.
5. Press on the ends of the Mem-Cal until the retaining clips snap into the ends of the

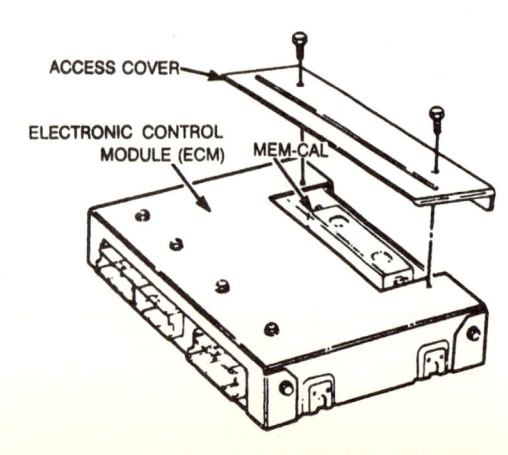

Removal and installation of the MEM-CAL assembly

# FUEL SYSTEM 175

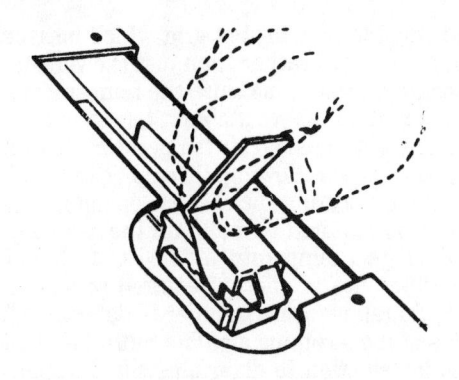

**PROM removal using special tool**

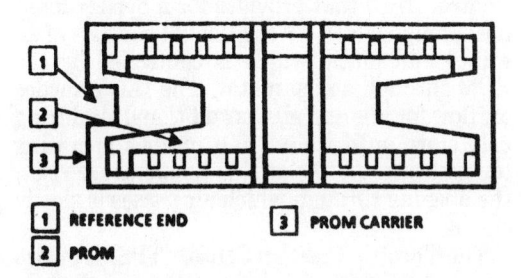

**Correct PROM-to-Carrier installation**
1. REFERENCE END
2. PROM
3. PROM CARRIER

Mem-Cal. Do not press on the middle of the Mem-Cal, only on the ends.

6. Install the Mem-Cal access cover and reinstall the ECM.

## PROM

### REMOVAL AND INSTALLATION

1. Remove the ECM.
2. Remove the PROM access panel.
3. Using the rocker type PROM removal tool, engage 1 end of the PROM carrier with the hook end of the tool. Press on the vertical bar end of the tool and rock the engaged end of the PROM carrier up as far as possible.
4. Engage the opposite end of the PROM carrier in the same manner and rock this end up as far as possible.
5. Repeat this process until the PROM carrier and PROM are free of the PROM socket. The PROM carrier with PROM in it should lift off of the PROM socket easily.
6. The PROM carrier should only be removed by using the special PROM removal tool. Other methods could cause damage to the PROM or PROM socket.
7. Before installing a new PROM, be sure the new PROM part number is the same as the old one or the as the updated number per a service bulletin.

**To install:**

8. Install the PROM with the small notch of the carrier aligned with the small notch in the socket. Press on the PROM carrier until the PROM is firmly seated, do not press on the PROM itself only on the PROM carrier.
9. Install the PROM access cover and reinstall the ECM.

### FUNCTIONAL CHECK

1. Turn the ignition switch to the **ON** position.
2. Enter the diagnostic mode.
3. Allow a Code 12 to flash 4 times to verify that no other codes are present. This indicates that the PROM is installed properly.
4. If trouble Code 51 occurs or if the SERVICE ENGINE SOON light in on constantly with no codes, the PROM is not fully seated, installed backwards, has bent pins or is defective.
5. If not fully seated press down firmly on the PROM carrier.
6. If installed backwards, replace the PROM.

NOTE: *Any time the PROM is installed backwards and the ignition switch is turned ON, the PROM is destroyed.*

7. If the pins are bent, remove the PROM straighten the pins and reinstall the PROM. If the bent pins break or crack during straightening, discard the PROM and replace with a new PROM.

NOTE: *To prevent possible electrostatic discharge damage to the PROM or Cal-Pak, do not touch the component leads and do not remove the integrated circuit from the carrier.*

## MULTI-PORT FUEL INJECTION SYSTEM
**(2.0L, 2.3L, 3.0L AND 3.3L ENGINES)**

### System Description

The Multi-Port Fuel Injection (MPI) system is controlled by an Electronic Control Module (ECM) which monitors engine operations and generates output signals to provide the correct air/fuel mixture, ignition timing and engine idle speed control. Input to the control unit is provided by an oxygen sensor, coolant temperature sensor, detonation (knock) sensor on some engines, hot film Mass Air Flow (MAF) sensor or Manifold Absolute Pressure (MAP) sensor and Throttle Position Sensor (TPS). The ECM also receives information concerning engine rpm, vehicle speed, transaxle selector position, power steering and air conditioning.

The injectors are located, one at each intake port, rather than the single injector found on the throttle body system. The injectors are mounted on a fuel rail and are activated by a signal from the Electronic Control Module (ECM). The injector is a solenoid-operated valve which remains open depending on the width of the electronic pulses (length of the signal) from the ECM; the longer the open time, the more fuel is injected. In this manner, the air/fuel mixture can be precisely controlled for maximum performance with minimum emissions. On all multi-port fuel injection systems, except the 2.3L engine, the ECM fires all of the injectors at once.

The system of 2.3L engines is slightly different in that the injectors are paired by companion cylinders and are fired in pairs. This system is called Alternating Synchronous Double Fire (ASDF) fuel injection and is similar in operation to the other injection systems except that each pair of cylinders fires once per crankshaft revolution. That means cylinders 1 and 4, and 2 and 3 fire once per crankshaft revolution. In this way, a cylinder's injector fires on the intake stroke and exhaust stroke. Firing the injector on the exhaust stroke (when the intake valve is closed) helps provide better fuel vaporization.

Fuel is pumped from the tank by a high pressure fuel pump, located inside the fuel tank. It is a positive displacement roller vane pump. The impeller serves as a vapor separator and pre-charges the high pressure assembly. A pressure regulator maintains 28–36 psi (193–248kpa) — 28–50 psi (193–345kpa) on turbocharged engines — in the fuel line to the injectors and the excess fuel is fed back to the tank. A fuel accumulator is used to dampen the hydraulic line hammer in the system created when all injectors open simultaneously.

The MAP sensor, used on all except the 3.0L and 3.3L engines, measures the changes in intake manifold pressure, which result from engine load and speed changes and converts this information to a voltage output. The MAP sensor reading is the opposite of a vacuum gauge reading: when manifold pressure is high, MAP sensor value is high and vacuum is low. A MAP sensor will produce a low output on engine coastdown with a closed throttle while a wide open throttle will produce a high output. The high output is produced because the pressure inside the manifold is the same as outside the manifold, so 100 percent of the outside air pressure is measured.

The MAP sensor is also used to measure barometric pressure under certain conditions, which allows the ECM to automatically adjust for different altitudes.

The MAP sensor changes the 5 volt signal supplied by the ECM, which reads the change and uses the information to control fuel delivery and ignition timing.

The Mass Air Flow (MAF) Sensor used on 3.0L and 3.3L engines, measures the mass of air that is drawn into the engine. It is located just ahead of the throttle in the intake system and consists of a heated grid which measures the mass of air, rather than just the volume. A resistor is used to measure the temperature of the film at 75° above ambient temperature. As the ambient (outside) air temperature rises and the rate of air flowing through the grid increases (indicating the throttle opening), more energy is required to maintain the heated grid at the higher temperature. The ECM calculates the difference in energy required to maintain the grid temperature in order to determine the mass of the incoming air. The control unit uses this information to determine the duration of fuel injection pulse, timing and EGR.

The throttle body incorporates an Idle Air Control (IAC) that provides for a bypass channel through which air can flow. It consists of an orifice and pintle which is controlled by the ECM through a step motor. The IAC provides air flow for idle and allows additional air during cold start until the engine reaches operating temperature. As the engine temperature rises, the opening through which air passes is slowly closed.

The Throttle Position Sensor (TPS) provides the control unit with information on throttle position, in order to determine injector pulse width and hence correct mixture. The TPS is connected to the throttle shaft on the throttle body and consists of as potentiometer with on end connected to a 5 volt source from the ECM and the other to ground. A third wire is connected to the ECM to measure the voltage output from the TPS which changes as the throttle valve angle is changed (accelerator pedal moves). At the closed throttle position, the output is low (approximately 0.4 volts); as the throttle valve opens, the output increases to a maximum 5 volts at Wide Open Throttle (WOT). The TPS can be misadjusted open, shorted, or loose and if it is out of adjustment, the idle quality or WOT performance may be poor. A loose TPS can cause intermittent bursts of fuel from the injectors and an unstable idle because the ECM thinks the throttle is moving. This should cause a trouble code to be set. Once a trouble code is set, the ECM will use a preset value for TPS and some vehicle performance may return. A small amount of engine coolant is routed through the throttle assembly to prevent freezing inside the throttle bore during cold operation.

## Service Precautions

When working around any part of the fuel system, take precautionary steps to prevent fire and/or explosion:

• Disconnect negative terminal from battery (except when testing with battery voltage is required).

# FUEL SYSTEM

- When ever possible, use a flashlight instead of a drop light.
- Keep all open flame and smoking material out of the area.
- Use a shop cloth or similar to catch fuel when opening a fuel system.
- Relieve fuel system pressure before servicing.
- Use eye protection.
- Always keep a dry chemical (class B) fire extinguisher near the area.

## Relieving Fuel System Pressure

### WITH FUEL RAIL TEST FITTING

1. Disconnect the negative battery cable.
2. Loosen the fuel filler cap to relieve fuel tank vapor pressure.
3. Connect a fuel pressure gauge with valve to the fuel pressure relief connection at the fuel rail.
4. Wrap a shop towel around the fittings while connecting the tool to prevent fuel spillage.
5. Install a bleed hose into an approved container and open the valve to bleed the system pressure.
6. Install the fuel filler cap.

### WITHOUT FUEL RAIL TEST FITTING

1. Remove the fuel filler cap to relieve fuel tank vapor pressure.
2. From under the vehicle, disconnect the fuel pump electrical connector. It should be the only connector coming from the fuel tank.
3. Start the engine and run until the engine stalls. Engage the starter an additional 3 seconds to assure complete relief.
4. Install the fuel filler cap.
5. Disconnect the negative battery cable and continue with fuel system work.

## Electric Fuel Pump

### FUEL PRESSURE CHECK

1. Connect pressure gauge J-34730-1, or equivalent, to fuel pressure test point on the fuel rail. Wrap a rag around the pressure tap to absorb any leakage that may occur when installing the gauge.
2. Turn the ignition **ON**. The fuel pump pressure should read as follows:
- 2.0L engine – 35-38 psi (245-256 kPa)
- 2.3L engine – 41-47 psi (280-325 kPa)
- 1985-86 3.0L engine – 37-43 psi (255-298 kPa)
- 1987-88 3.0L engine – 41-47 psi (280-325 kPa)
- 3.3L engine – 41-47 psi (280-325 kPa)

3. Start the engine and allow it to idle. The fuel pressure should drop no more than 3-10 psi (21-69kpa).

NOTE: *The idle pressure will vary somewhat depending on barometric pressure. Check for a drop in pressure indicating regulator control, rather than specific values.*

4. On turbocharged vehicles, use a low pressure air pump to apply air pressure to the regulator to simulate turbocharger boost pressure. Boost pressure should increase fuel pressure 1 psi (7kpa) for every lb. of boost. Again, look for changes rather than specific pressures. The maximum fuel pressure should not exceed 46 psi (317kpa).

5. If the fuel pressure drops, check the operation of the check valve, the pump coupling connection, fuel pressure regulator valve and the injectors. A restricted fuel line or filter may also cause a pressure drip. To check the fuel pump output, restrict the fuel return line and run 12 volts to the pump. The fuel pressure should rise to approximately 75 psi (517kpa) with the return line restricted.

6. Before attempting to remove or service any fuel system component, it is necessary to relieve the fuel system pressure.

### REMOVAL AND INSTALLATION

1. Disconnect the negative battery cable.
2. Relieve the fuel system pressure.
3. Raise and safely support the vehicle with jackstands.
4. Safely drain and remove the fuel tank assembly as outlined in the "Fuel tank" removal procedures in this Chapter.
5. Turn the fuel pump cam lock ring counterclockwise and lift the assembly out of the tank.
6. Remove the fuel pump from the level sensor unit as follows:
   a. Pull the pump up into the attaching hose or pulsator while pulling outward away from the bottom support.
   b. Take care to prevent damage to the rubber insulator and strainer during removal.
   c. When the pump assembly is clear of the bottom support, pull the pump out of the rubber connector for removal.

**To install:**

7. Replace any attaching hoses or rubber sound insulator that show signs of deterioration.
8. Push the fuel pump into the attaching hoses and install the pump/sensor assembly into the tank. Always use a new O-ring seal.

Be careful not to fold over or twist the strainer when installing the sensor unit. Also, make sure the strainer does not block full travel of the float arm.

# 178   FUEL SYSTEM

9. Install the cam lock and turn clockwise to lock.

10. Install the fuel tank as outlined in this Chapter.

11. Fill the tank with four gallons of gas and check for fuel leaks.

## Throttle Body

### REMOVAL AND INSTALLATION

CAUTION: *When draining the coolant, keep in mind that cats and dogs are attracted by the ethylene glycol antifreeze, and are quite likely to drink any that is left in an uncovered container or in puddles on the ground. This will prove fatal in sufficient quantity. Always drain the coolant into a sealable container. Coolant should be reused unless it is contaminated or several years old.*

### 2.3L Engine

1. Disconnect the negative battery cable. Drain the top half of the engine coolant into a suitable drain pan.

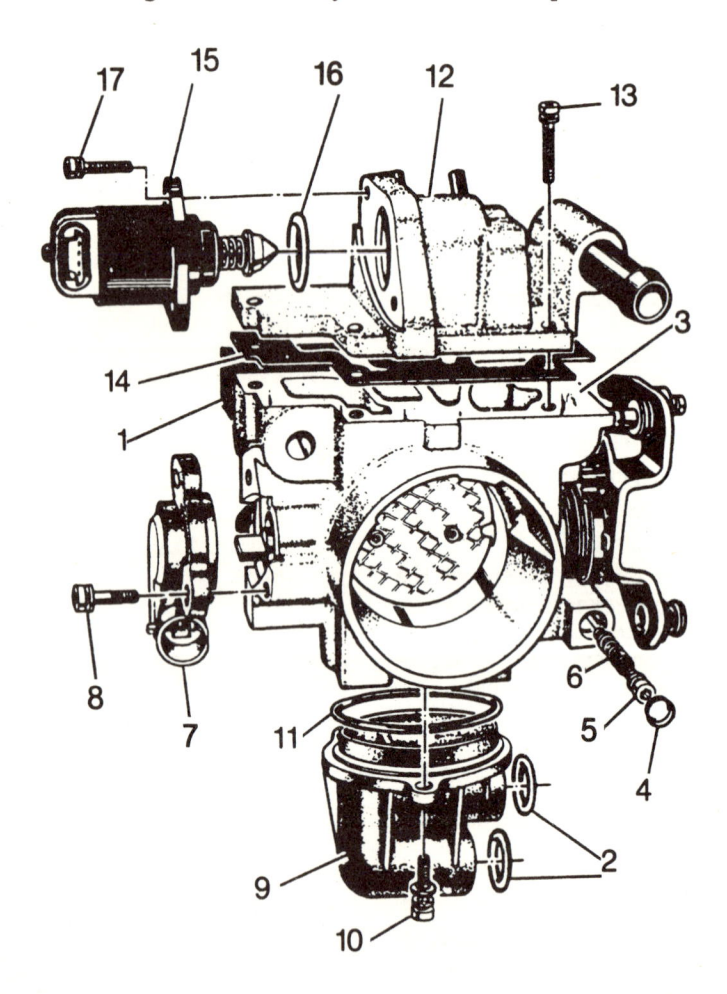

1. Flange gasket
2. Coolant line O-ring
3. Throttle body assembly
4. Idle stop crew plug
5. Idle stop screw assembly
6. Idle stop screw assembly spring
7. Throttle Position Sensor (TPS)
8. TPS attaching screw
9. Coolant passage cover
10. Coolant passage cover attaching screw
11. Coolant cover-to-throttle body O-ring
12. Idle air/vacuum signal housing assembly
13. Idle air/vacuum signal housing assembly screw
14. Idle air/vacuum signal housing assembly gasket
15. Idle Air Control (IAC) valve assembly
16. IAC valve O-ring
17. Idle air control valve attaching screw

**Throttle body assembly—2.3L engine**

# FUEL SYSTEM

2. Remove the air inlet duct. Disconnect the idle air control valve and throttle position sensor connectors.
3. Remove and mark all necessary vacuum lines. Remove and plug the 2 coolant hoses.
4. Remove the throttle, T.V. and cruise control cables. Remove the power steering pump brace.
5. Remove the throttle body retaining bolts and then remove the throttle body assembly. Discard the flange gasket.
6. Installation is the reverse order of the removal procedure. Torque the retaining bolts to 20 ft. lbs. (27 Nm).
7. Connect the negative battery cable. Refill the cooling system.

### Except 2.3L Engine

1. Disconnect the negative battery cable.
2. Partially drain the cooling system to allow the coolant hoses at the throttle body to be removed.
3. Remove the air inlet duct at the throttle body and crankcase vent pipe at the valve cover grommet.
4. Disconnect the TPS and IAC valve electrical connectors.
5. Disconnect the vacuum harness connector from the throttle body.
6. Disconnect the throttle, TV (transmission control) and cruise control cables.
7. Disconnect the coolant hoses from the throttle body.
8. Remove the throttle body attaching bolts.
9. Remove the throttle body assembly and flange gasket. Discard the gasket.

**To install:**
NOTE: *Use care in the cleaning of old gasket material from machined aluminum surfaces. Sharp tools may cause damage to sealing surfaces.*

10. Install the throttle body assembly with a new flange gasket. Install the throttle body attaching bolts. Tighten to 18–20 ft. lbs. (24–27 Nm).
11. Connect the coolant hoses to the throttle body.
12. Connect the throttle, TV and cruise cables.
   NOTE: *Ensure that the throttle and cruise control linkage does not hold the throttle open.*
13. Connect the vacuum harness connector to the throttle body.
14. Connect the TPS and IAC valve electrical connectors.
15. Connect the air inlet duct to the throttle body and crankcase vent pipe to the valve cover grommet.
16. Refill the radiator.
17. Connect the negative battery cable.
18. With the ignition switch in the **OFF** position, ensure that the movement of the accelerator is free.

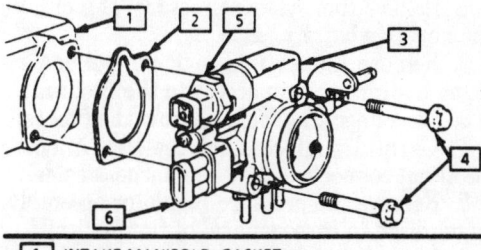

| 1 | INTAKE MANIFOLD GASKET |
| 2 | GASKET |
| 3 | THROTTLE BODY ASM |
| 4 | BOLTS 14–20 N·m (10–15 lb. ft.) |
| 5 | IDLE AIR CONTROL VALVE |
| 6 | THROTTLE POSITION SENSOR |

Throttle body assembly—2.0L engine

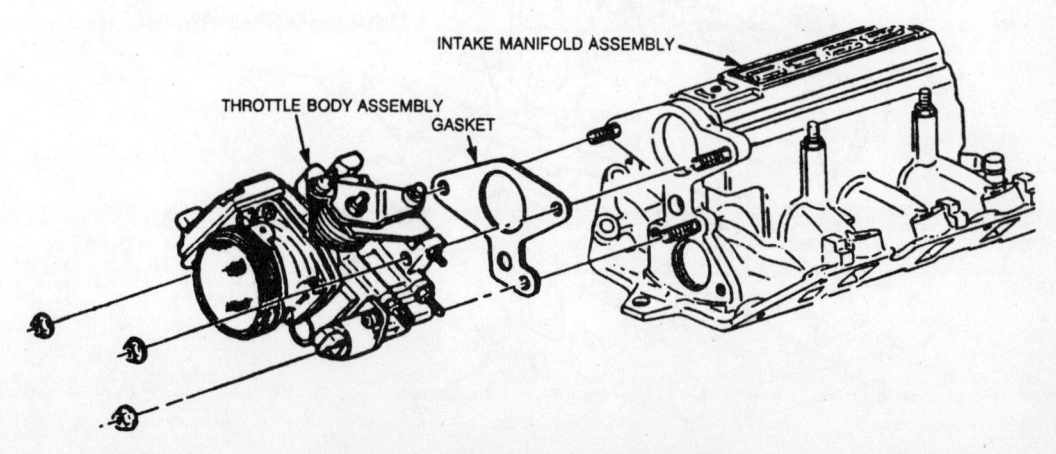

Throttle body assembly—3.0L and 3.3L engines

## Fuel Rail Assembly

When servicing the fuel rail assembly, be careful to prevent dirt and other contaminants from entering the fuel passages. Fittings should be capped and holes plugged during servicing. At any time the fuel system is opened for service, the O-ring seals and retainers used with related components should be replaced.

Before removing the fuel rail, the fuel rail assembly may be cleaned with a spray type cleaner, GM–30A or equivalent, following package instructions. Do not immerse fuel rails in liquid cleaning solvent. Be sure to always use new O-rings and seals when reinstalling the fuel rail assemblies.

There is an 8-digit number stamped on the under side of the fuel rail assembly on 4 cylinder engines and on the left hand fuel rail on dual rail assemblies (fueling even cylinders No. 2, 4, 6). Refer to this number if servicing or part replacement is required.

### REMOVAL AND INSTALLATION

#### 2.0L Engine

1. Relieve fuel system pressure. Disconnect the negative battery cable.
2. Remove the air intake ducts and/or passages in order to gain access to the fuel rail.
3. Disconnect the fuel line from the fuel rail.
4. Carefully, disconnect the fuel injector electrical connectors. Lay the harness aside.
5. Remove the pressure regulator assembly, as required to ease removal of the fuel rail.
6. Remove the fuel rail mounting hardware.
7. Carefully remove the fuel injectors from the intake manifold.
8. Remove the fuel rail from the vehicle.
9. Discard the fuel injector O-rings.

**To install:**

10. Install new fuel injector O-rings. Lubricate with a light coating of engine oil.
11. Carefully, install the fuel injectors to the intake manifold.
12. Install the fuel rail attaching hardware.
13. If removed, install the pressure regulator.
14. Connect the fuel injector electrical connectors.
15. Connect the fuel line to the fuel rail.
16. Install the air intake ducts and/or passages.
17. Connect the negative battery cable.
18. Turn the ignition key to the **ON** position. Check for fuel leaks.
19. Start the engine and allow to idle. Recheck for leaks.

#### 2.3L Engine

1. Relieve fuel system pressure. Disconnect the negative battery cable.
2. Remove the crankcase ventilation oil/air separator and the canister purge solenoid.
3. Disconnect the fuel feed line and return line from the fuel rail assembly, be sure to use a backup wrench on the inlet fitting to prevent turning.
4. Remove the vacuum line at the pressure regulator. Remove the fuel rail assembly retaining bolts.
5. Push in the wire connector clip, while pulling the connector away from the injector.
6. Remove the fuel rail assembly and cover all openings with masking tape to prevent dirt entry.

NOTE: *If any injectors become separated from the fuel rail and remain in the intake manifold, both O-ring seals and injector retaining clip must be replaced. Use care in re-*

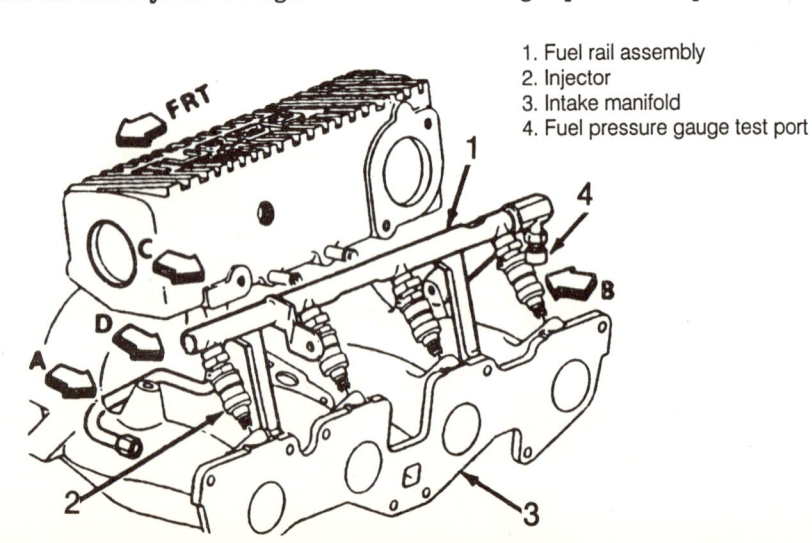

1. Fuel rail assembly
2. Injector
3. Intake manifold
4. Fuel pressure gauge test port

**Fuel rail assembly—2.0L engine**

# FUEL SYSTEM 181

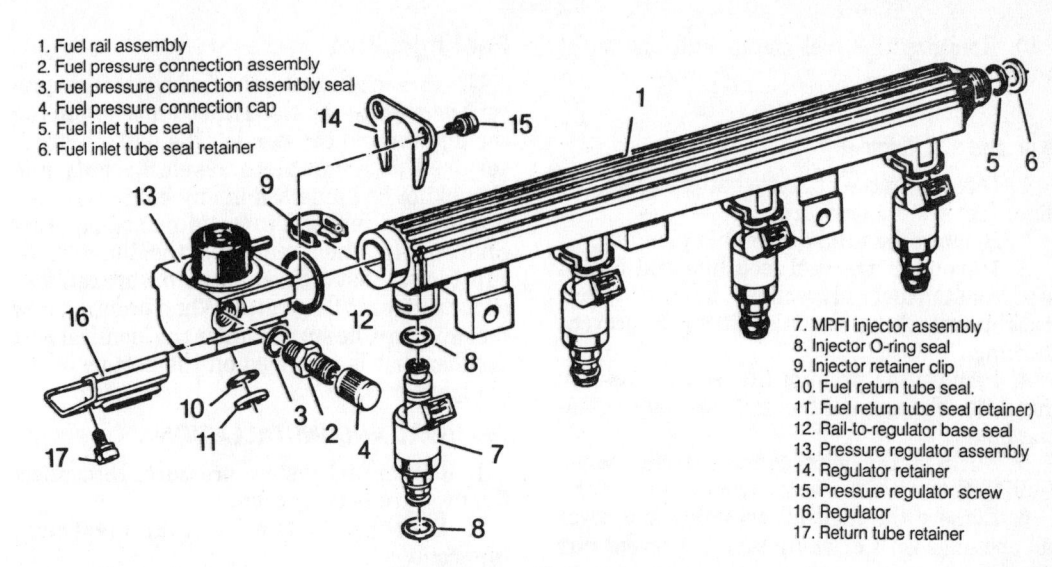

1. Fuel rail assembly
2. Fuel pressure connection assembly
3. Fuel pressure connection assembly seal
4. Fuel pressure connection cap
5. Fuel inlet tube seal
6. Fuel inlet tube seal retainer
7. MPFI injector assembly
8. Injector O-ring seal
9. Injector retainer clip
10. Fuel return tube seal.
11. Fuel return tube seal retainer)
12. Rail-to-regulator base seal
13. Pressure regulator assembly
14. Regulator retainer
15. Pressure regulator screw
16. Regulator
17. Return tube retainer

**Fuel rail assembly—2.3L engine**

moving the fuel rail assembly, to prevent damage to the injector electrical connector terminals and the injector spray tips. When removed, support the fuel rail to avoid damaging its components. The fuel injector is serviced as a complete unit only. Since it is an electrical component, it should not be immersed in any type of cleaner.

7. Be sure to lubricate all the O-rings and seals with clean engine oil. Carefully push the injectors into the cylinder head intake ports until the bolt holes on the fuel rail and manifold are aligned.

8. The remainder of the installation is the reverse order of the removal procedure.

9. Apply a coating of tread locking compound on the treads of the fittings. Torque the fuel rail retaining bolts to 19 ft. lbs. (26 Nm), the fuel feed line nut to 22 ft. lbs. (30 Nm) and the fuel pipe fittings to 20 ft. lbs. (26 Nm).

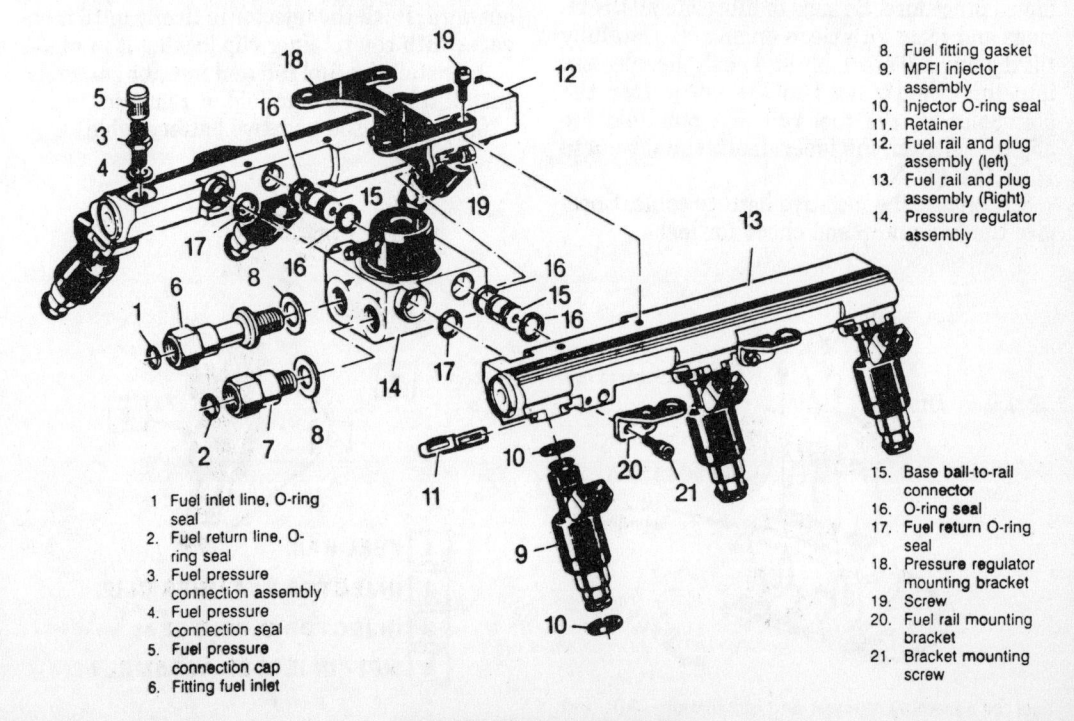

1. Fuel inlet line, O-ring seal
2. Fuel return line, O-ring seal
3. Fuel pressure connection assembly
4. Fuel pressure connection seal
5. Fuel pressure connection cap
6. Fitting fuel inlet
7. 
8. Fuel fitting gasket
9. MPFI injector assembly
10. Injector O-ring seal
11. Retainer
12. Fuel rail and plug assembly (left)
13. Fuel rail and plug assembly (Right)
14. Pressure regulator assembly
15. Base ball-to-rail connector
16. O-ring seal
17. Fuel return O-ring seal
18. Pressure regulator mounting bracket
19. Screw
20. Fuel rail mounting bracket
21. Bracket mounting screw

**Fuel rail assembly—V6 engine**

# FUEL SYSTEM

10. Energize the fuel pump and check for leaks.

### 3.0L and 3.3L Engines

1. Disconnect the negative battery cable. Relieve fuel system pressure.
2. Remove the intake manifold plenum.
3. Disconnect the fuel feed line and return line from the fuel rail assembly, be sure to use a backup wrench on the inlet fitting to prevent turning.
4. Remove the vacuum line at the pressure regulator. Remove the fuel rail assembly retaining bolts.
5. Push in the wire connector clip, while pulling the connector away from the injector.
6. Remove the fuel rail assembly and cover all openings with masking tape to prevent dirt entry.

NOTE: *If any injectors become separated from the fuel rail and remain in the intake manifold, both O-ring seals and injector retaining clip must be replaced. Use care in removing the fuel rail assembly, to prevent damage to the injector electrical connector terminals and the injector spray tips. When removed, support the fuel rail to avoid damaging its components. The fuel injector is serviced as a complete unit only. Since it is an electrical component, it should not be immersed in any type of cleaner.*

7. Installation is the reverse order of the removal procedure. Be sure to lubricate all the O-rings and seals with clean engine oil. Carefully tilt the fuel rail assembly and push the injectors into the cylinder head intake ports until the bolt holes on the fuel rail and manifold are aligned. Tighten the fuel rail attaching bolts to 20 ft. lbs. (27 Nm).
8. Connect the negative battery cable. Energize the fuel pump and check for leaks.

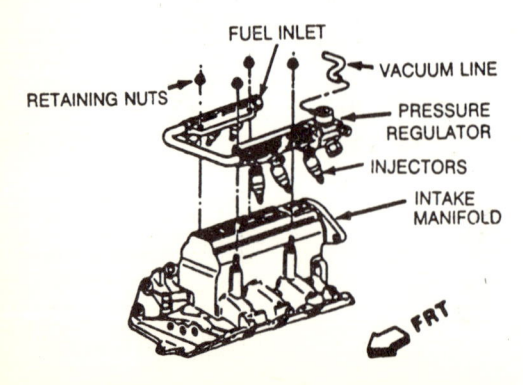

Fuel rail assembly removal and installation—3.0L and 3.3L engine

## Fuel Injectors

Use care in removing the fuel injectors to prevent damage to the electrical connector pins on the injector and the nozzle. The fuel injector is serviced as a complete assembly only and should not be immersed in any kind of cleaner. Support the fuel rail to avoid damaging other components while removing the injector. Be sure to note that different injectors are calibrated for different flow rates. When ordering new fuel injectors, be sure to order the identical part number that is inscribed on the bottom of the old injector.

### REMOVAL AND INSTALLATION

1. Relieve fuel system pressure. Disconnect the negative battery cable.
2. Disconnect the injector electrical connections.
3. Remove the fuel rail assembly.
4. Remove the injector retaining clip. Separate the injector from the fuel rail.
5. Remove both injector seals from the injector and discard.

**To install:**

6. Prior to installing the injectors, coat the new injector O-ring seals with clean engine oil. Install the seals on the injector assembly.
7. Use new injector retainer clips on the injector assembly. Position the open end of the clip facing the injector electrical connector.
8. Install the injector into the fuel rail injector socket with the electrical connectors facing outward. Push the injector in firmly until it engages with the retainer clip locking it in place.
9. Install the fuel rail and injector assembly. Install the intake manifold, if removed.
10. Connect the negative battery cable.

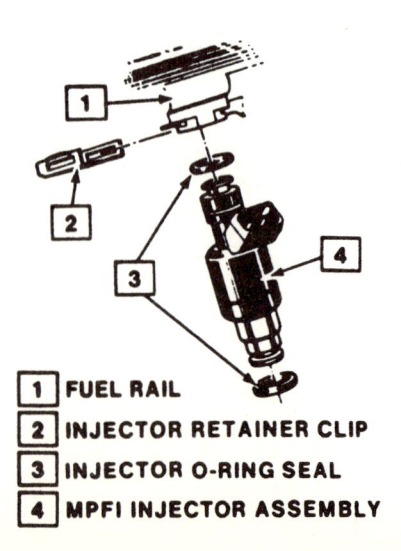

MPFI fuel injector assembly

## FUEL SYSTEM    183

11. Turn the ignition switch **ON** and **OFF** to allow fuel pressure back into system. Check for leaks.

### Fuel Pressure Regulator

NOTE: *On some applications, the pressure regulator and fuel rail are only available as an assembly. Check with your local parts retailer for parts availability and compatibility. Refer to the exploded views of the fuel rails.*

#### REMOVAL AND INSTALLATION

1. Relieve fuel system pressure.
2. Disconnect the negative battery cable.
3. Disconnect the fuel feed line and return line from the fuel rail assembly, be sure to use a backup wrench on the inlet fitting to prevent turning.
4. Remove the fuel rail assembly from the engine.
5. With the fuel rail assembly removed from the engine, remove the pressure regulator mounting screw or retainer.
6. Remove the pressure regulator from the rail assembly by twisting back and forth while pulling apart.

**To install:**

7. Prior to assembling the pressure regulator to the fuel rail, lubricate the new rail-to-regulator O-ring seal with clean engine oil.
8. Place the O-ring on the pressure regulator and install the pressure regulator to the fuel rail.
9. Install the retainer or coat the regulator mounting screws with an approved tread locking compound and secure the pressure regulator in place. Torque the mounting screws to 102 inch lbs. (11.5 Nm).
10. Install the fuel rail assembly to the engine.
11. Connect the fuel feed line and return line to the fuel rail assembly, use a backup wrench on the inlet fitting to prevent turning.
12. Connect the negative battery cable.
13. Turn the ignition switch **ON** and **OFF** to allow fuel pressure back into system. Check for leaks.

### Idle Air Control Valve

#### REMOVAL AND INSTALLATION

1. Disconnect the negative battery cable.
2. Disconnect electrical connector from idle air control valve.
3. Remove the screws retaining the idle air control valve. Remove the idle air control valve from mounting position.

**To install:**

4. Prior to installing the idle air control valve, measure the distance the valve plunger is extended. Measurement should be made from the edge of the valves mounting flange to the end of the cone. The distance should not exceed 1⅛ in. (28mm), or damage to the valve may occur when installed. If measuring distance is greater than specified above, press on the valve firmly to retract it, using a slight side to side motion to help it retract easier.
5. Use a new gasket and install the idle air control valve in mounting position.
6. Install the retaining screws. Torque the retaining screws to 27 inch lbs. (3 Nm). Connect the electrical connector.
7. The idle may be unstable for up to 7 minutes upon restarting while the ECM resets the IAC valve pintle to the correct position.

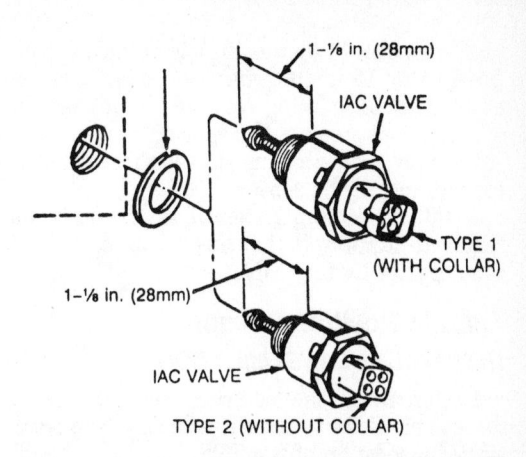

Removal and installation of the Idle Air Control (IAC) valve

### Coolant Temperature Sensor

The coolant temperature sensor is located on the intake manifold water jacket or near (or on) the thermostat housing. It may be necessary to drain some of the coolant from the coolant system.

#### REMOVAL AND INSTALLATION

CAUTION: *When draining the coolant, keep in mind that cats and dogs are attracted by the ethylene glycol antifreeze, and are quite likely to drink any that is left in an uncovered container or in puddles on the ground. This will prove fatal in sufficient quantity. Always drain the coolant into a sealable container. Coolant should be reused unless it is contaminated or several years old.*

1. Disconnect the negative battery cable and disconnect the electrical connector at the sensor.
2. Remove the threaded temperature sensor from the engine.
3. Check the sensor with the tip immersed in water at 50°F (15°C). The resistance across the

# 184  FUEL SYSTEM

terminals should approximately 5600Ω. Check Code 14 or 15 engine chart for specific resistance on vehicle being serviced. If not within specifications, replace the sensor.

4. Apply some pipe tape to the threaded sensor and install the sensor.

5. Fill the cooling system if any coolant was removed. Reconnect the sensor connector and the negative battery cable.

## Throttle Position Sensor

### REMOVAL AND INSTALLATION

1. Disconnect the electrical connector from the sensor. Refer to the throttle body exploded views for location of the TPS.

2. Remove the attaching screws, lock washers and retainers.

3. Remove the throttle position sensor. If necessary, remove the screw holding the actuator to the end of the throttle shaft.

4. With the throttle valve in the normal closed idle position, install the throttle position sensor on the throttle body assembly, making sure the sensor pickup lever is located above the tang on the throttle actuator lever.

5. Install the retainers, screws and lock washers using a thread locking compound. Tighten to 18 inch lbs. (2 Nm).

### ADJUSTMENT

#### 3.0L and 3.3L Engines

1. Connect SCAN tool and view throttle position

2. With the ignition in the **ON** position and the throttle closed, adjust the position of the throttle sensor to obtain a reading of 0.50–0.59 volts for a 3.0L engine and 0.38–0.42 volts for a 3.3L engine.

3. Tighten the screws to 18 inch lbs. (2.0 Nm).

4. Recheck reading.

### TPS Output Check Test

*WITH SCAN TOOL*

1. Use a suitable scan tool to read the TPS voltage.

2. With the ignition switch **ON** and the engine **OFF**, the TPS voltage should be less, than 1.25 volts.

3. If the voltage reading is higher than specified, replace the throttle position sensor.

*WITHOUT SCAN TOOL*

1. Disconnect the TPS harness from the TPS.

2. Using suitable jumper wires, connect a digital voltmeter to terminals A and B on the TPS.

3. With the ignition **ON** and the engine running, the TPS voltage should be 0.450–1.25 volts at base idle to approximately 4.5 volts at wide open throttle.

4. If the reading on the TPS is out of specification, replace it.

5. Turn ignition **OFF**, remove jumper wires, then reconnect harness to throttle position switch.

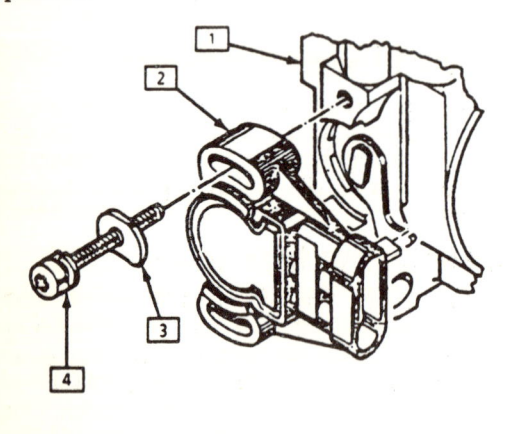

| | |
|---|---|
| 1 | THROTTLE BODY ASM. |
| 2 | THROTTLE POSITION SENSOR (TPS) |
| 3 | RETAINER (2) |
| 4 | SCREW (2) 2 N·m (18 lb. in.) |

Throttle Position Sensor (TPS) installation—3.0L and 3.3L engine

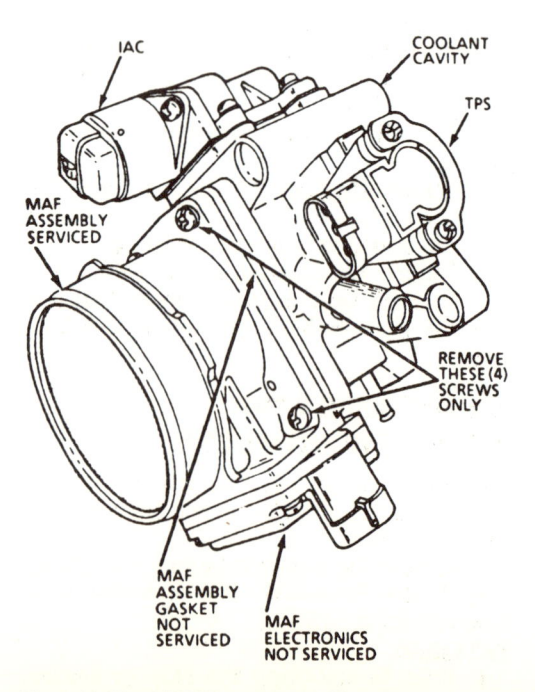

Mass Air Flow (MAF) sensor—3.3L engine

# FUEL SYSTEM

## Mass Air Flow Sensor
### REMOVAL AND INSTALLATION
1. Disconnect the negative battery cable.
2. Disconnect the electrical connector to the MAF sensor.
3. Remove the air cleaner and duct assembly. Remove the sensor retaining clamps and remove the sensor.
4. Installation is the reverse order of the removal procedure.

## Torque Converter Clutch Solenoid
### REMOVAL AND INSTALLATION
1. Remove the negative battery cable. Raise and support the vehicle safely.
2. Drain the transmission fluid into a suitable drain pan. Remove the transmission pan.
3. Remove the TCC solenoid retaining screws and then remove the electrical connector, solenoid and check ball.
4. Clean and inspect all parts. Replace defective parts as necessary.
**To install:**
5. Install the check ball, TCC solenoid and electrical connector. Install the solenoid retaining screws and torque them to 10 ft. lbs. (14 Nm).
6. Install the transmission pan with a new gasket and torque the pan retaining bolts to 10 ft. lbs. (14 Nm).
7. Lower the vehicle and refill the transmission with the proper amount of the automatic transmission fluid.

## MEM-CAL
### REMOVAL AND INSTALLATION
1. Remove the ECM.
2. Remove the Mem-Cal access panel.
3. Using 2 fingers, push both retaining clips back away from the Mem-Cal. At the same time, grasp it at both ends and lift it out of the socket. Do not remove the cover of the Mem-Cal. Use of an unapproved Mem-Cal removal procedures may cause damage to the Mem-Cal or the socket.
**To install:**
4. Install the new Mem-Cal by pressing only the ends of the Mem-Cal. Small notches in the Mem-Cal must be aligned with the small notches in the Mem-Cal socket.
5. Press on the ends of the Mem-Cal until the retaining clips snap into the ends of the Mem-Cal. Do not press on the middle of the Mem-Cal, only on the ends.
6. Install the Mem-Cal access cover and reinstall the ECM.

## PROM
### REMOVAL AND INSTALLATION
1. Remove the ECM.
2. Remove the PROM access panel.
3. Using the rocker type PROM removal tool, engage 1 end of the PROM carrier with the hook end of the tool. Press on the vertical bar end of the tool and rock the engaged end of the PROM carrier up as far as possible.
4. Engage the opposite end of the PROM carrier in the same manner and rock this end up as far as possible.
5. Repeat this process until the PROM carrier and PROM are free of the PROM socket. The PROM carrier with PROM in it should lift off of the PROM socket easily.
6. The PROM carrier should only be removed by using the special PROM removal tool. Other methods could cause damage to the PROM or PROM socket.
7. Before installing a new PROM, be sure the new PROM part number is the same as the old one or the as the updated number per a service bulletin.
**To install:**
8. Install the PROM with the small notch of the carrier aligned with the small notch in the socket. Press on the PROM carrier until the PROM is firmly seated, do not press on the PROM itself only on the PROM carrier.
9. Install the PROM access cover and reinstall the ECM.

### FUNCTIONAL CHECK
1. Turn the ignition switch to the **ON** position.
2. Enter the diagnostic mode.
3. Allow a Code 12 to flash 4 times to verify that no other codes are present. This indicates that the PROM is installed properly.
4. If trouble Code 51 occurs or if the SERVICE ENGINE SOON light in on constantly with no codes, the PROM is not fully seated, installed backwards, has bent pins or is defective.
5. If not fully seated press down firmly on the PROM carrier.
6. If installed backwards, replace the PROM.
NOTE: *Any time the PROM is installed backwards and the ignition switch is turned ON, the PROM is destroyed.*
7. If the pins are bent, remove the PROM straighten the pins and reinstall the PROM. If the bent pins break or crack during straightening, discard the PROM and replace with a new PROM.
NOTE: *To prevent possible electrostatic discharge damage to the PROM or Cal-Pak, do not touch the component leads and do not remove the integrated circuit from the carrier.*

# FUEL SYSTEM

## FUEL TANK

### DRAINING

1. Disconnect the negative battery cable.
CAUTION: *To reduce the risk of fire and personal injury, always keep a dry chemical (Class B) fire extinguisher near the work area.*
2. Remove the fuel cap.
3. Raise the vehicle and support with jackstands.
4. Disconnect the filler vent hose from the tank.
5. Use a hand operated pump approved for gasoline to drain as much fuel as possible through the filler vent hose.
6. Reconnect the filler vent hose and tighten the clamp.
7. Install any removed lines, hoses and cap. Connect the negative battery cable.

### REMOVAL AND INSTALLATION

1. Disconnect the negative battery cable.
2. Drain the fuel tank.
3. Remove the fuel filler door assembly and disconnect the screw retaining the filler pipe-to-body bracket.
4. Raise the vehicle and support with jackstands.
5. Disconnect the tank level sender lead connector.
6. Support the tank with a transmission jack or equivalent. Remove the two tank retaining straps.
7. Lower the tank far enough to disconnect the ground lead and fuel hoses from the pump assembly.
8. Remove the tank from the vehicle slowly to ensure all connections and hoses have been disconnected.
9. Remove the fuel pump/level sender assembly using a locking cam tool J-24187 or equivalent.

**To install:**

10. Using a new fuel pump O-ring gasket, install the pump/sender assembly into the tank.
CAUTION: *Do not twist the strainer when installing the pump/sender assembly. Make sure the strainer does not block the full travel of the float arm.*
11. Place the tank on the jack.
12. Position the tank sound insulators in their original positions and raise the tank far enough to connect the electrical and hose connectors.
13. Raise the tank to the proper position and loosely install the retaining straps. Make sure the tank is in the proper position before tightening the retaining straps.
14. Torque the straps to 26 ft. lbs. (35 Nm).
15. Connect the grounding strap and negative battery cable.
16. With the engine OFF, turn the ignition key to the ON position and check for fuel leaks at the tank.

# Chassis Electrical

## HEATER AND AIR CONDITIONING

### General Information

The heater and air conditioning systems are controlled manually. The manual system controls air temperature through a cable-actuated lever and air flow through a vacuum switching valve and vacuum actuators.

The heating system provides heating, ventilation and defrosting for the windshield and side windows. The heater core is a heat exchanger supplied with coolant from the engine cooling system. Temperature is controlled by the temperature valve which moves an air door that directs air flow through the heater core for more heat or bypasses the heater core for less heat.

Vacuum actuators control the mode doors which direct air flow to the outlet ducts. The mode selector on the control panel directs engine vacuum to the actuators. The position of the mode doors determines whether air flows from the floor, panel, defrost or panel and defrost ducts (bi-level mode).

### Blower Motor

#### REMOVAL AND INSTALLATION

1. Disconnect negative battery cable.
2. Remove the serpentine belt and/or the power steering pressure hose, as required.
3. Disconnect the connector to the blower motor and remove the cooling tube.
4. Remove the attaching screws and remove the blower from the case.

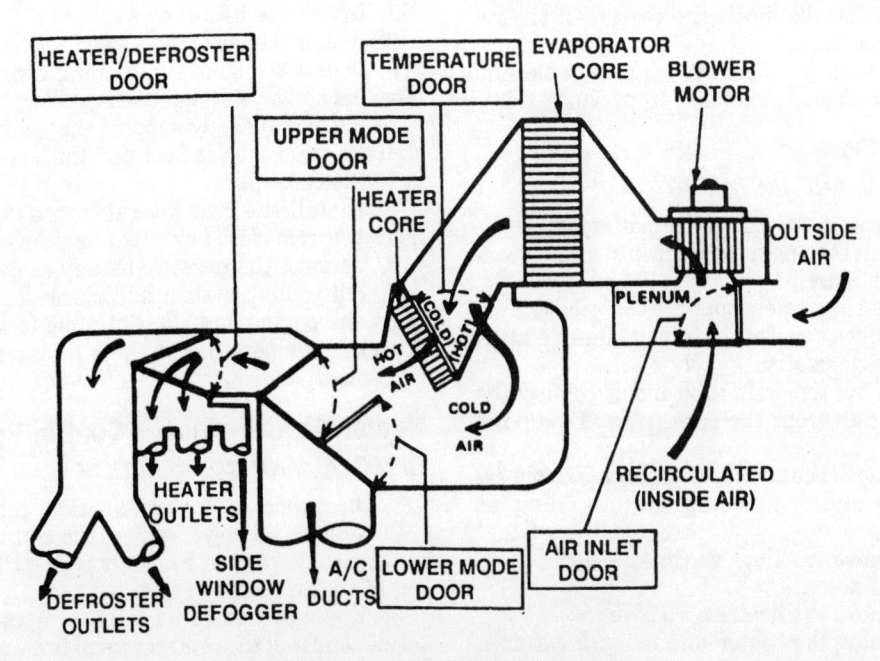

Typical heater/air conditioner air flow

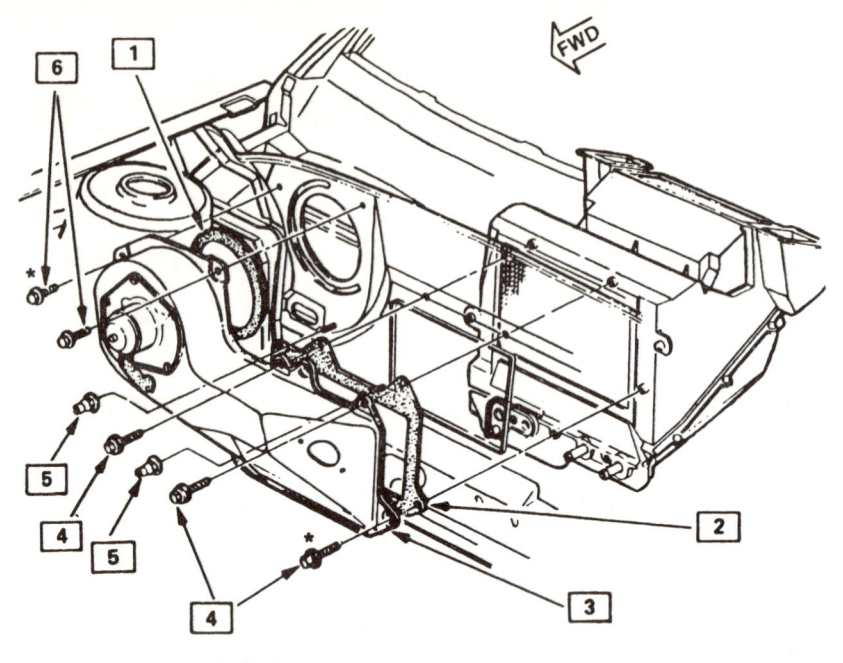

# 188  CHASSIS ELECTRICAL

1. Gasket
2. Gasket
3. Blower assembly
4. Bolt/screw (install this screw first)
5. Nut
6. Bolt/screw (install this screw second)

Blower motor and air inlet assembly

5. If necessary, remove the fan from the blower motor.
6. The installation is the reverse of the removal procedure.
7. Connect the negative battery cable and check the blower motor for proper operation.

## Heater Core

### REMOVAL AND INSTALLATION

1. Disconnect the negative battery cable.
2. Drain the engine coolant into a clean container for reuse.
3. Raise and safely support the vehicle.
4. Remove the rear lateral transaxle strut mount, if necessary.
5. Remove the drain tube and disconnect the heater hoses from the core tubes. Lower the vehicle.
6. Remove the sound insulators, console extensions and/or steering column filler, as required.
7. Remove the floor or console outlet ductwork and hoses.
8. Remove the heater core cover.
9. Remove the heater core mounting clamps and remove the heater core.

**To install:**
10. Install the heater core and clamps.
11. Install the heater core cover.
12. Install the outlet hoses and ducts.
13. Install the sound insulators, console extensions and/or steering column filler.
14. Raise and safely support the vehicle. Install the drain tube and connect the heater hoses to the core tubes.
15. Install the rear lateral transaxle strut mount, if removed. Lower the vehicle.
16. Connect the negative battery cable.
17. Fill cooling system and check for leaks. Start the engine and allow to come to normal operating temperature. Recheck for leaks. Top-up coolant.

## Heater/Air Conditioner Control Panel

### REMOVAL AND INSTALLATION

1. Disconnect the negative battery cable.
2. Remove the lower center trim plate by removing the screws or by gently prying the tabs out of the retainers.
3. Remove the control panel attaching screws and pull the control assembly away from the instrument panel.

## CHASSIS ELECTRICAL 189

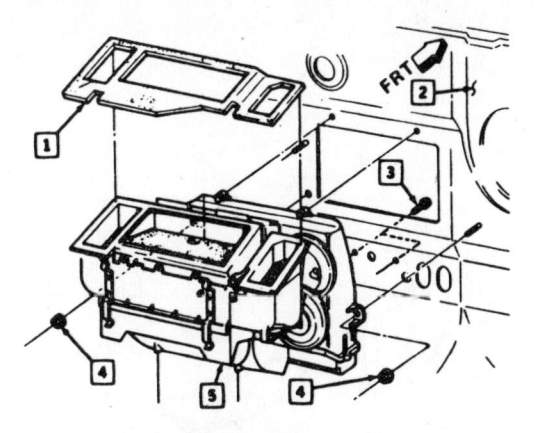

1. Module-to-air distributor seal assembly
2. Dash panel assembly
3. Screw
4. Nut
5. A/C and heater module

**Heater module assembly**

4. Disconnect the electrical connectors.
5. Label and disconnect the control cables.

**To install:**

6. Connect the control cables to the new control panel assembly.

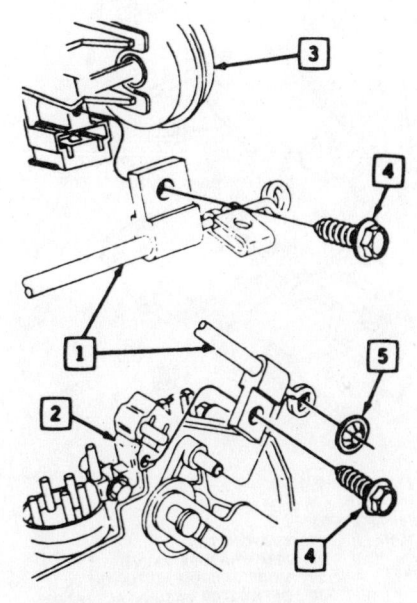

1. TEMPERATURE CONTROL CABLE
2. HEATER CONTROL
3. DEFROST VACUUM ACTUATOR
4. SCREW - 4.2 mm (8 - 18) FULLY DRIVEN, SEATED AND NOT STRIPPED
5. CABLE RETAINER

**Temperature control cable repair**

7. Connect the electrical connectors.
8. Reposition the control panel assembly and install the attaching screws.
9. Install the lower center trim plate by removing the screws or gently pressing on the plate until the tabs snap into the retainers.
10. Connect the negative battery cable.

## Control Cables

### REMOVAL AND INSTALLATION

1. Disconnect the negative battery cable.
2. Remove the screws securing the cluster trim plate to the instrument panel.
3. Tilt the top of the cluster trim plate downward releasing the clips that mount the bottom of the trim plate to the dash. Remove the trim plate.
4. Remove the screws attaching the accessory trim center plate to the dash.
5. Tilt the top of accessory trim plate downward releasing the clips that mount the bottom of the plate to the instrument panel. Remove the plate.
6. Remove the screws attaching the control assembly to the dash.
7. Remove the control assembly from the dash.
8. Disconnect the control assembly electrical connectors.
9. Remove the control assembly.

**To install:**

10. Install the control assembly.
11. Connect the control assembly electrical connectors.
12. Install the control assembly attaching screws.
13. Push the mounting clips into place and roll the top of the accessory trim plate upward into position.
14. Install the screws attaching the accessory trim plate to the dash.
15. Push the mounting clips into place and roll the top of the cluster trim plate upward into position.
16. Install the screws attaching the cluster trim plate to the instrument panel.
17. Connect the negative battery cable.

## Air Conditioner
## Evaporator Core

### REMOVAL AND INSTALLATION

NOTE: *R-12 refrigerant is a chlorofluorocarbon which, when released into the atmosphere, can contribute to the depletion of the protective ozone layer in the upper atmosphere. There are also several safety hazzards associated with handling R-12. It is essential that every effort be made to avoid discharging the refrigerant to the atmosphere.*

## 190 CHASSIS ELECTRICAL

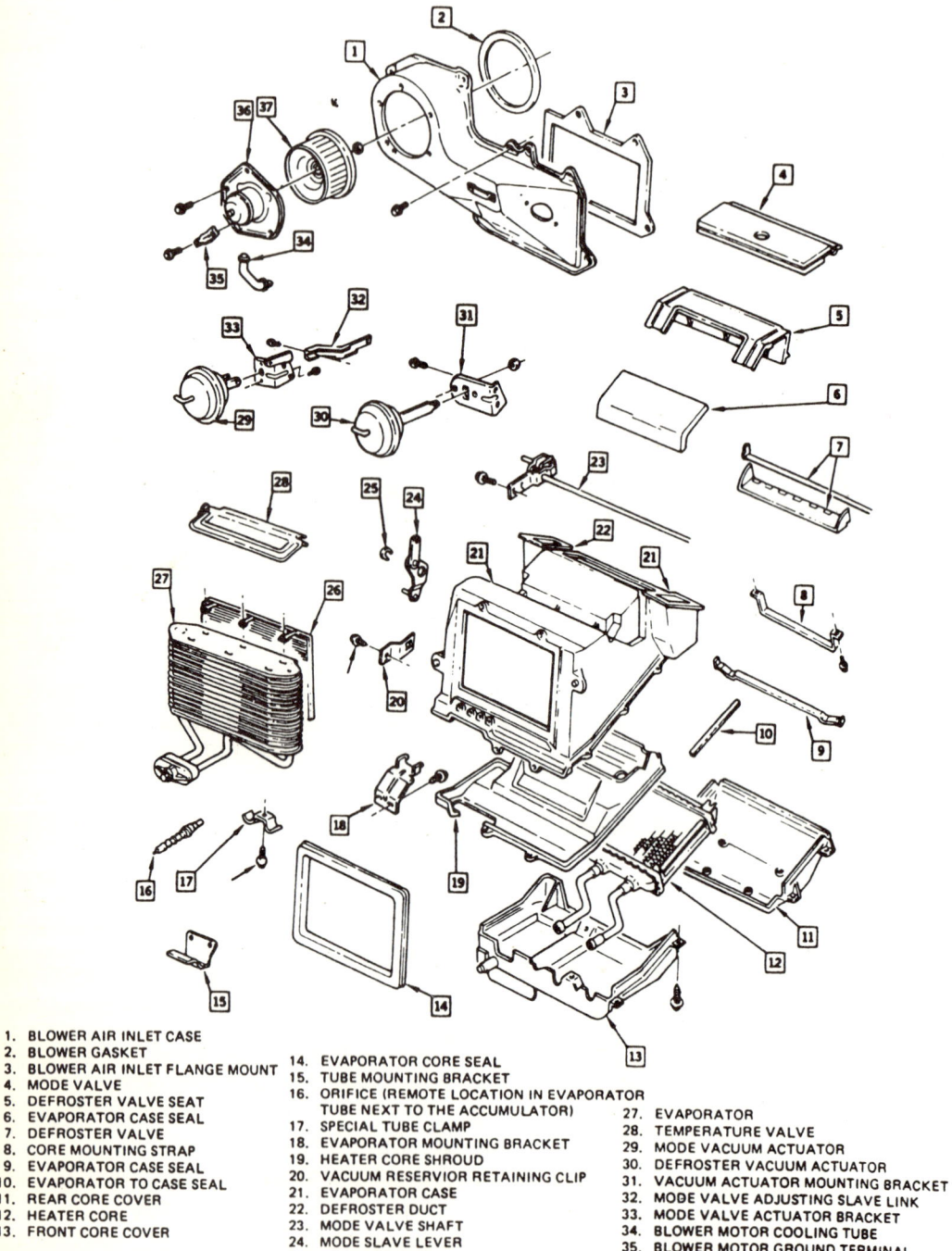

1. BLOWER AIR INLET CASE
2. BLOWER GASKET
3. BLOWER AIR INLET FLANGE MOUNT
4. MODE VALVE
5. DEFROSTER VALVE SEAT
6. EVAPORATOR CASE SEAL
7. DEFROSTER VALVE
8. CORE MOUNTING STRAP
9. EVAPORATOR CASE SEAL
10. EVAPORATOR TO CASE SEAL
11. REAR CORE COVER
12. HEATER CORE
13. FRONT CORE COVER
14. EVAPORATOR CORE SEAL
15. TUBE MOUNTING BRACKET
16. ORIFICE (REMOTE LOCATION IN EVAPORATOR TUBE NEXT TO THE ACCUMULATOR)
17. SPECIAL TUBE CLAMP
18. EVAPORATOR MOUNTING BRACKET
19. HEATER CORE SHROUD
20. VACUUM RESERVIOR RETAINING CLIP
21. EVAPORATOR CASE
22. DEFROSTER DUCT
23. MODE VALVE SHAFT
24. MODE SLAVE LEVER
25. RETAINER (PUSH ON)
26. WATER CORE FILTER
27. EVAPORATOR
28. TEMPERATURE VALVE
29. MODE VACUUM ACTUATOR
30. DEFROSTER VACUUM ACTUATOR
31. VACUUM ACTUATOR MOUNTING BRACKET
32. MODE VALVE ADJUSTING SLAVE LINK
33. MODE VALVE ACTUATOR BRACKET
34. BLOWER MOTOR COOLING TUBE
35. BLOWER MOTOR GROUND TERMINAL
36. BLOWER MOTOR
37. BLOWER FAN

**Heater and evaporator module**

Discharging and refilling the air conditioning system can only be done properly with approved freon recovery and evacuation equipment. Since this is specialized equipment not normally available outside a professional repair facility, all other air conditioning service that requires discharging the system is considered beyond the scope of this book. If it is necessary to remove a component from the air conditioning system, have the system properly discharged at a shop that has freon recovery equipment. Please refer to Chapter 1 for important instructions pertaining to safety hazzards and discharging the system.

1. Disconnect the negative battery cable.
2. Drain the cooling system into a clean container for reuse.
3. Properly discharge the air conditioning system using freon recovery equipment.
4. Raise and safely support the vehicle.
5. Disconnect the heater hoses at the heater core.
6. Remove the drain tube.
7. Disconnect the block fitting at the evaporator and discard the O-rings.

NOTE: *Cap the refrigerant lines when opening the system to prevent the entry of dirt and moisture and the loss of refrigerant lubricant.*

8. Lower the vehicle.
9. Remove the right and left sound insulators.
10. Remove the floor air outlet duct and hoses from the duct.
11. Remove the heater core cover.
12. Remove the heater core.
13. Remove the evaporator core cover.
14. Remove the evaporator core.

**To install:**

NOTE: *If replacing the evaporator or if the original evaporator was flushed during service, add 3 fluid oz. (90ml) of refrigerant lubricant to the system.*

15. Install the evaporator core.
16. Install the evaporator core cover.
17. Install the heater core.
18. Install the heater core cover.
19. Install the floor air outlet duct and hoses.
20. Install the right and left sound insulators.
21. Raise and safely support the vehicle.
22. Install new O-rings on the evaporator refrigerant lines. Lubricate with refrigerant oil.
23. Connect the block fitting to the evaporator.
24. Install the drain tube.
25. Connect the heater hoses to the heater core.
26. Lower the vehicle.
27. Evacuate, recharge and leak test the air conditioning system.
28. Connect the negative battery cable.
29. Fill cooling system and check for leaks. Start the engine and allow to come to normal operating temperature. Recheck for coolant leaks. Allow the engine to warm up sufficiently to confirm operation of cooling fan.

## ENTERTAINMENT SYSTEMS

### Radio Receiver/Amplifier/Tape Player

*REMOVAL AND INSTALLATION*

**Console Mounted**

NOTE: *If equipped with a compact disc player, removal and installation procedures are the same as for the radio.*

1. Disconnect the negative battery cable.
2. Remove the console bezel.
3. Remove the screws that attach the radio to the console.
4. Pull the radio out, disconnect the connectors, ground cable and antenna and remove the radio.
5. The installation is the reverse of the removal procedure.
6. Connect the negative battery cable and check the radio for proper operation.

**Dash Mounted**

1. Disconnect the negative battery cable.
2. Remove the instrument panel extension bezel.
3. Remove the radio bracket.
4. Remove the screws that attach the radio to the instrument panel.
5. Pull the radio out, disconnect the connectors, ground cable and antenna and remove the radio.

1. SCREW – FULLY DRIVEN, SEATED AND NOT STRIPPED
2. INSTRUMENT PANEL
3. SPEAKER – NOTE: HARNESS CONNECTOR MUST FACE FORWARD

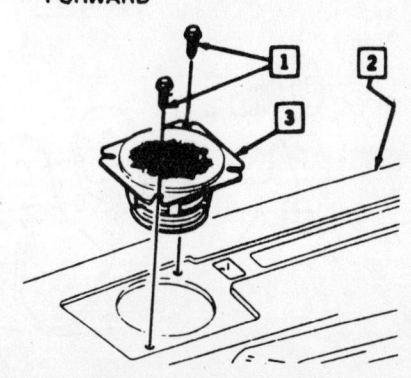

Instrument panel speaker installation

# 192  CHASSIS ELECTRICAL

6. The installation is the reverse of the removal procedure.
7. Connect the negative battery cable and check the radio for proper operation.

## Speakers

### REMOVAL AND INSTALLATION

#### Front Speakers

1. Remove the speaker/defroster grille from the instrument panel.
2. Remove the speaker attaching screws.
3. Lift the speaker and disconnect the electrical connectors.
4. Remove the speaker.

**To install:**

5. Connect the speaker electrical connector.
6. Place the speaker into position and install the attaching screws.
7. Install the speaker/defroster grille to the instrument panel.

#### Rear Speakers

1. Remove the rear seat cushion by removing the bolts from the bracket at the front of the seat.
2. Grasp the seat cushion and lift up and outward.

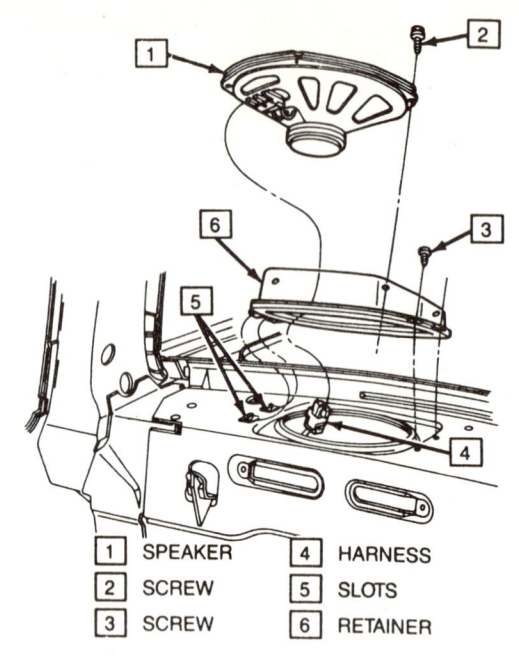

| 1 | SPEAKER | 4 | HARNESS |
| 2 | SCREW | 5 | SLOTS |
| 3 | SCREW | 6 | RETAINER |

Rear speaker installation

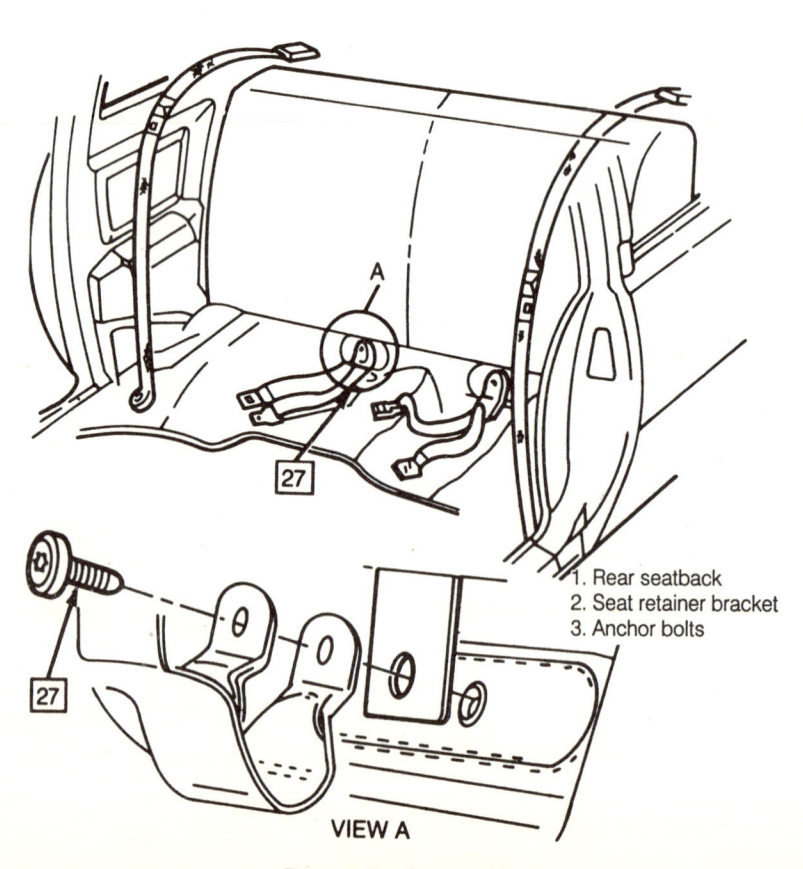

1. Rear seatback
2. Seat retainer bracket
3. Anchor bolts

VIEW A

Rear seatback assembly

# CHASSIS ELECTRICAL 193

1. WIPER ARM
2. TRANSMISSION SHAFT
3. WIPER ARM RETAINING LATCH
4. WIPER BLADE REMOVAL
5. WIPER INSERT REMOVAL
6. WIPER BLADE ASSEMBLY
7. WIPER INSERT
8. SCREWDRIVER
9. BLADE RETAINER
10. INSERT RETAINER

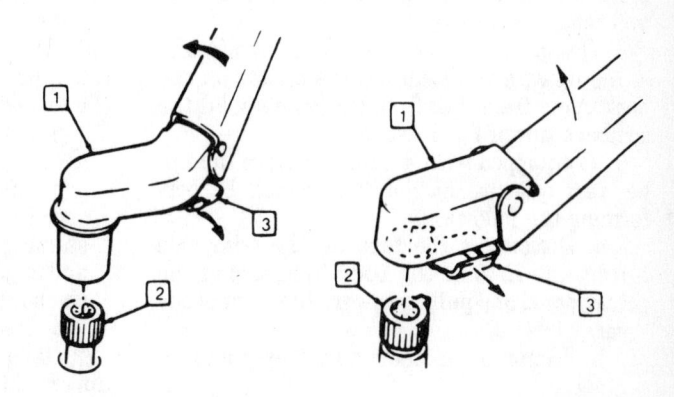

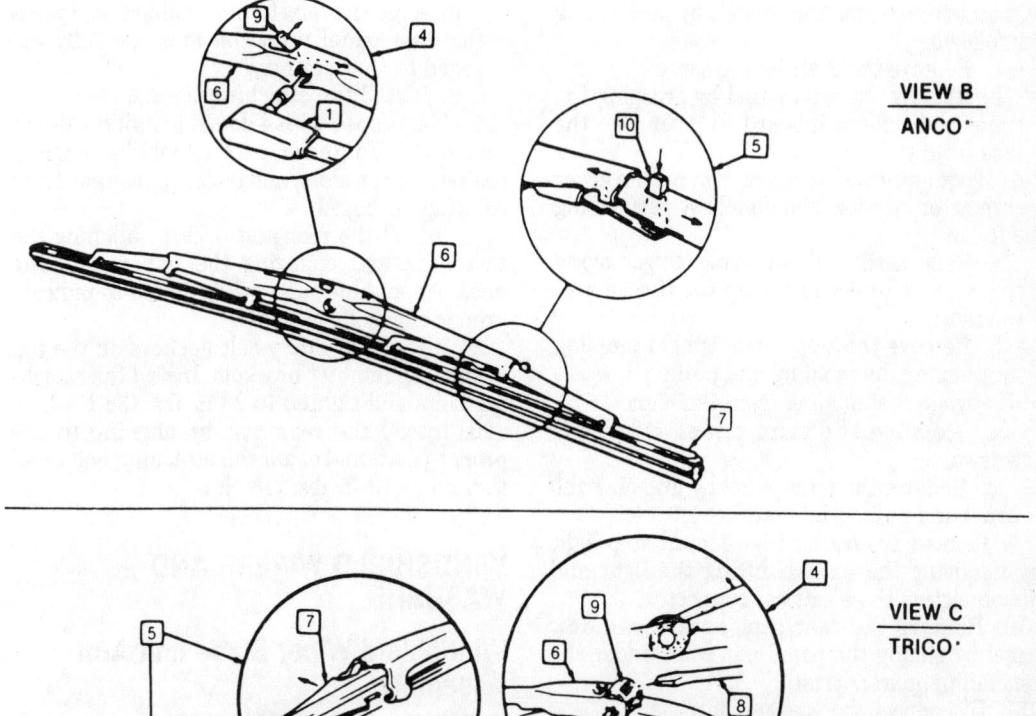

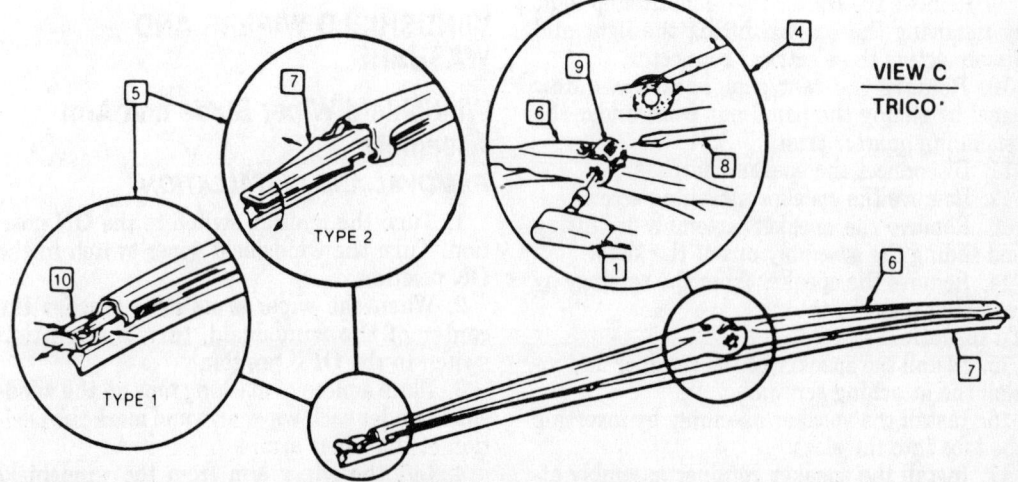

VIEW B
ANCO*

VIEW C
TRICO*

TYPE 2

TYPE 1

**Windshield wiper arm installation**

# CHASSIS ELECTRICAL

3. Remove the cushion from the vehicle.
4. Remove the anchor bolts from the bottom of the seatback securing the rear seat retainers and center seat safety belts.
5. Grasp the bottom of the seatback and swing upward to disengage the offsets on the back upper frame bar from the hangers; lift the seatback upward to remove.
6. If equipped with 4 doors, remove the upper rear quarter interior trim panels by performing the following:
    a. Disconnect the tabs on the trim pale from the slots in the body by grasping the trim panel and pulling toward the front of the car.
    b. Remove the trim panel by rotating inboard.
7. If equipped with 4 doors, remove the lower rear quarter interior trim panels by performing the following:
    a. Remove the 2 attaching screws.
    b. Remove the trim panel by grasping the panel and pulling inboard to disengage the tabs from the retainers.
8. If equipped with 2 doors, remove the lower rear quarter interior trim panels by performing the following:
    a. Remove the carpet retainer by removing the screws and lifting up on the carpet retainer.
    b. Remove the upper windshield molding by grasping the molding and pulling down to disengage the molding from the clips.
    c. Remove the trim panel attaching screws.
    d. Remove the trim panel by grasping the panel and pulling inboard.
9. Remove the center high-mount stop light by removing the screws, lifting the light and disconnecting the electrical connector.
10. Remove the rear seat back-to-window panel by sliding the panel out from under the remaining quarter trim.
11. Disconnect the speaker harness.
12. Remove the speaker attaching screws.
13. Remove the speaker assembly by lifting and sliding the assembly out of the slots.
14. Remove the speaker from the retainer by removing the screws.

**To install:**

15. Install the speaker to the retainer and install the attaching screws.
16. Install the speaker assembly by inserting the tabs into the slots.
17. Install the speaker retainer assembly attaching screws.
18. Connect the speaker electrical connectors.
19. Install the rear seat-to-back window trim panel by sliding the panel under the quarter trim.
20. Install the center high-mount stop light by connecting the electrical connector, positioning the assembly and installing the attaching screws.
21. If equipped with 2 doors, install the lower rear quarter interior trim panels by performing the following:
    a. Align the fasteners to the retainers in the body and pushing outboard on the panel.
    b. Install the 2 attaching screws.
    c. Install the upper windshield molding by starting at the top rear of the body lock pillar and engaging the tabs on the molding clips in the body.
    d. Install the carpet retainer.
22. If equipped with 4 doors, install the lower upper rear quarter interior trim panels by performing the following:
    a. Align the tabs to the retainers and press the trim panel until the tabs are fully engaged to the retainers.
    b. Install the attaching screws.
23. If equipped with 4 doors, install the upper rear quarter interior trim panels by aligning the tabs in the slots, and pushing rearward and rotating outboard.
24. Install the rear seat back by aligning the seat back and engaging the upper retaining hook. An audible snap will be heard to indicate proper engagement.
25. Install the safety belt anchors on the top of the seat retainer brackets. Install the attaching bolts and tighten to 28 ft. lbs. (38 Nm).
26. Install the rear seat by aligning to the proper position. Install the attaching bolts and tighten to 13 ft. lbs. (18 Nm).

## WINDSHIELD WIPERS AND WASHERS

### Windshield Wiper Blade and Arm Assembly

#### REMOVAL AND INSTALLATION

1. Turn the ignition switch to the **ON** position. Turn the windshield wiper switch to the **ON** position.
2. When the wiper arms have reaches the center of the windshield, turn the ignition switch to the **OFF** position.
3. Place a piece of masking tape on the windshield under each wiper arm and mark the position of the wiper arm.
4. Lift the wiper arm from the windshield and pull the retaining latch.
5. Remove the wiper arm from the transmission shaft.

**To install:**

6. Align the wiper arm with the marks made

# CHASSIS ELECTRICAL 195

before removal and slide the wiper arm onto the transmission shaft.

7. Push the retaining latch in and allow the wiper arm to return to the windshield. Make sure the marks are still in alignment.
8. Remove the masking tape.

## Windshield Wiper Motor
### REMOVAL AND INSTALLATION

1. Disconnect the negative battery cable.
2. Remove the wiper arm assembly(s) and cowl cover, if necessary.
3. Remove the wiper arm drive link from the crank arm.
4. Disconnect the connectors from the motor.
5. Remove the wiper motor attaching bolts.
6. Remove the wiper motor and crank arm by guiding the assembly through the access hole in the upper shroud panel.

**To install:**

7. Guide the wiper motor and crank arm assembly through the access hole and into position.
8. Install the wiper motor attaching bolts.
9. Connect the wiper motor electrical connector.
10. Install the wiper arm drive link to the crank arm.
11. If removed, install the wiper arm assembly(s) and cowl cover.
12. Connect the negative battery cable.

## Wiper Linkage
### REMOVAL AND INSTALLATION

1. Remove the wiper arms.
2. Remove the wiper motor.
3. Remove the bolts attaching the left and right side transmission assemblies.
4. Remove the wiper linkage.

**To install:**

5. Install the wiper linkage.
6. Install the bolts attaching the left and right side transmission assemblies.
7. Install the wiper motor.
8. Install the wiper arms.

## Windshield Washer Fluid Reservoir
### REMOVAL AND INSTALLATION

1. Disconnect the electrical connectors and washer hose from the reservoir.
2. Remove the reservoir attaching bolts.
3. Remove the reservoir from the vehicle.

**To install:**

4. Install the vehicle in its mounting location.
5. Install the attaching bolts.
6. Connect the washer hose and electrical connectors.

## Windshield Washer Pump Motor
### REMOVAL AND INSTALLATION

1. Remove the washer solvent from the reservoir.
2. Remove the brace.

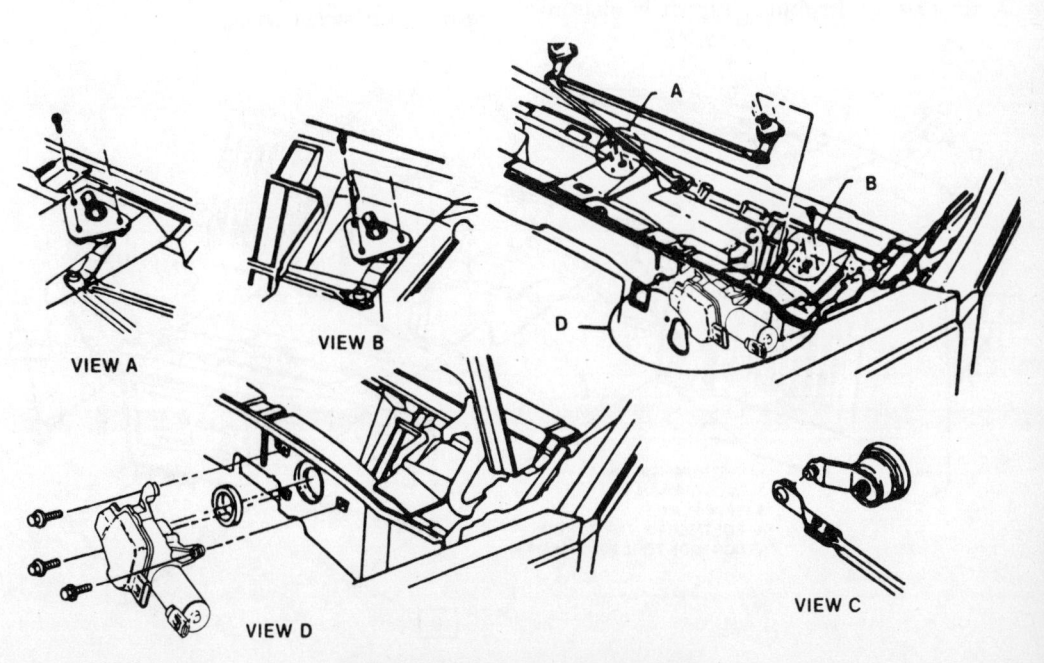

**Windshield wiper and motor installation**

# 196 CHASSIS ELECTRICAL

3. Remove the reservoir bolts.
4. Disconnect the electrical connectors and washer hose.
5. Remove the washer pump from the reservoir.

**To install:**

6. Install the washer pump motor to the reservoir.
NOTE: *Make sure the new washer pump is pushed all the way into the reservoir gasket.*
7. Connect the electrical connectors and washer hose.
8. Install the reservoir attaching screws.
9. Install the brace.
10. Refill the reservoir with washer solvent.

## INSTRUMENTS AND SWITCHES

### Instrument Cluster

#### REMOVAL AND INSTALLATION

NOTE: *For Instrument Panel and Console removal and installation, please refer to Chapter 10.*

### Skylark

#### 1985–89

1. Disconnect the negative battery cable.
2. Remove the cluster trim plate, headlight and wiper switch trim plates and the switches.
3. Remove the screws fastening the cluster to the instrument panel pad, pull the cluster out to unplug all connectors and remove the cluster.
4. Remove the lens and gauge trim plate to gain access to the speedometer assembly attaching screws and remove the speedometer or gauges. If equipped with digital gauges, replace them as an assembly.
5. The installation is the reverse of the removal procedure.
6. Connect the negative battery cable and check all cluster-related components for proper operation.

#### 1990–92

1. Disconnect the negative battery cable.
2. Remove the steering column opening filler.
3. Remove the cluster trim plate.
4. If equipped with a column-mounted shifter, disconnect the PRNDL cable clip from the shift collar on the column.

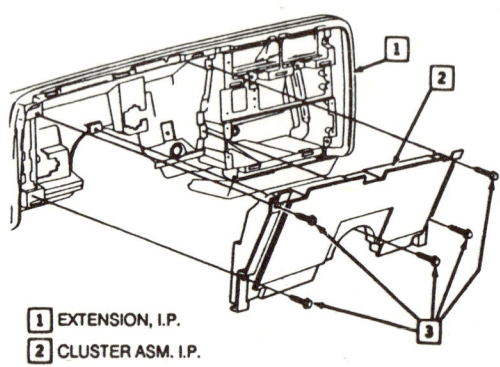

1 EXTENSION, I.P.
2 CLUSTER ASM. I.P.
3 SCREW - FULLY DRIVEN, SEATED AND NOT STRIPPED

**Instrument cluster mounting**

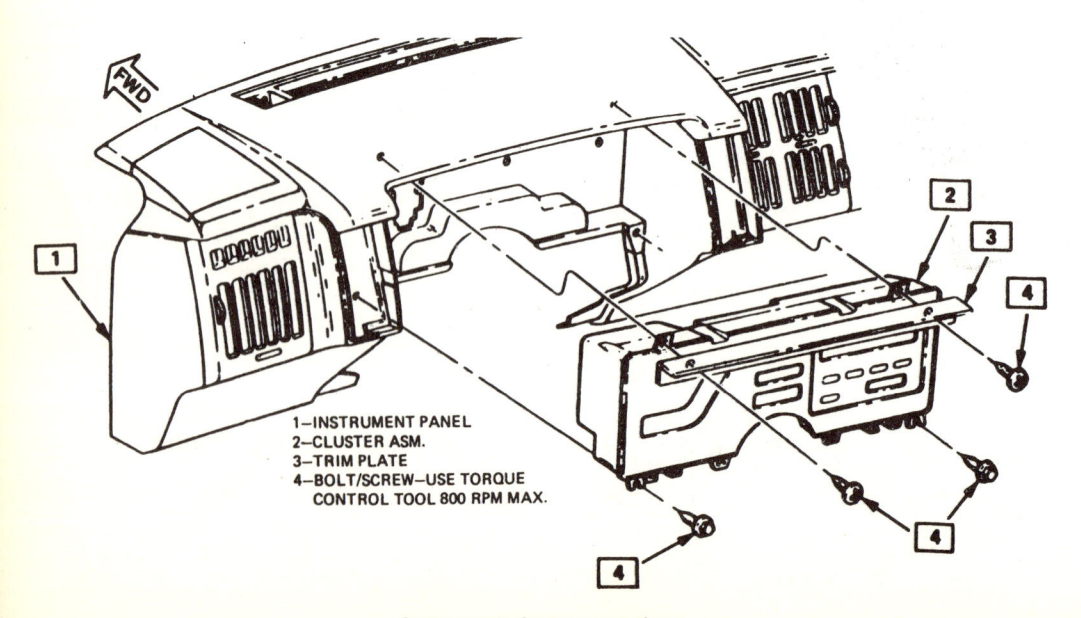

1—INSTRUMENT PANEL
2—CLUSTER ASM.
3—TRIM PLATE
4—BOLT/SCREW—USE TORQUE CONTROL TOOL 800 RPM MAX.

**Instrument cluster mounting**

# CHASSIS ELECTRICAL

5. Remove the screws fastening the cluster to the instrument panel pad, pull the cluster out to unplug all connectors and remove the cluster.
6. Remove the lens and gauge trim plate to gain access to the speedometer assembly attaching screws and remove the speedometer or gauges. If equipped with digital dash, replace it as an assembly.
7. The installation is the reverse of the removal procedure.
8. Connect the negative battery cable and check all cluster-related components for proper operation.

### Calais

1. Disconnect the negative battery cable.
2. Remove the steering column collar.
3. Remove the steering column and cluster trim plates.
4. Lower the steering column.
5. Remove the screws fastening the cluster to the instrument panel pad, pull the cluster out to unplug all connectors and remove the cluster.
6. Remove the lens and applique, if necessary, to gain access to the speedometer or gauges attaching screws and remove the speedometer or gauges.
7. The installation is the reverse of the removal procedure.
8. Connect the negative battery cable and check all cluster-related components for proper operation.

### Grand Am

1. Disconnect the negative battery cable.
2. Remove the 3 screws at the lower edge of the cluster and remove the trim plate.
3. Remove the steering column cover and lower the column, as required.
4. Remove the screws fastening the cluster to the instrument panel pad, pull the cluster out to unplug all connectors and remove the cluster.
5. Remove the lens and gauge trim plate to gain access to the speedometer assembly or gauges attaching screws and remove the speedometer or gauges. If equipped with digital dash, replace it as an assembly.
6. The installation is the reverse of the removal procedure.
7. Connect the negative battery cable and check all cluster-related components for proper operation.

## Speedometer

### REMOVAL AND INSTALLATION

NOTE: *If equipped with electronic instrumentation, the speedometer cannot be re-placed separately; the entire instrument cluster must be replaced.*

#### Standard Cluster

1. Remove the instrument cluster.
2. Remove the screws from the cluster lens.
3. Remove the cluster lens.
4. Carefully, lift the speedometer facing.
5. Unplug the odometer motor leads.

**To install:**

6. Plug the odometer motor leads.
7. Install the speedometer facing.
8. Install the cluster lens.
9. Install the cluster lens attaching screws.
10. Install the instrument cluster.

## Speedometer Cable

### REMOVAL AND INSTALLATION

NOTE: *Only vehicles equipped with standard gauge clusters have mechanically driven speedometers. Electronic gauges use a vehicle speed sensor to drive the speedometer.*

1. Remove the instrument cluster far enough to reach behind and disconnect the speedometer cable from the back of the cluster.
2. Remove the left side sound insulator panel.
3. Push the speedometer cable grommet through the fire wall.
4. Observe the routing of the speedometer cable from the firewall up to the instrument cluster. If possible, tape a length of wire or string to the cable to aid installation of the new cable. Feed the cable down and through the hole in firewall.
5. Disconnect the speedometer cable from the transaxle by removing the bolt attaching the cable to the drive assembly on the transaxle.
6. Remove the speedometer cable.

**To install:**

7. Attach the length of wire or string to the new speedometer cable and pull through the firewall and up behind the instrument panel.
8. Connect the speedometer cable to the speedometer drive assembly on the transaxle. Install the attaching bolt.

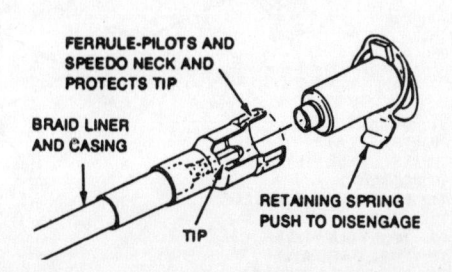

Speedometer cable disengagement at the speedometer

# 198  CHASSIS ELECTRICAL

9. Connect the speedometer cable to the speedometer.
10. Install the instrument cluster.
11. Make sure the speedometer cable is routed freely and has not kinks or sharp bends.
12. Install the grommet in the firewall.
13. Install the left side sound insulator panel.

## Printed Circuit Board
### REMOVAL AND INSTALLATION

1. Remove the instrument panel.
2. Remove the screws from the cluster lens.
3. Carefully, lift up on the lens and trim plate.
4. Remove the foam gasket from the trip odometer reset.
5. Remove the screws from the fuel gauge, speedometer and odometer.
6. Disconnect the fuel gauge.
7. Remove the speedometer and odometer.
8. Disconnect the odometer connector from the circuit board.
9. Remove the circuit board from inside the case.

**To install:**
10. Install the circuit board inside the case.
11. Connect the odometer connector to the circuit board.
12. Install the speedometer and odometer.
13. Connect the fuel gauge electrical connector.
14. Install the screws to the fuel gauge, speedometer and odometer.
15. Install the foam gasket on the trip odometer reset.
16. Install the trim plate and lens.
17. Install the screws through the lens and trim plate into the case.
18. Install the instrument cluster.

## Windshield Wiper Switch
### REMOVAL AND INSTALLATION
**Except Skylark**

1. Disconnect the negative battery cable.
2. Remove the cluster trim, instrument panel trim or wiper switch trim screws, as required.
3. Remove the wiper switch attaching screws.
4. Pull the switch out, unplug the connectors and remove the switch assembly.
5. The installation is the reverse of the removal procedure.
6. Connect the negative battery cable and check the wipers and washers for proper operation.

**Skylark**

1. Disconnect the negative battery cable.
2. Remove the lower instrument panel sound insulator, trim pad and steering column trim collar.
3. Straighten the steering wheel so the tires are pointing straight ahead.
4. Remove the steering wheel.
5. Remove the plastic wire protector from under the steering column.

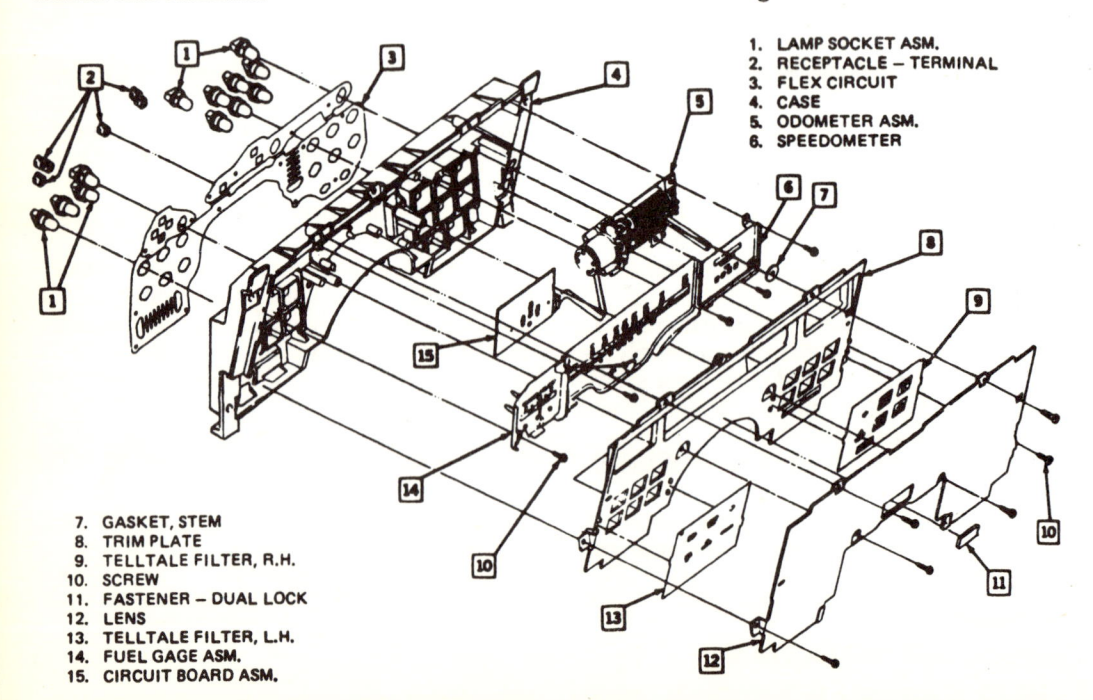

1. LAMP SOCKET ASM.
2. RECEPTACLE – TERMINAL
3. FLEX CIRCUIT
4. CASE
5. ODOMETER ASM.
6. SPEEDOMETER
7. GASKET, STEM
8. TRIM PLATE
9. TELLTALE FILTER, R.H.
10. SCREW
11. FASTENER – DUAL LOCK
12. LENS
13. TELLTALE FILTER, L.H.
14. FUEL GAGE ASM.
15. CIRCUIT BOARD ASM.

**Cluster disassembled**

## CHASSIS ELECTRICAL 199

6. Disconnect the turn signal switch, wiper switch and cruise control connectors, if equipped.

7. To disassemble the top of the column:

 a. Remove the shaft lock cover.

 b. If equipped with telescope steering, remove the first set of spacers, bumper, second set of spacers and carrier snapring retainer.

 c. Depress the lockplate with the proper depressing tool and remove the retaining ring from its groove.

 d. Remove the tool, retaining ring, lockplate, canceling cam and spring.

8. Pull the turn signal lever straight out of the wiper switch.

9. Remove the 3 screws and remove the turn signal switch and actuator lever.

10. Remove the ignition key light.

11. Place the key in the **RUN** position and use a thin suitable tool to remove the buzzer switch.

12. Remove the key lock cylinder attaching screw and remove the lock cylinder.

13. Remove the 3 housing cover screws and remove the housing cover assembly.

14. Remove the wiper switch pivot pin and remove the switch.

**To install:**

15. Run the wiring through the opening and down the steering column, position the switch and install the wiper switch pivot pin.

16. Install the housing cover assembly, making sure the dimmer switch actuator is properly aligned.

17. Install the key lock cylinder and place in the **RUN** position. Install the buzzer switch and key light.

18. Install the turn signal switch and lever.

19. To assemble the top end of the column:

 a. Install the spring, canceling cam, lockplate and retaining ring on the steering shaft.

 b. Depress the plate with the depressing tool and install the ring securely in the groove. Remove the tool slowly.

 c. If equipped with telescopic steering, install the carrier snapring retainer, lower set of spacers, bumper and upper set of spacers.

 d. Install the shaft lock cover.

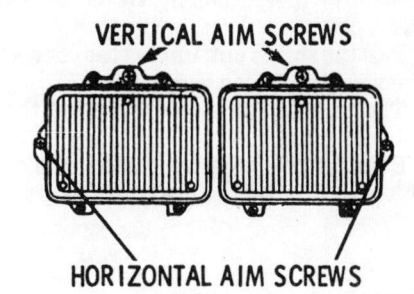

Location of the headlamp aiming scres

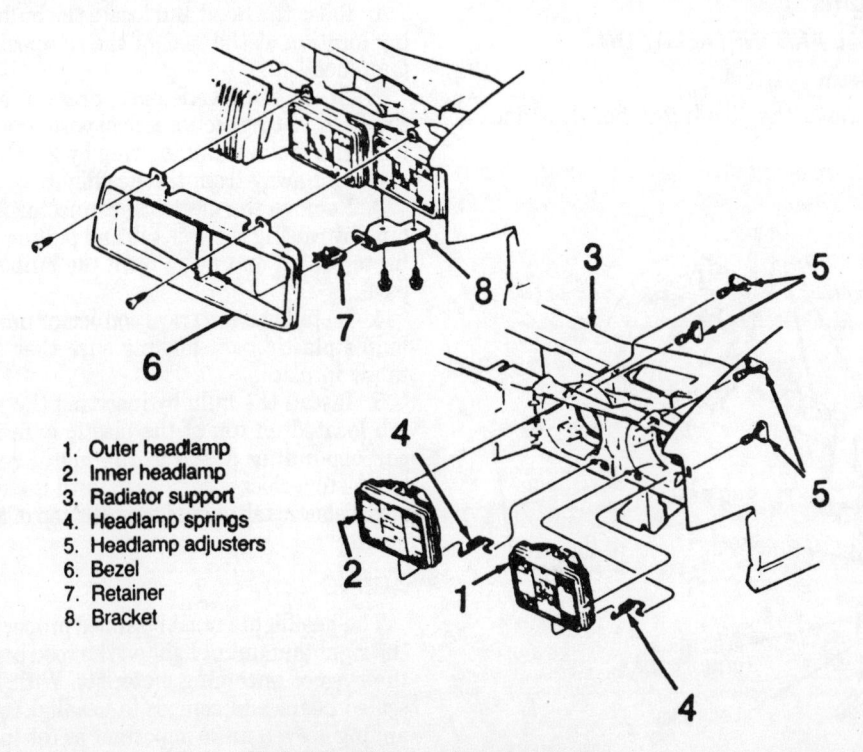

1. Outer headlamp
2. Inner headlamp
3. Radiator support
4. Headlamp springs
5. Headlamp adjusters
6. Bezel
7. Retainer
8. Bracket

Typical headlamp and bezel mounting

# 200  CHASSIS ELECTRICAL

20. Connect the turn signal switch, wiper switch and cruise control connectors. Install the wire protector.
21. Install and steering wheel.
22. Install the steering column trim collar, lower instrument panel trim pad and sound insulator.
23. Connect the negative battery cable and check the key lock cylinder, wiper and washer, cruise control, turn signal switch and dimmer switch for proper operation.

## Headlight Switch

### REMOVAL AND INSTALLATION

1. Disconnect the negative battery cable.
2. Remove the cluster trim, instrument panel trim or headlight switch trim screws, as required.
3. Remove the headlight switch attaching screws.
4. Pull the switch out, unplug the connectors and remove the switch assembly.
5. The installation is the reverse of the removal procedure.
6. Connect the negative battery cable and check the headlight switch for proper operation.

## LIGHTING

## Headlights

### REMOVAL AND INSTALLATION

#### Sealed Beam

1. Remove the headlight bezel attaching screws.
   NOTE: *To avoid turning the vertical or horizontal aiming screws, refer to the illustration before removing the headlight retainer.*
2. Remove the headlight retainer attaching screws.
3. Pull the headlight out and, carefully, disconnect the electrical connector.

**To install:**

4. Connect the electrical connector to the new headlamp.
5. Place the headlamp into the socket.
6. Install the retainer and attaching screws.
7. Turn the headlight switch on to confirm headlight operation.
8. Install the headlight bezel and attaching screws.

#### Composite

CAUTION: *Halogen bulbs contain gas under pressure. Improper handling of the bulb could cause it to shatter into flying glass fragments. To avoid possible personal injury, follow the safety precautions listed below.*

- Turn off the headlight switch and allow the bulb to cool before attempting to change.
- Always wear eye protection when changing a halogen bulb.
- Handle the bulb only by its base. Avoid touching the glass.
- Do not drop or scratch the bulb.
- Keep dirt and moisture off the bulb.
- Place the used bulb in the new bulb's carton and dispose of it properly.

1. Raise the hood and locate the bulb mounting location at the rear of the composite headlamp body.
2. Grasp the plastic base, press in and turn the base ¼ turn counterclockwise and remove from the metal retaining ring by gently pulling back and away from the headlight.
3. Remove the electrical connector from the bulb by raising the lock tab and pulling the connector down and away from the bulb's plastic base.
4. Install the electrical connector on the new bulb's plastic base making sure that the lock tab is in place.
5. Install the bulb by inserting the smallest tab located on top of the plastic base into the corresponding notch in the metal retaining ring. Turn clockwise ¼ turn until it stops. The small plastic tab should be at the top of the metal ring.

### AIMING

The headlights must be aimed properly to get the right amount of light on the road and out of the eyes of oncoming motorists. With halogen sealed beam and composite headlights, proper aiming is even more important as the increased range and power of these lights can make even

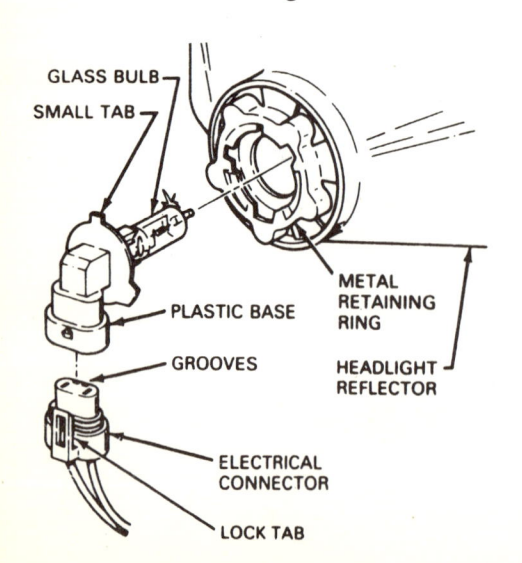

**Composite headlight bulb replacement**

# CHASSIS ELECTRICAL 201

slight variations from the recommended settings hazardous to approaching traffic. Accordingly, aiming of the headlights should be performed by a qualified service technician using the proper aiming equipment.

The headlights are aimed by turning the vertical or horizontal aiming screws. The vehicle should be at its normal weight with the spare tire stowed in the trunk, normal fluid levels and the fuel tank at least half full. Tires should be uniformly inflated to the proper pressure. If the car normally carries an unusual load in the trunk or tows a trailer, these loads should be on the car when the headlamps are aimed.

## Signal and Marker Lights

### REMOVAL AND INSTALLATION

#### Front Turn Signal and Parking Lights

1. Remove the socket from the lamp housing by turning counterclockwise.
2. Remove the lamp from the socket by pressing in and turning counterclockwise.

**To install:**

3 Install the replacement lamp into the socket, matching the directional alignment pins on the base of the bulb with the complementary slots in the socket. This will assure that the proper filament is energized at the right time; i.e.: the turn signal filament and not the parking lamp filament is energized when the turn signal is turned on.

4. Push the lamp into the socket and turn clockwise.
5. Install the socket to the lamp housing by turning clockwise.
6. Check operation of the parking lamp and turn signal.

#### Front Side Marker Lights

1. Remove the side marker housing attaching screws.
2. Remove the housing far enough to remove the socket from the housing by turning 45 degrees counterclockwise.
3. Remove the bulb and socket from the housing.
4. Remove the bulb.

**To install:**

5. Install the bulb into the socket.
6. Install the socket to the lamp housing.
7. Secure the socket to the lamp housing by turning 45 degrees clockwise.
8. Install the side marker housing and attaching screws.

#### Rear Side Marker, Turn, Stop, Parking and Back-Up Lights

1. Open the trunk.
2. Remove the nuts from the rear trim.
3. Remove the housing cover nuts.
4. Remove the lamp socket by turning counterclockwise.
5. Remove the lamp from the socket by pressing in and turning counterclockwise.

**To install:**

6. Install the lamp to the socket and pressing in and turning clockwise.
7. Install the socket and turn clockwise.
8. Install the housing cover nuts.
9. Install the rear trim.
10. Check operation of the rear lights.

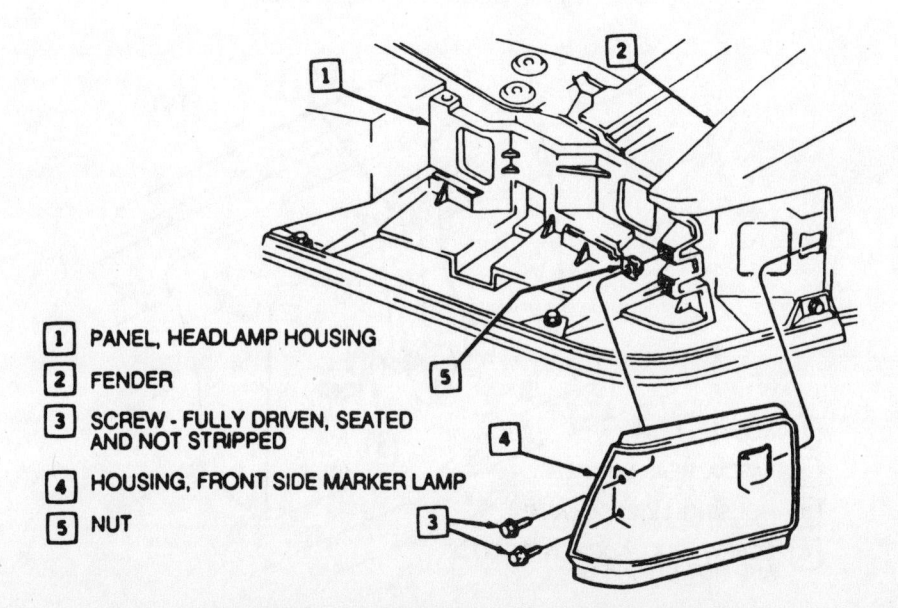

|1| PANEL, HEADLAMP HOUSING
|2| FENDER
|3| SCREW - FULLY DRIVEN, SEATED AND NOT STRIPPED
|4| HOUSING, FRONT SIDE MARKER LAMP
|5| NUT

**Front side marker lamp housing—Grand Am shown**

## CHASSIS ELECTRICAL

### High-Mount Brake Light
1. Remove the 2 lens screws.
2. Remove the lens.
3. Remove the bulb from the socket.

**To install:**
4. Install the bulb to the socket.
5. Install the lens.
6. Install the 2 lens screws.
7. Check operation of the light.

### Dome Light
1. Carefully, pry the lens from the housing.
2. Remove the bulb.

**To install:**
3. Install the bulb to the socket.
4. Install the lens.

### License Plate Lights
1. Remove the 2 screws from the lamp assembly.
2. Carefully, pull the assembly down.
3. Remove the bulb from the socket by turning counterclockwise.

**To install:**
4. Install the bulb to the socket by pressing in and turning clockwise.

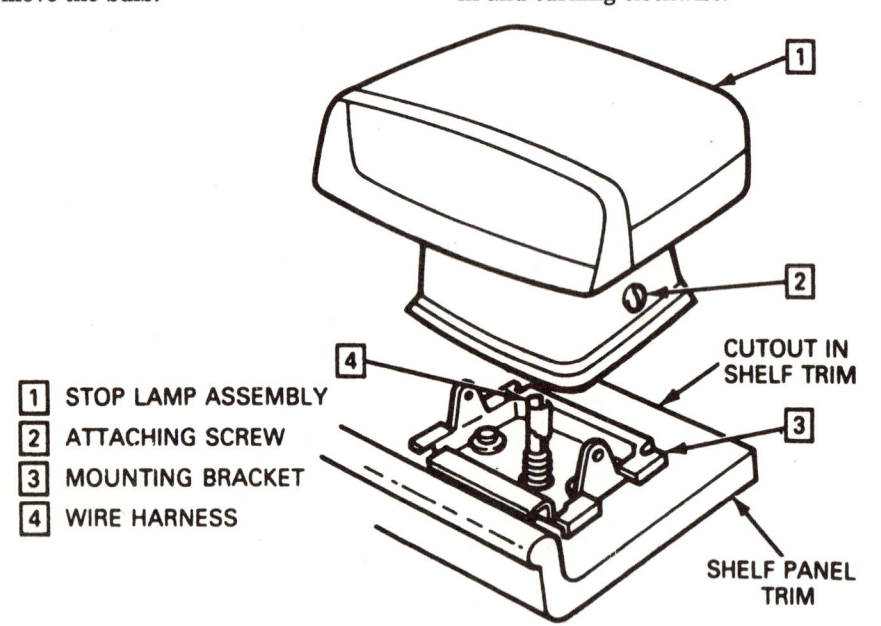

[1] STOP LAMP ASSEMBLY
[2] ATTACHING SCREW
[3] MOUNTING BRACKET
[4] WIRE HARNESS

CUTOUT IN SHELF TRIM
SHELF PANEL TRIM

**Center high-mount stop lamp replacement**

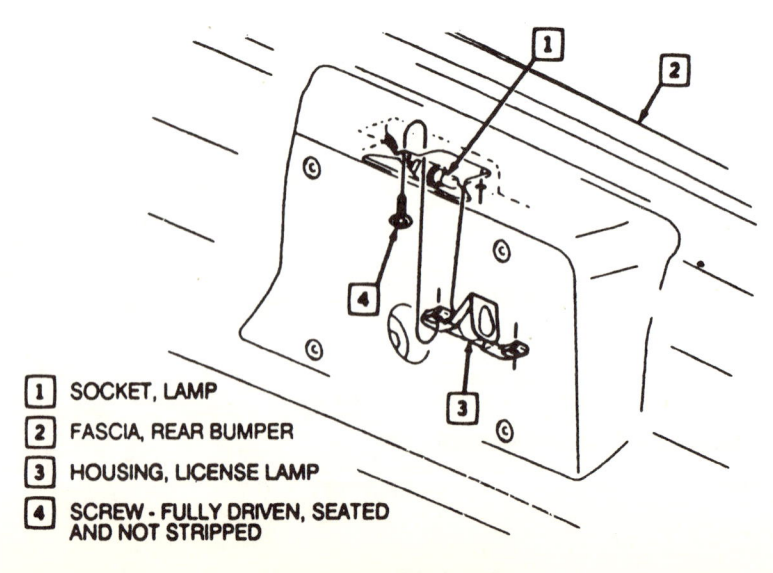

[1] SOCKET, LAMP
[2] FASCIA, REAR BUMPER
[3] HOUSING, LICENSE LAMP
[4] SCREW - FULLY DRIVEN, SEATED AND NOT STRIPPED

**License plate light housing**

5. Reposition the lamp assembly.
6. Install the mounting screws.

## Fog Lights

CAUTION: *Halogen bulbs contain gas under pressure. Improper handling of the bulb could cause it to shatter into flying glass fragments. To avoid possible personal injury, follow the safety precautions listed below.*

- Turn off the headlight switch and allow the bulb to cool before attempting to change.
- Always wear eye protection when changing a halogen bulb.
- Handle the bulb only by its base. Avoid touching the glass.
- Do not drop or scratch the bulb.
- Keep dirt and moisture off the bulb.
- Place the used bulb in the new bulb's carton and dispose of it properly.

### REMOVAL AND INSTALLATION

1. Remove the screw and nut behind the assembly
2. Remove the upper screw and spring.
3. Disconnect the electrical connector.

**To install:**

4. Connect the electrical connector.
5. Install the upper screw and spring.
6. Install the screw and spring behind the assembly
7. Check the aim of the fog lamps.

### AIMING

1. Park the car on level ground facing, perpendicular to, and about 25 ft. from a flat wall.
2. Remove any stone shields and switch on the fog lights.
3. Loosen the mounting hardware and aim as follows:
   a. The horizontal distance between the light beams on the wall should be the same as between the lights themselves.
   b. The vertical height of the light beams above the ground should be 4 in. (102mm) less than the distance between the ground and the center of the lamp lenses.
4. Tighten the mounting hardware.

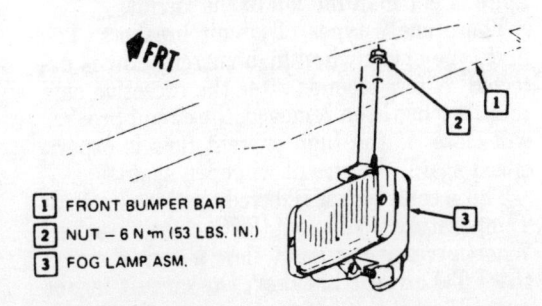

| 1 | FRONT BUMPER BAR |
| 2 | NUT — 6 N·m (53 LBS. IN.) |
| 3 | FOG LAMP ASM. |

**Fog lamp mounting**

## TRAILER WIRING

Wiring the car for towing is fairly easy. There are a number of good wiring kits available and these should be used, rather than trying to design your own. All trailers will need brake lights and turn signals as well as tail lights and side marker lights. Most states require extra marker lights for overly wide trailers. Also, most states have recently required back-up lights for trailers, and most trailer manufacturers have been building trailers with back-up lights for several years.

Additionally, some Class I, most Class II and just about all Class III trailers will have electric brakes.

Add to this number an accessories wire, to operate trailer internal equipment or to charge the trailer's battery, and you can have as many as seven wires in the harness.

Determine the equipment on your trailer and buy the wiring kit necessary. The kit will contain all the wires needed, plus a plug adapter set which included the female plug, mounted on the bumper or hitch, and the male plug, wired into, or plugged into the trailer harness.

When installing the kit, follow the manufacturer's instructions. The color coding of the wires is standard throughout the industry.

One point to note: some domestic vehicles, and most imported vehicles, have separate turn signals. On most domestic vehicles, the brake lights and rear turn signals operate with the same bulb. For those vehicles with separate turn signals, you can purchase an isolation unit so that the brake lights won't blink whenever the turn signals are operated, or, you can go to your local electronics supply house and buy four diodes to wire in series with the brake and turn signal bulbs. Diodes will isolate the brake and turn signals. The choice is yours. The isolation units are simple and quick to install, but far more expensive than the diodes. The diodes, however, require more work to install properly, since they require the cutting of each bulb's wire and soldering in place of the diode.

One final point, the best kits are those with a spring loaded cover on the vehicle mounted socket. This cover prevents dirt and moisture from corroding the terminals. Never let the vehicle socket hang loosely; always mount it securely to the bumper or hitch.

## CIRCUIT PROTECTION

### Fuses

#### REPLACEMENT

1. Locate the fuse for the circuit in question.
2. Check the fuse by removing it and observ-

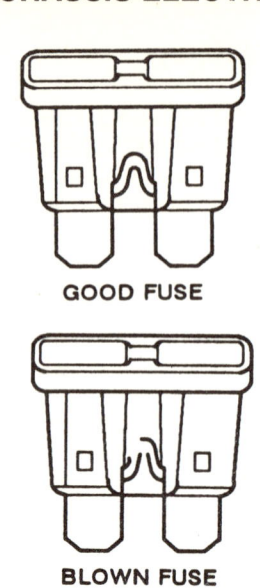

# CHASSIS ELECTRICAL

**GOOD FUSE**

**BLOWN FUSE**

Blown fuse

| CURRENT RATING AMPERES | COLOR |
|---|---|
| **AUTO-FUSES, MINI FUSES** ||
| 3 | VIOLET |
| 5 | TAN |
| 7.5 | BROWN |
| 10 | RED |
| 15 | BLUE |
| 20 | YELLOW |
| 25 | WHITE |
| 30 | GREEN |
| **MAXI FUSES** ||
| 20 | YELLOW |
| 30 | LIGHT GREEN |
| 40 | ORANGE |
| 60 | BLUE |

Fuse rating and color

ing the fuse element. If it is broken, replace the fuse. If the fuse blows again, check the circuit for a short to ground or faulty device in the circuit protected by the fuse.

3. Continuity can also be checked with the fuse installed in the fuse block with the use of a test light connected across the 2 test points on the end of the fuse. If the test light lights, replace the fuse. Check the circuit for a short to ground or faulty device in the circuit protected by the fuse.

## Fusible Links

Like fuses, fusible links are one-time circuit protectors. They are usually installed to protect circuits between the battery and the fuse panel.

When a fusible link burns out, it generally creates a great deal of smoke which is intended partially to get your attention. Since the device in the circuit it protects could be destroyed if the problem is not rectified, the problem in the circuit must be diagnosed and corrected before replacing the fusible link.

### REPLACEMENT

1. Disconnect the negative battery cable.
2. Locate the burned out link.
3. Strip away all the melted harness insulation.
4. Cut the burned link ends from the circuit wire.
5. Strip the circuit wire back approximately ½ in. (13mm) to allow soldering of the new link.
6. Using fusible link about 10 in. (254mm) long and 4 gauges smaller than the wire in the circuit to be protected, solder a new link into the circuit.

NOTE: *Use only resin core solder. Do not use acid core solder as corrosion could result. Do not connect the fusible link in any other manner than soldering.*

7. Tape the soldered ends securely using electrical tape.
8. After taping the wire, tape the harness, leaving an exposed loop of wire approximately 5 in. (127mm) in length.
9. Connect the negative battery cable.

## Circuit Breakers

### REPLACEMENT

Circuit breakers differ from fuses in that they are reusable. Circuit breakers open when the flow of current exceeds specified value and will close after a few seconds when current flow returns to normal. Some of the circuits protected by circuit breakers include electric windows and power accessories. Circuits breakers are used in these applications due to the fact that they must operated at times under prolonged high current flow due to demand even though there is not malfunction in the circuit.

There are 2 types of circuit breakers. The first type opens when high current flow is detected. A few seconds after the excessive current flow has been removed, the circuit breaker will close. If the high current flow is experienced again, the circuit will open again.

The second type is referred to as the Positive Temperature Coefficient (PTC) circuit breaker. When excessive current flow passes through the PTC circuit breaker, the circuit is not opened but its resistance increases. As the device heats ups with the increase in current flow, the resistance increases to the point where the circuit is effectively open. Unlike other circuit breakers, the PTC circuit breaker will not reset until the circuit is opened, removing voltage from the terminals. Once the voltage is removed, the circuit breaker will re-close within a few seconds.

Replace the circuit breaker by unplugging the old one and plugging in the new one. Confirm proper circuit operation.

## Flashers
### REPLACEMENT

The hazard flasher is located forward of the console on all N-Body vehicles. The turn signal flasher is located behind the instrument panel, on the left side of the steering column bracket. Replace the flasher by unplugging the old one and plugging in the new one. Confirm proper flasher operation.

# Drive Train 7

## 5-SPEED MANUAL TRANSAXLE

### Identification

The Hydra-matic Muncie 282 (HM-282) transaxle name was changed to the 5TM40 in 1990. This is a 5 speed unit with gearing that provides for 5 synchronized forward speeds, a reverse speed, a final drive with differential output and speedometer drive. The Isuzu MT2 transaxle is also used in some models, depending on the engine.

The transaxle identification stamp on the 5TM40 transaxle is located at the center top of the case. The transaxle identification tag is located on the left side near the left side cover.

The identification number on the Isuzu transaxle is stamped into a tag mounted on the shift quadrant box on the left side.

### Metric Fasteners

The metric fastener dimensions are very close to the dimensions of the familiar inch system fasteners and, for this reason, replacement fasteners must have the same measurement and strength as those removed.

Do not attempt to interchange metric fasteners with standard fasteners. Mismatched or incorrect fasteners can result in damage to the transaxle unit through malfunctions, breakage

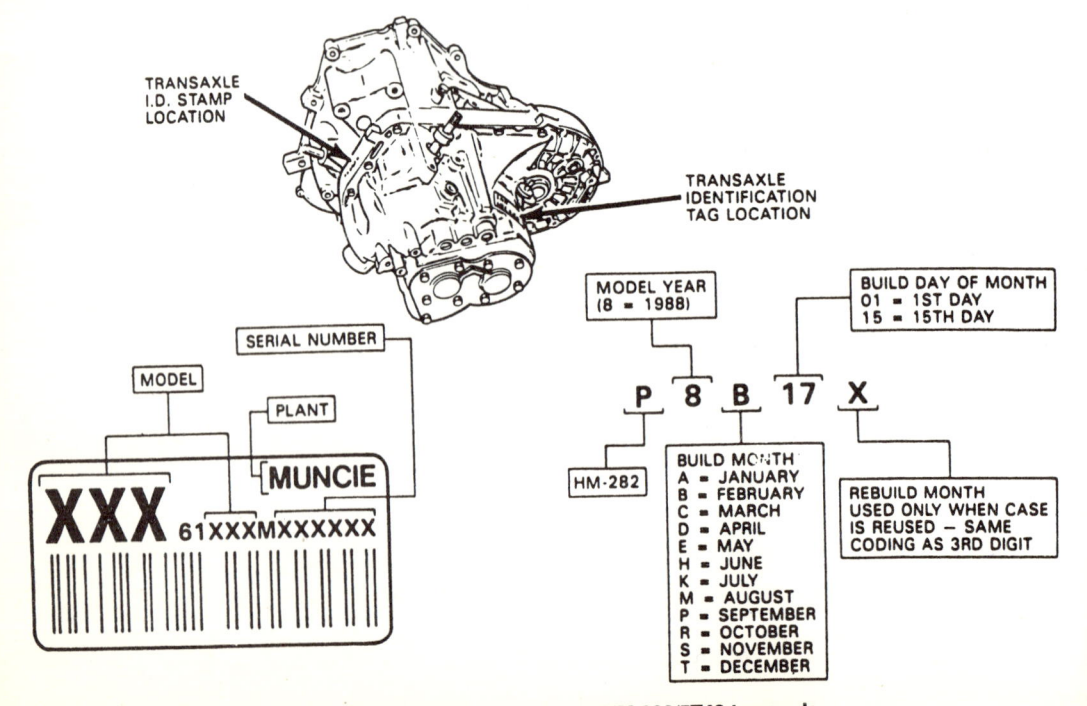

**Transaxle identification location—HM-282/5T40 transaxle**

## ISUZU 5-SPEED TRANSAXLE

**TRANSAXLE I.D. NAMEPLATE**

5 0 0 0 0 1

SEQUENCE NUMBER
LAST NUMBER OF CALENDAR YEAR

FRONT OF VEHICLE

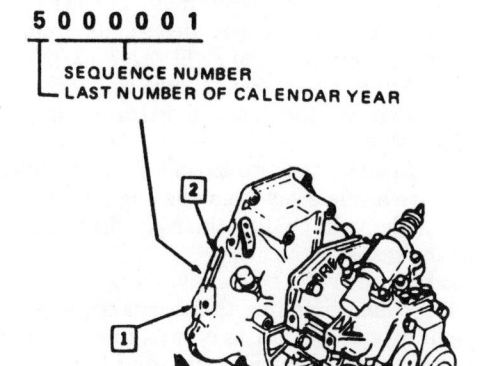

[1] VIN LOCATION
[2] OPTIONAL VIN LOCATION

Transaxle identification location—Isuzu transaxle

or possible personal injury. Care should be taken to re-use the fasteners in the same locations as removed.

## Capacities

To fill a dry transaxle on N-body, add 5 pints (2.1L) of 5W-30 manual transaxle oil, part number 1052931 or equivalent. On 1988-92 vehicles, use syncromesh transaxle fluid, part number 12345349 or equivalent.

## Adjustments

### SHIFT LINKAGE

The shift linkage procedure shown in the illustration is for 1985-87 vehicles equipped with an Isuzu 5 speed transaxle.

## Backup Light Switch

### REMOVAL AND INSTALLATION

1. Disconnect the negative battery cable.
2. Disconnect the back-up light connector.
3. Remove the back-up light switch assembly.

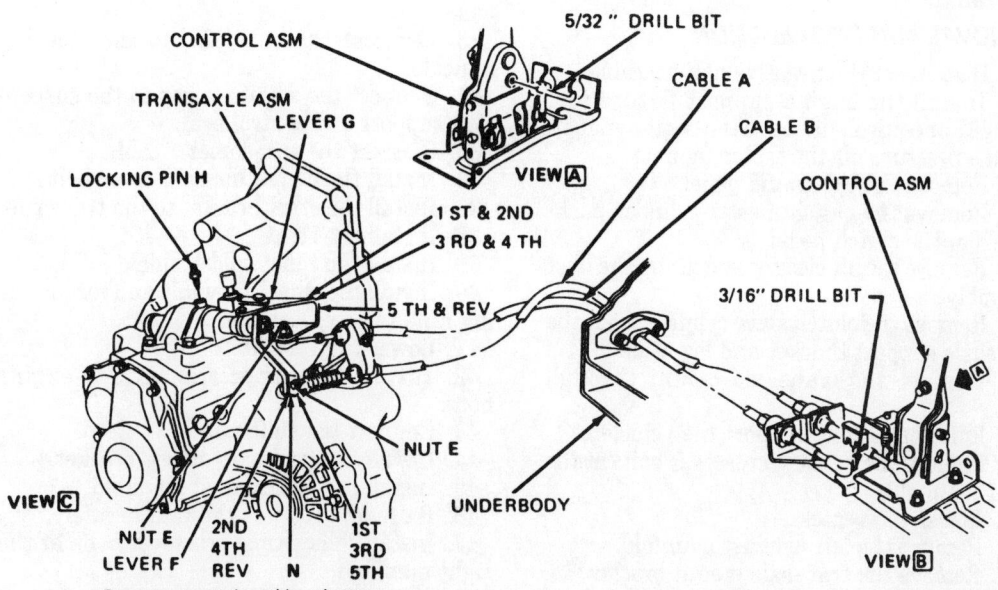

1. Disconnect negative cable at battery.
2. Shift transaxle into third gear. Remove lock pin (H) and reinstall with tapered end down. This will lock transaxle in third gear.
3. Loosen shift cable attaching nuts (E) at transaxle levers (G) and (F).
4. Remove console trim plate and slide shifter boot up shifter handle. Remove console.
5. Install a 5/32" or No. 22 drill bit into alignment hole at side of shifter assembly, as shown in View A.
6. Align the hole in the select lever (View B) with the slot in the shifter plate and install a 3/16" drill bit.
7. Tighten nuts E at levers G and F. Remove drill bits from alignments holes at the shifter. Remove lockpin (H) and reinstall with tapered end up.
8. Install console, shifter boot and trim plate.
9. Connect negative cable at battery.
10. Road test vehicle to check for a good neutral gate feel during shifting. It may be necessary to fine tune the adjustment after testing.

Manual shift linkage adjustment—Isuzu transaxle

## DRIVE TRAIN

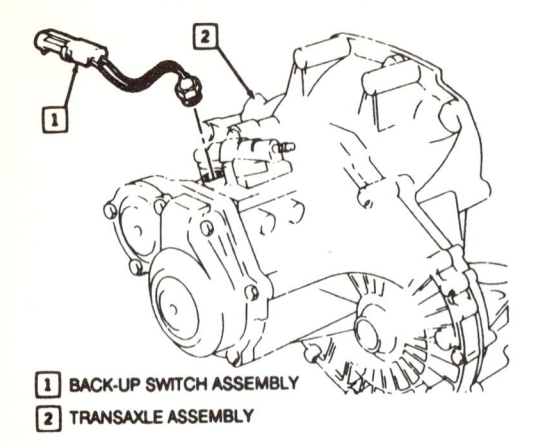

Back-up light switch installation—Isuzu transaxle

**To install:**
4. Install the back-up light switch assembly using a suitable pipe sealant compound. Tighten to 24 ft. lbs. (33 Nm).
5. Connect the back-up light switch connector.
6. Connect the negative battery cable.

## Transaxle

### REMOVAL AND INSTALLATION

1. Disconnect the negative battery cable.
2. Install the engine support fixture tool J-28467 or equivalent. Raise the engine enough to take pressure off the motor mounts.
3. Remove the left sound panel.
4. Remove the clutch master cylinder pushrod from the clutch pedal.
5. Remove the air cleaner and air intake duct assembly.
6. Remove the clutch slave cylinder from the transaxle support bracket and lay aside.
7. Remove the transaxle mount through bolt.
8. Raise and safely support the vehicle.
9. Remove the exhaust crossover bolts at the right manifold.
10. Lower the vehicle.
11. Remove the left exhaust manifold.
12. Remove the transaxle mount bracket.
13. Disconnect the shift cables.
14. Remove the upper transaxle-to-engine bolts.
15. Raise the vehicle and support the safely.
16. Remove the left wheel assembly.
17. Remove the left front inner splash shield.
18. Remove the transaxle strut and bracket.
19. Drain the transaxle.
20. Remove the clutch housing cover bolts.
21. Disconnect the speedometer cable.
22. Disconnect the stabilizer bar at the left suspension support and control arm.
23. Disconnect the ball joint from the steering knuckle.
24. Remove the left suspension support attaching bolts and remove the support and control arm as an assembly.
25. Disconnect the driveshafts at the transaxle and remove the left driveshaft from the transaxle. Support the right driveshaft.
26. Attach the transaxle case to a jack.
27. Remove the remaining transaxle-to-engine bolts.
28. Remove the transaxle by sliding toward the drive side away from the engine. Carefully lower the jack, guiding the right driveshaft out of the transaxle.

**To install:**
29. When installing the transaxle, guide the right driveshaft into its bore as the transaxle is being raised. The right driveshaft can not be readily installed after the transaxle is connected to the engine.
30. Install the transaxle-to-engine mounting bolts and tighten to specifications.
31. Install the left driveshaft into its bore at the transaxle and seat both driveshafts at the transaxle.
32. Install the suspension support-to-body bolts.
33. Connect the ball joint to the steering knuckle.
34. Connect the stabilizer bar to the suspension support and control arm.
35. Connect the speedometer cable.
36. Install the clutch housing cover bolts.
37. Install the strut bracket to the transaxle.
38. Install the strut.
39. Install the inner splash shield.
40. Install the wheel assembly and torque the lug nuts to specifications.
41. Lower the vehicle.
42. Install the upper transaxle-to-engine bolts.
43. Connect the shift cables.
44. Install the transaxle mount bracket.
45. Install the left exhaust manifold.
46. Raise and support the vehicle safely.
47. Install the exhaust crossover bolts at the right manifold.
48. Lower the vehicle.
49. Install the transaxle mount through bolt.
50. Install the clutch slave cylinder to the support bracket.
51. Install the air cleaner and air intake duct assembly.
52. Remove the engine support fixture.
52. Install the clutch master cylinder push rod to the clutch pedal.
54. Install the left sound panel.
55. Fill the transaxle with 5 pints (2.1L) of 5W–30 manual transaxle oil, part number

## DRIVE TRAIN

1052931 or equivalent. (On 1988–89 vehicles, use syncromesh transaxle fluid, part number 12345349 or equivalent.)

56. Connect the negative battery cable.

## Halfshafts

### REMOVAL AND INSTALLATION

NOTE: *If equipped with tri-pot joints, care must be exercised not to allow joints to become overextended. Overextending the joint could result in separation of internal components.*

**1985–88 Vehicles**

1. Disconnect the negative battery cable.
2. Raise and safely support the vehicle under the body lift points. Do not support under lower control arms. Remove wheel assemblies.
3. Remove the shaft nut and washer.
4. Remove caliper bolts and support caliper; do not let the caliper hang by its brake hose.
5. Remove the rotor and ball joint nut.
6. Remove the stabilizer bolt from lower control arm.
7. Remove the ball joint attaching nut and separate the control arm from the steering knuckle.
8. Pry the halfshaft from the transaxle or intermediate shaft.
9. Install a halfshaft pressing tool and press halfshaft in and away from hub. The halfshaft should only be pressed in until the press fit between the halfshaft and hub is loose.
10. To remove the intermediate shaft:
    a. Remove the detonation sensor.
    b. Remove the power steering pump brace.
    c. Remove the intermediate shaft bracket bolts and remove the assembly.

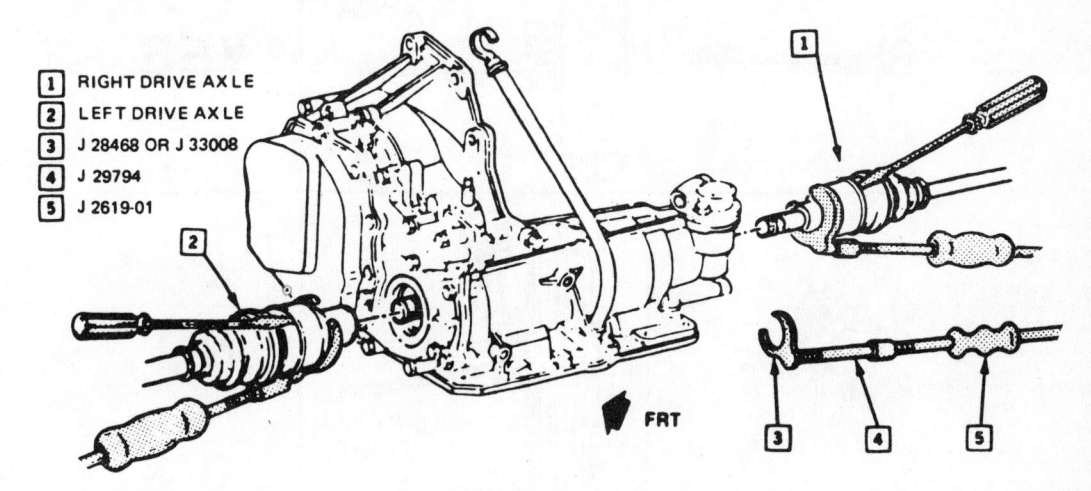

1. RIGHT DRIVE AXLE
2. LEFT DRIVE AXLE
3. J 28468 OR J 33008
4. J 29794
5. J 2619-01

Removing and installing drive axle

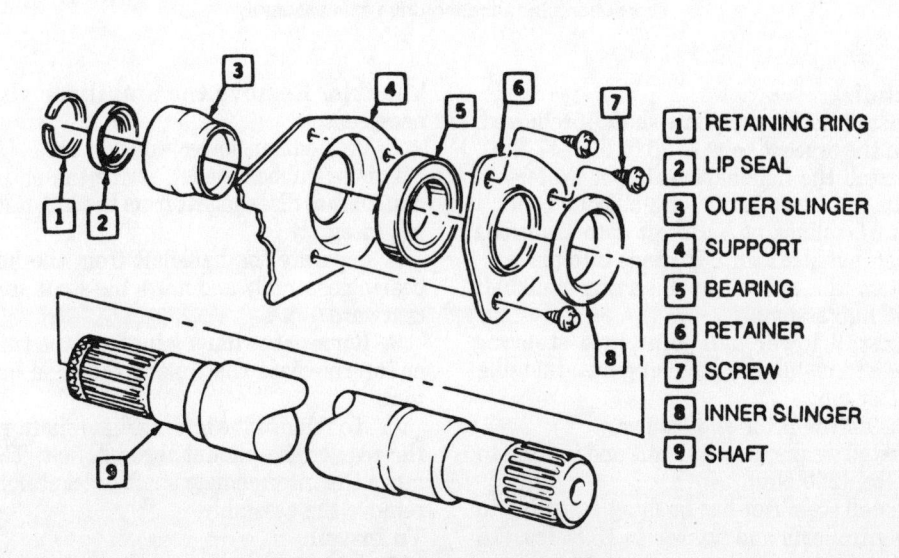

1. RETAINING RING
2. LIP SEAL
3. OUTER SLINGER
4. SUPPORT
5. BEARING
6. RETAINER
7. SCREW
8. INNER SLINGER
9. SHAFT

Intermediate shaft disassembled view

# 210 DRIVE TRAIN

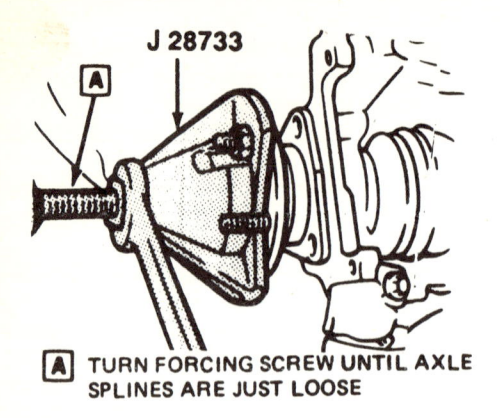

**A** TURN FORCING SCREW UNTIL AXLE SPLINES ARE JUST LOOSE

Removing drive axle from the hub

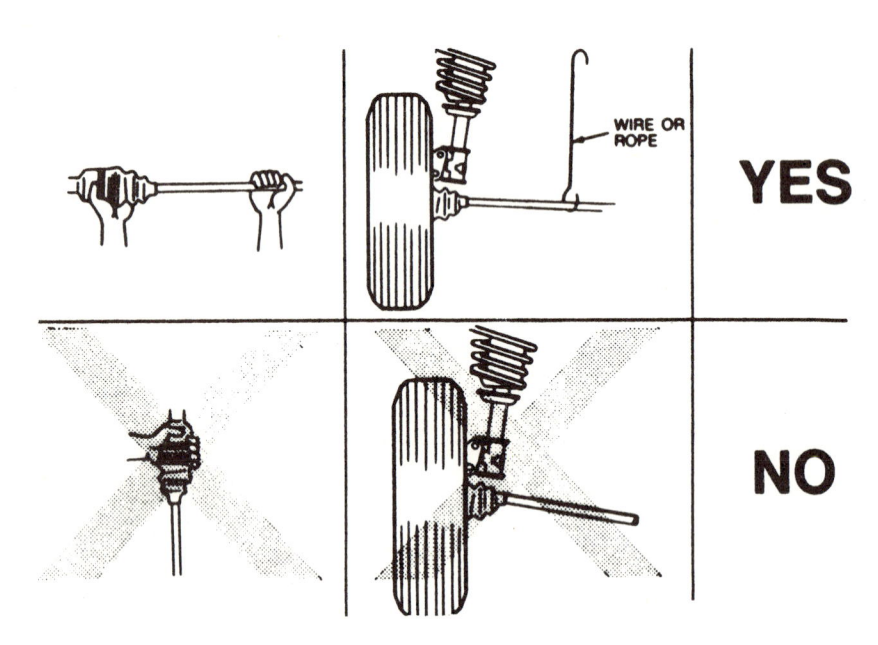

Precautions for handling drive axle assembly

19. Remove halfshaft seal boot protector, if used.
20. Install the wheels.
21. Connect the negative battery cable and check for proper operation.

**1989–92 Vehicles**

1. Disconnect the negative battery cable.
2. Raise and safely support the vehicle.
3. Remove the wheels.
4. Install the halfshaft seal protector on the outer joint.
5. Remove the shaft nut and washer.
6. Remove the ball joint attaching nut and separate the control arm from the steering knuckle. Remove the stabilizer shaft, if necessary.
7. Pull out on lower knuckle area. Using a plastic or rubber mallet, strike the end of the halfshaft to disengage it from the hub and bearing assembly.
8. Separate the halfshaft from the hub and bearing assembly and move the strut assembly rearward.
9. Remove the inner joint from the transaxle or intermediate shaft using the slide hammer tool.
10. To remove the intermediate shaft, remove the rear engine mount through bolt. Then remove the intermediate shaft bracket bolts and remove the assembly.

**To install:**

11. Install the seal protector to the transaxle.

**To install:**

11. Install the intermediate shaft, if removed. Tighten the bracket bolts to 35 ft. lbs. (47 Nm).
12. Install the halfshaft seal boot protectors on all tri-pot inner joints with silicone boots.
13. Start splines of halfshaft into transaxle and push halfshaft until it snaps into place.
14. Start the splines by inserting halfshaft into the hub assembly.
15. Install lower ball joint into steering knuckle and install the attaching nut. Install a new cotter pin.
16. Install the rotor and caliper.
17. Install washer and hub nut and tighten to 191 ft. lbs. (260 Nm).
18. Install stabilizer bar bushing assembly to lower control arm and tighten to 13 ft. lbs. (18 Nm).

# DRIVE TRAIN

Install the intermediate shaft, if removed. Tighten the bracket bolts to 35 ft. lbs. (47 Nm).

12. Drive the halfshaft into the transaxle or intermediate shaft by placing a suitable tool into the groove on the joint housing and tapping until seated. Be careful not to damage the axle seal or spring. Verify that the axle is seated by grasping the inner joint housing and pulling outboard.

13. Install the axle to the hub and bearing assembly.

14. Install the washer and nut and tighten to 185 ft. lbs. (260 Nm).

15. Install the ball joint to the steering knuckle. Install the stabilizer shaft, if removed.

16. Remove the seal protectors.

17. Install the wheels.

18. Connect the negative battery cable and check for proper operation.

## CLUTCH

CAUTION: *The clutch driven disc contains asbestos, which has been determined to be a cancer causing agent. Never clean clutch surfaces with compressed air! Avoid inhaling any dust from any clutch surface! When cleaning clutch surfaces, use a commercially available brake cleaning fluid.*

## Adjustments

### CLUTCH CABLE

The adjusting mechanism is mounted to the clutch pedal and bracket assembly. The cable is a fixed length and cannot be lengthened or shortened; however, the position of the cable can be changed by adjusting the position of the quadrant in relation to the clutch pedal. This mechanism makes adjustments in the quadrant position which changes the effective cable length. This is done by lifting the clutch pedal to disengage the pawl from the quadrant. The spring in the hub of the quadrant applies a tension load to the cable and keeps the release bearing in contact with the clutch levers. This

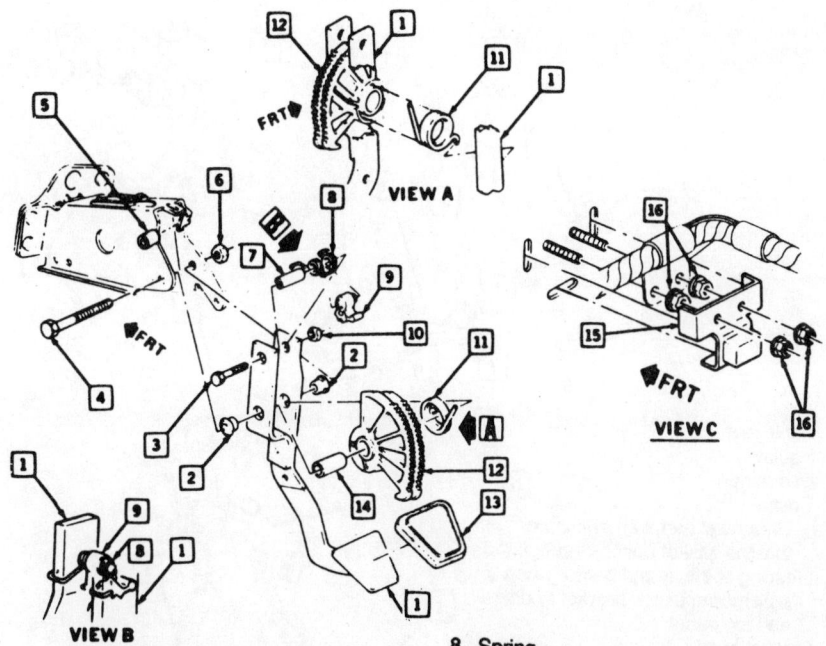

**VIEW B**
1. Pedal assembly
Pedal must swing freely after assembling. Pedal must have a minimum travel of 46° without contacting carpet or sound barrier.
2. Bushing
3. Bolt/screw
4. Bolt/screw
5. Bumper
Assemble bumper past both tangs on clutch pedal bracket assembly
6. 35 N·m (26 lbs. ft.)
7. Spacer
8. Spring
9. Pawl
With pedal against bumper, pawl teeth must clear O.D. of detent teeth and snap into engagement when pedal is moved.
10. 5 N·m (44 lbs. in.)
11. Spring
12. Detent
13. Cover
14. Spacer
15. Bracket
16. Nut

**Exploded view of the clutch pedal assembly**

## DRIVE TRAIN

results in a balanced condition, with the correct tension applied to the cable.

As the clutch friction material wears, the cable must be lengthened. This is accomplished by simply pulling the clutch pedal up to its rubber bumper. This action forces the pawl against its stop and rotates it out of mesh with the quadrant teeth, allowing the cable to play out until the quadrant spring load is balanced against the load applied by the release bearing. This adjustment procedure is required approximately every 5000 miles.

### HYDRAULIC CLUTCH

The hydraulic clutch release system consists of a clutch master cylinder with an integral or remote reservoir and a slave cylinder connected to the master cylinder by a hydraulic line, much like the brake system. The clutch master cylinder is mounted to the front of the dash and the slave cylinder is mounted to the transaxle support bracket. The clutch master cylinder is operated directly off the clutch pedal by the pushrod.

When the clutch pedal is depressed, hydraulic fluid under pressure from the master cylinder flows into the slave cylinder. As the hydraulic force reaches the slave cylinder, the pushrod movement rotates the clutch fork which forces the release bearing into the clutch diaphragm and disengages the clutch. The hydraulic clutch system provides automatic clutch adjustment, so no periodic adjustment of the clutch linkage or pedal is required.

NOTE: *When adding fluid to the clutch master cylinder, use Delco Supreme 11 brake fluid or an equivalent that meets DOT 3 specifications. Do not use mineral or paraffin based oil in the clutch hydraulic system as these fluids will damage the rubber components in the cylinders.*

1. Cable asm.
2. Insulator
3. Dampener
4. Gasket
   Care must be taken to ensure that the gasket passes through the facing of the sound barrier when assembling clutch bracket to dash and toe panel.
5. Bracket asm.
6. Nut
7. Insulator
   Coat insulator O.D. with grease prior to installation into bracket asm.
8. Washer
9. Secure pedal in up position to hold pedal against bumper during cable assembly to trans. lever and engine mount bracket.
10. Care must be taken to ensure that nylon tube on cable asm., is pushed to bottom of rubber slot in bracket assembly.

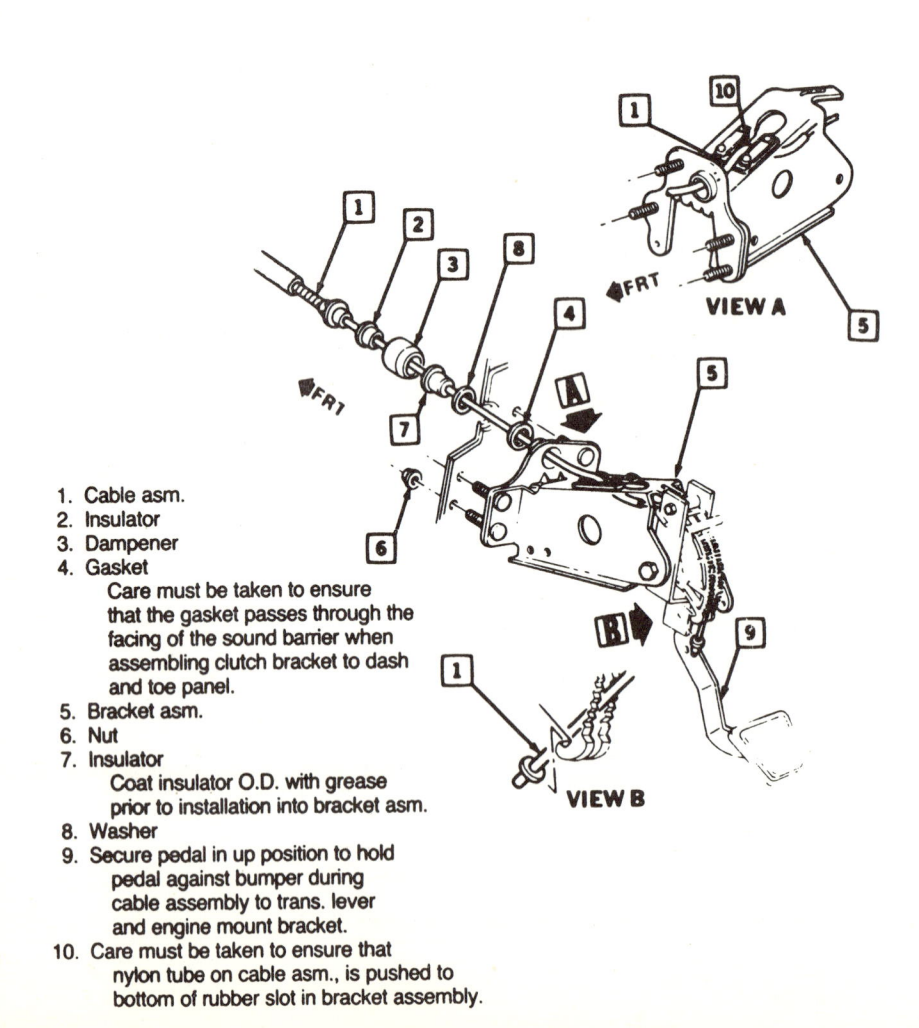

**Clutch bracket and cable**

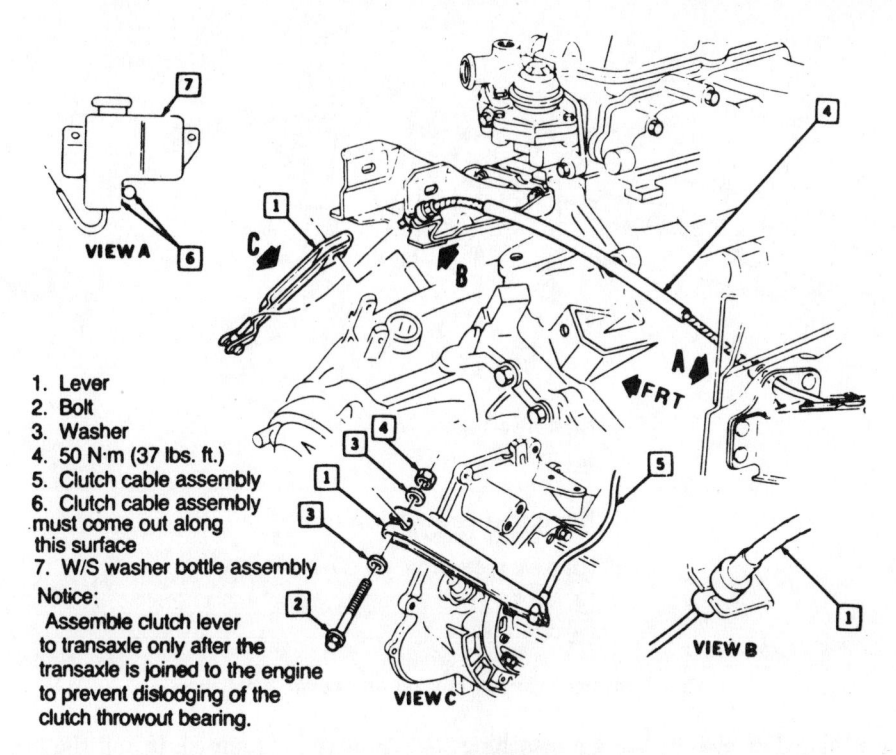

1. Lever
2. Bolt
3. Washer
4. 50 N·m (37 lbs. ft.)
5. Clutch cable assembly
6. Clutch cable assembly must come out along this surface
7. W/S washer bottle assembly

Notice:
Assemble clutch lever to transaxle only after the transaxle is joined to the engine to prevent dislodging of the clutch throwout bearing.

Clutch cable routing

## Clutch Cable

### REMOVAL AND INSTALLATION

1. Support the clutch pedal upward against the bumper stop to release the pawl from the quadrant.
2. Disconnect the end of the cable from the clutch release lever at the transaxle. Be careful to prevent the cable from snapping toward the rear of the car. The quadrant in the adjusting mechanism can be damaged by allowing the cable to snap back.
3. Disconnect the clutch cable from the quadrant. Lift the locking pawl away from the quadrant, then slide the cable out on the right side of the quadrant.
4. From the engine side of the cowl, disconnect the 2 upper nuts holding the cable retainer to the upper studs. Disconnect the cable from the bracket mounted to the transaxle and remove the cable.
5. Inspect the clutch cable from signs of fraying, kinks, worn ends or excessive cable friction. Replace the cable if any of these problems are noted.

**To install:**

6. Place the gasket into position on the 2 upper studs, then position the cable with the retaining flange against the bracket.
7. Attach the end of the cable to the quadrant, being sure to route the cable underneath the pawl. Attach the 2 upper nuts to the retainer mounting studs and tighten.
8. Attach the cable to the bracket mounted to the transaxle.
9. Support the clutch pedal upward against the bumper to release the pawl from the quadrant. Attach the outer end of the cable to the clutch release lever.

NOTE: *Be sure NOT to yank on the cable, since overloading the cable could damage the quadrant.*

10. Check clutch operation and adjust by lifting the clutch pedal up to allow the mechanism to adjust the cable length. Depress the pedal slowly several times to set the pawl into mesh with the quadrant teeth.

## Clutch Pedal

### REMOVAL AND INSTALLATION

1. Disconnect the negative battery cable.
2. Remove the right side sound insulator.
3. Disconnect the clutch cable or master cylinder pushrod from the clutch pedal.
4. If the clutch pedal pivot is mounted using a nut and bolt, remove from the bracket and remove the clutch pedal. Remove the spaces and bushings from the pedal.
5. If the clutch pedal pivot is mounted using a rivet, the pedal and bracket must be removed

# 214 DRIVE TRAIN

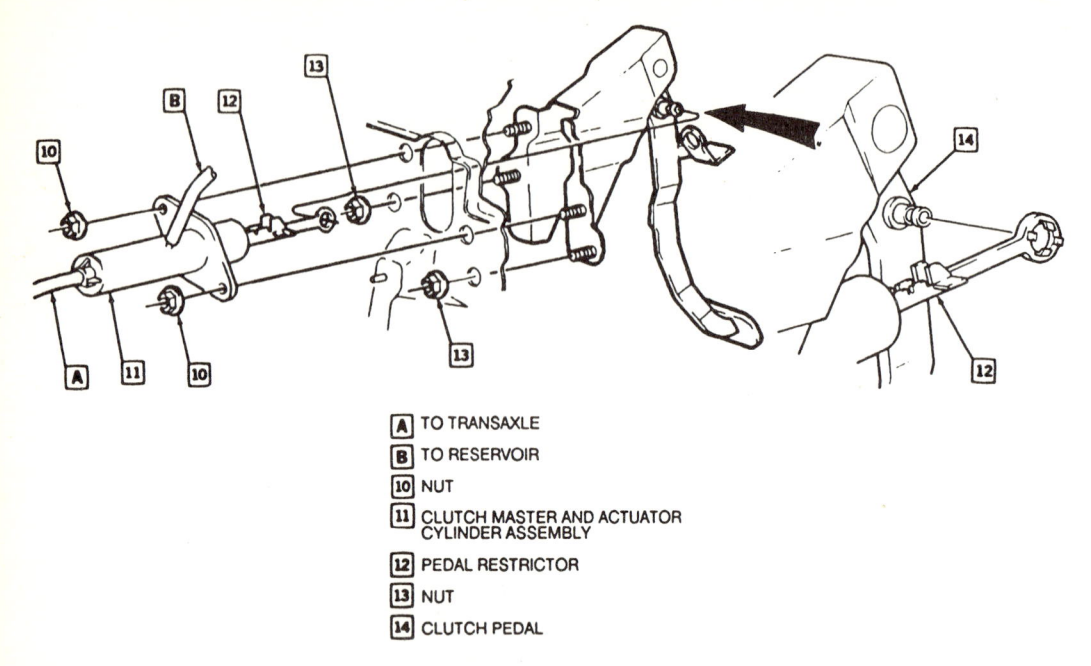

**A** TO TRANSAXLE
**B** TO RESERVOIR
**10** NUT
**11** CLUTCH MASTER AND ACTUATOR CYLINDER ASSEMBLY
**12** PEDAL RESTRICTOR
**13** NUT
**14** CLUTCH PEDAL

Clutch master cylinder, bracket and pedal installation

as an assembly. Remove the bracket attaching nuts from inside the engine compartment and remove the bracket and pedal assembly.

**To install:**
6. If mounted with a nut and bolt, perform the following;
   a. Install the spacer and bushings on the pedal. Lubricate the bushings before installing on the pedal.
   b. Position the clutch pedal to the mounting bracket and install the pivot bolt and retaining nut. Tighten to 23 ft. lbs. (31 Nm).

7. If rivet mounted, install the bracket and pedal assembly. Install the attaching nuts. Tighten to 16 ft. lbs. (22 Nm) starting with the upper left nut and moving clockwise.
8. Lubricate the master cylinder pushrod busing
9. Install the pushrod on the pedal or connect the cable. If equipped with cruise control, check the switch adjustment at the clutch pedal bracket.
10. Install the right side sound insulator.
11. Connect the negative battery cable.

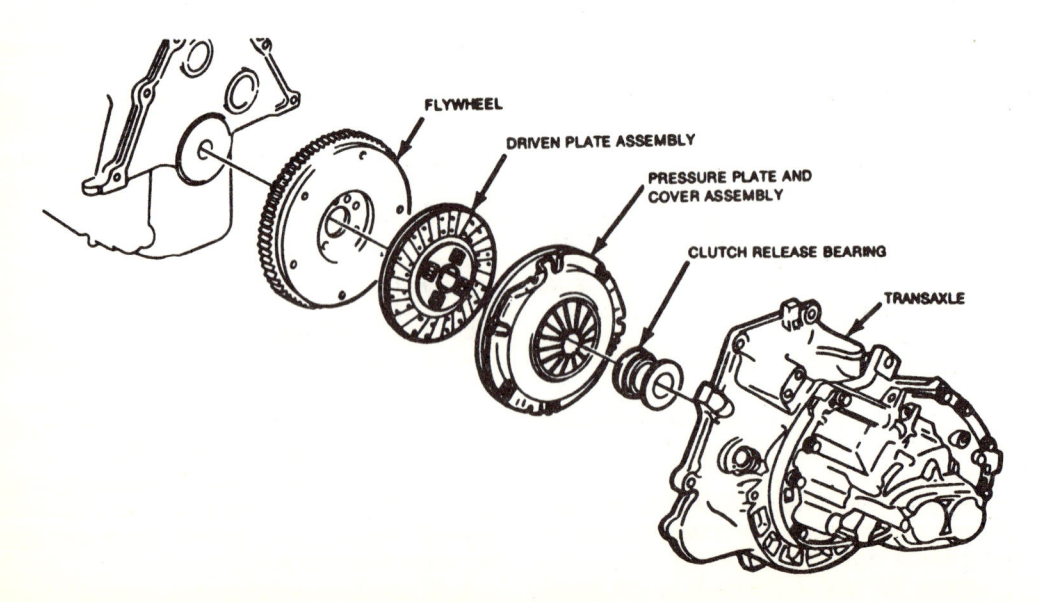

Clutch components

# DRIVE TRAIN

## Drive Disc and Pressure Plate
### REMOVAL AND INSTALLATION

1. Disconnect the negative battery cable. Remove the transaxle.
2. Matchmark the clutch/pressure plate cover and flywheel, if reinstalling old parts. Insert a clutch plate alignment tool into the clutch disc hub.
3. Loosen the flywheel to pressure plate bolts gradually and evenly to avoid warpage.
4. Remove the pressure plate/clutch assembly from the flywheel.
5. Sand the flywheel or replace it, if scored, cracked or heat damaged.
6. Sparingly apply anti-seize compound to the input shaft and clutch disc splines. Install a new release bearing.

### To install:
7. Using a clutch disc alignment tool, tighten the pressure plate bolts to center the disc.
8. Tighten the pressure plate/clutch assembly mounting bolts to the flywheel gradually and evenly to 20-25 ft. lbs. (27-34 Nm).
9. Install the transaxle.
10. Connect the negative battery cable and check the clutch and reverse lights for proper operation.

## Clutch Master and Slave Cylinders
### REMOVAL AND INSTALLATION

1. Disconnect the negative battery cable.
2. Remove the steering column opening filler from inside the vehicle.
3. Disconnect the clutch master cylinder pushrod from the clutch pedal.
4. Remove the clutch master cylinder attaching nuts at the front of the dash and disconnect the remote fluid reservoir, if equipped.
5. Remove the actuator cylinder attaching nuts at the transaxle.
6. Remove the hydraulic actuating system as an assembly.

### To install:
7. Bleed the system, if necessary.
8. Install the actuator cylinder to the transaxle, aligning the pushrod into the pocket on the lever. Tighten the attaching nuts evenly to prevent damage.

NOTE: *New actuators are packaged with plastic straps to retain the pushrod. Do not break the strap off; it will break upon the first clutch application.*

9. Install the master cylinder. Tighten the attaching nuts evenly to prevent damage. Connect the remote fluid reservoir, if equipped. If equipped with a bleed screw and bleeding is necessary, bleed the system.
10. Remove the pushrod restrictor from the master cylinder pushrod. Lubricate the bushing on the clutch pedal. Connect the pushrod to the pedal and install the retaining clip. Make sure the cruise control switch is operating properly.

NOTE: *When adjusting the cruise control switch, do not use a force of more than 20 lbs. to pull the pedal up, or damage to the master cylinder pushrod retaining ring could result.*

11. Install the steering column opening filler from inside the vehicle.
12. Push the clutch pedal down a few times. This will break the plastic straps on the actuator.
13. Connect the negative battery cable and check for proper operation.

### Adjustment

The hydraulic system used provides automatic clutch adjustment, therefore no adjustment to any portion of the system is required.

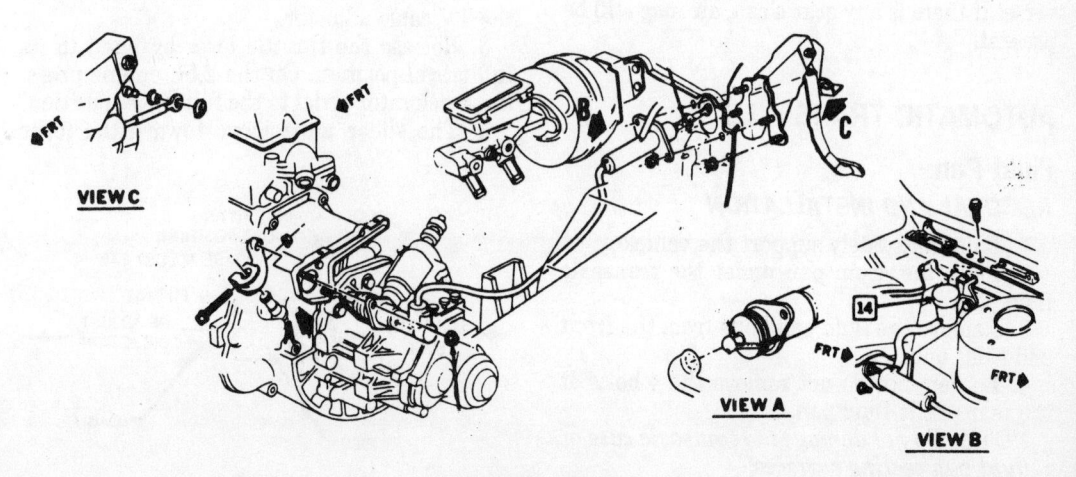

**Hydraulic system**

# DRIVE TRAIN

## Hydraulic Clutch System Bleeding

### WITH BLEED SCREW

1. Make sure the reservoir is full of DOT 3 fluid and is kept topped off throughout this procedure.
2. Loosen the bleed screw, located on the actuator cylinder body next to the inlet connection.
3. When a steady stream of fluid comes out the bleeder, tighten it to 17 inch lbs. (2 Nm).
4. Refill the fluid reservoir.
5. To check the system, start the engine and wait 10 seconds.
6. Depress the clutch pedal and shift into Reverse. If there is any gear clash, air may still be present.

### WITHOUT BLEED SCREW

1. Remove the actuator cylinder from the transaxle.
2. Loosen the master cylinder attaching nuts to the ends of the studs.
3. Remove the reservoir cap and diaphragm.
4. Depress the actuator cylinder pushrod about ¾ in. into its bore and hold the position.
5. Install the reservoir diaphragm and cap while holding the actuator pushrod.
6. Release the pushrod when the diaphragm and cap are properly installed.
7. With the actuator lower than the master cylinder, hold the actuator vertically with the pushrod end facing the ground.
8. Press the actuator pushrod into its bore with ½ in. strokes. Check the reservoir for bubbles. Continue until no bubbles enter the reservoir.
9. Install the master cylinder and actuator.
10. Refill the fluid reservoir.
11. To check the system, start the engine and wait 10 seconds.
12. Depress the clutch pedal and shift into reverse. If there is any gear clash, air may still be present.

## AUTOMATIC TRANSAXLE

## Fluid Pan

### REMOVAL AND INSTALLATION

1. Raise and safely support the vehicle.
2. Place the drain pan under the transaxle fluid pan.
3. Remove the fluid pan bolts from the front and sides only.
4. Loosen, but do not remove the 4 bolts at the rear of the fluid pan.
   NOTE: *Do not damage the transaxle case or fluid pan sealing surfaces.*
5. Lightly tap the fluid pan with a rubber mallet or pry to allow the fluid to partially drain from the pan.
6. Remove the remaining fluid pan bolts, fluid pan and gasket.

**To install:**

7. Install a new gasket to the fluid pan.
8. Install the fluid pan to the transaxle.
   NOTE: *Apply a suitable sealant compound to the bolt shown in the illustration to prevent fluid leaks.*
9. Install the pan bolts. Tighten to 133 inch lbs. (11 Nm).
10. Lower the vehicle.
11. Fill the transaxle to the proper level with Dexron® II fluid. Check cold level reading. Do not overfill.
12. Follow the fluid check procedure in this Chapter.
13. Check the pan for leaks.

### FILTER SERVICE

1. With the pan removed from the vehicle and the fluid completely drained, thoroughly clean the inside of the pan to remove all old fluid and residue.
2. Inspect the gasket sealing surface on the fluid pan and remove any remaining gasket fragments with a scraper.
3. Remove the fluid filter, O-ring and seal from the case.

**To install:**

4. Apply a small amount of Transjel to the new seal and install the seal.
5. Install a new filter O-ring and filter.
6. Install the new gasket to the pan.

## Adjustments

### TV CABLE ADJUSTMENT

**Except 2.3L Engine**

1. Disconnect the negative battery cable.
2. Depress and hold the adjustment tap at the TV cable adjuster.
3. Release the throttle lever by hand to its full travel position. On the 2.5L engine press, the accelerator pedal to the full travel position.
4. The slider must move toward the lever

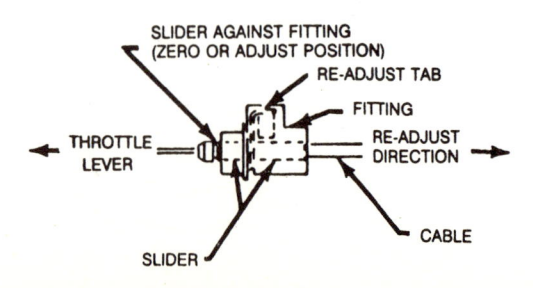

TV cable adjuster—with slider

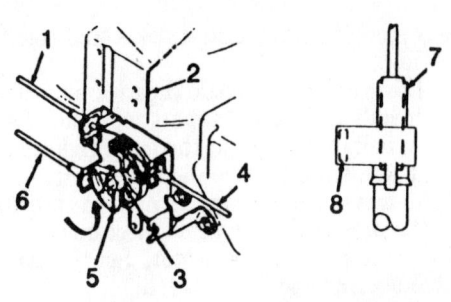

# DRIVE TRAIN

**TV cable adjuster—without slider**

| | |
|---|---|
| 1 Accelerator cable | 5 Spool assembly |
| 2 Accelerator bracket | 6 Throttle value assembly |
| 3 Hex nut | 7 Adjuster |
| 4 Throttle body cable | 8 Adjuster button |

when the lever is rotated to the full travel position or when the accelerator pedal is pressed to the full travel position on the 2.5L engine.

5. Inspect the cable for freedom of movement. The cable may appear to function properly with the engine stopped and cold. Recheck the cable after the engine is warm.
6. Road test the vehicle and check for proper shifting.

### 2.3L Engine

1. Disconnect the negative battery cable.
2. Rotate the TV cable adjuster body at the transaxle 90 degrees and pull the cable conduit out until the slider mechanism contacts the stop.
3. Rotate the adjuster body back to the original position.
4. Using a torque wrench, rotate the TV cable adjuster until 75 inch lbs. (9 Nm) is reached.
5. Road test the vehicle and check for proper shifting.

### SHIFT CABLE ADJUSTMENT

1. Place the selector in the **N** detent.
2. Raise the locking tab on the cable adjuster.
3. Place the shift control assembly on the transaxle in the neutral position.
4. Push the locking tab back into position.

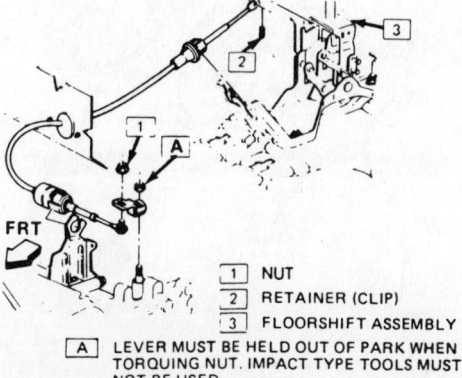

## Neutral Safety and Back-Up Switch

### REMOVAL AND INSTALLATION

1. Disconnect the negative battery cable. Place the shifter in the **N** detent.
2. Disconnect the shifter linkage.
3. Disconnect the switch.
4. Remove the mounting bolts and remove the switch from the transaxle.

**To install:**

5. If not already done, place the shifter shaft in the **N** detent.
6. Align the flats of the shift shaft with those of the switch.
7. If replacing the switch, tighten the installation bolts and remove the pre-installed alignment pin.
8. If reusing the old switch, install the mounting bolts loosely and adjust the switch.
9. Connect the negative battery cable and check the switch for proper operation. The reverse lights should come on when the transaxle is shifted into **R**. If the engine can be started in any gear except **P** or **N**, readjust the switch.

### ADJUSTMENT

1. Place the shifter in the **N** detent.
2. The switch is located on the shift shaft on the top of the automatic transaxle. Loosen the switch attaching bolts.
3. Rotate the switch on the shifter assembly to align the service adjustment hole with the carrier tang hole.
4. Insert a $3/32$ in. maximum diameter gauge pin into the hole to a depth of $5/8$ in.
5. Tighten the mounting bolts and remove the pin.

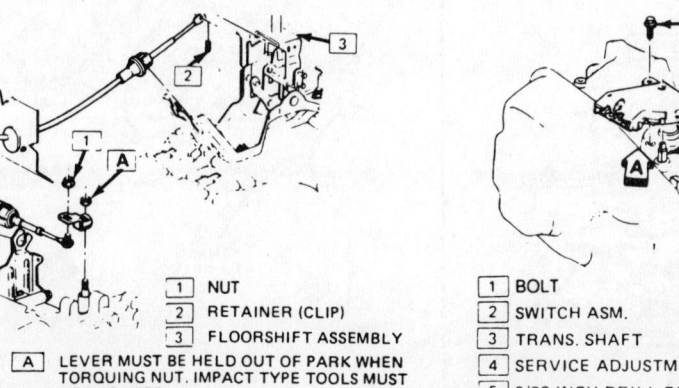

**Floorshift cable routing**

| | |
|---|---|
| 1 | NUT |
| 2 | RETAINER (CLIP) |
| 3 | FLOORSHIFT ASSEMBLY |
| A | LEVER MUST BE HELD OUT OF PARK WHEN TORQUING NUT. IMPACT TYPE TOOLS MUST NOT BE USED. |

**Neutral start and back-up light switch**

| | |
|---|---|
| 1 | BOLT |
| 2 | SWITCH ASM. |
| 3 | TRANS. SHAFT |
| 4 | SERVICE ADJUSTMENT HOLE |
| 5 | 3/32 INCH DRILL BIT OR 2.34 DIA. GAGE PIN |

# DRIVE TRAIN

## Transaxle

### REMOVAL AND INSTALLATION

1. Disconnect the negative battery cable. If necessary, drain the coolant and disconnect the heater core hoses.
2. Remove the air cleaner assembly. If equipped with a 3.0L or 3.3L engine, remove the mass air flow sensor and air intake duct.
3. Disconnect the throttle valve cable from the throttle lever and the transaxle.
4. If equipped with a 2.3L engine, remove the power steering pump and bracket and position it aside.
5. Remove the transaxle dipstick and tube.
6. Install an engine support tool. Insert a ¼ × 2 in. bolt in the hole at the front right motor mount to maintain driveline alignment.
7. Remove the wiring harness-to-transaxle nut. Disconnect the wiring connectors from the speed sensor, TCC connector, neutral safety switch and reverse light switch.
8. Disconnect the shift linkage from the transaxle.

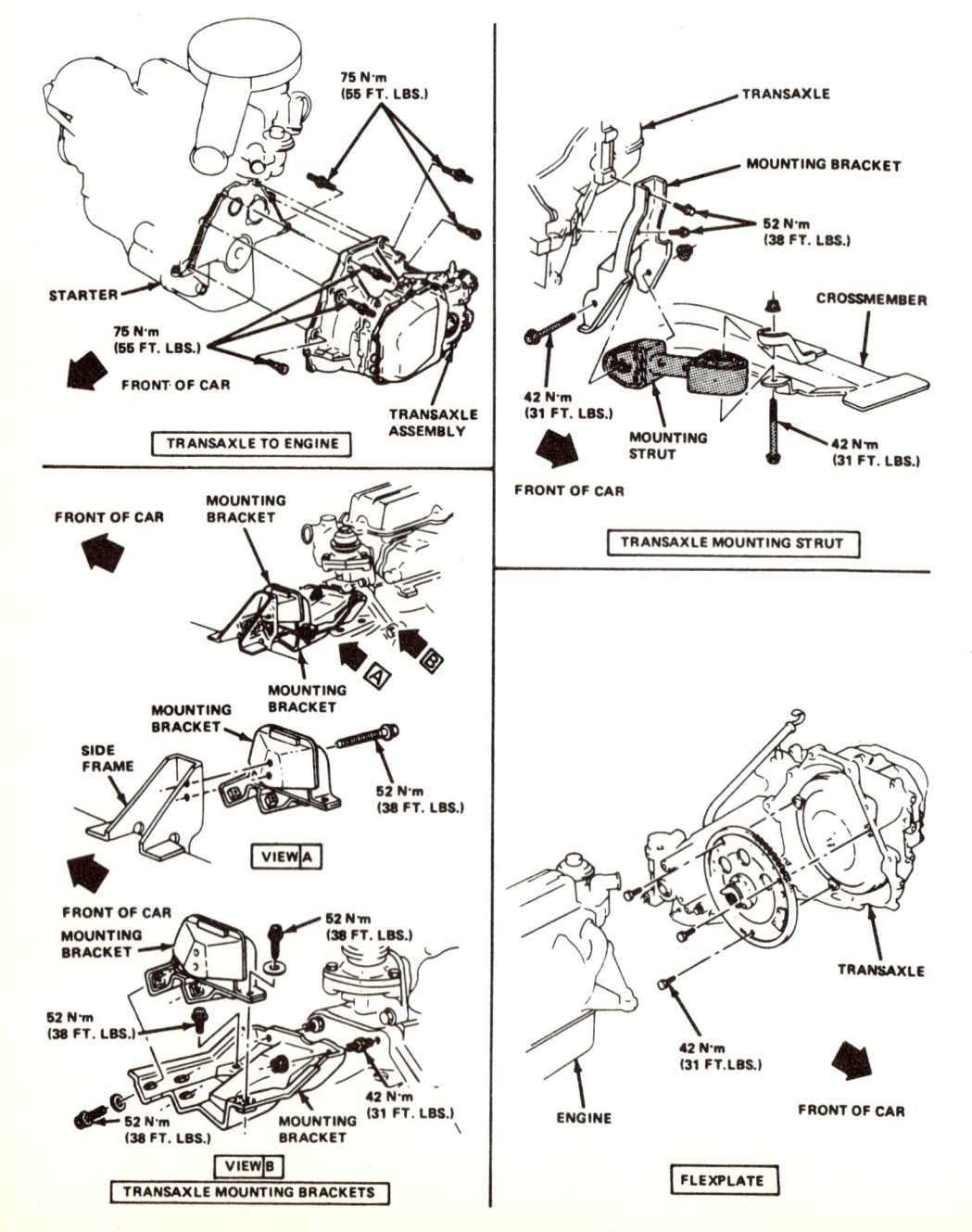

**Typical transaxle mounts**

9. Remove the upper 2 transaxle-to-engine bolts and the upper left transaxle mount along with the bracket assembly.
10. Remove the rubber hose from the transaxle vent pipe. Remove the remaining upper engine-to-transaxle bolts.
11. Raise and safely support the vehicle. Remove both front wheels.
12. If equipped with a 2.3L engine, remove both lower ball joints and stabilizer shafts links.
13. Drain the transaxle fluid.
14. Remove the shift linkage bracket from the transaxle.
15. Install a halfshaft boot seal protector on the inner seals.

NOTE: *Some vehicles may use a gray silicone boot on the inboard axle joint. Use boot protector tool on these boots. All other boots are made from a black thermo-plastic material and do not require the use of a boot seal protector.*

16. Remove both ball joint-to-control arm nuts and separate the ball joints from the control arms.
17. Remove both halfshafts and support them with a cord or wire.
18. Remove the transaxle mounting strut.
19. Remove the left stabilizer bar link pin bolt, left frame bushing clamp nuts and left frame support assembly.
20. Remove the torque converter cover. Matchmark the flexplate and torque converter for installation purposes. Remove the torque converter-to-flexplate bolts.
21. Disconnect and plug the transaxle oil cooler lines.
22. Remove the transaxle-to-engine support bracket and install the transaxle removal jack.
23. Remove the remaining transaxle-to-engine attaching bolts and the transaxle from the vehicle.

**To install:**
24. Securely mount the transaxle on the jack.
25. Apply a small amount of grease on the torque converter hub and seat in the oil pump.
26. Position the transaxle in the vehicle and install the lower engine to transaxle bolts.
27. Install the transaxle to engine support bracket. Once the transaxle is securely held in place, remove the jack. Connect the cooler lines.
28. Install the torque converter bolts and tighten to specification.
29. Install the torque converter cover.
30. Install the left frame support assembly.
31. Install the left stabilizer shaft frame busing nuts and link pin bolt.
32. Install the transaxle mounting strut.
33. Install the halfshafts. Install the ball joints.
34. Install the shift linkage bracket to the transaxle.
35. Install the wheels and lower the vehicle.
36. Install the upper transaxle to engine bolts.
37. Install the left side transaxle mount.
38. Connect the shift linkage to the transaxle.
39. Connect the wiring connectors to their switches on the transaxle.
40. Remove the ¼ × 2 in. bolt that was placed in the hole at the front right motor mount to maintain driveline alignment. Remove an engine support tool.
41. Replace the O-ring, lubricate it and install the dipstick tube and dipstick.
42. Install the TV cable and rubber vent tube.
43. Install the air cleaner assembly and air tubes.
44. Connect the heater hoses, if disconnected.
45. Fill all fluids to their proper levels. Adjust cables as required.
46. Connect the negative battery cable and check the transaxle for proper operation and leaks.

# Suspension and Steering

## 8

## WHEELS

### Front and Rear Wheels
#### REMOVAL AND INSTALLATION

1. Remove the wheel cover.
2. Loosen, but do not remove the lug nut.
3. Raise and safely support the vehicle so the tire is clear of the ground.
4. Remove the lug nuts.
5. Remove the wheel.

**To install:**

6. Install the wheel.
7. Install the lug nuts and tighten in a star pattern.
8. Lower the vehicle.
9. Tighten the lug nuts in a star pattern to 100 ft. lbs. (140 Nm).
10. Install the wheel cover.

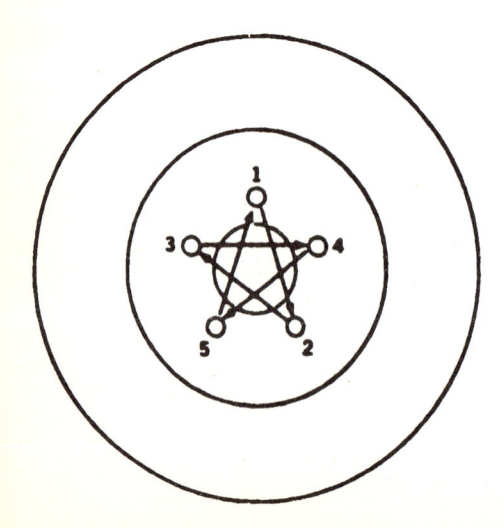

Five hole lug nut tightening sequence

#### INSPECTION

1. Inspect the wheels for dents, excess corrosion and build-up of dried mud, especially on the inside surface of the wheel.
2. Inspect the tires for uneven wear, tread separation and cracks in the sidewalls due to dry rotting or curb damage.
3. Inspect the tire valve for leaking and proper sealing in the wheel assembly.
4. Take corrective action or replace as necessary.

### Wheel Lug Studs
#### REPLACEMENT
**Front Wheels**

1. Remove the tire and wheel assembly.
2. Remove the wheel stud using a wheel stud removal tool.

**To install:**

5. Insert the new stud from the rear of the hub.
6. Install 4 flat washers onto the stud.
7. Install the wheel nut with the flat side toward the washers.
8. Tighten the nut until the stud head is properly seated in the hub flange.
9. Remove the nut and washers.
10. Install the tire and wheel assembly.

**Rear Wheels**

1. Remove the tire and wheel assembly.
2. Remove the brake drum.
3. Remove the wheel stud using a wheel stud removal tool.

**To install:**

4. Insert the new stud from the rear of the hub.
5. Install 4 flat washers onto the stud.
6. Install the wheel nut with the flat side toward the washers.
7. Tighten the nut until the stud head is properly seated in the hub flange.

## SUSPENSION AND STEERING    221

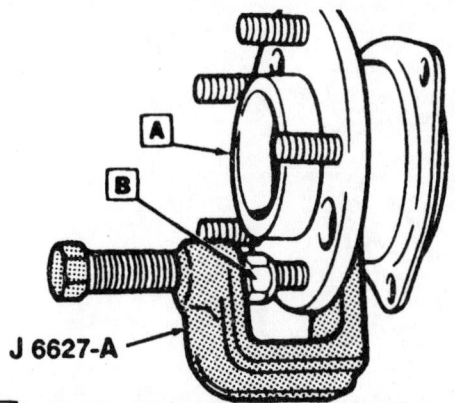

**A** HUB AND BEARING ASSEMBLY REMOVED FROM VEHICLE

**B** WHEEL NUT INSTALLED ON WHEEL STUD

Removing the wheel stud

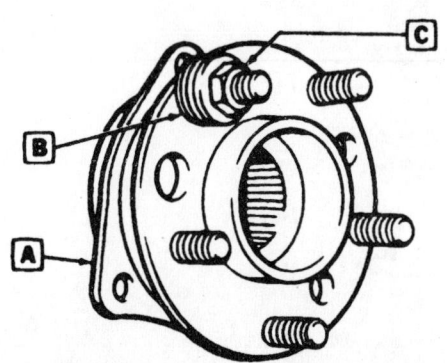

**A** HUB AND BEARING ASSEMBLY REMOVED FROM VEHICLE

**B** INSERT WASHERS OVER WHEEL STUD

**C** TIGHTEN NUT TO DRAW WHEEL STUD INTO CORRECT POSITION

Install the wheel stud

8. Remove the nut and washers.
9. Install the brake drum.
10. Install the tire and wheel assembly.

## FRONT SUSPENSION

The front suspension on all N-Body models is a MacPherson strut design. This combination strut and shock absorber adapts to front wheel drive. The lower control arm pivots from the engine cradle, which has isolation mounts to the body and conventional rubber bushings for the lower control arm pivots. The upper end of the strut is isolated by a rubber mount which contains a nonserviceable bearing for wheel turning.

The lower end of the wheel steering knuckle pivots on a ball stud for wheel turning. The ball stud is retained in the lower control arm and the steering knuckle clamps to the stud portion.

All front suspension fasteners are an important attaching part in that it could affect the performance of vital parts and systems and/or could result in major repair expense. They must be replaced with one of the same part number or with an equivalent part if replacement becomes necessary. Do not use a replacement part of lesser quality or substitute design. Never attempt to heat, quench or straighten any front suspension part. If bent or damaged, the part should be replaced.

### MacPherson Strut

#### REMOVAL AND INSTALLATION

NOTE: *Before removing front suspension components, their positions should be marked so they may assembled correctly. Scribe the knuckle along the lower outboard strut radius (A), the strut flange on the inboard side along the curve of the knuckle (B) and make a chisel mark across the strut/knuckle interface (C). When reassembling, carefully match the marks to the components.*

1. Remove the three nuts attaching the top of the strut assembly to the body.
2. Raise the car and support it safely.
3. Place jackstands under the frame.
4. Lower the car slightly so that the weight rests on the jackstands and not on the control arms.
5. Remove the front tire.

CAUTION: *Whenever working near the drive axles, take care to prevent the inner Tri-Pot joints from being overextended. Overextension of the joint could result in separation of internal components which could go undetected and result in failure of the joint.*

6. Some vehicles may use a silicone (gray) boot on the inboard axle joint. Use boot protector J-33162 or equivalent on these boots. All other boots are made from a thermoplastic ma-

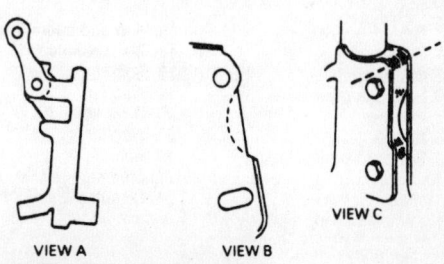

VIEW A    VIEW B    VIEW C

Scribing the strut and knuckle

Scribing the strut and knuckle

## 222 SUSPENSION AND STEERING

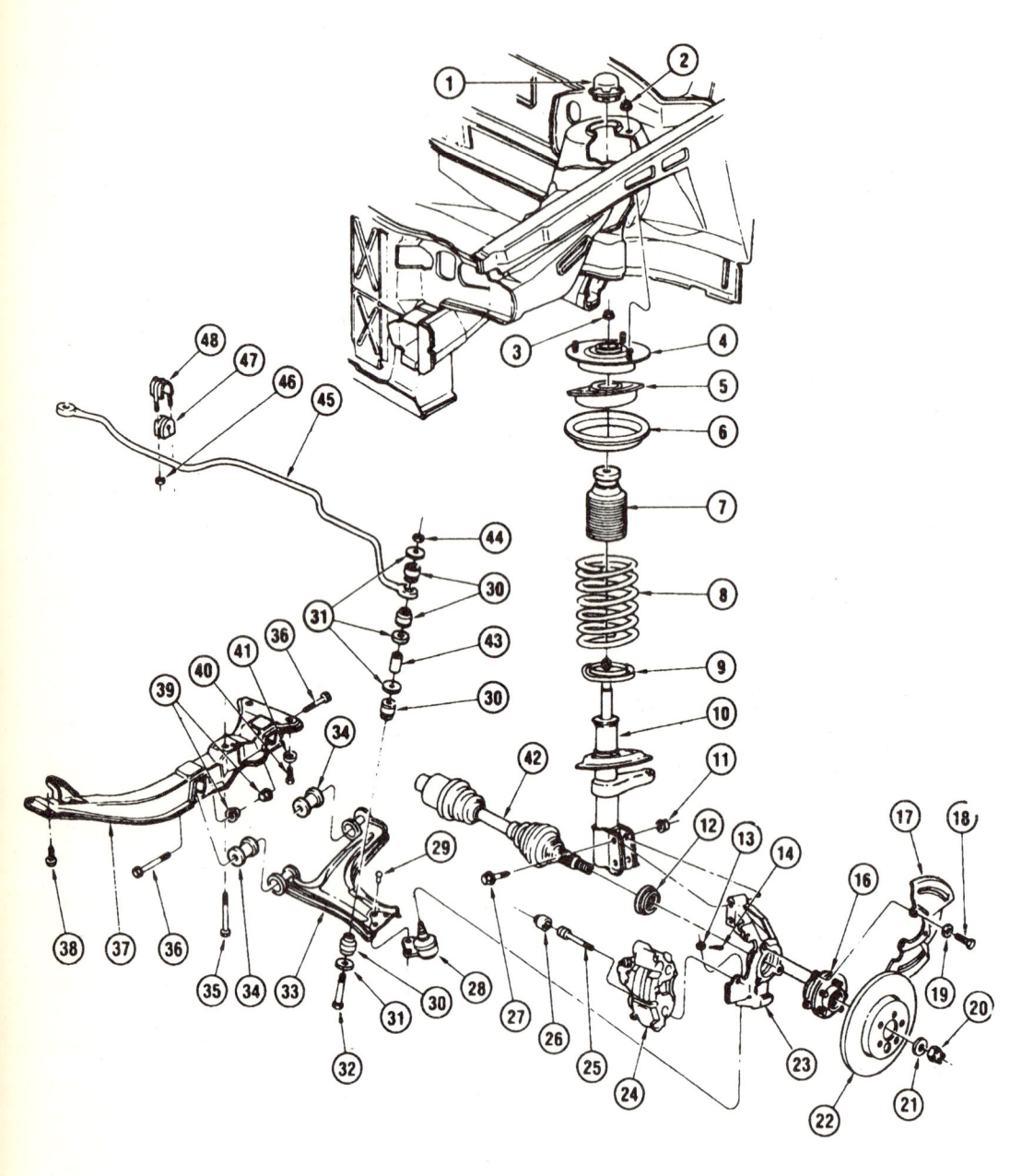

1. Strut mount cover
2. Nut
3. Nut
4. Strut mount
5. Spring seat
6. Spring upper insulator
7. Bumper
8. Spring
9. Spring lower insulator
10. Strut
11. Nut
12. Wheel bearing seal
13. Nut
14. Pin
16. Hub and bearing assembly
17. Disc brake splash shield
18. Bolt
19. Washer
20. Drive shaft nut
21. Washer
22. Rotor
23. Steering knuckle
24. Disc brake caliper
25. Bolt
26. Cover
27. Bolt
28. Lower ball joint
29. Rivet
30. Insulator
31. Washer
32. Bolt
33. Lower control arm
34. Bushing
35. Bolt
36. Bolt
37. Support
38. Bolt
39. Nut
40. Bolt
41. Washer
42. Drive shaft
43. Spacer
44. Nut
45. Stabilizer shaft
46. Nut
47. Insulator
48. Clamp

**Front suspension assembly**

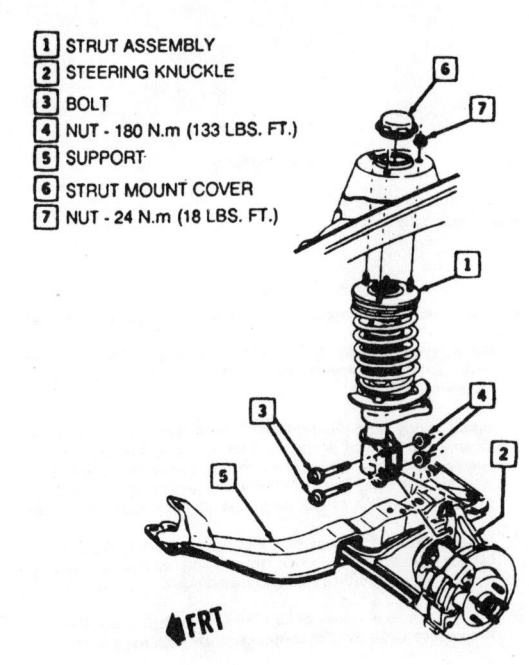

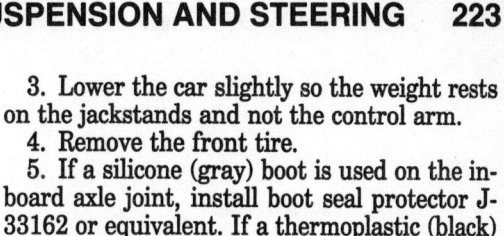

# SUSPENSION AND STEERING 223

1. STRUT ASSEMBLY
2. STEERING KNUCKLE
3. BOLT
4. NUT - 180 N.m (133 LBS. FT.)
5. SUPPORT
6. STRUT MOUNT COVER
7. NUT - 24 N.m (18 LBS. FT.)

**Strut assembly mounting**

terial (black) and do not require the use of a boot seal protector.

7. Disconnect the brake line bracket from the strut assembly.
8. Remove the strut to steering knuckle bolts.
9. Remove the strut assembly from the vehicle. Care should be taken to avoid chipping or cracking the spring coating when handling the front suspension coil spring assembly.
10. Installation is the reverse of removal.

## Lower Ball Joint

### INSPECTION

1. Raise and safely support the vehicle on jackstands. Allow the suspension to hang freely.
2. Grasp the tire at the top and bottom and move the top of the tire in and out.
3. Observe for any horizontal movement of the steering knuckle relative to the front lower control arm. If any movement is detected, replace the ball joint.
4. If the ball stud is disconnected from the steering knuckle and any looseness is detected, or if the ball stud can be twisted in its socket using finger pressure, replace the ball joint.

### REMOVAL AND INSTALLATION

1. Raise and safely support the vehicle.
2. Place jackstands under the frame.

3. Lower the car slightly so the weight rests on the jackstands and not the control arm.
4. Remove the front tire.
5. If a silicone (gray) boot is used on the inboard axle joint, install boot seal protector J-33162 or equivalent. If a thermoplastic (black) boot is used, no protector is necessary.
6. Remove the cotter pin from the ball joint castellated nut.
7. Remove the castellated nut and disconnect the ball joint from the steering knuckle using ball joint separator J-34505 or equivalent.
8. Drill out the three rivets retaining the ball joint.
NOTE: *Be careful not to damage the drive axle boot when drilling out the ball joint rivets.*
9. Loosen the stabilizer shaft bushing assembly nut.
10. Remove the ball joint from the control arm.
**To install:**
12. Install the ball joint to the control arm.
13. Tighten the stabilizer shaft bushing assembly nut to 15 ft. lbs. (20 Nm).
14. Install the 3 ball joint attaching bolts and tighten to 50 ft. lbs. (68 Nm).
15. Connect the ball joint to the steering knuckle. Install the castellated nut and tighten to 41–50 ft. lbs. (55–65 Nm).
16. Install the cotter pin to the ball joint castellated nut.
17. If installed, remove the boot protector.
18. Install the front tire.
19. Raise the vehicle and remove the jackstands.
20. Lower the vehicle.
NOTE: *The front end alignment should be checked and adjusted whenever the strut assemblies are removed.*

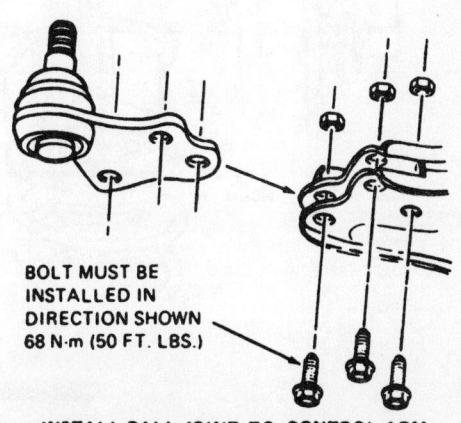

BOLT MUST BE
INSTALLED IN
DIRECTION SHOWN
68 N·m (50 FT. LBS.)

**INSTALL BALL JOINT TO CONTROL ARM**

**Removing ball joint assembly**

# 224 SUSPENSION AND STEERING

## DISASSEMBLY

NOTICE: Care should be taken to avoid chipping or cracking the spring coating when handling the front suspension coil spring.

1. Mount Strut Compressor J-34013 in Holding Fixture J-3289-20.
2. Mount strut into Strut Compressor. Notice that Strut Compressor has strut mounting holes drilled for specific car lines.
3. Compress strut approx. ½ its height after initial contact with top cap. NEVER BOTTOM SPRING OR DAMPENER ROD.
4. Remove the nut from the strut dampener shaft and place the J-34013-27 Guiding Rod on top of the dampener shaft. Use this rod to guide the dampener shaft straight down through the bearing cap while decompressing the spring. Remove components.
5. Perform services as required.

## ASSEMBLY

1. Install bearing cap into Strut Compressor if previously removed.
2. Mount strut into Strut Compressor using bottom locking pin only. Extend dampener shaft and install clamp J-34013-20 on dampener shaft.
3. Install spring over dampener and swing assembly up so upper locking pin can be installed. Install upper insulator, shield, bumper, and upper spring seat. Be sure flat on upper spring seat is facing in proper direction. The spring seat flat should be facing the same direction as the centerline of strut assembly spindle.
4. Install Guiding Rod and turn forcing screw while Guiding Rod centers the assembly. When threads on dampener shaft are visible, remove Guiding Rod and install nut.
5. Tighten nut to a torque of 85 N·m (65 lbs. ft.). Use a crowsfoot line wrench while holding dampener shaft with socket.
6. Remove clamp.

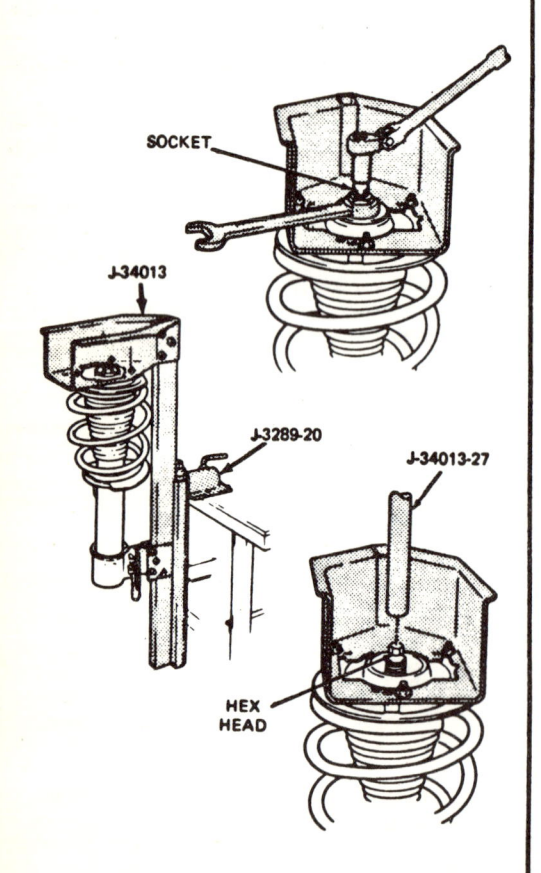

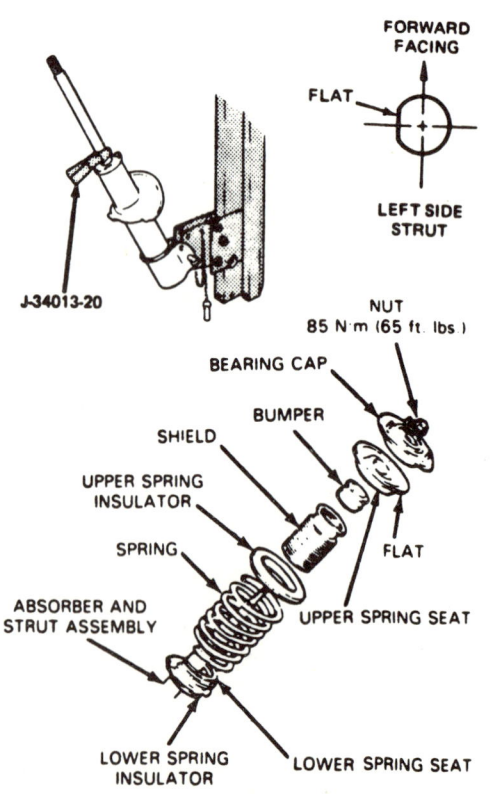

**Strut assembly overhaul**

# SUSPENSION AND STEERING 225

## Stabilizer Shaft and Bushings
### REMOVAL AND INSTALLATION

1. Raise and safely support the vehicle with jackstands, allowing the front suspension to hang freely.
2. Remove the front tire.
3. Disconnect the stabilizer shaft from the control arms.
4. Disconnect the stabilizer shaft from the suspension support assemblies.
5. Loosen the front bolts and remove the rear and center bolts from the support assemblies to lower them enough to remove the stabilizer shaft.
6. Remove the stabilizer shaft and bushings.

**To install:**

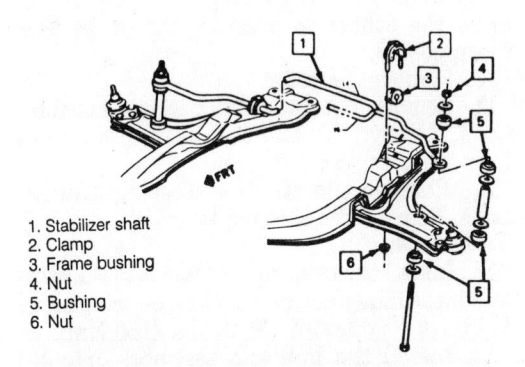

7. Install the stabilizer shaft with bushings and insulators.
8. Raise the front suspension assemblies and install the center and rear bolts. Loosely assembly all components while ensuring that the stabilizer shaft is centered side-to-side.
9. Install the shaft to front suspension support assemblies and loosely install the insulators and clamps.
10. Install the stabilizer shaft to control arms and loosely install the bolts.
11. Tighten the suspension support bolts as follows and in sequence:
- First—center bolts to 66 ft. lbs. (90 Nm)
- Second—front bolts to 65 ft. lbs. (88 Nm)
- Third—rear bolts to 65 ft. lbs. (88 Nm)
- Stabilizer shaft to support assembly nuts to 16 ft. lbs. (22 Nm)
- Stabilizer shaft to control arm nuts to 13 ft. lbs. (17 Nm).

12. Install the wheels.
13. Lower the vehicle.

## Lower Control Arm
### REMOVAL AND INSTALLATION

1. Raise and safely support the vehicle on jackstands. Place the jackstands under the frame so that the suspension hangs freely.
2. Remove the tire.
3. Disconnect the stabilizer shaft from the control arm and/or support assembly.
4. Disconnect the ball joint from the steering

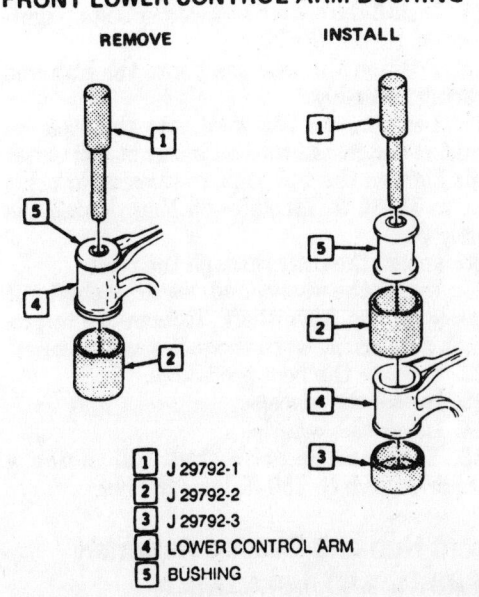

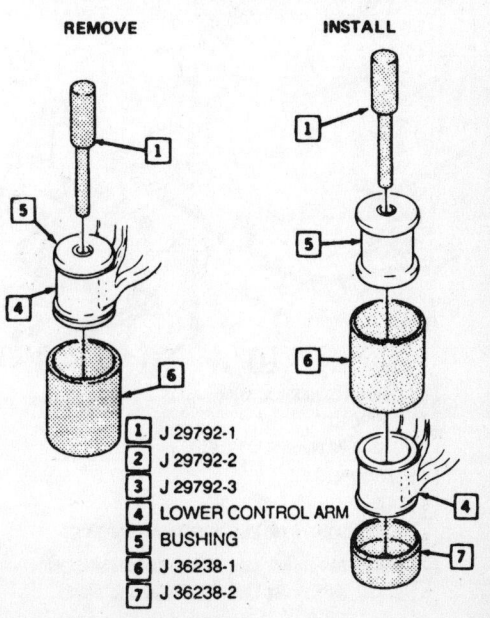

1. Stabilizer shaft
2. Clamp
3. Frame bushing
4. Nut
5. Bushing
6. Nut

**Stabilizer shaft mounting**

**FRONT LOWER CONTROL ARM BUSHING**

REMOVE    INSTALL

1. J 29792-1
2. J 29792-2
3. J 29792-3
4. LOWER CONTROL ARM
5. BUSHING

**REAR LOWER CONTROL ARM BUSHING**

REMOVE    INSTALL

1. J 29792-1
2. J 29792-2
3. J 29792-3
4. LOWER CONTROL ARM
5. BUSHING
6. J 36238-1
7. J 36238-2

**Control arm and suspension support assembly**

# SUSPENSION AND STEERING

knuckle using separator tool J-29330 or equivalent. See "Ball Joint Removal."

5. To remove the support assembly with the control arm attached, remove the bolts mounting the support assembly to the car. To remove the control arm only, remove the control arm to support assembly bolts.

6. Installation is the reverse of the removal procedure. Tighten the ball joint castellated nut to 45 ft.lbs. (60 Nm).

7. If the support assembly was removed, tighten the rear bolts first to 65 ft.lbs. (88 Nm); the center bolts second to 66 ft.lb. (90 Nm); and the front bolts last to 65 ft.lb. (88 Nm). Tighten the control arm pivot bolts to 60 ft.lb. (85 Nm) with the weight of the car on the control arm.

## CONTROL ARM BUSHING REPLACEMENT

1. Remove the lower control arm.
2. Install bushing removal tool.
3. Coat the threads of the tool with extreme pressure lubricant.
4. Remove the lower control arm bushings.

**To install:**

5. Install the bushing installation tools.
6. Coat the outer case of the bushing with a light coating of a suitable lubricant.
7. Install the lower control arm bushings.
8. Install the lower control arm.

## Steering Knuckle

### REMOVAL AND INSTALLATION

1. Raise and safely support the vehicle.
2. Remove the front wheels.

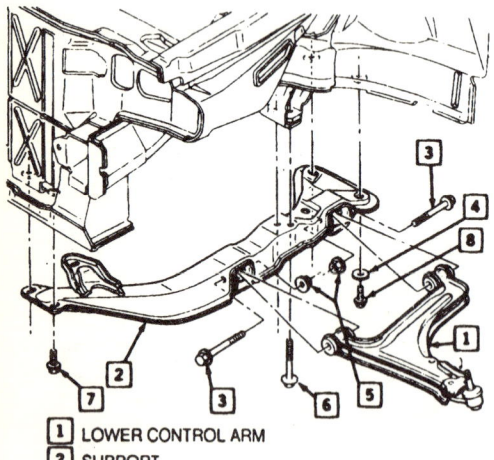

[1] LOWER CONTROL ARM
[2] SUPPORT
[3] BOLT - 83 N.m (61 LBS. FT.)
[4] WASHER
[5] NUT
[6] BOLT - 90 N.m (66 LBS. FT.) TIGHTEN FIRST
[7] BOLT - 88 N.m (65 LBS. FT.) TIGHTEN SECOND
[8] BOLT - 88 N.m (65 LBS. FT.) TIGHTEN THIRD

**Removal and installation of control arm bushings**

NOTE: *When drive axles are disconnected, care must be taken to avoid over-extending Tri-pot joints which could result in separation of internal joint components and possible joint failure. Also, the use of CV-joint boot protectors is recommended.*

3. Install outer boot protector.
4. Insert a drift punch through the rotor cooling vanes to lock the rotor in place and remove the hub nut. Clean the drive axle threads of all dirt and grease.
5. Remove the drive shaft nut and washer.
6. Disengage the axle from the hub and bearing.
7. Disconnect the ball joint from the steering knuckle.
8. Move the axle shaft inward.
9. Remove the caliper bolts and caliper. Support the caliper using a length of wire. Do not allow the caliper to hang by the brake hose unsupported.
10. Remove the rotor.
11. Remove the hub and bearing assembly bolts. Remove the hub and bearing assembly from the knuckle.
12. Remove the strut-to-steering knuckle bolts. Remove the steering knuckle.

**To install:**

13. Install the steering knuckle into the strut and install the steering knuckle-to-strut assembly bolts. Tighten to 133 ft. lbs. (180 Nm).
14. Install the hub and assembly onto the knuckle and install the hub and bearing assembly bolts. Tighten to 70 ft. lbs. (95 Nm).
15. Install a new hub and bearing seal.
16. Install the rotor.
17. Install the caliper and caliper bolts. Tighten to 38 ft. lbs. (51 Nm).
18. Position the axle shaft into the hub and bearing assembly.
19. Position the ball joint into the steering knuckle and install the ball joint nut and cotter pin. Tighten the ball joint-to-steering knuckle nut to 41–50 ft. lbs. (55–65 Nm). Install the cotter pin.
20. Insert the drift through the rotor.
21. Install the washer and new drive shaft nut loosely on the drive shaft. Tighten the nut as much as possible until the axle starts to turn.
22. Remove the boot protectors.
23. Install the wheels.
24. Lower the vehicle.
25. Tighten the drive shaft nut, using a torque wrench to 180 ft. lbs. (260 Nm).

## Front Hub and Bearing Assembly

### REMOVAL AND INSTALLATION

NOTE: *This procedure requires the use of a number of special tools.*

## SUSPENSION AND STEERING 227

1. Raise and safely support the vehicle with jackstands. Place the jackstands under the frame so that the front suspension hangs freely.
2. Remove the front tire.
3. If a silicone (gray) boot is used on the inboard axle joint, place boot seal protector J-33162 or equivalent. If a thermoplastic (black) boot is used, no seal protector is necessary.
4. Insert a drift punch through the rotor cooling vanes to lock the rotor in place and remove the hub nut. Clean the drive axle threads of all dirt and grease.
5. Remove the brake caliper mounting bolts and remove the caliper from the spindle assembly. Support the caliper with string or wire. Do not allow it to hang by the brake hose.
6. Remove the brake rotor.
7. Attach tool J-28733 or equivalent and separate the hub and drive axle.
8. Remove the three hub and bearing retaining bolts, shield, hub and bearing assembly and O-ring.

NOTE: *The hub and bearing are replaced as an assembly*

9. Using a punch, tap the seal toward the engine. When the seal is removed from the steering knuckle, cut it off the drive axle using wire cutters. The factory seal is installed from the engine side of the steering knuckle, but the service replacement is installed from the wheel side of the steering knuckle.
10. Install the new hub and bearing seal in the steering knuckle using a suitable hub seal installer tool.
11. The remainder of the installation is in reverse order of removal. Lubricate the hub and bearing seal with grease and install a new O-ring around the hub and bearing assembly. Tighten the hub and bearing bolts to 70 ft.lbs. (95 Nm). Tighten the hub nut to 180 ft.lb. (260 Nm).

## Front End Alignment

Front alignment refers to the angular relationship between the front wheels, the front suspension attaching parts and the ground. Camber is the tilting of the front wheels from the vertical when viewed from the front of the car. When the wheels tilt outward at the top, the camber is said to be positive (+); when the wheels tilt inward at the top, the camber is said

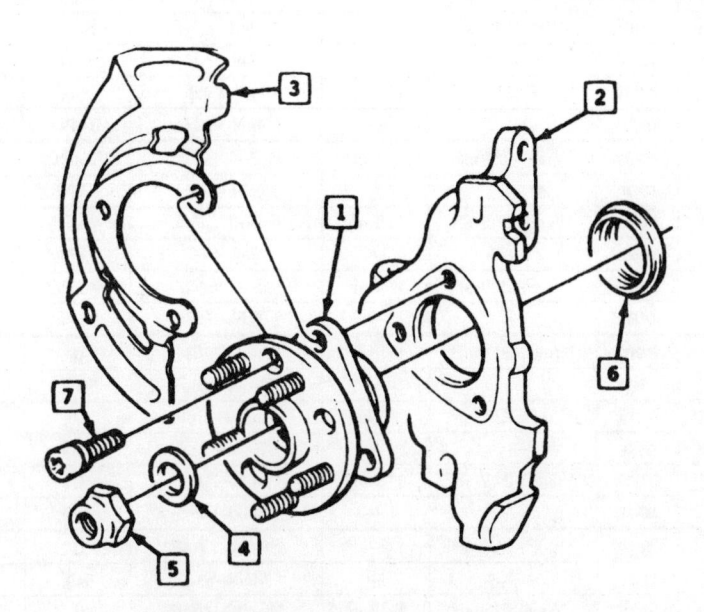

| 1 | HUB AND BEARING ASSEMBLY |
| 2 | STEERING KNUCKLE |
| 3 | SHIELD |
| 4 | WASHER |
| 5 | DRIVE SHAFT NUT |
| 6 | WHEEL BEARING SEAL |
| 7 | HUB AND BEARING RETAINING BOLT |

**Hub and bearing assembly replacement**

## 228 SUSPENSION AND STEERING

## WHEEL ALIGNMENT

| Year | Model | | Caster Range (deg.) | Caster Preferred Setting (deg.) | Camber Range (deg.) | Camber Preferred Setting (deg.) | Toe-in (in.) | Steering Axis Inclination (deg.) |
|---|---|---|---|---|---|---|---|---|
| 1985 | Somerset | | 1P–3P | 2P | 1/2N–1/2P | 0 | 0 | NA |
| | Calais | | 11/16P–2 11/16P | 1 11/16P | 7/32N–1 13/32P | 13/16P | 1/16N | 13 1/2 |
| | Grand Am | | 11/16P–2 11/16P | 1 11/16P | 7/32N–1 13/32P | 13/16P | 1/16N | 13 1/2 |
| 1986 | Somerset | | 23/34P–2 23/32P | 1 23/32P | 1/4P–1 7/16P | 27/32P | 0 | 13 1/2 |
| | Calais | | 11/16P–2 11/16P | 1 11/16P | 7/32N–1 13/32P | 13/16P | 1/16N | 13 1/2 |
| | Grand Am | | 11/16P–2 11/16P | 1 11/16P | 7/32N–1 13/32P | 13/16P | 1/16N | 13 1/2 |
| 1987 | Skylark | | 23/34P–2 23/32P | 1 23/32P | 1/4P–1 7/16P | 27/32P | 0 | 13 1/2 |
| | Somerset | | 23/34P–2 23/32P | 1 23/32P | 1/4P–1 7/16P | 27/32P | 0 | 13 1/2 |
| | Calais | | 11/16P–2 11/16P | 1 11/16P | 7/32N–1 13/32P | 13/16P | 1/16N | 13 1/2 |
| | Grand Am | | 11/16P–2 11/16P | 1 11/16P | 7/32N–1 13/32P | 13/16P | 1/16N | 13 1/2 |
| 1988 | Skylark | | 13/16N–4 3/16P | 1 11/16P | 3/16N–1 13/16P | 13/16 | 0 | 13 1/2 |
| | Calais | | 13/16N–4 3/16P | 1 11/16P | 3/16N–1 13/16P | 13/16 | 0 | 13 1/2 |
| | Grand Am | | 13/16N–4 3/16P | 1 11/16P | 3/16N–1 13/16P | 13/16 | 0 | 13 1/2 |
| 1989 | Calais | front | 11/16P–2 11/16P | 1 11/16P | 1/8P–1 1/2P ② | 13/16P ① | 0 | 13 1/2 |
| | | rear | — | — | 3/4N–1/4P | 1/4N | 1/4 | — |
| | Grand Am | front | 11/16P–2 11/16P | 1 11/16P | 1/8P–1 1/2P ② | 13/16P ① | 0 | 13 1/2 |
| | | rear | — | — | 3/4N–1/4P | 1/4N | 1/4 | — |
| | Skylark | front | 11/16P–2 11/16P | 1 11/16P | 1/8P–1 1/2P | 13/16P | 0 | 13 1/2 |
| | | rear | — | — | 3/4N–1/4P | 1/4N | 1/4 | — |
| 1990 | Calais | front | 11/16P–2 11/16P | 1 11/16P | 1/8P–1 1/2P ② | 13/16P ① | 0 | 13 1/2 |
| | | rear | — | — | 3/4N–1/4P | 1/4N | 1/4 | — |
| | Grand Am | front | 11/16P–2 11/16P | 1 11/16P | 1/8P–1 1/2P ② | 13/16P ① | 0 | 13 1/2 |
| | | rear | — | — | 3/4N–1/4P | 1/4N | 1/4 | — |
| | Skylark | front | 11/16P–2 11/16P | 1 11/16P | 1/8P–1 1/2P ② | 13/16P ① | 0 | 13 1/2 |
| | | rear | — | — | 3/4N–1/4P | 1/4N | 1/4 | — |
| 1991 | Calais | front | 11/16P–2 11/16P | 1 11/16P | 11/16N–1 1/16P | 0 | 0 | 13 1/2 |
| | | rear | — | — | 13/16N–5/16P | 1/4N | 1/8 | — |
| | Grand Am | front | 11/16P–2 11/16P | 1 11/16P | 1/16N–1 1/16P | 0 | 0 | 13 1/2 |
| | | rear | — | — | 13/16N–5/16P | 1/4N | 1/8 | — |
| | Skylark | front | 11/16P–2 11/16P | 1 11/16P | 11/16N–1 1/16P | 0 | 0 | 13 1/2 |
| | | rear | — | — | 3/4N–1/4P | 1/4N | 1/8 | — |
| 1992 | Achieva | front | 11/16P–2 11/16P | 1 11/16P | 11/16N–1 1/16P | 0 | 0 | — |
| | | rear | — | — | 13/16N–5/16P | 1/4N | 1/8 | — |
| | Grand Am | front | 11/16P–2 11/16P | 1 11/16P | 11/16N–1 1/16P | 0 | 0 | — |
| | | rear | — | — | 13/16N–5/16P | 1/4N | 1/8 | — |
| | Skylark | front | 11/16P–2 11/16P | 1 11/16P | 11/16N–1 1/16P | 0 | 0 | 13 1/2 |
| | | rear | — | — | 3/4N–1/2P | 1/4N | 1/8 | — |

N—Negative
P—Positive
① with 16 in. wheels: 0
② with 16 in. wheels: 11/16N–11/16P

## SUSPENSION AND STEERING

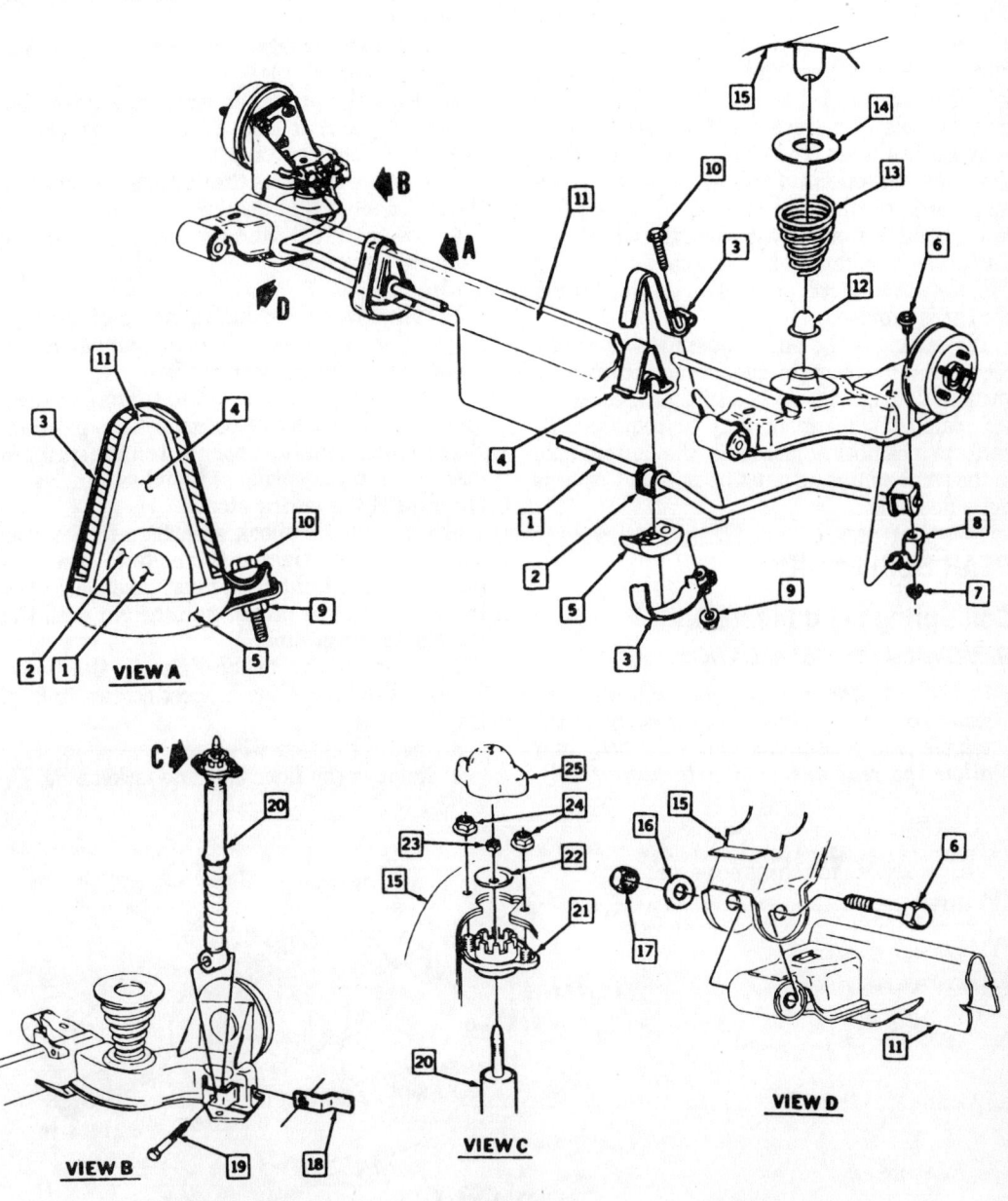

1. Stabilizer shaft
2. Stabilizer shaft insulator
3. Stabilizer shaft clamp
4. Upper spacer
5. Lower spacer
6. Bolt
7. Nut
8. Stabilizer shaft clamp
9. Nut
10. 
11. Axle
12. Axle bumper
13. Spring
14. Spring upper insulator
15. Underbody
16. Washer
17. Nut
18. Shock absorber nut
19. Bolt
20. Shock absorber
21. Shock absorber upper mount
22. Retainer
23. Nut
24. Nut
25. Shock absorber upper cover

**Rear axle assembly**

## 230  SUSPENSION AND STEERING

to be negative (–). The amount of tilt is measured in degrees from the vertical and this measurement is called camber angle.

Toe-in is the turning in of the front wheels. The actual amount of toe-in is normally only a fraction of one degree. The purpose of the toe-in specification is to insure parallel rolling of the front wheels. Excessive toe-in or toe-out may increase tire wear. Toe-in also serves to offset the small deflections of the wheel support system which occur when the car is rolling forward. In other words, even when the wheels are set to toe-in slightly when the car is standing still, they tend to roll parallel on the road when the car is moving.

Toe setting is the only adjustment normally required. However, in special circumstances such as damage due to road hazard, collision, etc., camber adjustment may be required. To perform a camber adjustment, the bottom hole in the strut mounting must be slotted. Caster is not adjustable.

## REAR SUSPENSION

### Coil Springs and Insulators

#### REMOVAL AND INSTALLATION

CAUTION: *The coil springs are under tension. To avoid personal injury, support the vehicle with jackstands under the body and allow the rear suspension to hang freely.*

*Then, support the rear axle assembly with a floor jack. When the axle bolts have been removed, lower the jack to relax the spring tension*

1. Raise and safely support the vehicle. Remove the rear wheels.
2. Using the proper equipment, support the weight of the rear axle. Disconnect the brake lines from the rear axle.
3. Remove the bolts that attach the shock to the lower mounting bracket.
4. Lower the axle and remove the coil spring from the vehicle.

**To install:**

NOTE: *Prior to installing the coil springs, install the insulators in their seats using an adhesive to hold them in place.*

5. Install the springs and insulators in their seats and raise the axle assembly into position. Ensure the end of the upper coil on the spring is positioned in the spring seat and within $9/16$ in. (15 mm) of the spring stop.
6. Connect the shock absorbers to the rear axle, but do not tighten the bolts to specification. The final tightening must take place with the vehicle at the proper trim height with the wheels on the ground.
7. Connect the brake lines to the body. Tighten the brake line bracket screws to 8 ft. lbs. (11 Nm).
8. Install the rear wheels.
9. Remove the floor jack and jackstands.

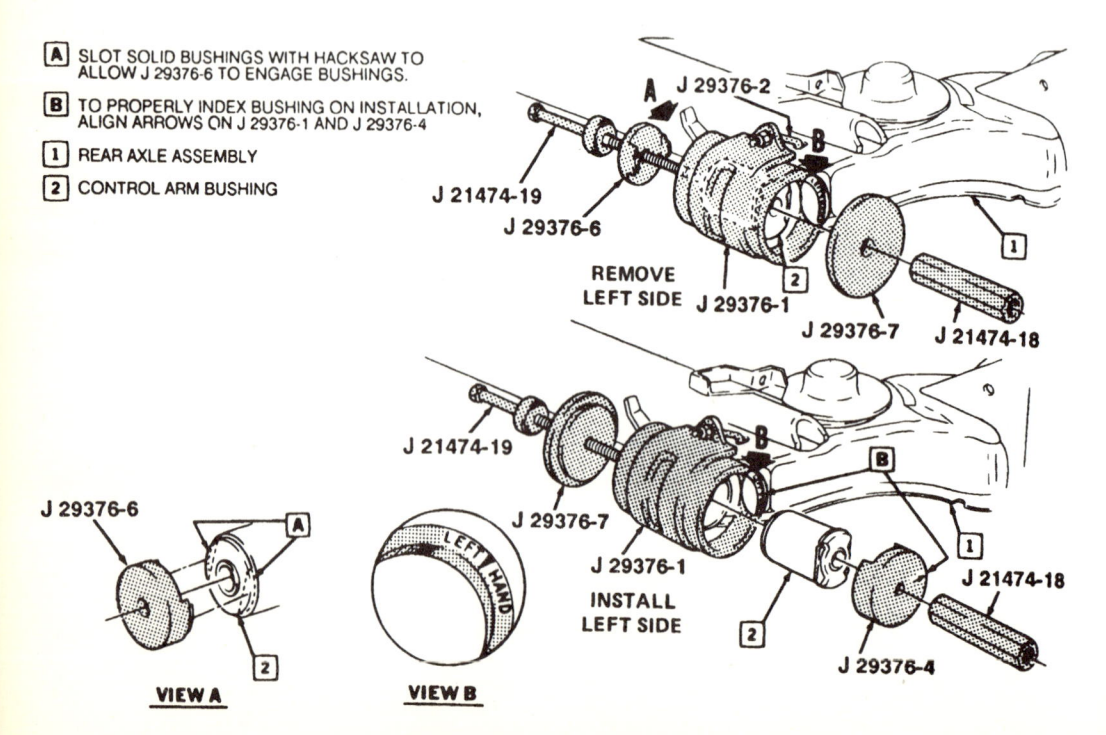

[A] SLOT SOLID BUSHINGS WITH HACKSAW TO ALLOW J 29376-6 TO ENGAGE BUSHINGS.
[B] TO PROPERLY INDEX BUSHING ON INSTALLATION, ALIGN ARROWS ON J 29376-1 AND J 29376-4
[1] REAR AXLE ASSEMBLY
[2] CONTROL ARM BUSHING

**Control arm bushing replacement**

# SUSPENSION AND STEERING

10. Lower the vehicle.
11. With all 4 wheels on the ground, tighten the rear axle attaching bolts to 35 ft. lbs. (47 Nm)

## Shock Absorber

### REMOVAL AND INSTALLATION

1. Disconnect the negative battery cable.
2. Open the deck lid and remove the trim cover.
3. Remove the upper shock attaching nut. Remove 1 shock at a time if removing both.
4. Raise and safely support the vehicle.
5. Remove the lower mounting bolt.
6. Remove the shock from the vehicle.

**To install:**

7. Connect the shock absorbers at the lower attachment and install the attaching bolt.
8. Lower the vehicle enough to guide the shock absorber upper stud through the body opening and install the upper shock absorber attaching nut loosely. Tighten the lower shock absorber mounting bolt to 35 ft. lbs. (47 Nm).
9. Remove the axle support and lower the vehicle. Tighten the shock absorber upper nut to 21 ft. lbs. (29 Nm).
10. Replace the rear trim cover.

## Control Arm Bushing

### REMOVAL AND INSTALLATION

1. Raise and safely support the vehicle.
2. Remove the rear wheels.
3. Replace 1 bushing at a time. If the right side bushing is being replaced, disconnect the brake lines from the body. If the left busing is being removed, disconnect the brake line bracket from the body and parking brake cable from the hook guide on the body.
4. Remove the nut, bolt and washer from the control arm and bracket attachment and rotate the control arm downward.
5. Remove the bushing by performing the following:
    a. Install tool J-29376-1 receiver on the control arm over the bushing and tighten the attaching nuts until the tool is securely in place.
    b. Install tool J-21474-19 bolt through plate J-29376-7 and install into J-29376-1 receiver.
    c. Place tool J-29376-6 remover into position on the bushing and install nut J-21474-18 onto J-21474-19 bolt.
    d. Remove the bushing from the control arm by turning the bolt.

**To install:**

6. Install the bushing by performing the following:
    a. Install tool J-29376-1 receiver onto the control arm
    b. Install tool J-21474-19 bolt through plate J-29376-7 and install into J-29376-1 receiver.
    c. Install bushing onto bolt and position into housing. Align bushing installer arrow with the arrow onto the receiver for proper indexing of the bushing.
    d. Install nut J-21474-18 onto bolt J-21474-19.
    e. Press the bushing into the control arm by turning the bolt. When the bushing is in proper position, the end flange will be flush against the face of the control arm.
7. Raise the control arm into position and install the bolt, washer and nut. Do not tighten to specification at this time.
8. Connect the brake line bracket to the frame. Tighten to 8 ft. lbs. (11 Nm).
9. If the left side was disconnected, reconnect the brake cables to the bracket and reinstall the brake cable to the hook. Adjust the parking brake cable as necessary.
10. Install the rear wheels.
11. Lower the vehicle.
12. With the vehicle at proper trim height, tighten the control arm bushing bolts to 68 ft. lbs. (93 Nm).

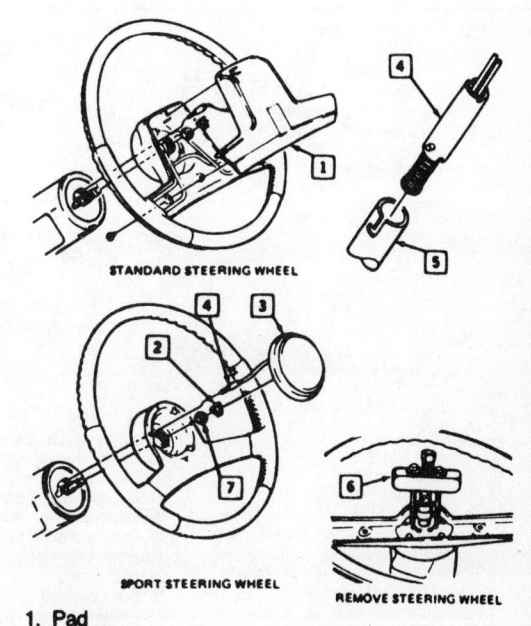

STANDARD STEERING WHEEL

SPORT STEERING WHEEL

REMOVE STEERING WHEEL

1. Pad
2. Retainer
3. Cap
4. Horn lead
5. Cam tower
6. J-1859-03 or BT-61-9
7. Nut—41 N·m (30 ft. lbs.)

Steering wheel mounting

## 232 SUSPENSION AND STEERING

## Stabilizer Bar

### REMOVAL AND INSTALLATION

1. Raise the vehicle and support it safely with jackstands.
2. Remove the nuts and bolts at both the axle and control arm attachments and remove the bracket, insulator and stabilizer bar.

**To install:**
3. Install the U-bolts, upper clamp, spacer and insulator in the trailing axle. Position the stabilizer bar in the insulators and loosely install the lower clamp and nuts.
4. Attach the end of the stabilizer bar to the control arms and torque all nuts to 15 ft.lb. (20 Nm).
5. Tighten the axle attaching nut, then lower the vehicle.

## Rear End Alignment

Rear wheel alignment is not adjustable. If a check of the rear alignment is determined to be out of specification, check for bent or broken rear suspension parts.

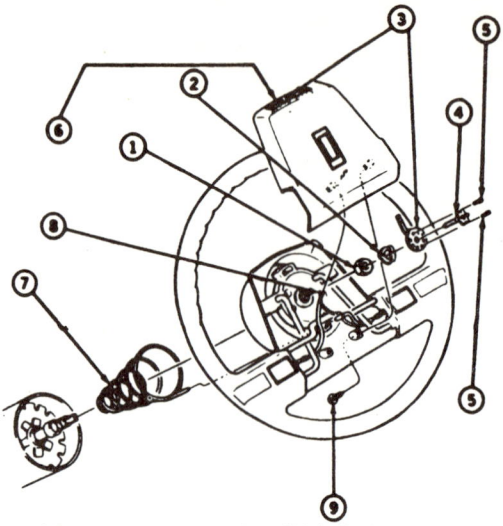

1. Steering wheel nut 41 N·m (30 ft. lbs.)
2. Steering wheel nut retainer
3. Telescoping adjuster lever
4. Steering shaft lock knob bolt
5. Steering shaft lock knob bolt positioning screw (2)
6. Steering wheel pad
7. Horn contact spring
8. Horn lead
9. Fully driven, seated and not stripped

**Tilt-wheel mounting**

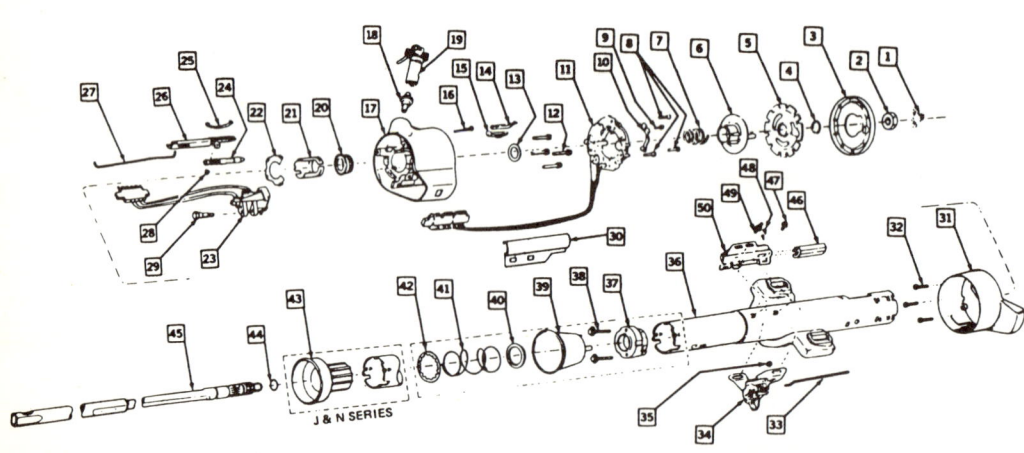

1. Retainer
2. Hexagon jam nut
3. Shaft lock cover
4. Retaining ring
5. Steering shaft lock
6. Turn signal canceling cam assembly
7. Upper bearing spring
8. Binding head cross recess screw
9. Round washer head screw
10. Switch actuator arm assembly
11. Turn signal switch assembly
12. Hex washer head tapping screw
13. Thrust washer
14. Buzzer switch assembly
15. Buzzer switch retaining clip
16. Lock retaining screw
17. Steering column housing
18. Switch actuator sector
19. Steering column lock cylinder set
20. Bearing assembly
21. Bearing retaining bushing
22. Upper bearing retainer
23. Pivot and switch assembly (windshield wiper switch)
24. Lock bolt
25. Rack preload spring
26. Switch actuator rack
27. Switch actuator rod
28. Spring thrust washer
29. Switch actuator pivot pin
30. Wiring protector
31. Floor shift bowl
32. Binding head cross recess screw
33. Dimmer switch actuator rod
34. Dimmer switch assembly
35. Hexagon nut
36. Steering column jacket assembly
37. Adapter and bearing assembly
38. Hex washer head tapping screw
39. Bearing retainer
40. Lower bearing seat
41. Lower bearing spring
42. Lower spring retainer
43. Steering column jacket bushing
44. Retaining ring
45. Steering shaft assembly
46. Ignition switch housing assembly
47. Washer head screw
48. Pan head screw
49. Dimmer and ignition switch mounting stud
50. Ignition switch assembly

**Park lock standard steering column for automatic floor shift shown—others similar**

## SUSPENSION AND STEERING

# STEERING

## Steering Wheel

### REMOVAL AND INSTALLATION

1. Disconnect the negative battery cable.
2. Remove the 2 screws that retain the steering pad.
3. Disconnect the horn lead and remove the horn pad.
4. Remove the retainer, nut and dampener, if equipped.
5. Matchmark the steering wheel to the shaft and remove the steering wheel from the vehicle.
6. The installation is the reverse of the removal procedure. Tighten the attaching nut to 30 ft. lbs. (41 Nm).

## Turn Signal Switch

### REMOVAL AND INSTALLATION

1. Disconnect the negative battery cable.
2. Remove the lower instrument panel sound insulator, trim pad and steering column trim collar.
3. Straighten the steering wheel so the tires are pointing straight ahead.
4. Remove the steering wheel.
5. Remove the plastic wire protector from under the steering column.
6. Disconnect the turn signal switch connector at the bottom of the column.
7. To disassemble the top of the column:
    a. Remove the shaft lock cover.
    b. If equipped with telescope steering, remove the first set of spacers, bumper, second set of spacers and carrier snapring retainer.
    c. Depress the lockplate with the proper depressing tool and remove the retaining ring from its groove.
    d. Remove the tool, ring, lockplate, canceling cam and spring.

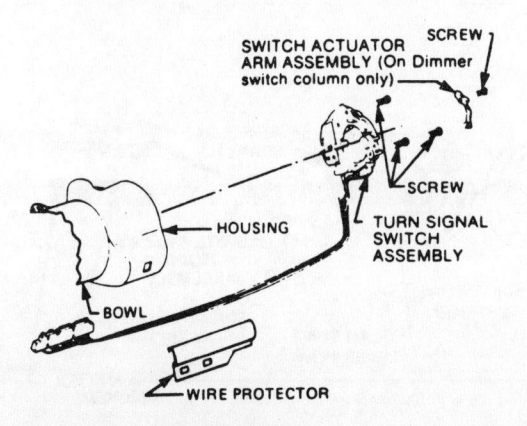

8. Remove the 3 screws, the turn signal switch and actuator lever.

### To install:

9. Install the turn signal switch and lever.
10. To assemble the top end of the column:
    a. Install the spring, canceling cam, lockplate and retaining ring on the steering shaft.
    b. Depress the plate with the depressing tool and install the ring securely in the groove. Remove the tool slowly.
    c. If equipped with telescope steering, install the carrier snapring retainer, lower set of spacers, bumper and upper set of spacers.
    d. Install the shaft lock cover.
11. Connect the turn signal switch connector and install the wire protector.
12. Install the steering wheel.
13. Install the steering column trim collar, lower instrument panel trim pad and sound insulator.
14. Connect the negative battery cable and check the turn signal switch for proper operation.

## Ignition Switch

### REMOVAL AND INSTALLATION

1. Disconnect the negative battery cable.
2. Remove the left instrument panel insulator.
3. Remove the left instrument panel trim pad and the steering column trim collar.
4. Remove the steering column upper support bracket bolts and remove the support bracket.
5. Lower the steering column and support it safely.
6. Disconnect the wiring from the ignition switch.
7. Remove the ignition switch-to-steering column screws. Remove the ignition switch from the steering column.

### To install:

8. Before installing, place the slider in the proper position (switch viewed with the terminals pointing up), according to the steering column and accessories:
    a. Standard column with key release – extreme left detent.
    b. Standard column with PARK/LOCK – 1 detent from extreme left.
    c. All other standard columns – 2 detents from extreme left.
    d. Tilt column with key release – extreme right detent.
    e. Tilt column with PARK/LOCK – 1 detent from extreme right.
    f. All other tilt columns – 2 detents from extreme right.

Turn signal switch installation

## 234 SUSPENSION AND STEERING

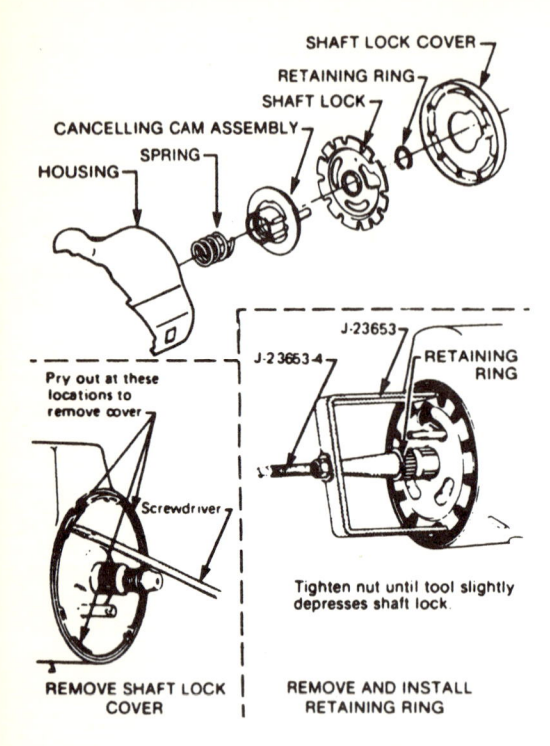

*Lock plate and canceling cam installation*

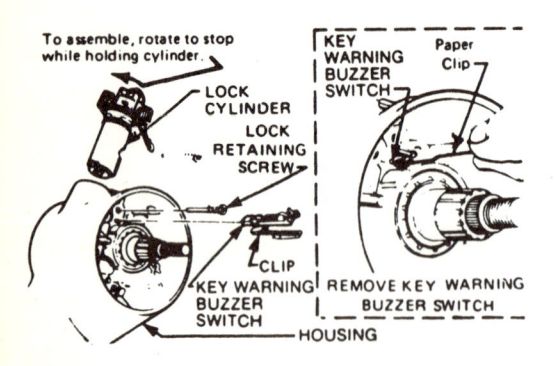

*Ignition lock cylinder installation*

*Ignition switch installation*

9. Install the activating rod into the switch and install the switch to the column. Do not use oversized screws as they could impair the collapsibility of the column.
10. Connect the wiring to the ignition switch. Adjust the switch, as required.
11. Install the steering column.
12. Install the steering column trim collar, instrument panel trim pad and insulator.
13. Connect the negative battery cable and check the ignition switch for proper operation.

### Ignition Lock Cylinder
*REMOVAL AND INSTALLATION*

1. Disconnect the negative battery cable.
2. Remove the lower instrument panel sound insulator, trim pad and steering column trim collar.
3. Straighten the steering wheel so the tires are pointing straight ahead.
4. Remove the steering wheel.
5. Remove the plastic wire protector from under the steering column.
6. Disconnect the turn signal switch.
7. To disassemble the top of the column:
    a. Remove the shaft lock cover.
    b. If equipped with telescope steering, remove the first set of spacers, bumper, second set of spacers and carrier snapring retainer.
    c. Depress the lock plate with the proper depressing tool and remove the retaining ring from its groove.
    d. Remove the tool, retaining ring, lockplate, canceling cam and spring.
8. Remove the 3 screws and pull the turn signal switch out from its mount as far as possible.
9. Place the key in the **RUN** position and use a thin suitable tool to remove the buzzer switch.

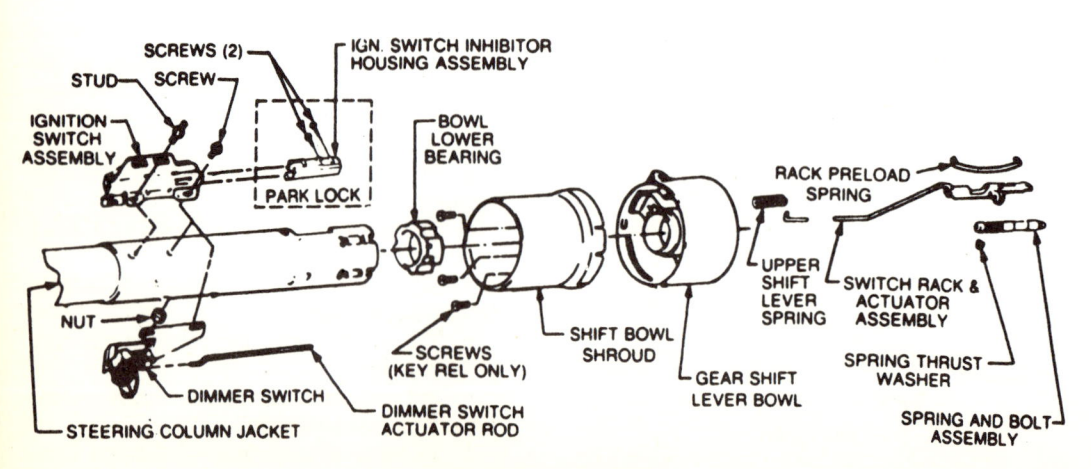

10. Remove the key lock cylinder attaching screw and remove the lock cylinder.

**To install:**

11. Install the key lock cylinder and place in the **RUN** position. Install the buzzer switch and key light.
12. Install the turn signal switch and lever.
13. To assemble the top end of the column:

   a. Install the spring, canceling cam, lock plate and retaining ring on the steering shaft.

   b. Depress the plate with the depressing tool and install the ring securely in the groove. Remove the tool slowly.

   c. If equipped with telescope steering, install the carrier snapring retainer, lower set of spacers, bumper and upper set of spacers.

   d. Install the shaft lock cover.

14. Connect the turn signal switch connector. Install the wire protector.
15. Install the steering wheel.
16. Install the steering column trim collar, lower instrument panel trim pad and sound insulator.
17. Connect the negative battery cable and check the key lock cylinder and turn signal switch for proper operation.

## Steering Column

### REMOVAL AND INSTALLATION

1. Disconnect the negative battery cable.
2. If column repairs are to be made, remove the steering wheel.
3. Remove the steering column-to-intermediate shaft coupling pinch bolt. Remove the safety strap and bolt, if equipped.
4. Remove the steering column trim shrouds and column covers.
5. Disconnect all wiring harness connectors. If equipped with column shift, disconnect the shift indicator cable. Remove the dust boot mounting screws and steering column-to-dash bracket bolts.
6. Lower the column to clear the mounting bracket and carefully remove from the vehicle.

**To install:**

7. Carefully, install the steering column into the vehicle.
8. If equipped with column shift, connect the shift indicator cable.
9. Connect the electrical harness connectors.
10. Install the column bracket bolts.
11. Install the flange and upper steering coupling upper pinch bolt. Tighten the column bracket support bolts to 22 ft. lbs. (30 Nm) and the upper pinch bolt to 30 ft. lbs. (41 Nm).
12. Adjust the shift indicator, if equipped.
13. If removed, install the steering wheel.
14. If removed, install the steering wheel pad.
15. Connect the negative battery cable.

## DISASSEMBLY

### Steering Linkage

#### REMOVAL AND INSTALLATION

**Tie Rod Ends**

*INNER TIE ROD*

1. Disconnect the negative battery cable. Remove the rack and pinion gear from the vehicle.
2. Remove the lock plate from the inner tie rod bolts.
3. If removing both tie rods, remove both bolts, the bolt support plate and 1 of the tie rod assemblies. Reinstall the removed tie rod's bolt to keep inner parts of the rack aligned. Remove the remaining tie rod.
4. If only removing 1 tie rod, slide the assembly out from between the support plate and the center housing cover washer.

**To install:**

5. Install the center housing cover washer fitted into the rack and pinion boot.
6. Install the inner tie rod bolts through the holes in the bolt support plate, inner pivot bushing, center housing cover washer, rack housing and into the threaded holes.
7. Tighten the bolts to 65 ft. lbs. (90 Nm).
8. Install a new lock plate with its notches over the bolt flats.
9. Install the rack and pinion gear.
10. Fill the power steering pump with fluid and bleed the system.
11. Connect the negative battery cable and check the rack for proper operation and leaks.

*OUTER TIE ROD*

1. Disconnect the negative battery cable.
2. Remove the cotter pin and the nut from the tie rod ball stud at the steering knuckle.
3. Loosen the pinch bolts.
4. Using the proper tools, separate the tie rod taper from the steering knuckle.
5. Remove the tie rod from the adjuster.
6. The installation is the reverse of the removal procedure.
7. Perform a front end alignment.

## Power Rack and Pinion Steering Gear

### ADJUSTMANT

*RACK BEARING PRELOAD*

1. Center the steering wheel. Raise and safely support the vehicle.
2. Loosen the locknut and turn the adjuster plug clockwise until it bottoms in the housing. Then back off about ⅛ turn and tighten the locknut while holding the position of the adjuster plug.

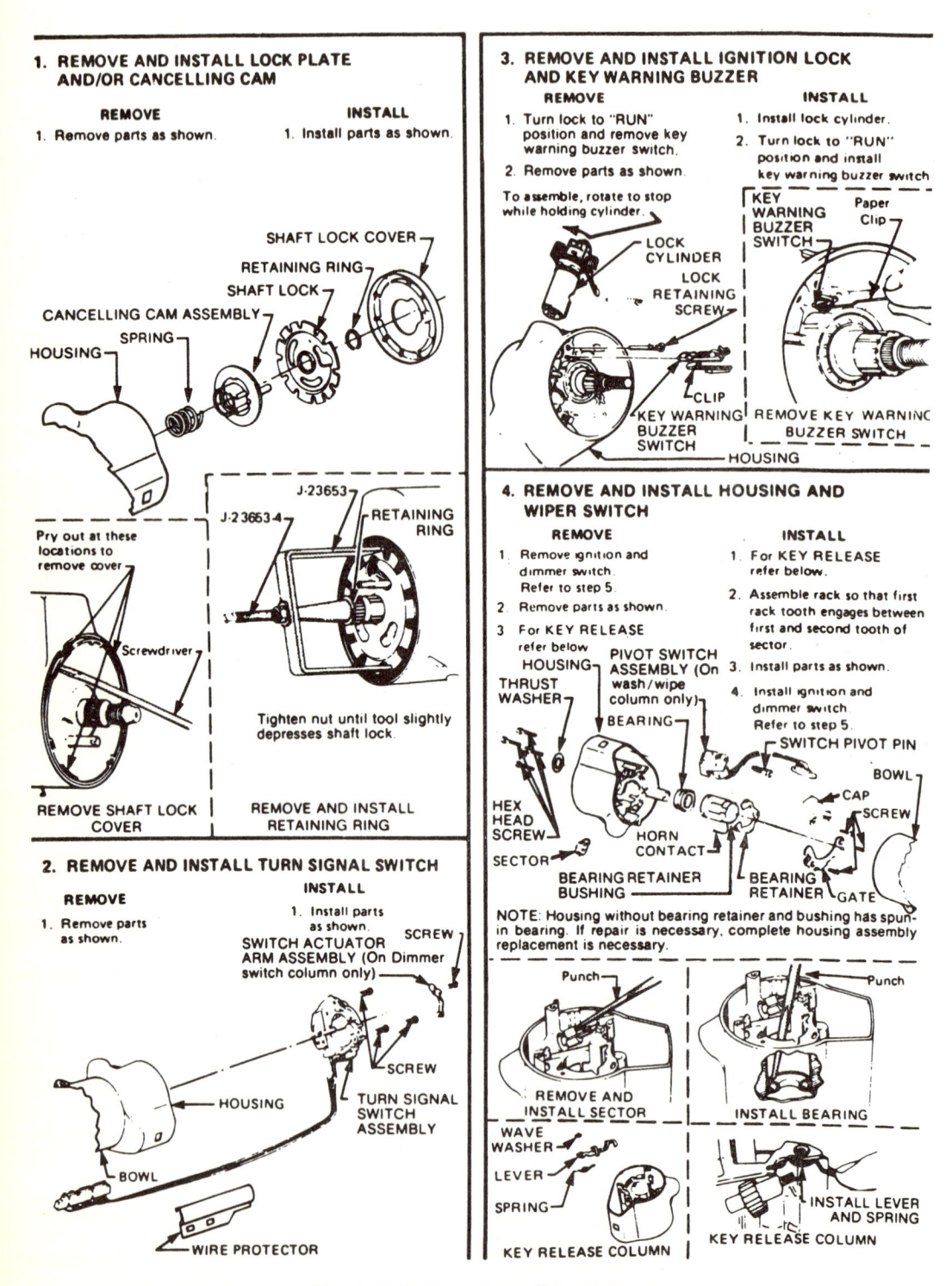

## 236 SUSPENSION AND STEERING

### 1. REMOVE AND INSTALL LOCK PLATE AND/OR CANCELLING CAM

**REMOVE**
1. Remove parts as shown.

**INSTALL**
1. Install parts as shown.

### 3. REMOVE AND INSTALL IGNITION LOCK AND KEY WARNING BUZZER

**REMOVE**
1. Turn lock to "RUN" position and remove key warning buzzer switch.
2. Remove parts as shown.

To assemble, rotate to stop while holding cylinder.

**INSTALL**
1. Install lock cylinder.
2. Turn lock to "RUN" position and install key warning buzzer switch.

### 4. REMOVE AND INSTALL HOUSING AND WIPER SWITCH

**REMOVE**
1. Remove ignition and dimmer switch. Refer to step 5.
2. Remove parts as shown.
3. For KEY RELEASE refer below.

**INSTALL**
1. For KEY RELEASE refer below.
2. Assemble rack so that first rack tooth engages between first and second tooth of sector.
3. Install parts as shown.
4. Install ignition and dimmer switch. Refer to step 5.

NOTE: Housing without bearing retainer and bushing has spun-in bearing. If repair is necessary, complete housing assembly replacement is necessary.

### 2. REMOVE AND INSTALL TURN SIGNAL SWITCH

**REMOVE**
1. Remove parts as shown.

**INSTALL**
1. Install parts as shown.

**Standard steering column disassembly**

# SUSPENSION AND STEERING 237

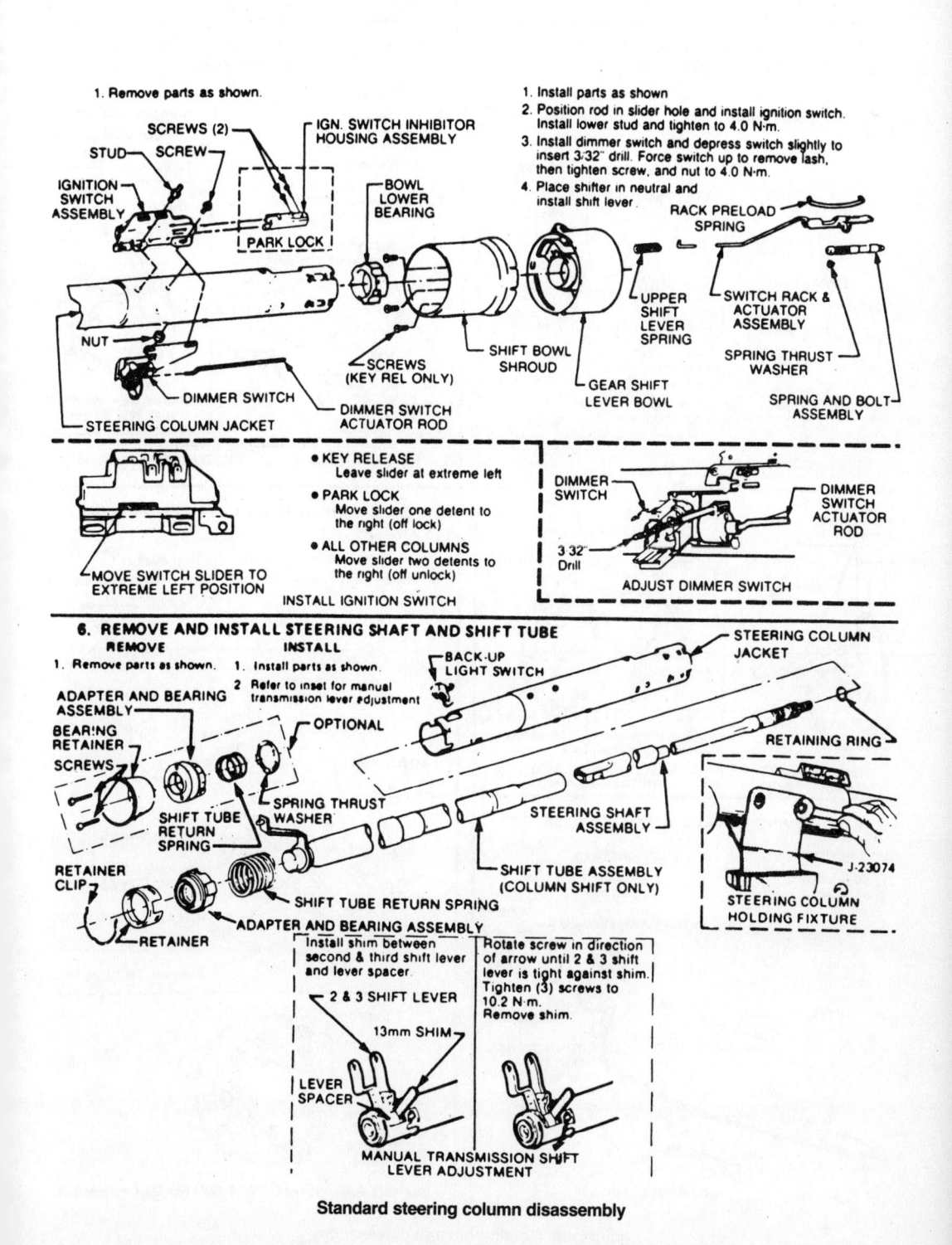

**Standard steering column disassembly**

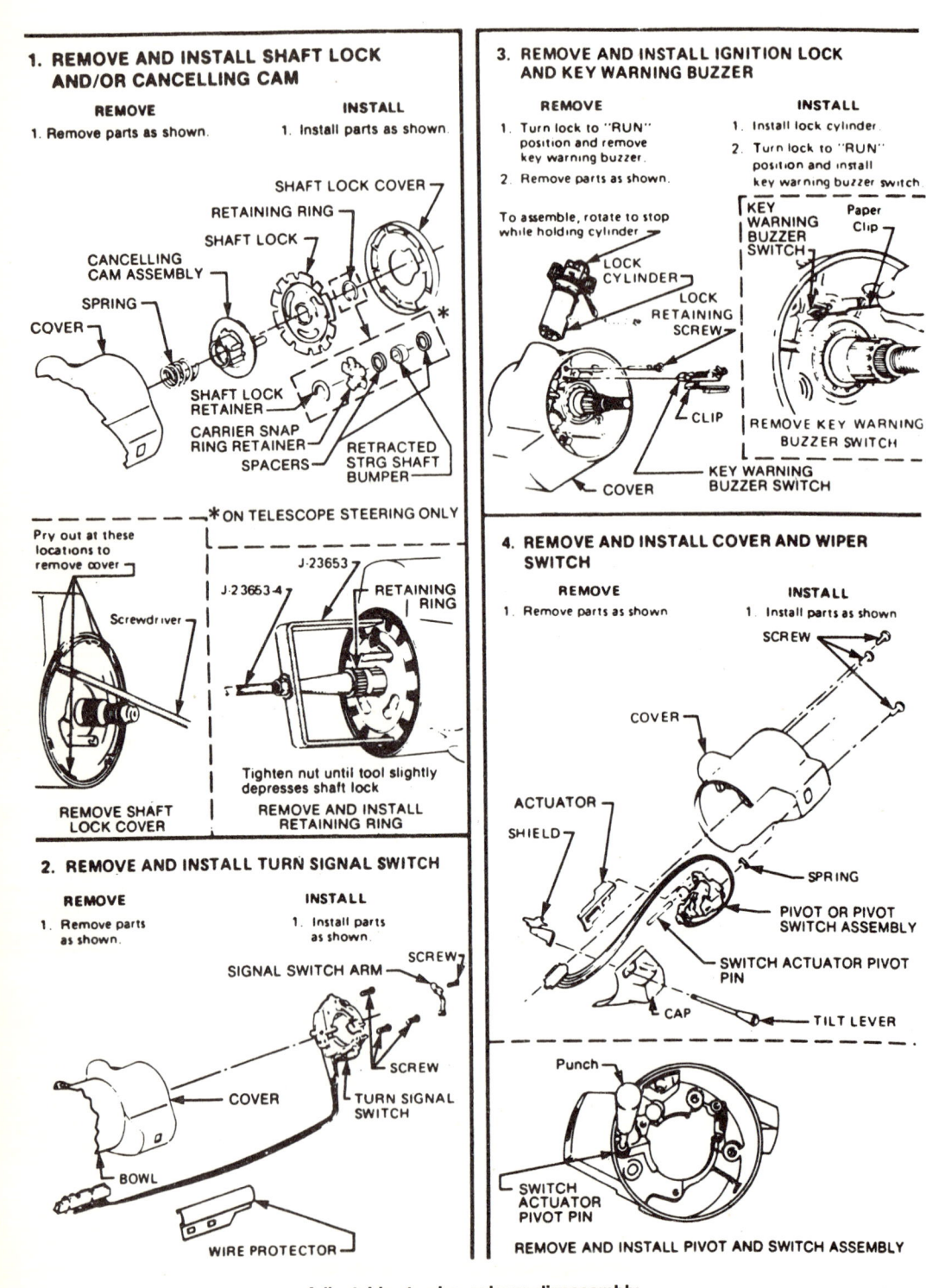

## 238 SUSPENSION AND STEERING

### 1. REMOVE AND INSTALL SHAFT LOCK AND/OR CANCELLING CAM

**REMOVE**
1. Remove parts as shown.

**INSTALL**
1. Install parts as shown.

- SHAFT LOCK COVER
- RETAINING RING
- SHAFT LOCK
- CANCELLING CAM ASSEMBLY
- SPRING
- COVER
- SHAFT LOCK RETAINER
- CARRIER SNAP RING RETAINER
- SPACERS
- RETRACTED STRG SHAFT BUMPER

*ON TELESCOPE STEERING ONLY

- Pry out at these locations to remove cover
- Screwdriver

**REMOVE SHAFT LOCK COVER**

- J-23653
- J-23653-4
- RETAINING RING

Tighten nut until tool slightly depresses shaft lock

**REMOVE AND INSTALL RETAINING RING**

### 2. REMOVE AND INSTALL TURN SIGNAL SWITCH

**REMOVE**
1. Remove parts as shown.

**INSTALL**
1. Install parts as shown.

- SIGNAL SWITCH ARM
- SCREW
- COVER
- SCREW
- TURN SIGNAL SWITCH
- BOWL
- WIRE PROTECTOR

### 3. REMOVE AND INSTALL IGNITION LOCK AND KEY WARNING BUZZER

**REMOVE**
1. Turn lock to "RUN" position and remove key warning buzzer.
2. Remove parts as shown.

**INSTALL**
1. Install lock cylinder.
2. Turn lock to "RUN" position and install key warning buzzer switch.

To assemble, rotate to stop while holding cylinder

- LOCK CYLINDER
- LOCK RETAINING SCREW
- CLIP
- COVER
- KEY WARNING BUZZER SWITCH
- KEY WARNING BUZZER SWITCH
- Paper Clip

**REMOVE KEY WARNING BUZZER SWITCH**

### 4. REMOVE AND INSTALL COVER AND WIPER SWITCH

**REMOVE**
1. Remove parts as shown.

**INSTALL**
1. Install parts as shown.

- SCREW
- COVER
- ACTUATOR
- SHIELD
- SPRING
- PIVOT OR PIVOT SWITCH ASSEMBLY
- SWITCH ACTUATOR PIVOT PIN
- CAP
- TILT LEVER

- Punch
- SWITCH ACTUATOR PIVOT PIN

**REMOVE AND INSTALL PIVOT AND SWITCH ASSEMBLY**

**Adjustable steering column disassembly**

# SUSPENSION AND STEERING 239

## REMOVE

1. Reinstall tilt lever and place column in full "UP" position.
2. Remove tilt spring and pivot pins.
3. Remove housing by pulling upward on tilt lever and pull housing upward until it stops. Move housing to the right to disengage rack from actuator.
4. Remove tilt lever.
5. Remove parts as shown.

## INSTALL

1. Install parts as shown.
2. While holding up on tilt lever to disengage lock shoes install over steering shaft. Move rack downward and hold. Tip housing to the left until rack engages pin on actuator rod. Push housing down until pivot pin holes are in alignment.

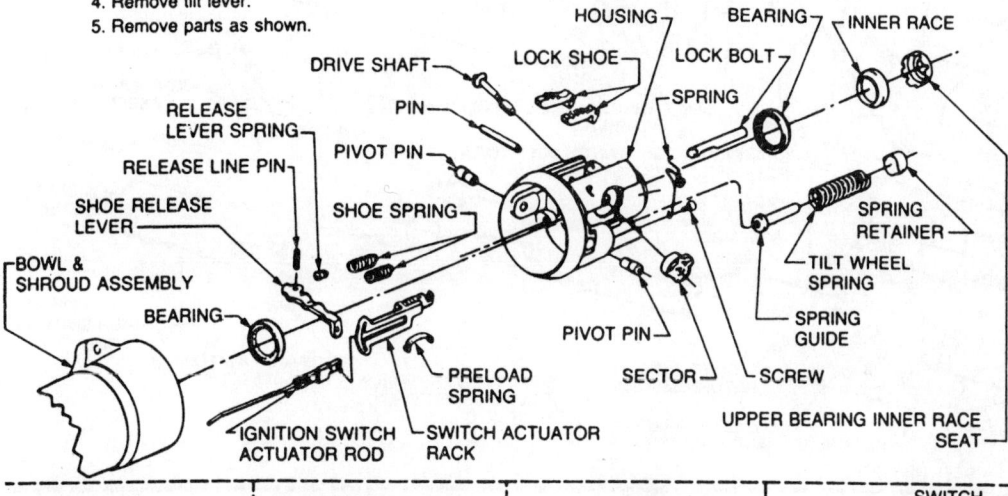

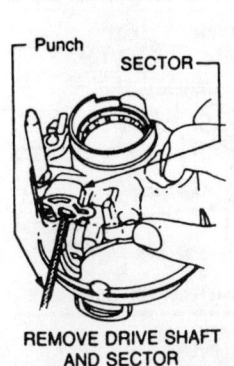

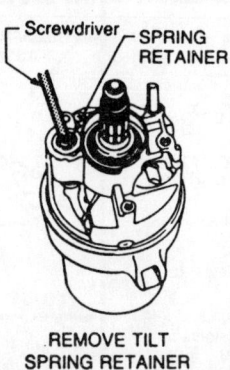

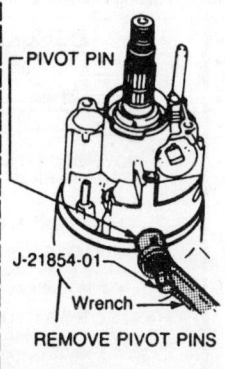

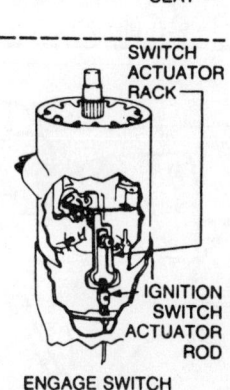

Parts labeled: DRIVE SHAFT, PIN, RELEASE LEVER SPRING, PIVOT PIN, RELEASE LINE PIN, SHOE RELEASE LEVER, SHOE SPRING, BOWL & SHROUD ASSEMBLY, BEARING, IGNITION SWITCH ACTUATOR ROD, PRELOAD SPRING, SWITCH ACTUATOR RACK, HOUSING, LOCK SHOE, LOCK BOLT, SPRING, BEARING, INNER RACE, PIVOT PIN, SECTOR, SCREW, SPRING RETAINER, TILT WHEEL SPRING, SPRING GUIDE, UPPER BEARING INNER RACE SEAT

Sub-images:
- REMOVE DRIVE SHAFT AND SECTOR (Punch, SECTOR)
- REMOVE TILT SPRING RETAINER (Screwdriver, SPRING RETAINER)
- REMOVE PIVOT PINS (PIVOT PIN, J-21854-01 Wrench)
- ENGAGE SWITCH ACTUATOR RACK (SWITCH ACTUATOR RACK, IGNITION SWITCH ACTUATOR ROD)

## 6. REMOVE AND INSTALL LOWER STEERING SHAFT ASSEMBLY

**REMOVE**
1. Remove parts as shown.

ON DISASSEMBLY, OBSERVE ALIGNMENT OF BOLT SLOT AND INDEX MARK. REASSEMBLE IN SAME MANNER.

**INSTALL**
1. Install parts as shown.

Parts labeled: BOWL & SHROUD ASSEMBLY, LOWER STEERING SHAFT ASSEMBLY, CENTERING SPHERE, RACE AND UPPER SHAFT ASSEMBLY, BOLT SLOT, JOINT PRELOAD SPRING, INDEX MARK

**Adjustable steering column disassembly**

## 240 SUSPENSION AND STEERING

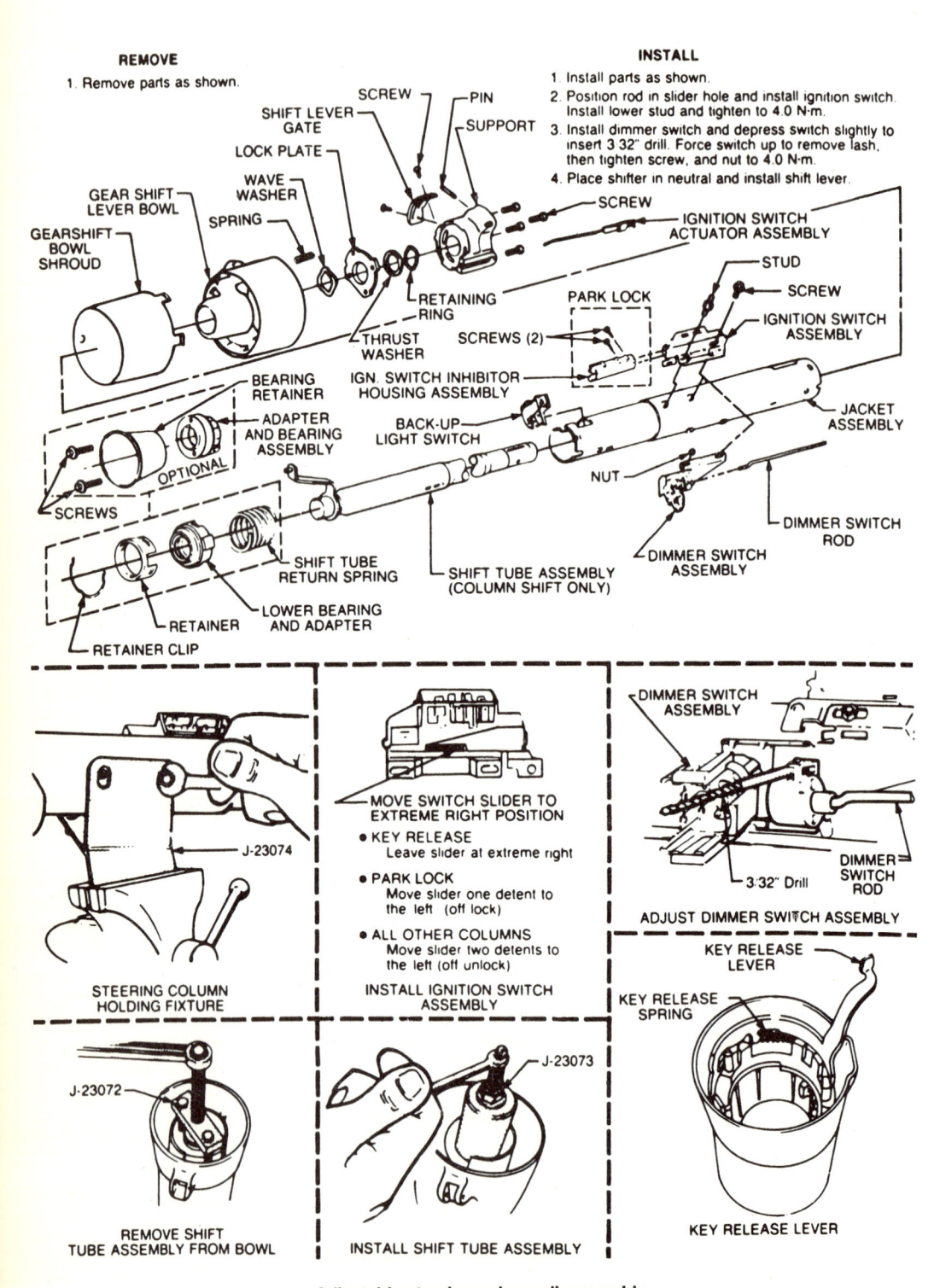

**REMOVE**
1. Remove parts as shown.

**INSTALL**
1. Install parts as shown.
2. Position rod in slider hole and install ignition switch. Install lower stud and tighten to 4.0 N·m.
3. Install dimmer switch and depress switch slightly to insert 3/32" drill. Force switch up to remove lash, then tighten screw, and nut to 4.0 N·m.
4. Place shifter in neutral and install shift lever.

Labels (exploded view):
- SCREW
- PIN
- SHIFT LEVER GATE
- SUPPORT
- LOCK PLATE
- WAVE WASHER
- GEAR SHIFT LEVER BOWL
- SPRING
- GEARSHIFT BOWL SHROUD
- SCREW
- IGNITION SWITCH ACTUATOR ASSEMBLY
- RETAINING RING
- THRUST WASHER
- PARK LOCK
- STUD
- SCREW
- IGNITION SWITCH ASSEMBLY
- BEARING RETAINER
- IGN. SWITCH INHIBITOR HOUSING ASSEMBLY
- SCREWS (2)
- ADAPTER AND BEARING ASSEMBLY
- BACK-UP LIGHT SWITCH
- JACKET ASSEMBLY
- OPTIONAL
- NUT
- SCREWS
- DIMMER SWITCH ASSEMBLY
- DIMMER SWITCH ROD
- SHIFT TUBE RETURN SPRING
- SHIFT TUBE ASSEMBLY (COLUMN SHIFT ONLY)
- RETAINER
- LOWER BEARING AND ADAPTER
- RETAINER CLIP

---

J-23074

**STEERING COLUMN HOLDING FIXTURE**

---

MOVE SWITCH SLIDER TO EXTREME RIGHT POSITION
- **KEY RELEASE** Leave slider at extreme right
- **PARK LOCK** Move slider one detent to the left (off lock)
- **ALL OTHER COLUMNS** Move slider two detents to the left (off unlock)

**INSTALL IGNITION SWITCH ASSEMBLY**

---

DIMMER SWITCH ASSEMBLY
DIMMER SWITCH ROD
3/32" Drill

**ADJUST DIMMER SWITCH ASSEMBLY**

---

J-23072

**REMOVE SHIFT TUBE ASSEMBLY FROM BOWL**

---

J-23073

**INSTALL SHIFT TUBE ASSEMBLY**

---

KEY RELEASE LEVER
KEY RELEASE SPRING

**KEY RELEASE LEVER**

---

**Adjustable steering column disassembly**

# SUSPENSION AND STEERING 241

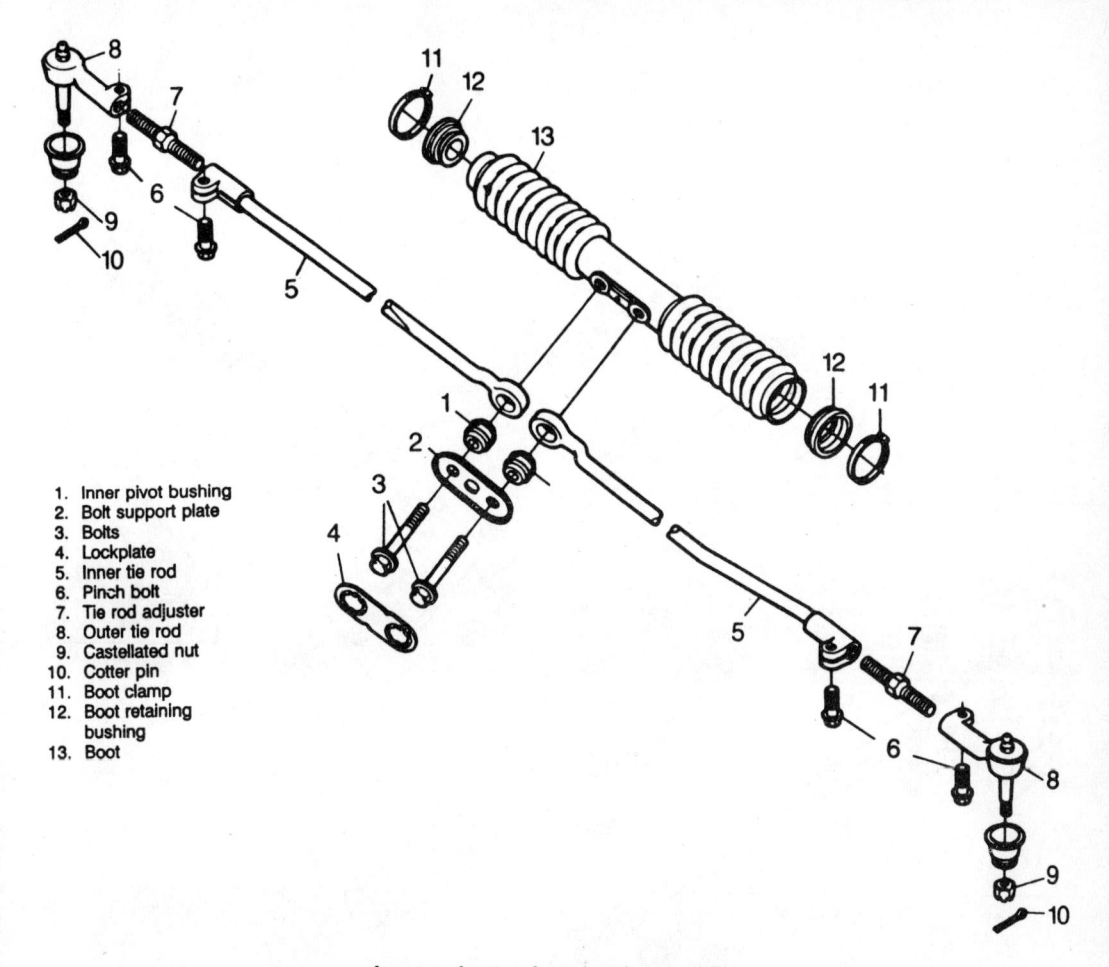

1. Inner pivot bushing
2. Bolt support plate
3. Bolts
4. Lockplate
5. Inner tie rod
6. Pinch bolt
7. Tie rod adjuster
8. Outer tie rod
9. Castellated nut
10. Cotter pin
11. Boot clamp
12. Boot retaining bushing
13. Boot

**Inner and outer tie rod end assemblies**

3. Check the steering for ability to return to center after the adjustment has been completed.

## REMOVAL AND INSTALLATION

1. Disconnect the negative battery cable. Remove the left side sound insulator.
2. Disconnect the upper pinch bolt on the steering coupling assembly.
3. Disconnect the clamp nuts.
4. Raise and safely support the vehicle. Remove both front wheel assemblies.
5. Remove the clamp nut and the fluid line retainer.
6. Remove the tie rod end-to-steering knuckle cotter pin and castle nut. Using a puller tool, disconnect the tie rod ends from the steering knuckles.
7. Lower the vehicle.
8. Disconnect and plug the fluid lines from the power steering rack.
9. Remove the mounting clamps. Move the steering rack forward and remove the lower pinch bolt on the coupling assembly.

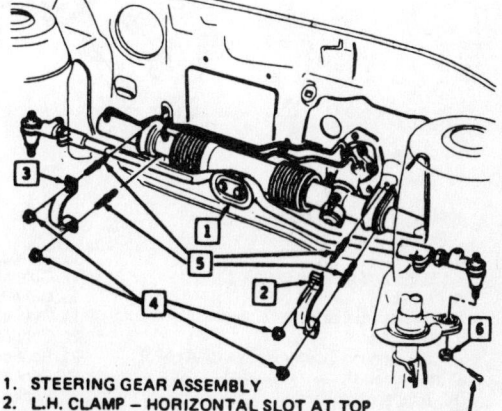

1. STEERING GEAR ASSEMBLY
2. L.H. CLAMP – HORIZONTAL SLOT AT TOP
3. R.H. CLAMP – HORIZONTAL SLOT AT TOP
4. NUT – 30 N·m (22 LBS. FT.) – HAND START ALL NUTS. TIGHTEN LEFT SIDE CLAMP NUTS FIRST, THEN TIGHTEN RIGHT SIDE NUTS.
5. STUD – 20 N·m (15 LBS. FT.) AFTER SECOND REUSE OF STUD, THREAD LOCKING KIT NO. 1052624 MUST BE USED.
6. NUT – 50 N·m (35 LBS. FT.)
   75 N·m (50 LBS. FT.) MAXIMUM TO INSTALL COTTER PIN.
7. COTTER PIN

**Exploded view of the power rack and pinion assembly**

## 242 SUSPENSION AND STEERING

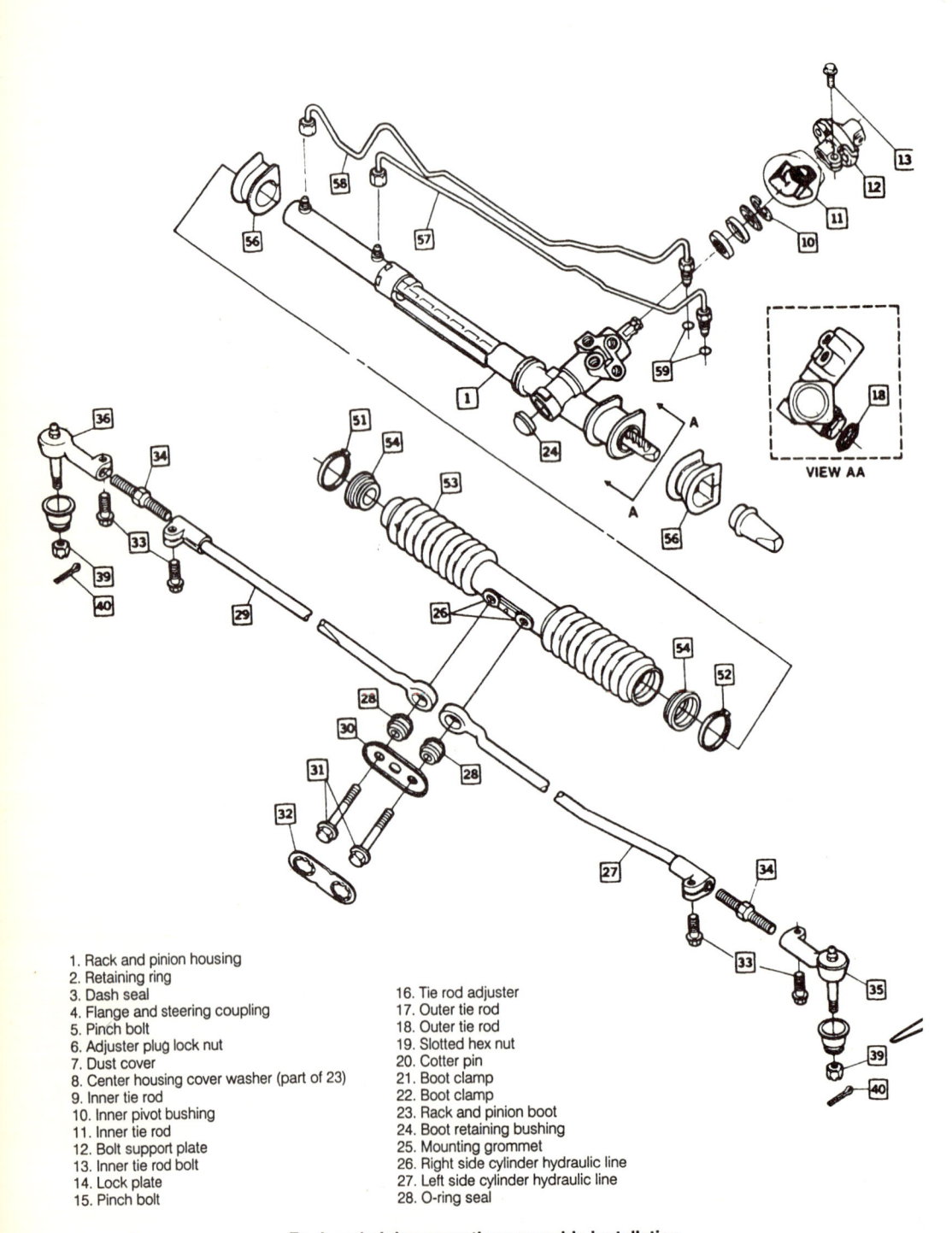

1. Rack and pinion housing
2. Retaining ring
3. Dash seal
4. Flange and steering coupling
5. Pinch bolt
6. Adjuster plug lock nut
7. Dust cover
8. Center housing cover washer (part of 23)
9. Inner tie rod
10. Inner pivot bushing
11. Inner tie rod
12. Bolt support plate
13. Inner tie rod bolt
14. Lock plate
15. Pinch bolt
16. Tie rod adjuster
17. Outer tie rod
18. Outer tie rod
19. Slotted hex nut
20. Cotter pin
21. Boot clamp
22. Boot clamp
23. Rack and pinion boot
24. Boot retaining bushing
25. Mounting grommet
26. Right side cylinder hydraulic line
27. Left side cylinder hydraulic line
28. O-ring seal

**Rack and pinion mounting assembly installation**

## SUSPENSION AND STEERING 243

10. Disconnect the coupling from the steering rack.
11. Remove the rack and pinion assembly with the dash seal through the left wheel opening.

**To install:**
12. If the studs were removed with the mounting clamps, reinstall the studs into the cowl. If the stud is being reused, use Loctite® to secure the threads.
13. Slide the rack and pinion assembly through the left side wheel housing opening and secure the dash seal.
14. Move the assembly forward and install the coupling.
15. Install the lower pinch bolt and tighten to 29 ft. lbs. (40 Nm).
16. Connect the fluid lines.
17. Install the clamp nuts. Tighten the left side clamp first, then tighten the right side. Raise and safely support the vehicle.
18. Connect the tie rod ends to the steering knuckle, tighten the nut to 35 ft. lbs. (47 Nm) and install a new cotter pin. Install the wheels.
19. Install the line retainer and lower the vehicle.
20. Install the upper pinch bolt on the coupling assembly. Tighten to 29 ft. lbs. (40 Nm).
21. Install the sound insulator.

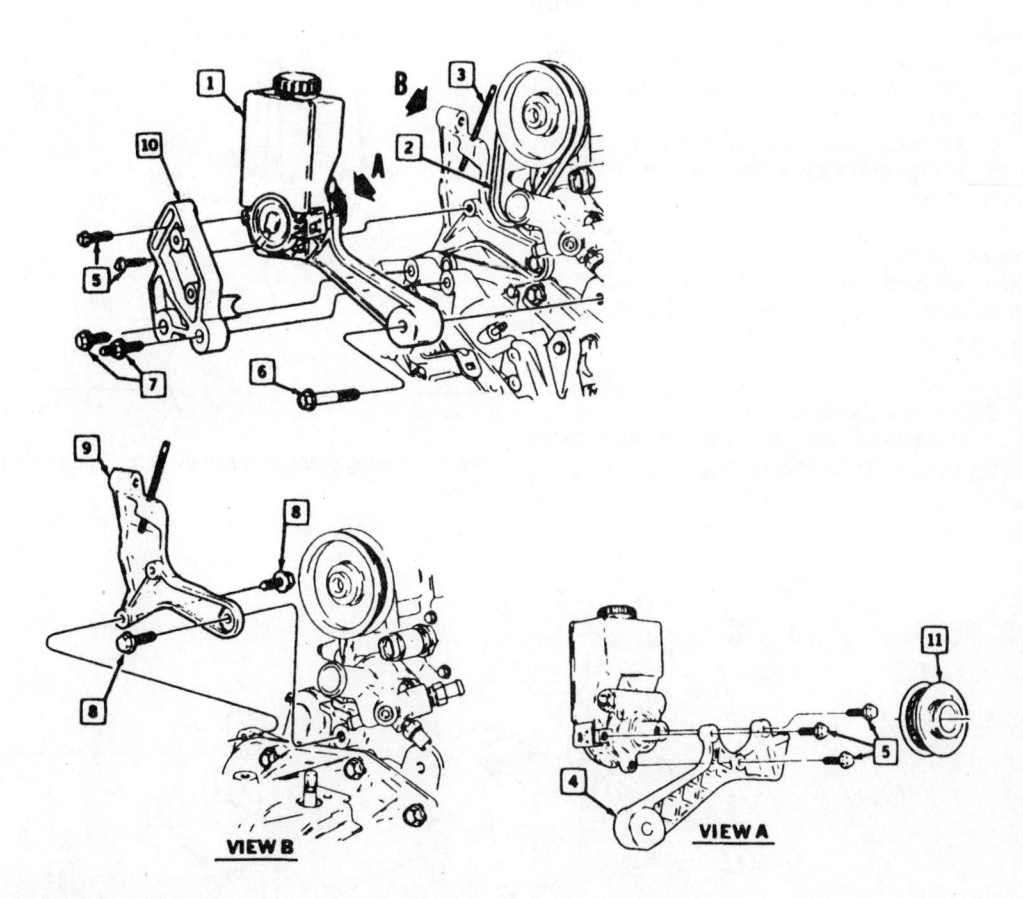

1. Power steering pump
2. Drive belt
3. Adjustment screw
4. Front bracket
5. Bolt
6. Bolt
7. Bolt/stud
8. Bolt
9. Rear support
10. Front support
11. Pulley — Note: when tensioning belt, tighten rear bracket adjustment belt first, then the bolt just below it. Tighten bolt 6 last.

**Power steering pump installation—2.3L engine**

## 244 SUSPENSION AND STEERING

22. Fill the power steering pump with fluid and bleed the system.
23. Connect the negative battery cable and check the rack for proper operation and leaks.
24. Check and adjust front end alignment, as required.

## Power Steering Pump

### REMOVAL AND INSTALLATION

#### 2.3L ENGINE

1. Disconnect the negative battery cable.
2. Disconnect the pressure and return lines from the pump.
3. Remove the rear bracket to pump bolts.
4. Remove the drive belt and position aside.
5. Remove the rear bracket to transaxle bolts.
6. Remove the front bracket to engine bolt.
7. Remove the pump and bracket as an assembly.
8. Transfer pulley and bracket, as necessary.
9. The installation is the reverse of the removal procedure.
10. Fill the power steering pump with fluid and bleed the system.
11. Connect the negative battery cable and check the pump for proper operation and leaks.

#### 2.5L ENGINE

1. Disconnect the negative battery cable.
2. Remove the drive belt.
3. Disconnect and plug the pressure tubes from the power steering pump.
4. Remove the front adjustment bracket-to-rear adjustment bracket bolt.
5. Remove the front adjustment bracket-to-engine bolt and spacer.
6. Remove the pump with the front adjustment bracket.
7. If installing a new pump, transfer the pulley and front adjustment bracket to the new pump.

**To install:**

8. The installation is the reverse of the removal procedure.
9. Adjust the drive belt tension.
10. Fill the power steering pump with fluid and bleed the system.

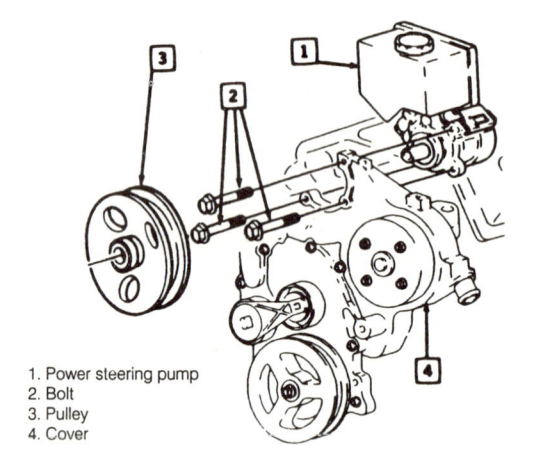

1. Power steering pump
2. Bolt
3. Pulley
4. Cover

**Power steering pump installation—2.0L, 3.0L and 3.3L engines**

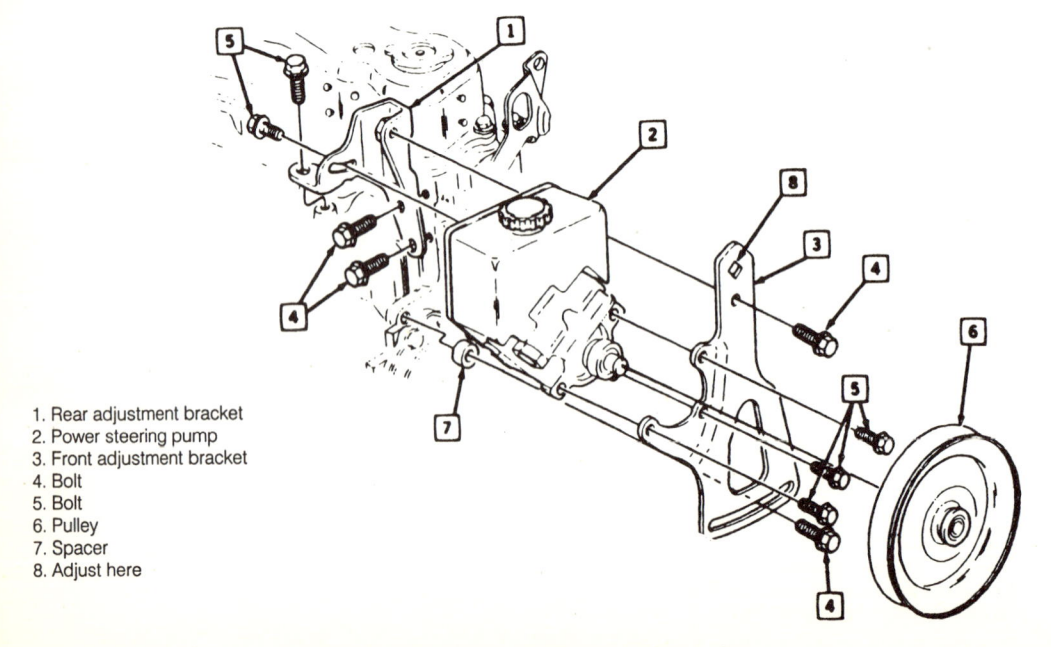

1. Rear adjustment bracket
2. Power steering pump
3. Front adjustment bracket
4. Bolt
5. Bolt
6. Pulley
7. Spacer
8. Adjust here

**Power steering pump installation—2.5L engine**

11. Connect the negative battery cable and check the pump for proper operation and leaks.

### 2.0L, 3.0L AND 3.3L ENGINES

1. Disconnect the negative battery cable.
2. Remove the serpentine drive belt.
3. Remove the power steering pump-to-engine bolts.
4. Pull the pump forward and disconnect the pressure tubes.
5. Remove the pump and transfer the pulley, as necessary.
6. The installation is the reverse of the removal procedure.
7. Adjust the drive belt tension.
8. Fill the power steering pump with fluid and bleed the system.
9. Connect the negative battery cable and check the pump for proper operation and leaks.

### Belt Adjustment

NOTE: *Serpentine belt driven power steering pumps do not require adjustment. If the belt is stretched beyond usable limits, replace it.*

1. Place the appropriate gauge on the belt and measure the tension. The specifications are:
- 2.3L engine, new and used belt—110 lbs.
- 2.5L and 3.0L engine, used belt—100 lbs; new belt—180 lbs.

2. If the tension is not at specifications, loosen the mounting bolts and move the pump or turn the adjustment stud.
3. Tighten the mounting bolts while holding the adjusted position of the pump.
4. Run the engine for 2 minutes and recheck the tension.

### System Bleeding

1. Raise the vehicle so the wheels are off the ground. Turn the wheels all the way to the left. Add power steering fluid to the **COLD** or **FULL COLD** mark on the fluid level indicator.
2. Start the engine and check the fluid level at fast idle. Add fluid, if necessary to bring the level up to the mark.
3. Bleed air from the system by turning the wheels from side-to-side without hitting the stops. Keep the fluid level at the **COLD** or **FULL COLD** mark. Fluid with air in it has a tan appearance.
4. Return the wheels to the center position and continue running the engine for 2–3 minutes.
5. Lower the vehicle and road test to check steering function and recheck the fluid level with the system at its normal operating temperature. Fluid should be at the **HOT** mark when finished.

# Brakes

# 9

## BRAKE OPERATING SYSTEM

### Adjustments

#### DRUM BRAKES

1. Raise and safely support the vehicle.
2. Remove the rear wheels.
3. Remove the brake drum.
4. Using a H-gauge, measure the inside diameter of the brake drum
5. Turn the star wheel to adjust the shoe and lining diameter to be 0.030 in. (0.76mm) less than the inside diameter of the drum for each wheel.
6. Install the drums and wheels.
7. Tighten the wheel nuts.
8. Make several alternate forward and reverse stops applying firm force to the brake pedal. Repeat this procedure until ample pedal reserve is built up.

### Brake Light Switch

#### REMOVAL AND INSTALLATION

1. Disconnect the negative battery cable.
2. Remove the left sound insulator.
3. Disconnect the wiring from the switch.
4. Pull the switch out of the retainer in the bracket.

**To install:**

5. Install the retainer in the bracket, at the underside of the bracket.
6. Depress the brake pedal and insert the switch into the retainer until the switch seats. Allow the pedal to return.
7. Connect the connector.
8. To adjust the switch, pull the pedal up against the switch until no more clicks are heard. The switch will automatically move up in the retainer providing adjustment. Repeat a few times to ensure that the switch is properly adjusted.
9. Connect the negative battery cable and check the switch for proper operation.

### Brake Pedal

#### REMOVAL AND INSTALLATION

1. Remove the left side sound insulator.
2. Remove the brake pedal bracket.
3. Disconnect the pushrod from the brake pedal.

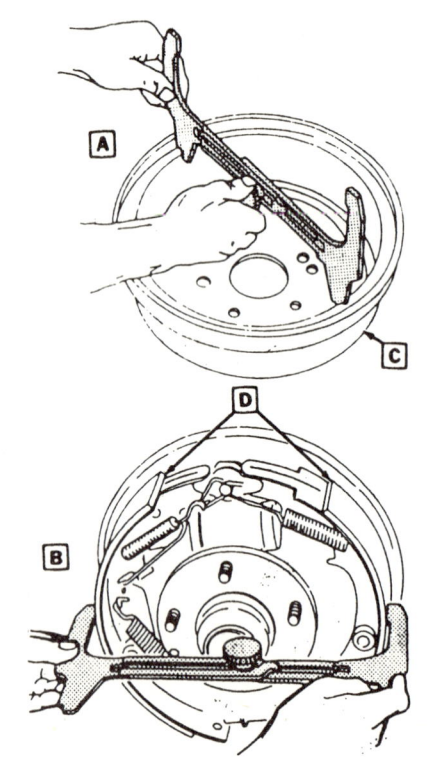

A SETTING TOOL TO DRUM
B SETTING BRAKE SHOES TO TOOL
C BRAKE DRUM
D BRAKE LININGS

**Adjusting rear brakes**

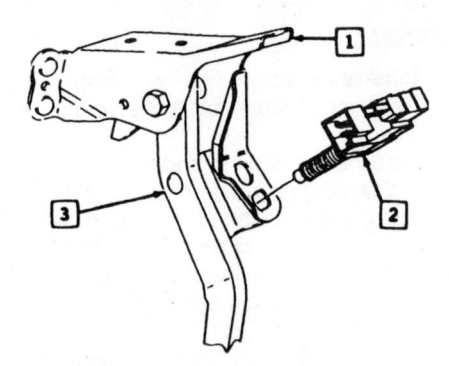

# BRAKES 247

4. Remove the master cylinder from the mounting studs.
5. Remove the retaining roll pins and remove the fluid reservoir from the cylinder, if necessary.

**To install:**

6. Replace the reservoir O-rings and bench bleed the master cylinder.
7. Install to the booster and install the nuts.
8. Install the brake lines to the master cylinder.
9. Fill the reservoir with brake fluid.
10. Connect the negative battery cable and check the brakes for proper operation.

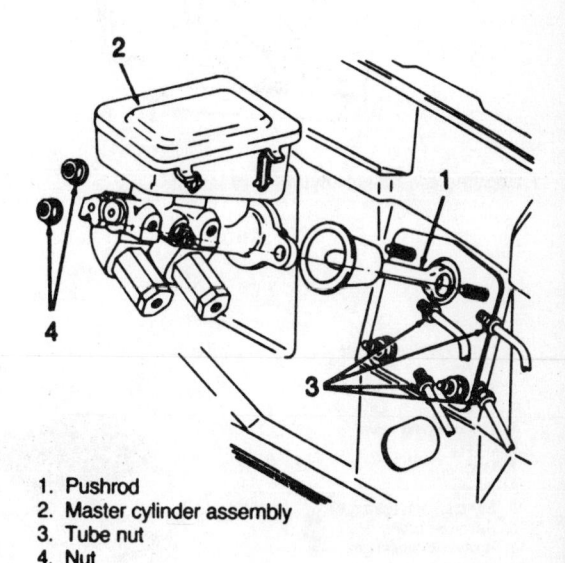

**1** BRACKET, BRAKE PEDAL
**2** SWITCH, STOP LAMP AND T.C.C.
**3** PEDAL ASM., BRAKE

Brake light switch installation

4. Remove the pivot bolt and bushing.
5. Remove the brake pedal.

**To install:**

6. Install the brake pedal.
7. Install the brake pedal bushing and pivot bolt. Tighten to 25 ft. lbs. (34 Nm).
8. Install the brake pedal bracket.
9. Install the left side sound insulator.

## Master Cylinder

### REMOVAL AND INSTALLATION

**Except Anti-Lock Brakes**

1. Disconnect the negative battery cable. Unplug the fluid level sensor connector.
2. Disconnect and plug the brake lines from the master cylinder.
3. Remove the nuts attaching the master cylinder to the power booster.

1. Pushrod
2. Master cylinder assembly
3. Tube nut
4. Nut

Master cylinder mounting

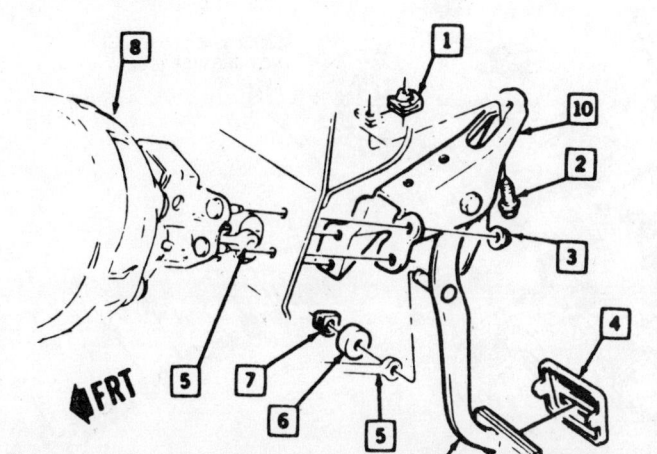

1. Clip nut
2. Bolt
3. Nut
4. Pedal cover
5. Booster push rod
6. Washer
7. Retainer
8. Vacuum booster
9. Brake pedal
10. Bracket

Brake pedal mounting

# 248  BRAKES

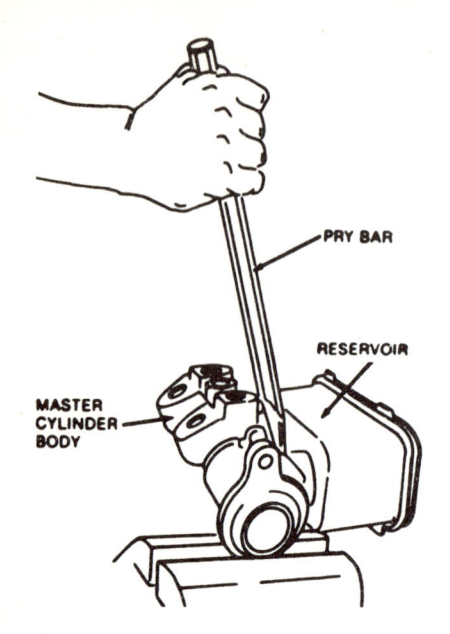

Removing the master cylinder reservoir

## OVERHAUL

1. Remove the master cylinder from the car.
2. Empty any remaining brake fluid from the reservoir.
3. Secure the master cylinder in a soft-jawed vise by clamping it on the mounting flange.
4. Using a small prybar, carefully lever the reservoir from the master cylinder body.
5. Remove the lockring while depressing the primary piston with a suitable blunt drift.
6. Use compressed air applied at the rear outlet to force out the pistons, retainer and spring.
7. Wash all parts in denatured alcohol and inspect for wear, scoring or other defects. Replace any parts found to be suspect. If any defect is found in the master cylinder bore, the entire cylinder must be replaced.

NOTE: *The master cylinder cannot be honed and no abrasives are to be used in the bore.*

8. Assemble the master cylinder components in reverse order of disassembly. Lubricate all parts and seals with clean brake fluid. Install the reservoir by pushing in with a rocking motion.

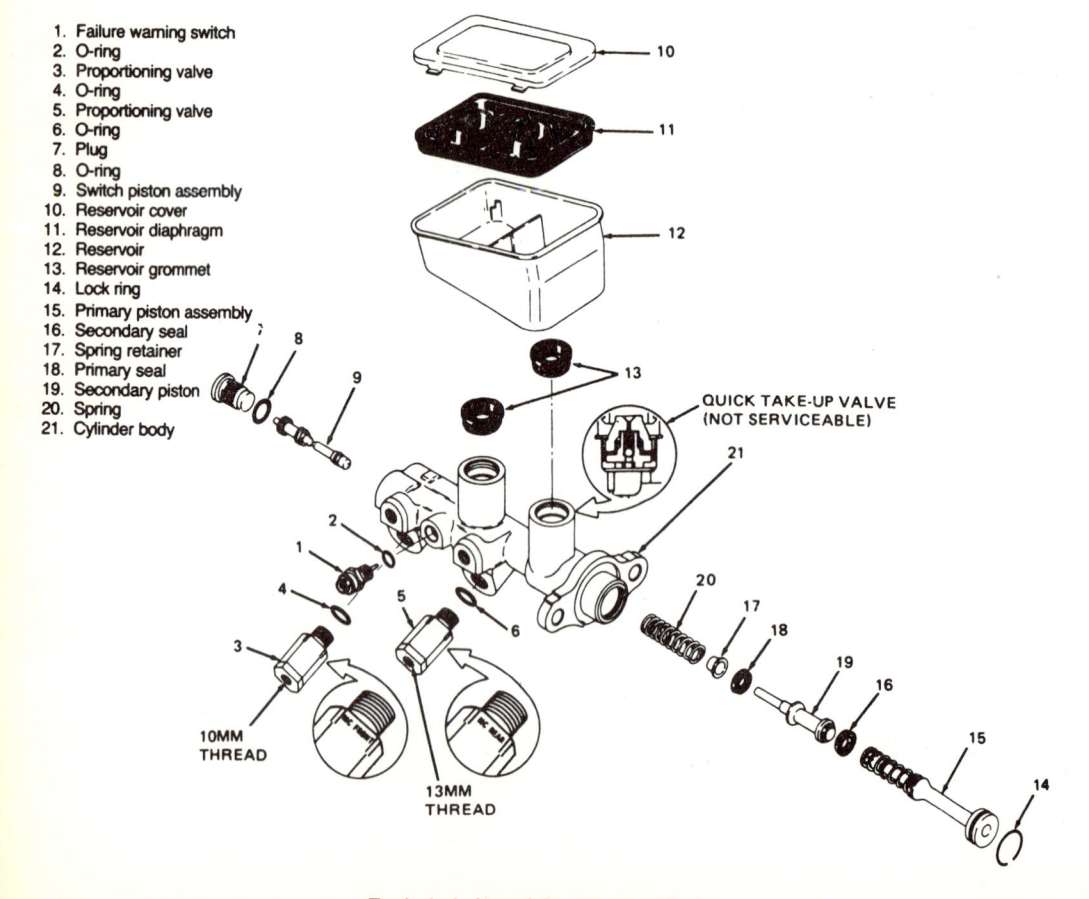

1. Failure warning switch
2. O-ring
3. Proportioning valve
4. O-ring
5. Proportioning valve
6. O-ring
7. Plug
8. O-ring
9. Switch piston assembly
10. Reservoir cover
11. Reservoir diaphragm
12. Reservoir
13. Reservoir grommet
14. Lock ring
15. Primary piston assembly
16. Secondary seal
17. Spring retainer
18. Primary seal
19. Secondary piston
20. Spring
21. Cylinder body

Exploded view of the master cylinder

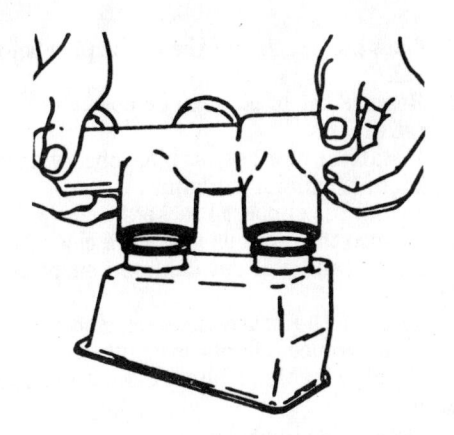

# BRAKES

**Install the master cylinder body to the reservoir with a rocking motion**

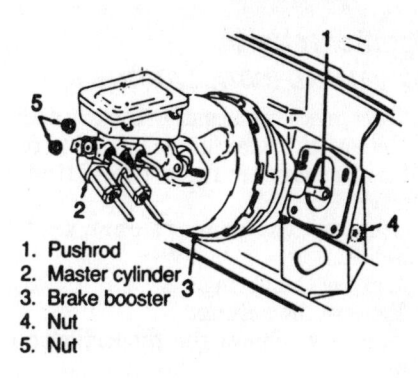

**Brake booster location**
1. Pushrod
2. Master cylinder
3. Brake booster
4. Nut
5. Nut

9. Bench bleeding the master cylinder reduces the possibility of getting air into the lines when the unit is installed. Connect two short pieces of brake line to the outlet fittings, then bend them until the free end is below the fluid level in the master cylinder reservoirs.
10. Fill the reservoirs with fresh brake fluid, then slowly pump the piston with a suitable blunt drift until no more air bubbles appear in the reservoirs.
11. Disconnect the two short lines, top up the brake fluid level and install the reservoir cap.
12. Install the master cylinder on the car. Attach the lines, but do not tighten them. Force out any air that might have been trapped at the connection by slowly depressing the brake pedal, then tighten the lines before releasing the pedal. Bleed the brake system as described below.

## Power Brake Booster

### REMOVAL AND INSTALLATION

1. Disconnect the negative battery cable.
2. Disconnect the vacuum hose(s) from the booster.
3. Remove the master cylinder.
4. From inside of the vehicle, remove the booster pushrod from the brake pedal.
5. Remove the nuts that attach the booster to the dash panel and remove it from the vehicle.
6. Transfer the necessary parts to the new booster.
7. The installation is the reverse of the removal procedure.
8. Bleed the brake system, connect the negative battery cable and check the brakes for proper operation.

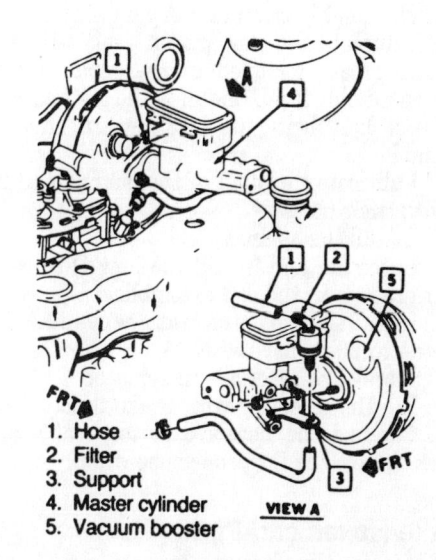

**Vacuum booster and hoses on 4 cylinder engine**
1. Hose
2. Filter
3. Support
4. Master cylinder
5. Vacuum booster

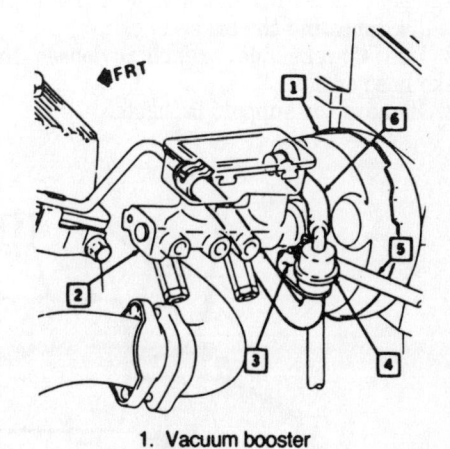

**Vacuum booster and hoses on V6 engine**
1. Vacuum booster
2. Master cylinder
3. Support
4. Filter
5. Brace
6. Hose

# 250 BRAKES

## Proportioner Valve
### REMOVAL AND INSTALLATION
1. Disconnect the negative battery cable.
2. Remove the retaining roll pins and remove the fluid reservoir from the cylinder, if necessary.
3. Remove the proportioner valve cap assemblies.
4. Remove the O-rings.
5. Remove the springs.
6. Carefully remove the proportioner valve pistons.
7. Remove the seals from the pistons.

**To install:**
8. Thoroughly clean and dry all parts.
9. Lubricate the new piston seals with the silicone grease included in the repair kit or brake assembly fluid. Install to the pistons with the seal lips facing upward toward the cap assembly.
10. Lubricate the stem of the pistons and install to their bores.
11. Install the springs.
12. Lubricate and install the new O-rings in their grooves in the cap assemblies.
13. Install the caps to the master cylinder and tighten to 20 ft. lbs. (27 Nm).
14. Install the reservoir, if replaced.
15. Fill the reservoir with brake fluid.
16. Connect the negative battery cable and check the brakes for proper operation.

## Brake Hoses and Pipes
### REMOVAL AND INSTALLATION
1. If brake line fittings are corroded, apply a coating of penetrating oil and allow to stand before disconnecting the brake lines.
2. Use a brake line wrench to loosen the brake hose or pipe.
3. Remove the support brackets.
4. Note the location of the brake pipe before removal.
5. Remove the brake pipe or hose.

**To install:**
6. Install the new hose or pipe, observing the location of original installation.
7. Install the support brackets.
8. Ensure the pipes or hoses are clear of rotating parts and will not chafe on suspension parts.
9. Tighten the brake hose or pipe using a brake line wrench. Do not overtighten.
10. Properly bleed the brake hydraulic system.
11. Test drive the vehicle.

### BRAKE PIPE FLARING
**Precautions:**
Always use double walled steel brake pipe.
Carefully route and retain replacement pipes.
Always use the correct fasteners and mount in the original location.
Use only double lap flaring tools. The use of single lap flaring tools produces a flare which may not withstand system pressure.

1. Obtain the recommended pipe and steel fitting nut of the correct size. Use the outside diameter of the pipe to specify size.
2. Cut the pipe to the appropriate length with a pipe cutter. Do not force the cutter. Correct length of pipe is determined by measuring the old pipe using a string and adding approximately 1/8 in. (3mm) for each flare.
3. Make sure the fittings are installed before starting the flare.
4. Chamfer the inside and outside diameter of the pipe with the de-burring tool.
5. Remove all traces of lubricant from the brake pipe and flaring tool.
6. Clamp the flaring tool body in a vise.
7. Select the correct size collet and forming mandrel for the pipe size used.

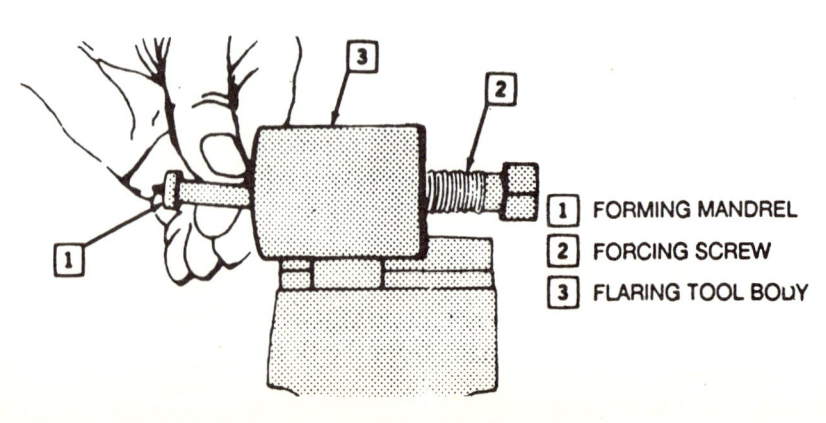

1 FORMING MANDREL
2 FORCING SCREW
3 FLARING TOOL BODY

**Forming mandrel and forcing screw**

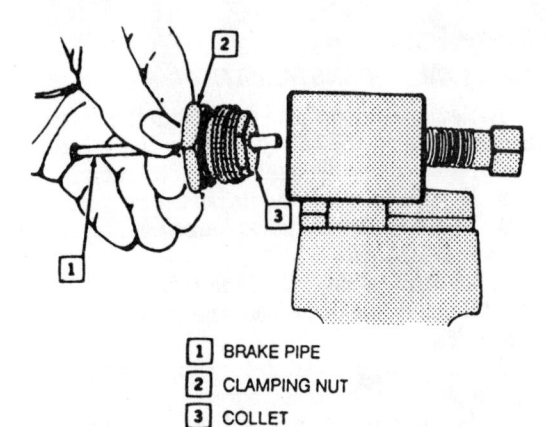

# BRAKES 251

## Bleeding

### EXCEPT ANTI-LOCK BRAKES

NOTE: *If using a pressure bleeder, follow the instructions furnished with the unit and choose the correct adaptor for the application. Do not substitute an adapter that "almost fits" as it will not work and could be dangerous.*

**Master Cylinder**

If the master cylinder is off the vehicle it can be bench bled.

1. Connect 2 short pieces of brake line to the outlet fittings, bend them until the free end is below the fluid level in the master cylinder reservoirs.
2. Fill the reservoir with fresh brake fluid. Pump the piston slowly until no more air bubbles appear in the reservoirs.
3. Disconnect the 2 short lines, refill the master cylinder and securely install the cylinder caps.
4. If the master cylinder is on the vehicle, it can still be bled, using a flare nut wrench.
5. Open the brake lines slightly with the flare nut wrench while pressure is applied to the brake pedal by a helper inside the vehicle.
6. Be sure to tighten the line before the brake pedal is released.
7. Repeat the process with both lines until no air bubbles come out.

**Calipers and Wheel Cylinders**

1. Fill the master cylinder with fresh brake fluid. Check the level often during the procedure.
2. Starting with the right rear wheel, remove

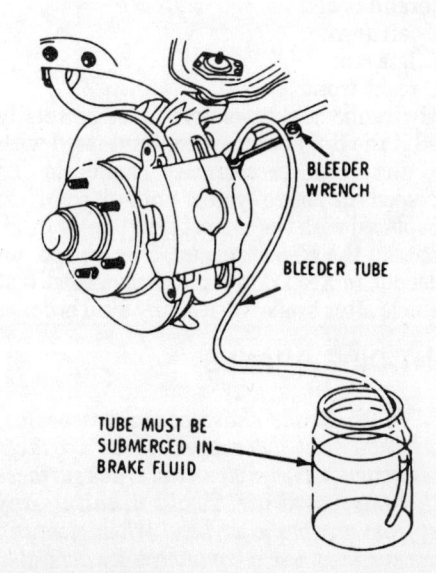

[1] BRAKE PIPE
[2] CLAMPING NUT
[3] COLLET

Clamping nut and collet

[1] FLARE

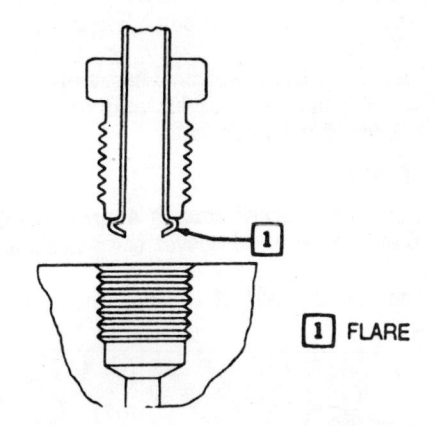

ISO flare

8. Insert the proper forming mandrel into the tool body. While holding forming mandrel in place with your finger, thread in the forcing screw until it makes contact and begins to move the forming mandrel. When contact is made, turn the forcing screw back 1 complete turn.
9. Slide the clamping nut over the brake pipe and insert the prepared brake pipe into the correct collet. Leave approximately 0.750 in. (19mm) of tubing extending out of the collet. Insert the assembly into the tool body. The brake pipe end must contact the face of the forming mandrel.
10. Tighten the clamping nut into the tool body very tight or the pipe may push out.
11. Wrench tighten the forcing screw in until it bottoms. Do not over-tighten the forcing screw or the flare may become over-sized.
12. Back the clamping nut out of the toll body and disassemble the clamping the clamping nut and collet assembly. The flare is now ready for use.
13. Bend the pipe assembly to match the old pipe. Clearance of 0.750 in. (19mm) must be maintained to all moving or vibrating parts.

BLEEDER WRENCH
BLEEDER TUBE
TUBE MUST BE SUBMERGED IN BRAKE FLUID

Bleeding the brakes

# 252  BRAKES

the protective cap from the bleeder, if equipped, and place where it will not be lost. Clean the bleed screw.

CAUTION: *When bleeding the brakes, keep face away from the brake area. Spewing fluid may cause facial and/or visual damage. Do not allow brake fluid to spill on the car's finish; it will remove the paint.*

3. If the system is empty, the most efficient way to get fluid down to the wheel is to loosen the bleeder about ½–¾ turn, place a finger firmly over the bleeder and have a helper pump the brakes slowly until fluid comes out the bleeder. Once fluid is at the bleeder, close it before the pedal is released inside the vehicle.

NOTE: *If the pedal is pumped rapidly, the fluid will churn and create small air bubbles, which are almost impossible to remove from the system. These air bubbles will eventually congregate and a spongy pedal will result.*

4. Once fluid has been pumped to the caliper or wheel cylinder, open the bleed screw again, have the helper press the brake pedal to the floor, lock the bleeder and have the helper slowly release the pedal. Wait 15 seconds and repeat the procedure (including the 15 second wait) until no more air comes out of the bleeder upon application of the brake pedal. Remember to close the bleeder before the pedal is released inside the vehicle each time the bleeder is opened. If not, air will be induced into the system.

5. If a helper is not available, connect a small hose to the bleeder, place the end in a container of brake fluid and proceed to pump the pedal from inside the vehicle until no more air comes out the bleeder. The hose will prevent air from entering the system.

6. Repeat the procedure on remaining wheel cylinders in order:
   a. left front
   b. left rear
   c. right front

7. Hydraulic brake systems must be totally flushed if the fluid becomes contaminated with water, dirt or other corrosive chemicals. To flush, bleed the entire system until all fluid has been replaced with the correct type of new fluid.

8. Install the bleeder cap(s), if equipped, on the bleeder to keep dirt out. Always road test the vehicle after brake work of any kind is done.

## FRONT DISC BRAKES

CAUTION: *Brake shoes contain asbestos, which has been determined to be a cancer causing agent. Never clean the brake surfaces with compressed air! Avoid inhaling any dust from any brake surface! When cleaning brake surfaces, use a commercially available brake cleaning fluid.*

## Brake Pads

### REMOVAL AND INSTALLATION

1. Remove some of the fluid from the master cylinder. Raise and safely support the vehicle.
2. Remove the tire and wheel assembly.
3. Bottom the piston in its bore for clearance.
4. Remove the caliper mounting bolt and sleeve assemblies.
5. Lift the caliper off of the rotor.
6. Remove the pads from the caliper.

**To install:**

7. Use a large C-clamp to compress the piston back into the caliper bore.
8. Install the pads and anti-rattle clip to the caliper. Adjust the bent-over tabs for a tight fit.
9. Position the caliper over the rotor so the caliper engages the adaptor correctly. Lubricate and install the sleeves and bolts. Tighten to 38 ft. lbs. (51 Nm).
10. Install the tire and wheel assembly.
11. Fill the master cylinder and check the brakes for proper operation.

### INSPECTION

1. Inspect the brake linings approximately every 6,000 miles or whenever the wheels are removed.
2. Check both ends of the pad for uneven wear.

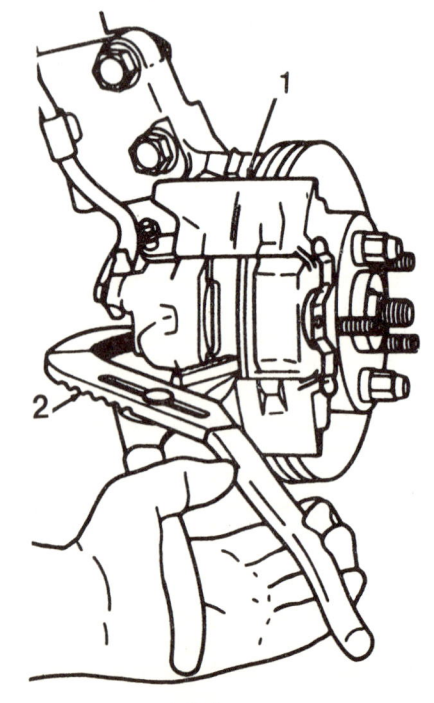

1. Caliper
2. Pliers

**Compressing the piston**

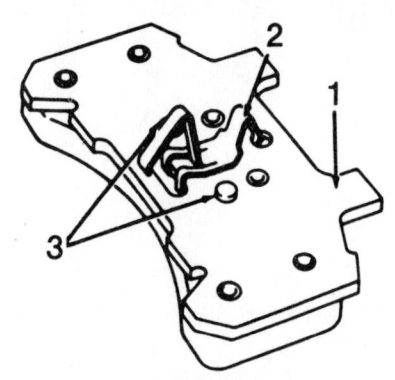

# BRAKES 253

1. Inboard shoe and lining
2. Shoe retainer spring
3. Retention lug

**Inboard pad and retainer**

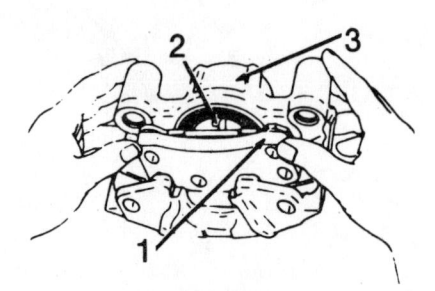

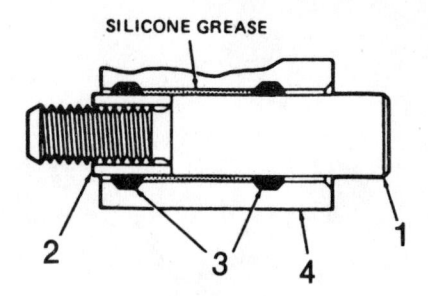

1. Mounting sleeve
2. Sleeve
3. Bushing
4. Caliper housing

**Lubrication points**

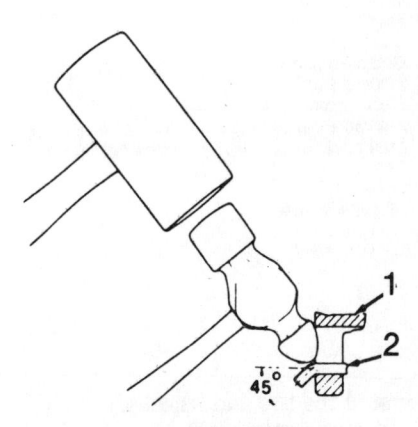

1. Inboard shoe and lining
2. Shoe retainer spring
3. Caliper housing

**Installing the inboard pad**

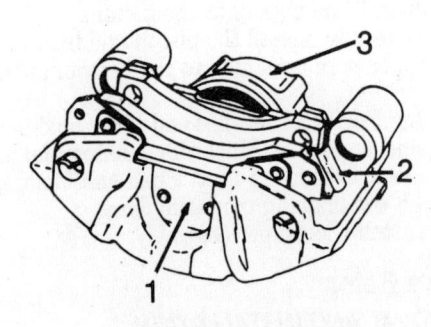

1. Caliper body
2. Outboard shoe tab

**Bending the outboard pad tabs**

4. Whenever the thickness of the lining is worn to the wear indicator, replace the pads on both sides.

## Brake Caliper

### REMOVAL AND INSTALLATION

1. Raise and safely support the vehicle.
2. Remove the tire and wheel assembly.
3. Bottom the piston in its bore for clearance.
4. Remove the bolt that attaches the brake hose from the caliper.
5. Remove the caliper mounting bolt and sleeve assemblies.
6. Lift the caliper off of the rotor.

**To install:**

7. Install the brake hose to the caliper using new copper washers.
8. Position the caliper over the rotor so the caliper engages the adaptor correctly. Lubricate and install the sleeves and bolts. Tighten to 38 ft. lbs. (51 Nm).

1. Outboard shoe and lining
2. Wear sensor
3. Caliper housing

**Installing the outboard pad**

3. Check the lining thickness on the inner shoe to make sure it is wearing evenly.

NOTE: *Some inboard shoes have a thermal lining against the shoe, molded integrally with the lining. Do not confuse this lining with uneven inboard-outboard lining wear.*

# 254 BRAKES

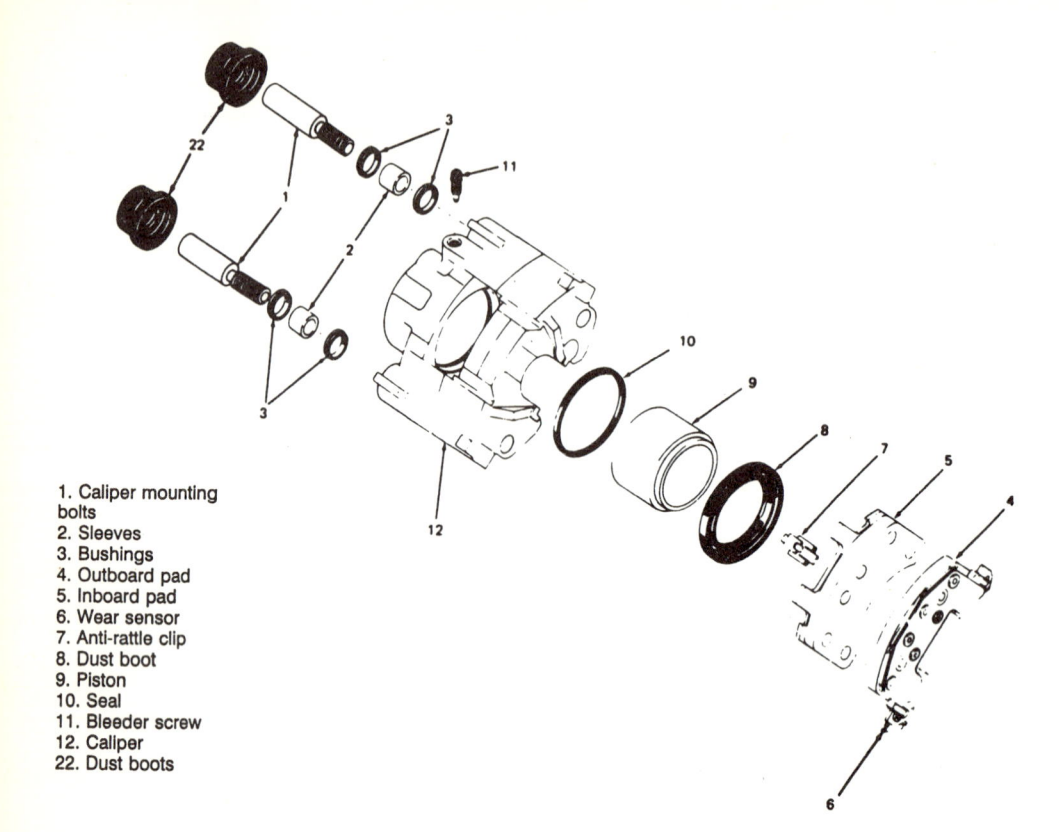

1. Caliper mounting bolts
2. Sleeves
3. Bushings
4. Outboard pad
5. Inboard pad
6. Wear sensor
7. Anti-rattle clip
8. Dust boot
9. Piston
10. Seal
11. Bleeder screw
12. Caliper
22. Dust boots

**Caliper exploded view**

9. Install the tire and wheel assembly.
10. Fill the master cylinder and bleed the brakes.

## OVERHAUL

1. Remove the caliper from the vehicle.
2. Remove the bushings. Inspect for cuts and nicks. Replace as necessary.
3. Stuff a shop towel into the caliper to catch the piston and apply compressed air to the inlet hole.

CAUTION: *Do not try to catch the piston with your hands when removing from the caliper as personal injury could occur.*

4. Inspect the piston for scoring, nicks, corrosion and worn chrome plating. Replace as necessary.
5. Remove the boot from the caliper housing bore.
6. Remove the piston seal from the groove with a small wooden or plastic tool.
7. Inspect the housing bore and seal groove for scoring, nicks, corrosion and wear. Crocus cloth can be used to polish out light corrosion.
8. Remove the bleeder valve and bleeder valve cap.

**To install:**

9. Install the bleeder valve and bleeder valve cap into the caliper.
10. Lubricate all rubber parts with clean brake fluid.
11. Install the piston seal into the caliper seal groove. Make sure it is not twisted.
12. Install the boot onto the piston.
13. Carefully, install the piston and boot into the caliper bore and push to the bottom of the bore.
14. Lubricate the bevelled end of the bushings with silicone grease. Pinch the bushing and install the bevelled end first. Push the bushing through the housing mounting bore.
15. Install the caliper assembly.

## Brake Rotor

### REMOVAL AND INSTALLATION

1. Raise and safely support the vehicle. Remove the tire and wheel assembly.
2. Remove the caliper and brake pads.
3. Remove the rotor from the hub.
4. The installation is the reverse of the removal procedure.

### INSPECTION

**Thickness Variation**

1. Measure the thickness at 4 points on the rotor. Make all measure measurements at the same distance in from the edge of the rotor.

2. If the variation from lowest to highest reading is greater than 0.0005 in. (0.013mm), the rotor should be resurfaced or replaced.

**Lateral Runout**

1. Remove the caliper and install 2 lug nuts to hold the rotor in position.
2. Secure a dial indicator to the steering knuckle so the indicator stylus contacts the rotor at about 1 in. (25mm) from the outer edge of the rotor.
3. Zero the dial indicator.
4. Move the rotor 1 complete revolution and observe the total indicated runout.
5. If the runout exceeds 0.0031 in. (0.08mm), resurface or replace the rotor.

# REAR DRUM BRAKES

CAUTION: *Brake shoes contain asbestos, which has been determined to be a cancer causing agent. Never clean the brake surfaces with compressed air! Avoid inhaling any dust from any brake surface! When cleaning brake surfaces, use a commercially available brake cleaning fluid.*

## Brake Drums

### REMOVAL AND INSTALLATION

1. Raise and safely support the vehicle.
2. Remove the wheel and tire assembly.
3. Remove the drum. If the drum is difficult to remove, the plug from the rear of the backing plate and push the self-adjuster lever away from the star wheel. Rotate the star wheel to retract the shoes.
4. The installation is the reverse of the removal procedure.
5. Adjust the brakes as required.

### INSPECTION

1. Inspect the brake drum for scoring, cracking or grooving. Light scoring of the drum not exceeding 0.020 in. (0.51mm) in depth will not affect brake operation.
2. Inspect the brake drum for excessive taper and out-of-round. When measuring a drum for out-of-round, taper and wear, take measurements at the open and closed edges of the machined surface and at right angles to each other.

## Brake Shoes

### INSPECTION

1. Remove the wheel and drum.
2. Inspect the shoes for proper thickness. The lining should be at least $1/32$ in. (0.8mm) above the rivet head for riveted brakes and $1/16$ in. (1.6mm) above the mounting surface for bonded brake linings.
3. Inspect the linings for even wear, cracking and scoring. Replace as necessary.

### REMOVAL AND INSTALLATION

NOTE: *If unsure of spring positioning, finish one side before starting the other and use the untouched side as a guide.*

1. Remove the wheels and drums. Remove the primary and secondary shoe return springs

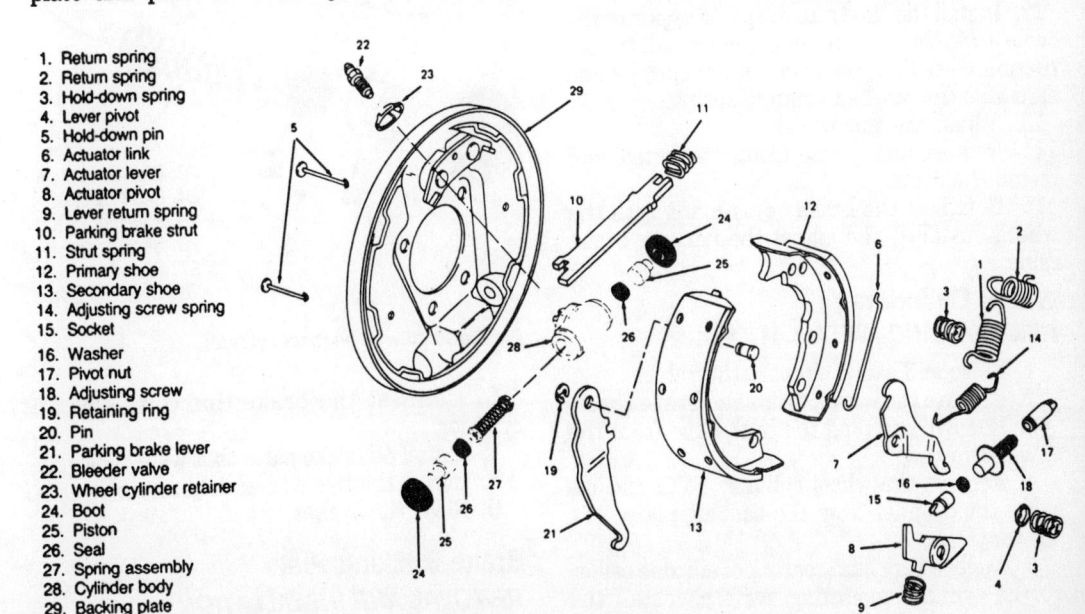

1. Return spring
2. Return spring
3. Hold-down spring
4. Lever pivot
5. Hold-down pin
6. Actuator link
7. Actuator lever
8. Actuator pivot
9. Lever return spring
10. Parking brake strut
11. Strut spring
12. Primary shoe
13. Secondary shoe
14. Adjusting screw spring
15. Socket
16. Washer
17. Pivot nut
18. Adjusting screw
19. Retaining ring
20. Pin
21. Parking brake lever
22. Bleeder valve
23. Wheel cylinder retainer
24. Boot
25. Piston
26. Seal
27. Spring assembly
28. Cylinder body
29. Backing plate

Drum brake components

# BRAKES

from the anchor pin but leave them installed in the shoes.

2. Lift on the adjuster lever and remove the adjuster cable. Remove the actuating lever link and pawl return spring.

3. Remove the hold-down pin return springs and cups. Remove the parking brake strut and spring. Remove the actuating lever and pawl.

4. Remove the shoes, held together by the lower spring, while separating the parking brake actuating lever from the shoe with a twisting motion.

5. Lift the wheel cylinder dust boots and inspect for fluid leakage.

6. Thoroughly clean and dry the backing plate.

**To install:**

7. Remove, clean and dry all parts still on the old shoes. Lubricate the star wheel shaft threads and transfer all the parts to the new shoes in their proper locations.

8. To prepare the backing plate, lubricate the bosses, anchor pin and parking brake actuating lever pivot surface lightly with the brake-compatible lubricant.

9. Spread the shoes apart, engage the parking brake actuating lever and position them on the backing plate so the wheel cylinder pins engage properly and the anchor pin holds the shoes up.

10. Install the parking brake strut and the hold-down pin assemblies. Install the actuating lever with the hold-down pin assembly.

11. Install the anchor plate. Lubricate the sliding surface of the adjuster cable plate and install the adjuster cable.

12. Install the shoe return spring opposite the cable, then the remaining spring. Install the actuating lever link, the shoe return springs and assemble the pawl and return spring.

13. Adjust the star wheel.

14. Remove any grease from the linings and install the drum.

15. Complete the brake adjustment with the wheels installed and adjust the parking brake cable.

## Wheel Cylinders

### REMOVAL AND INSTALLATION

1. Raise and safely support the vehicle.
2. Remove the wheel, drum and brake shoes.
3. Remove and plug the brake line from the wheel cylinder.
4. Remove the wheel cylinder bolts and remove the cylinder from the backing plate.

**To install:**

5. Apply a very thin coating of silicone sealer to the cylinder mounting surface, install the cylinder to the backing plate and install the attaching bolts.

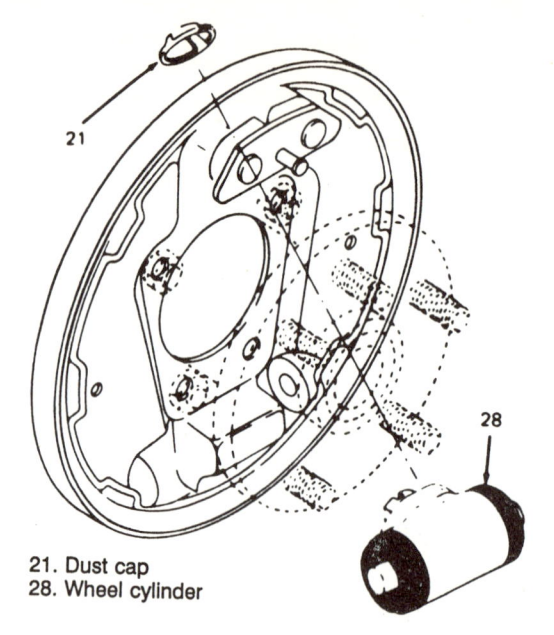

6. Connect the brake line to the wheel cylinder.
7. Install all brake parts that were removed.
8. Install the tire and wheel assembly.
9. Bleed the brakes.

## Brake Backing Plate

### REMOVAL AND INSTALLATION

1. Raise and safely support the vehicle. Remove the rear wheel(s).

---

21. Dust cap
28. Wheel cylinder

**Wheel cylinder mounting**

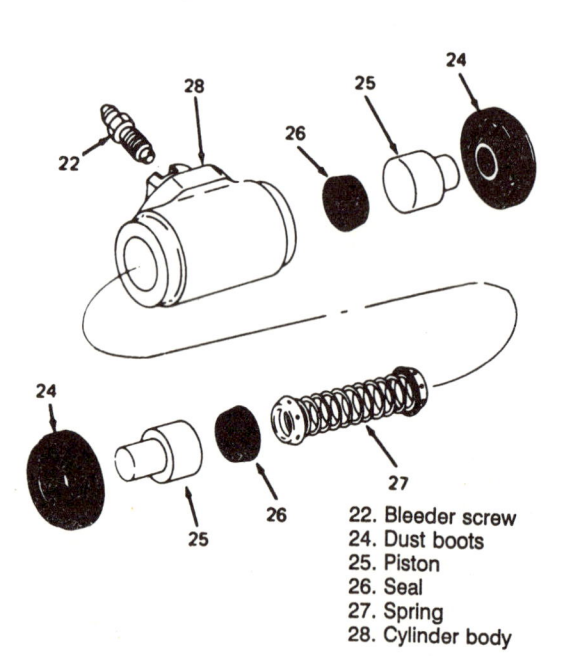

22. Bleeder screw
24. Dust boots
25. Piston
26. Seal
27. Spring
28. Cylinder body

**Exploded view of a wheel cylinder**

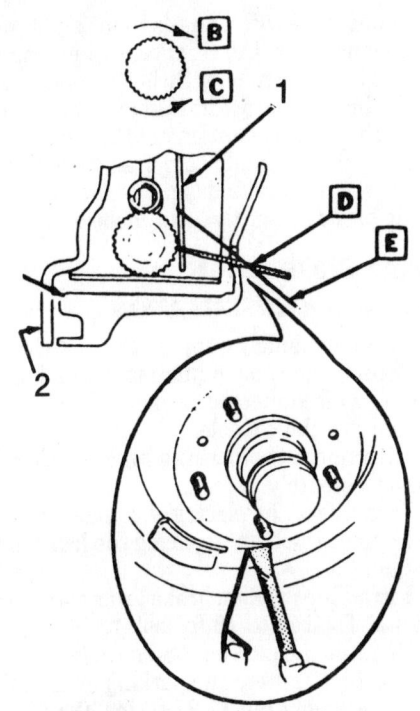

# BRAKES 257

2. Remove the brake components.
3. Disconnect the inlet tube and nut from the wheel cylinder.
4. Disconnect the parking brake cable from the backing plate.
5. Remove the hub and bearing assembly bolts.
6. Remove the backing plate.

**To install:**
7. Install the backing plate to the axle assembly.
8. Install the hub and bearing assembly bolts.
9. Connect the parking brake cable to the backing plate.
10. Connect the inlet tube and nut to the wheel cylinder. Tight to 12 ft. lbs. (17 Nm).
11. Install the brake system components. Check the brake adjustment.
12. Bleed the brake system.
13. Install the rear wheel(s).
14. Lower the vehicle.
15. Adjust the parking brake.

## PARKING BRAKE

### Cables

#### REMOVAL AND INSTALLATION

#### FRONT CABLE

1. Disconnect the negative battery cable. Raise and safely support the vehicle.

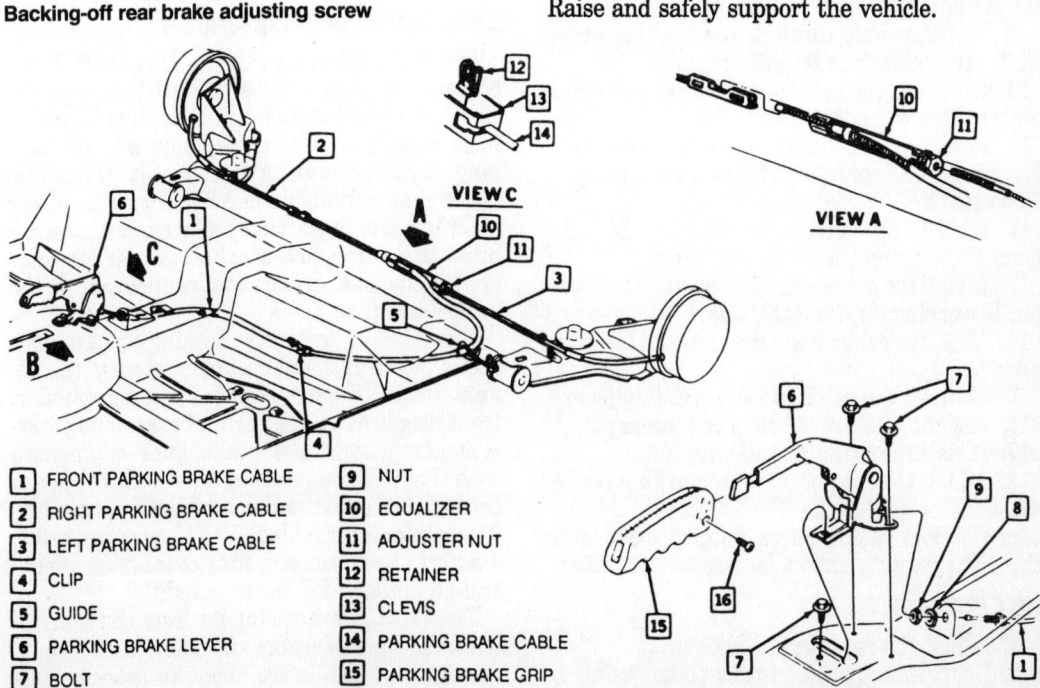

1. Brake drum
2. Star wheel rotation to retract brake shoes
3. Star wheel rotation to expand brake shoes
4. Screwdriver
5. Wire hook used only when backing off adjustment
6. Parking brake lever
7. Backing plate

**Backing-off rear brake adjusting screw**

| | |
|---|---|
| 1 FRONT PARKING BRAKE CABLE | 9 NUT |
| 2 RIGHT PARKING BRAKE CABLE | 10 EQUALIZER |
| 3 LEFT PARKING BRAKE CABLE | 11 ADJUSTER NUT |
| 4 CLIP | 12 RETAINER |
| 5 GUIDE | 13 CLEVIS |
| 6 PARKING BRAKE LEVER | 14 PARKING BRAKE CABLE |
| 7 BOLT | 15 PARKING BRAKE GRIP |
| 8 WASHER | 16 SCREW |

**Parking brake cables and lever assembly**

# BRAKES

2. Loosen or remove the equalizer nut. Lower the vehicle.
3. Remove the console.
4. Disconnect the parking brake cable from the lever.
5. Remove the nut that secures the front cable to the floor pan.
6. Loosen the catalytic converter shield and the parking brake cable from the body.
7. Remove the cable from the equalizer, guide and underbody clips.
8. The installation is the reverse of the removal procedure.
9. Adjust the cable.
10. Connect the negative battery cable and check the parking brakes for proper operation.

### REAR CABLES

1. Disconnect the negative battery cable. Raise and safely support the vehicle.
2. Loosen or remove the equalizer nut.
3. Remove the wheel(s) and drum(s).
4. Insert a suitable tool between the brake shoe and the top part of the brake adjuster bracket. Push the bracket to the front and release the top adjuster bracket rod.
5. Remove the hold-down spring, actuator lever and lever return spring.
6. Remove the adjuster spring.
7. Remove the top rear brake shoe return spring.
8. Disconnect the parking brake cable from the actuating lever.
9. Pull the cable through the backing plate while depressing the retaining tangs.
10. On the right side, remove the cable end button from the connector.
11. Remove the conduit fitting from the axle bracket while depressing the retaining tangs.

**To install:**

12. Install the conduit fitting into the axle bracket, securing the retaining tangs.
13. Install the cable end button to the connector, if working on the right side.
14. Click the cable assembly into the backing plate.
15. Connect the cable to the actuating lever.
16. Assemble the rear brake components.
17. Install the drum(s) and wheel(s).
18. Adjust the rear brakes and parking brake cable.
19. Connect the negative battery cable and check the parking brakes for proper operation.

### ADJUSTMENT

1. Adjust the rear brake shoes.
2. Depress the parking brake pedal exactly 3 ratchet clicks.
3. Raise and safely support the vehicle.
4. Check that the equalizer nut groove is liberally lubricated with chassis lube. Tighten the adjusting nut until the right rear wheel can just be turned to the rear with both hands but is locked when forward rotation is attempted.
5. With the mechanism totally disengaged, both rear wheels should turn freely in either direction with no brake drag. Do not adjust the parking brake so tightly as to cause brake drag.

## Parking Brake Lever

### REMOVAL AND INSTALLATION

1. Raise and safely support the vehicle.
2. Loosen the cable adjustment to allow the cable to be disconnected from the lever.
3. Remove the console.
4. Disconnect the parking brake cable from the lever assembly.
5. Disconnect the electrical connector.
6. Remove the bolts securing the lever to the floor pan.
7. Install the parking brake lever and attaching bolts. Tighten to 18 ft. lbs. (25 Nm).
8. Connect the parking brake cable to the lever assembly. Tighten the parking brake cable-to-lever assembly nut to 21 ft. lbs. (28 Nm).
9. Install the console.
10. Adjust the parking brake cable.
11. Lower the vehicle.

# ANTI-LOCK BRAKE SYSTEM (ABS)

## Description and Operation

Anti-lock brakes provide the driver with 3 important benefits over standard braking systems: increased vehicle stability, improved vehicle steerability and potentially reduced stopping distances during braking. It should be noted that although the ABS-VI system offers definite advantages, the system cannot increase brake pressure above master cylinder pressure applied by the driver and cannot apply the brakes itself.

The ABS-VI Anti-lock Braking System consist of a conventional braking system with vacuum power booster, compact master cylinder, front disc brakes, rear drum brakes and interconnecting hydraulic brake lines augmented with the ABS components. The ABS-VI system consists of a hydraulic modulator assembly, Electronic Control Unit (ECU), a system relay, 4 wheel speed sensors, interconnecting wiring and an amber ABS warning light.

The ECU monitors inputs from the individual wheel speed sensors and determines when a wheel or wheels is/are about to lock-up. The ECU controls the motors on the hydraulic modulator assembly to reduce brake pressure to the wheel about to lock-up. When the wheel regains traction, the brake pressure is increased until the wheel again approaches lock-up. The cycle repeats until either the vehicle comes to a stop, the brake pedal is released or no wheels are about to lock-up. The ECU also has the ability to monitor itself and can store diagnostic codes in a non-volatile (will not be erased if the battery is disconnected) memory. The ECU is serviced as an assembly.

The ABS-VI braking system employs 2 modes: base (conventional) braking and anti-lock braking. Under normal braking, the conventional part of the system stops the vehicle. When in the ABS mode, the Electromagnetic Brakes (EMB) action of the ABS system controls the 2 front wheels individually and the rear wheels together. If the 1 rear wheel is about to lock-up, the hydraulic pressure to both wheels is reduced, controlling both wheels together. Since the vast majority of the braking is controlled by the front wheels, there is no adverse effect on vehicle control during hard braking.

## ONBOARD DIAGNOSTICS

The ABS-VI contains sophisticated onboard diagnostics that, when accessed with a bidirectional "Scan" tool, are designed to identify the source of any system fault as specifically as possible, including whether or not the fault is intermittent. There are 58 diagnostic fault codes to assist the service technician with diagnosis. The last diagnostic fault code to occur is specifically identified, and specific ABS data is stored at the time of this fault, also, the first five codes set. Additionally, using a bidirectional "Scan" tool, each input and output can be monitored, thus enabling fault confirmation and repair verification. Manual control of components and automated functional tests are also available when using a GM approved "Scan" tool. Details of many of these functions are contained in the following sections.

## ENHANCED DIAGNOSTICS

Enhanced Diagnostic Information, found in the CODE HISTORY function of the bidirectional "Scan" tool, is designed to provide the service technician with specific fault occurrence information. For each of the first five (5) and the very last diagnostic fault codes stored, data is stored to identify the specific fault code number, the number of failure occurrences, and the number of drive cycles since the failure first and last occurred (a drive cycle occurs when the ignition is turned "ON" and the vehicle is driven faster than 10 mph). However, if a fault is present, the drive cycle counter will increment by turning the ignition "ON" and "OFF". These first five (5) diagnostic fault codes are also stored in the order of occurrence. The order in which the first 5 faults occurred can be useful in determining if a previous fault is linked to the most recent faults, such as an intermittent wheel speed sensor which later becomes completely open.

During difficult diagnosis situations, this information can be used to identify fault occurrence trends. Does the fault occur more frequently now than it did during the last time when it only failed 1 out of 35 drive cycles? Did the fault only occur once over a large number of drive cycles, indication an unusual condition present when the fault occurred? Does the fault occur infrequently over a large number of drive cycles, indication special diagnosis techniques may be required to identify the source of the fault?

If a fault occurred 1 out of 20 drive cycles, the fault is intermittent and has not reoccurred for 19 drive cycles. This fault may be difficult or impossible to duplicate and may have been caused by a severe vehicle impact (large pot hole, speed bump at high speed, etc.) that momentarily opened an electrical connector or caused unusual vehicle suspension movement. Problem resolution is unlikely, and the problem may never reoccur (check diagnostic aids proved for that code). If the fault occurred 3 out of 15 drive cycles, the odds of finding the cause are still not good, but you know how often it occurs and you can determine whether or not the fault is becoming more frequent based on an additional or past occurrences visit if the source of the problem can not or could not be found. If the fault occurred 10 out of 20 drive cycles, the odds of finding the cause are very good, as the fault may be easily reproduced.

By using the additional fault data, you can also determine if a failure is randomly intermittent or if it has not reoccurred for long periods of time due to weather changes or a repair prior to this visit. Say a diagnostic fault code occurred 10 of 20 drive cycles but has not reoccurred for 10 drive cycles. This means the failure occurred 10 of 10 drive cycles but has not reoccurred since. A significant environmental change or a repair occurred 10 drive cycles ago. A repair may not be necessary if a recent repair can be confirmed. If no repair was made, the service can focus on diagnosis techniques used to locate difficult to recreate problems.

## DIAGNOSTIC PROCESS

When servicing the ABS-VI, the following steps should be followed in order. Failure to follow these steps may result in the loss of important diagnostic data and may lead to difficult and time consuming diagnosis procedures.

# BRAKES

1. Using a bidirectional "Scan" tool, read all current and history diagnostic codes. Be certain to note which codes are current diagnostic code failures. DO NOT CLEAR CODES unless directed to do so.
2. Using a bidirectional "Scan" tool, read the CODE HISTORY data. Note the diagnostic fault codes stored and their frequency of failure. Specifically note the last failure that occurred and the conditions present when this failure occurred. This "last failure" should be the starting point for diagnosis and repair.
3. Perform a vehicle preliminary diagnosis inspection. This should include:
    a. Inspection of the compact master cylinder for proper brake fluid level.
    b. Inspection of the ABS hydraulic modulator for any leaks or wiring damage.
    c. Inspection of brake components at all four (4) wheels. Verify no drag exists. Also verify proper brake apply operation.
    d. Inspection for worn or damaged wheel bearings that allow a wheel to "wobble."
    e. Inspection of the wheel speed sensors and their wiring. Verify correct air gap range, solid sensor attachment, undamaged sensor toothed ring, and undamaged wiring, especially at vehicle attachment points.
    f. Verify proper outer CV joint alignment and operation.
    g. Verify tires meet legal tread depth requirements.
4. If no codes are present, or mechanical component failure codes are present, perform the automated modulator test using the Tech 1 or T-100 to isolate the cause of the problem. If the failure is intermittent and not reproducible, test drive the vehicle while using the automatic snapshot feature of the bidirectional "Scan" tool.

Perform normal acceleration, stopping, and turning maneuvers. If this does not reproduce the failure, perform an ABS stop, on a low coefficient surface such as gravel, from approximately 30 - 50 mph while triggering on any ABS code. If the failure is still not reproducible, use the enhanced diagnostic information found in CODE HISTORY to determine whether or not this failure should be further diagnosed.
5. Once all system failures have been corrected, clear the ABS codes.

The Tech 1 and T-100, when plugged into the

## ABS SYMPTOM AND TROUBLE CODE TABLE

| TROUBLE CODE | DESCRIPTION |
| --- | --- |
| A064 | Rear Axle Motor Circuit Open |
| A065 | Rear Axle Motor Circuit Shorted to Ground |
| A066 | Rear Axle Motor Circuit Shorted to Battery or Motor Shorted |
| A067 | Left Front EMB Circuit Open or Shorted to Ground |
| A068 | Left Front EMB Circuit Shorted to Battery or EMB Shorted |
| A071 | Right Front EMB Circuit Open or Shorted to Ground |
| A072 | Right Front EMB Circuit Shorted to Battery or EMB Shorted |
| A076 | Left Front Solenoid Circuit Shorted to Battery or Open |
| A077 | Left Front Solenoid Circuit Shorted to Ground or Driver Open |
| A078 | Right Front Solenoid Circuit Shorted to Battery or Open |
| A081 | Right Front Solenoid Circuit Shorted to Ground or Driver Open |
| A082 | Calibration Memory Failure |
| A086 | Red Brake Warning Light Activated by ABS |
| A087 | Red Brake Warning Light Circuit Open |
| A088 | Red Brake Warning Light Circuit Shorted to Battery |
| A091 | Open Brake Switch Contacts During Deceleration |
| A092 | Open Brake Switch Contacts When ABS Was Required |
| A093 | Code 91 or 92 Set in Current or Previous Ignition Cycle |
| A094 | Brake Switch Contacts Always Closed |
| A095 | Brake Switch Circuit Open |
| A096 | Brake Lights Circuit Open |

ABS-VI trouble codes

## ABS SYMPTOM AND TROUBLE CODE TABLE

| CHART | SYMPTOM |
|---|---|
| A | ABS (Amber) Warning Light "ON" Constantly, No Codes Stored |
| B | ABS (Amber) Warning Light "ON" Intermittently, No Codes Stored |

| TROUBLE CODE | DESCRIPTION |
|---|---|
| A011 | ABS Warning Light Circuit Open or Shorted to Ground |
| A013 | ABS Warning Light Circuit Shorted to Battery |
| A014 | Enable Relay Contacts Or Fuse Open |
| A015 | Enable Relay Contacts Shorted to Battery |
| A016 | Enable Relay Coil Circuit Open |
| A017 | Enable Relay Coil Circuit Shorted to Ground |
| A018 | Enable Relay Coil Circuit Shorted to Battery |
| A021 | Left Front Wheel Speed = 0 (1 of 2) |
| A022 | Right Front Wheel Speed = 0 (1 of 2) |
| A023 | Left Rear Wheel Speed = 0 (1 of 2) |
| A024 | Right Rear Wheel Speed = 0 (1 of 2) |
| A025 | Left Front Excessive Wheel Speed Variation (1 of 2) |
| A026 | Right Front Excessive Wheel Speed Variation (1 of 2) |
| A027 | Left Rear Excessive Wheel Speed Variation (1 of 2) |
| A028 | Right Rear Excessive Wheel Speed Variation (1 of 2) |
| A031 | Two Wheel Speeds = 0 (1 of 2) (Non-Tubular Rear Axle) |
| A031 | Two Wheel Speeds = 0 (1 of 2) (Tubular Rear Axle) |
| A036 | Low System Voltage |
| A037 | High System Voltage |
| A038 | Left Front EMB Will Not Hold Motor |
| A041 | Right Front EMB Will Not Hold Motor |
| A042 | Rear Axle ESB Will Not Hold Motor |
| A044 | Left Front Channel Will Not Move |
| A045 | Right Front Channel Will Not Move |
| A046 | Rear Axle Channel Will Not Move |
| A047 | Left Front Motor Free Spins |
| A048 | Right Front Motor Free Spins |
| A051 | Rear Axle Motor Free Spins |
| A052 | Left Front Channel in Release Too Long |
| A053 | Right Front Channel In Release Too Long |
| A054 | Rear Axle Channel in Release Too Long |
| A055 | Motor Driver Fault Detected |
| A056 | Left Front Motor Circuit Open |
| A057 | Left Front Motor Circuit Shorted to Ground |
| A058 | Left Front Motor Circuit Shorted to Battery or Motor Shorted |
| A061 | Right Front Motor Circuit Open |
| A062 | Right Front Motor Circuit Shorted to Ground |
| A063 | Right Front Motor Circuit Shorted to Battery or Motor Shorted |

**ABS-VI trouble codes**

# BRAKES

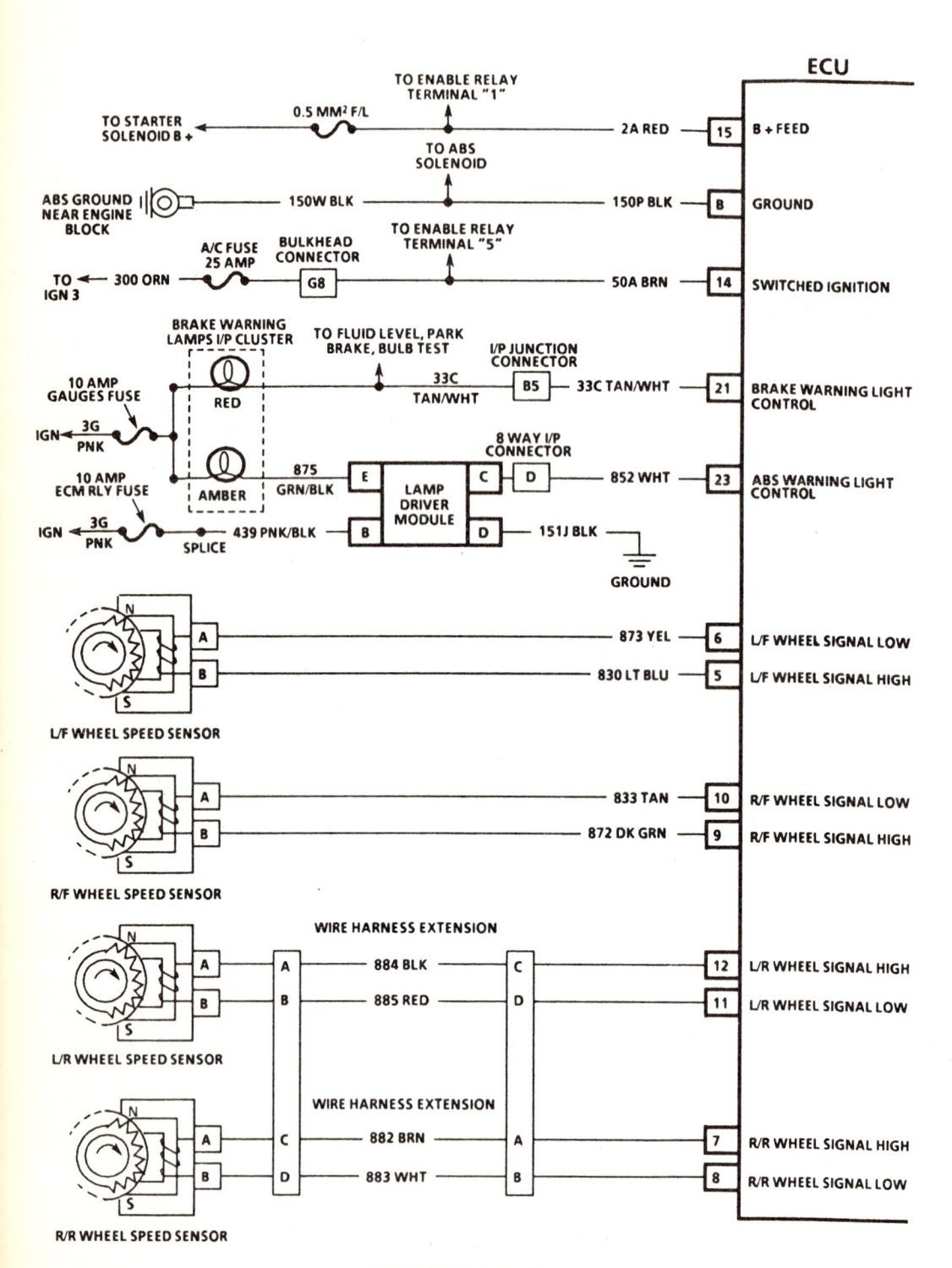

**ABS-VI ECU wiring diagram**

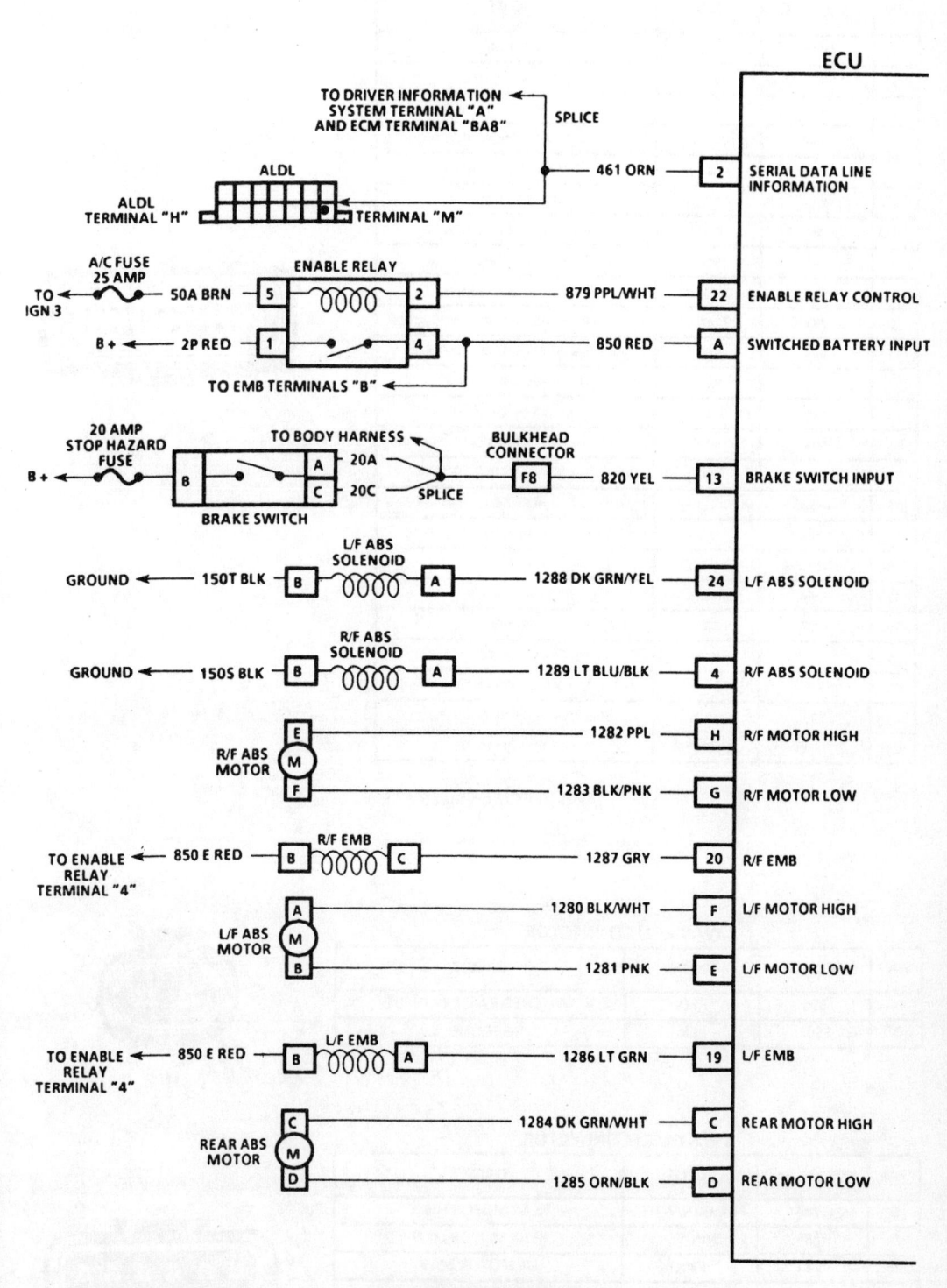

# BRAKES 263

**ABS-VI ECU wiring diagram**

# BRAKES

## ECU 24 PIN WORLD CONNECTOR

| PIN | CIRCUIT NO. | COLOR | CIRCUIT |
|---|---|---|---|
| 1 | OPEN | | NOT USED |
| 2 | 461 | ORN | SERIAL DATA LINE |
| 3 | OPEN | | NOT USED |
| 4 | 1289 | LT BLU/BLK | R/F ABS SOLENOID |
| 5 | 830 | LT BLU | L/F WHEEL SIGNAL HIGH |
| 6 | 873 | YEL | L/F WHEEL SIGNAL LOW |
| 7 | 882 | BRN | R/R WHEEL SIGNAL HIGH |
| 8 | 883 | WHT | R/R WHEEL SIGNAL LOW |
| 9 | 872 | DK GRN | R/F WHEEL SIGNAL HIGH |
| 10 | 833 | TAN | R/F WHEEL SIGNAL LOW |
| 11 | 885 | RED | L/R WHEEL SIGNAL LOW |
| 12 | 884 | BLK | L/R WHEEL SIGNAL HIGH |
| 13 | 820 | YEL | BRAKE SWITCH INPUT |
| 14 | 50A | BRN | SWITCH IGNITION |
| 15 | 2A | RED | B + FEED |
| 16 | OPEN | | NOT USED |
| 17 | OPEN | | NOT USED |
| 18 | VENT TUBE | BLK | VENT TUBE |
| 19 | 1286 | LT GRN | L/F EMB |
| 20 | 1287 | GRY | R/F EMB |
| 21 | 33C | TAN/WHT | BRAKE TELLTALE |
| 22 | 879 | PPL/WHT | ENABLE RELAY CONTROL |
| 23 | 852 | WHT | ABS WARNING LIGHT CONTROL |
| 24 | 1288 | DK GRN/YEL | L/F ABS SOLENOID |

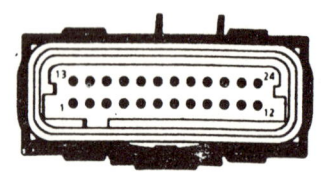

**ABS-VI ECU connector view**

## 2 WAY ECU CONNECTOR

| PIN | CIRCUIT No. | COLOR | CIRCUIT |
|---|---|---|---|
| A | 850 | RED | SWITCHED BATTERY INPUT |
| B | 150P | BLK | GROUND |

## 6 WAY ECU CONNECTOR

| PIN | CIRCUIT No. | COLOR | CIRCUIT |
|---|---|---|---|
| C | 1284 | DK GRN/WHT | REAR MOTOR HIGH |
| D | 1285 | ORN/BLK | REAR MOTOR LOW |
| E | 1281 | PNK | L/F MOTOR LOW |
| F | 1280 | BLK/WHT | L/F MOTOR HIGH |
| G | 1283 | BLK/PNK | R/F MOTOR LOW |
| H | 1282 | PPL | R/F MOTOR HIGH |

**ABS-VI ECU connector view**

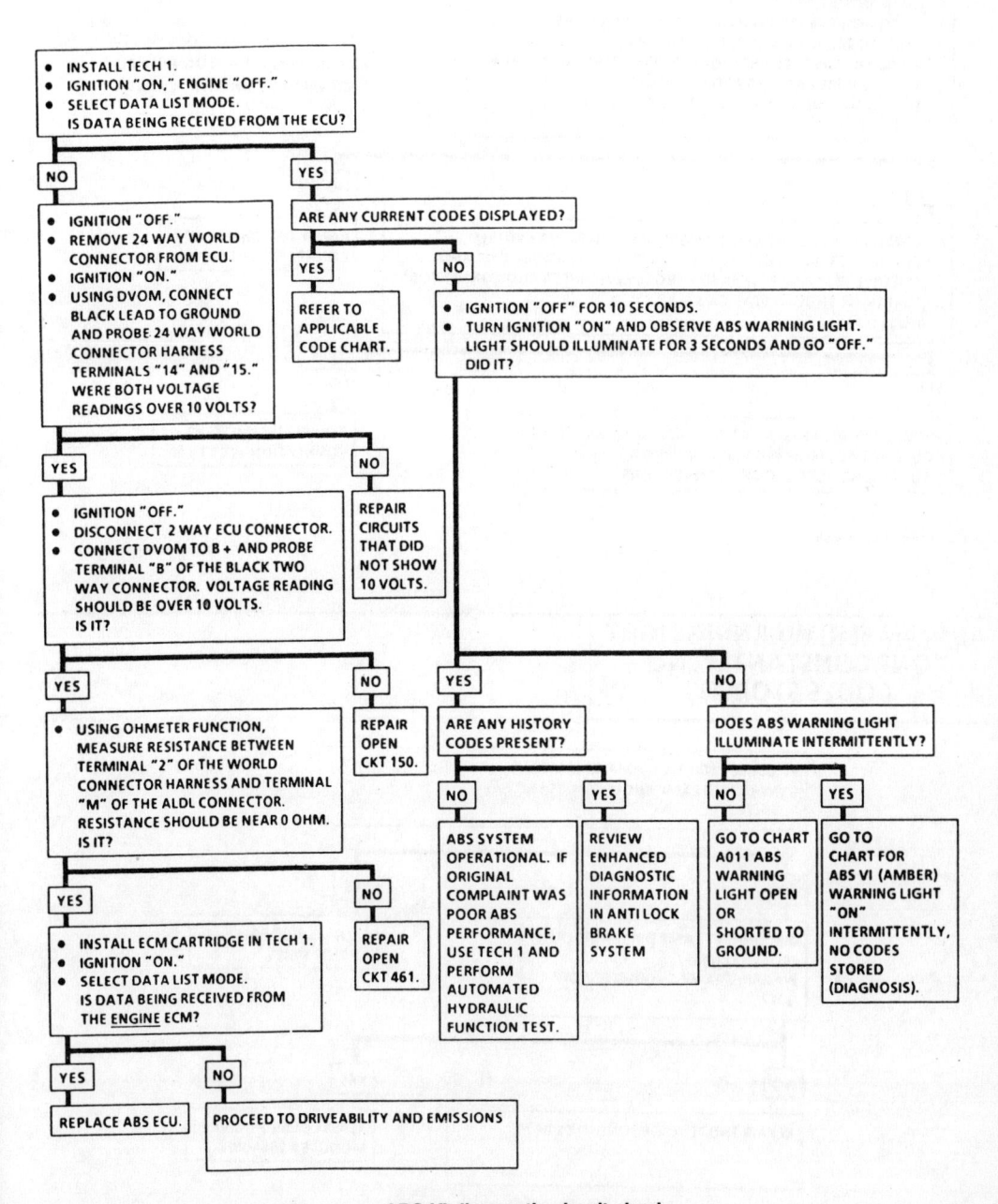

**BRAKES** 265

## ABS-VI
### DIAGNOSTIC CIRCUIT CHECK

- INSTALL TECH 1.
- IGNITION "ON," ENGINE "OFF."
- SELECT DATA LIST MODE.
  IS DATA BEING RECEIVED FROM THE ECU?

**NO**
- IGNITION "OFF."
- REMOVE 24 WAY WORLD CONNECTOR FROM ECU.
- IGNITION "ON."
- USING DVOM, CONNECT BLACK LEAD TO GROUND AND PROBE 24 WAY WORLD CONNECTOR HARNESS TERMINALS "14" AND "15." WERE BOTH VOLTAGE READINGS OVER 10 VOLTS?

**YES**
ARE ANY CURRENT CODES DISPLAYED?

**YES** → REFER TO APPLICABLE CODE CHART.

**NO**
- IGNITION "OFF" FOR 10 SECONDS.
- TURN IGNITION "ON" AND OBSERVE ABS WARNING LIGHT. LIGHT SHOULD ILLUMINATE FOR 3 SECONDS AND GO "OFF." DID IT?

**YES**
- IGNITION "OFF."
- DISCONNECT 2 WAY ECU CONNECTOR.
- CONNECT DVOM TO B+ AND PROBE TERMINAL "B" OF THE BLACK TWO WAY CONNECTOR. VOLTAGE READING SHOULD BE OVER 10 VOLTS. IS IT?

**NO** → REPAIR CIRCUITS THAT DID NOT SHOW 10 VOLTS.

**YES**
USING OHMETER FUNCTION, MEASURE RESISTANCE BETWEEN TERMINAL "2" OF THE WORLD CONNECTOR HARNESS AND TERMINAL "M" OF THE ALDL CONNECTOR. RESISTANCE SHOULD BE NEAR 0 OHM. IS IT?

**NO** → REPAIR OPEN CKT 150.

**YES** (from DID IT? YES branch)
ARE ANY HISTORY CODES PRESENT?

**NO** → ABS SYSTEM OPERATIONAL. IF ORIGINAL COMPLAINT WAS POOR ABS PERFORMANCE, USE TECH 1 AND PERFORM AUTOMATED HYDRAULIC FUNCTION TEST.

**YES** → REVIEW ENHANCED DIAGNOSTIC INFORMATION IN ANTI LOCK BRAKE SYSTEM

**NO** (from DID IT?)
DOES ABS WARNING LIGHT ILLUMINATE INTERMITTENTLY?

**NO** → GO TO CHART A011 ABS WARNING LIGHT OPEN OR SHORTED TO GROUND.

**YES** → GO TO CHART FOR ABS VI (AMBER) WARNING LIGHT "ON" INTERMITTENTLY, NO CODES STORED (DIAGNOSIS).

**YES**
- INSTALL ECM CARTRIDGE IN TECH 1.
- IGNITION "ON."
- SELECT DATA LIST MODE.
  IS DATA BEING RECEIVED FROM THE ENGINE ECM?

**NO** → REPAIR OPEN CKT 461.

**YES** → REPLACE ABS ECU.

**NO** → PROCEED TO DRIVEABILITY AND EMISSIONS

**ABS-VI diagnostic circuit check**

# BRAKES

## ABS (AMBER) WARNING LIGHT "ON" INTERMITTENTLY, NO CODES STORED

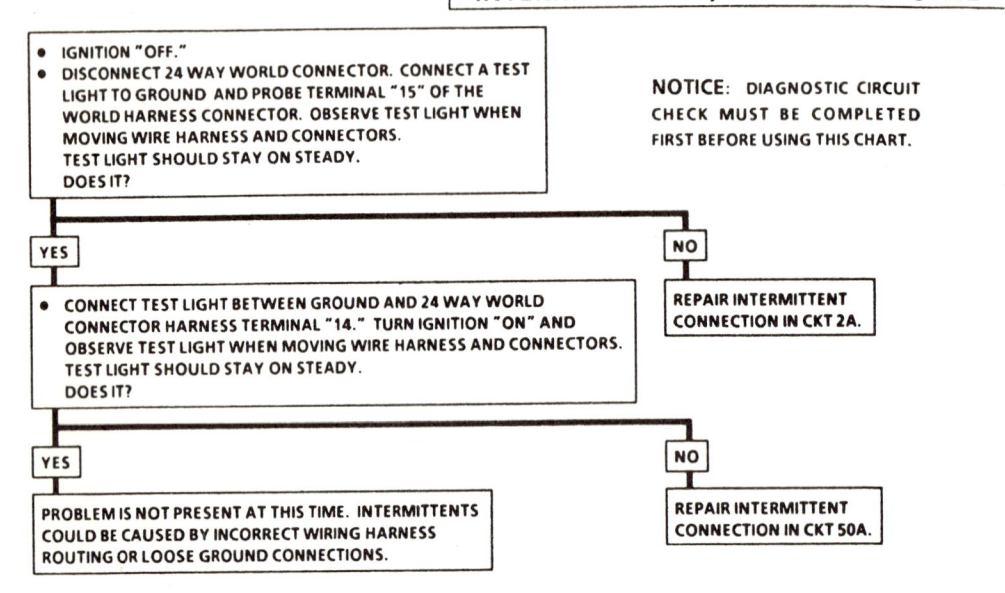

NOTICE: DIAGNOSTIC CIRCUIT CHECK MUST BE COMPLETED FIRST BEFORE USING THIS CHART.

- IGNITION "OFF."
- DISCONNECT 24 WAY WORLD CONNECTOR. CONNECT A TEST LIGHT TO GROUND AND PROBE TERMINAL "15" OF THE WORLD HARNESS CONNECTOR. OBSERVE TEST LIGHT WHEN MOVING WIRE HARNESS AND CONNECTORS.
TEST LIGHT SHOULD STAY ON STEADY.
DOES IT?

**YES** →
- CONNECT TEST LIGHT BETWEEN GROUND AND 24 WAY WORLD CONNECTOR HARNESS TERMINAL "14." TURN IGNITION "ON" AND OBSERVE TEST LIGHT WHEN MOVING WIRE HARNESS AND CONNECTORS.
TEST LIGHT SHOULD STAY ON STEADY.
DOES IT?

**NO** → REPAIR INTERMITTENT CONNECTION IN CKT 2A.

**YES** → PROBLEM IS NOT PRESENT AT THIS TIME. INTERMITTENTS COULD BE CAUSED BY INCORRECT WIRING HARNESS ROUTING OR LOOSE GROUND CONNECTIONS.

**NO** → REPAIR INTERMITTENT CONNECTION IN CKT 50A.

FIG. 34 ABS-VI diagnosis

## ABS (AMBER) WARNING LIGHT "ON" CONSTANTLY, NO CODES STORED

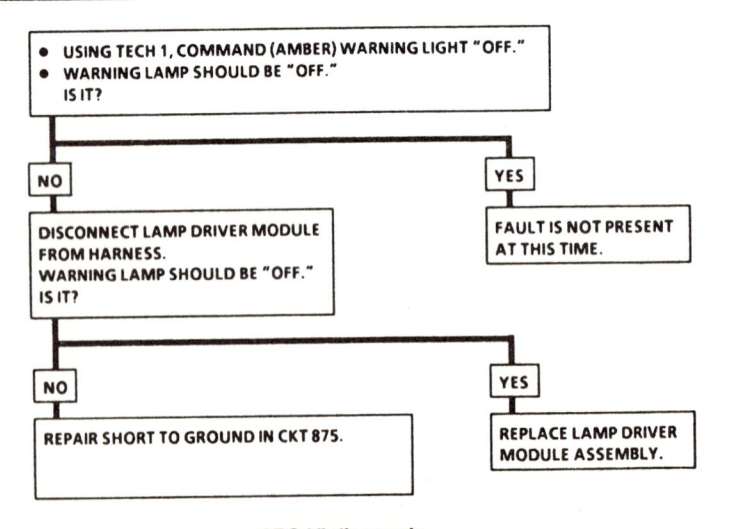

- USING TECH 1, COMMAND (AMBER) WARNING LIGHT "OFF."
- WARNING LAMP SHOULD BE "OFF."
IS IT?

**NO** → DISCONNECT LAMP DRIVER MODULE FROM HARNESS.
WARNING LAMP SHOULD BE "OFF."
IS IT?

**YES** → FAULT IS NOT PRESENT AT THIS TIME.

**NO** → REPAIR SHORT TO GROUND IN CKT 875.

**YES** → REPLACE LAMP DRIVER MODULE ASSEMBLY.

ABS-VI diagnosis

ALDL connector, becomes part of the vehicle's electronic system. The Tech 1 and T-100 can also perform the following functions on components linked by the Serial Data Link (SDL):
- Display ABS data
- Display and clear ABS trouble codes
- Control ABS components
- Perform extensive ABS diagnosis
- Provide diagnostic testing for "Intermittent" ABS conditions.

Each test mode has specific diagnosis capabilities which depend upon various keystrokes. In general, five (5) keys control sequencing: "YES," "NO," "EXIT," "UP" arrow and "DOWN" arrow. The F0 through F9 keys select operating modes, perform functions within an operating mode, or enter trouble code or model year designations.

In general, the Tech 1 has five (5) test modes for diagnosing the anti-lock brake system. The five (5) test modes are as follows:

**MODE F0: DATA LIST** - In this test mode, the Tech 1 continuously monitors wheel speed data, brake switch status and other inputs and outputs.

**MODE F1: CODE HISTORY** - In this mode, fault code history data is displayed. This data includes how many ignition cycles since the fault code occurred, along with other ABS information. The first five (5) and last fault codes set are included in the ABS history data.

**MODE F2: TROUBLE CODES** - In this test mode, trouble codes stored by the EBCM, both current ignition cycle and history, may be displayed or cleared.

**MODE F3: ABS SNAPSHOT** - In this test mode, the Tech 1 captures ABS data before and after a fault occurrence or a forced manual trigger.

**MODE F4: ABS TESTS** - In this test mode, the Tech 1 performs hydraulic modulator functional tests to assist in problem isolation during troubleshooting. Included here is manual control of the motors which is used prior to bleeding the brake system.

Press F7 to covert from English to metric.

## DISPLAYING CODES

Diagnostic fault codes can only be read through the use of a bidirectional "Scan" tool. There are no provisions for "Flash Code" diagnostics.

## CLEARING CODES

The trouble codes in EBCM memory are erased in one of two ways:
1. Tech 1 "Clear Codes" selection.
2. Ignition cycle default.

These two methods are detailed below. Be sure to verify proper system operation and absence of codes when clearing procedure is completed.

The EBCM will not permit code clearing until all of the codes have been displayed. Also, codes cannot be cleared by unplugging the EBCM, disconnecting the battery cables, or turning the ignition "OFF" (except on an ignition cycle default).

### Tech 1 "Clear Codes" Method

Select F2 for trouble codes. After codes have been viewed completely, Tech 1 will display CLEAR ABS CODES. Answer YES; the Tech 1 will then read, DISPLAY CODE HIST. DATA? "LOST" IF CODES CLEARED. "NO" TO CLEAR CODES. Answer NO and codes will be cleared.

### Ignition Cycle Default

If no diagnostic fault code occurs for 100 drive cycles (a drive cycle occurs when the ignition is turned ON and the vehicle is driven faster than 10 mph), any existing fault codes are cleared from the EBCM memory.

## INTERMITTENT FAILURES

As with most electronic systems, intermittent failures may be difficult to accurately diagnose. The following is a method to try to isolate an intermittent failure especially wheel speed circuitry failures.

If an ABS fault occurs, the ABS warning light indicator will be on during the ignition cycle in which the fault was detected. If it is an intermittent problem which seems to have corrected itself (ABS warning light off), a history trouble code will be stored. Also stored will be the history data of the code at the time the fault occurred. The Tech 1 must be used to read ABS history data.

## INTERMITTENTS AND POOR CONNECTIONS

Most intermittents are caused by faulty electrical connections or wiring, although occasionally a sticking relay or solenoid can be a problem. Some items to check are:

1. Poor mating of connector halves, or terminals not fully seated in the connector body (backed out).
2. Dirt or corrosion on the terminals. The terminals must be clean and free of any foreign material which could impede proper terminal contact.
3. Damaged connector body, exposing the terminals to moisture and dirt, as well as not maintaining proper terminal orientation with the component or mating connector.
4. Improperly formed or damaged terminals. All connector terminals in problem circuits

should be checked carefully to ensure good contact tension. Use a corresponding mating terminal to check for proper tension. Refer to "Checking Terminal Contact" in this Chapter for the specific procedure.

5. The J 35616-A Connector Test Adapter Kit must be used whenever a diagnostic procedure requests checking or probing a terminal. Using the adapter will ensure that no damage to the terminal will occur, as well as giving an idea of whether contact tension is sufficient. If contact tension seems incorrect, refer to "Checking Terminal Contact" in this Chapter for specifics.

6. Poor terminal-to-wire connection. Checking this requires removing the terminal from the connector body. Some conditions which fall under this description are poor crimps, poor solder joints, crimping over wire insulation rather than the wire itself, corrosion in the wire-to-terminal contact area, etc.

7. Wire insulation which is rubbed through, causing an intermittent short as the bare area touches other wiring or parts of the vehicle.

8. Wiring broken inside the insulation. This condition could cause a continuity check to show a good circuit, but if only 1 or 2 strands of a multi-strand-type wire are intact, resistance could be far too high.

### Checking Terminal Contact

When diagnosing an electrical system that uses Metri-Pack 150/280/480/630 series terminals (refer to Terminal Repair Kit J 38125-A instruction manual J 38125-4 for terminal identification), it is important to check terminal contact between a connector and component, or between in-line connectors, before replacing a suspect component.

Frequently, a diagnostic chart leads to a step that reads "Check for poor connection". Mating terminals must be inspected to ensure good terminal contact. A poor connection between the male and female terminal at a connector may be the result of contamination or deformation.

Contamination is caused by the connector halves being improperly connected, a missing or damaged connector seal, or damage to the connector itself, exposing the terminals to moisture and dirt. Contamination, usually in underhood or underbody connectors, leads to terminal corrosion, causing an open circuit or an intermittently open circuit.

Deformation is caused by probing the mating side of a connector terminal without the proper adapter, improperly joining the connector halves or repeatedly separating and joining the connector halves. Deformation, usually to the female terminal contact tang, can result in poor terminal contact causing an open or intermittently open circuit.

Follow the procedure below to check terminal contact.

1. Separate the connector halves. Refer to Terminal Repair Kit J 38125-A instruction manual J 38125-4, if available.

2. Inspect the connector halves for contamination. Contamination will result in a white or green buildup within the connector body or between terminals, causing high terminal resistance, intermittent contact or an open circuit. An underhood or underbody connector that shows signs of contamination should be replaced in its entirety: terminals, seals, and connector body.

3. Using an equivalent male terminal from the Terminal Repair Kit J 38125-A, check the retention force of the female terminal in question by inserting and removing the male terminal to the female terminal in the connector body. Good terminal contact will require a certain amount of force to separate the terminals.

4. Using an equivalent female terminal from the Terminal Repair Kit J 38125-A, compare the retention force of this terminal to the female terminal in question by joining and separating the male terminal to the female terminal in question. If the retention force is significantly different between the two female terminals, replace the female terminal in question, using a terminal from Terminal Repair Kit J 38125-A.

## Anti-Lock Brake System Service

### Precautions

Failure to observe the following precautions may result in system damage.

- Performing diagnostic work on the ABS-VI requires the use of a Tech I Scan diagnostic tool or equivalent. If unavailable, please refer diagnostic work to a qualified technician.
- Before performing electric arc welding on the vehicle, disconnect the Electronic Brake Control Module (EBCM) and the hydraulic modulator connectors.
- When performing painting work on the vehicle, do not expose the Electronic Brake Control Module (EBCM) to temperatures in excess of 185°F (85°C) for longer than 2 hrs. The system may be exposed to temperatures up to 200°F (95°C) for less than 15 min.
- Never disconnect or connect the Electronic Brake Control Module (EBCM) or hydraulic modulator connectors with the ignition switch ON.
- Never disassemble any component of the Anti-Lock Brake System (ABS) which is designated non-serviceable; the component must be replaced as an assembly.

# BRAKES 269

- When filling the master cylinder, always use Delco Supreme 11 brake fluid or equivalent, which meets DOT-3 specifications; petroleum base fluid will destroy the rubber parts.

## ABS Hydraulic Modulator Assembly

### Removal and Installation

CAUTION: *To avoid personal injury, use the Tech I Scan tool to relieve the gear tension in the hydraulic modulator. This procedure must be performed prior to removal of the brake control and motor assembly.*

1. Disconnect the negative battery cable.
2. Disconnect the 2 solenoid electrical connectors and the fluid level sensor connector.
3. Disconnect the 6-pin and 3-pin motor pack electrical connectors.
4. Wrap a shop towel around the hydraulic brake lines and disconnect the 4 brake lines from the modulator.

NOTE: *Cap the disconnected lines to prevent the loss of fluid and the entry of moisture and contaminants.*

5. Remove the 2 nuts attaching the ABS hydraulic modulator assembly to the vacuum booster.
6. Remove the ABS hydraulic modulator assembly from the vehicle.

**To install:**

7. Install the ABS hydraulic modulator assembly to the vehicle. Install the 2 attaching nuts and tighten to 20 ft. lbs. (27 Nm).
8. Connect the 4 brake pipes to the modulator assembly. Tighten to 13 ft. lbs. (17 Nm).
9. Connect the 6-pin and 3-pin electrical connectors and the fluid level sensor connector.
10. Properly bleed the system.
11. Connect the negative battery cable.

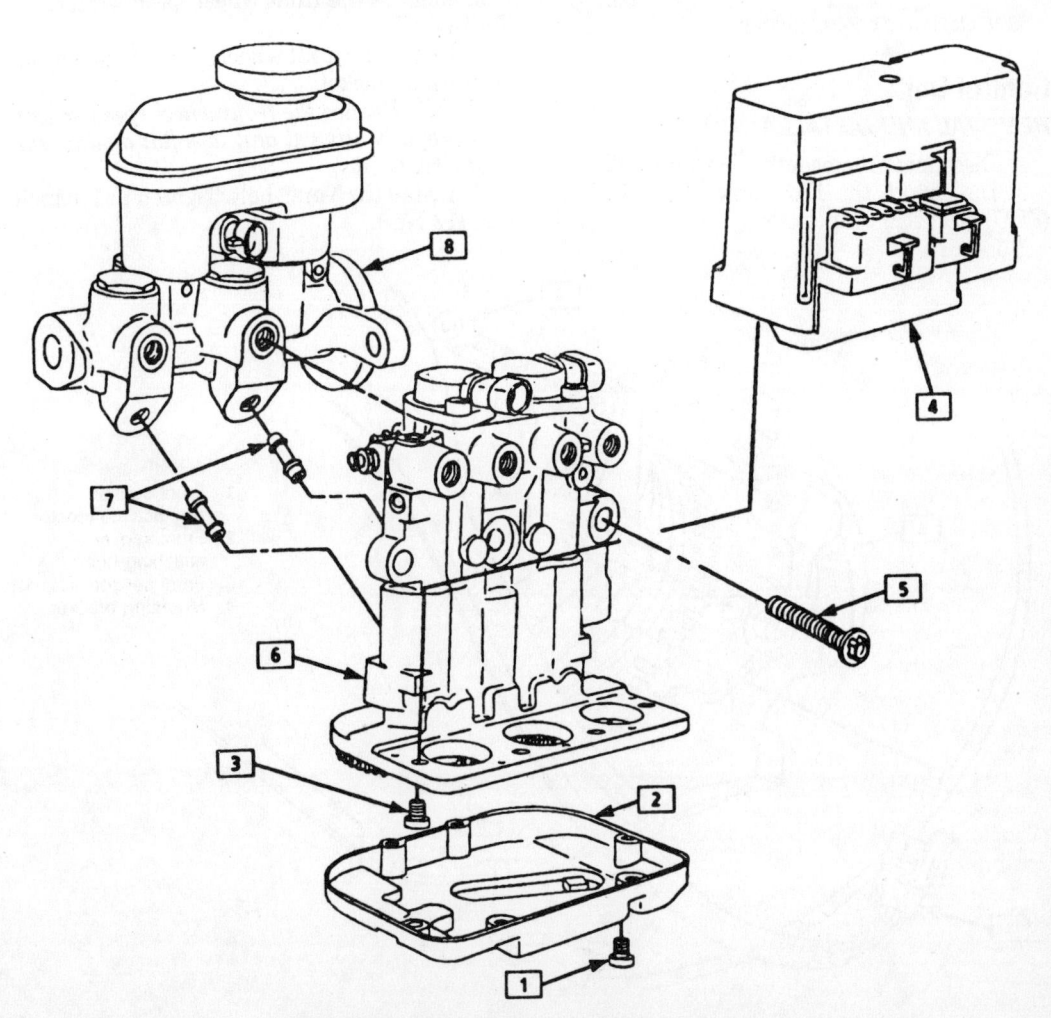

ABS-VI hydraulic modulator assembly components

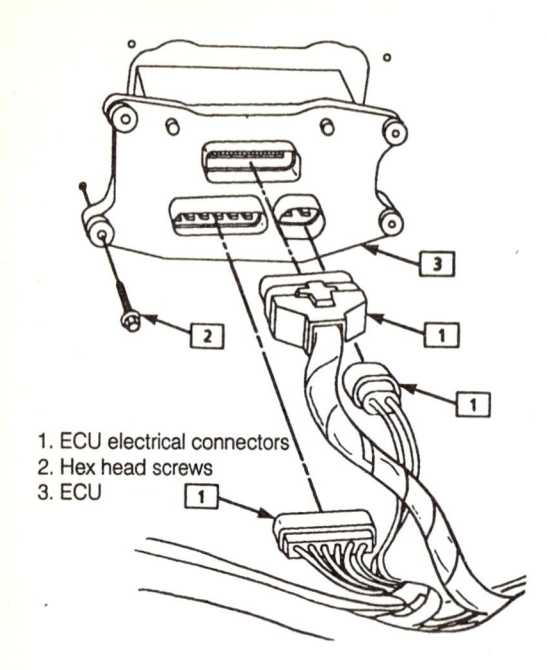

# 270 BRAKES

3. Remove the hex head screws attaching the ECU to the dash panel.
4. Remove the ECU from the dash panel.

**To install:**

5. Ensure all plastic grommets are properly located.
6. Install the ECU to the dash panel, aligning screw holes.
7. Install the hex head screws attaching the ECU.
8. Connect the ECU electrical connectors.
9. Connect the negative battery cable.

## Speed Sensors

### REMOVAL AND INSTALLATION

#### Front Wheel Speed Sensor

1. Disconnect the negative battery cable.
2. Raise and safely support the vehicle.
3. Disconnect the front sensor electrical connector.
4. Remove the Torx® bolt.
5. Remove the front wheel speed sensor.

**To install:**

6. Install the front wheel speed sensor on the mounting bracket.

NOTE: *Ensure the front wheel speed sensor is properly aligned and lays flat against the bracket bosses.*

7. Install the Torx® bolt. Tighten to 106 inch lbs. (12 Nm).

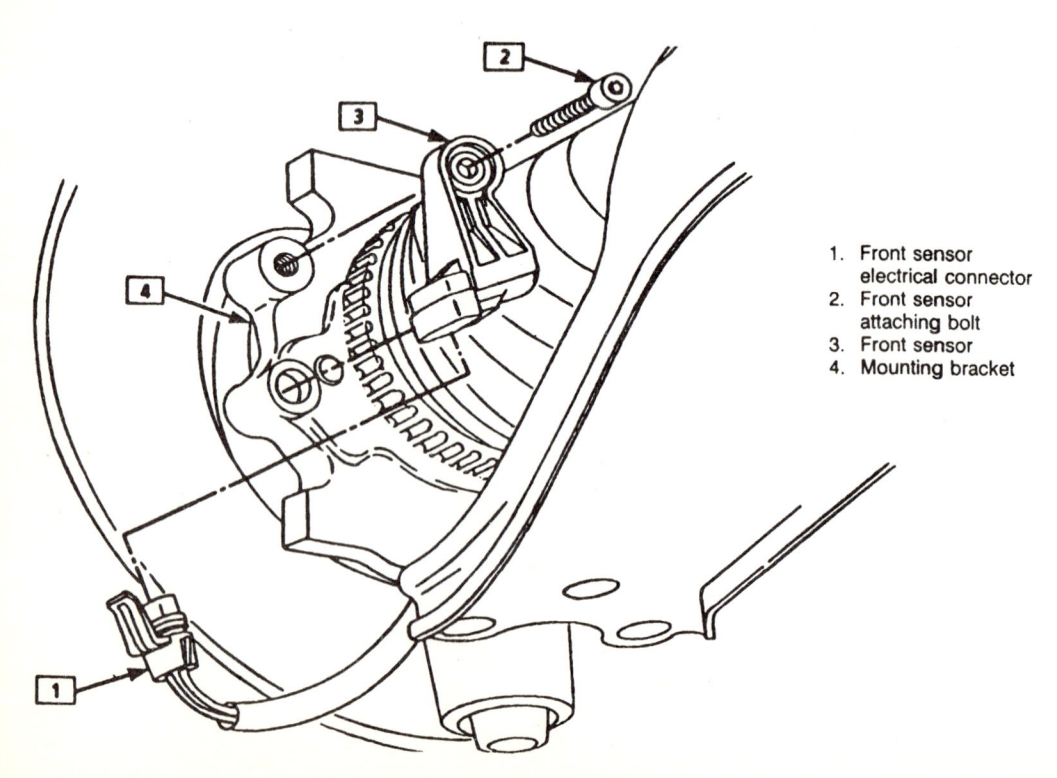

1. ECU electrical connectors
2. Hex head screws
3. ECU

**ABS-VI electronic control unit removal**

## Control Unit

### REMOVAL AND INSTALLATION

1. Disconnect the negative battery cable.
2. Disconnect the Electronic Control Unit (ECU) electrical connectors.

1. Front sensor electrical connector
2. Front sensor attaching bolt
3. Front sensor
4. Mounting bracket

**Front wheel speed sensor removal**

# BRAKES

8. Connect the front sensor electrical connector.
9. Lower the vehicle.
10. Connect the negative battery cable.

**Rear Wheel Bearing And Speed Sensor Assembly**

NOTE: *The rear integral wheel bearing and sensor assembly must be replaced as a unit.*

1. Disconnect the negative battery cable.
2. Raise and safely support the vehicle.
3. Remove the rear wheel.
4. Remove the brake drum.
5. Disconnect the rear sensor electrical connector.
6. Remove the bolts and nuts attaching the rear wheel bearing and speed sensor assembly to the backing plate.

NOTE: *With the rear wheel bearing and speed sensor attaching bolts and nuts removed, the drum brake assembly is supported only by the brake line connection. To avoid bending or damage to the brake line, do not bump or exert force on the assembly.*

7. Remove the rear wheel bearing and speed sensor assembly.

**To install:**

8. Install the rear wheel bearing and speed sensor assembly by aligning the bolt hoses in the wheel bearing and speed sensor assembly, drum brake assembly and rear suspension bracket. Install the attaching bolts and nuts. Tighten to 37 ft. lbs. (50 Nm).
9. Connect the rear speed sensor electrical connector.
10. Install the brake drum.
11. Install the rear wheel.
12. Lower the vehicle.
13. Connect the negative battery cable.

## Brake Control Solenoid Assembly

### REMOVAL AND INSTALLATION

1. Disconnect the negative battery cable.
2. Disconnect the solenoid electrical connector.
3. Remove the Torx® head bolts.
4. Remove the solenoid assembly.

**To install:**

5. Lubricate the O-rings on the new solenoid with clean brake fluid.
6. Position the solenoid so the connectors face each other.
7. Press down firmly by hand until the solenoid assembly flange seats on the modulator assembly.
8. Install the Torx® head bolts. Tighten to 39 inch lbs. (5 Nm).

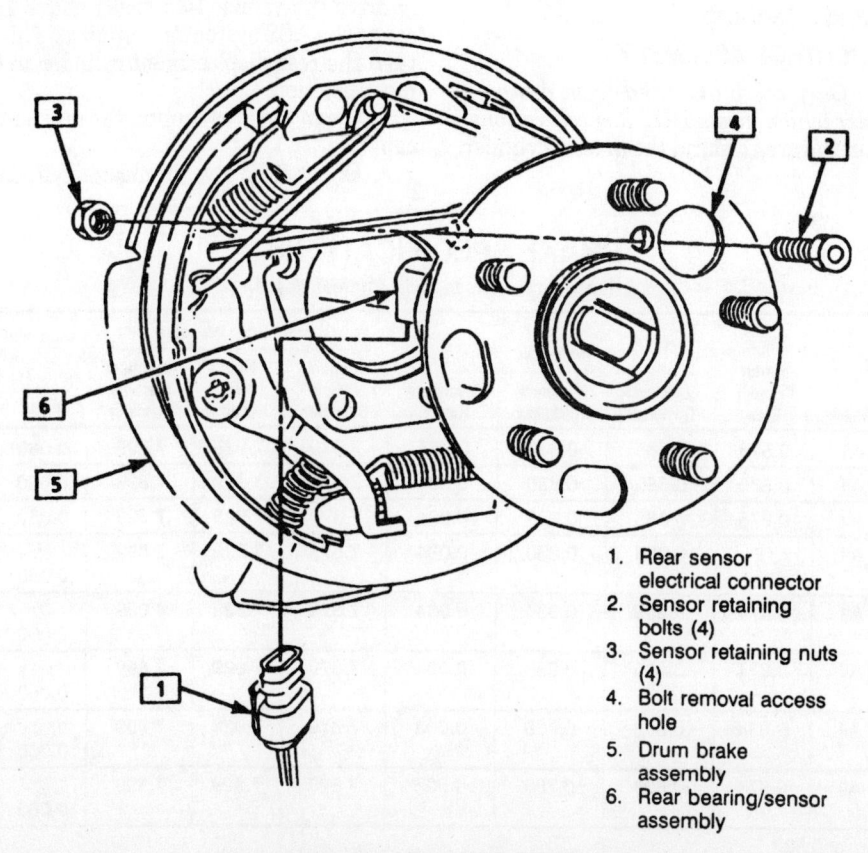

1. Rear sensor electrical connector
2. Sensor retaining bolts (4)
3. Sensor retaining nuts (4)
4. Bolt removal access hole
5. Drum brake assembly
6. Rear bearing/sensor assembly

**Rear wheel bearing and speed sensor removal**

## 272　BRAKES

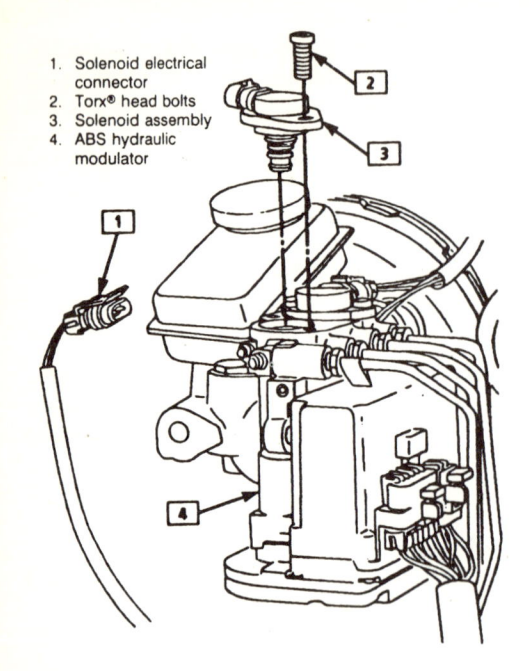

1. Solenoid electrical connector
2. Torx® head bolts
3. Solenoid assembly
4. ABS hydraulic modulator

**Brake control solenoid removal**

9. Connect the solenoid electrical connector.
10. Properly bleed the brake system.
11. Connect the negative battery cable.

## Filling and Bleeding

### BRAKE CONTROL ASSEMBLY

NOTE: *Only use brake fluid from a sealed container which meets DOT 3 specifications.*

1. Clean the area around the master cylinder cap.
2. Check fluid level in master cylinder reservoir and top-up, as necessary. Check fluid level frequently during bleeding procedure.
3. Attach a bleeder hose to the rear bleeder valve on the brake control assembly. Slowly open the bleeder valve.
4. Depress the brake pedal slowly until fluid begins to flow.
5. Close the valve and release the brake pedal.
6. Repeat for the front bleeder valve on the brake control assembly.

NOTE: *When fluid flows from both bleeder valves, the brake control assembly is sufficiently full of fluid. However, it may not be completely purged of air. Bleed the individual wheel calipers/cylinders and return to the control assembly to purge the remaining air.*

### WHEEL CALIPERS/CYLINDERS

NOTE: *Prior to bleeding the rear brakes, the rear displacement cylinder must be returned to the top-most position. This can be accomplished using the Tech I Scan tool or T-100 (CAMS), by entering the manual control function and applying the rear motor.*

If a Tech I or T-100 are unavailable, bleed the front brakes. Ensure the pedal is firm. Carefully drive the vehicle to a speed above 4 mph to cause the ABS system to initialize. This will return the rear displacement cylinder to the top-most position.

1. Clean the area around the master cylinder cap.
2. Check fluid level in master cylinder reser-

## BRAKE SPECIFICATIONS
All measurements in inches unless noted.

| Year | Model | Master Cylinder Bore | Brake Disc Original Thickness | Brake Disc Minimum Thickness | Brake Disc Maximum Runout | Brake Drum Diameter Original Inside Diameter | Brake Drum Diameter Max. Wear Limit | Brake Drum Diameter Maximum Machine Diameter | Minimum Lining Thickness Front | Minimum Lining Thickness Rear |
|---|---|---|---|---|---|---|---|---|---|---|
| 1985 | All | 0.875 | 0.885 | 0.830 | 0.004 | 7.879 | 7.929 | 7.899 | 0.030 | 0.030 |
| 1986 | All | 0.875 | 0.885 | 0.830 | 0.004 | 7.879 | 7.929 | 7.899 | 0.030 | 0.030 |
| 1987 | All | 0.875 | 0.885 | 0.830 | 0.004 | 7.879 | 7.929 | 7.899 | 0.030 | 0.030 |
| 1988 | All | ① | 0.885 | 0.830 | 0.004 | 7.879 | 7.929 | 7.899 | ② 0.060 | ② 0.060 |
| 1989 | All | 0.874 | 0.885 | 0.830 | 0.004 | 7.879 | 7.929 | 7.899 | ② 0.060 | ② 0.060 |
| 1990 | All | 0.874 | 0.885 | 0.830 | 0.004 | 7.879 | 7.929 | 7.899 | ② 0.060 | ② 0.060 |
| 1991 | All | 0.874 | 0.806 | 0.786 | 0.003 | 7.879 | 7.929 | 7.899 | ② 0.060 | ② 0.060 |
| 1992 | All | 0.874 | 0.806 | 0.786 | 0.003 | 7.879 | 7.929 | 7.899 | ② 0.060 | ② 0.060 |

① 0.874 in. or 0.937
② Measured above the rivet head

voir and top-up, as necessary. Check fluid level frequently during bleeding procedure.

3. Raise and safely support the vehicle.
4. Attach a bleeder hose to the bleeder valve of the right rear wheel and submerge the opposite hose in a clean container partially filled with brake fluid.
5. Open the bleeder valve.
6. Slowly depress the brake pedal.
7. Close the bleeder valve and release the brake pedal.
8. Wait 5 seconds.
9. Repeat Steps 5–8 until the pedal begins to feel firm and no air bubbles appear in the bleeder hose.
10. Repeat Steps 5–9, until the pedal is firm and no air bubbles appear in the brake hose, for the remaining wheels in the following order:
   a. left rear
   b. right front
   c. left front.
11. Lower the vehicle.

# Body 10

## EXTERIOR

### Doors

#### REMOVAL AND INSTALLATION

1. If equipped with power door components, disconnect the negative battery cable.
2. Remove the inner door trim panel.
3. If equipped with power door components, disconnect the electrical connectors and remove the harness.
4. Using a suitable tool mark the location of the door hinges in relation to the door and remove the door detent bolt.
5. With an assistant supporting the door, remove the hinge to door bolts and remove the door from the vehicle.

**To install:**

6. With the aid of an assistant, reposition the door and install the hinge to door bolts. Torque the bolts to 18 ft. lbs. (24 Nm).
7. If so equipped, install the electrical harness and connect the electrical connectors to the power door components.
8. Install the inner door trim panel and install the door detent bolt.
9. Connect the negative battery cable.

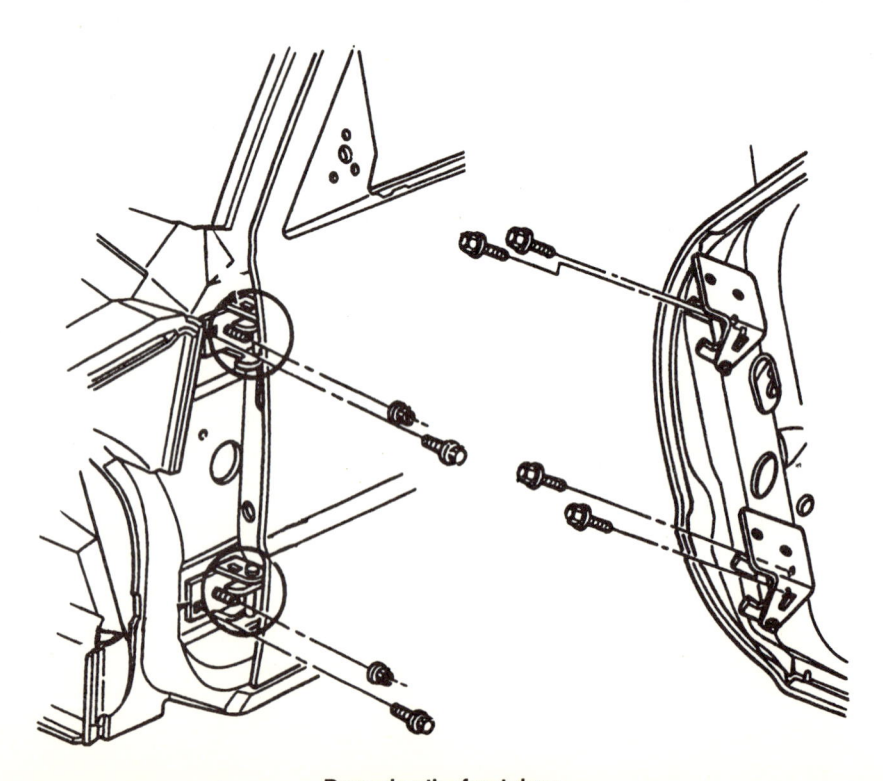

**Removing the front door**

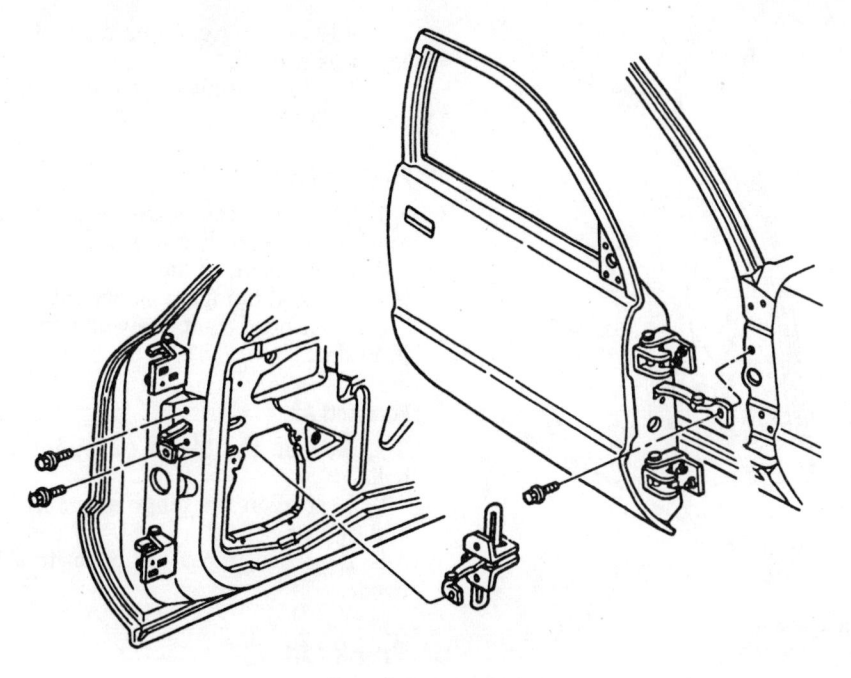

BODY 275

*Door detent removal*

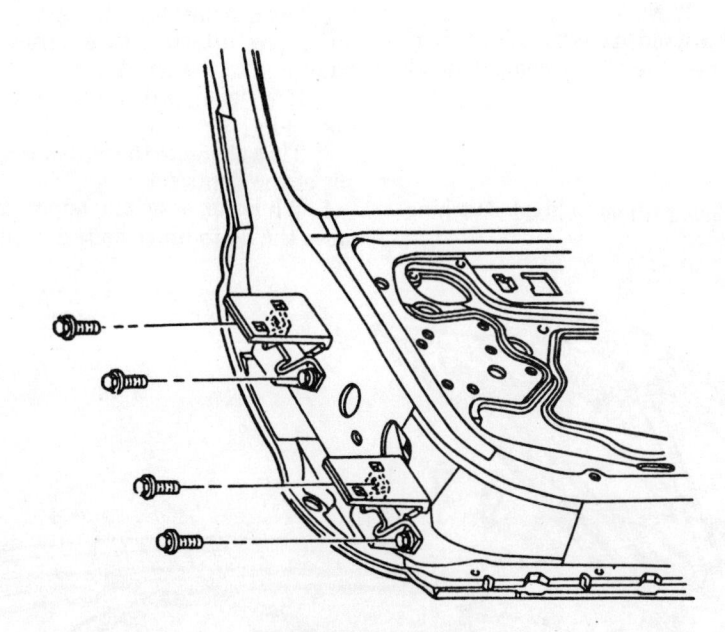

*Removing the rear door*

## ADJUSTMENT

1. Adjust the door so that the door to body and lock to striker align properly.
2. The hinge to door bolts may need to be loosened to adjust the alignment properly.

## Hood

### REMOVAL AND INSTALLATION

1. Raise the hood and remove the engine compartment lamp.
2. Using a suitable tool, mark the position of the hinges in relation to the hood.
3. Disconnect the hood assist rod strut, if equipped.
4. With an assistant supporting the hood, remove the bolts attaching the hinge to the hood and remove the hood from the vehicle.

**To install:**

5. With the aid of an assistant align the hood to the hinges and install the retaining bolts.

# BODY

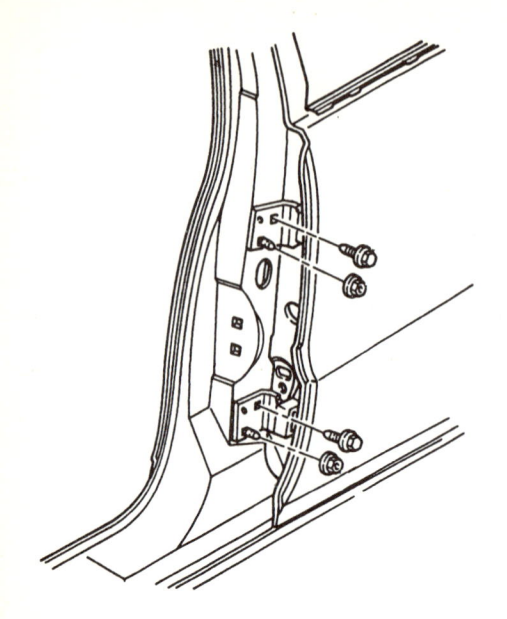

**Rear door hinge removal**

6. Check alignment marks and tighten the bolts to 20 ft. lbs. (27 Nm).
7. Connect the hood assist rod strut, if equipped and connect the engine compartment lamp.

## ALIGNMENT
### Rear Corners

1. Loosen the lower hinge to hood attaching bolts.
2. Add or remove shims under the hinge to adjust as needed.
3. Tighten the hinge to hood bolts to 20 ft. lbs. (27 Nm).

### Front Corners

1. Close hood completely and determine how much adjustment is required.
2. Open the hood and raise or lower the adjustable hood bumpers as needed.
3. Close hood completely and inspect, repeat if needed.

### Fore and Aft

1. Loosen the hinge to fender attaching bolts.
2. Reposition the hinge assembly as needed and tighten bolts.
3. If needed, repeat on opposite side of the hood.

## Trunk Lid
### REMOVAL AND INSTALLATION

1. Open trunk and disconnect all electrical connectors attached to electrical components connected to the trunk lid.
2. If so equipped, disconnect the lock out solenoid.
3. Tie a string to the wire harness and pull it out of the trunk lid.
4. While an assistant supports the lid, remove the lid to hinge bolts and remove the lid.

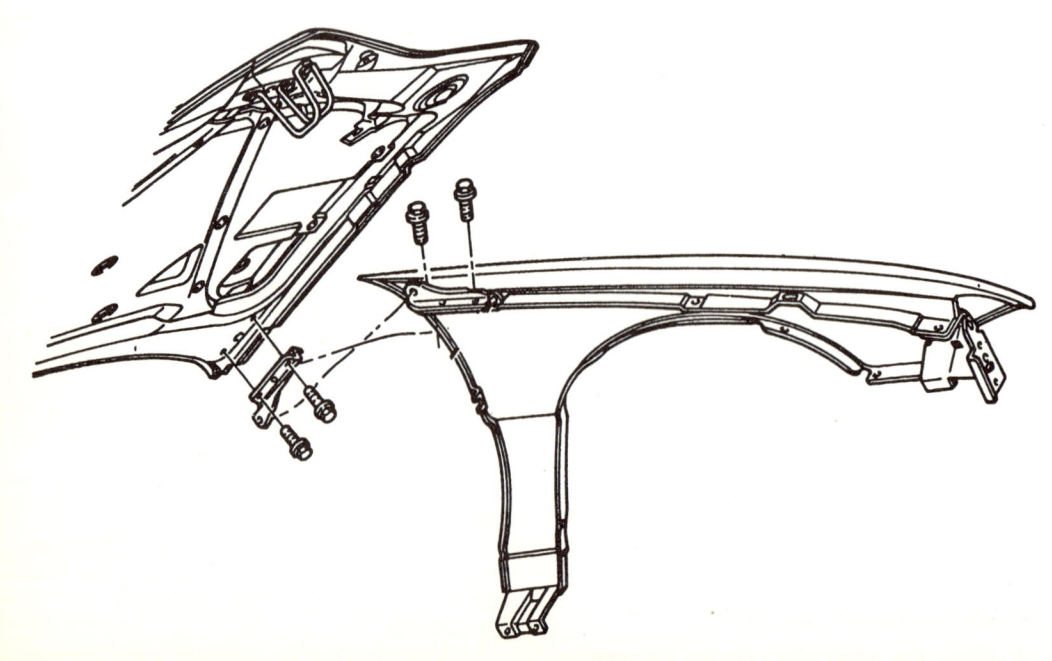

**Hood removal and installation**

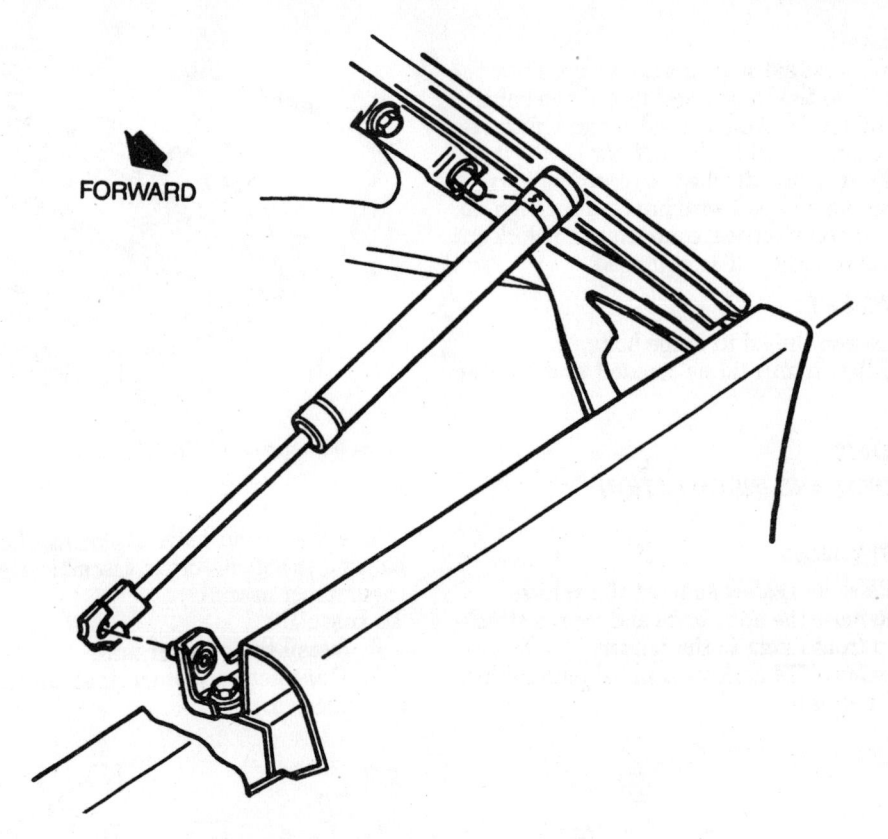

BODY 277

FORWARD

Hood open assist rod removal and installation

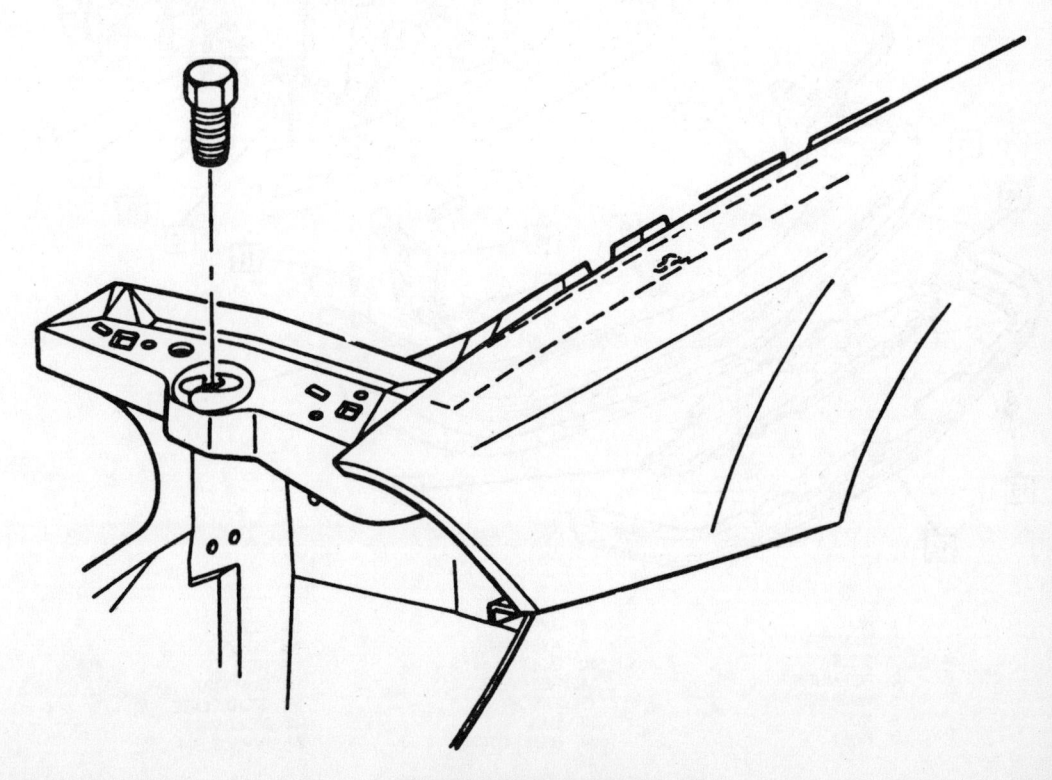

Hood bumper adjustment

**278** **BODY**

**To install:**
5. With the aid of an assistant, reposition the trunk lid to the hinges and install the bolts.
6. Adjust the hood as needed and tighten retaining bolts to 18 ft. lbs. (24 Nm).
7. Feed string attached to electrical harness through lid and pull wire harness through lid.
8. Connect electrical connectors and lock out solenoid connector if so equipped.

**ALIGNMENT**
1. Loosen the lid to hinge bolts.
2. Align trunk lid as needed and tighten bolts.

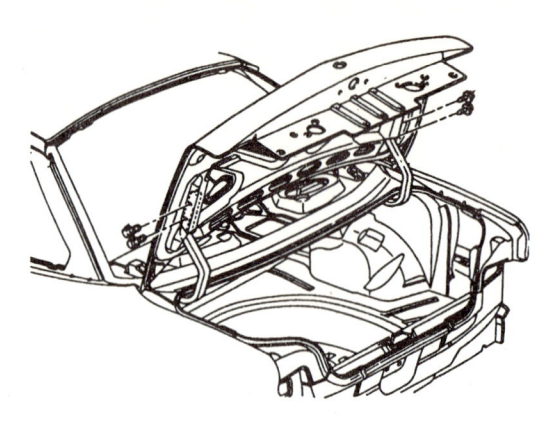

Trunk lid removal and installation

## Bumpers

### REMOVAL AND INSTALLATION

**Front**
**1985-91 Vehicles**
1. Raise and safely support the vehicle.
2. Remove the nuts, bolts and screws attaching the front fascia to the fender.
3. Remove the park/turn signal bulb connectors if necessary.
4. Remove the bolts attaching the bumper bar and energy absorber assembly and remove the bumper assembly.

**To install:**
6. Install the bumper unit.
7. Connect any electrical connectors if disconnected.

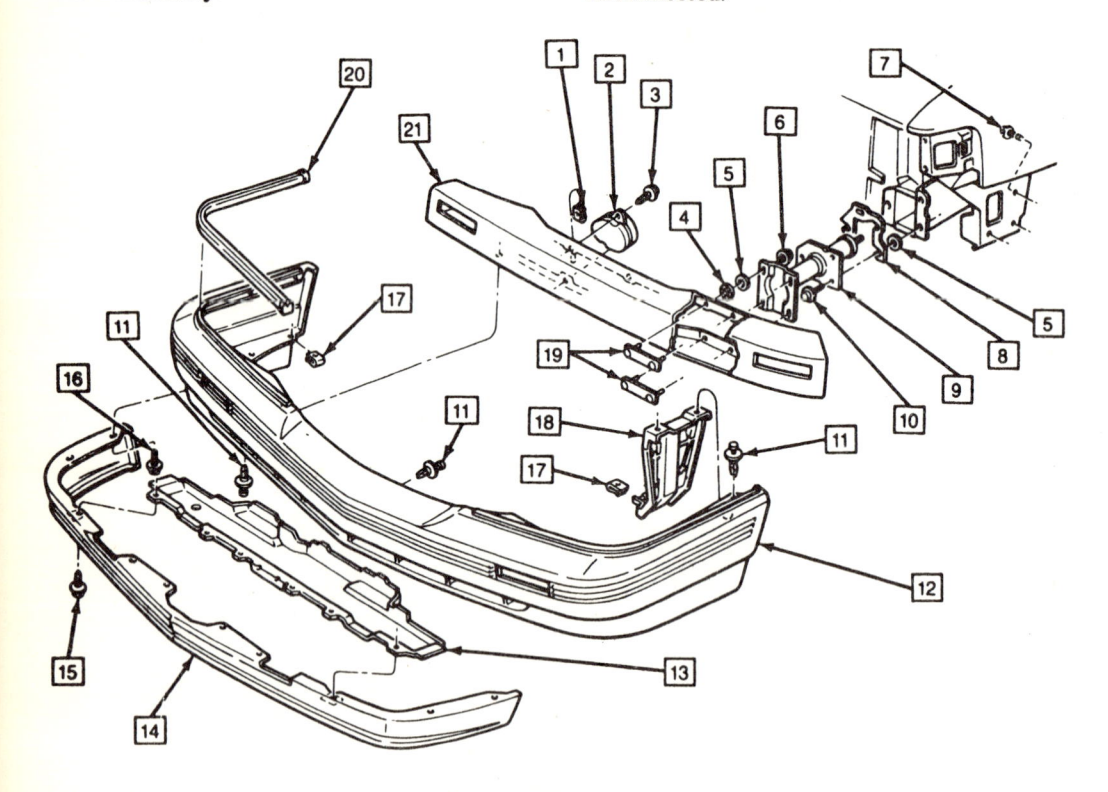

| | | |
|---|---|---|
| 1. NUT | 8. SHIM | 15. BOLT |
| 2. DAMPER | 9. ABSORBER | 16. BOLT |
| 3. BOLT | 10. BOLT | 17. NUT |
| 4. RETAINER | 11. RETAINER | 18. SUPPORT |
| 5. WASHER | 12. FASCIA | 19. STUD PLATE |
| 6. NUT | 13. BAR | 20. MOLDING |
| 7. BOLT | 14. DEFLECTOR | 21. IMPACT BAR |

1985-91 typical front bumper assembly

BODY 279

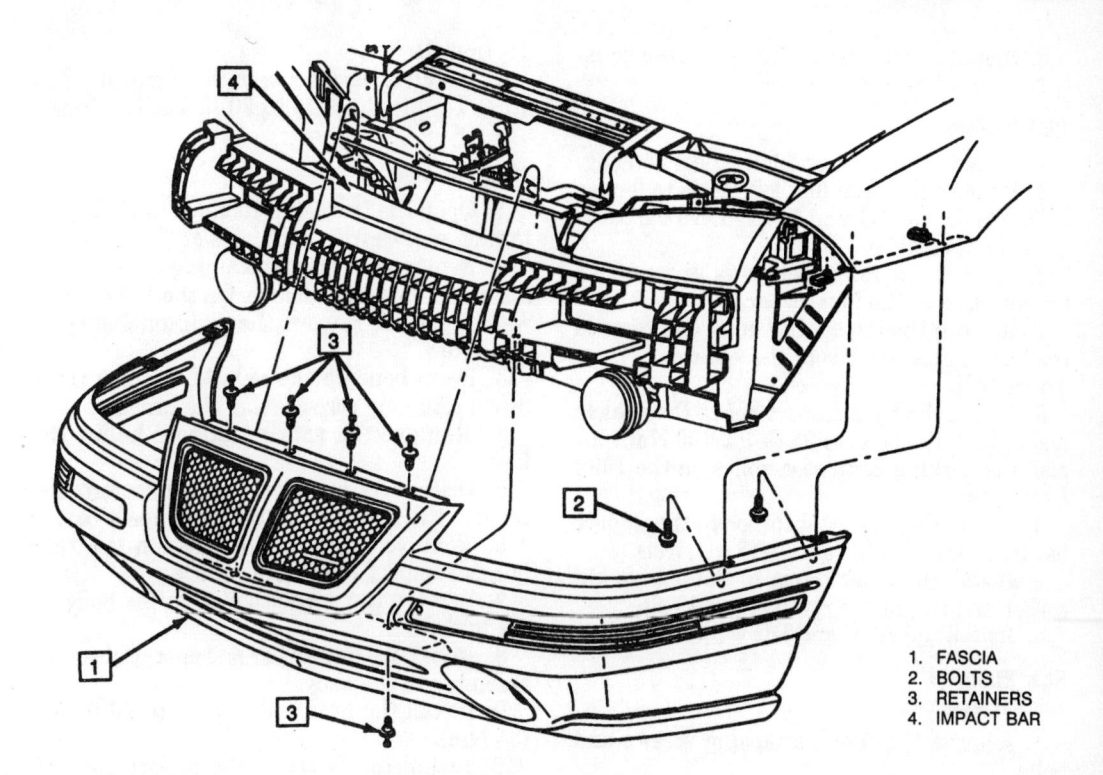

1. FASCIA
2. BOLTS
3. RETAINERS
4. IMPACT BAR

1992 Grand Am front bumper fascia

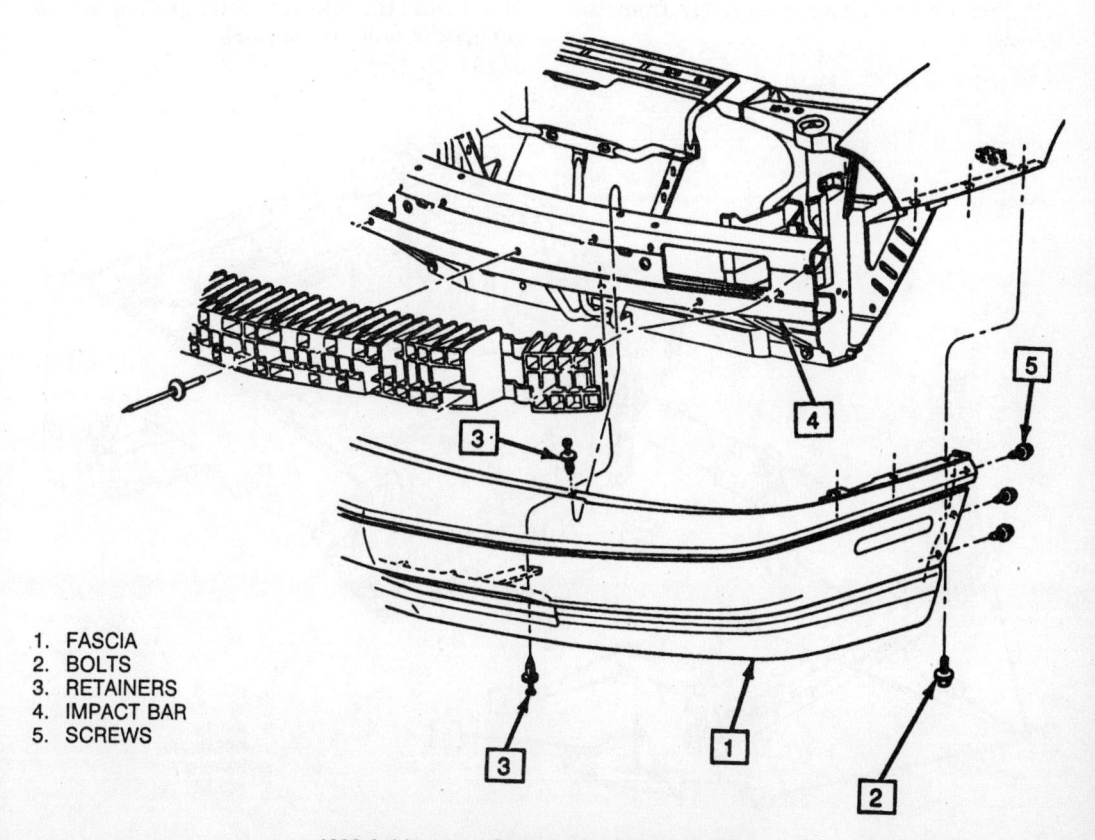

1. FASCIA
2. BOLTS
3. RETAINERS
4. IMPACT BAR
5. SCREWS

1992 Achieva and Skylark front bumper fascia

# 280 BODY

8. Install all nuts, bolts and screws previously removed. Lower the vehicle.

### 1992 Vehicles

1. Remove the right and left wheel housing.
2. Remove the right and left fascia to fender bolts. On the 1992 Grand Am, remove the parking lamp assemblies.
3. Remove the fascia retainers and remove the fascia from the impact bar.
4. Remove the impact bar bolts and remove the front impact bar from the vehicle.

**To install:**

5. Install the front impact bar to the vehicle and tighten the bolts to 22 ft. lbs. (30 Nm). Install the parking lamp assemblies on the 1992 Grand Am.
6. Install the energy absorber to the impact bar and connect with nine 3/16 in. rivets.
7. Install the front fascia to the energy absorber and install the retainers and bolts.
8. Install the right and left wheel housings.

### Rear Bumpers
### 1985-91 Vehicles

1. Remove the fascia attaching screws and bolts.
2. From inside the trunk, remove the bumper attaching nuts and washers.
3. Remove the bumper assembly from the vehicle.

**To install:**

4. Install is the reverse of the removal procedure. Torque the nuts to 20 ft. lbs. (27 Nm).

### 1992 Vehicles

1. Open the trunk lid. Remove the fascia retaining screws from each side of the trunk.
2. Remove the fascia retaining screws from inside the rear wheelhouse. On the 1992 Grand Am GT model, remove the additional support and screw.
3. From beneath the vehicle, remove the 4 fascia retaining screws from the bracket.
4. Remove the retainers from below the fascia.
5. Disconnect any electrical connectors and remove the rear fascia from the impact bar.
6. Remove the nuts that attach the rear bumper impact bar to the vehicle.
7. Remove the impact bar from the body.

**To install:**

8. Install the impact bar and energy absorber assembly to the body.
9. Install the nuts and tighten to 26 ft. lbs. (35 Nm).
10. Install the fascia to the impact bar and connect any electrical connectors that were disconnected.
11. Install the retainers and attaching screws in opposite order of removal.

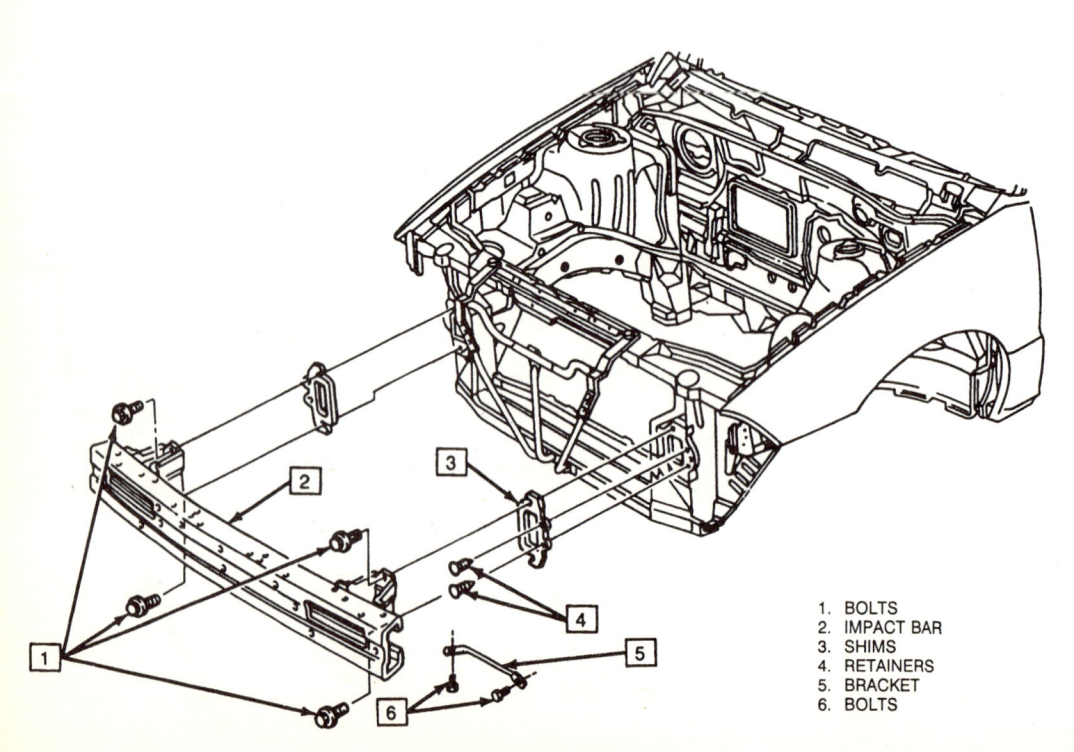

1. BOLTS
2. IMPACT BAR
3. SHIMS
4. RETAINERS
5. BRACKET
6. BOLTS

**1992 front bumper impact bar**

BODY 281

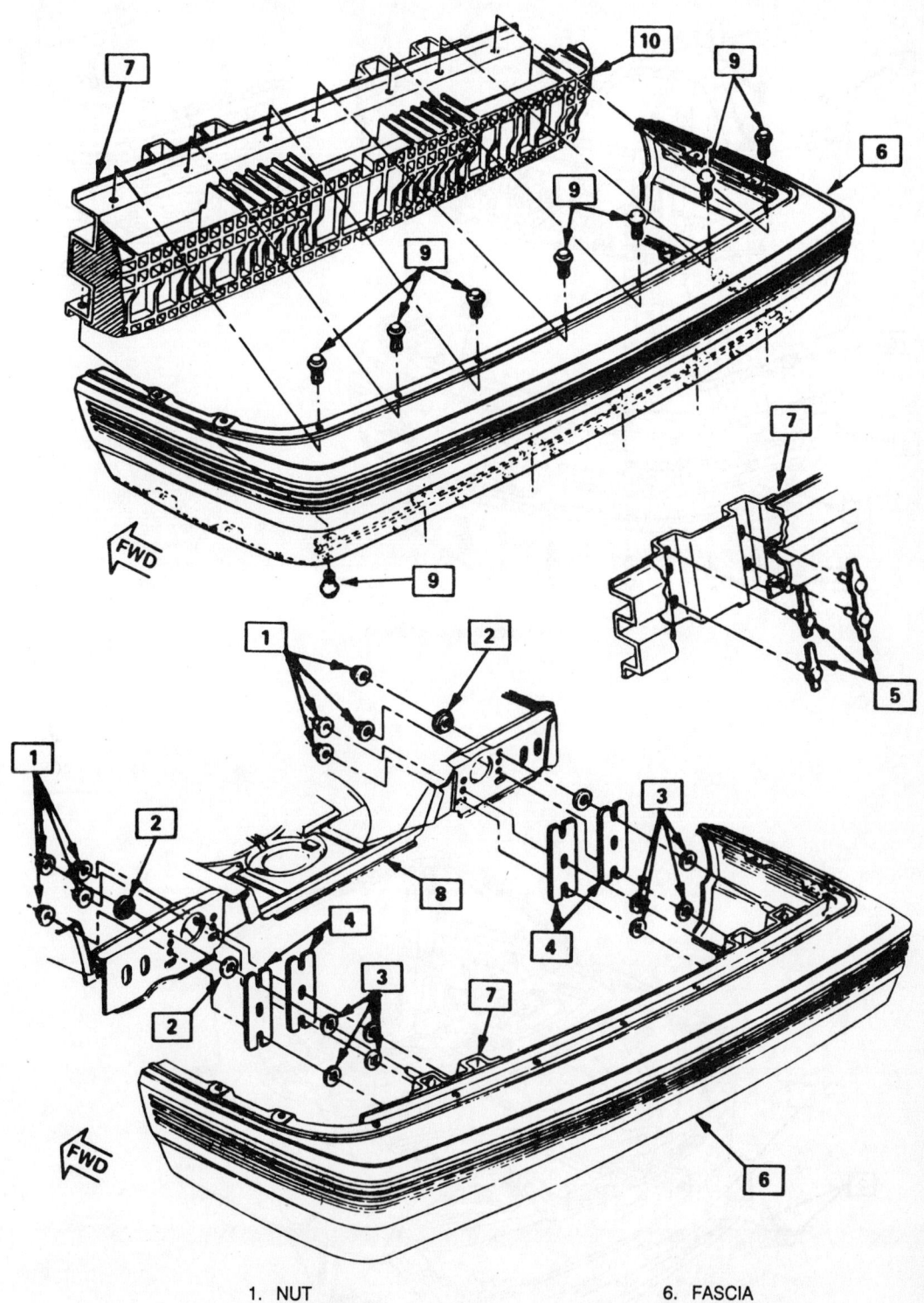

1. NUT
2. WASHER
3. RETAINER
4. SHIM
5. PLATE ASSEMBLY
6. FASCIA
7. BAR ASSEMBLY
8. PANEL
9. RETAINER
10. ENERGY ABSORBER

**1985–91 typical rear bumper assembly**

## 282 BODY

GT MODEL ONLY

1. BUMPER FASCIA
2. SCREWS
3. SCREW
4. RETAINERS
5. SCREW
6. BRACKET
7. RETAINER
8. SCREW
9. SUPPORT

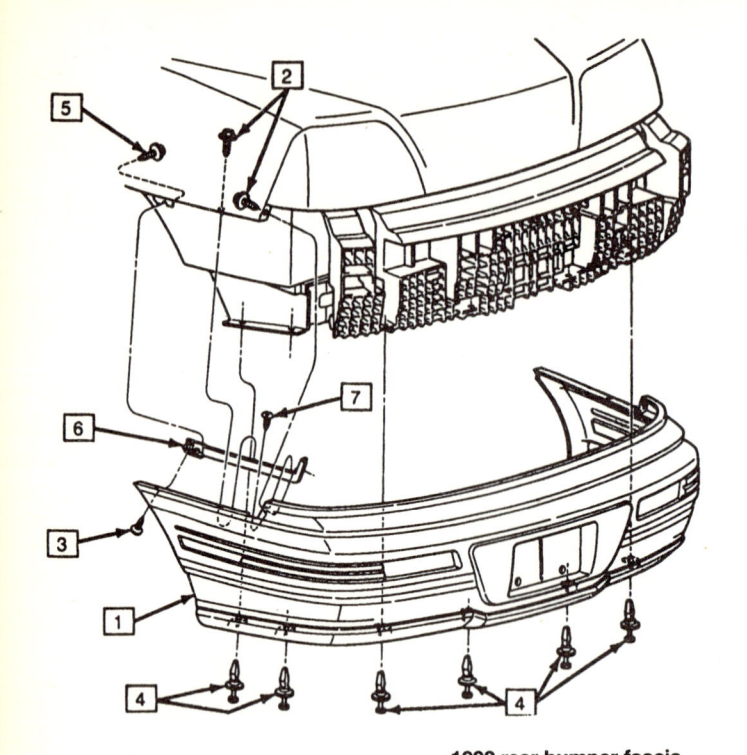

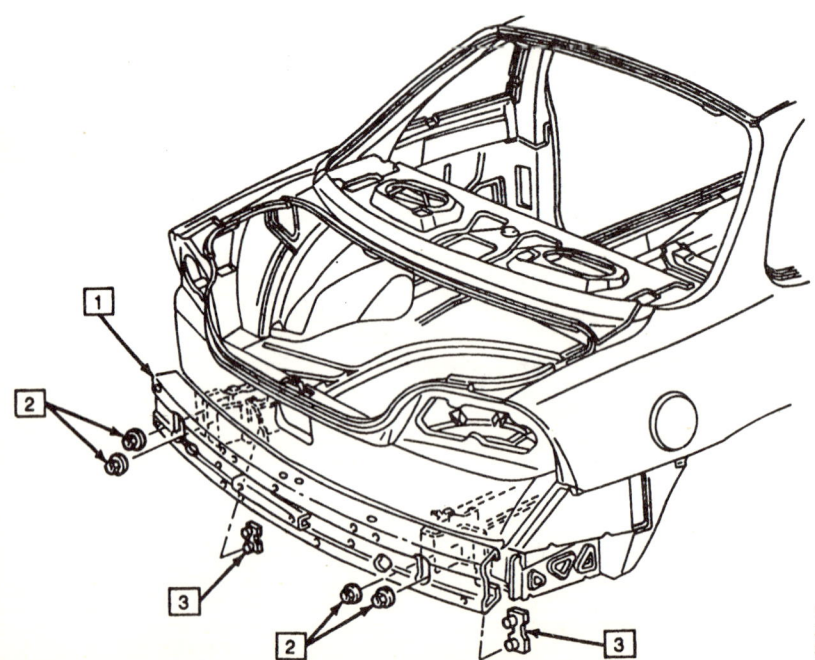

1992 rear bumper fascia

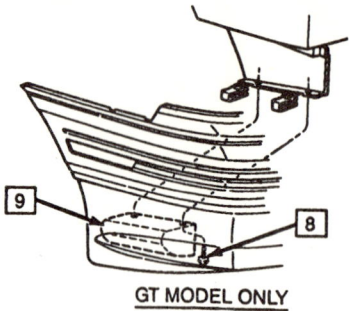

1. IMPACT BAR
2. NUTS
3. STUD PLATES

1992 rear bumper impact bar

BODY **283**

# Grille

## REMOVAL AND INSTALLATION

### 1985-91 Vehicles
### Except 1989-91 Grand Am

1. Remove the screws from the grille.
2. Remove the grill assembly.

**To install:**

3. Installation is the reverse of the removal procedure.

### 1989-91 Grand Am

To remove grille, just release the tabs and pull grille outward. Installation is done by inserting grille and locking tabs.

### 1992 Achleva and Skylark

1. Remove the screws along the top of the grille.
2. Pull out on the grille to release the lower tabs.

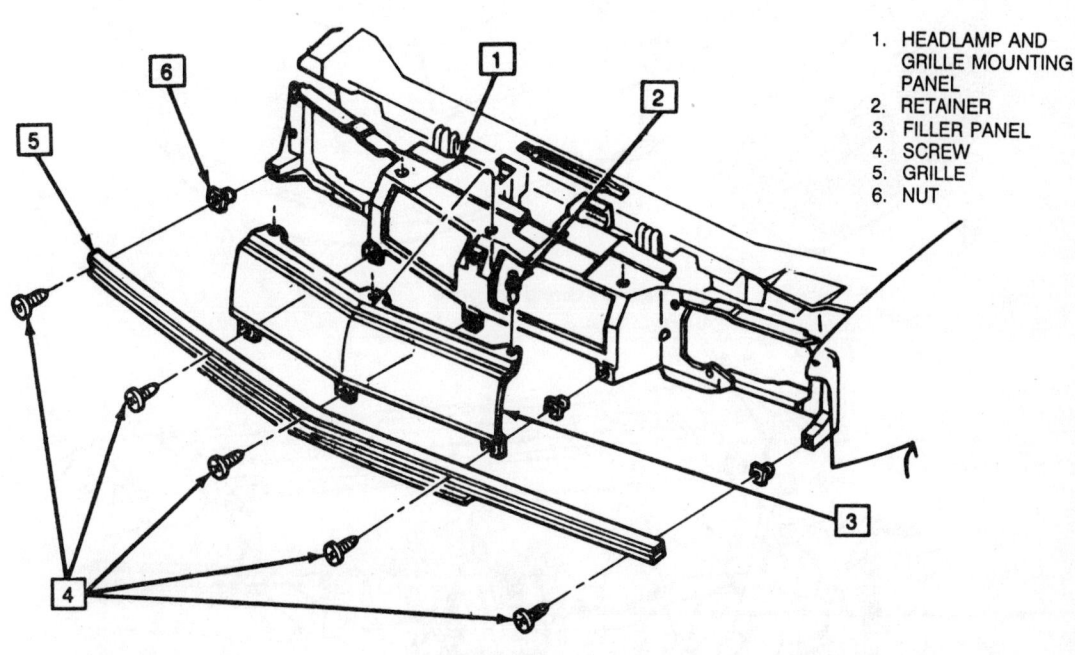

1. HEADLAMP AND GRILLE MOUNTING PANEL
2. RETAINER
3. FILLER PANEL
4. SCREW
5. GRILLE
6. NUT

1985-91 Cutlass Calais grille

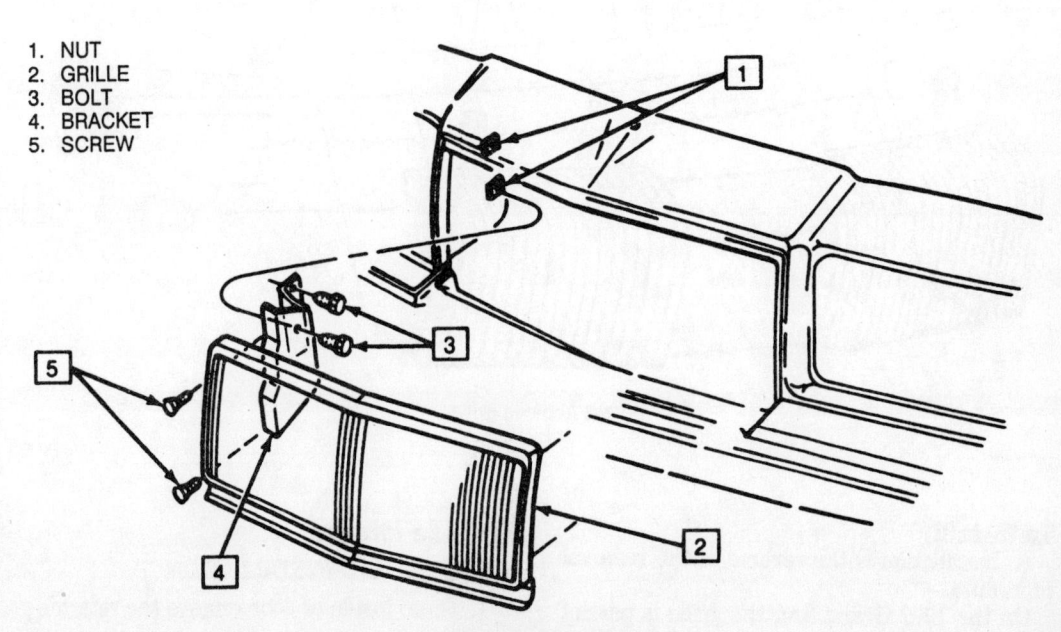

1. NUT
2. GRILLE
3. BOLT
4. BRACKET
5. SCREW

1985-91 Skylark grille

## 284 BODY

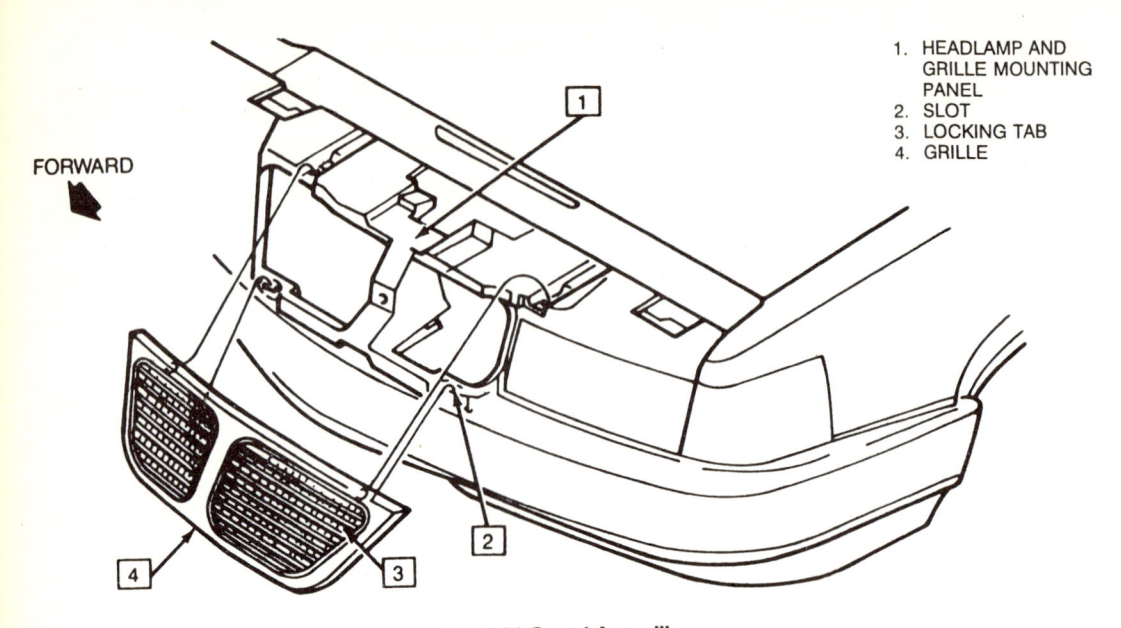

1. HEADLAMP AND GRILLE MOUNTING PANEL
2. SLOT
3. LOCKING TAB
4. GRILLE

FORWARD

**1989–91 Grand Am grille**

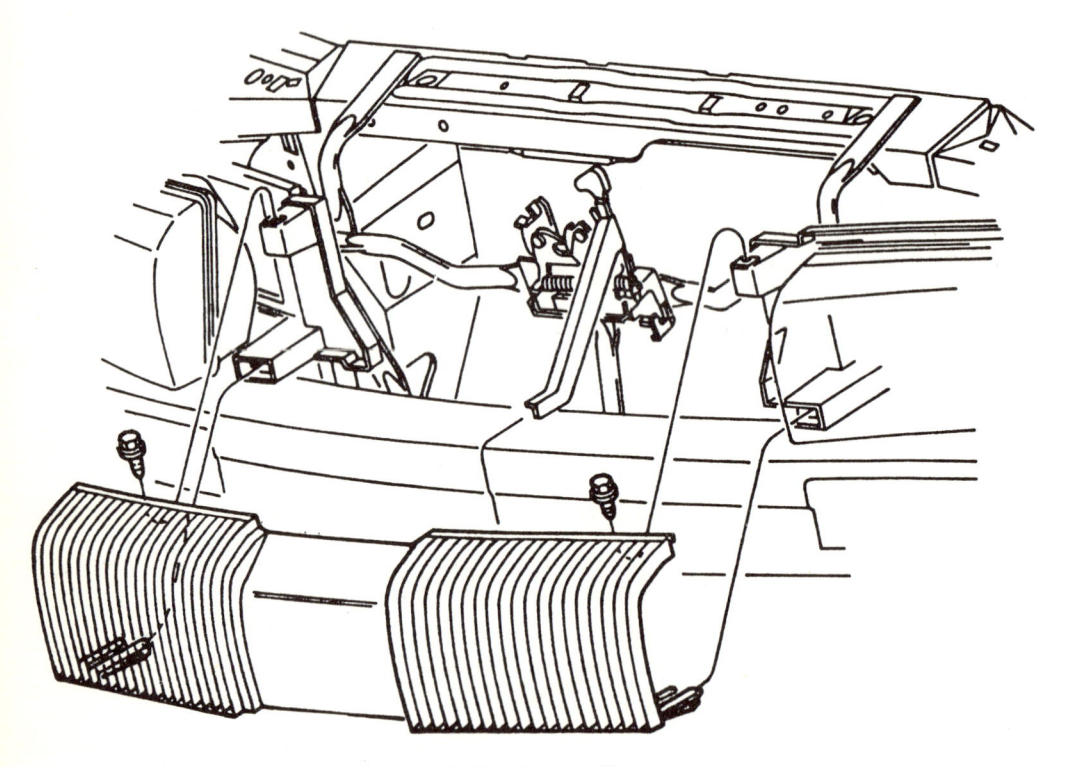

**1992 Achieva grille**

**To install:**
3. Installation is the reverse of the removal procedure.
On the 1992 Grand Am, the grille is part of the bumper fascia.

## Outside Mirrors
### REMOVAL AND INSTALLATION

1. From inside of door remove the retaining screw.

# BODY 285

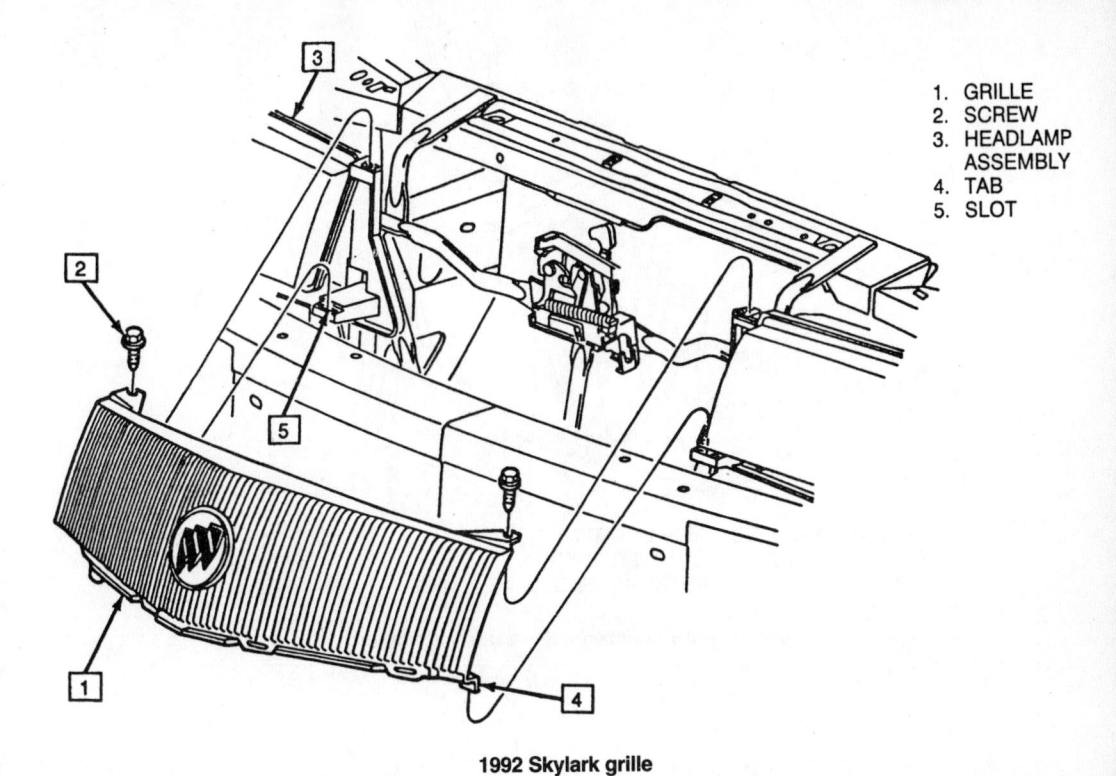

1. GRILLE
2. SCREW
3. HEADLAMP ASSEMBLY
4. TAB
5. SLOT

**1992 Skylark grille**

2. Remove the outside mirror escutcheon by pulling inward.
3. Remove mirror control handle and remove escutcheon.
4. If equipped with power mirrors, disconnect the electrical connector.
5. Remove the gasket and the retaining nuts.
6. Remove the mirror from the door.

**To install:**

7. Install the mirror to the door and tighten the nuts to 45 in. lbs. (5 Nm).
8. Install the gasket and if equipped with power mirrors connect the electrical connector.
9. Slide the escutcheon onto handle shaft and install handle onto shaft.
10. Snap escutcheon into place and install the screw.

## Antenna

### REPLACEMENT

**Fixed Antenna**
**Rear fender mount**

1. Remove rear compartment trim.
2. Remove the antenna mast from the base.

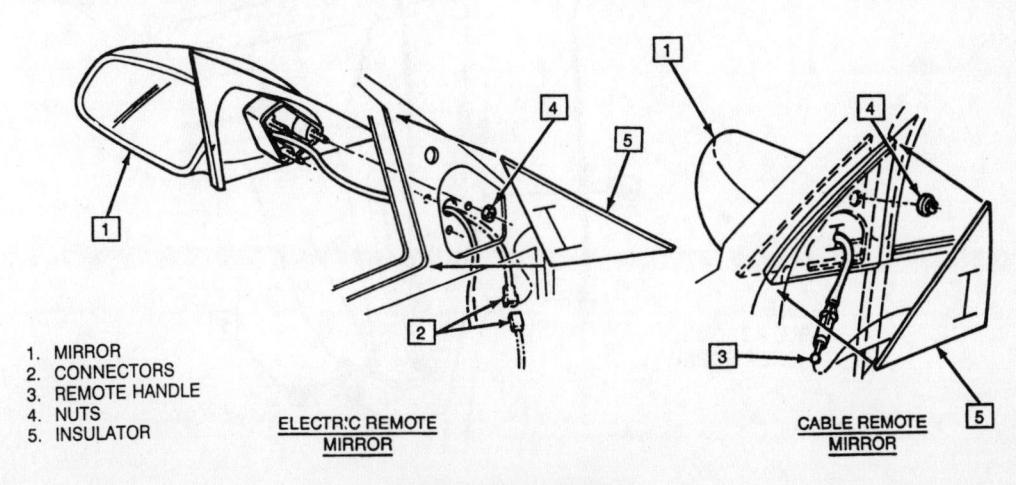

1. MIRROR
2. CONNECTORS
3. REMOTE HANDLE
4. NUTS
5. INSULATOR

ELECTRIC REMOTE MIRROR

CABLE REMOTE MIRROR

**Typical mirror installation**

286  BODY

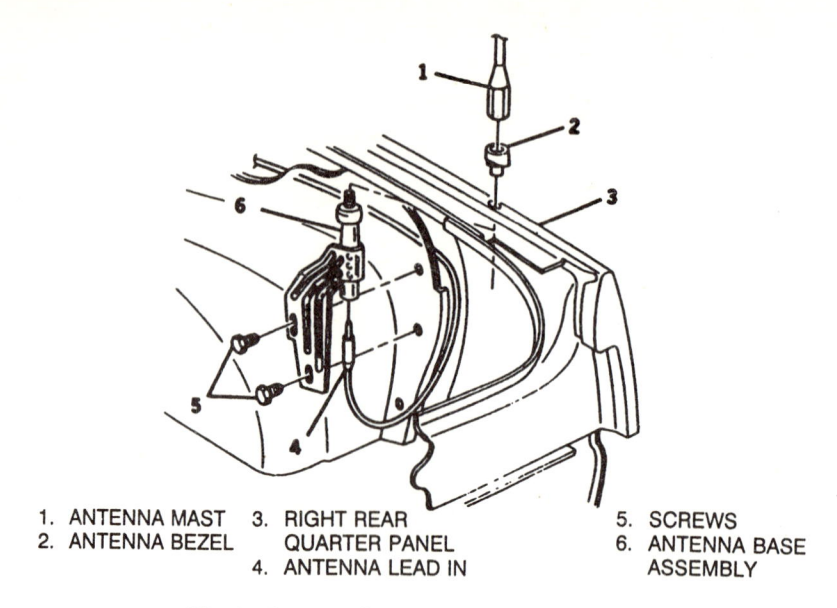

1. ANTENNA MAST
2. ANTENNA BEZEL
3. RIGHT REAR QUARTER PANEL
4. ANTENNA LEAD IN
5. SCREWS
6. ANTENNA BASE ASSEMBLY

Fixed antenna replacement—rear fender mount

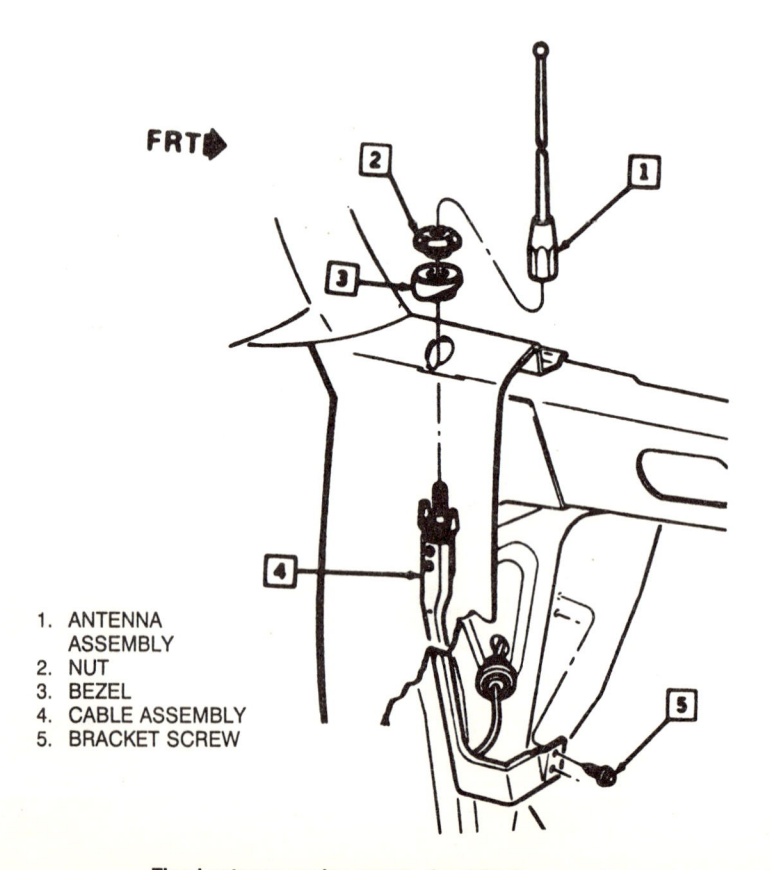

1. ANTENNA ASSEMBLY
2. NUT
3. BEZEL
4. CABLE ASSEMBLY
5. BRACKET SCREW

Fixed antenna replacement—front fender mount

BODY    287

3. Remove the screws that secure the antenna base to the brace.
4. Disconnect the lead-in cable from the base and remove the base from the vehicle.

**To install:**
5. Install the antenna base into the vehicle and connect the lead-in cable.
6. Install the base to panel screws and tighten to 18 in. lbs. (2 Nm).
7. Install the antenna mast to the base and install the rear compartment trim.

**Front fender mount**

1. Remove the radio trim and the radio.
2. Disconnect the antenna cable and connect a peice of wire or string to the cable.
3. Remove the antenna nut and bezel.
4. Remove the wheelhouse inner shield.
5. Remove the kick panel door sill trim screws nearest the door hinge.
6. Pull carpet away to gain access to the radio cable.
7. Remove the antenna base mounting screws and remove the assembly.

**To install:**
8. Install the antenna base assembly and install the mounting screws.
9. Install the carpet to the kick panel.
10. Install the panel door sill trim screws.
11. Install the wheelhouse inner shield.
12. Install the antenna nut and bezel.
13. Connect the antenna cable and install the radio and radio trim.

**Power Antenna**
**Rear fender mount**

1. Disconnect the negative battery cable.
2. Remove the rear compartment trim.
3. Disconnect the relay connector from the antenna assembly.
4. Remove the screws that secure the antenna assembly to the brace.
5. Remove the antenna insulator and disconnect the lead-in cable from the antenna assembly.
6. Remove antenna assembly from the vehicle.

**To install:**
7. Connect the lead-in cable to the antenna assembly.
8. Install the base to panel screws and tighten to 18 in. lbs. (2 Nm).
9. Install the antenna insulator and connect the electrical connector to the antenna.
10. Install the rear compartment trim and connect the negative battery cable.

**Front fender mount**

1. Disconnect the negative battery cable.
2. Remove the right side, under dash, inner panel, sound insulator.

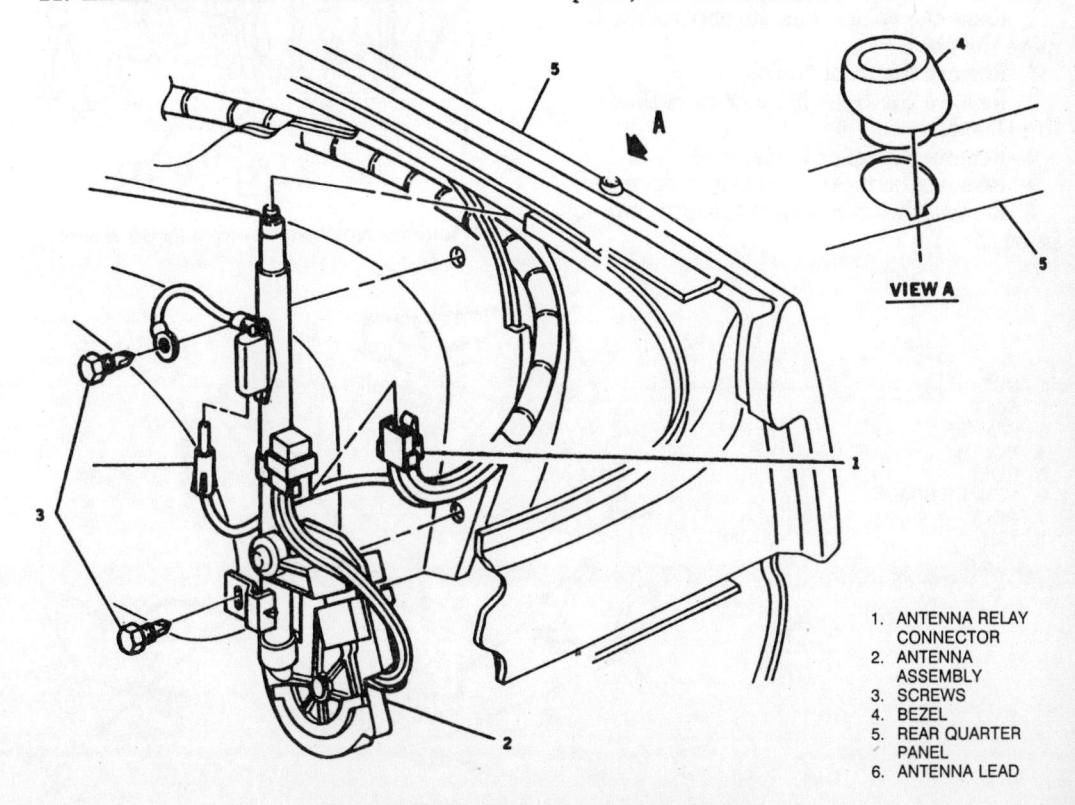

1. ANTENNA RELAY CONNECTOR
2. ANTENNA ASSEMBLY
3. SCREWS
4. BEZEL
5. REAR QUARTER PANEL
6. ANTENNA LEAD

**Power antenna replacement—rear fender mount**

# 288  BODY

3. Disconnect the antenna lead-in cable from extension cable.
4. Disconnect the antenna wiring connector.
5. Remove the grommet from the right cowl.
6. Remove the screws from the right inner fender splash shield.
7. Remove the screws from the antenna motor bracket.
8. Remove the nut and bezel holding the antenna to the fender and remove the assembly from the vehicle.

**To install:**

9. Install the antenna assembly to the vehicle and install the nut and bezel to the antenna.
10. Install the screws to the antenna motor and bracket.
11. Connect the wiring connector.
12. Connect the antenna lead-in cable to the extension cable.
13. Install the right side sound insulator.
14. Connect the negative battery cable.

## Fenders

### REMOVAL AND INSTALLATION

NOTE: *Use masking tape and heavy rags to protect the painted surfaces around the fender area. This procedure will help avoid expensive paint damage during fender removal and installation.*

1. Raise the vehicle and support safely. Remove the hood.
2. Remove the front wheel.
3. Remove the front bumper as outlined in this Chapter.
4. Remove the inner fender well.
5. Remove the rocker molding, if equipped.
6. Remove the grille and headlamp mounting panel.
7. Remove the bolts from along the top of the fender.
8. Remove the bolts that attach the bottom of the fender to the rocker panel.
9. Remove the front brace attaching bolts.
10. Remove the fender from the vehicle.

**To install:**

11. Connect the braces and hardware to the fender.

1. NUT
2. ANTENNA ASSEMBLY
3. ANTENNA WIRING HARNESS
4. ANTENNA CABLE
5. SCREW
6. BRACKET
7. GROMMET

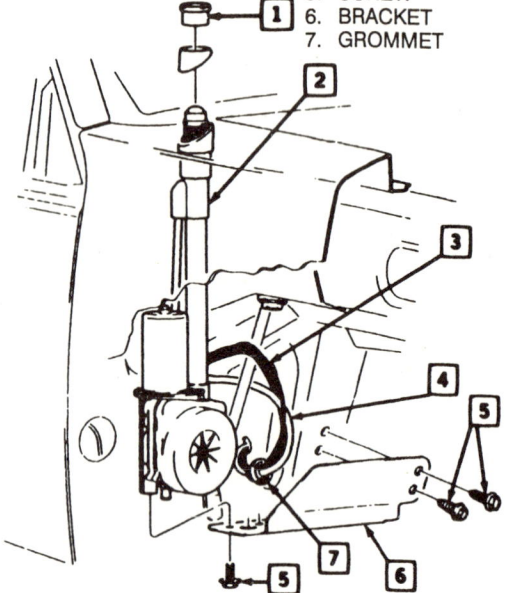

**Power antenna replacement—front fender mount**

1. NUT
2. BOLT
3. FENDER
4. BOLT
5. BOLT
6. FENDER BRACE
7. BOLT
8. NUT

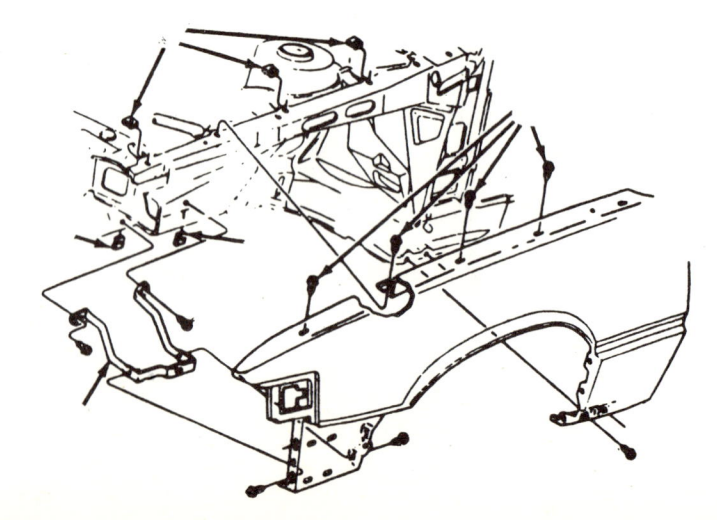

**Typical front fender—1985–91 vehicles**

BODY    289

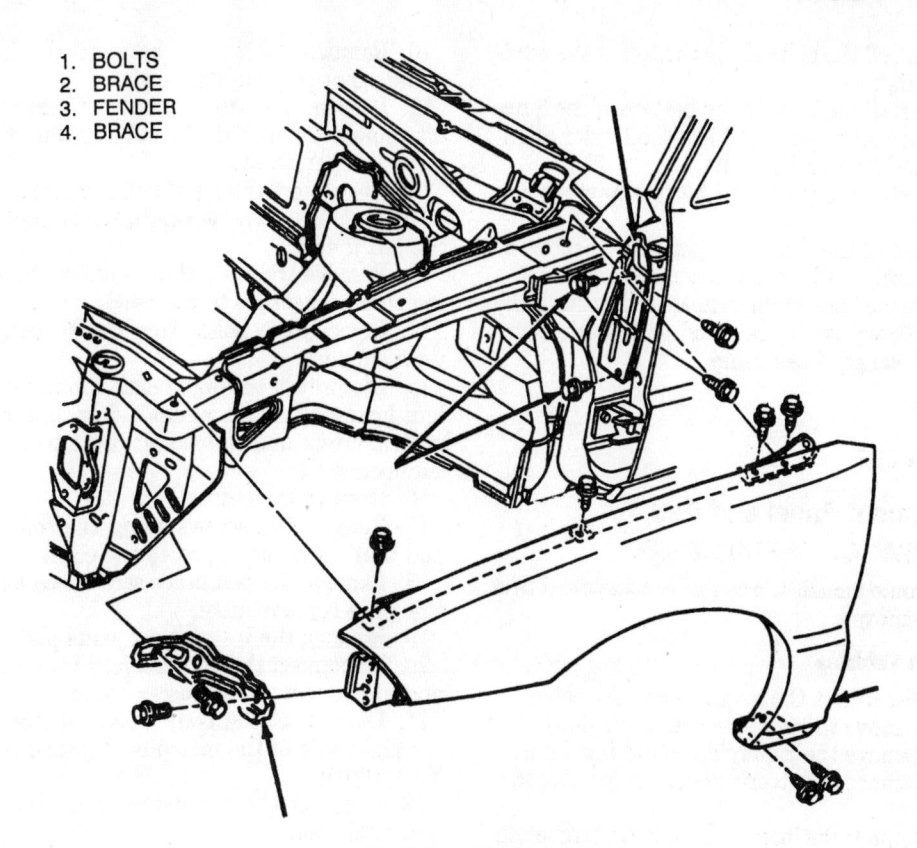

1. BOLTS
2. BRACE
3. FENDER
4. BRACE

**Front fender—1992 Grand Am**

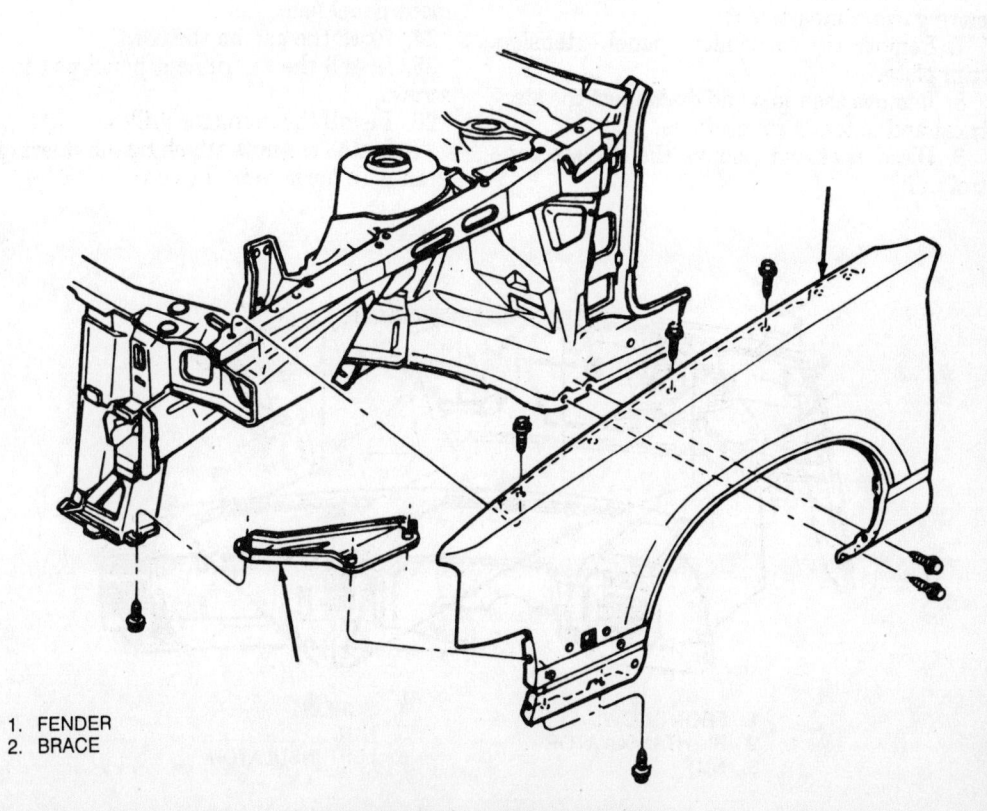

1. FENDER
2. BRACE

**Front fender—1992 Achieva**

# 290 BODY

12. Install the bolts along the top of the fender and tighten.
13. Install the bolts to the bottom of the fender at the rocker panel. Check the fender alignment and tighten the bolts.
14. Install the grille and headlamp mounting panel.
15. Install the front bumper and wheel well.
16. Connect all electrical connectors.
17. Install the front wheel and install the hood. Slowly lower the hood and check alignment. Realign if necessary.

## INTERIOR

### Instrument Panel and Pad

#### REMOVAL AND INSTALLATION

On some models the center console must first be removed.

**1985-91 Vehicles**

1. Disconnect the negative battery cable.
2. Remove the left side sound insulator.
3. Remove the right side sound insulator.
4. Remove the steering column opening trim plate.
5. Remove the instrument cluster trim plate.
6. Open the glove compartment door and remove glove compartment.
7. Remove the instrument panel extension trim plate.
8. Remove the radio and disconnect the electrical and antenna connections.
9. Disconnect and remove the climate control unit.
10. Remove the 2 nuts between the instrument panel pad and the cowl.
11. Loosen the panel attaching screws and disconnect the electrical connectors under the glove compartment.
12. Disconnect the bulkhead connector located under the hood between the wiper motor and the left fender.
13. Remove the nuts that connect the steering column harness to the cowl.
14. Remove the bolts from the steering column support.
15. Disconnect the high beam dimmer switch, ignition switch, turn signal switch, brake light switch, cruise and clutch start switch electrical connectors.
16. Remove the defroster grilles.
17. Remove the screws along the top of the pad that connect the pad to the cowl.
18. Remove the pad brace screw located near the glove compartment.
19. Remove the instrument panel pad.
20. Disconnect the antenna lead from the pad and disconnect the defroster hoses.
21. Disconnect the body electrical lead from the right side of the instrument panel.

**To install:**

22. Connect the defroster hoses and body electrical lead.
23. Connect the antenna lead to the instrument panel pad.
24. Place the pad on the cowl.
25. Install the instrument panel pad to cowl screws.
26. Install the defroster grilles.
27. Install the nuts attaching the steering column wire harness to the cowl.

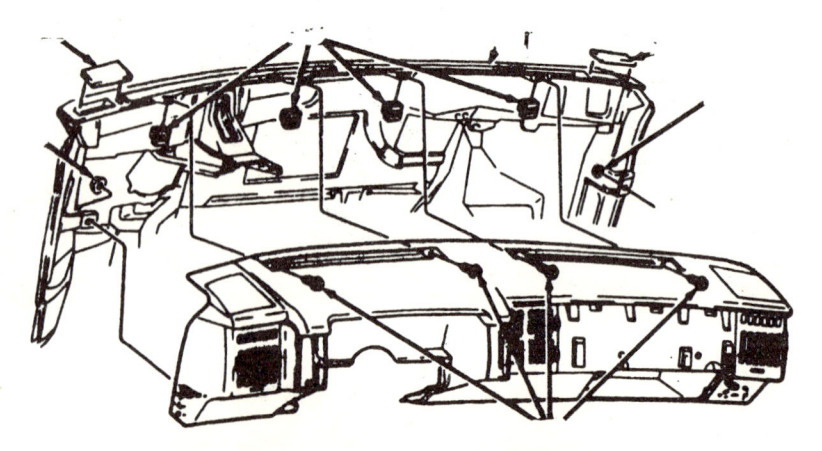

1. FRONT COWL
2. RIGHT INSULATOR
3. NUT
4. SCREW
5. NUT
6. LEFT INSULATOR

1985-91 instrument panel pad mounting

# BODY 291

28. Connect the electrical connectors and install the steering column mounting bolts.
29. Connect the bulkhead connector.
30. Install the nuts from each side of the instrument panel pad.
31. Connect the instrument panel connectors and tighten the bolts.
32. Connect the radio connectors and install the radio.
33. Install the climate control unit.
34. Install the glove compartment and slide the instrument panel assembly into the pad and tighten the screws.
35. Install the instrument panel trim plate.
36. Install the steering column trim plate.
37. Install the left and right side sound insulation panels.
38. Connect the negative battery cable.

**1992 Vehicles**

1. Disconnect the negative battery cable.
2. Remove the left side sound insulator.
3. Remove the steering column filler.
4. Remove the instrument panel cover.
5. Remove the left side instrument panel trim plate.
6. Remove the upper glove compartment screws and remove the compartment.
7. Remove the lower glove compartment screws and remove the compartment.
8. Remove the radio from the vehicle.
9. Remove the heater and A/C control.
10. Remove the defroster grille.
11. Remove the upper instrument panel screw covers and remove the screws.
12. Remove the left side lower support screw.
13. Disconnect the brake switches.
14. Disconnect the bulkhead harness under the hood.
15. Remove the upper and lower steering column covers. Remove the steering column bolts.

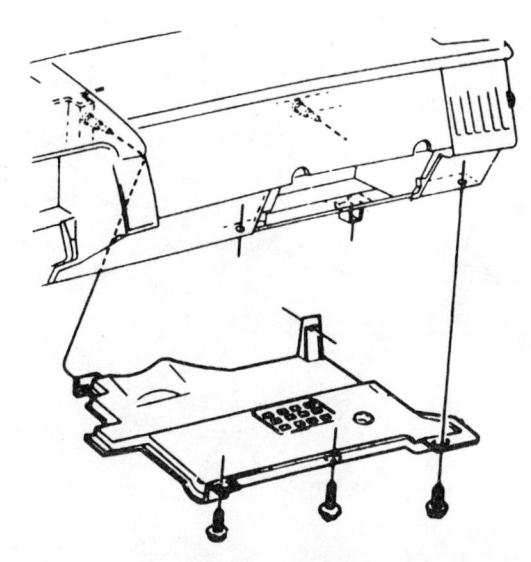

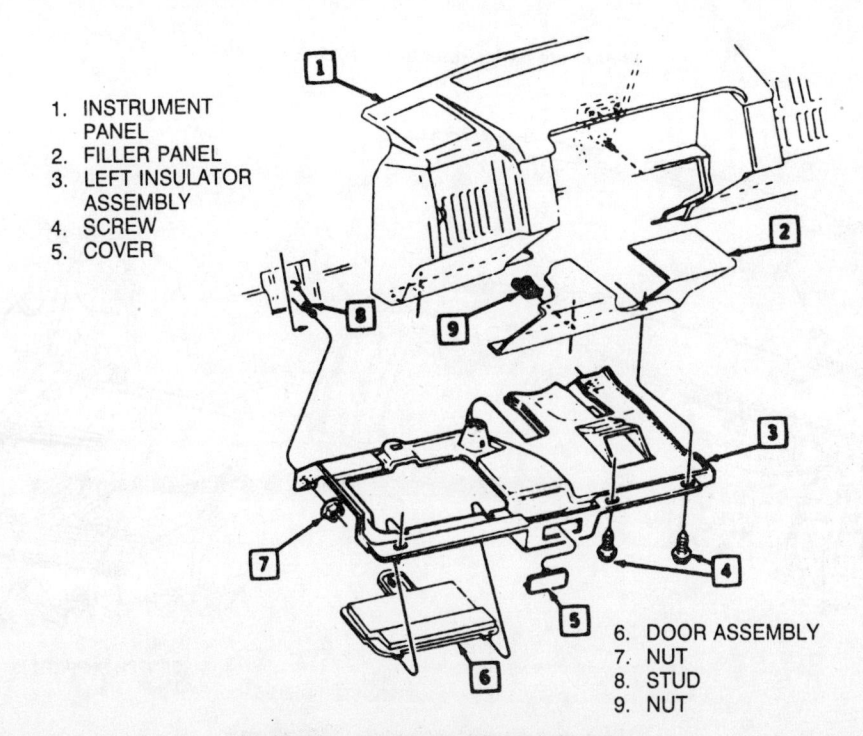

**1985–91 Right and left sound insulation panels**

1. INSTRUMENT PANEL
2. FILLER PANEL
3. LEFT INSULATOR ASSEMBLY
4. SCREW
5. COVER
6. DOOR ASSEMBLY
7. NUT
8. STUD
9. NUT

**Instrument filler and lower panel removal**

## 292  BODY

16. Remove the right side center support screw at the glove compartment opening.
17. Remove the right sound insulator panel and right side 23 pin electrical connector.
18. Remove the lower instrument panel screws and remove the instrument panel from the vehicle.

**To install:**
19. Install the instrument panel to the cowl.
20. Insert the upper instrument panel screws but do not tighten.
21. Install the lower instrument panel screws and tighten to 17 in. lbs.(2 Nm).
22. Connect the body electrical connector.
23. Install the right side sound insulator and the right center support screw.
24. Install the steering column bolts and install the column covers.
25. Connect the bulkhead electrical connector.
26. Connect the brake switch connectors.
27. Install the left support screws.

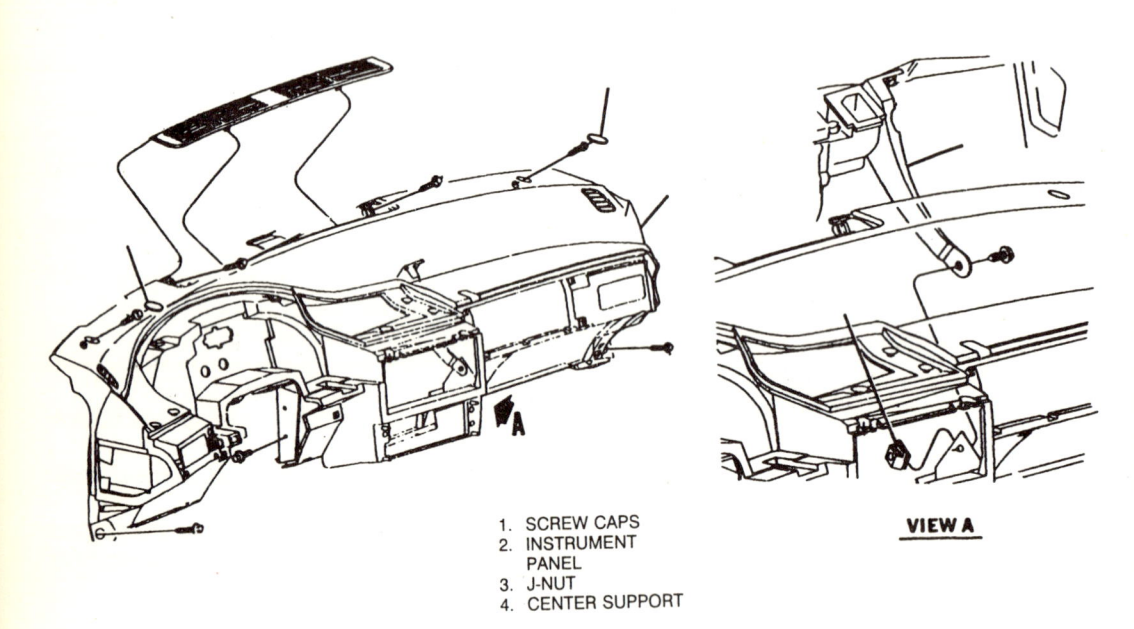

1. SCREW CAPS
2. INSTRUMENT PANEL
3. J-NUT
4. CENTER SUPPORT

VIEW A

**Instrument panel mounting—1992 Grand Am**

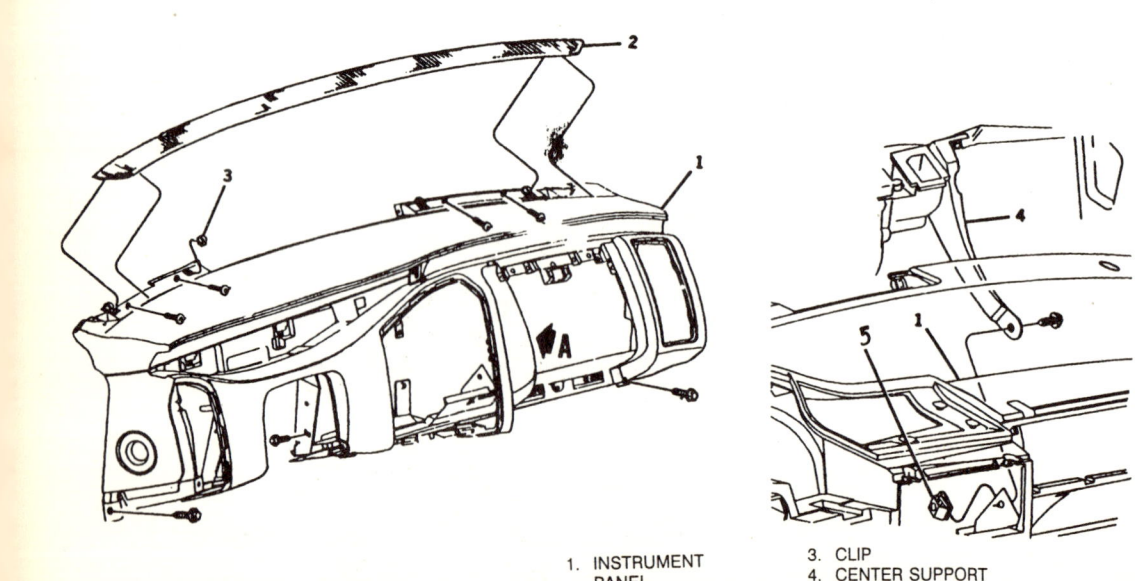

1. INSTRUMENT PANEL
2. DEFROSTER GRILLE
3. CLIP
4. CENTER SUPPORT
5. J-NUT

**Instrument panel mounting—1992 Skylark**

BODY 293

28. Tighten the upper instrument panel screws to 17 in. lbs. (2 Nm).
29. Install the upper instrument panel screw covers.
30. Install the defroster grilles.
31. Install the heater and A/C control and install the radio.
32. Install the upper and lower glove compartments.
33. Install the instrument panel trim plate.
34. Install the steering column filler and the left side sound insulator.
35. Connect the negative battery cable.

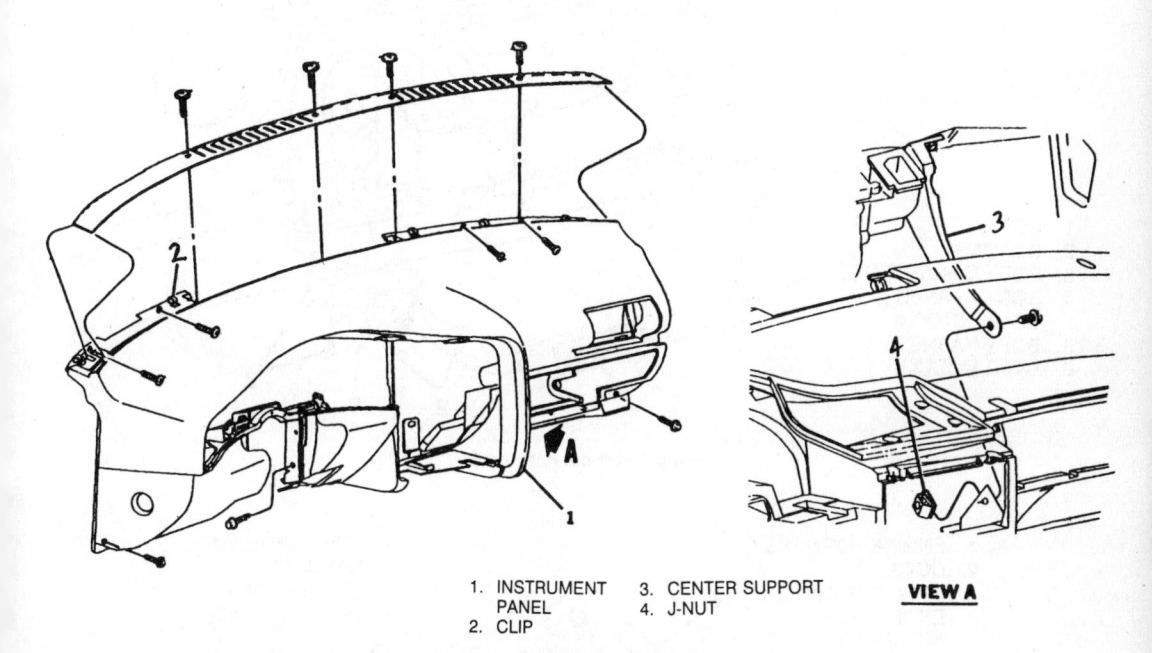

1. INSTRUMENT PANEL
2. CLIP
3. CENTER SUPPORT
4. J-NUT

VIEW A

**Instrument panel mounting—1992 Achieva**

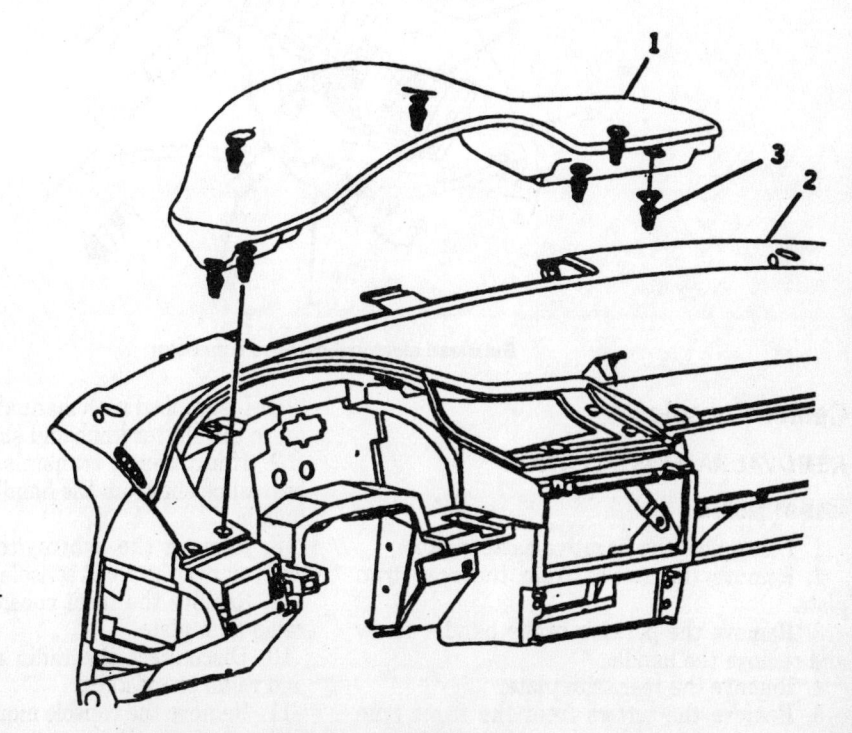

1. I/P TRIM PANEL
2. INSTRUMENT PANEL
3. RETAINERS

**Instrument panel cover—1992 Grand Am**

# 294 BODY

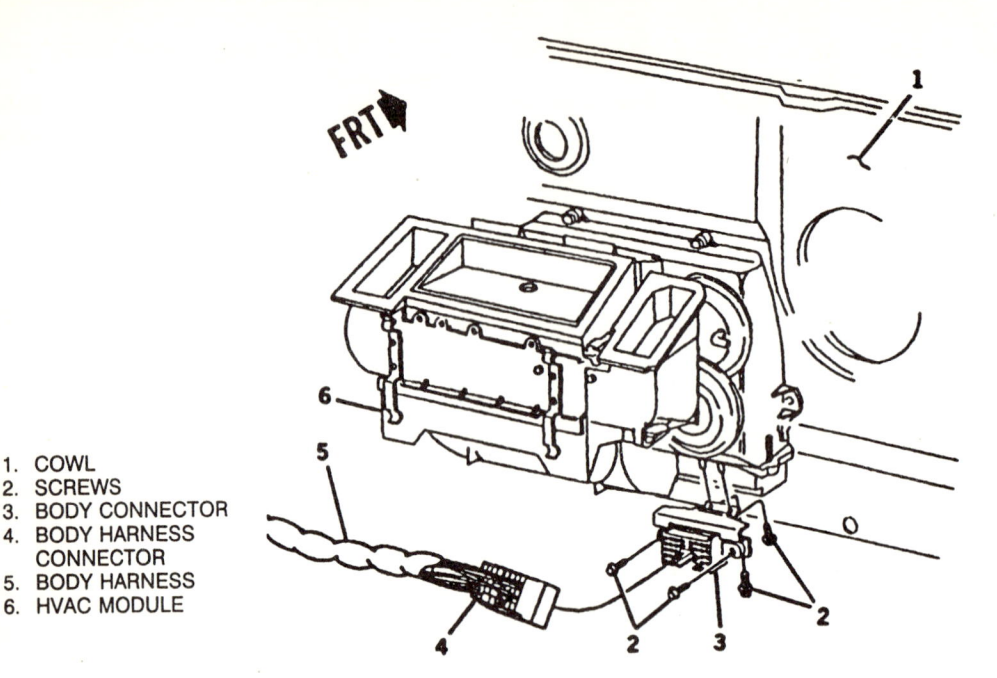

1. COWL
2. SCREWS
3. BODY CONNECTOR
4. BODY HARNESS CONNECTOR
5. BODY HARNESS
6. HVAC MODULE

*Body electrical connector*

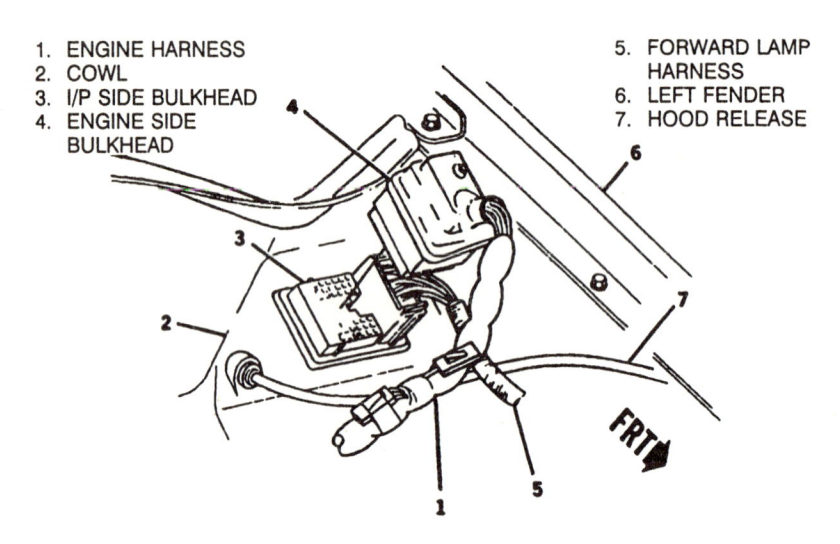

1. ENGINE HARNESS
2. COWL
3. I/P SIDE BULKHEAD
4. ENGINE SIDE BULKHEAD
5. FORWARD LAMP HARNESS
6. LEFT FENDER
7. HOOD RELEASE

*Bulkhead electrical harness connector*

## Center Console

### REMOVAL AND INSTALLATION

#### 1985-91 Models

1. Disconnect the negative battery cable.
2. Remove the screws from the rear trim plate.
3. Remove the parking brake handle screw and remove the handle.
4. Remove the rear trim plate.
5. Remove the screws from the front trim plate.
6. If equipped with manual transmission, remove the shifter knob and shifter boot screws.
7. If automatic transmission, remove the horseshoe clip from the handle and remove the handle.
8. Remove the ashtray/coin compartment and remove the front console trim plate screw.
9. Remove the front console trim plate and radio trim plate.
10. Disconnect the radio mounting screws and radio connectors.
11. Remove the console mounting screws and disconnect the electrical connectors.

BODY    295

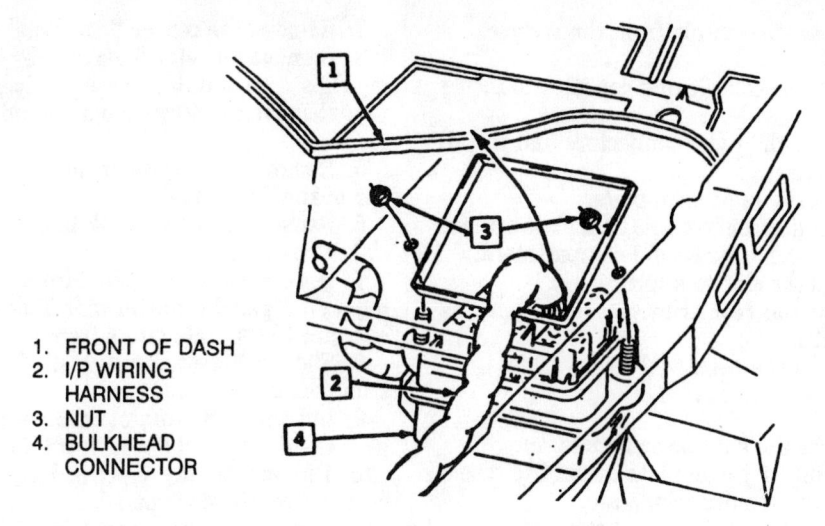

1. FRONT OF DASH
2. I/P WIRING HARNESS
3. NUT
4. BULKHEAD CONNECTOR

**Bulkhead**

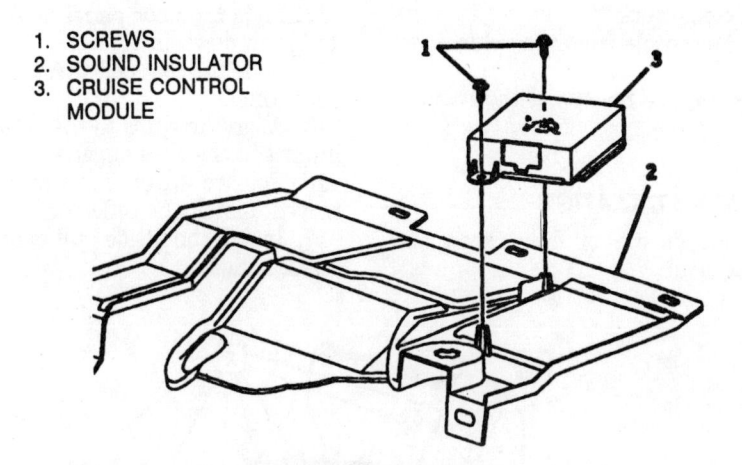

1. SCREWS
2. SOUND INSULATOR
3. CRUISE CONTROL MODULE

**Left insulator panel—1992 models**

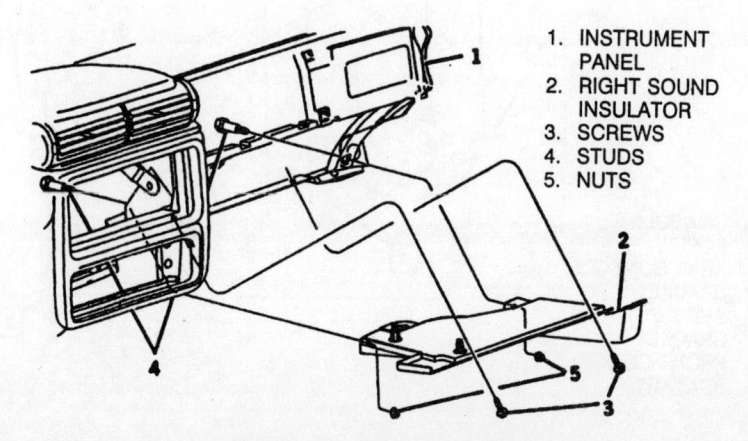

1. INSTRUMENT PANEL
2. RIGHT SOUND INSULATOR
3. SCREWS
4. STUDS
5. NUTS

**Right insulator panel—1992 models**

12. Remove the console from the vehicle.

**To install:**

13. Install the console and console mounting screws.
14. Connect the radio connectors and install the radio screws.
15. Install the radio trim plate.
16. Install the front console trim plate screws.
17. Install the ashtray/coin compartment.
18. Install the shifter knob.
19. Install the rear trim plate and parking brake handle.
20. Connect the negative battery cable.

**1992 Models**

1. Remove the shift lever handle.
2. Carefully pry trim plate upward to disengage clips and remove trim plate.
3. Remove the console compartment.
4. Remove the screws at the rear compartment.
5. Pull console towards the rear and disconnect electrical connectors.
6. Remove the console from the vehicle.

**To install:**

7. Installation is the reverse of the removal procedure.

## Door Panels

### REMOVAL AND INSTALLATION

1. Remove outside mirror escutcheon and seat belt escutcheon.
2. Remove the center door panel screw.
3. Remove reflector from door by disconnecting clips with thin blade screwdriver.
4. Remove the screw from behind the reflector base.
5. Remove the screws at the lower front corner of the door panel.
6. Remove window crank handle using special remover tool.
7. Separate the door panel from the door using a door panel removal tool. Pull door panel outward to separate studs from the retainers.
8. Slide seat belt through slit in bottom of trim panel.
9. Lift up on bottom of trim panel to disengage the door panel hooks from the slots.
10. Disconnect any electrical connectors to switches on the door panel.
11. Remove the trim panel from the vehicle.

**To install:**

12. Connect any electrical connectors to switches on the door panel.
13. Slide the door panel hooks into the slots and push down to engage.
14. Slide the seat belt through the slits in the door panel.
15. Align the studs to the retainers and push inward so the clips engage.
16. Replace all of the screws that were removed. Install the reflector.
17. Install the inside pull handle and window crank handle.

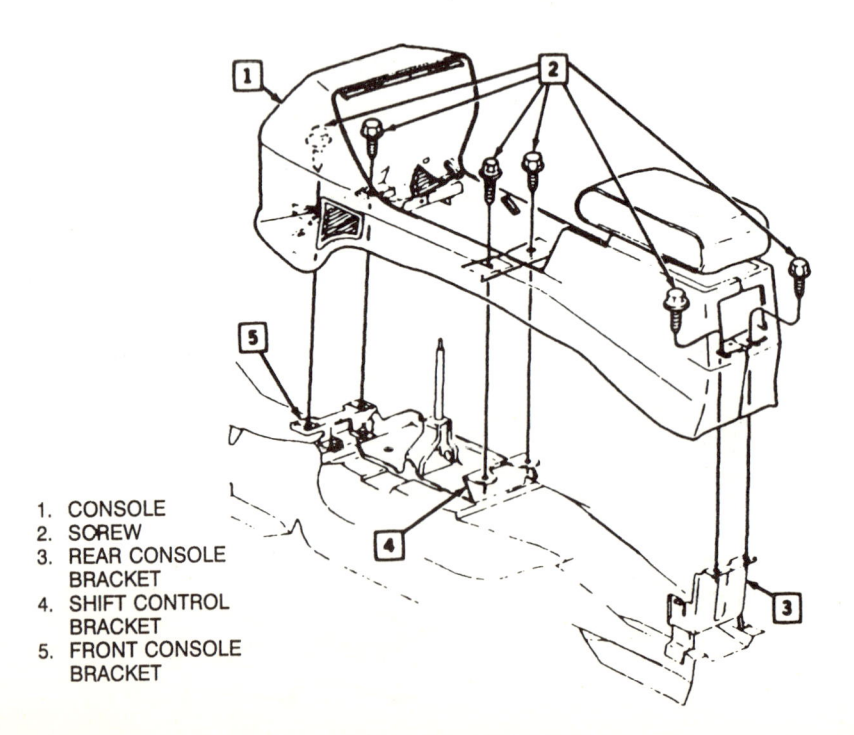

1. CONSOLE
2. SCREW
3. REAR CONSOLE BRACKET
4. SHIFT CONTROL BRACKET
5. FRONT CONSOLE BRACKET

1985–91 typical center console mounting

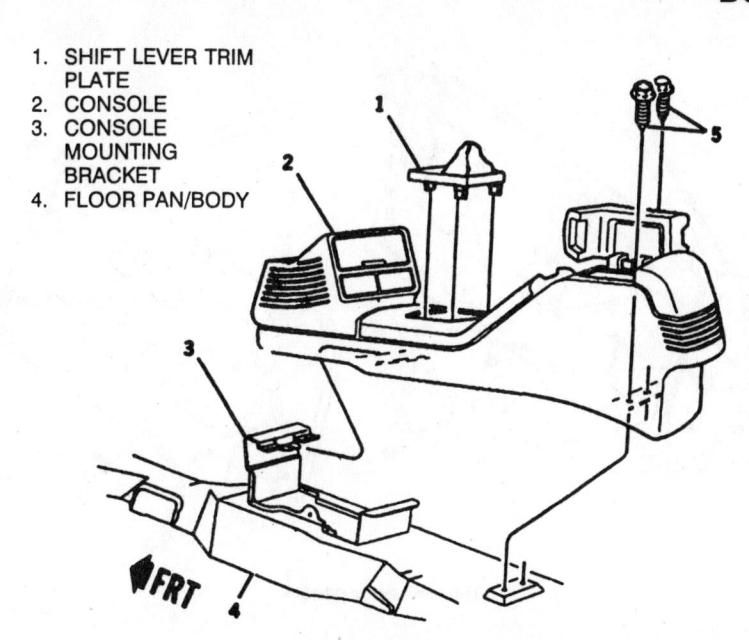

1. SHIFT LEVER TRIM PLATE
2. CONSOLE
3. CONSOLE MOUNTING BRACKET
4. FLOOR PAN/BODY

*1992 typical center console mounting*

18. Install the outside mirror escutcheon and seat belt opening escutcheon.

## Interior Trim Panels
### REMOVAL AND INSTALLATION
#### Upper and Lower Inside Door Trim Panels

1. Remove the inside door panel as detailed above.
2. Remove the nuts securing the trim panel to the door panel.
3. Separate the trim panel from the door panel.
4. Installation is the reverse of the removal procedure.

#### Rear Quarter Interior Trim Panel
#### 2-door

1. Remove the rear seat back and rear seat cushion
2. Disconnect carpet retainer by removing the screws and lifting up on carpet retainer.
3. Remove windshield side upper molding by grasping molding and pulling down to disengage molding.
4. Remove the trim panel screws.
5. Pull outward on the trim panel to disengage the fasteners from the retainers.
6. Remove the seat belt from the slit in the panel and remove the panel.

**To install:**

7. Install the seat belt through the slit in the panel.
8. Align the fasteners to the retainers and push in on panel to engage.
9. Install the panel screw.
10. Install windshield side upper molding.
11. Install carpet retainers and install rear seat back and cushion.

#### Rear Quarter Interior Trim Panel
#### 4-door

1. Remove rear seat cushion and rear seat back.
2. Remove the panel screws and remove trim panel by pulling downward to disengage clips.

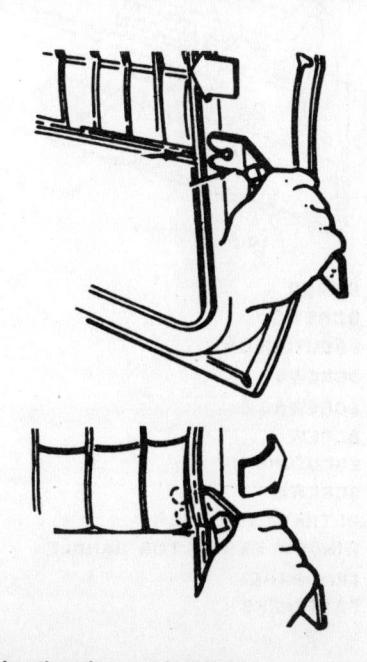

*Releasing the trim panel retainers*

## 298  BODY

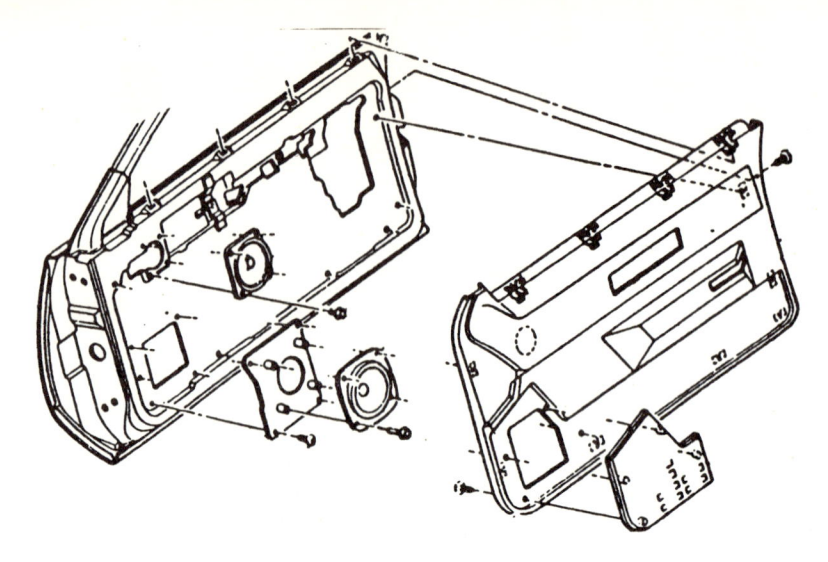

*1985–87 door panels*

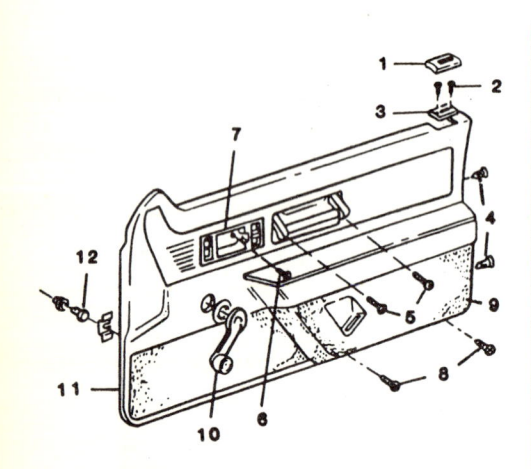

1. COVER
2. SCREWS
3. ESCUTCHEON
4. SCREWS
5. SCREWS
6. SCREW
7. ESCUTCHEON
8. SCREWS
9. RETRACTOR COVER
10. WINDOW REGULATOR HANDLE
11. TRIM PANEL
12. FASTENERS

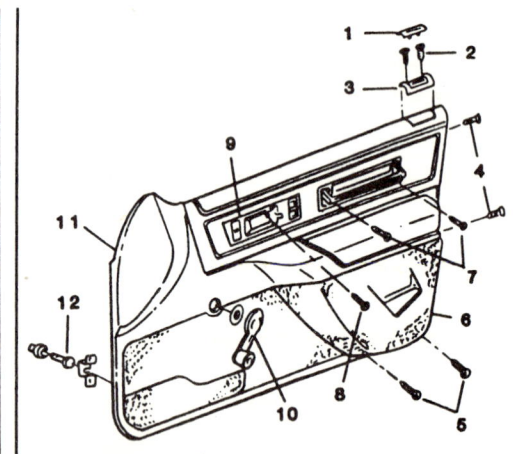

1. COVER
2. SCREWS
3. ESCUTCHEON
4. SCREWS
5. SCREWS
6. RETRACTOR COVER OR MAP POCKET
7. SCREWS
8. SCREWS
9. ESCUTCHEON
10. WINDOW REGULATOR HANDLE
11. TRIM PANEL
12. FASTENER

*1988 Grand Am and 1988–91 Calais and Skylark door panels*

# BODY 299

1. ESCUTCHEON
2. RETAINER
3. TRIM PANEL
4. ARM REST
5. ESCUTCHEON
6. FASTENERS
7. MAP POCKET
8. COVER
9. SCREWS
10. SCREW
11. SCREW
12. SCREW
13. SCREWS
14. RETRACTOR COVER
15. SCREWS

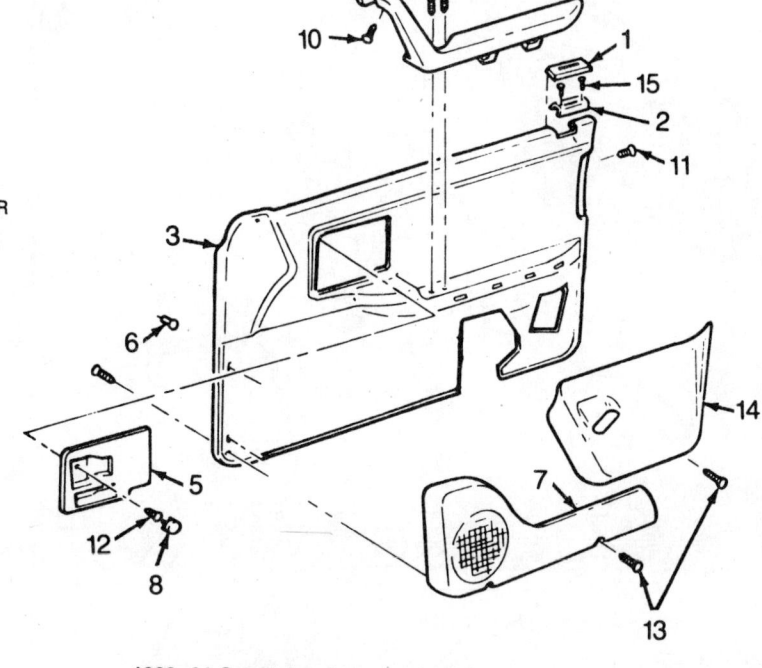

*1989–91 Grand Am door panel*

## To install:

3. Install the trim panel by aligning tabs and retainers and pressing upward until secure.
4. Install panel screws and install rear seat back and rear seat cushion.

## Headliner

### REMOVAL AND INSTALLATION

1. Pull inward on inside upper garnish molding to release tabs from the retainers and remove the moldings from the vehicle.

2. On the 2 door model, remove the rear quarter trim panel. On the 4 door model, remove the center pillar trim panel.
3. On the 4 door model, remove both the upper and lower quarter trim panels.
4. Remove the left side instrument panel sound insulator and disconnect the electrical connector from the side of the instrument panel.
5. Disconnect the electrical harness connectors.

1. TRIM PANEL
2. ESCUTCHEON
3. SCREW
4. SCREW
5. REFLECTOR
6. CLIPS
7. SCREWS
8. STUD
9. RETAINER
10. HOOK
11. SLOTS

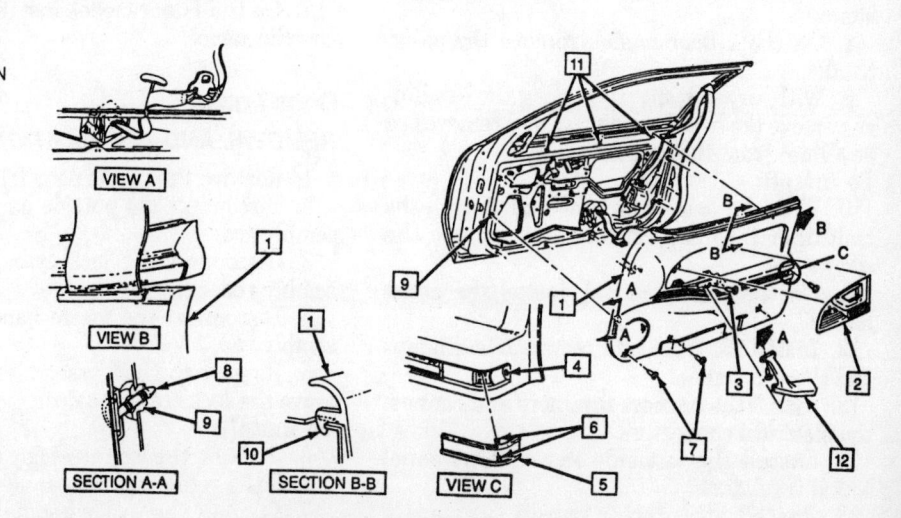

*1992 Skylark door panel*

# 300 BODY

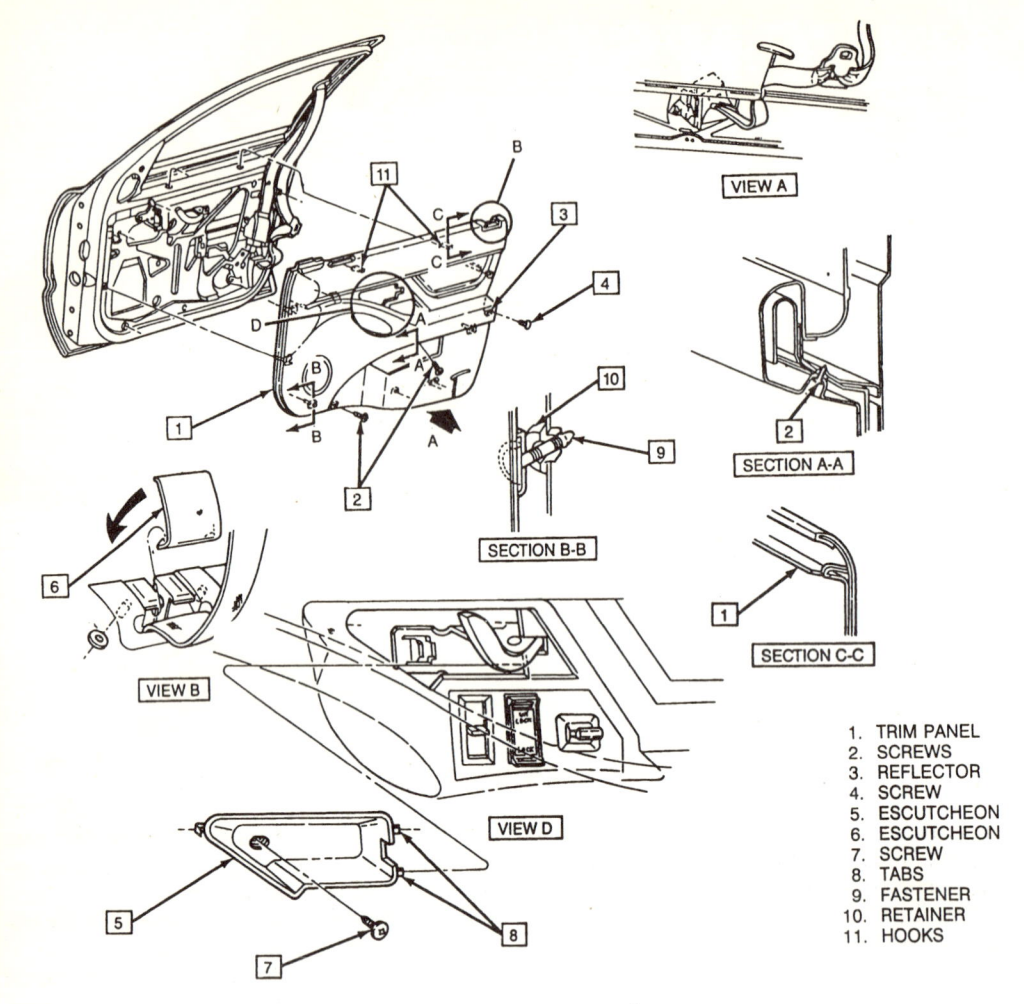

*1992 Achieva door panel*

1. TRIM PANEL
2. SCREWS
3. REFLECTOR
4. SCREW
5. ESCUTCHEON
6. ESCUTCHEON
7. SCREW
8. TABS
9. FASTENER
10. RETAINER
11. HOOKS

6. Remove both sunshades.
7. Remove the front and rear courtesy lamps.
8. On the 4 door model, remove the assist handle.
9. With an assistant supporting the headliner, remove the headliner screws and remove the headliner from the vehicle.

**To install:**

10. With the help of an assistant, install the headliner into the vehicle and replace the screws.
11. On the 4 door model, install the assist handle.
12. Install the front and rear courtesy lamps and the sunshades.
13. Install the harness retainers and connect the electrical connectors.
14. Install the left side instrument panel sound insulator.
15. Install all interior panels previously removed.
16. Install the windshield side upper garnish moldings.
17. On the 4 door model, install the center pillar trim panel.

## Door Locks

### REMOVAL AND INSTALLATION

1. Remove the inside door trim panel.
2. Disconnect the outside handle to lock assembly rod.
3. Disconnect the lock cylinder to lock assembly rod.
4. Disconnect the inside handle to lock assembly rod.
5. Remove the lock assembly screws and remove the lock from the door.

**To install:**

6. Position the lock assembly to the door and install the retaining screws.
7. Connect the inside handle to the lock assembly rod.

# CHILTON'S
# AUTO BODY REPAIR TIPS

**Tools and Materials • Step-by-Step Illustrated Procedures
How To Repair Dents, Scratches and Rust Holes
Spray Painting and Refinishing Tips**

**EASY STEP-BY-STEP TIPS FROM PROS**

With a little practice, basic body repair procedures can be mastered by any do-it-yourself mechanic. The step-by-step repairs shown here can be applied to almost any type of auto body repair.

## TOOLS & MATERIALS

You may already have basic tools, such as hammers and electric drills. Other tools unique to body repair — body hammers, grinding attachments, sanding blocks, dent puller, half-round plastic file and plastic spreaders — are relatively inexpensive and can be obtained wherever auto parts or auto body repair parts are sold. Portable air compressors and paint spray guns can be purchased or rented.

### Auto Body Repair Kits

The best and most often used products are available to the do-it-yourselfer in kit form, from major manufacturers of auto body repair products. The same manufacturers also merchandise the individual products for use by pros.

Kits are available to make a wide variety of repairs, including holes, dents and scratches and fiberglass, and offer the advantage of buying the materials you'll need for the job. There is little waste or chance of materials going bad from not being used. Many kits may also contain basic body-working tools such as body files, sanding blocks and spreaders. Check the contents of the kit before buying your tools.

## BODY REPAIR TIPS

### Safety

Many of the products associated with auto body repair and refinishing contain toxic chemicals. Read all labels before opening containers and store them in a safe place and manner.

• Wear eye protection (safety goggles) when using power tools or when performing any operation that involves the removal of any type of material.

• Wear lung protection (disposable mask or respirator) when grinding, sanding or painting.

### Sanding

**1** Sand off paint before using a dent puller. When using a non-adhesive sanding disc, cover the back of the disc with an overlapping layer or two of masking tape and trim the edges. The disc will last considerably longer.

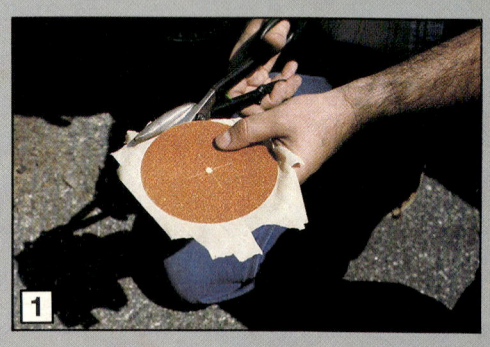

**2** Use the circular motion of the sanding disc to grind *into* the edge of the repair. Grinding or sanding away from the jagged edge will only tear the sandpaper.

**3** Use the palm of your hand flat on the panel to detect high and low spots. Do not use your fingertips. Slide your hand slowly back and forth.

# WORKING WITH BODY FILLER

## Mixing The Filler

**C**leanliness and proper mixing and application are extremely important. Use a clean piece of plastic or glass or a disposable artist's palette to mix body filler.

**1** Allow plenty of time and follow directions. No useful purpose will be served by adding more hardener to make it cure (set-up) faster. Less hardener means more curing time, but the mixture dries harder; more hardener means less curing time but a softer mixture.

**2** Both the hardener and the filler should be thoroughly kneaded or stirred before mixing. Hardener should be a solid paste and dispense like thin toothpaste. Body filler should be smooth, and free of lumps or thick spots.

Getting the proper amount of hardener in the filler is the trickiest part of preparing the filler. Use the same amount of hardener in cold or warm weather. For contour filler (thick coats), a bead of hardener twice the diameter of the filler is about right. There's about a 15% margin on either side, but, if in doubt use less hardener.

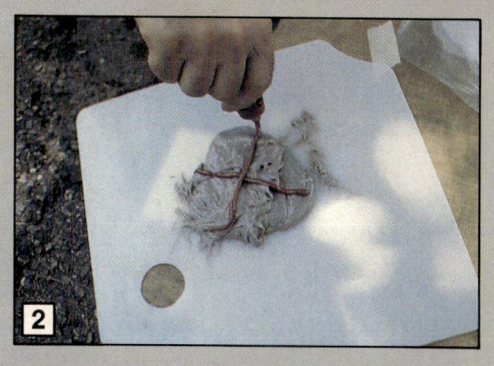

**3** Mix the body filler and hardener by wiping across the mixing surface, picking the mixture up and wiping it again. Colder weather requires longer mixing times. Do not mix in a circular motion; this will trap air bubbles which will become holes in the cured filler.

## Applying The Filler

**1** For best results, filler should not be applied over ¼" thick.

Apply the filler in several coats. Build it up to above the level of the repair surface so that it can be sanded or grated down.

The first coat of filler must be pressed on with a firm wiping motion.

Apply the filler in one direction only. Working the filler back and forth will either pull it off the metal or trap air bubbles.

# REPAIRING DENTS

**B**efore you start, take a few minutes to study the damaged area. Try to visualize the shape of the panel before it was damaged. If the damage is on the left fender, look at the right fender and use it as a guide. If there is access to the panel from behind, you can reshape it with a body hammer. If not, you'll have to use a dent puller. Go slowly and work the metal a little at a time. Get the panel as straight as possible before applying filler.

**1** This dent is typical of one that can be pulled out or hammered out from behind. Remove the headlight cover, headlight assembly and turn signal housing.

**2** Drill a series of holes ½ the size of the end of the dent puller along the stress line. Make some trial pulls and assess the results. If necessary, drill more holes and try again. Do not hurry.

**3** If possible, use a body hammer and block to shape the metal back to its original contours. Get the metal back as close to its original shape as possible. Don't depend on body filler to fill dents.

**4** Using an 80-grit grinding disc on an electric drill, grind the paint from the surrounding area down to bare metal. Use a new grinding pad to prevent heat buildup that will warp metal.

**5** The area should look like this when you're finished grinding. Knock the drill holes in and tape over small openings to keep plastic filler out.

**6** Mix the body filler (see Body Repair Tips). Spread the body filler evenly over the entire area (see Body Repair Tips). Be sure to cover the area completely.

**7** Let the body filler dry until the surface can just be scratched with your fingernail. Knock the high spots from the body filler with a body file ("Cheesegrater"). Check frequently with the palm of your hand for high and low spots.

**8** Check to be sure that trim pieces that will be installed later will fit exactly. Sand the area with 40-grit paper.

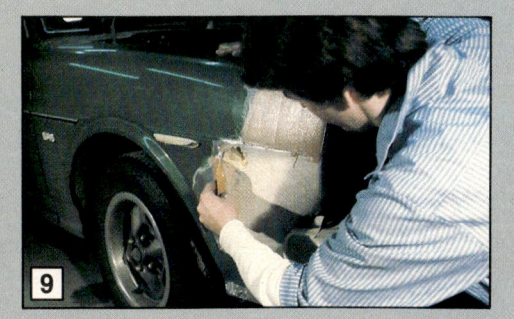

**9** If you wind up with low spots, you may have to apply another layer of filler.

**10** Knock the high spots off with 40-grit paper. When you are satisfied with the contours of the repair, apply a thin coat of filler to cover pin holes and scratches.

**11** Block sand the area with 40-grit paper to a smooth finish. Pay particular attention to body lines and ridges that must be well-defined.

**12** Sand the area with 400 paper and then finish with a scuff pad. The finished repair is ready for priming and painting (see Painting Tips).

Materials and photos courtesy of Ritt Jones Auto Body, Prospect Park, PA.

# REPAIRING RUST HOLES

There are many ways to repair rust holes. The fiberglass cloth kit shown here is one of the most cost efficient for the owner because it provides a strong repair that resists cracking and moisture and is relatively easy to use. It can be used on large and small holes (with or without backing) and can be applied over contoured areas. Remember, however, that short of replacing an entire panel, no repair is a guarantee that the rust will not return.

**1** Remove any trim that will be in the way. Clean away all loose debris. Cut away all the rusted metal. But be sure to leave enough metal to retain the contour or body shape.

**2** Grind away all traces of rust with a 24-grit grinding disc. Be sure to grind back 3-4 inches from the edge of the hole down to bare metal and be sure all traces of paint, primer and rust are removed.

**3** Block sand the area with 80 or 100 grit sandpaper to get a clear, shiny surface and feathered paint edge. Tap the edges of the hole inward with a ball peen hammer.

**4** If you are going to use release film, cut a piece about 2-3" larger than the area you have sanded. Place the film over the repair and mark the sanded area on the film. Avoid any unnecessary wrinkling of the film.

**5** Cut 2 pieces of fiberglass matte to match the shape of the repair. One piece should be about 1" smaller than the sanded area and the second piece should be 1" smaller than the first. Mix enough filler and hardener to saturate the fiberglass material (see Body Repair Tips).

**6** Lay the release sheet on a flat surface and spread an even layer of filler, large enough to cover the repair. Lay the smaller piece of fiberglass cloth in the center of the sheet and spread another layer of filler over the fiberglass cloth. Repeat the operation for the larger piece of cloth.

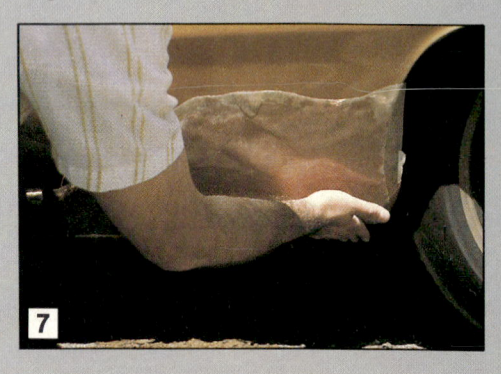

**7** Place the repair material over the repair area, with the release film facing outward. Use a spreader and work from the center outward to smooth the material, following the body contours. Be sure to remove all air bubbles.

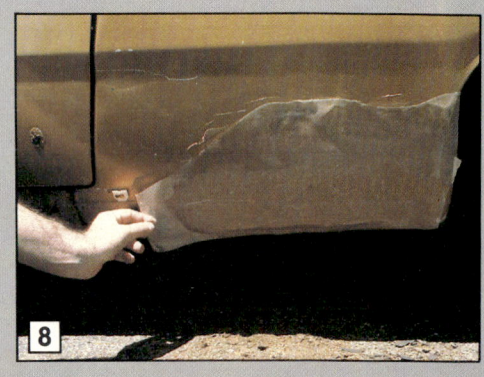

**8** Wait until the repair has dried tack-free and peel off the release sheet. The ideal working temperature is 60°-90° F. Cooler or warmer temperatures or high humidity may require additional curing time. Wait longer, if in doubt.

**9** Sand and feather-edge the entire area. The initial sanding can be done with a sanding disc on an electric drill if care is used. Finish the sanding with a block sander. Low spots can be filled with body filler; this may require several applications.

**10** When the filler can just be scratched with a fingernail, knock the high spots down with a body file and smooth the entire area with 80-grit. Feather the filled areas into the surrounding areas.

**11** When the area is sanded smooth, mix some topcoat and hardener and apply it directly with a spreader. This will give a smooth finish and prevent the glass matte from showing through the paint.

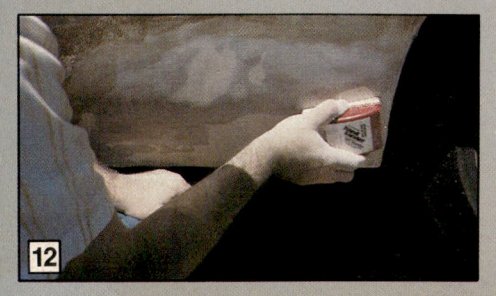

**12** Block sand the topcoat smooth with finishing sandpaper (200 grit), and 400 grit. The repair is ready for masking, priming and painting (see Painting Tips).

Materials and photos courtesy Marson Corporation, Chelsea, Massachusetts

# PAINTING TIPS

## Preparation

**1** SANDING — Use a 400 or 600 grit wet or dry sandpaper. Wet-sand the area with a 1/4 sheet of sandpaper soaked in clean water. Keep the paper wet while sanding. Sand the area until the repaired area tapers into the original finish.

**2** CLEANING — Wash the area to be painted thoroughly with water and a clean rag. Rinse it thoroughly and wipe the surface dry until you're sure it's completely free of dirt, dust, fingerprints, wax, detergent or other foreign matter.

**3** MASKING — Protect any areas you don't want to overspray by covering them with masking tape and newspaper. Be careful not get fingerprints on the area to be painted.

**4** PRIMING — All exposed metal should be primed before painting. Primer protects the metal and provides an excellent surface for paint adhesion. When the primer is dry, wet-sand the area again with 600 grit wet-sandpaper. Clean the area again after sanding.

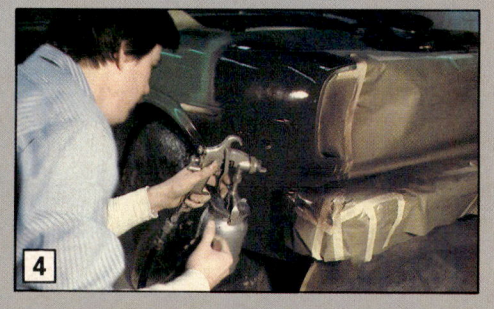

## Painting Techniques

**P**aint applied from either a spray gun or a spray can (for small areas) will provide good results. Experiment on an old piece of metal to get the right combination before you begin painting.

**SPRAYING VISCOSITY (SPRAY GUN ONLY)** — Paint should be thinned to spraying viscosity according to the directions on the can. Use only the recommended thinner or reducer and the same amount of reduction regardless of temperature.

**AIR PRESSURE (SPRAY GUN ONLY)** — This is extremely important. Be sure you are using the proper recommended pressure.

**TEMPERATURE** — The surface to be painted should be approximately the same temperature as the surrounding air. Applying warm paint to a cold surface, or vice versa, will completely upset the paint characteristics.

**THICKNESS** — Spray with smooth strokes. In general, the thicker the coat of paint, the longer the drying time. Apply several thin coats about 30 seconds apart. The paint should remain wet long enough to flow out and no longer; heavier coats will only produce sags or wrinkles. Spray a light (fog) coat, followed by heavier color coats.

**DISTANCE** — The ideal spraying distance is 8"-12" from the gun or can to the surface. Shorter distances will produce ripples, while greater distances will result in orange peel, dry film and poor color match and loss of material due to overspray.

**OVERLAPPING** — The gun or can should be kept at right angles to the surface at all times. Work to a wet edge at an even speed, using a 50% overlap and direct the center of the spray at the lower or nearest edge of the previous stroke.

**RUBBING OUT (BLENDING) FRESH PAINT** — Let the paint dry thoroughly. Runs or imperfections can be sanded out, primed and repainted.

Don't be in too big a hurry to remove the masking. This only produces paint ridges. When the finish has dried for at least a week, apply a small amount of fine grade rubbing compound with a clean, wet cloth. Use lots of water and blend the new paint with the surrounding area.

**WRONG**
*Thin coat. Stroke too fast, not enough overlap, gun too far away.*

**CORRECT**
*Medium coat. Proper distance, good stroke, proper overlap.*

**WRONG**
*Heavy coat. Stroke too slow, too much overlap, gun too close.*

BODY 301

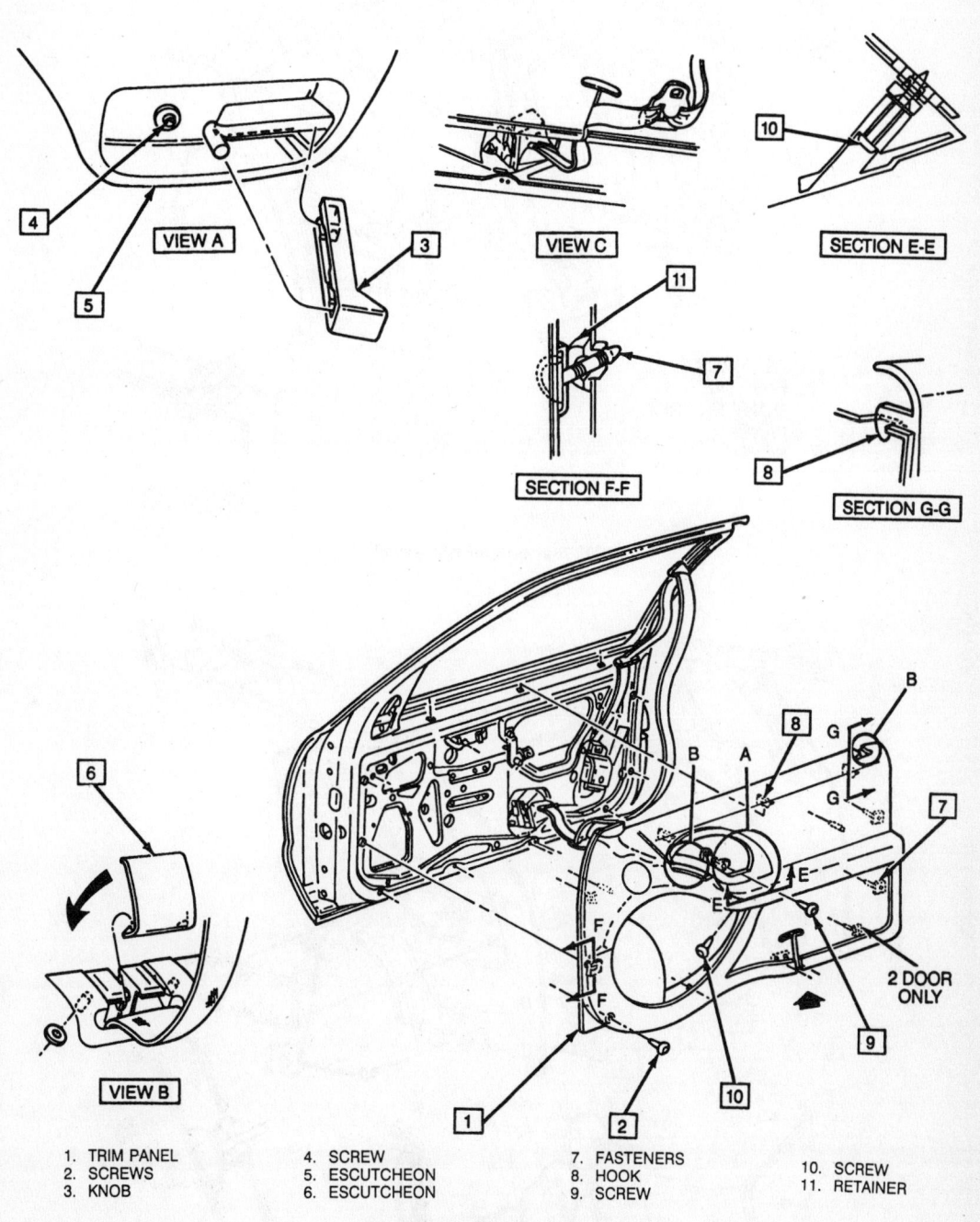

1. TRIM PANEL
2. SCREWS
3. KNOB
4. SCREW
5. ESCUTCHEON
6. ESCUTCHEON
7. FASTENERS
8. HOOK
9. SCREW
10. SCREW
11. RETAINER

**1992 Grand Am door panel**

## 302 BODY

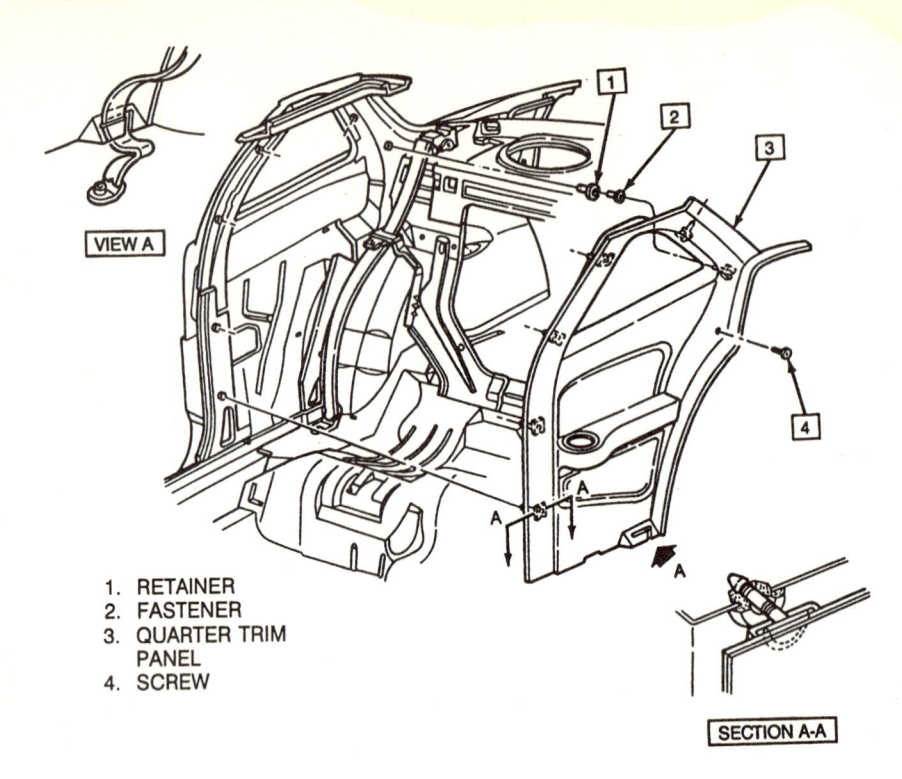

VIEW A

1. RETAINER
2. FASTENER
3. QUARTER TRIM PANEL
4. SCREW

SECTION A-A

**1992 rear quarter trim panel**

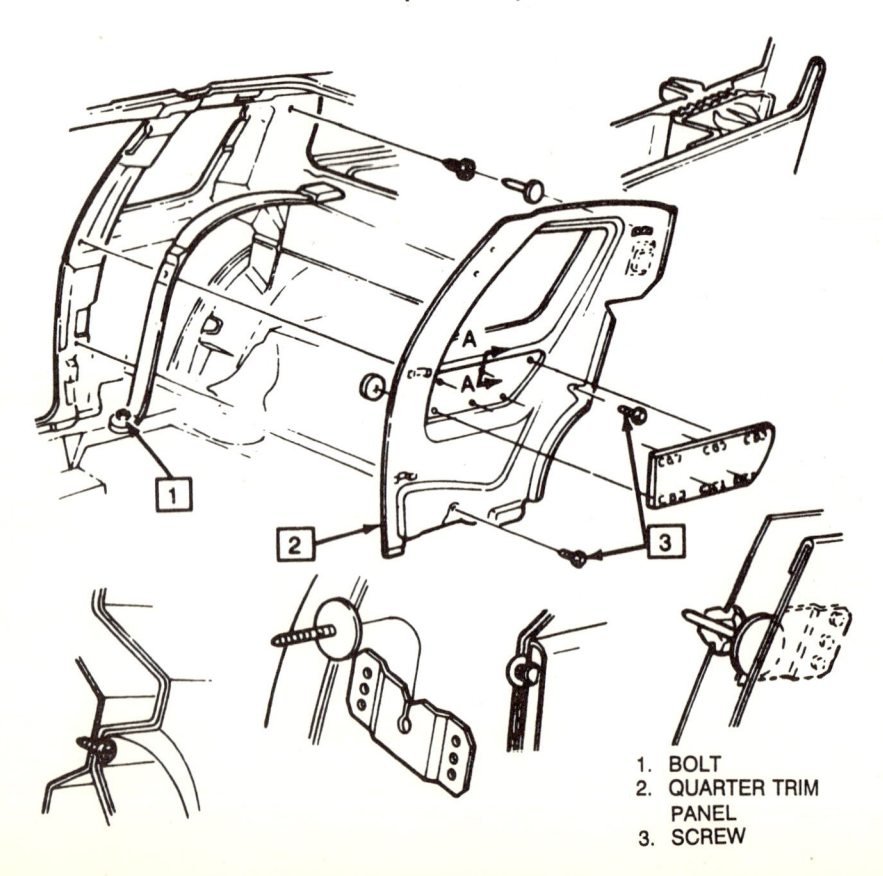

1. BOLT
2. QUARTER TRIM PANEL
3. SCREW

**1985–91 rear quarter trim panel**

# BODY

8. Connect the lock cylinder to the lock assembly rod.
9. Connect the outside handle to the lock assembly rod.
10. Install the inside door trim panel.

## Door Glass

### REMOVAL AND INSTALLATION

1. Remove the door trim panel.
2. Remove inside plastic lining from door.
3. Lower window to full down position and remove window run channel.
4. Move window to the half down position.
5. Remove the window retaining nuts.
6. While holding onto the window, lower the regulator to the full down position.
7. Remove the window by sliding towards the rear and rotating front of window upward and out of door.

**To install:**

8. Install the window to the door and align regulator with the glass.
9. While holding onto window move regulator to half up position.
10. Install the nuts. Roll the window to the full up position.
11. Install the rear run channel.
12. Install the plastic door lining and secure with waterproof adhesive.
13. Install the door trim panel.

## Window Regulator

### REMOVAL AND INSTALLATION

1. Remove the door trim panel.
2. Remove the inside plastic door liner.

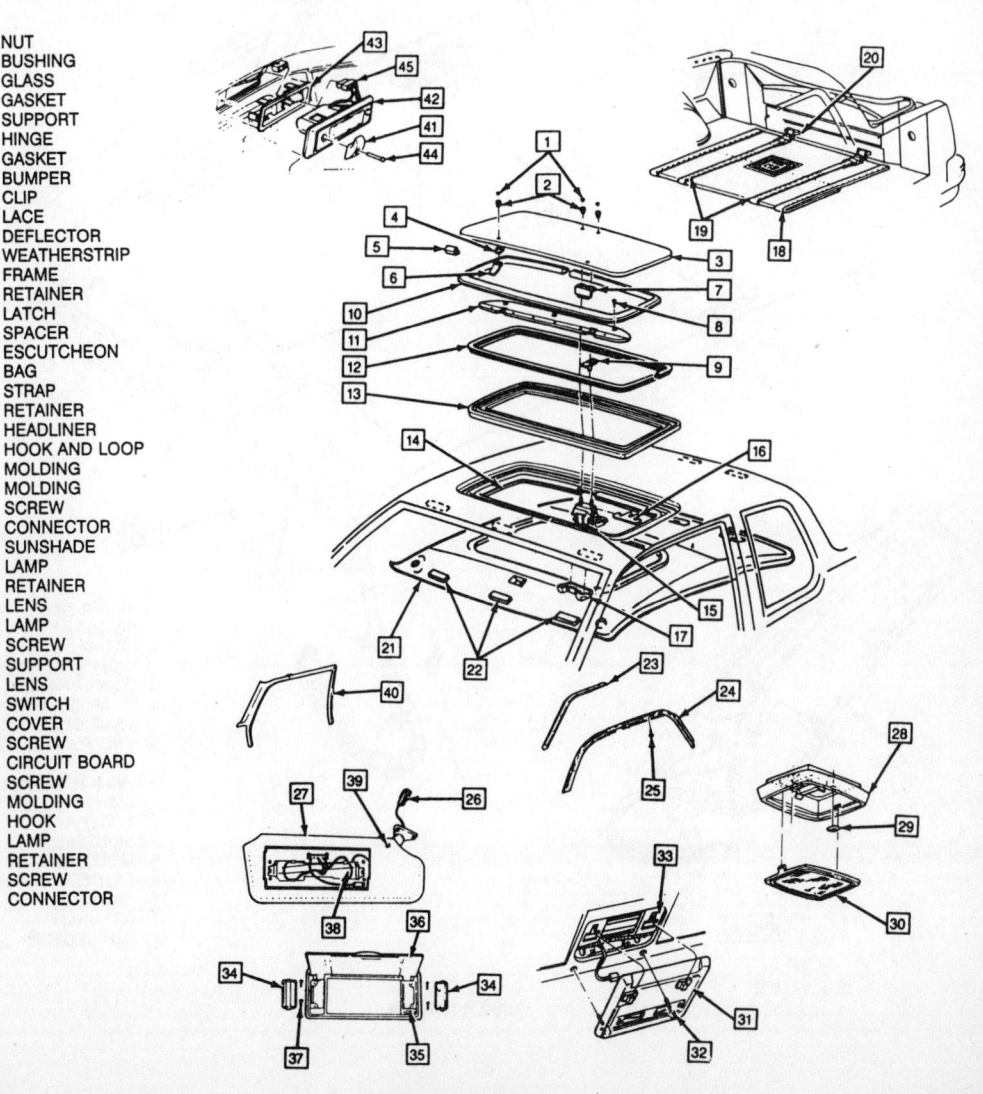

1. NUT
2. BUSHING
3. GLASS
4. GASKET
5. SUPPORT
6. HINGE
7. GASKET
8. BUMPER
9. CLIP
10. LACE
11. DEFLECTOR
12. WEATHERSTRIP
13. FRAME
14. RETAINER
15. LATCH
16. SPACER
17. ESCUTCHEON
18. BAG
19. STRAP
20. RETAINER
21. HEADLINER
22. HOOK AND LOOP
23. MOLDING
24. MOLDING
25. SCREW
26. CONNECTOR
27. SUNSHADE
28. LAMP
29. RETAINER
30. LENS
31. LAMP
32. SCREW
33. SUPPORT
34. LENS
35. SWITCH
36. COVER
37. SCREW
38. CIRCUIT BOARD
39. SCREW
40. MOLDING
41. HOOK
42. LAMP
43. RETAINER
44. SCREW
45. CONNECTOR

1985–91 headliner

304  BODY

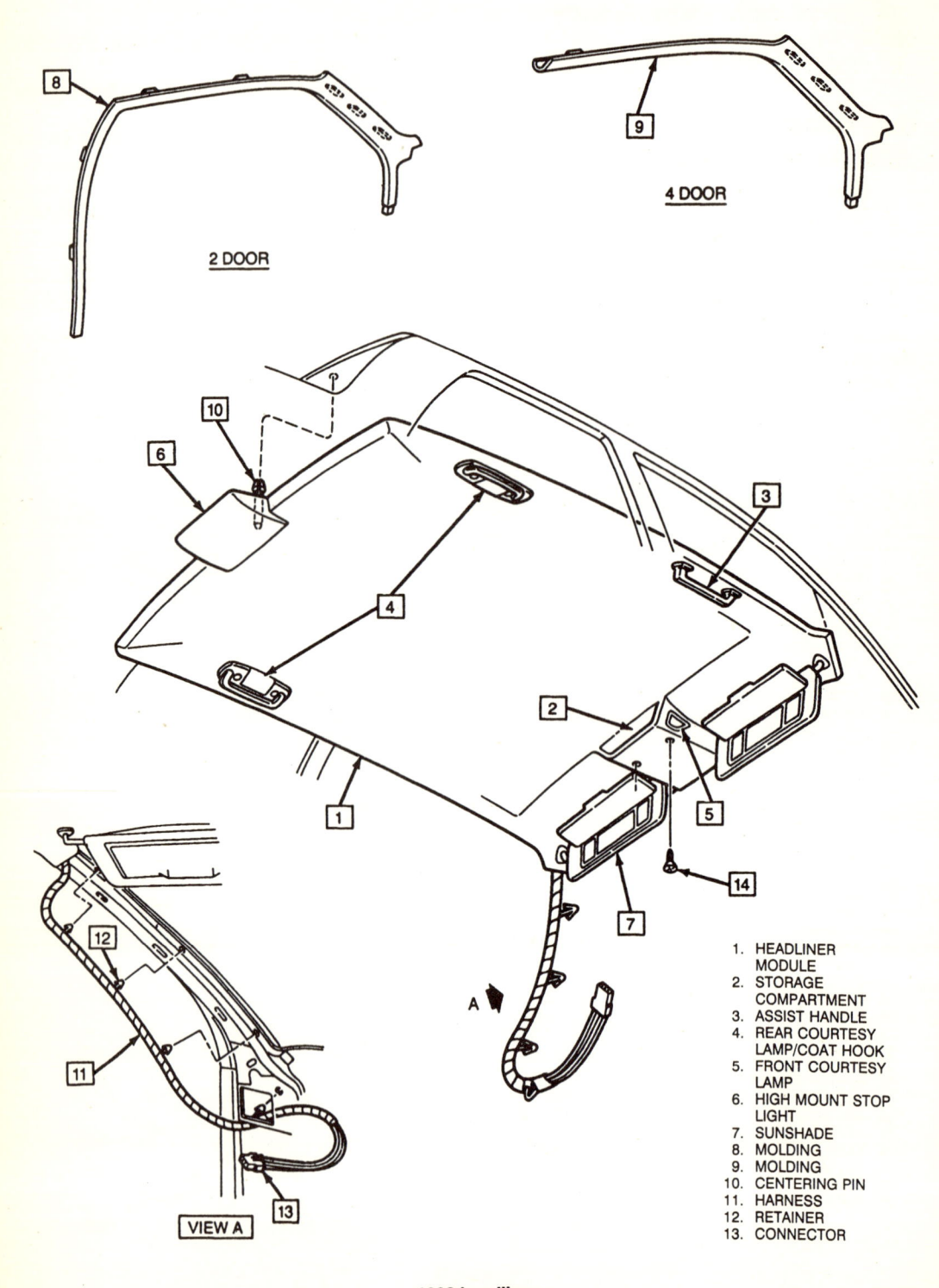

2 DOOR

4 DOOR

VIEW A

1. HEADLINER MODULE
2. STORAGE COMPARTMENT
3. ASSIST HANDLE
4. REAR COURTESY LAMP/COAT HOOK
5. FRONT COURTESY LAMP
6. HIGH MOUNT STOP LIGHT
7. SUNSHADE
8. MOLDING
9. MOLDING
10. CENTERING PIN
11. HARNESS
12. RETAINER
13. CONNECTOR

**1992 headliner**

## BODY 305

3. Remove the door window assembly- refer to previous section.

4. Remove the bolts securing the regulator to the door.

5. Remove the nuts securing the upper regulator guide.

6. Using a 1/4 in. drill, drill out the regulator rivets.

7. Disconnect the electrical connector if power windows.

8. Remove the regulator through the large access hole in door.

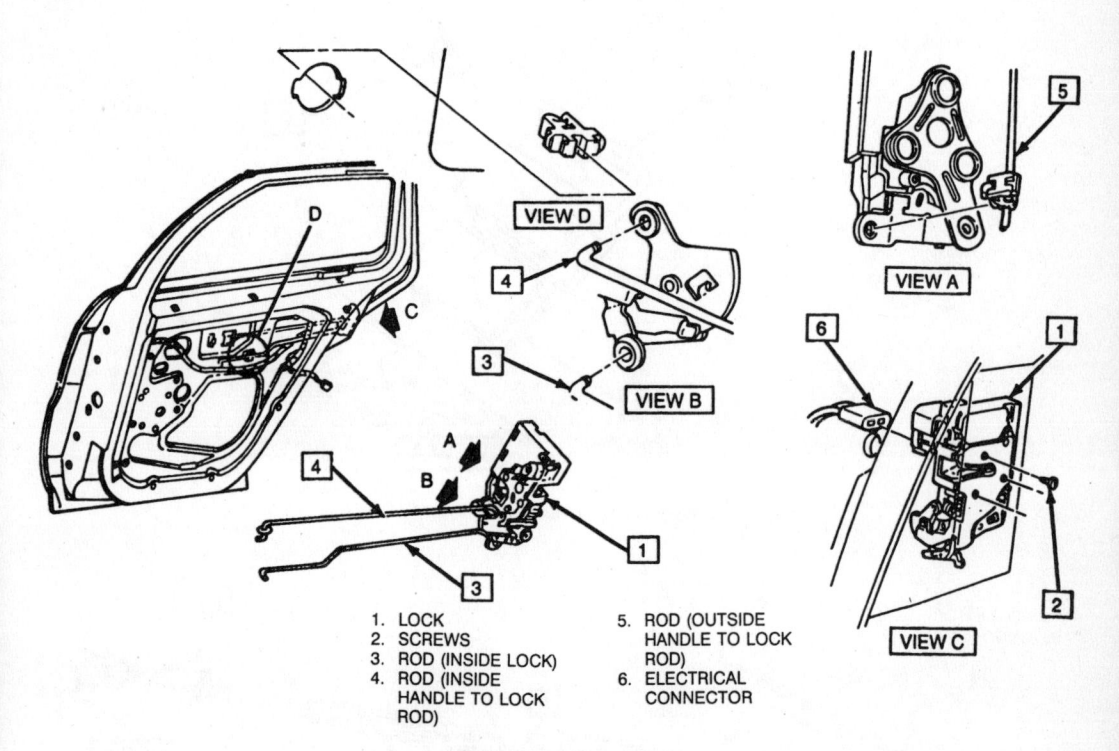

1. LOCK
2. SCREWS
3. ROD (INSIDE LOCK)
4. ROD (INSIDE HANDLE TO LOCK ROD)
5. ROD (OUTSIDE HANDLE TO LOCK ROD)
6. ELECTRICAL CONNECTOR

**Typical lock assembly**

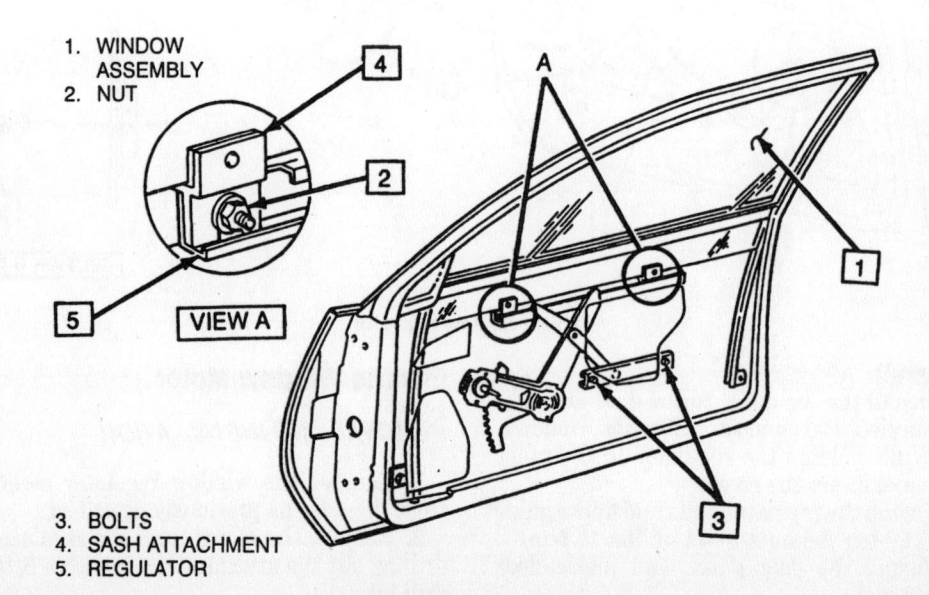

1. WINDOW ASSEMBLY
2. NUT
3. BOLTS
4. SASH ATTACHMENT
5. REGULATOR

**Typical window attachment**

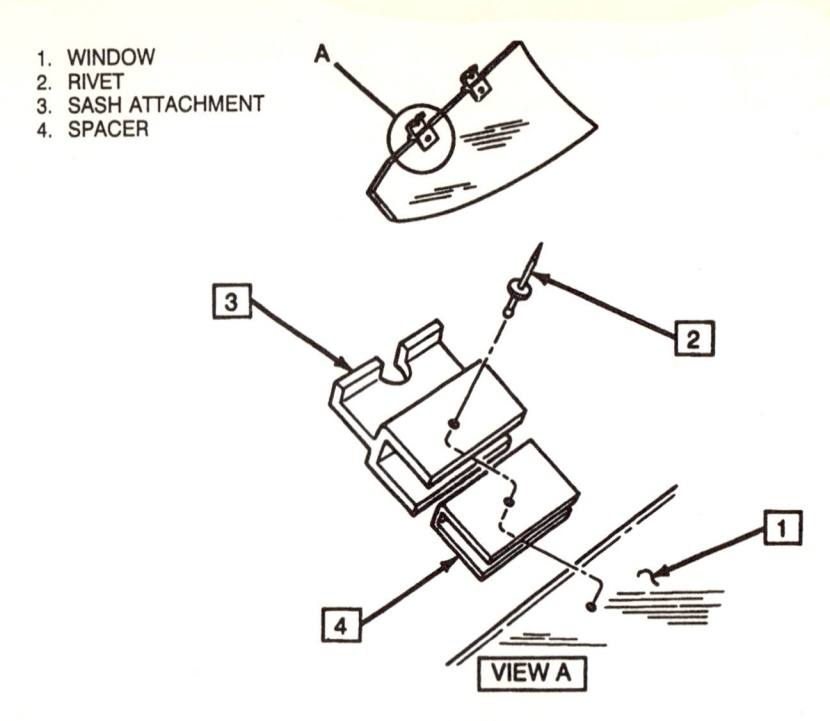

# 306 BODY

1. WINDOW
2. RIVET
3. SASH ATTACHMENT
4. SPACER

**Lower window sash attachment**

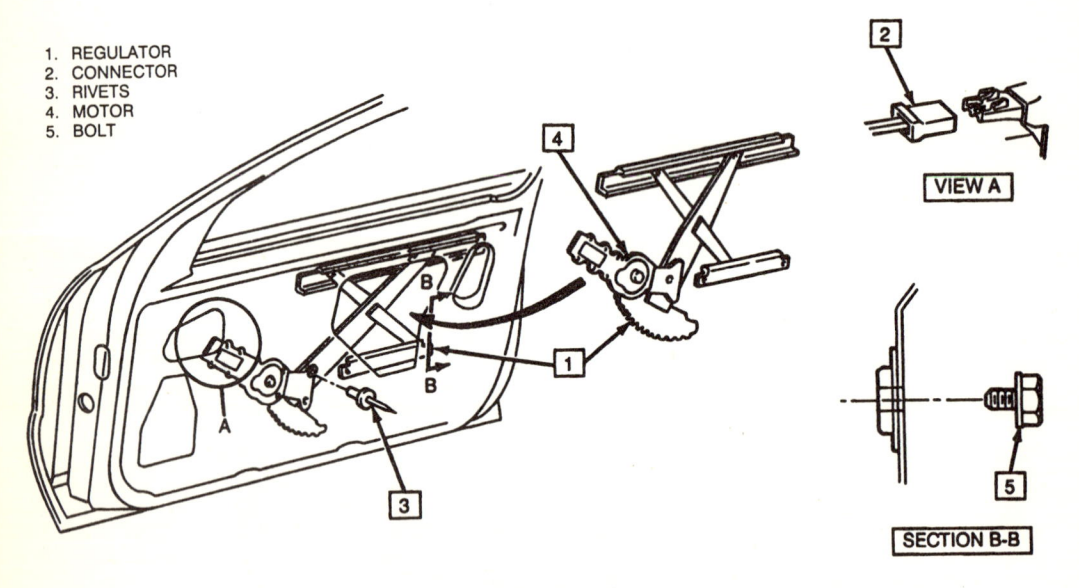

1. REGULATOR
2. CONNECTOR
3. RIVETS
4. MOTOR
5. BOLT

**Typical window regulator**

**To install:**
9. Install the regulator to the door and connect the electrical connector if power windows.
10. While holding the regulator to the inner door panel insert the rivets.
11. Install the regulator bolts and upper guide nuts. Tighten the nuts to 44 in. lbs. (5 Nm)
12. Install the door glass, and inside door plastic panel.
13. Install the inside door trim panel.

## Electric Window Motor

### REMOVAL AND INSTALLATION

1. Remove the window regulator assembly from the door as previously described.
2. Remove the motor from the regulator by drilling out the attaching rivets with a 3/16 in. drill bit.

**To install:**

3. Connect the window motor to the regulator with 3/16 in. rivets.
4. Install the window regulator assembly.

## Windshield and Rear Window
### REMOVAL AND INSTALLATION
NOTE: *The windshield is a very delicate and expensive piece of glass. During the procedure the glass can break very easily. Removal and installation is recommended to be performed by a qualified glass installation shop.*
1. Remove the wiper arms and the shroud top vent grille panel.
2. Remove the reveal moldings from around the glass. To do this follow the steps below:
    a. On 1992 models, remove the screws securing the side reveal moldings and slide the molding down to disengage it from the top molding.
    b. Grasp the end of the top molding and slowly pull away from the body.
    c. On 1991 and older models, pry the end of the molding out approx. 3 in. and slowly pull away from around the perimeter of the windshield.
    d. Remove the glass supports on the 1991 and older models.
3. Apply masking tape around the windshield area to protect the painted areas.
4. Using tool J24402A or a power tool with a reciprocating blade, cut around the entire perimeter of the windshield. Be sure that the blade of the tool is kept as close to the windshield as is possible.
5. Remove the glass from the vehicle.

**To install:**
6. If reusing the old glass, clean all traces of urethane and primer from the glass. Install the windshield supports, if removed.
7. Inspect window frame for any metal damage, repair if any present.
8. On 1992 models, insert the acoustic sealing strip around the perimeter of the windshield opening.
9. Apply the clear primer to the perimeter of the windshield and apply a smooth continuous bead of adhesive around the glass. Replace spacers, if removed.
10. With the aid of an assistant, install the windshield into the vehicle.
11. Check windshield alignment and reposition if needed.
12. Press firmly on the glass to set adhesive. Smooth the adhesive out around the windshield to ensure a watertight seal.

1. MOLDING
2. TOOL

**Removal of reveal molding 1985–91**

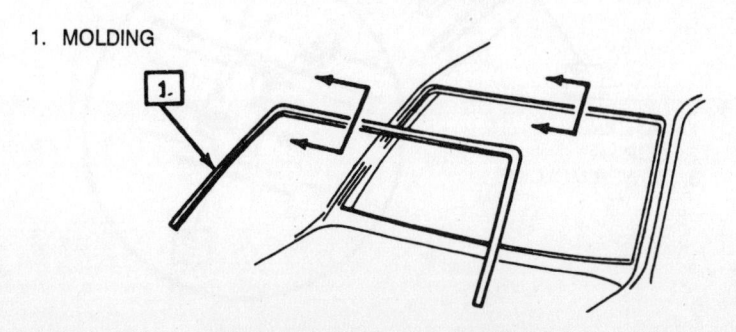

1. MOLDING

**1985–91 windshield reveal molding**

308  **BODY**

1. WINDSHIELD
2. REVEAL MOLDING

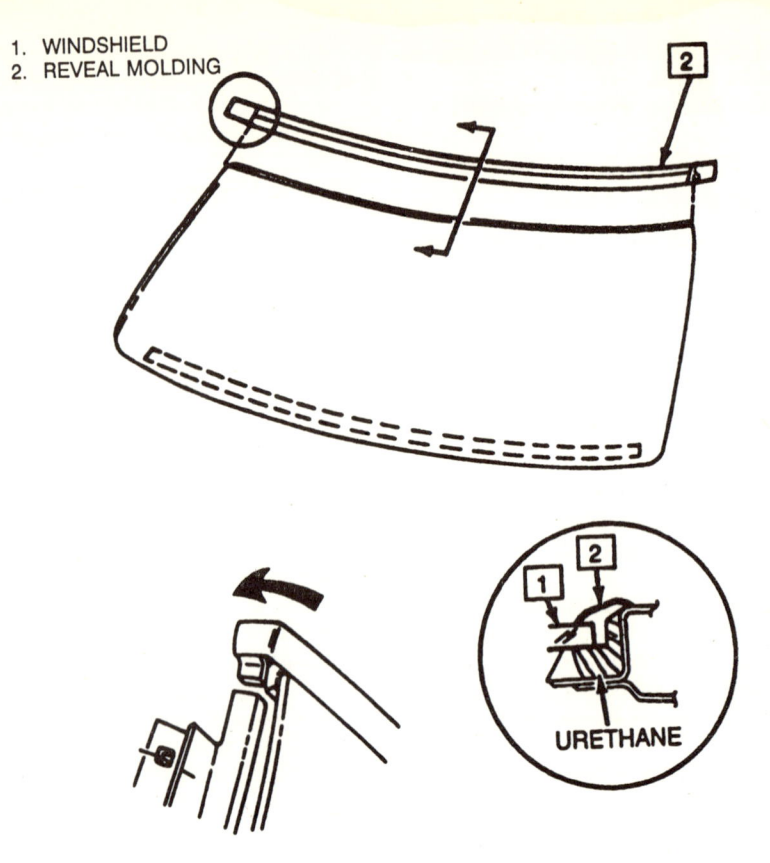

URETHANE

1992 Grand Am top reveal molding

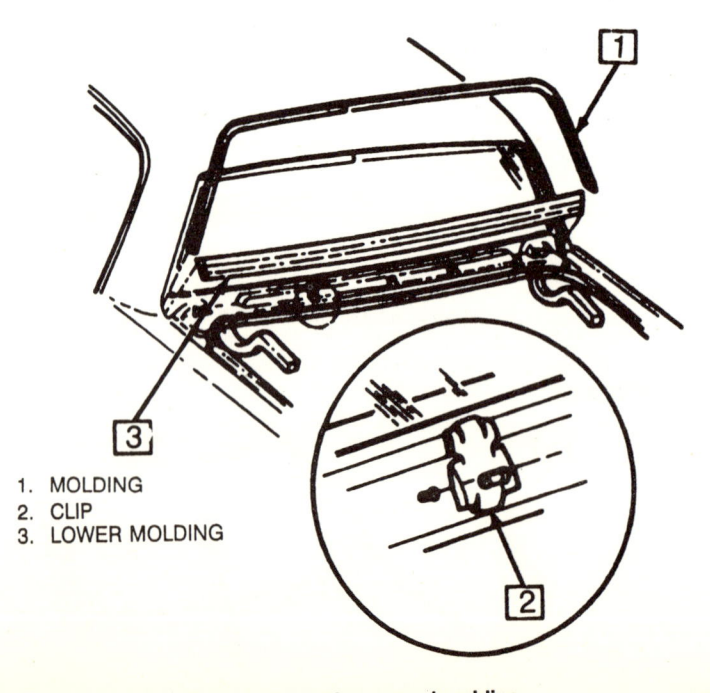

1. MOLDING
2. CLIP
3. LOWER MOLDING

1985–91 back glass reveal molding

# BODY 309

1. SIDE REVEAL MOLDING
2. SCREWS
3. TOP REVEAL MOLDING

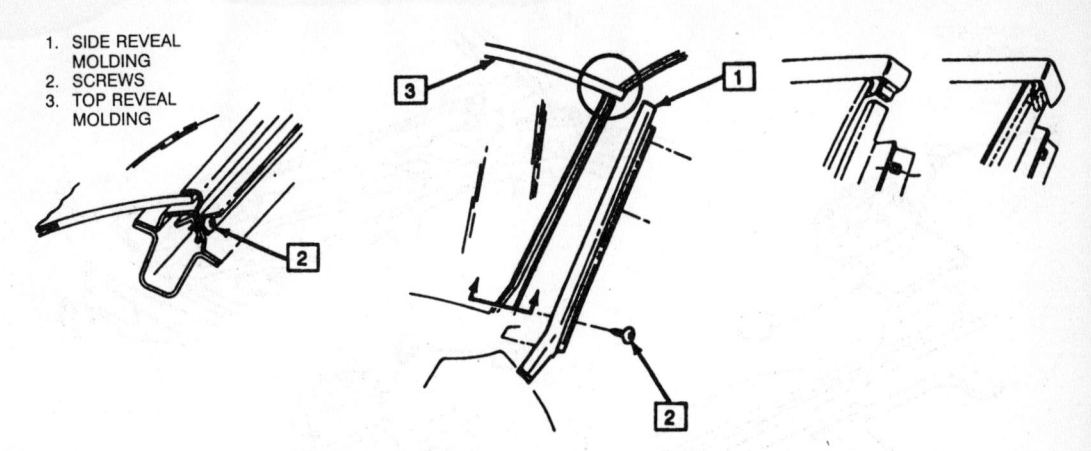

*1992 Grand Am windshield side reveal moldings*

13. Water Test the seal with soft spray. Do not direct hard spray at fresh adhesive.
14. Install all reveal moldings and vent grille panel if removed. Connect the rear window defroster connectors, if disconnected.

## Rear Quarter Window 2-Door

### REMOVAL AND INSTALLATION

**1992 Models**

1. Remove the screws securing the body lock applique panel to the door frame and remove the panel.
2. Remove the upper and lower quarter trim panels.
3. Using tool J24402A or a power tool with a oscillating blade, cut around the entire perimeter of the window. Be sure that the blade of the tool is kept as close to the window as possible.
4. Remove window from the vehicle. Clean all traces of adhesive from the window and from the frame.

**To install:**

5. Apply black primer from urethane adhesive kit around the pinch weld flange.
6. Using a caulking gun, apply a smooth, continuous bead of adhesive material around the entire mounting surface of the window.
7. Place the window into the opening and press firmly to set the glass.
8. Check quarter window for any water leaks by spraying water onto window area while having an assistant watching inside for leakage.
9. Remove any excessive urethane from around the window.
10. Install the upper and lower quarter trim finish panels.
11. Install the body lock pillar applique panel.

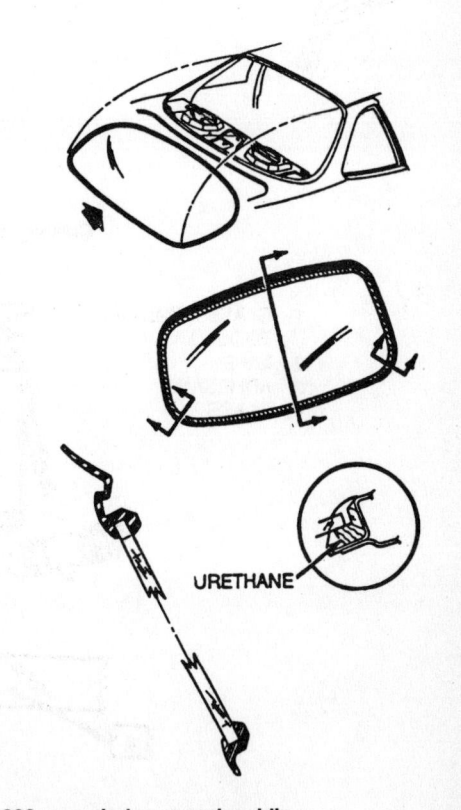

*1992 rear window reveal molding*

**1985-91 Models**

1. Apply tape to body of vehicle around the rear quarter window to protect the body.
2. Remove the roof drip molding.
3. Remove the screws from the quarter window reveal molding frame, at the body lock pillar.
4. Using a putty knife carefully release the molding from the retainer clips.
5. Carefully cut the urethane bond between the reveal molding and the glass.

# 310 BODY

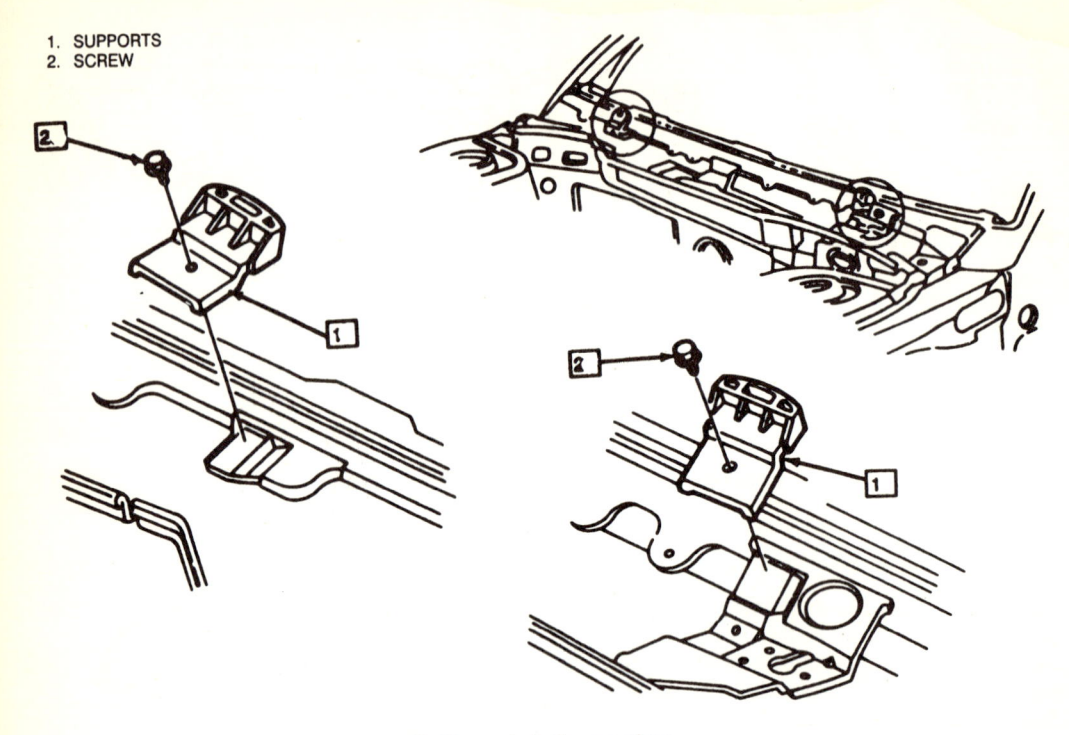

1. SUPPORTS
2. SCREW

**Cutting out stationary glass**

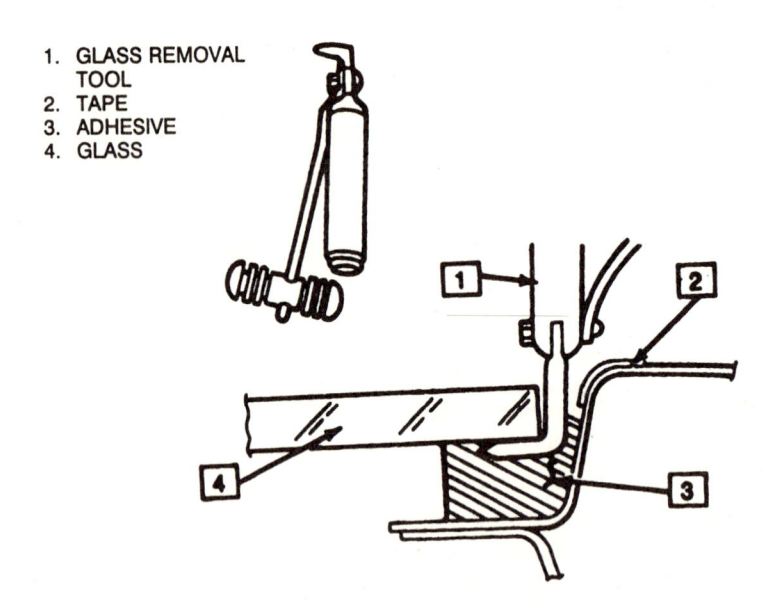

1. GLASS REMOVAL TOOL
2. TAPE
3. ADHESIVE
4. GLASS

**Rear glass supports 1985–91**

6. Apply tape to the inside and outside of the glass to minimize scattering of broken glass.

7. Break the glass with a hammer and cut the module from the vehicle.

**To install:**

8. Apply the black primer to the pinch weld flange and apply the clear primer to the perimeter of the quarter window. Allow the primer to dry for approx. 5 minutes.

9. Apply a continuous bead of adhesive around the glass module, making sure to fill the grooves with the adhesive.

10. Install the module and press until clips become engaged.

BODY   311

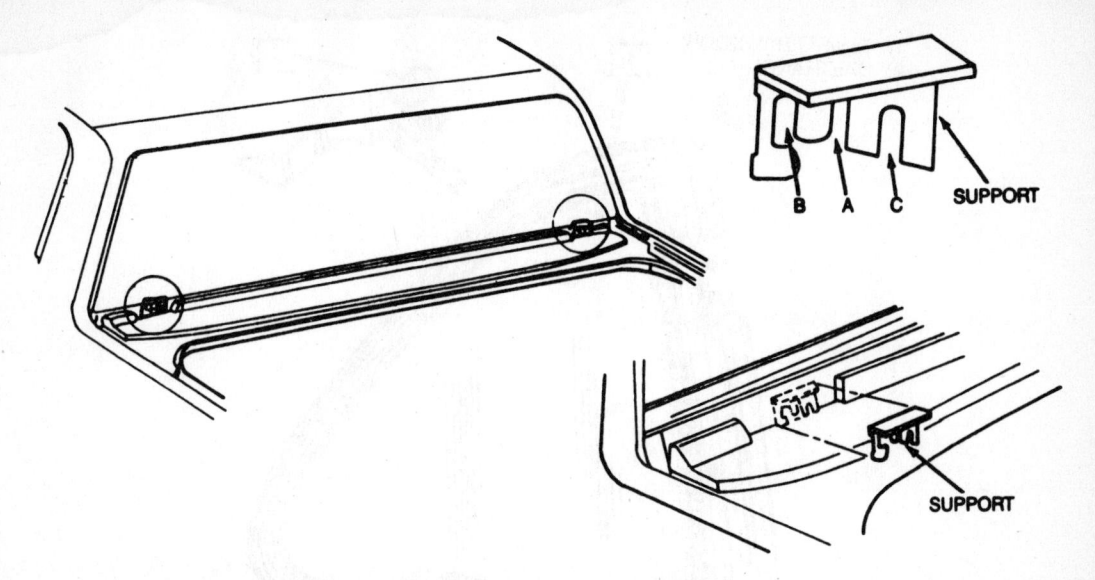

Windshield glass supports 1985–91

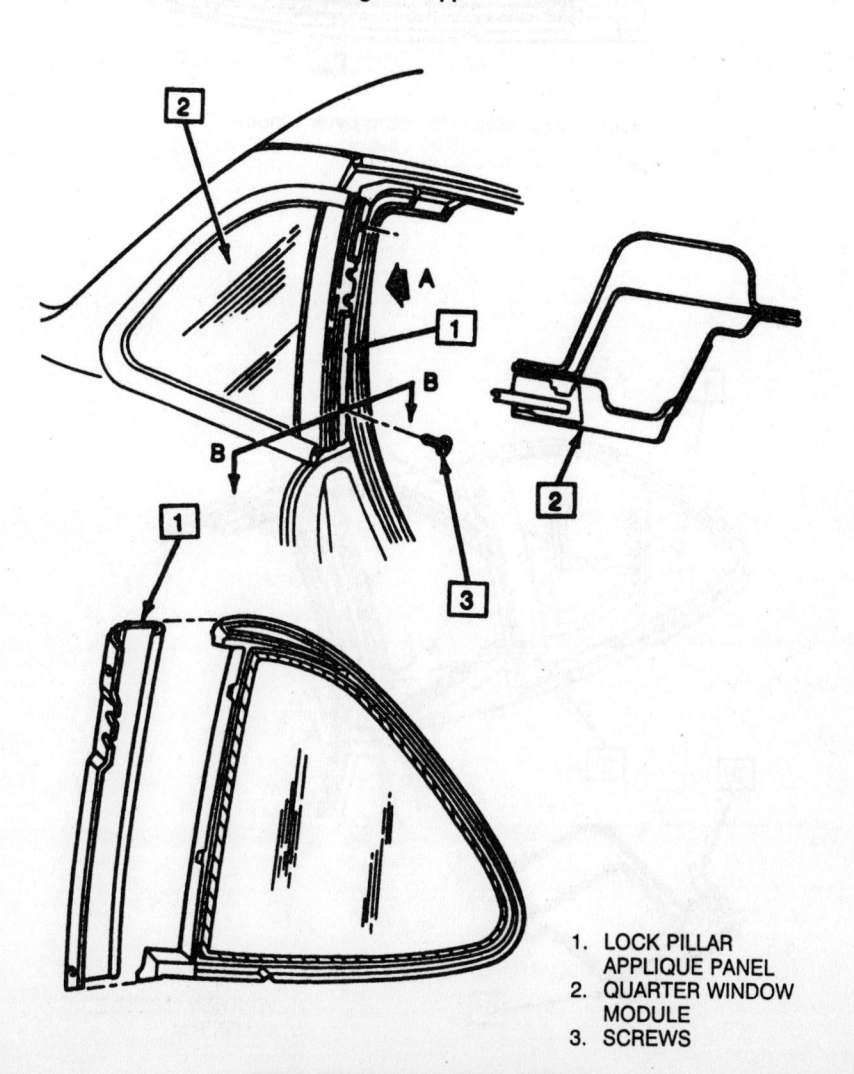

1. LOCK PILLAR APPLIQUE PANEL
2. QUARTER WINDOW MODULE
3. SCREWS

1992 Grand Am rear quarter window

## 312 BODY

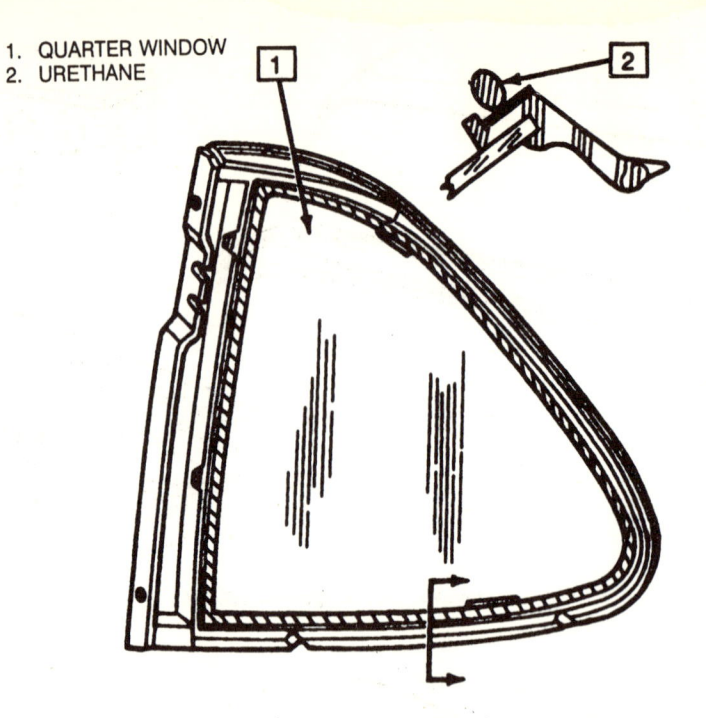

1. QUARTER WINDOW
2. URETHANE

**Applying urethane to rear quarter window**

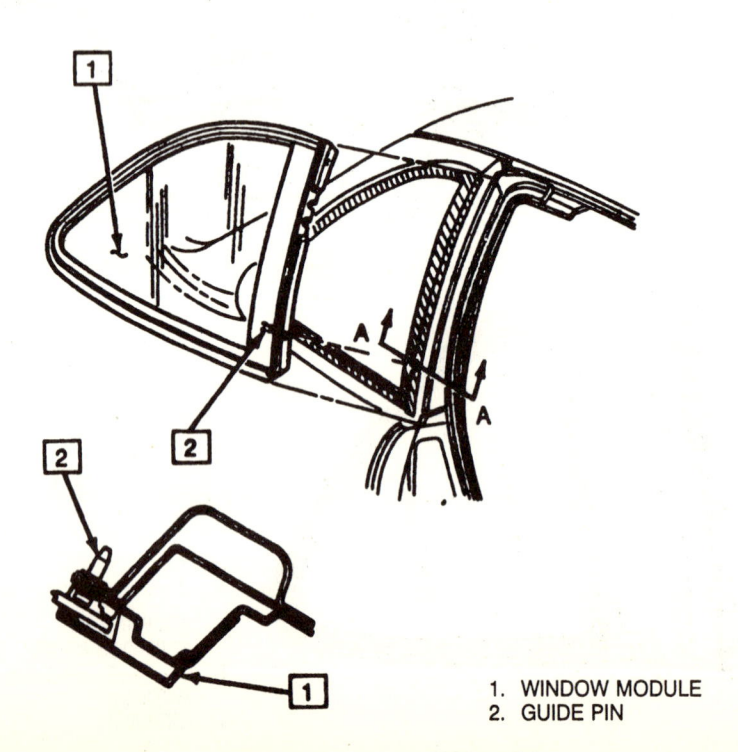

1. WINDOW MODULE
2. GUIDE PIN

**Installing rear quarter 1992 model**

BODY 313

11. Check for water leaks and install all previously removed moldings.

## Inside Rear View Mirror
### REPLACEMENT
The rearview mirror is attached to a support with a retaining screw. The support is secured to the windshield glass by using a plastic polyvinyl butyl adhesive. To reinstall a mirror support arm to the windshield, follow the instructions included with an outside mirror installation kit. This kit may be purchased at most auto supply stores.

1. PINCHWELD FLANGE
2. CURVED BLADE KNIFE

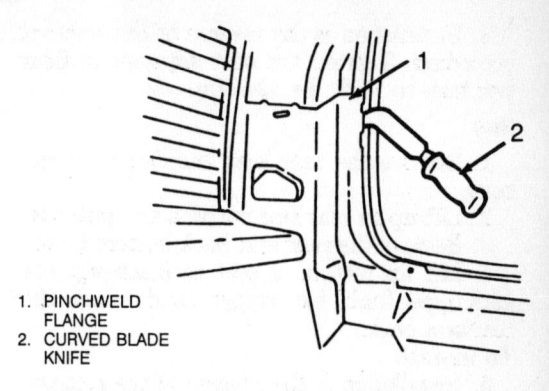

Cutting out rear window module 1985–91

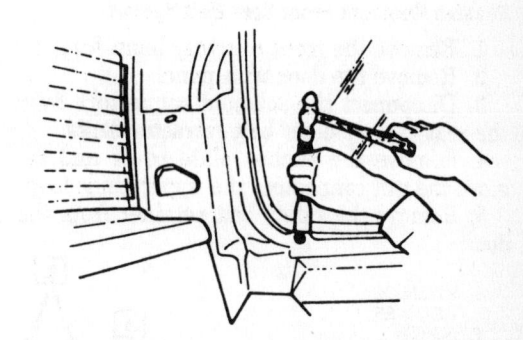

## Seats
### REMOVAL AND INSTALLATION
**Front**

1. Move the seats to the full-forward position.
2. Remove the rear foot covers and carpet retainers to gain access to the rear nuts.
3. Remove the track covers and remove the nuts securing the adjuster to the floor.
4. Move the seat to the full-rearward position.
5. Remove the adjuster front foot covers and remove the adjuster to front floor pan nuts.
6. If power seats, tilt forward and disconnect the electrical connectors.
7. Remove the seat assembly from the vehicle.

**To install:**

Cutting plastic studs—rear quarter window 1985–91

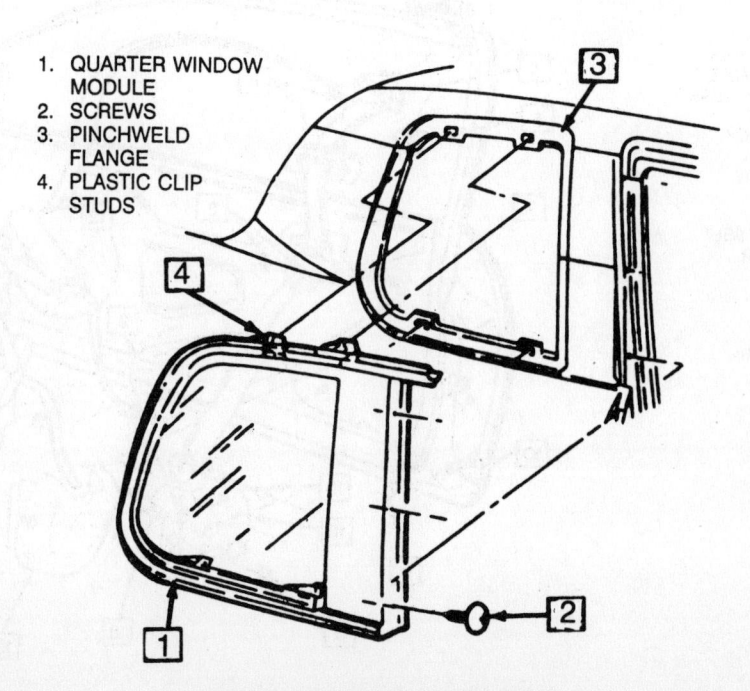

1. QUARTER WINDOW MODULE
2. SCREWS
3. PINCHWELD FLANGE
4. PLASTIC CLIP STUDS

Rear quarter window module 1985–91

# 314 BODY

8. Installation is the reverse of the removal procedure. Tighten the seat adjuster to floor pan nuts to 18 ft. lbs. (24 Nm).

**Rear**

1. Remove the rear seat cushion retaining bolts.
2. Lift up on rear seat cushion and pull out.
3. Remove the rear seat back bottom bolts.
4. Lift up bottom of seat to disengage the back upper frame bar hangers, and remove the rear seat back.

**To install:**

5. Installation is the reverse of the removal procedure.

## Seat Belts

### REMOVAL AND INSTALLATION

**Passive Restraint Front Seat Belt System**

1. Remove the front courtesy lamp fuse.
2. Remove the door trim panel.
3. Disconnect the solenoid connectors from the seat and shoulder belt retractor units.
4. Remove the anchor plate cover and remove the nut connecting the upper guide loop.
5. Remove the safety belt retainer from the door.
6. Remove the top screw from the shoulder safety belt retractor.
7. Remove the nuts from the seat and shoulder safety belt retractors.

**To install:**

8. Insert the retaining tab of the seat belt into the inner door panel while seating the bottom of the retainer over the stud.
9. Place the lap belt retractor on the inner door panel studs. Install the nuts and tighten.
10. Install the seat belt retainer and install the retaining screws.
11. Install the anchor plate to the upper guide loop and install the nut.
12. Install the anchor plate cover.
13. Connect the solenoid electrical connectors.
14. Install the door trim panel and the courtesy lamp fuse.
15. Inspect seat belt operation.

**Active Restraint Front Seat Belt System**

1. Remove the carpet retainer.
2. Remove the windshield upper side garnish molding.

1. INTERLOCK RETAINER
2. SCREW
3. NUT
4. UPPER GUIDE LOOP
5. ANCHOR PLATE COVER
6. SCREW
7. SEAT BELT RETAINER
8. SCREWS
9. COMFORT LOCK RELEASE CABLE
10. COMFORT RELEASE
11. NYLON NUT
12. SPLITTER BOX COVER
13. LATCH PLATE
14. SOLENOID
15. SCREW
16. SHOULDER BELT RETRACTOR
17. NUT
18. SOLENOID
19. COVER
20. SEAT BELT RETRACTOR
21. NUT

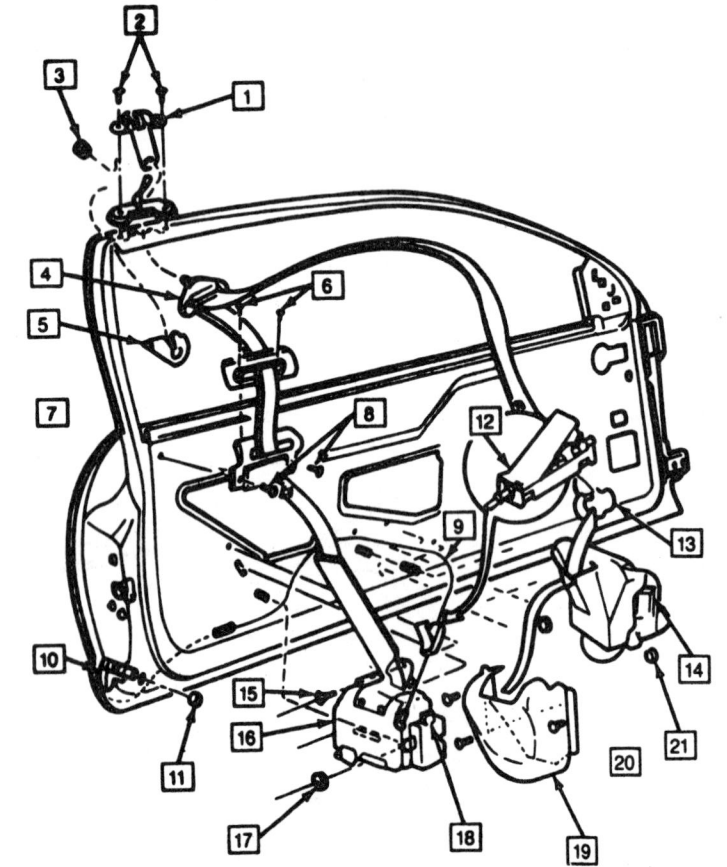

Typical front seat belt system

3. Remove the rear seat back and rear seat cushion.
4. Remove the shoulder belt guide cover and upper bolt.
5. Remove the outboard belt assembly lower bolt.
6. Remove the inner quarter trim panel.
7. Using tool J23457 remove the retractor bolts and anchor bolts as required.

**To install:**
8. Installation is the reverse of the removal procedure.

### Rear Seat Belts

Rear seat belt removal and installation is only a matter of removing the rear seats and removing the seat belt retaining bolts.

## Power Seat Motor
### REMOVAL AND INSTALLATION

1. Remove the seat assembly from the vehicle.
2. Disconnect the motor feed wires from the motors.
3. Remove the nut that attaches the front of the motor support bracket to the inboard adjuster.
4. Disconnect the drive cables and completely remove the bracket and motor assembly.
5. Grind off the grommet that secures the motor to the bracket and separate the motor from the bracket.

**To install:**
6. Installation is the reverse of the removal procedure.

# Mechanic's Data 11

## General Conversion Table

| Multiply By | To Convert | To | |
|---|---|---|---|
| **LENGTH** | | | |
| 2.54 | Inches | Centimeters | .3937 |
| 25.4 | Inches | Millimeters | .03937 |
| 30.48 | Feet | Centimeters | .0328 |
| .304 | Feet | Meters | 3.28 |
| .914 | Yards | Meters | 1.094 |
| 1.609 | Miles | Kilometers | .621 |
| **VOLUME** | | | |
| .473 | Pints | Liters | 2.11 |
| .946 | Quarts | Liters | 1.06 |
| 3.785 | Gallons | Liters | .264 |
| .016 | Cubic inches | Liters | 61.02 |
| 16.39 | Cubic inches | Cubic cms. | .061 |
| 28.3 | Cubic feet | Liters | .0353 |
| **MASS (Weight)** | | | |
| 28.35 | Ounces | Grams | .035 |
| .4536 | Pounds | Kilograms | 2.20 |
| — | To obtain | From | Multiply by |

| Multiply By | To Convert | To | |
|---|---|---|---|
| **AREA** | | | |
| .645 | Square inches | Square cms. | .155 |
| .836 | Square yds. | Square meters | 1.196 |
| **FORCE** | | | |
| 4.448 | Pounds | Newtons | .225 |
| .138 | Ft./lbs. | Kilogram/meters | 7.23 |
| 1.36 | Ft./lbs. | Newton-meters | .737 |
| .112 | In./lbs. | Newton-meters | 8.844 |
| **PRESSURE** | | | |
| .068 | Psi | Atmospheres | 14.7 |
| 6.89 | Psi | Kilopascals | .145 |
| **OTHER** | | | |
| 1.104 | Horsepower (DIN) | Horsepower (SAE) | .9861 |
| .746 | Horsepower (SAE) | Kilowatts (KW) | 1.34 |
| 1.60 | Mph | Km/h | .625 |
| .425 | Mpg | Km/1 | 2.35 |
| — | To obtain | From | Multiply by |

## Tap Drill Sizes

### National Coarse or U.S.S.

| Screw & Tap Size | Threads Per Inch | Use Drill Number |
|---|---|---|
| No. 5 | 40 | 39 |
| No. 6 | 32 | 36 |
| No. 8 | 32 | 29 |
| No. 10 | 24 | 25 |
| No. 12 | 24 | 17 |
| 1/4 | 20 | 8 |
| 5/16 | 18 | F |
| 3/8 | 16 | 5/16 |
| 7/16 | 14 | U |
| 1/2 | 13 | 27/64 |
| 9/16 | 12 | 31/64 |
| 5/8 | 11 | 17/32 |
| 3/4 | 10 | 21/32 |
| 7/8 | 9 | 49/64 |

### National Coarse or U.S.S.

| Screw & Tap Size | Threads Per Inch | Use Drill Number |
|---|---|---|
| 1 | 8 | 7/8 |
| 1 1/8 | 7 | 63/64 |
| 1 1/4 | 7 | 1 7/54 |
| 1 1/2 | 6 | 1 11/32 |

### National Fine or S.A.E.

| Screw & Tap Size | Threads Per Inch | Use Drill Number |
|---|---|---|
| No. 5 | 44 | 37 |
| No. 6 | 40 | 33 |
| No. 8 | 36 | 29 |
| No. 10 | 32 | 21 |

### National Fine or S.A.E.

| Screw & Tap Size | Threads Per Inch | Use Drill Number |
|---|---|---|
| No. 12 | 28 | 15 |
| 1/4 | 28 | 3 |
| 6/16 | 24 | 1 |
| 3/8 | 24 | Q |
| 7/16 | 20 | W |
| 1/2 | 20 | 29/64 |
| 9/16 | 18 | 33/64 |
| 5/8 | 18 | 37/64 |
| 3/4 | 16 | 11/16 |
| 7/8 | 14 | 13/16 |
| 1 1/8 | 12 | 1 3/64 |
| 1 1/4 | 12 | 1 11/64 |
| 1 1/2 | 12 | 1 27/64 |

# MECHANIC'S DATA

## Drill Sizes In Decimal Equivalents

| Inch | Decimal | Wire | mm | Inch | Decimal | Wire | mm | Inch | Decimal | Wire & Letter | mm | Inch | Decimal | Letter | mm | Inch | Decimal | mm |
|---|---|---|---|---|---|---|---|---|---|---|---|---|---|---|---|---|---|---|
| 1/64 | .0156 | | .39 | | .0730 | 49 | | | .1614 | | 4.1 | | .2717 | | 6.9 | | .4331 | 11.0 |
| | .0157 | | .4 | | .0748 | | 1.9 | | .1654 | | 4.2 | | .2720 | I | | 7/16 | .4375 | 11.11 |
| | .0160 | 78 | | | .0760 | 48 | | | .1660 | 19 | | | .2756 | | 7.0 | | .4528 | 11.5 |
| | .0165 | | .42 | | .0768 | | 1.95 | | .1673 | | 4.25 | | .2770 | J | | 29/64 | .4531 | 11.51 |
| | .0173 | | .44 | 5/64 | .0781 | | 1.98 | | .1693 | | 4.3 | | .2795 | | 7.1 | 15/32 | .4688 | 11.90 |
| | .0177 | | .45 | | .0785 | 47 | | | .1695 | 18 | | | .2810 | K | | | .4724 | 12.0 |
| | .0180 | 77 | | | .0787 | | 2.0 | 11/64 | .1719 | | 4.36 | 9/32 | .2812 | | 7.14 | 31/64 | .4844 | 12.30 |
| | .0181 | | .46 | | .0807 | | 2.05 | | .1730 | 17 | | | .2835 | | 7.2 | | .4921 | 12.5 |
| | .0189 | | .48 | | .0810 | 46 | | | .1732 | | 4.4 | | .2854 | | 7.25 | 1/2 | .5000 | 12.70 |
| | .0197 | | .5 | | .0820 | 45 | | | .1770 | 16 | | | .2874 | | 7.3 | | .5118 | 13.0 |
| | .0200 | 76 | | | .0827 | | 2.1 | | .1772 | | 4.5 | | .2900 | L | | 33/64 | .5156 | 13.09 |
| | .0210 | 75 | | | .0846 | | 2.15 | | .1800 | 15 | | | .2913 | | 7.4 | 17/32 | .5312 | 13.49 |
| | .0217 | | .55 | | .0860 | 44 | | | .1811 | | 4.6 | | .2950 | M | | | .5315 | 13.5 |
| | .0225 | 74 | | | .0866 | | 2.2 | | .1820 | 14 | | | .2953 | | 7.5 | 35/64 | .5469 | 13.89 |
| | .0236 | | .6 | | .0886 | | 2.25 | | .1850 | 13 | | 19/64 | .2969 | | 7.54 | | .5512 | 14.0 |
| | .0240 | 73 | | | .0890 | 43 | | | .1850 | | 4.7 | | .2992 | | 7.6 | 9/16 | .5625 | 14.28 |
| | .0250 | 72 | | | .0906 | | 2.3 | | .1870 | | 4.75 | | .3020 | N | | | .5709 | 14.5 |
| | .0256 | | .65 | | .0925 | | 2.35 | 3/16 | .1875 | | 4.76 | | .3031 | | | 37/64 | .5781 | 14.68 |
| | .0260 | 71 | | | .0935 | 42 | | | .1890 | | 4.8 | | .3051 | | 7.75 | | .5906 | 15.0 |
| | .0276 | | .7 | 3/32 | .0938 | | 2.38 | | .1890 | 12 | | | .3071 | | 7.8 | 19/32 | .5938 | 15.08 |
| | .0280 | 70 | | | .0945 | | 2.4 | | .1910 | 11 | | | .3110 | | 7.9 | 39/64 | .6094 | 15.47 |
| | .0292 | 69 | | | .0960 | 41 | | | .1929 | | 4.9 | 5/16 | .3125 | | 7.93 | | .6102 | 15.5 |
| | .0295 | | .75 | | .0965 | | 2.45 | | .1935 | 10 | | | .3150 | | 8.0 | 5/8 | .6250 | 15.87 |
| | .0310 | 68 | | | .0980 | 40 | | | .1960 | 9 | | | .3160 | O | | | .6299 | 16.0 |
| 1/32 | .0312 | | .79 | | .0981 | | 2.5 | | .1969 | | 5.0 | | .3189 | | 8.1 | 41/64 | .6406 | 16.27 |
| | .0315 | | .8 | | .0995 | 39 | | | .1990 | 8 | | | .3228 | | 8.2 | | .6496 | 16.5 |
| | .0320 | 67 | | | .1015 | 38 | | | .2008 | | 5.1 | | .3230 | P | | 21/32 | .6562 | 16.66 |
| | .0330 | 66 | | | .1024 | | 2.6 | | .2010 | 7 | | | .3248 | | 8.25 | | .6693 | 17.0 |
| | .0335 | | .85 | | .1040 | 37 | | 13/64 | .2031 | | 5.16 | | .3268 | | 8.3 | 43/64 | .6719 | 17.06 |
| | .0350 | 65 | | | .1063 | | 2.7 | | .2040 | 6 | | 21/64 | .3281 | | 8.33 | 11/16 | .6875 | 17.46 |
| | .0354 | | .9 | | .1065 | 36 | | | .2047 | | 5.2 | | .3307 | | 8.4 | | .6890 | 17.5 |
| | .0360 | 64 | | | .1083 | | 2.75 | | .2055 | 5 | | | .3320 | Q | | 45/64 | .7031 | 17.85 |
| | .0370 | 63 | | 7/64 | .1094 | | 2.77 | | .2067 | | 5.25 | | .3346 | | 8.5 | | .7087 | 18.0 |
| | .0374 | | .95 | | .1100 | 35 | | | .2087 | | 5.3 | | .3386 | | 8.6 | 23/32 | .7188 | 18.25 |
| | .0380 | 62 | | | .1102 | | 2.8 | | .2090 | 4 | | | .3390 | R | | | .7283 | 18.5 |
| | .0390 | 61 | | | .1110 | 34 | | | .2126 | | 5.4 | | .3425 | | 8.7 | 47/64 | .7344 | 18.65 |
| | .0394 | | 1.0 | | .1130 | 33 | | | .2130 | 3 | | 11/32 | .3438 | | 8.73 | | .7480 | 19.0 |
| | .0400 | 60 | | | .1142 | | 2.9 | | .2165 | | 5.5 | | .3445 | | 8.75 | 3/4 | .7500 | 19.05 |
| | .0410 | 59 | | | .1160 | 32 | | 7/32 | 2188 | | 5.55 | | .3465 | | 8.8 | 49/64 | .7656 | 19.44 |
| | .0413 | | 1.05 | | .1181 | | 3.0 | | .2205 | | 5.6 | | .3480 | S | | | .7677 | 19.5 |
| | .0420 | 58 | | | .1200 | 31 | | | .2210 | 2 | | | .3504 | | 8.9 | 25/32 | .7812 | 19.84 |
| | .0430 | 57 | | | .1220 | | 3.1 | | .2244 | | 5.7 | | .3543 | | 9.0 | | .7874 | 20.0 |
| | .0433 | | 1.1 | 1/8 | .1250 | | 3.17 | | .2264 | | 5.75 | | .3580 | T | | 51/64 | .7969 | 20.24 |
| | .0453 | | 1.15 | | .1260 | | 3.2 | | .2280 | 1 | | | .3583 | | 9.1 | | .8071 | 20.5 |
| | .0465 | 56 | | | .1280 | | 3.25 | | .2283 | | 5.8 | 23/64 | .3594 | | 9.12 | 13/16 | .8125 | 20.63 |
| 3/64 | .0469 | | 1.19 | | .1285 | 30 | | | .2323 | | 5.9 | | .3622 | | 9.2 | | .8268 | 21.0 |
| | .0472 | | 1.2 | | .1299 | | 3.3 | | .2340 | A | | | .3642 | | 9.25 | 53/64 | .8281 | 21.03 |
| | .0492 | | 1.25 | | .1339 | | 3.4 | 15/64 | .2344 | | 5.95 | | .3661 | | 9.3 | 27/32 | .8438 | 21.43 |
| | .0512 | | 1.3 | | .1360 | 29 | | | .2362 | | 6.0 | | .3680 | U | | | .8465 | 21.5 |
| | .0520 | 55 | | | .1378 | | 3.5 | | .2380 | B | | | .3701 | | 9.4 | 55/64 | .8594 | 21.82 |
| | .0531 | | 1.35 | | .1405 | 28 | | | .2402 | | 6.1 | | .3740 | | 9.5 | | .8661 | 22.0 |
| | .0550 | 54 | | 9/64 | .1406 | | 3.57 | | .2420 | C | | 3/8 | .3750 | | 9.52 | 7/8 | .8750 | 22.22 |
| | .0551 | | 1.4 | | .1417 | | 3.6 | | .2441 | | 6.2 | | .3770 | V | | | .8858 | 22.5 |
| | .0571 | | 1.45 | | .1440 | 27 | | | .2460 | D | | | .3780 | | 9.6 | 57/64 | .8906 | 22.62 |
| | .0591 | | 1.5 | | .1457 | | 3.7 | | .2461 | | 6.25 | | .3819 | | 9.7 | | .9055 | 23.0 |
| | .0595 | 53 | | | .1470 | 26 | | | .2480 | | 6.3 | | .3839 | | 9.75 | 29/32 | .9062 | 23.01 |
| | .0610 | | 1.55 | | .1476 | | 3.75 | 1/4 | .2500 | E | 6.35 | | .3858 | | 9.8 | 59/64 | .9219 | 23.41 |
| 1/16 | .0625 | | 1.59 | | .1495 | 25 | | | .2520 | | 6. | | .3860 | W | | | .9252 | 23.5 |
| | .0630 | | 1.6 | | .1496 | | 3.8 | | .2559 | | 6.5 | | .3898 | | 9.9 | 15/16 | .9375 | 23.81 |
| | .0635 | 52 | | | .1520 | 24 | | | .2570 | F | | 25/64 | .3906 | | 9.92 | | .9449 | 24.0 |
| | .0650 | | 1.65 | | .1535 | | 3.9 | | .2598 | | 6.6 | | .3937 | | 10.0 | 61/64 | .9531 | 24.2 |
| | .0669 | | 1.7 | | .1540 | 23 | | | .2610 | G | | | .3970 | X | | | .9646 | 24.5 |
| | .0670 | 51 | | 5/32 | .1562 | | 3.96 | | .2638 | | 6.7 | | .4040 | Y | | 31/64 | .9688 | 24.6 |
| | .0689 | | 1.75 | | .1570 | 22 | | 17/64 | .2656 | | 6.74 | 13/32 | .4062 | | 10.31 | | .9843 | 25.0 |
| | .0700 | 50 | | | .1575 | | 4.0 | | .2657 | | 6.75 | | .4130 | Z | | 63/64 | .9844 | 25.0 |
| | .0709 | | 1.8 | | .1590 | 21 | | | .2660 | H | | | .4134 | | 10.5 | 1 | 1.0000 | 25.4 |
| | .0728 | | 1.85 | | .1610 | 20 | | | .2677 | | 6.8 | 27/64 | .4219 | | 10.71 | | | |

# GLOSSARY OF TERMS

**AIR/FUEL RATIO**: The ratio of air to gasoline by weight in the fuel mixture drawn into the engine.

**AIR INJECTION**: One method of reducing harmful exhaust emissions by injecting air into each of the exhaust ports of an engine. The fresh air entering the hot exhaust manifold causes any remaining fuel to be burned before it can exit the tailpipe.

**ALTERNATOR**: A device used for converting mechanical energy into electrical energy.

**AMMETER**: An instrument, calibrated in amperes, used to measure the flow of an electrical current in a circuit. Ammeters are always connected in series with the circuit being tested.

**AMPERE**: The rate of flow of electrical current present when one volt of electrical pressure is applied against one ohm of electrical resistance.

**ANALOG COMPUTER**: Any microprocessor that uses similar (analogous) electrical signals to make its calculations.

**ARMATURE**: A laminated, soft iron core wrapped by a wire that converts electrical energy to mechanical energy as in a motor or relay. When rotated in a magnetic field, it changes mechanical energy into electrical energy as in a generator.

**ATMOSPHERIC PRESSURE**: The pressure on the Earth's surface caused by the weight of the air in the atmosphere. At sea level, this pressure is 14.7 psi at 32°F (101 kPa at 0°C).

**ATOMIZATION**: The breaking down of a liquid into a fine mist that can be suspended in air.

**AXIAL PLAY**: Movement parallel to a shaft or bearing bore.

**BACKFIRE**: The sudden combustion of gases in the intake or exhaust system that results in a loud explosion.

**BACKLASH**: The clearance or play between two parts, such as meshed gears.

**BACKPRESSURE**: Restrictions in the exhaust system that slow the exit of exhaust gases from the combustion chamber.

**BAKELITE**: A heat resistant, plastic insulator material commonly used in printed circuit boards and transistorized components.

**BALL BEARING**: A bearing made up of hardened inner and outer races between which hardened steel ball roll.

**BALLAST RESISTOR**: A resistor in the primary ignition circuit that lowers voltage after the engine is started to reduce wear on ignition components.

**BEARING**: A friction reducing, supportive device usually located between a stationary part and a moving part.

**BIMETAL TEMPERATURE SENSOR**: Any sensor or switch made of two dissimilar types of metal that bend when heated or cooled due to the different expansion rates of the alloys. These types of sensors usually function as an on/off switch.

**BLOWBY**: Combustion gases, composed of water vapor and unburned fuel, that leak past the piston rings into the crankcase during normal engine operation. These gases are removed by the PCV system to prevent the buildup of harmful acids in the crankcase.

**BRAKE PAD**: A brake shoe and lining assembly used with disc brakes.

**BRAKE SHOE**: The backing for the brake lining. The term is, however, usually applied to the assembly of the brake backing and lining.

**BUSHING**: A liner, usually removable, for a bearing; an anti-friction liner used in place of a bearing.

**BYPASS**: System used to bypass ballast resistor during engine cranking to increase voltage supplied to the coil.

**CALIPER**: A hydraulically activated device in a disc brake system, which is mounted straddling the brake rotor (disc). The caliper contains at least one piston and two brake pads. Hydraulic pressure on the piston(s) forces the pads against the rotor.

**CAMSHAFT**: A shaft in the engine on which are the lobes (cams) which operate the valves. The camshaft is driven by the crankshaft, via a

# GLOSSARY

belt, chain or gears, at one half the crankshaft speed.

**CAPACITOR**: A device which stores an electrical charge.

**CARBON MONOXIDE (CO)**: a colorless, odorless gas given off as a normal byproduct of combustion. It is poisonous and extremely dangerous in confined areas, building up slowly to toxic levels without warning if adequate ventilation is not available.

**CARBURETOR**: A device, usually mounted on the intake manifold of an engine, which mixes the air and fuel in the proper proportion to allow even combustion.

**CATALYTIC CONVERTER**: A device installed in the exhaust system, like a muffler, that converts harmful byproducts of combustion into carbon dioxide and water vapor by means of a heat-producing chemical reaction.

**CENTRIFUGAL ADVANCE**: A mechanical method of advancing the spark timing by using flyweights in the distributor that react to centrifugal force generated by the distributor shaft rotation.

**CHECK VALVE**: Any one-way valve installed to permit the flow of air, fuel or vacuum in one direction only.

**CHOKE**: A device, usually a moveable valve, placed in the intake path of a carburetor to restrict the flow of air.

**CIRCUIT**: Any unbroken path through which an electrical current can flow. Also used to describe fuel flow in some instances.

**CIRCUIT BREAKER**: A switch which protects an electrical circuit from overload by opening the circuit when the current flow exceeds a predetermined level. Some circuit breakers must be reset manually, while other reset automatically

**COIL (IGNITION)**: A transformer in the ignition circuit which steps of the voltage provided to the spark plugs.

**COMBINATION MANIFOLD**: An assembly which includes both the intake and exhaust manifolds in one casting.

**COMBINATION VALVE**: A device used in some fuel systems that routes fuel vapors to a charcoal storage canister instead of venting them into the atmosphere. The valve relieves fuel tank pressure and allows fresh air into the tank as fuel level drops to prevent a vapor lock situation.

**COMPRESSION RATIO**: The comparison of the total volume of the cylinder and combustion chamber with the piston at BDC and the piston at TDC.

**CONDENSER**: 1. An electrical device which acts to store an electrical charge, preventing voltage surges.
2. A radiator-like device in the air conditioning system in which refrigerant gas condenses into a liquid, giving off heat.

**CONDUCTOR**: Any material through which an electrical current can be transmitted easily.

**CONTINUITY**: Continuous or complete circuit. Can be checked with an ohmmeter.

**COUNTERSHAFT**: An intermediate shaft which is rotated by a mainshaft and transmits, in turn, that rotation to a working part.

**CRANKCASE**: The lower part of an engine in which the crankshaft and related parts operate.

**CRANKSHAFT**: The main driving shaft of an engine which receives reciprocating motion from the pistons and converts it to rotary motion.

**CYLINDER**: In an engine, the round hole in the engine block in which the piston(s) ride.

**CYLINDER BLOCK**: The main structural member of an engine in which is found the cylinders, crankshaft and other principal parts.

**CYLINDER HEAD**: The detachable portion of the engine, fastened, usually, to the top of the cylinder block, containing all or most of the combustion chambers. On overhead valve engines, it contains the valves and their operating parts. On overhead cam engines, it contains the camshaft as well.

**DEAD CENTER**: The extreme top or bottom of the piston stroke.

**DETONATION**: An unwanted explosion of the air fuel mixture in the combustion chamber caused by excess heat and compression, advanced timing, or an overly lean mixture. Also referred to as "ping".

**DIAPHRAGM**: A thin, flexible wall separating two cavities, such as in a vacuum advance unit.

**DIESELING**: A condition in which hot spots in the combustion chamber cause the engine to run on after the key is turned off.

**DIFFERENTIAL**: A geared assembly which allows the transmission of motion between drive axles, giving one axle the ability to turn faster than the other.

**DIODE**: An electrical device that will allow current to flow in one direction only.

**DISC BRAKE**: A hydraulic braking assembly consisting of a brake disc, or rotor, mounted on an axle, and a caliper assembly containing, usually two brake pads which are activated by hydraulic pressure. The pads are forced against the sides of the disc, creating friction which slows the vehicle.

**DISTRIBUTOR**: A mechanically driven device on an engine which is responsible for electrically firing the spark plug at a predetermined point of the piston stroke.

**DOWEL PIN**: A pin, inserted in mating holes in two different parts allowing those parts to maintain a fixed relationship.

**DRUM BRAKE**: A braking system which consists of two brake shoes and one or two wheel cylinders, mounted on a fixed backing plate, and a brake drum, mounted on an axle, which revolves around the assembly. Hydraulic action applied to the wheel cylinders forces the shoes outward against the drum, creating friction and slowing the vehicle.

**DWELL**: The rate, measured in degrees of shaft rotation, at which an electrical circuit cycles on and off.

**ELECTRONIC CONTROL UNIT (ECU)**: Ignition module, module, amplifier or igniter. See Module for definition.

**ELECTRONIC IGNITION**: A system in which the timing and firing of the spark plugs is controlled by an electronic control unit, usually called a module. These systems have not points or condenser.

**ENDPLAY**: The measured amount of axial movement in a shaft.

**ENGINE**: A device that converts heat into mechanical energy.

**EXHAUST MANIFOLD**: A set of cast passages or pipes which conduct exhaust gases from the engine.

**FEELER GAUGE**: A blade, usually metal, of precisely predetermined thickness, used to measure the clearance between two parts. These blades usually are available in sets of assorted thicknesses.

**F-Head**: An engine configuration in which the intake valves are in the cylinder head, while the camshaft and exhaust valves are located in the cylinder block. The camshaft operates the intake valves via lifters and pushrods, while it operates the exhaust valves directly.

**FIRING ORDER**: The order in which combustion occurs in the cylinders of an engine. Also the order in which spark is distributed to the plugs by the distributor.

**FLATHEAD**: An engine configuration in which the camshaft and all the valves are located in the cylinder block.

**FLOODING**: The presence of too much fuel in the intake manifold and combustion chamber which prevents the air/fuel mixture from firing, thereby causing a no-start situation.

**FLYWHEEL**: A disc shaped part bolted to the rear end of the crankshaft. Around the outer perimeter is affixed the ring gear. The starter drive engages the ring gear, turning the flywheel, which rotates the crankshaft, imparting the initial starting motion to the engine.

**FOOT POUND (ft.lb. or sometimes, ft. lbs.)**: The amount of energy or work needed to raise an item weighing one pound, a distance of one foot.

**FUSE**: A protective device in a circuit which prevents circuit overload by breaking the circuit when a specific amperage is present. The device is constructed around a strip or wire of a lower amperage rating than the circuit it is designed to protect. When an amperage higher than that stamped on the fuse is present in the circuit, the strip or wire melts, opening the circuit.

**GEAR RATIO**: The ratio between the number of teeth on meshing gears.

# GLOSSARY

**GENERATOR**: A device which converts mechanical energy into electrical energy.

**HEAT RANGE**: The measure of a spark plug's ability to dissipate heat from its firing end. The higher the heat range, the hotter the plug fires.

**HUB**: The center part of a wheel or gear.

**HYDROCARBON (HC)**: Any chemical compound made up of hydrogen and carbon. A major pollutant formed by the engine as a byproduct of combustion.

**HYDROMETER**: An instrument used to measure the specific gravity of a solution.

**INCH POUND (in.lb. or sometimes, in. lbs.)**: One twelfth of a foot pound.

**INDUCTION**: A means of transferring electrical energy in the form of a magnetic field. Principle used in the ignition coil to increase voltage.

**INJECTION PUMP**: A device, usually mechanically operated, which meters and delivers fuel under pressure to the fuel injector.

**INJECTOR**: A device which receives metered fuel under relatively low pressure and is activated to inject the fuel into the engine under relatively high pressure at a predetermined time.

**INPUT SHAFT**: The shaft to which torque is applied, usually carrying the driving gear or gears.

**INTAKE MANIFOLD**: A casting of passages or pipes used to conduct air or a fuel/air mixture to the cylinders.

**JOURNAL**: The bearing surface within which a shaft operates.

**KEY**: A small block usually fitted in a notch between a shaft and a hub to prevent slippage of the two parts.

**MANIFOLD**: A casting of passages or set of pipes which connect the cylinders to an inlet or outlet source.

**MANIFOLD VACUUM**: Low pressure in an engine intake manifold formed just below the throttle plates. Manifold vacuum is highest at idle and drops under acceleration.

**MASTER CYLINDER**: The primary fluid pressurizing device in a hydraulic system. In automotive use, it is found in brake and hydraulic clutch systems and is pedal activated, either directly or, in a power brake system, through the power booster.

**MODULE**: Electronic control unit, amplifier or igniter of solid state or integrated design which controls the current flow in the ignition primary circuit based on input from the pickup coil. When the module opens the primary circuit, the high secondary voltage is induced in the coil.

**NEEDLE BEARING**: A bearing which consists of a number (usually a large number) of long, thin rollers.

**OHM**: ($\Omega$) The unit used to measure the resistance of conductor to electrical flow. One ohm is the amount of resistance that limits current flow to one ampere in a circuit with one volt of pressure.

**OHMMETER**: An instrument used for measuring the resistance, in ohms, in an electrical circuit.

**OUTPUT SHAFT**: The shaft which transmits torque from a device, such as a transmission.

**OVERDRIVE**: A gear assembly which produces more shaft revolutions than that transmitted to it.

**OVERHEAD CAMSHAFT (OHC)**: An engine configuration in which the camshaft is mounted on top of the cylinder head and operates the valve either directly or by means of rocker arms.

**OVERHEAD VALVE (OHV)**: An engine configuration in which all of the valves are located in the cylinder head and the camshaft is located in the cylinder block. The camshaft operates the valves via lifters and pushrods.

**OXIDES OF NITROGEN (NOx)**: Chemical compounds of nitrogen produced as a byproduct of combustion. They combine with hydrocarbons to produce smog.

**OXYGEN SENSOR**: Used with the feedback system to sense the presence of oxygen in the exhaust gas and signal the computer which can reference the voltage signal to an air/fuel ratio.

**PINION**: The smaller of two meshing gears.

# GLOSSARY

**PISTON RING**: An open ended ring which fits into a groove on the outer diameter of the piston. Its chief function is to form a seal between the piston and cylinder wall. Most automotive pistons have three rings: two for compression sealing; one for oil sealing.

**PRELOAD**: A predetermined load placed on a bearing during assembly or by adjustment.

**PRIMARY CIRCUIT**: Is the low voltage side of the ignition system which consists of the ignition switch, ballast resistor or resistance wire, bypass, coil, electronic control unit and pick-up coil as well as the connecting wires and harnesses.

**PRESS FIT**: The mating of two parts under pressure, due to the inner diameter of one being smaller than the outer diameter of the other, or vice versa; an interference fit.

**RACE**: The surface on the inner or outer ring of a bearing on which the balls, needles or rollers move.

**REGULATOR**: A device which maintains the amperage and/or voltage levels of a circuit at predetermined values.

**RELAY**: A switch which automatically opens and/or closes a circuit.

**RESISTANCE**: The opposition to the flow of current through a circuit or electrical device, and is measured in ohms. Resistance is equal to the voltage divided by the amperage.

**RESISTOR**: A device, usually made of wire, which offers a preset amount of resistance in an electrical circuit.

**RING GEAR**: The name given to a ring-shaped gear attached to a differential case, or affixed to a flywheel or as part a planetary gear set.

**ROLLER BEARING**: A bearing made up of hardened inner and outer races between which hardened steel rollers move.

**ROTOR**: 1. The disc-shaped part of a disc brake assembly, upon which the brake pads bear; also called, brake disc.
2. The device mounted atop the distributor shaft, which passes current to the distributor cap tower contacts.

**SECONDARY CIRCUIT**: The high voltage side of the ignition system, usually above 20,000 volts. The secondary includes the ignition coil, coil wire, distributor cap and rotor, spark plug wires and spark plugs.

**SENDING UNIT**: A mechanical, electrical, hydraulic or electromagnetic device which transmits information to a gauge.

**SENSOR**: Any device designed to measure engine operating conditions or ambient pressures and temperatures. Usually electronic in nature and designed to send a voltage signal to an on-board computer, some sensors may operate as a simple on/off switch or they may provide a variable voltage signal (like a potentiometer) as conditions or measured parameters change.

**SHIM**: Spacers of precise, predetermined thickness used between parts to establish a proper working relationship.

**SLAVE CYLINDER**: In automotive use, a device in the hydraulic clutch system which is activated by hydraulic force, disengaging the clutch.

**SOLENOID**: A coil used to produce a magnetic field, the effect of which is produce work.

**SPARK PLUG**: A device screwed into the combustion chamber of a spark ignition engine. The basic construction is a conductive core inside of a ceramic insulator, mounted in an outer conductive base. An electrical charge from the spark plug wire travels along the conductive core and jumps a preset air gap to a grounding point or points at the end of the conductive base. The resultant spark ignites the fuel/air mixture in the combustion chamber.

**SPLINES**: Ridges machined or cast onto the outer diameter of a shaft or inner diameter of a bore to enable parts to mate without rotation.

**TACHOMETER**: A device used to measure the rotary speed of an engine, shaft, gear, etc., usually in rotations per minute.

**THERMOSTAT**: A valve, located in the cooling system of an engine, which is closed when cold and opens gradually in response to engine heating, controlling the temperature of the coolant and rate of coolant flow.

**TOP DEAD CENTER (TDC)**: The point at which the piston reaches the top of its travel on the compression stroke.

**TORQUE**: The twisting force applied to an object.

**TORQUE CONVERTER**: A turbine used to transmit power from a driving member to a driven member via hydraulic action, providing changes in drive ratio and torque. In automotive use, it links the driveplate at the rear of the engine to the automatic transmission.

**TRANSDUCER**: A device used to change a force into an electrical signal.

**TRANSISTOR**: A semi-conductor component which can be actuated by a small voltage to perform an electrical switching function.

**TUNE-UP**: A regular maintenance function, usually associated with the replacement and adjustment of parts and components in the electrical and fuel systems of a vehicle for the purpose of attaining optimum performance.

**TURBOCHARGER**: An exhaust driven pump which compresses intake air and forces it into the combustion chambers at higher than atmospheric pressures. The increased air pressure allows more fuel to be burned and results in increased horsepower being produced.

**VACUUM ADVANCE**: A device which advances the ignition timing in response to increased engine vacuum.

**VACUUM GAUGE**: An instrument used to measure the presence of vacuum in a chamber.

**VALVE**: A device which control the pressure, direction of flow or rate of flow of a liquid or gas.

**VALVE CLEARANCE**: The measured gap between the end of the valve stem and the rocker arm, cam lobe or follower that activates the valve.

**VISCOSITY**: The rating of a liquid's internal resistance to flow.

**VOLTMETER**: An instrument used for measuring electrical force in units called volts. Voltmeters are always connected parallel with the circuit being tested.

**WHEEL CYLINDER**: Found in the automotive drum brake assembly, it is a device, actuated by hydraulic pressure, which, through internal pistons, pushes the brake shoes outward against the drums.

# ABBREVIATIONS AND SYMBOLS

A: Ampere
AC: Alternating current
A/C: Air conditioning
A-h: Ampere hour
AT: Automatic transmission
ATDC: After top dead center
μA: Microampere
bbl: Barrel
BDC: Bottom dead center
bhp: Brake horsepower
BTDC: Before top dead center
BTU: British thermal unit
C: Celsius (Centigrade)
CCA: Cold cranking amps
cd: Candela
$cm^2$: Square centimeter
$cm^3$, cc: Cubic centimeter
CO: Carbon monoxide
$CO_2$: Carbon dioxide
cu.in., $in^3$: Cubic inch
CV: Constant velocity
Cyl.: Cylinder
DC: Direct current
ECM: Electronic control module
EFE: Early fuel evaporation
EFI: Electronic fuel injection
EGR: Exhaust gas recirculation
Exh.: Exhaust
F: Fahrenheit

F: Farad
pF: Picofarad
μF: Microfarad
FI: Fuel injection
ft.lb., ft. lb., ft. lbs.: foot pound(s)
gal: Gallon
g: Gram
HC: Hydrocarbon
HEI: High energy ignition
HO: High output
hp: Horsepower
Hyd.: Hydraulic
Hz: Hertz
ID: Inside diameter
in.lb.; in. lb.; in. lbs: inch pound(s)
Int.: Intake
K: Kelvin
kg: Kilogram
kHz: Kilohertz
km: Kilometer
km/h: Kilometers per hour
kΩ: Kilohm
kPa: Kilopascal
kV: Kilovolt
kW: Kilowatt
l: Liter
l/s: Liters per second
m: Meter
mA: Milliampere

# ABBREVIATIONS

mg: Milligram

mHz: Megahertz

mm: Millimeter

mm$^2$: Square millimeter

m$^3$: Cubic meter

M$\Omega$: Megohm

m/s: Meters per second

MT: Manual transmission

mV: Millivolt

μm: Micrometer

N: Newton

N-m: Newton meter

NOx: Nitrous oxide

OD: Outside diameter

OHC: Over head camshaft

OHV: Over head valve

$\Omega$: Ohm

PCV: Positive crankcase ventilation

psi: Pounds per square inch

pts: Pints

qts: Quarts

rpm: Rotations per minute

rps: Rotations per second

R-12: A refrigerant gas (Freon)

SAE: Society of Automotive Engineers

SO$_2$: Sulfur dioxide

T: Ton

t: Megagram

TBI: Throttle Body Injection

TPS: Throttle Position Sensor

V: 1. Volt; 2. Venturi

μV: Microvolt

W: Watt

∞: Infinity

<: Less than

>: Greater than

# Index

## A

Abbreviations and Symbols, 324
Air cleaner, 9
Air conditioning
    Blower, 187
    Control panel, 188
    Evaporator, 189
    Safety precautions, 24
Alternator
    Alternator precautions, 77
    Operation, 77
    Removal and installation, 79
Alignment, wheel
    Camber, 227
    Caster, 227
    Toe, 228
Antenna, 285
Anti-lock brake system, 258
Automatic transaxle
    Application chart, 11
    Back-up light switch, 217
    Filter change, 30, 216
    Fluid change, 30, 216
    Linkage adjustments, 216
    Neutral safety switch, 217
    Pan removal, 216
    Removal and installation, 218

## B

Back-up light switch
    Automatic transaxle, 217
    Manual transaxle, 207
Ball joints
    Inspection, 223
    Removal and installation, 223
Battery
    Fluid level and maintenance, 15
    Jump starting, 17
    Removal and installation, 80
Bearings
    Engine, 148
    Wheel, 220
Belts, 18, 21

Brakes
    Anti-lock brake system, 258
    Bleeding, 251
    Brake light switch, 246
    Disc brakes (Front)
        Caliper, 253
        Pads, 252
        Rotor (Disc), 254
    Drum brakes (Rear)
        Adjustment, 246
        Drum, 255
        Shoes, 255
        Wheel cylinder, 256
    Fluid level, 31
    Hoses and lines, 250
    Master cylinder, 247
    Parking brake
        Adjustment, 258
        Removal and installation, 257
    Power booster, 249
    Proportioning valve, 250
    Specifications, 272
Bumpers, 278

## C

Calipers
    Overhaul, 254
    Removal and installation, 253
Camber, 227
Camshaft and bearings
    Service, 139
    Specifications, 88
Capacities Chart, 36
Caster, 227
Catalytic converter, 152, 161
Charging system, 77
Chassis electrical system
    Circuit protection, 203
    Heater and air conditioning, 187
    Instrument panel, 290
    Lighting, 200
    Windshield wipers, 25, 193
Chassis lubrication, 33

## INDEX

Circuit breakers, 204
Circuit protection, 203
Clutch
    Adjustment, 211
    Cable, 213
    Hydraulic system bleeding, 216
    Master cylinder, 215
    Pedal, 213
    Removal and installation, 215
    Slave cylinder, 215
Coil (ignition), 73
Compression testing, 91
Connecting rods and bearings
    Service, 144
    Specifications, 89
Console, 294
Control arm
    Lower, 225
Cooling system, 30
Crankcase ventilation valve, 15, 154
Crankshaft
    Service, 148
    Specifications, 89
Crankshaft damper, 133
Cylinder head, 120

## D

Disc brakes, 252
Distributor, 76
Door glass, 303
Door locks, 300
Doors
    Glass, 303
    Locks, 300
    Removal and installation, 274
Door trim panel, 297
Dome light, 202
Drive Train, 206
Drum brakes, 255

## E

EGR valve, 158
Electric cooling fan, 116
Electrical
    Chassis
        Battery, 15, 80
        Circuit breakers, 204
        Fuses, 203
        Fusible links, 204
        Heater and air conditioning, 187
        Jump starting, 17
        Spark plug wires, 41
    Engine
        Alternator, 77
        Coil, 73
        Distributor, 76
        Electronic engine controls, 161
        Ignition module, 54, 64, 67
Electronic engine controls, 161
Electronic Ignition, 43, 49, 56, 65

Emission controls
    Catalytic Converter, 152, 161
    Evaporative canister, 15, 157
    Exhaust Gas Recirculation (EGR) system, 158
    Oxygen sensor, 84
    PCV valve, 14, 154
Engine
    Camshaft, 139
    Compression testing, 91
    Connecting rods and bearings, 144
    Crankshaft, 144
    Crankshaft damper, 133
    Cylinder head, 120
    Electronic controls, 161
    Exhaust manifold, 109
    Fluids and lubricants, 28-29
    Flywheel, 150
    Front (timing) cover, 133, 134, 135
    Front seal, 135
    Identification, 7, 8
    Intake manifold, 105
    Lifters, 127
    Main bearings, 148
    Oil pan, 129
    Oil pump, 131
    Overhaul tips, 85
    Piston pin, 145
    Pistons, 144
    Rear main seal, 147
    Removal and installation, 91
    Rings, 144
    Rocker cover, 102
    Rocker arms, 103
    Spark plug wires, 41
    Specifications, 86-92
    Thermostat, 104
    Timing belt, 135
    Timing chain and gears, 136
    Tools, 85
    Valve lifters, 127
    Valves, 125
    Valve springs, 126
    Valve stem oil seals, 126
    Water pump, 118
Evaporative canister, 15, 157
Exhaust Manifold, 109
Exhaust pipe, 151
Exhaust system, 150

## F

Fan, 116
Fenders, 288
Filters
    Air, 9
    Fuel, 14
    Oil, 29
Firing orders, 43
Flashers, 205
Fluids and lubricants
    Automatic transaxle, 29
    Battery, 15

# 328　INDEX

Fluids and lubricants (*continued*)
  Chassis greasing, 33
  Coolant, 30
  Engine oil, 28-29
  Fuel, 28
  Manual transaxle, 29
  Master cylinder
    Brake, 31
    Clutch, 32
  Power steering pump, 32
Flywheel, 150
Fog lights, 203
Front brakes, 252
Front hubs, 226
Front suspension
  Ball joints, 223
  Knuckles, 226
  Lower control arm, 225
  Stabilizer bar, 225
  Struts, 221
  Wheel alignment, 227
Front wheel bearings, 226
Fuel injection
  Fuel body, 171
  Fuel pressure regulator, 172, 183
  Fuel pump, 169, 177
  Idle air control valve, 173, 183
  Injectors, 172, 182
  Operation, 162, 169, 175
  Relieving fuel system pressure, 169, 177
  Throttle body, 170, 178
  Throttle position sensor, 174, 184
Fuel filter, 14
Fuel pump, 169, 177
Fuel system, 169
Fuel tank, 186
Fuses and circuit breakers, 203, 204
Fusible links, 204

# G

Generator (see alternator)
Glass
  Door, 303
  Side window, 309
  Windshield, 307
Glossary, 318
Grille, 283

# H

Halfshaft, 209
Hazard flasher, 205
Headlights, 200
Headliner, 299
Heater
  Blower, 187
  Control panel, 188
  Core, 188
Hood, 275
Hoses
  Brake, 250
  Coolant, 20, 23
How to Use This Book, 1

# I

Identification
  Engine, 7, 8
  Model, 4
  Serial number, 4
  Transaxle, 7, 11
  Vehicle, 4
Idle speed and mixture adjustment, 70
Ignition
  Coil, 47, 48, 54, 57, 67, 73, 75
  Lock cylinder, 234
  Module, 48, 54, 64, 67
  Switch, 233
  Timing, 69
Injectors, fuel, 172, 182
Instrument cluster, 196
Instrument panel
  Cluster, 196
  Console, 294
  Panel removal, 290
  Radio, 191
  Speedometer cable, 197
Intake manifold, 105

# J

Jacking points, 34
Jump starting, 17

# L

Lighting
  Dome light, 202
  Fog lights, 203
  Headlights, 200
  Signal and marker lights, 201
Lower ball joint, 223
Lower control arm, 225
Lubrication
  Automatic transaxle, 29
  Body, 34
  Chassis, 33
  Engine, 28-29
  Manual transaxle, 29

# M

MacPherson struts, 221
Main bearings, 148
Manifolds
  Intake, 105
  Exhaust, 109
Manual transaxle
  Application chart, 11
  Linkage adjustment, 207
  Removal and installation, 208
Marker lights, 201
Master cylinder
  Brake, 247
  Clutch, 215
Mechanic's data, 316
Mirrors, 284, 313
Model identification, 4

# INDEX

Module (ignition), 48, 54, 64, 67
Muffler, 152
Multi-function switch, 233

## N

Neutral safety switch, 217

## O

Oil and fuel recommendations, 28
Oil and filter change (engine), 29
Oil level check
    Engine, 28
    Transaxle
        Automatic, 29
        Manual, 29
Oil pan, 129
Oil pump, 130
Oxygen sensor, 84

## P

Parking brake, 257
Piston pin, 145
Pistons, 144
PCV valve, 14, 150
Power brake booster, 249
Power seat motor, 315
Power steering gear (rack and pinion)
    Removal and installation, 235
Power steering pump
    Fluid level, 32
    Removal and installation, 244
Power windows, 306
Printed circuit board, 198
Pushing, 34

## R

Radiator, 113
Radio, 191
Rear brakes, 255
Rear main oil seal, 146
Rear suspension
    Shock absorbers, 231
    Springs, 230
    Sway bar, 232
Regulator, 80
Rings, 144
Rocker cover, 102
Rocker arms, 103
Rotor (Brake disc), 254
Routine maintenance, 9

## S

Safety notice, 1
Seats, 313
Seat belts, 314
Serial number location, 4
Shock absorbers, 231
Slave cylinder, 215
Spark plugs, 38

Spark plug wires, 41
Special tools, 2
Specifications Charts
    Brakes, 272
    Camshaft, 88
    Capacities, 36
    Crankshaft and connecting rod, 89
    General engine, 86
    Piston and ring, 90
    Starter, 83
    Torque, 92
    Tune-up, 39
    Valves, 87
    Wheel alignment, 228
Speedometer, 197
Speedometer cable, 197
Springs, 230
Stabilizer bar, 225
Starter
    Removal and installation, 81
    Specifications, 83
Steering column, 235
Steering gear
    Power, 235
Steering linkage
    Tie rod ends, 235
Steering lock, 234
Steering wheel, 233
Stripped threads, 86
Suspension, 221, 230
Switches
    Back-up light, 207, 217
    Brake light switch, 246
    Headlight, 200
    Ignition switch, 233
    Multi-function switch
    Neutral safety switch, 217
    Turn signal switch, 233
    Windshield wiper, 196

## T

Tailpipe, 152
Thermostat, 104
Throttle body, 170, 178
Tie rod ends, 235
Timing (ignition), 69
Timing belt, 135
Timing chain and gears, 137
Timing gear cover, 133, 134, 135
Tires
    Design, 27
    Inflation, 28
    Rotation, 27
    Storage, 28
Toe-in, 228
Tools, 2
Torque specifications, 92
Towing, 34
Trailer towing, 33
Transaxle
    Application charts, 11
    Automatic, 216

## INDEX

Transaxle (*continued*)
  Manual, 206
  Routine maintenance, 29
Trouble codes, 45
Trunk lid, 276
Tune-up
  Distributor, 77
  Idle speed, 70
  Ignition timing, 69
  Procedures, 38
  Spark plugs and wires, 38, 41
  Specifications, 39
Turbocharger, 112
Turn signal flasher, 205
Turn signal switch, 233

## V

Valve lash adjustment, 70
Valve lifters, 127
Valve service, 126
Valve specifications, 87
Valve springs, 126
Vehicle identification, 4

## W

Water pump, 118
Wheel alignment
  Adjustment, 227
  Specifications, 228
Wheel bearings
  Front wheel, 226
Wheel cylinders, 256
Wheels, 28, 220
Window glass, 309
Window regulator, 303
Windshield, 307
Windshield wipers
  Arm, 193-194
  Blade, 193-194
  Motor, 195
  Refill, 25
  Windshield wiper switch, 198
Wiring
  Spark plug, 41
  Trailer, 203

# Chilton's Repair & Tune-Up Guides

The Complete line covers domestic cars, imports, trucks, vans, RV's and 4-wheel drive vehicles.

| RTUG Title | Part No. |
|---|---|
| **AMC 1975-82** <br> Covers all U.S. and Canadian models | 7199 |
| **Aspen/Volare 1976-80** <br> Covers all U.S. and Canadian models | 6637 |
| **Audi 1970-73** <br> Covers all U.S. and Canadian models. | 5902 |
| **Audi 4000/5000 1978-81** <br> Covers all U.S. and Canadian models including turbocharged and diesel engines | 7028 |
| **Barracuda/Challenger 1965-72** <br> Covers all U.S. and Canadian models | 5807 |
| **Blazer/Jimmy 1969-82** <br> Covers all U.S. and Canadian 2- and 4-wheel drive models, including diesel engines | 6931 |
| **BMW 1970-82** <br> Covers U.S. and Canadian models | 6844 |
| **Buick/Olds/Pontiac 1975-85** <br> Covers all U.S. and Canadian full size rear wheel drive models | 7308 |
| **Cadillac 1967-84** <br> Covers all U.S. and Canadian rear wheel drive models | 7462 |
| **Camaro 1967-81** <br> Covers all U.S. and Canadian models | 6735 |
| **Camaro 1982-85** <br> Covers all U.S. and Canadian models | 7317 |
| **Capri 1970-77** <br> Covers all U.S. and Canadian models | 6695 |
| **Caravan/Voyager 1984-85** <br> Covers all U.S. and Canadian models | 7482 |
| **Century/Regal 1975-85** <br> Covers all U.S. and Canadian rear wheel drive models, including turbocharged engines | 7307 |
| **Champ/Arrow/Sapporo 1978-83** <br> Covers all U.S. and Canadian models | 7041 |
| **Chevette/1000 1976-86** <br> Covers all U.S. and Canadian models | 6836 |
| **Chevrolet 1968-85** <br> Covers all U.S. and Canadian models | 7135 |
| **Chevrolet 1968-79 Spanish** | 7082 |
| **Chevrolet/GMC Pick-Ups 1970-82 Spanish** | 7468 |
| **Chevrolet/GMC Pick-Ups and Suburban 1970-86** <br> Covers all U.S. and Canadian $1/2$, $3/4$, and 1 ton models, including 4-wheel drive and diesel engines | 6936 |
| **Chevrolet LUV 1972-81** <br> Covers all U.S. and Canadian models | 6815 |
| **Chevrolet Mid-Size 1964-86** <br> Covers all U.S. and Canadian models of 1964-77 Chevelle, Malibu and Malibu SS; 1974-77 Laguna; 1978-85 Malibu; 1970-86 Monte Carlo; 1964-84 El Camino, including diesel engines | 6840 |
| **Chevrolet Nova 1986** <br> Covers all U.S. and Canadian models | 7658 |
| **Chevy/GMC Vans 1967-84** <br> Covers all U.S. and Canadian models of $1/2$, $3/4$, and 1 ton vans, cutaways, and motor home chassis, including diesel engines | 6930 |
| **Chevy S-10 Blazer/GMC S-15 Jimmy 1982-85** <br> Covers all U.S. and Canadian models | 7383 |
| **Chevy S-10/GMC S-15 Pick-Ups 1982-85** <br> Covers all U.S. and Canadian models | 7310 |
| **Chevy II/Nova 1962-79** <br> Covers all U.S. and Canadian models | 6841 |
| **Chrysler K- and E-Car 1981-85** <br> Covers all U.S. and Canadian front wheel drive models | 7163 |
| **Colt/Challenger/Vista/Conquest 1971-85** <br> Covers all U.S. and Canadian models | 7037 |
| **Corolla/Carina/Tercel/Starlet 1970-85** <br> Covers all U.S. and Canadian models | 7036 |
| **Corona/Cressida/Crown/Mk.II/Camry/Van 1970-84** <br> Covers all U.S. and Canadian models | 7044 |

| RTUG Title | Part No. |
|---|---|
| **Corvair 1960-69** <br> Covers all U.S. and Canadian models | 6691 |
| **Corvette 1953-62** <br> Covers all U.S. and Canadian models | 6576 |
| **Corvette 1963-84** <br> Covers all U.S. and Canadian models | 6843 |
| **Cutlass 1970-85** <br> Covers all U.S. and Canadian models | 6933 |
| **Dart/Demon 1968-76** <br> Covers all U.S. and Canadian models | 6324 |
| **Datsun 1961-72** <br> Covers all U.S. and Canadian models of Nissan Patrol; 1500, 1600 and 2000 sports cars; Pick-Ups; 410, 411, 510, 1200 and 240Z | 5790 |
| **Datsun 1973-80 Spanish** | 7083 |
| **Datsun/Nissan F-10, 310, Stanza, Pulsar 1977-86** <br> Covers all U.S. and Canadian models | 7196 |
| **Datsun/Nissan Pick-Ups 1970-84** <br> Covers all U.S. and Canadian models | 6816 |
| **Datsun/Nissan Z & ZX 1970-86** <br> Covers all U.S. and Canadian models | 6932 |
| **Datsun/Nissan 1200, 210, Sentra 1973-86** <br> Covers all U.S. and Canadian models | 7197 |
| **Datsun/Nissan 200SX, 510, 610, 710, 810, Maxima 1973-84** <br> Covers all U.S. and Canadian models | 7170 |
| **Dodge 1968-77** <br> Covers all U.S. and Canadian models | 6554 |
| **Dodge Charger 1967-70** <br> Covers all U.S. and Canadian models | 6486 |
| **Dodge/Plymouth Trucks 1967-84** <br> Covers all $1/2$, $3/4$, and 1 ton 2- and 4-wheel drive U.S. and Canadian models, including diesel engines | 7459 |
| **Dodge/Plymouth Vans 1967-84** <br> Covers all $1/2$, $3/4$, and 1 ton U.S. and Canadian models of vans, cutaways and motor home chassis | 6934 |
| **D-50/Arrow Pick-Up 1979-81** <br> Covers all U.S. and Canadian models | 7032 |
| **Fairlane/Torino 1962-75** <br> Covers all U.S. and Canadian models | 6320 |
| **Fairmont/Zephyr 1978-83** <br> Covers all U.S. and Canadian models | 6965 |
| **Fiat 1969-81** <br> Covers all U.S. and Canadian models | 7042 |
| **Fiesta 1978-80** <br> Covers all U.S. and Canadian models | 6846 |
| **Firebird 1967-81** <br> Covers all U.S. and Canadian models | 5996 |
| **Firebird 1982-85** <br> Covers all U.S. and Canadian models | 7345 |
| **Ford 1968-79 Spanish** | 7084 |
| **Ford Bronco 1966-83** <br> Covers all U.S. and Canadian models | 7140 |
| **Ford Bronco II 1984** <br> Covers all U.S. and Canadian models | 7408 |
| **Ford Courier 1972-82** <br> Covers all U.S. and Canadian models | 6983 |
| **Ford/Mercury Front Wheel Drive 1981-85** <br> Covers all U.S. and Canadian models Escort, EXP, Tempo, Lynx, LN-7 and Topaz | 7055 |
| **Ford/Mercury/Lincoln 1968-85** <br> Covers all U.S. and Canadian models of FORD Country Sedan, Country Squire, Crown Victoria, Custom, Custom 500, Galaxie 500, LTD through 1982, Ranch Wagon, and XL; MERCURY Colony Park, Commuter, Marquis through 1982, Gran Marquis, Monterey and Park Lane; LINCOLN Continental and Towne Car | 6842 |
| **Ford/Mercury/Lincoln Mid-Size 1971-85** <br> Covers all U.S. and Canadian models of FORD Elite, 1983-85 LTD, 1977-79 LTD II, Ranchero, Torino, Gran Torino, 1977-85 Thunderbird; MERCURY 1972-85 Cougar, | 6696 |

*continued on next page*

| RTUG Title | Part No. |
|---|---|
| 1983-85 Marquis, Montego, 1980-85 XR-7; LINCOLN 1982-85 Continental, 1984-85 Mark VII, 1978-80 Versailles | |
| **Ford Pick-Ups 1965-86** | 6913 |
| Covers all ½, ¾ and 1 ton, 2- and 4-wheel drive U.S. and Canadian pick-up, chassis cab and camper models, including diesel engines | |
| **Ford Pick-Ups 1965-82 Spanish** | 7469 |
| **Ford Ranger 1983-84** | 7338 |
| Covers all U.S. and Canadian models | |
| **Ford Vans 1961-86** | 6849 |
| Covers all U.S. and Canadian ½, ¾ and 1 ton van and cutaway chassis models, including diesel engines | |
| **GM A-Body 1982-85** | 7309 |
| Covers all front wheel drive U.S. and Canadian models of BUICK Century, CHEVROLET Celebrity, OLDSMOBILE Cutlass Ciera and PONTIAC 6000 | |
| **GM C-Body 1985** | 7587 |
| Covers all front wheel drive U.S. and Canadian models of BUICK Electra Park Avenue and Electra T-Type, CADILLAC Fleetwood and deVille, OLDSMOBILE 98 Regency and Regency Brougham | |
| **GM J-Car 1982-85** | 7059 |
| Covers all U.S. and Canadian models of BUICK Skyhawk, CHEVROLET Cavalier, CADILLAC Cimarron, OLDSMOBILE Firenza and PONTIAC 2000 and Sunbird | |
| **GM N-Body 1985-86** | 7657 |
| Covers all U.S. and Canadian models of front wheel drive BUICK Somerset and Skylark, OLDSMOBILE Calais, and PONTIAC Grand Am | |
| **GM X-Body 1980-85** | 7049 |
| Covers all U.S. and Canadian models of BUICK Skylark, CHEVROLET Citation, OLDSMOBILE Omega and PONTIAC Phoenix | |
| **GM Subcompact 1971-80** | 6935 |
| Covers all U.S. and Canadian models of BUICK Skyhawk (1975-80), CHEVROLET Vega and Monza, OLDSMOBILE Starfire, and PONTIAC Astre and 1975-80 Sunbird | |
| **Granada/Monarch 1975-82** | 6937 |
| Covers all U.S. and Canadian models | |
| **Honda 1973-84** | 6980 |
| Covers all U.S. and Canadian models | |
| **International Scout 1967-73** | 5912 |
| Covers all U.S. and Canadian models | |
| **Jeep 1945-87** | 6817 |
| Covers all U.S. and Canadian CJ-2A, CJ-3A, CJ-3B, CJ-5, CJ-6, CJ-7, Scrambler and Wrangler models | |
| **Jeep Wagoneer, Commando, Cherokee, Truck 1957-86** | 6739 |
| Covers all U.S. and Canadian models of Wagoneer, Cherokee, Grand Wagoneer, Jeepster, Jeepster Commando, J-100, J-200, J-300, J-10, J20, FC-150 and FC-170 | |
| **Laser/Daytona 1984-85** | 7563 |
| Covers all U.S. and Canadian models | |
| **Maverick/Comet 1970-77** | 6634 |
| Covers all U.S. and Canadian models | |
| **Mazda 1971-84** | 6981 |
| Covers all U.S. and Canadian models of RX-2, RX-3, RX-4, 808, 1300, 1600, Cosmo, GLC and 626 | |
| **Mazda Pick-Ups 1972-86** | 7659 |
| Covers all U.S. and Canadian models | |
| **Mercedes-Benz 1959-70** | 6065 |
| Covers all U.S. and Canadian models | |
| **Mercedes-Benz 1968-73** | 5907 |
| Covers all U.S. and Canadian models | |

| RTUG Title | Part No. |
|---|---|
| **Mercedes-Benz 1974-84** | 6809 |
| Covers all U.S. and Canadian models | |
| **Mitsubishi, Cordia, Tredia, Starion, Galant 1983-85** | 7583 |
| Covers all U.S. and Canadian models | |
| **MG 1961-81** | 6780 |
| Covers all U.S. and Canadian models | |
| **Mustang/Capri/Merkur 1979-85** | 6963 |
| Covers all U.S. and Canadian models | |
| **Mustang/Cougar 1965-73** | 6542 |
| Covers all U.S. and Canadian models | |
| **Mustang II 1974-78** | 6812 |
| Covers all U.S. and Canadian models | |
| **Omni/Horizon/Rampage 1978-84** | 6845 |
| Covers all U.S. and Canadian models of DODGE omni, Miser, 024, Charger 2.2; PLYMOUTH Horizon, Miser, TC3, TC3 Tourismo; Rampage | |
| **Opel 1971-75** | 6575 |
| Covers all U.S. and Canadian models | |
| **Peugeot 1970-74** | 5982 |
| Covers all U.S. and Canadian models | |
| **Pinto/Bobcat 1971-80** | 7027 |
| Covers all U.S. and Canadian models | |
| **Plymouth 1968-76** | 6552 |
| Covers all U.S. and Canadian models | |
| **Pontiac Fiero 1984-85** | 7571 |
| Covers all U.S. and Canadian models | |
| **Pontiac Mid-Size 1974-83** | 7346 |
| Covers all U.S. and Canadian models of Ventura, Grand Am, LeMans, Grand LeMans, GTO, Phoenix, and Grand Prix | |
| **Porsche 924/928 1976-81** | 7048 |
| Covers all U.S. and Canadian models | |
| **Renault 1975-85** | 7165 |
| Covers all U.S. and Canadian models | |
| **Roadrunner/Satellite/Belvedere/GTX 1968-73** | 5821 |
| Covers all U.S. and Canadian models | |
| **RX-7 1979-81** | 7031 |
| Covers all U.S. and Canadian models | |
| **SAAB 99 1969-75** | 5988 |
| Covers all U.S. and Canadian models | |
| **SAAB 900 1979-85** | 7572 |
| Covers all U.S. and Canadian models | |
| **Snowmobiles 1976-80** | 6978 |
| Covers Arctic Cat, John Deere, Kawasaki, Polaris, Ski-Doo and Yamaha | |
| **Subaru 1970-84** | 6982 |
| Covers all U.S. and Canadian models | |
| **Tempest/GTO/LeMans 1968-73** | 5905 |
| Covers all U.S. and Canadian models | |
| **Toyota 1966-70** | 5795 |
| Covers all U.S. and Canadian models of Corona, MkII, Corolla, Crown, Land Cruiser, Stout and Hi-Lux | |
| **Toyota 1970-79 Spanish** | 7467 |
| **Toyota Celica/Supra 1971-85** | 7043 |
| Covers all U.S. and Canadian models | |
| **Toyota Trucks 1970-85** | 7035 |
| Covers all U.S. and Canadian models of pick-ups, Land Cruiser and 4Runner | |
| **Valiant/Duster 1968-76** | 6326 |
| Covers all U.S. and Canadian models | |
| **Volvo 1956-69** | 6529 |
| Covers all U.S. and Canadian models | |
| **Volvo 1970-83** | 7040 |
| Covers all U.S. and Canadian models | |
| **VW Front Wheel Drive 1974-85** | 6962 |
| Covers all U.S. and Canadian models | |
| **VW 1949-71** | 5796 |
| Covers all U.S. and Canadian models | |
| **VW 1970-79 Spanish** | 7081 |
| **VW 1970-81** | 6837 |
| Covers all U.S. and Canadian Beetles, Karmann Ghia, Fastback, Squareback, Vans, 411 and 412 | |

Chilton's Repair Manuals are available at your local retailer or by mailing a check or money order for **$15.95** per book plus **$3.50** for 1st book and **$.50** for each additional book to cover postage and handling to:

## Chilton Book Company
### Dept. DM
### Radnor, PA 19089

NOTE: When ordering be sure to include your name & address, book part No. & title.